Lecture Notes in Computer Science

Lecture Notes in Artificial Intelligence   13955

Founding Editor

Jörg Siekmann

Series Editors

Randy Goebel, *University of Alberta, Edmonton, Canada*
Wolfgang Wahlster, *DFKI, Berlin, Germany*
Zhi-Hua Zhou, *Nanjing University, Nanjing, China*

The series Lecture Notes in Artificial Intelligence (LNAI) was established in 1988 as a topical subseries of LNCS devoted to artificial intelligence.

The series publishes state-of-the-art research results at a high level. As with the LNCS mother series, the mission of the series is to serve the international R & D community by providing an invaluable service, mainly focused on the publication of conference and workshop proceedings and postproceedings.

Philippe Mathieu · Frank Dignum ·
Paulo Novais · Fernando De la Prieta
Editors

Advances in Practical Applications of Agents, Multi-Agent Systems, and Cognitive Mimetics

The PAAMS Collection

21st International Conference, PAAMS 2023
Guimarães, Portugal, July 12–14, 2023
Proceedings

 Springer

Editors
Philippe Mathieu 🆔
University of Lille
Lille, France

Paulo Novais 🆔
Universidade do Minho
Braga, Portugal

Frank Dignum 🆔
Umeå University
Umeå, Sweden

Fernando De la Prieta 🆔
University of Salamanca
Salamanca, Spain

ISSN 0302-9743   ISSN 1611-3349 (electronic)
Lecture Notes in Artificial Intelligence
ISBN 978-3-031-37615-3   ISBN 978-3-031-37616-0 (eBook)
https://doi.org/10.1007/978-3-031-37616-0

LNCS Sublibrary: SL7 – Artificial Intelligence

This Springer imprint is published by the registered company Springer Nature Switzerland AG
The registered company address is: Gewerbestrasse 11, 6330 Cham, Switzerland

Preface

Research on agents and multi-agent systems has matured during the last thirty years and many effective applications of this technology are now deployed. An international forum to present and discuss the latest scientific developments and their effective applications, to assess the impact of the approach, and to facilitate technology transfer, became a necessity and was created almost two decades ago.

PAAMS, the International Conference on Practical Applications of Agents and Multi-Agent Systems, is the international yearly conference to present, discuss, and disseminate the latest developments and the most important outcomes related to real-world applications. It provides a unique opportunity to bring multi-disciplinary experts, academics, and practitioners together to exchange their experience in the development and deployment of agents and multi-agent systems.

This volume presents the papers that were accepted for the 2023 edition of PAAMS. These articles report on the application and validation of agent-based models, methods, and technologies in a number of key application areas, including: cognitive mimetic, simulating complex systems, agents for social good, advanced models for learning, agent-based programming, distributed data analysis, automatic planning, decision-making, social interactions, formal and theoretic models, self-adaptation, mobile edge computing, swarms, and task allocation. Each paper submitted to PAAMS went through a stringent peer-review process by three members of the Program Committee composed of 120 internationally renowned researchers from 29 countries. From the 70 submissions received, 19 were selected for full presentation at the conference; another 13 papers were accepted as short presentations. In addition, a demonstration track featuring innovative and emergent applications of agent and multi-agent systems and technologies in real-world domains was organized. In all, 5 demonstrations were shown, and this volume contains a description of each of them.

This edition of the conference is organized by the LASI and Centro Algoritmi of the University of Minho (Portugal). We would like to thank all the contributing authors, the members of the Program Committee, and the sponsors (AIR Institute, and Camara Municipal de Guimarães) for their hard and highly valuable work. We thank the funding supporting with the project "*COordinated intelligent Services for Adaptive Smart areaS (COSASS)*", Id. PID2021-123673OB-C33 funded by MCIN /AEI /10.13039/501100011033 / FEDER, UE.

Thanks for your help – PAAMS 2023 would not exist without your contribution.

July 2023

Philippe Mathieu
Frank Dignum
Paulo Novais
Fernando De la Prieta

Organization

General Co-chairs

Philippe Mathieu   University of Lille, France
Frank Dignum   Umeå University, Sweden
Paulo Novais   University of Minho, Portugal
Fernando De la Prieta   University of Salamanca, Spain

Workshop Chairs

Dalila Durães   University of Minho, Portugal
Alfonso González Briones   University of Salamanca, Spain

Advisory Board

Bo An   Nanyang Technological University, Singapore
Paul Davidsson   Malmö University, Sweden
Keith Decker   University of Delaware, USA
Yves Demazeau   Centre National de la Recherche Scientifique, France
Tom Holvoet   KU Leuven, Belgium
Toru Ishida   Kyoto University, Japan
Takayuki Ito   Nagoya Institute of Technology, Japan
Eric Matson   Purdue University, USA
Jörg P. Müller   Clausthal Technical University, Germany
Michal Pěchouček   Technical University in Prague, Czech Republic
Franco Zambonelli   University of Modena and Reggio Emilia, Italy

Local Organizing Committee

Paulo Novais (Chair)   University of Minho, Portugal
José Manuel Machado (Co-chair)   University of Minho, Portugal
Hugo Peixoto   University of Minho, Portugal
Regina Sousa   University of Minho, Portugal
Pedro José Oliveira   University of Minho, Portugal

Francisco Marcondes	University of Minho, Portugal
Manuel Rodrigues	University of Minho, Portugal
Filipe Gonçalves	University of Minho, Portugal
Dalila Durães	University of Minho, Portugal
Sérgio Gonçalves	University of Minho, Portugal

Organizing Committee

Juan M. Corchado Rodríguez	University of Salamanca and AIR Institute, Spain
Fernando De la Prieta	University of Salamanca, Spain
Sara Rodríguez González	University of Salamanca, Spain
Javier Prieto Tejedor	University of Salamanca and AIR Institute, Spain
Ricardo S. Alonso Rincón	AIR Institute, Spain
Alfonso González Briones	University of Salamanca, Spain
Pablo Chamoso Santos	University of Salamanca, Spain
Javier Parra	University of Salamanca, Spain
Liliana Durón	University of Salamanca, Spain
Marta Plaza Hernández	University of Salamanca, Spain
Belén Pérez Lancho	University of Salamanca, Spain
Ana Belén Gil González	University of Salamanca, Spain
Ana De Luis Reboredo	University of Salamanca, Spain
Angélica González Arrieta	University of Salamanca, Spain
Angel Luis Sánchez Lázaro	University of Salamanca, Spain
Emilio S. Corchado Rodríguez	University of Salamanca, Spain
Raúl López	University of Salamanca, Spain
Beatriz Bellido	University of Salamanca, Spain
María Alonso	University of Salamanca, Spain
Yeray Mezquita Martín	AIR Institute, Spain
Sergio Márquez	AIR Institute, Spain
Andrea Gil	University of Salamanca, Spain
Albano Carrera González	AIR Institute, Spain

Program Committee

Emmanuel Adam	Université Polytechnique Hauts-de-France, France
Analia Amandi	CONICET, Argentina
Fred Amblard	IRIT - University Toulouse 1 Capitole, France
Francesco Amigoni	Politecnico di Milano, Italy
Luis Antunes	University of Lisbon, Portugal

Faruk Polat	Middle East Technical University, Turkey
David Pynadath	University of Southern California, USA
Zinovi Rabinovic	Nanyang Technological University, Singapore
Alessandro Ricci	University of Bologna, Italy
David Robertson	University of Edinburgh, UK
Sebastian Rodriguez	GITIA-UTN, Argentina
Juan Rodriguez Aguilar	IIIA-CSIC, Spain
Kristin Yvonne Rozier	Iowa State University, USA
Yuko Sakurai	National Institute of Advanced Industrial Science and Technology, Japan
Ken Satoh	National Institute of Informatics and Sokendai, Japan
Silvia Schiaffino	CONICET, Argentina
Holger Schlingloff	Fraunhofer Institute for Open Communication Systems, Germany
Michael Ignaz Schumacher	University of Applied Sciences Western Switzerland, Switzerland
Franciszek Seredynski	Cardinal Stefan Wyszynski University, Poland
Emilio Serrano	Universidad Politécnica de Madrid, Spain
Jaime Sichman	University of São Paulo, Brazil
Kostas Stathis	Royal Holloway, University of London, UK
Toshiharu Sugawara	Waseda University, Japan
Andreas Theodorou	Umeå universitet, Sweden
Viviane Torres da Silva	IBM, Brazil
Ali Emre Turgut	IRIDIA-ULB, Belgium
Suguru Ueda	Saga University, Japan
Domenico Ursino	Università Politecnica delle Marche, Italy
Lois Vanhee	Umeå Universitet, Sweden
László Zsolt	Varga ELTE IK, Hungary
Laurent Vercouter	LITIS Lab, INSA, Rouen, France
Harko Verhagen	Stockholm University, Sweden
José Ramón Villar	University of Oviedo, Spain
Gerhard Weiss	University of Maastricht, Netherlands
Wayne Wobcke	University of New South Wales, Australia
Gaku Yamamoto	IBM Software Group, Tokyo Institute of Technology, Japan
Neil Yorke-Smith	Delft University of Technology, Netherlands
Franco Zambonelli	Università Modena e Reggio Emilia, Italy
Laura Zavala	City University of New York, USA
Jinyu Zhang	NJU, China

PAAMS 2023 Sponsors

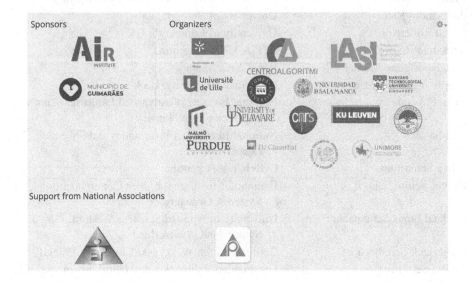

Contents

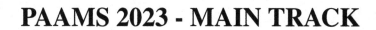

PAAMS 2023 - MAIN TRACK

Brain Waves Classification Using a Single-Channel Dry EEG Headset: An Application for Controlling an Intelligent Wheelchair

Patricia Almeida[1], Brigida Monica Faria[2,3(✉)], and Luis Paulo Reis[1,3]

[1] Faculty of Engineering of University of Porto (FEUP), Rua Dr. Roberto Frias, sn, 4200-465 Porto, Portugal
up201605165@edu.fe.up.pt
[2] ESS, Polytechnic of Porto (ESS-P.PORTO), Rua Dr. António Bernardino de Almeida, 400, 4200-072 Porto, Portugal
monica.faria@ess.ipp.pt
[3] Artificial Intelligence and Computer Science Laboratory (LIACC - Member of LASI LA), Rua Dr. Roberto Frias, sn, 4200-465 Porto, Portugal
lpreis@fe.up.pt

Abstract. Assistive technologies such as Intelligent Wheelchairs (IWs) can improve mobility and independence among elders and disabled people. To achieve this, various adapted sensors can be employed. In this study, the NeuroSky Mindwave Mobile 2 sensor is utilized to interpret the user's intentions into one of four commands: forward, right turn, left turn, or stop. By collecting brainwave data, specifically rhythms associated with imagining specific actions, the sensor enables the recognition of user desires. Data acquisition experiments were conducted, where individuals imagined different directions under four distinct conditions. Among the four datasets, the most effective classification was achieved when participants imagined the desired direction after being presented with the respective cue. Feature standardization leads to higher performances when compared to other scaling techniques. In conclusion, the findings suggest promising prospects for the control of intelligent wheelchairs through brainwave analysis.

Keywords: Intelligent Wheelchair · Brain-Computer Interface · NeuroSky Mindwave Mobile 2

1 Introduction

Independence and autonomy are fundamental concepts with special importance for elders and disabled people. Moreover, wheelchairs have proven to be fundamental for the movement of these people with physical disabilities in the lower limbs, paralysis or other type of restrictive diseases. Consequently, the increase in life expectancy combined with the ageing of the population has created the

P. Mathieu et al. (Eds.): PAAMS 2023, LNAI 13955, pp. 3–14, 2023.
https://doi.org/10.1007/978-3-031-37616-0_1

ideal conditions for the introduction of a new wheelchair concept, the Intelligent Wheelchair. Hence, a new form of navigation, more customized and easy to use, promoting inclusion and subsequently enhancing the quality of life of everyone with some mobility restrictions, has been developed. The importance of providing multifaceted wheelchairs which can be adapted to the most diverse conditions of their users is thus emphasised. Different interfaces are being developed enabling to overcome existing barriers of use [1]. However brain-computer interface (BCI) systems are proving to be extremely successful methods of wheelchair control due to their accessible price and non-invasiveness. The present study intends to introduce insights into this field of intelligent wheelchairs in order to overcome this perceived problem.

2   Human Machine Interface

Communication between human beings and machines, specifically computers, has been facilitated by the newest innovations in electronics and wearable technologies [2]. This Human Machine Interface (HMI) system will be increasingly relevant to the Internet of Things (IoT) and universal computing [3]. Commonly, communication begins when an object/machine, collects and interprets a human's desire. Therefore, the HMI, is essentially an input device, for example, an adaptive sensor, which can capture the user's intention [4]. BCIs could be considered a communication system to convert humans' minds or wills into commands to manipulate devices [5]. Consequently, these interfaces are immensely helpful to support people with motor disabilities or completely paralyzed people [6,7], since communication has a direct pathway between the brain and external devices. For the purpose of providing a BCI, a presence of a device is imperative to collect information about brain activity. Several options for EEG devices are available on the market. However, the Neurosky MindWave Mobile 2, Muse 2, Ultracortex Mark IV, and the Emotiv Epoc are highlighted for being non-invasive EEG headsets, and for measuring multiple parameters [8]. These properties make their use more convenient and comfortable for operators. The NeuroSky MindWave is a single-channel, dry EEG headset that measures and transmits data via Bluetooth Low Energy or classic Bluetooth [9]. Muse 2 is a brain-sensing headband that offers measurements of EEG and photo-plethysmography (PPG) and provides instant feedback of brain activity [10]. The Ultracortex Mark IV is an open-source, 3D-printable headset designed to operate with any OpenBCI Board [11]. It can evaluate different parameters such as EEG, muscle activity, and heart activity. Emotiv EPOC X is an EEG headset that features two electrode arms allowing coverage of the temporal, parietal and occipital lobes [12]. For this work, the NeuroSky MindWave's importance stems from its single-channel, dry EEG design, which simplifies the user experience, enhances portability, and expands its potential applications. Its ease of use, convenience, affordability, and versatility make it an invaluable tool for various fields, ranging from neuroscience research to personal cognitive enhancement.

3   Methodology

Driving an IW requires several commands. In this work, the four basic commands, forward, stop, go to the left and to the right will be assumed as the desired classes. Analysing the specificities of the wheelchair area and considering the properties of the sensors, Neurosky MindWave Mobile 2 demonstrated to be an interesting option for being incorporated in the interface of an IW. NeuroSky MindWave Mobile 2 is an EEG headset capable of recording brain waves. When a movement is imagined, even without being performed, it produces brain rhythms [13]. These types of imagination-based activities, commonly known as motor-imagery (MI), will be the ones used in this work.

3.1   Data Sets Description

Considering this type of sensor, only data from one data channel is collected. For this reason, it is important to record data when subjects perform different tasks to understand the approach that leads to better results. In this context, four data sets were created, each one acquired under a specific condition, as next described.

– **Data set A**
   Based on the acquisition protocol of BCI Competition 2008 (IV) Graz data set B [14], this data set consists of imagining one of four directions (front, left, right or stop) after the respective cue be displayed on the screen.
   This data set includes EEG data of twelve different healthy subjects, all right-handed and with ages ranging from 20 to 24 years. Participants were seated comfortably in a chair, observing a flat screen monitor situated about 1 m away at eye level.
   Each experimental trial was approximately 22 s long per direction, as shown in Fig. 1. The first 2 s correspond to a preparation phase in which the subject is adjusting the sensor to his head. After that, a visual cue is presented for 4 s on the screen, followed by the 16 s of the imaginary period. In order to restrict and indicate the imagination period, there is also an acoustic sound at the beginning and at the end of this phase.

Fig. 1. Timing schedule of the acquisition protocol for Data set A

– **Data set B & Data set C**
   Data sets B and C were created to investigate how a different visual stimulus could lead to an improved performance in wheelchair driving. According to this and motivated by Turnip et al., 2016 [15] work, participants were asked to

imagine the wheelchair moving in a direction while watching that respective direction on a video format stimulus. For an easy and fast identification of which direction they should imagine at each moment of the video, it contained an arrow with the corresponding movement, as can be seen in Fig. 2.

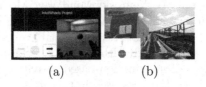

(a)   (b)

Fig. 2. Example of a frame from the video stimulus used for the acquisition of: (a) Data set B; (b) Data set C.

For data set B, this video involves a wheelchair simulator [16], while in data set C the video represents a roller coaster ride, as a stronger stimulus.

Regarding the Acquisition Protocol (Fig. 3), it started with a preparation phase, similar to data set A, followed by a warning sound and, after that, a 2-minute video was exhibited. Each video included three simulations per direction, being randomly alternated between them and having a duration of approximately 10 s each. Lastly, a sound was emitted to signaling the end of the data collection.

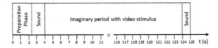

Fig. 3. Timing schedule of the acquisition protocol for Data sets B and C.

This experimental acquisition comprises EEG data from the same twelve subjects described in data set A.

- **Data set D**

  These data arise to study the different classification classes through EEG data collected while participants drive a wheelchair on a predefined route (Fig. 4). For this acquisition, volunteers were first asked to fit the sensor and minimise their head movements. Next, a brief explanation was given on how to drive the wheelchair used, the one from the Intellwheels project, as well as the path to follow. All participants performed the route once for familiarization and training, and only then performed two repetitions of the route where EEG was recorded. Ten participants took part in this test, all of them healthy and without previous experience in driving a wheelchair.

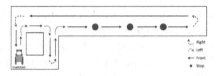

Fig. 4. Top view of the route used for Data set D acquisition.

3.2 Training and Testing Data

During this analysis all data sets (from A to D) follow a structure of 80% for training and 20% for testing. In addition, to increase the number of data and taking into account that classification is sensitive to epoch length [13,17], each extracted EEG signal was divided into non-overlapping segments with different time windows, 2, 3 and 4 s.

3.3 Pre-processing

After epoching the EEG data to the desired time windows, a resampling was required to ensure that all data had the same sampling rate [18]. Next, the EEG signal is recognised to have a significant amount of noise and ocular artefacts typically present at low and high frequencies. Hence, a bandpass filter, more specifically a Butterworth filter, was applied to remove all this noise. Finally, the signal comprises only the bands of interest, alpha and beta, in which the features will be extracted.

3.4 Feature Extraction

Obtaining features that could efficiently associate the EEG segments to the respective thought direction is the main goal of the feature extraction step. For this reason, features are extracted from several domains, namely time domain (Statistical and Fractal Dimension (FD) features), frequency domain (Power features) and time-frequency domain (Empirical Mode Decomposition (EMD) and Entropy features). All the extracted features, which are further described below, have been widely used for EEG-based MI recognition [19–22].

Statistical Features: In order to characterise the time series of EEG signals six features (Mean, Standard Deviation, Mean Absolute deviation, Hjorth Parameters, Skewness, Kurtosis) were extracted, which are adapted from [23,24]. **Power Features**: The power spectrum feature was estimated using the modified periodogram algorithm, named the Welch method. In order to compute this feature, the data is first decomposed into successive blocks and then a periodogram is built up for each one. Lastly, the mean is calculated by assuming the average over the blocks. **Entropy Features**: The EEG signal is non-linear in nature, thus it is equally important to extract features, such as entropy, that represent this dynamic [18]. Five variants of entropy were considered in this analysis: Permutation entropy (PE), Spectral entropy (SE), Singular value decomposition entropy

(SVDE) and Approximate entropy (ApEn) & Sample entropy (SampEn). **FD Features**: In FD the EEG signals are considered as a geometric figure, thus the geometric complexity, its correlation and evolutionary features are estimated by quantifying the fractal spaces occupied [18]. Within the several existing algorithms to compute FD, those proposed by Katz [25], Petrosian [26] and Higuchi [27] are extensively used for EEG signal characterization [28] and therefore, were the ones applied in this study. **EMD Features**: EMD separates EEG signals into a set of Intrinsic Mode Functions (IMFs) using an automatic shifting process. It is intended that each IMF represents different frequency components of the original signals so that the number of endpoints and zero-crossings must be equal or different at most by one and, at each point, the mean value estimated through the upper and lower envelope must be null [29]. During this study, three features that describe the IMF over time, frequency and energy domain were extracted: First Difference of IMF Time Series, First Difference of IMF's Phase and Normalized Energy of IMF.

3.5   Feature Selection and Dimensionality Reduction and Classification

Feature selection, Dimensionality reduction and classification are crucial points that contribute to the achievement of better outcomes. These procedures are based on the ones described in [30].

3.6   Application

For this sensor a real time test is required. In a first instance, the development of an application where it could be possible to control a robot using the sensor was chosen. This was the first technique followed, however due to the incompatibility felt between the Python versions of acquisition and processing, this could not reach conclusive results. Consequently, a new alternative was found to validate the proposed model, perform a new data acquisition, and determine the respective label. For this test it was intended to use the participant that could have a more statistically significant data set, and then implement its model with better performance for the classification.

4   Results and Discussion

NeuroSky Mindwave Mobile 2 captured EEG data from different subjects while performing multiple tasks. Considering that different epochs can result in improved classifications, the results obtained for each data set as well as for each epoch are presented below. It should be clarified that in Tables 1 and 2, when the term "all" is mentioned, it corresponds to training the classifiers with data from all subjects. Furthermore, the terms "Stand" and "Norm" are the simplified versions of Standardization and Normalization, respectively. When a "-" appears in the feature scaling cell, it indicates that the best result was achieved without these types of techniques.

4.1 Data Sets

Given all the results obtained and summarised in Table 1, data set A appears as being the best approach to develop a model that enables users to drive an intelligent wheelchair. In this data set for all three epoch lengths, the F1-Score reaches the maximum value.

Table 1. Comparison of the best participant from each data set.

	Epoch 4s				Epoch 3s				Epoch 2s			
	Subject	F1 - Score	Classifier	Feature Scaling	Subject	F1 - Score	Classifier	Feature Scaling	Subject	F1 - Score	Classifier	Feature Scaling
Data set A	1,2,4,6,7,9,11,12	1	MLP, LDA	Stand	10, 12	1	RF, GNB	Stand, -	2	1	SVM	-
Data set B	6, 10, 12	0,88	DTC, RF, MLP	-, Norm, Stand	11	0,75	LSVM	Stand	10	0,8	LR	-
Data set C	9	1	MLP	-	2	0,81	LR	Stand	9	0,75	GNB	-
Data set D	8	1	LDA	Stand	8	0,89	LDA	Stand	1	0,79	KNN	-

Concerning the classifiers or the feature scaling, these changed based on the subject. However, surprisingly for a 2 s epoch for all the data sets, the highest performance was provided without feature scaling. Feature scaling is usually required to suppress the effect of different magnitudes or amplitudes on features. Although the classification overall seems to be great, the data set sizes are relatively small, which could represent a statistically non-significant sample for inferring conclusions. Consequently, one of the participants, in this case, the 12 for having greater availability and being within those with better results in one of the data sets, repeated the acquisition protocol for data set A six more times. This resulted in training and test sets with new sizes, as described in Table 2.

Table 2. Size of the training and test set for the new acquisition of subject 12 to the data set A.

	Epoch 4s	Epoch 3s	Epoch 2s
Train Set	75	108	162
Test Set	19	27	41

After training these new data, new performances were generated, as can be seen by the F1-Score values shown in Table 3.

Table 3. Results of the F1-score for the new acquisition of subject 12 to the data set A.

		Data set A (Subject 12)								
		Epoch 4s			Epoch 3s			Epoch 2s		
		F1 - Score	Classifier	Feature Scaling	F1 - Score	Classifier	Feature Scaling	F1 - Score	Classifier	Feature Scaling
1 model		0,48	KNN	Stand	0,39	RF	Stand	0,38	RF	-
Voting	Hard	0,48	KNN + SVM	Stand	0,37	RF + GNB	Stand	0,33	LDA + RF	Stand
	Soft	0,4			0,39			0,43		
AdaBoost		0,27	SVM	Stand	0,37	RF	Stand	0,35	RF	-

The classification was less efficient which was reflected in lower values of the evaluation parameter. To illustrate how the assignment of classes was carried out, the confusion matrix for the best result was represented, in this case the 4 s epoch with the K-NN classifier, which consists of an F1-Score value of 0.48. It can be concluded that the front and right classes were the most easily identified while the left and stop directions were more challenging. During this study F1-Score was used as the evaluation metric, due to the fact that FN and FP play a key role. However, to compare with other authors' work, accuracy was also estimated. Thereby for the F1-Score result of 0.48 with the K-NN classifier (subject 12 epoch of 4 s) a total accuracy of 47% was achieved, or more specifically 80%, 33%, 43% and 25% for the classes Front, Left, Right and Stop. Permana et al., 2019 [31] proposed a wheelchair controlled by also using this sensor where the four classes consisted of: move forward (think forward), backward (think backward), turn left (think backward while constantly moving their eyes) and turn right (think forward while continuously moving their eyes). This approach enabled them to have a total accuracy rate of 52–56% (depending on the participant) and 82%, 70%, 73%, 47% and 18% when the success rate for each class was considered. These results, not as satisfactory as desired, may stem from several factors. Firstly, the acquisition was conducted on different days, i.e. the first acquisition protocol was done on one day and then the repetitions were consecutively performed on another day, which could have caused brain exhaustion. Secondly, a higher level of fatigue could have occurred on the repetition day leading to a greater difficulty in concentration and consequently a poorer data quality. Thirdly, the extracted features may still not be the most suitable for this patient. In the literature it is also possible to find some studies with higher levels of accuracy for the classification, however, most of them used attention and concentration levels as features, which was not the goal of this study.

4.2 Real Time Application

Having into account the different data sets, classifiers and participants, subject 12 was the one selected to perform this test in real-time. Firstly, it was with him that the new data acquisition was carried out in order to have a statistically significant data set. Secondly, he was among the most available for continuing to contribute to this study, although the performance of his best model is medium (Table 3). Once the model is verified to work minimally on a patient where performance is not the highest this will validate the proof of concept. Therefore, 24 samples of 4 s were recorded following the acquisition protocol for data set A (Sect. 3.1). After that, the samples were classified using the K-NN model and feature standardization, the combination that appears to be the best for this participant (Table 3). The class allocated to each sample, and its true label, are presented in Table 4.

Table 4. Classification of the data set for validation of participant 12 with an epoch length of 4 s.

Epoch 4s		
Test Set File	Label	Predict
1	Front	Front
2	Right	Left
3	Left	Stop
4	Stop	Left
5	Front	Left
6	Right	Right
7	Left	Right
8	Stop	Right
9	Front	Front
10	Right	Stop
11	Left	Stop
12	Stop	Front
13	Front	Left
14	Right	Right
15	Left	Right
16	Stop	Right
17	Front	Front
18	Right	Left
19	Left	Front
20	Stop	Front
21	Front	Left
22	Right	Left
23	Left	Front
24	Stop	Stop

Front: 3 / 6
Right: 2 / 6
Left: 0 / 6
Stop: 1 / 6

Total: 6 / 24

It can be observed that the classification was not satisfactory, only 6 of the 24 samples were classified correctly. Having verified a greater ability to hit the classifications Front and Right, which was already expected since in the confusion matrix were also the most identified classes. Nevertheless, during the acquisition, the subject presented some problems in thinking about direction because it was a period of time so short that he could not concentrate appropriately. For this reason, just to evaluate the performance in longer temporal segments where the subject could be more focused, data acquisition for 10 s was also collected. Table 5 displays the results obtained for this epoch length.

Although the model was trained for 4 s it appears to be more effective in larger temporal segments, it was able to classify 6 from the 16 samples. This could be explained by the fact that in a longer temporal segment, the participant is able to be more conscious to imagine the direction. During the acquisition of the data for training, this limitation was not felt since 15 s was acquired and then these were divided into the intended temporal segments. In summary, this could be a promising approach, but it still requires some improvements. Firstly, misclassifications cannot occur in real time, this could endanger the life of the IW user. Moreover, 10 s segments are too long for real-time implementation.

Table 5. Classification of the data set for validation of participant 12 with an epoch length of 10 s.

Epoch 10s		
Test Set File	Label	Predict
1	Front	Front
2	Right	Right
3	Left	Right
4	Stop	Left
5	Front	Right
6	Right	Right
7	Left	Front
8	Stop	Front
9	Front	Front
10	Right	Left
11	Left	Front
12	Stop	Left
13	Front	Front
14	Right	Right
15	Left	Front
16	Stop	Left

Front:	3 / 4
Right:	3 / 4
Left:	0 / 4
Stop:	0 / 4

Total:	6 / 16

5   Conclusions and Future Work

Different health conditions imply the existence of multiple alternatives for the interaction between a human and a machine, replacing the traditional modes of communication. Consequently, manual wheelchairs are no longer viable solutions for everyone; therefore, with the trend towards an increasingly technological world, different options have emerged, especially that of IW. Comparing the data sets created, the one that showed the best results, suggests that imagining a certain direction after observing an arrow indicating the direction provides a better classification than having no stimulus or having a stimulus in video format. In general, it is noticed that feature standardization leads to higher performances when compared to other scaling techniques. The possibility of controlling an IW using brainwave analysis is promising and with improvements, could be incorporated into a real IW. For future work, it will be important to gather a broader range of participants and to investigate the effectiveness of alternative stimuli or cues for brainwave analysis and control. The integration process should also consider continuous user feedback.

Acknowledgements. This work was financially supported by: Base Funding - UIDB/00027/2020 of the Artificial Intelligence and Computer Science Laboratory (LIACC) funded by national funds through the FCT/MCTES (PIDDAC) and Intell-Wheels2.0: Intelligent Wheelchair with Flexible Multimodal Interface and Realistic Simulator (POCI-01-0247-FEDER-39898), supported by NORTE 2020, under PT2020.

References

1. Faria, B.M., Reis, L.P., Lau, N.: A survey on intelligent wheelchair prototypes and simulators. In: Rocha, Á., Correia, A.M., Tan, F.B., Stroetmann, K.A. (eds.) New Perspectives in Information Systems and Technologies, Volume 1. AISC, vol. 275, pp. 545–557. Springer, Cham (2014). https://doi.org/10.1007/978-3-319-05951-8_52

2. Nogueira, P., et al.: A review of commercial and medical-grade physiological monitoring devices for biofeedback-assisted quality of life improvement studies. J. Med. Syst. **42**(6), 101 (2018)
3. Pavlovic, V.I., Sharma, R., Huang, T.S.: Visual interpretation of hand gestures for human-computer interaction: a review. IEEE Trans. Pattern Anal. Mach. Intell. **19**(7), 677–695 (1997)
4. Han, H., Yoon, S.W.: Gyroscope-based continuous human hand gesture recognition for multi-modal wearable input device for human machine interaction. Sensors **19**(11), 2562 (2019)
5. Faria, B.M., Reis, L.P., Lau, N.: Cerebral palsy EEG signals classification: facial expressions and thoughts for driving an intelligent wheelchair. In: IEEE 12th International Conference on Data Mining Workshops, pp. 33–40. IEEE (2012)
6. Faria, B.M., Reis, L.P., Lau, N., Soares, J.C., Vasconcelos, S.: Patient classification and automatic configuration of an intelligent wheelchair. In: Filipe, J., Fred, A. (eds.) ICAART 2012. CCIS, vol. 358, pp. 268–282. Springer, Heidelberg (2013). https://doi.org/10.1007/978-3-642-36907-0_18
7. Faria, B.M., et al.: A methodology for creating intelligent wheelchair users' profiles. In: International Conference on Agents and Artificial Intelligence (2012)
8. LaRocco, J., Le, M.D., Paeng, D.-G.: A systemic review of available low-cost EEG headsets used for drowsiness detection. Front. Neuroinformatics **14** (2020)
9. MindWave. https://store.neurosky.com/pages/mindwave
10. Muse 2: Brain Sensing Headband - Technology Enhanced Meditation. https://choosemuse.com/muse-2/
11. Ultracortex "Mark IV" EEG Headset - OpenBCI Online Store. https://shop.openbci.com/collections/frontpage/products/ultracortex-mark-iv?variant=43568381966
12. EMOTIV EPOC X 14 Channel Mobile Brainwear® | EMOTIV. https://www.emotiv.com/product/emotiv-epoc-x-14-channel-mobile-brainwear/
13. Banerjee, S., Chatterjee, R.: Temporal window based feature extraction technique for motor-imagery EEG signal classification. bioRxiv (2021)
14. Leeb, R., et al.: BCI competition 2008–Graz data set B. In: Graz University of Technology, Austria, pp. 1–6 (2008)
15. Turnip, A., et al.: EEG-based brain-controlled wheelchair with four different stimuli frequencies. Int. Indonesia J. **8**(1), 65–69 (2016)
16. Faria, B.M., Reis, L.P., Lau, N., Moreira, A.P., Petry, M., Ferreira, L.M.: Intelligent wheelchair driving: bridging the gap between virtual and real intelligent wheelchairs. In: Pereira, F., Machado, P., Costa, E., Cardoso, A. (eds.) EPIA 2015. LNCS (LNAI), vol. 9273, pp. 445–456. Springer, Cham (2015). https://doi.org/10.1007/978-3-319-23485-4_44
17. Fraschini, M., et al.: The effect of epoch length on estimated EEG functional connectivity and brain network organisation. Journal Neural Eng. **13**(3), 036015 (2016)
18. Nawaz, R., et al.: Comparison of different feature extraction methods for EEG-based emotion recognition. Biocybern. Biomed. Eng. **40**(3), 910–926 (2020)
19. Monori, F., Oniga, S.: Processing EEG signals acquired from a consumer grade BCI device. Carpathian J. Electron. Comput. Eng. **11**(2), 29–34 (2018)
20. Ji, N., et al.: EEG signals feature extraction based on DWT and EMD combined with approximate entropy. Brain Sci. **9**(8), 201 (2019)
21. Bashar, S.K., Bhuiyan, M.I.H.: Classification of motor imagery movements using multivariate empirical mode decomposition and short time Fourier transform based hybrid method. Eng. Sci. Technol. Int. J. **19**(3), 1457–1464 (2016)

22. Padfield, N., et al.: EEG-based brain-computer interfaces using motor-imagery: techniques and challenges. Sensors **19**(6), 1423 (2019)
23. Kant, P., Hazarika, J., Laskar, S.H.: Wavelet transform based approach for EEG feature selection of motor imagery data for braincomputer interfaces. In: 2019 Third ICISC, pp. 101–105. IEEE (2019)
24. Monori, F., Oniga, S.: Processing EEG signals acquired from a consumer grade BCI device. Carpathian J. Electron. Comput. Eng. **11**(2), 29–34 (2018). https://doi.org/10.2478/cjece-2018-0015
25. Esteller, R., et al.: A comparison of waveform fractal dimension algorithms. IEEE Trans. Circuits Syst. I: Fundam. Theory Appl. **48**(2), 177–183 (2001)
26. Petrosian, A.: Kolmogorov complexity of finite sequences and recognition of different preictal EEG patterns. In: Proceedings Eighth IEEE Symposium on Computer-Based Medical Systems, pp. 212–217. IEEE (1995)
27. Higuchi, T.: Approach to an irregular time series on the basis of the fractal theory. Physica D: Nonlinear Phenomena **31**(2), 277–283 (1988)
28. García-Martínez, B., et al.: A review on nonlinear methods using electroencephalographic recordings for emotion recognition. IEEE Trans. Affect. Comput. **12**, 801–820 (2019)
29. Huang, N.E., et al.: The empirical mode decomposition and the Hilbert spectrum for nonlinear and non-stationary time series analysis. Proc. R. Soc. Lond. Seri. A: Math. Phys. Eng. Sci. **454**(1971), 903–995 (1998)
30. Almeida, P.M.: Intellwheels - Controlling an Intelligent Wheelchair using a Multimodal Interface (2021)
31. Permana, K., Wijaya, S.K., Prajitno, P.: Controlled wheelchair based on brain computer interface using Neurosky Mindwave Mobile 2. In: AIP Conference Proceedings, vol. 2168, p. 020022. AIP Publishing LLC (2019)

AJAN: An Engineering Framework for Semantic Web-Enabled Agents and Multi-Agent Systems

André Antakli[(✉)], Akbar Kazimov, Daniel Spieldenner,
Gloria Elena Jaramillo Rojas, Ingo Zinnikus, and Matthias Klusch

German Research Center for Artificial Intelligence, Saarland Informatics Campus,
Saarbruecken, Germany
{andre.antakli,akbar.kazimov,daniel.spieldenner,gloria.rojas,
ingo.zinnikus,matthias.klusch}@dfki.de

Abstract. The development of Semantic Web-enabled intelligent agents and multi-agent systems still remains a challenge due to the fact that there are hardly any agent engineering frameworks available for this purpose. To address this problem, we present AJAN, a modular framework for the engineering of agents that builds on Semantic Web standards and Behavior Tree technology. AJAN provides a web service-based execution and modeling environment in addition to an RDF-based modeling language for deliberative agents where SPARQL-extended behavior trees are used as a scripting language to define their behavior. In addition, AJAN supports the modeling of multi-agent coordination protocols while its architecture, in general, can be extended with other functional modules as plugins, data models, and communication layers as appropriate and not restricted to the Semantic Web.

Keywords: Semantic Web · Agent Engineering Framework ·
Multi-Agent Systems

1 Introduction

The idea of Semantic Web-enabled intelligent agents and multi-agent systems (MAS) has been around for almost as long as the idea of the Semantic Web itself, as indicated in [9]. Nonetheless, as mentioned in [8], web-based MAS has been somewhat neglected until recently. The situation has changed with the emergence of new standards such as Linked Data (LD) or Web of Things (WoT), which aim to improve the interoperability of heterogeneous environments and provide a solid foundation for building autonomous intelligent and distributed systems. For example, [9] presents agents for manufacturing using said standards, or show, as in [13], how those can be combined with machine learning.

However, these approaches are isolated solutions that only show how agents can be used in and implemented for the Semantic Web but without some agent engineering framework for this purpose. In fact, the development of semantic

P. Mathieu et al. (Eds.): PAAMS 2023, LNAI 13955, pp. 15–27, 2023.
https://doi.org/10.1007/978-3-031-37616-0_2

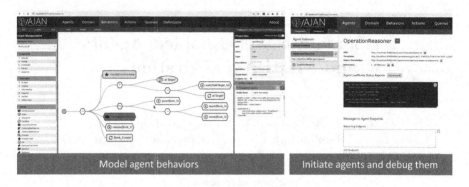

Fig. 1. The AJAN editor to model, create and debug AJAN agents

web-enabled agents and multi-agent systems still requires considerable manual effort from the agent engineer. Established agent engineering frameworks such as Jason, JaCaMo and JACK are simply not natively designed to interact with Semantic Web environments, let alone to provide an agent modeling language and environment that embeds itself homogeneously into the Semantic Web. [4] is taking a step in the right direction with a proposed OWL-based agent model language that can be combined with frameworks such as JADE. Or even [14], in which the behavior of reflexive agents can be described and executed via N3 rules. However, these approaches are insufficient in describing an agent's interaction with its environment or knowledge base, or do not even provide one. Additionally, they fail to support the engineer with templates for implementing multi-agent coordination protocols.

To address these challenges, we present AJAN, a novel, modular and extensible framework for the engineering of Semantic Web-enabled agents and multi-agent systems. AJAN relies on the SPARQL-BT paradigm to describe the event-based behavior of agents and enables them to natively interact with Semantic Web-based environments or coordinate themselves with other AJAN agents. The AJAN agent model including agent knowledge and behavior is described in RDF and SPARQL in direct support of the development of agents when they are intended for the Semantic Web. Due to its architecture, AJAN can be extended with other AI approaches but also data models as well as communication layers, allowing it to be used in various domains such as Industry 4.0, pedestrian simulation, smart living, or social services.

This paper is structured as follows. Section 2 describes the AJAN Framework. In Sect. 3, various application areas are presented in which AJAN is used. After discussing the related work in Sect. 4, we conclude the paper in Sect. 5.

2   The AJAN Framework

AJAN (Accessible Java Agent Nucleus) is an agent and multi-agent system framework primarily designed for the use in the Semantic Web. This framework

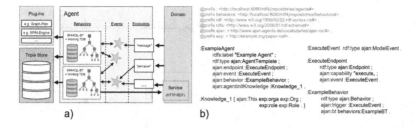

Fig. 2. a) Agent Model Overview; b) RDF example of an agent template

consists of multiple RDF based languages to model agents, a RDF triplestore for data management, the AJAN-service to execute agents and the AJAN-editor to model them. In general, with AJAN, Linked Data (LD) based deliberative agents can be modeled and executed. These agents are equipped with a RDF-based agent knowledge. The behavioral model of an AJAN agent is defined through SPARQL-extended Behavior Trees, known as SPARQL-BT. With this graphical scripting language designed for the Semantic Web, the internal decision-making process of an agent as well as its interaction with LD environments and RDF triplestores can be realized. Due to the modular nature of the SPARQL-BT approach (see Sect. 2.2), it can be easily extended with additional primitives for the use in various domains or to integrate other AI approaches. One goal is not only to realize agents interacting with LD-resources, the whole AJAN system has to act as one. Therefore, with the AJAN-service, agents can be created, executed, monitored and deleted via LD-interfaces. Furthermore, the whole agent model, including SPARQL-BTs and the knowledge of individual agents, are completely defined in RDF and accessible via a RDF triplestore. Through the chosen architecture, an AJAN agent can basically interact with its own service, e.g. to create new agents, but it is also possible to give the agent a kind of 'self-awareness', since it can access its own model and monitor running behaviors at any time via SPARQL-BTs and adapt these dynamically. The AJAN-editor (see Fig. 1) offers a GUI for agent and behavior modeling, which can be used at design time but also runtime, to create or delete agents and to monitor their knowledge and behaviors. A detailed description of AJAN can be found in the AJAN Wiki[1].

2.1 AJAN Agent Model

The agent model used in AJAN follows the principles of the BDI [12] paradigm, in which agents have a knowledge base and autonomously attempt to achieve agent goals using its plan library. While processing these goals, the agent can also set itself new context-based intermediate goals in order to be able to react dynamically to its agent environment. As shown in Fig. 2a, an AJAN agent has a plan or behavior library in which the respective behaviors are linked to events. When an event is created, it triggers the behavior associated with it. In addition to events, an AJAN agent also has semantic goals, a subclass of events,

---

[1] AJAN Agent Model Wiki: https://github.com/aantakli/AJAN-service/wiki.

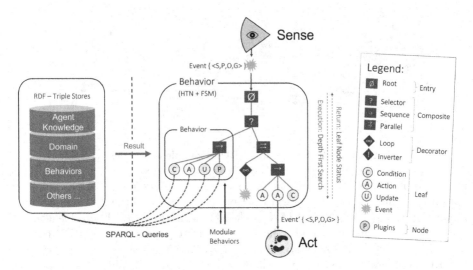

Fig. 3. SPARQL Behavior Tree Overview

described with pre- and postconditions. Depending on the agent's state, events and goals can be created via behaviors, thus the behavior execution can be seen as a Hierarchical Task Network. As an interface to the agent environment, an agent can have multiple LD endpoints (REST/RDF) that, when they receive data, also generate events and goals. The beliefs of an agent are stored in a RDF based agent knowledge base (KB), which can be accessed and updated through agent behaviors, implemented as SPARQL-BTs. Figure 2b shows an example of a RDF-based agent template. An AJAN agent template can be seen as a blueprint for an AJAN agent, and thus reflects the AJAN agent model. In addition to the specification of endpoints, events or goals and behaviors, initial knowledge can also be defined. This knowledge is available to an agent from the beginning via its local knowledge base. In addition to providing domain-specific assertional knowledge, the agent model itself can be extended via the initial knowledge. For example, an agent can be assigned additional properties such as organizational affiliation or roles via the 'keyword' *ajan:This*. To model agent templates the AJAN Agent Vocabulary[2] is used. These templates are stored in an RDF triplestore as well as the local agent knowledge, terminological knowledge about the domain in which the agent acts and the plan library. Event data is also represented in RDF and is available to the triggered behaviors, via SPARQL queries. SPARQL queries (ASK queries) are also used to represent the pre- and postconditions of goals, which are validated directly on the agent knowledge.

2.2 SPARQL-BT

For modeling AJAN agent behavior, the SPARQL-BT (SBT in short) approach is used. As shown in Fig. 3, SBTs are SPARQL extended Behavior Trees (BT, see

---

[2] AJAN agent vocabulary: http://ajan-agents.de/vocabularies/ajan-ns.

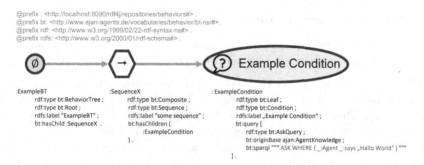

Fig. 4. Example SPARQL Behavior Tree

[10]), for which Spieldenner et al. presented a formal specification based on the Milner Calculus in [17]. Basically, SBTs are used as an agent behavior scripting language to perform contextual SPARQL queries and to execute functionalities through nodes. In depth-first execution of these nodes, they only communicate their status such as RUNNING, SUCCEEDED or FAILED to their parent nodes. Thus, SBTs are processed like typical BTs[3] and use standard BT composite and decorator nodes, with the difference that SBTs are executed via events or goals. In general SPARQL is used in SBTs for state checking, knowledge retrieval, and manipulation. To reduce agent knowledge base requests, each SBT has its own KB to store behavior specific data. To model AJAN behaviors the SPARQL-BT vocabulary[4] was defined. An example of a simple SBT, consisting of a *Root*, *Sequence* and a *Condition* node is shown in Fig. 4. *:ExampleBT* is the root RDF resource of the SBT. If an AJAN *Event* appears which is triggering an initiated SBT, the child of the *Root* node is executed first. This node points to its child via *bt:hasChild*, and therefore to the RDF resource *:SequenceX* which is from type *bt:Composite* and *bt:Sequence*. If this sequence is executed, it executes its children (*bt:hasChildren*) one after the other until all children SUCCEEDED or one FAILED. In this example, its only child is from type *bt:Condition*, which executes for state checking a SPARQL ASK Query (*bt:query*) on the agent knowledge (*ajan:AgentKnowledge*). In AJAN, there are a number of other SBT nodes. For example the *Update* node, which manipulates the agent knowledge via SPARQL UPDATE; or the *Handle Event* node, which reads event and goal information via a CONSTRUCT query. Since AJAN behavior models are stored in RDF triplestores, the *Load Behavior* node can access them via a SELECT query and then initiate and execute them. Thus, an AJAN agent has the ability to dynamically generate new SBTs using *Update* nodes and subsequently execute these SBTs.

---

[3] Used BT lib.: https://github.com/libgdx/gdx-ai/wiki/Behavior-Trees.

[4] SPARQL-BT vocabulary: http://ajan-agents.de/vocabularies/behavior/bt-ns.

2.3 Agent Environment Interaction

There are two ways to implement an interaction between AJAN agents and their environment: **passively** via AJAN agent endpoints; or **actively** via SBT nodes:

Passive Interaction: An AJAN agent is primarily designed to interact with and as a LD resource and thus, offers multiple HTTP/RDF endpoints. In addition to a general LD endpoint to query the current agent state, including behavioral and knowledge state information, further endpoints can be defined. Such endpoints generate internal events after receiving data, which are triggering linked SBTs. Standard events are linked RDF graphs, which are available to the respective SBT for querying. To access event information within a executed SBT and store it in an agent KB, the aforementioned *Handle Event* node must be used.

Active Interaction: With the SBT *Query Domain* node a selected LD resource can be actively requested using HTTP GET. The received RDF-based data is then stored in a selected knowledge base. The SBT *Message* node can be used to configure a detailed HTTP request. Besides selecting the HTTP method to be used, additional HTTP headers can be defined, using a SPARQL SELECT query. Additionally, the *Message* node can generate a RDF-based message payload via a SPARQL CONSTRUCT query and control which data received from the requested LD resource should be stored. The *Action* node is a message node, but with pre- and postconditions like a AJAN goal. After the RDF based payload is created via CONSTRUCT, it is validated via the precondition before being sent to the LD resource, and the response is validated via the postcondition. If the validations are failing, the node status is FAILED otherwise SUCCEEDED.

2.4 Interaction Between Agents

To enable communication between agents within AJAN, the *Message* node previously described is required, as it allows to send HTTP/RDF requests to LD resources like AJAN agents. Accordingly, each AJAN agent can directly (peer-to-peer) communicate with other AJAN agents via their individual endpoints. Each agent can make use of its agent knowledge which can contain information, e.g. originating from an agents registry, about other agents in the cloud (endpoints, roles and activity status) with which they can communicate. By default, an agent has knowledge of the AJAN-service in which the agent 'lives'. With this knowledge in form of a URI, an agent can not only query its own agent model via the service's LD interface, but also other AJAN agents for communication purposes or to create or delete agents with a *Message* node.

Implementing Protocols: To ensure that agents speak the same 'language' among themselves and follow the same communication rules, the used ontologies to formulate exchanged data must not only be coordinated within the MAS the interacting agents should also use same communication protocols. In the agent context, reference must be made to FIPA, which has standardized protocols for the use in MAS to improve the interoperation of heterogeneous agents and services that they can represent [18]. For the purpose of communication of agents,

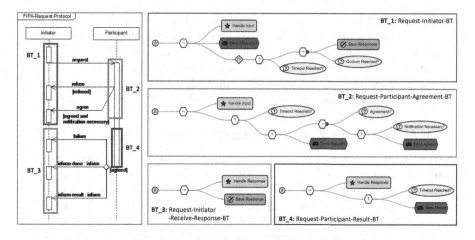

Fig. 5. FIPA Request Interaction Protocol implemented as SPARQL-BTs

these standards include e.g., speech act theory-based communicative acts or content languages. As an example of how a FIPA protocol can be modeled in AJAN, the Request Interaction protocol is implemented using four SBTs, see Fig. 5[5]. The Request-Initiator-BT (*BT_1*) sends a request to given agents via a SBT *Message* node (purple node), listens for responses via a SBT *Handle Event* node (green node), and checks for a quorum (minimum number of agents required to execute and proceed with the coordination protocol) via a SBT *Condition* node. The Request-Participant-Agreement-BT (*BT_2*) is used by the participant agent to accept or reject the request. The Request-Initiator-Receive-Response-BT (*BT_3*) receives and saves the results, and the Request-Participant-Result-BT (*BT_4*) sends the results back to the initiator agent.

2.5   Plug-In System

In order to be able to react flexibly to domain-specific circumstances and to extend the reactive planning of an agent, AJAN has a JAVA-based *Plug-In* system (see Fig. 2a). This system uses several SBT and SPARQL related interface definitions with which new SBT nodes or new SPARQL functions can be implemented and integrated into AJAN. In [3] for example Answer Set Programming (ASP) is integrated to solve combinatorial problems and to extend SBTs with foresighted action sequences. In addition, classical action planning is integrated, where new SBTs are generated to achieve an RDF-described goal state. Therefore, AJAN actions and goals are translated into PDDL operators, and the agent knowledge is interpreted as the initial state. To avoid having to implement the logic of a new SBT node in JAVA, a Python interpreter is integrated as a SBT node, allowing the implementation of new SBT nodes in Python. To enable

---

[5] The presented SBTs are available under https://github.com/AkbarKazimov/MAJAN.

AJAN to interact not only with LD domains and thus not only via RDF messages, the *Mapping* plug-in can be used to map incoming JSON, XML or CSV information to RDF data via RML (RDF Mapping Language). To send messages with native JSON-based content, mapped from a RDF dataset, POSER [16] is used. To process telemetry data in low-bandwidth networks, MQTT (Message Queuing Telemetry Transport) SBT nodes have been integrated as well.

2.6 MAJAN: Multi-Agent Coordination Plug-In

MAJAN[6] is an extension of the agent engineering tool AJAN which provides features to implement and evaluate SPARQL-BT-based coordination of AJAN agents. As an example, we discuss how the coordination problem class Optimal Coalition Structure Generation (CSGP) can be solved with MAJAN. CSGP is defined as follows: Given a coalition game (A, v) with set A of agents, real-valued coalition values $v(C)$ for all non-empty coalitions C among agents in A, then find a partition (coalition structure) $CS*$ of A (out of all possible coalition structures CS) with maximum social welfare:

$$CS^* = argmax_{CS \in A} \sum_{m=1}^{|CS|} cv(CS_m) \tag{1}$$

The value $v(C)$ of coalition C is the utility its members can jointly attain calculated as the sum of weighted individual utilities of coalition members, and the social welfare of a coalition structure is the sum of its coalition values. To solve CSGP problems, the BOSS algorithm [6] is used in MAJAN. As shown in Fig. 6, the protocol implemented in *MAJAN* with template SPARQL-BTs for solving the clustering problem of the above-mentioned type is an appropriate adaptation of the standard FIPA-Request-Interaction protocol (see Sect. 2.4) for multi-agent coordination. The initiator agent of the coordination process collects profile information (e.g. individual agent properties) from all other participating agents (steps 1, 2). It then generates possible coalitions C of agents (step 3) subject to given constraints on coalition size and broadcasts them together with the collected profile information to all other participating agents (step 4). To constitute the coalition game (A, v) of the CSGP to be solved, the value of each of these coalitions must be determined. For this purpose, each agent locally computes its individual utility values for only those coalitions it is a member of and returns them to the initiator agent (steps 5, 6). Each individual utility value of an agent in some coalition is calculated only by this agent as the extent to which (the profile information of) other members of this coalition satisfy its individual preferences (that are not shared with any agent). Finally, the initiator agent computes the coalition values as the sum of relevant individual utility values collected from participating agents, calls a given CSGP solver (in *MAJAN* that is the BOSS algorithm, which is executed with the yellow-colored *CSGP* node) to compute the optimal coalition structure for the actual coalition game, and broadcasts the solution to participating agents (steps 7, 8).

---

[6] *MAJAN* plug-in with documentation: https://github.com/AkbarKazimov/MAJAN.

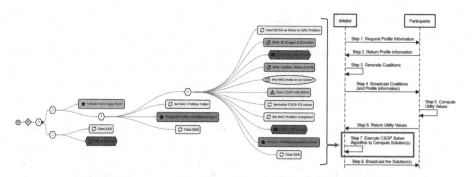

Fig. 6. Generic MAJAN MAC protocol for agent coalition structure generation

2.7   AJAN Implementation

The AJAN framework consists of the AJAN-service[7] and the AJAN-editor[8], which are available on GitHub as open source software under the LGPL 2.1 and MIT licenses, respectively. Both components are executable on Windows, Linux and Mac OS. The AJAN-service is JAVA 11-based and uses Spring Boot[9] to realize it as a web service. RDFBeans[10] translates the RDF-based AJAN agent model into executable JAVA code, and with PF4J[11], plug-ins are integrated into AJAN. With RDF4J[12] the interaction with RDF triplestores and data processing is realized. With it, W3C standards like OWL, SPIN (SPARQL Inferencing Notation) or SHACL (Shapes Constraint Language) can be used natively for e.g., building an agent knowledge graph with the corresponding reasoning techniques. The individual agent models and knowledge bases are stored in external triplestores which are accessible through standardized SPARQL endpoints[13]. Thus, RDF triplestores like RDF4J-server or GraphDB[14] can be used. To decrease the execution time of SBTs, and to allow that only the individual SBT has access to its own SBT knowledge base, the SBT KBs are kept in-memory RDF repositories and not externally like the agent KB. Access authorization to the AJAN-service and single triplestores, is realized using JSON Web Tokens (JWT)[15] The AJAN-editor is based on NodeJS[16] and Ember[17].

---

[7] AJAN-service on GitHub: https://github.com/aantakli/AJAN-service.

[8] AJAN-editor on GitHub: https://github.com/aantakli/AJAN-editor.

[9] Spring Boot: https://spring.io/.

[10] RDFBeans: https://rdfbeans.github.io/.

[11] PF4J: https://pf4j.org/.

[12] RDF4J: https://rdf4j.org/.

[13] SPARQL HTTP Protocol: https://www.w3.org/TR/sparql11-http-rdf-update/.

[14] GraphDB: https://www.ontotext.com/products/graphdb.

[15] JWT for Apache tomcat: https://github.com/andreacomo/tomcat-jwt-security.

[16] NodeJS: https://nodejs.org/en.

[17] EmberJS: https://emberjs.com/.

3   Selected Applications

AJAN has already been used in various LD and non-LD based domains to implement agent and multi-agent systems. For example, AJAN has been used to control simulated humans, to act in a Smart Living environment or to optimize production in an Industry 4.0 context.

Human Simulation. AJAN was used to control simulated entities in virtual production and traffic environments. In a human-robot collaboration scenario presented in [2], AJAN agents control simulated workers and mobile robots with LD interfaces to coordinate them for joint fulfillment of production steps. As presented in [3], AJAN was used to simulate pedestrians based on real human behavior. To realize this, an ML-based imitation model is integrated into AJAN to generate new trajectories, based on the simulated pedestrian's history and inferred targets, to steer the imitated pedestrian in a game engine.

Smart Living Environments. In [1], a smart living environment with AJAN agents uses the W3C Web of Things (WoT) architecture, where IoT resources have RDF-based Thing descriptions. In this scenario, AJAN agents are generating and executing new SBTs based on WoT resource descriptions to dynamically interact with these resources. For example to orchestrate them, to notify caregivers when a resident needs help.

Production Optimisation. The paper [17] describes a scenario where the production within a virtual factory floor is optimized. The factory floor, production units, product plans, and available products are all represented as web resources using the Linked Data Platform[18] specification. In this scenario AJAN agents represent these units and can initialize additional agents to distribute the production load. Coordination between agents is achieved through the LD environment as the communication layer, which allows agents to store RDF information that other agents can indirectly perceive. This approach is elaborated further in [15].

Language Course Coordination. In this application, AJAN agents help to coordinate language courses for third-country nationals (TCNs) as social services in the European project WELCOME[19] Each TCN is registered at a mobile cloud-based MyWELCOME app with an AJAN agent as personal assistant for service provision and coordination. The agents perform semantic service selection with an appropriate OWL-S service matchmaker, and can coordinate with each other to plan optimal groupings of TCNs for each lesson of a Language Learning Course (LLC, cf. Fig. 7). The goal is to assign TCNs to working groups that optimize their language learning based on individual preferences, progress, and teacher-specified constraints, such as group size and course progress level. Such constraints can be set in a *teacher panel*, and participants can set their individual preferences in their app. The agents aim to coordinate a maximally suitable

---

[18] Linked Data Platform: https://www.w3.org/TR/ldp/.
[19] WELCOME Project: https://welcome-h2020.eu/.

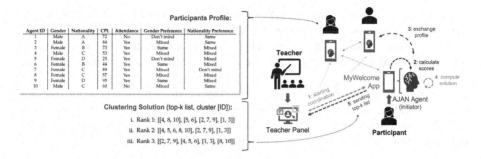

Fig. 7. Language course coordination by AJAN agents

working group structure for each lesson, which can be mapped to the multi-agent coalition structure generation problem. The MAJAN plug-in of AJAN (cf. Sect. 2.6) was used to enable agents to solve this problem with the corresponding BT-based multi-agent coordination protocol where each agent has a protocol-specific SBT executed in an event-based distributed fashion. The multi-agent coordination is performed in two phases initiated by the teacher at the end of each course lesson: In the *Assessment* phase, the MyWELCOME app used during the lesson by participants calculates appropriate scores and reports them to the respective agent of a participant, which, in turn, stores the overall course progress level of its TCN in its agent knowledge. In the *Coordination* phase, the agents coordinate to compute an optimal working group assignment and send the top-k ranked list of participants working group structures to the teacher for approval. This application has been implemented and evaluated successfully by user partners with selected TCNs.

4   Related Work

Semantic Web standards have been incorporated into agents and MAS since the idea of a Semantic Web appeared [9]. For example, in [13], OWL and RDF knowledge graphs have been utilized to train machine learning-based systems to interface a learning agent with the Semantic Web. [9], on the other hand, presents a web-based MAS for manufacturing, that interacts with LD and WoT environments to derive new behaviors from the semantic environment.

However, these systems are implemented for specific applications. In general, established agent system and MAS frameworks need to be adapted for use in the Semantic Web, as they have not been developed natively for it. To address this issue, [4] introduced an OWL-based ontology to describe agents and their agent-to-agent interaction, which can be translated into JADE agents, where basic FIPA specifications can be used. Other related works present ontologies and interpreters needed to translate semantically described agents into executable code for different BDI frameworks, such as [7] for JaCaMo, [11] for Jason, and [5] for JACK. However, these approaches limit the agent engineer's ability to specify behavior using Semantic Web standards and achieve a homogeneous modeling of the agent's interaction with its environment or knowledge, such as using SPARQL. Additionally, they lack flexibility in extending the agent model, necessitating adaptations to the interpreter, framework, and ontology used. An agent engineering framework that was developed specifically for the use in the Semantic Web is presented in [14]. Here, the agent behavior and its interaction with LD environments is described and executed via N3 rules, where even HTTP messages are defined in RDF. However, this framework allows to model only reflexive agents that can act only in an LD environment.

5 Conclusion

We presented AJAN, an open-source, modular and highly extensible agent engineering framework that particularly allows for the development of semantic web-enabled agents and MAS. AJAN relies on the paradigm of event-based SPARQL Behavior Tree processing and RDF for the modeling of deliberative agents and their interaction with the environment. Moreover, AJAN offers predefined Behavior Tree templates for implementing multi-agent coordination protocols such as clustering and coalition formation. AJAN has already been used for the development of agent-based applications in various domains such as human simulation, social services and production optimization.

Acknowledgement. This work has been supported by the German Federal Ministry of Education and Research (BMBF) in MOMENTUM project (01IW22001), and the European Commission in WELCOME project (870930).

References

1. Alberternst, S., et al.: From things into clouds-and back. In: 2021 IEEE/ACM 21st International Symposium on Cluster, Cloud and Internet Computing (CCGrid), pp. 668–675. IEEE (2021)
2. Antakli, A., et al.: Agent-based web supported simulation of human-robot collaboration. In: Proceedings of the 15th International Conference on Web Information Systems and Technologies (WEBIST), pp. 88–99 (2019)
3. Antakli, A., Vozniak, I., Lipp, N., Klusch, M., Müller, C.: HAIL: modular agent-based pedestrian imitation learning. In: Dignum, F., Corchado, J.M., De La Prieta, F. (eds.) PAAMS 2021. LNCS (LNAI), vol. 12946, pp. 27–39. Springer, Cham (2021). https://doi.org/10.1007/978-3-030-85739-4_3
4. Bella, G., Cantone, D., Asmundo, M.N., Santamaria, D.F.: The ontology for agents, systems and integration of services: recent advancements of oasis. In: Proceedings of the 23th Workshop From Objects to Agents, pp. 1–2 (2022)
5. Challenger, M., Tezel, B.T., Alaca, O.F., Tekinerdogan, B., Kardas, G.: Development of semantic web-enabled BDI multi-agent systems using SEA_ML: an electronic bartering case study. Appl. Sci. **8**(5), 688 (2018)
6. Changder, N., Aknine, S., Ramchurn, S.D., Dutta, A.: Boss: a bi-directional search technique for optimal coalition structure generation with minimal overlapping. In: Proceedings of the AAAI Conference on Artificial Intelligence, vol. 35, pp. 15765–15766 (2021)

7. Charpenay, V., Zimmermann, A., Lefrançois, M., Boissier, O.: Hypermedea: a framework for web (of things) agents. In: Companion Proceedings of the Web Conference 2022, pp. 176–179 (2022)

8. Ciortea, A., Mayer, S., Gandon, F., Boissier, O., Ricci, A., Zimmermann, A.: A decade in hindsight: the missing bridge between multi-agent systems and the world wide web. In: AAMAS (2019)

9. Ciortea, A., Mayer, S., Michahelles, F.: Repurposing manufacturing lines on the fly with multi-agent systems for the web of things. In: AAMAS, pp. 813–822 (2018)

10. Colledanchise, M., Ögren, P.: Behavior Trees in Robotics and AI: An Introduction. CRC Press (2018)

11. Demarchi, F., Santos, E.R., Silveira, R.A.: Integration between agents and remote ontologies for the use of content on the semantic web. In: ICAART, pp. 125–132 (2018)

12. Rao, A.S., Georgeff, M.P.: BDI agents: from theory to practice. In: Proceedings of the First International Conference on Multi-Agent Systems (ICMAS 1995), pp. 312–319. AAAI (1995)

13. Sabbatini, F., Ciatto, G., Omicini, A.: Semantic web-based interoperability for intelligent agents with PSyKE. In: Calvaresi, D., Najjar, A., Winikoff, M., Främling, K. (eds.) EXTRAAMAS 2022. LNCS, vol. 13283, pp. 124–142. Springer, Cham (2022). https://doi.org/10.1007/978-3-031-15565-9_8

14. Schraudner, D.: Stigmergic multi-agent systems in the semantic web of things. In: Verborgh, R., et al. (eds.) ESWC 2021. LNCS, vol. 12739, pp. 218–229. Springer, Cham (2021). https://doi.org/10.1007/978-3-030-80418-3_34

15. Schubotz, R., Spieldenner, T., Chelli, M.: stigLD: stigmergic coordination of linked data agents. In: Pan, L., Cui, Z., Cai, J., Li, L. (eds.) BIC-TA 2021. CCIS, vol. 1566, pp. 174–190. Springer, Singapore (2022). https://doi.org/10.1007/978-981-19-1253-5_13

16. Spieldenner, D.: Poser: a semantic payload lowering service. In: Proceedings of the 18th International Conference on Web Information Systems and Technologies (WEBIST). SCITEPRESS (2022)

17. Spieldenner, T., Antakli, A.: Behavior trees as executable representation of Milner calculus notations. In: 2022 IEEE/WIC/ACM International Joint Conference on Web Intelligence and Intelligent Agent Technology (WI-IAT). IEEE (2022)

18. Suguri, H.: A standardization effort for agent technologies: the foundation for intelligent physical agents and its activities. In: Proceedings of the 32nd Annual Hawaii International Conference on Systems Sciences (HICSS-32), p. 10. IEEE (1999)

Adaptive Consumption by Continuous Negotiation

Ellie Beauprez, Anne-Cécile Caron⬤, Maxime Morge$^{(\boxtimes)}$⬤,
and Jean-Christophe Routier⬤

Univ. Lille, CNRS, Centrale Lille, UMR 9189 CRIStAL, 59000 Lille, France
`maxime.morge@univ-lille.fr`

Abstract. In this paper, we study the problem of allocating concurrent jobs composed of situated tasks, underlying the distributed deployment of the MapReduce design pattern on a cluster. In order to implement our multi-agent strategy which aims at minimising the mean flowtime of jobs, we propose a modular agent architecture that allows the concurrency of negotiation and consumption. Our experiments show that our reallocation strategy, when executed continuously during the consumption process: (1) improves the flowtime; (2) does not penalise the consumption; (3) is robust against execution hazards.

Keywords: Distributed problem solving · Agent cooperation and negotiation

1 Introduction

Data sciences exploit large datasets on which computations are performed in parallel by different nodes. These applications challenge distributed computing in terms of task allocation and load-balancing. This is the case for the practical application that we consider in this paper: the most common model for processing massive data on a cluster, i.e. the MapReduce design pattern [8]. The execution of jobs, that need be completed as soon as possible, consists of processing resources located on nodes. Since multiple resources are required to perform a task on a node, its execution may require the retrieval of resources available on other nodes, thereby incurring additional cost.

Many works adopt the multi-agent paradigm to address the problem of task reallocation and load-balancing [9]. The individual-centred approach allows the distribution of heuristics for problems that are impractical due to the combinatorial scheduling, thus allowing for scaling. Moreover, multi-agent reallocation methods are inherently reactive and adapt to imprecise estimates of runtimes and to perturbations (e.g. node slowdowns).

In [2], we have proposed a multi-agent reallocation strategy for a set of jobs to be executed as soon as possible. In order to minimise the flowtime, the agents, which are cooperative, negotiate to determine the next tasks to delegate or even swap. This strategy requires the distributed deployment of autonomous agents that consume tasks and continuously exchange some of them to balance the current allocation. In this paper, we formalize the task consumption and reallocation operations and we propose a modular agent architecture that allows for the concurrency of negotiation and consumption.

P. Mathieu et al. (Eds.): PAAMS 2023, LNAI 13955, pp. 28–39, 2023.
https://doi.org/10.1007/978-3-031-37616-0_3

According to the principle of separation of concerns, a first component agent is dedicated to the consumption (i.e. the execution) of tasks, a second to the negotiations and a third one to the local coordination of these operations through the management of the task bundle. The difficulty lies in designing the behaviour of agents that do not share a global state of the system (e.g. allocation) but they have local and partial knowledge. Our experiments show that our reallocation strategy, when executed continuously during the consumption process, does not penalise consumption and it can improve the flowtime by up to 37%, even when the agents have an imperfect knowledge of the environment, such as execution hazards.

After a review of related work in Sect. 2, we recall in Sect. 3 the formalization of the problem of job allocation composed of situated tasks. Section 4 formalizes the consumption/reallocation operations. Then, we describe in Sect. 5 how the consumption and reallocation processes are intertwined. We detail our agent architecture in Sect. 6. Section 7 presents our experimental results. Section 8 summarises our contribution and presents our perspectives.

2 Related Work

Many papers have addressed the problem of task reassignment. The individual-centred approach overcomes the limitations of centralised solutions: the impossibility of solving large-scale problems and the low responsiveness to changes [9]. In particular, the dynamic task allocation problems require to propose processes that continuously adapt to changes in the execution environment or the performance of the executors [10]. Most of these works are based on the consensus-based bundle algorithm [5] which is a multi-agent task assignment method that: (a) selects the tasks to be negotiated through an auction process; (b) determines the bids that win these auctions by resolving potential conflicts. In particular, our modular agent architecture is largely inspired by [1]. However, our agents do not aim at minimising the makespan but the flowtime. Furthermore, we prefer here a bilateral protocol which allows, through the choice of the interlocutor, to make targeted proposals and thus to reduce the computational and communication costs associated with the negotiation. Finally, the simulation of the execution environment allows us to control its perturbations.

Chen *et al.* consider dynamic task allocation problems where tasks are released at uncertain times [4]. They propose to continuously adjust the task allocation by combining the local rescheduling of agents with task reallocation between agents. Similarly, our multi-agent strategy relies on a consumption strategy to define the local task scheduling and on a negotiation strategy for the tasks to be reallocated. Contrary to [4], we assume that the set of jobs is initially known, but our agents may have imperfect knowledge of the execution environment.

Most of the work, that considers that perturbations in the execution environment vary the task costs, rely on operations research techniques such as sensitivity analysis to assess the robustness of optima to perturbations, incremental methods to repair the initial optimal allocation when costs change, or combinatorial optimisation to exploit the measures of degradation [12]. Similarly, our strategy measures the gap between expected and observed progress in order to modify the allocation. However, our individual-centred approach allows us to solve large-scale problems.

Creech *et al.* address the problem of resource allocation and task hierarchy in distributed multi-agent systems for dynamic environments [6]. They propose an algorithm that combines updating and prioritisation algorithms, as well as reinforcement learning techniques. Contrary to learning techniques, our solution requires no prior model of either the data or the environment, and no exploration phase as this would not be relevant for the practical applications we are concerned with. In fact, the volume of data makes preprocessing and exploration too expensive. Moreover, the variability of the data makes it quickly obsolete.

Our previous experiments have shown that the flowtime achieved by our strategy is better than that achieved with distributed constrained optimisation (DCOP) techniques and remains close to that obtained with a classical heuristic, with in all cases a significantly reduced rescheduling time [2]. In this paper, we show how to deploy this strategy in a continuous way during the consumption process.

3   Problem

This section recalls the formalisation introduced in [2] of the task allocation problem with concurrent jobs composed of situated tasks. A distributed system consists of a set of computing nodes. These tasks require transferable and non-consumable resources that are distributed among different resource nodes.

Definition 1. *A **distributed system** is quadruple* $\mathcal{D} = \langle \mathcal{P}, \mathcal{N}_r, \mathcal{E}, \mathcal{R} \rangle$ *where:*

- $\mathcal{P}$ *is a set of p computing nodes;*
- $\mathcal{N}_r$ *is a set of de r resource nodes;*
- $\mathcal{E} : \mathcal{P} \times \mathcal{N}_r \to \{\top, \bot\}$ *is a neighborhood property that evaluates whether a computing node of $\mathcal{P}$ is local to a resource node in $\mathcal{N}_r$;*
- $\mathcal{R} = \{\rho_1, \ldots, \rho_k\}$ *is a set of resources of size $|\rho_i|$. The location of resources, which are eventually replicated, is determined by the function $l : \mathcal{R} \to 2^{\mathcal{N}_r}$.*

A resource can be local or remote to a computing node, depending on whether it is present on a resource node in the vicinity of the node. From this, we define the locality predicate: $\forall v_c \in \mathcal{P}, \forall \rho \in \mathcal{R}$, $\mathrm{local}(\rho, v_c)$ iff $\exists v_r \in l(\rho)$ s.t. $\mathcal{E}(v_c, v_r)$. Resources are accessible to all computing nodes, including those on remote resource nodes.

A job is a set of independent, non-divisible and non-preemptible tasks. The execution of each task requires access to resources distributed on the nodes of the system. The execution of a job (without a deadline) consists of the execution all its tasks.

Definition 2. *Let $\mathcal{D}$ be a distributed system. We consider a set of ℓ **jobs** $\mathcal{J} = \{J_1, \ldots, J_\ell\}$. Each job J_i, with the release time $t_{J_i}^0$, is a non-empty set of k_i **tasks** $J_i = \{\tau_1, \ldots, \tau_{k_i}\}$.*

We denote $\mathcal{T} = \cup_{1 \leq i \leq \ell} J_i$ the set of n tasks for $\mathcal{J}$ and $\mathcal{R}_\tau \subseteq \mathcal{R}$ the set of resources required by the task τ. For the sake of brevity, we note $\mathrm{job}(\tau)$ the job containing the task τ. We assume that that the number of jobs is negligible compared to the number of tasks, $|\mathcal{J}| << |\mathcal{T}|$.

The cost of a task for a node v_i is an estimate *a priori* of its runtime.

Definition 3. *Let $\mathcal{D}$ be a distributed system and $\mathcal{T}$ be a set of tasks. The **cost function** $c : \mathcal{T} \times \mathcal{N} \mapsto \mathbb{R}^*_+$ is such that:*

$$c(\tau, v_j) = \sum_{\rho_j \in \mathcal{R}_\tau} c(\rho_j, v_j) \text{ with } c(\rho_j, v_i) = \begin{cases} |\rho_j| \text{ if } local(\rho_j, v_i) \\ \kappa \times |\rho_j| \text{ with } \kappa > 1 \text{ otherwise.} \end{cases} \quad (1)$$

Since gathering remote resources is an additional cost, a task is more expensive if the resources required are "less local". The cost function can be extended to a set of tasks : $\forall T \subseteq \mathcal{T}, \ c(T, v_i) = \Sigma_{\tau \in T} c(\tau, v_i)$.

Essentially, we consider the problem of allocating jobs consisting of situated tasks.

Definition 4. *A **situated task allocation problem** is a quadruple $STAP = \langle \mathcal{D}, \mathcal{T}, \mathcal{J}, c \rangle$ where:*

- *$\mathcal{D}$ is a distributed system of m computing nodes;*
- *$\mathcal{T} = \{\tau_1, \ldots, \tau_n\}$ is a set of n tasks;*
- *$\mathcal{J} = \{J_1, \ldots, J_\ell\}$ is a partitioning of tasks in ℓ jobs;*
- *$c : \mathcal{T} \times \mathcal{N} \mapsto \mathbb{R}^*_+$ is the cost function.*

A task allocation is an assignment of sorted bundles to different nodes.

Definition 5. *An **allocation** for a STAP problem at time t is a vector of m sorted bundles $\overrightarrow{A_t} = ((B_{1,t}, \prec_1), \ldots, (B_{m,t}, \prec_m))$ where each bundle $(B_{i,t}, \prec_i)$ is the set of tasks $(B_{i,t} \subseteq \mathcal{T})$ assigned to the node v_i at time t, associated with a strict and total scheduling order $(\prec_i \subseteq \mathcal{T} \times \mathcal{T})$. $\tau_j \prec_i \tau_k$ means that if $\tau_j, \tau_k \in B_{i,t}$ then τ_j is executed before τ_k by v_i. The allocation $\overrightarrow{A_t}$ is such that:*

$$\forall \tau \in \mathcal{T}, \ \exists v_i \in \mathcal{N}, \ \tau \in B_{i,t} \quad (2)$$

$$\forall v_i \in \mathcal{N}, \forall v_j \in \mathcal{N} \setminus \{v_i\}, \ B_{i,t} \cap B_{j,t} = \emptyset \quad (3)$$

All the tasks are assigned (Eq. 2) and each task is assigned to a single node (Eq. 3). For the sake of brevity, we denote $\overrightarrow{B_{i,t}} = (B_{i,t}, \prec_i)$, the sorted bundle of v_i; $\min_{\prec_i} B_{i,t}$, the next task to be executed by v_i; and $v(\tau, \overrightarrow{A_t})$, the node whose bundle contains τ in $\overrightarrow{A_t}$.

In order to assess the quality of a job allocation, we consider the mean flowtime which measures the average time elapsed between the release date of the jobs and their completion date.

Definition 6. *Let STAP be a problem and $\overrightarrow{A_t}$ be an allocation at time t. We define:*

- *the waiting time of the task τ in the bundle $\overrightarrow{B_{i,t}}$,*
  $\Delta(\tau, v_i) = \Sigma_{\tau' \in B_{i,t} | \tau' \prec_i \tau} c(\tau', v_i)$
- *the completion time of the task $\tau \in \mathcal{T}$ for the allocation $\overrightarrow{A_t}$,*
  $C_\tau(\overrightarrow{A_t}) = \Delta(\tau, v(\tau, \overrightarrow{A_t})) + t - t^0_{job(\tau)} + c(\tau, v(\tau, \overrightarrow{A_t}))$
- *the completion time of the job $J \in \mathcal{J}$ for $\overrightarrow{A_t}$,*
  $C_J(\overrightarrow{A_t}) = \max_{\tau \in J} \{C_\tau(\overrightarrow{A_t})\}$
- *the **mean flowtime** of $\mathcal{J}$ for $\overrightarrow{A_t}$,*

$$C_{mean}(\overrightarrow{A_t}) = \frac{1}{\ell} C(\overrightarrow{A_t}) \text{ with } C(\overrightarrow{A_t}) = \Sigma_{J \in \mathcal{J}} C_J(\overrightarrow{A_t}) \quad (4)$$

The waiting time measures the time from the current time t until the task τ is executed.

4 Operations

Here we formalise the operations of task consumption and reallocation. A task consumption by a node consists in the latter removing this task from its bundle to execute it. The completion of a task is a disruptive event that changes not only the allocation of tasks but also the underlying problem.

Definition 7. *Let STAP = $\langle \mathcal{D}, \mathcal{T}, \mathcal{J}, c \rangle$ be a problem and $\overrightarrow{A_t}$ be an allocation. The **consumption at time** t **by the node** v_i, whose bundle is not empty ($B_{i,t} \neq \emptyset$), leads to the allocation $\overrightarrow{A_t}' = \lambda(v_i, \overrightarrow{B_{i,t}})$ for the problem STAP' = $\langle \mathcal{D}, \mathcal{T}', \mathcal{J}', c \rangle$ where:*

$$\mathcal{T}' = \mathcal{T} \setminus \{\min_{\prec_i} B_{i,t}\} \tag{5}$$

$$\mathcal{J}' = \begin{cases} \mathcal{J} \setminus \{job(\min_{\prec_i} B_{i,t})\} & if\ job(\min_{\prec_i} B_{i,t}) = \{\min_{\prec_i} B_{i,t}\} \\ \mathcal{J} & otherwise \end{cases} \tag{6}$$

In the latter case:

$$\forall J_j \in \mathcal{J}\ \exists J'_j \in \mathcal{J}'\ s.t.\ J'_j = \begin{cases} J_j \setminus \{\min_{\prec_i} B_{i,t}\}\ if\ job(\min_{\prec_i} B_{i,t}) = J_j \\ J_j\ otherwise \end{cases} \tag{7}$$

and $\overrightarrow{A_t}' = (\overrightarrow{B_{1,t}}', ..., \overrightarrow{B_{m,t}}')$ *with* $\overrightarrow{B_{j,t}}' = \begin{cases} \overrightarrow{B_{i,t} \ominus \min_{\prec_i} B_{i,t}} & if\ j = i \\ \overrightarrow{B_{j,t}} & otherwise \end{cases} \tag{8}$

When a task is consumed, it is removed not only from the resulting problem in the task set but also from the corresponding job. The latter can also be removed if the task was the only (last) task in the job. The resulting allocation is also changed. The task is removed from the bundle it was in. The tasks are intended to be consumed one by one until the empty allocation is reached.

A task consumption causes the *flowtime* to decrease locally, at time t:
$\Sigma_{J \in \mathcal{J}} C_J(\lambda(v_i, \overrightarrow{B_{i,t}})) < \Sigma_{J \in \mathcal{J}} C_J(\overrightarrow{B_{i,t}})$. This is not always the case over time since the effective costs of tasks may differ from the estimated costs. If a task turns out to be more expensive than expected when it is performed, the flowtime may increase after a task has been consumed, as in Example 1.

Example 1. Let STAP = $\langle \mathcal{D}, \mathcal{T}, \mathcal{J}, c \rangle$ be a problem with:

- $\mathcal{D} = \langle \mathcal{P}, \mathcal{N}_r, \mathcal{E}, \mathcal{R} \rangle$, a distributed system with a single computing node $\mathcal{P} = \{v_1\}$ associated with a single resource node $\mathcal{N}_r = \{v_1^r\}$, such that $\mathcal{E}(v_1, v_1^r) = \top$ and a single resource $\mathcal{R} = \{\rho_1\}$ over the resource node v_1^r;
- two tasks $\mathcal{T} = \{\tau_1, \tau_2\}$;
- a single job $\mathcal{J} = \{J_1\}$ released at $t_{J_1}^0 = 0$ composed of the two tasks $J_1 = \{\tau_1, \tau_2\}$;
- the cost functions c such that $c(\tau_1, v_1) = 2$ and $c(\tau_2, v_1) = 4$.

The allocation $\overrightarrow{A_0} = (\overrightarrow{B_{1,t}})$ with $\overrightarrow{B_{1,t}} = (\tau_1, \tau_2)$. According to Eq. 4, the flowtime is $C_{mean}(\overrightarrow{A_0}) = C_{J_1}(\overrightarrow{A_0}) = C_{\tau_2}(\overrightarrow{A_0}) = \Delta(\tau_2, v_1) + t + t_{J_1}^0 + c(\tau_2, v_1) = c(\tau_1, \overrightarrow{A_t}) + 0 + 0 + c(\tau_2, v_1) = 2 + 4 = 6$.

If the consumption of τ_1 ends at time $t_1 = 3$, it means that this task turns out to be more expensive than expected when running. Therefore, the flowtime of $\overrightarrow{A_{t_1}} = (\overrightarrow{B_{v_1, t_1}})$ with $B_{v_1, t_1} = (\tau_2)$ is $C_{mean}(\overrightarrow{A_{t_1}}) = C_{J_1}(\overrightarrow{A_{t_1}}) = t_1 + t_{J_1}^0 + c(\tau_2, v_1) = 3 + 0 + 4 = 7 > C_{mean}(\overrightarrow{A_0})$.

We consider an operation where some tasks are moved from one bundle to another.

Definition 8. *Let* $\overrightarrow{A_t} = (\overrightarrow{B_{1,t}}, \ldots, \overrightarrow{B_{m,t}})$ *be an allocation of the problem STAP =* $\langle \mathcal{D}, \mathcal{J}, \mathcal{J}, c \rangle$ *at time t. The **bilateral reallocation** ot the non-empty list of tasks* T_1 *assigned to the proposer* v_i *in exchange for the list of tasks* T_2 *assigned to the responder* v_j *in* $\overrightarrow{A_t}$ *($T_1 \subseteq B_{i,t}$ and $T_2 \subseteq B_{j,t}$) leads to the allocation* $\gamma(T_1, T_2, v_i, v_j, \overrightarrow{A_t})$ *with m bundles s.t.:*

$$\gamma(T_1, T_2, v_i, v_j, \overrightarrow{B_{k,t}}) = \begin{cases} \overrightarrow{B_{i,t} \ominus T_1 \oplus T_2} & if\ k = i, \\ \overrightarrow{B_{j,t} \ominus T_2 \oplus T_1} & if\ k = j, \\ \overrightarrow{B_{k,t}} & otherwise \end{cases} \tag{9}$$

If T_2 *is empty, the reallocation is called a delegation. Otherwise, it is a swap.*

We restrict ourselves here to bilateral reallocations, but multilateral reallocations deserve to be explored.

Contrary to most other works (e.g. [7]), our agents are not individually rational but they have a common goal that overrides their individual interests: to reduce the flowtime.

Definition 9. *Let* $\overrightarrow{A_t}$ *be an allocation at time t for the problem STAP =* $\langle \mathcal{D}, \mathcal{J}, \mathcal{J}, c \rangle$*. The bilateral reallocation* $\gamma(T_1, T_2, v_i, v_j, \overrightarrow{A_t})$ *is **socially rational** iff the flowtime decreases,* $C(\gamma(T_1, T_2, v_i, v_j, \overrightarrow{A_t})) < C(\overrightarrow{A_t})$.

An allocation is said to be **stable** if there is no socially rational reallocation. In [2], we have shown the termination of the process that iterates this type of reallocation.

5   Process

In order to carry out the consumption and reallocation processes simultaneously, we consider two types of agents: (a) node agents, each of which represents a computing node (cf Sect. 6); (b) the supervisor, which synchronises the phases of the negotiation process.

The consumption process consists of the concurrent or sequential execution of the different tasks by the computing nodes under the supervision of their agent. The reallocation process consists of multiple local reallocations that are the results of bilateral negotiations between node agents, performed sequentially or concurrently. These processes are complementary. While consumption is continuous, agents negotiate their task bundles up to the point where a stable allocation is reached. A task consumption can make an allocation unstable and thus trigger new negotiations. The consumption process ends when all tasks have been executed. It is worth noting that this multi-agent system is inherently adaptive. Indeed, if a task turns out to be more expensive than expected, because the runtime was underestimated or the running node is slowed down, then the reallocation process, which runs continuously, allows the allocation to be balanced by taking into account the actual cost of the task.

The **consumption strategy** of node agents, detailed in [2], specifies the scheduling of tasks executed by the node for which they are responsible. In order to reduce the flowtime, this strategy executes the tasks of the least expensive jobs before those of the most expensive jobs.

The **negotiation strategy** of node agents, also detailed in [2], which is based on a peer model, in particular a belief base built from the messages exchanged, determines whether a reallocation is socially rational according to the agent's beliefs. The agents have: (a) an offer strategy which proposes bilateral reallocations; (b) an acceptance rule that evaluates whether a proposal is socially rational before accepting or rejecting it; and (c) a counteroffer strategy that selects a counterparty to a delegation to propose a task swap.

The negotiation process consists of two successive stages: (1) agents propose the delegations which they consider socially rational and which are accepted or rejected by their peers; (2) agents propose delegations which are not necessarily socially rational but which are likely to trigger counter-offers and thus socially rational swap. The stages of negotiation alternate successively in a way that is concurrent with consumption.

6   Architecture

For the design of a node agent, we adopt a modular architecture that allows concurrent negotiation and consumption. A node agent is a composite agent consisting of 3 component ones (cf Fig. 2a), each with a limited role: the **worker** executes (consumes) tasks; the **negotiator** updates a belief base for negotiating tasks with peers; the **manager** handles the task bundle of the computing node to schedule the worker by adding or deleting tasks according to the bilateral reallocations bargained by the negotiator.

In order to prioritise task consumption, as soon as the manager is informed that the worker is free, the manager gives to the worker the next task to run in accordance with the consumption strategy, even if this means cancelling the reallocation of this task during the negotiation. This task is then no longer eligible for a potential reallocation.

We represent here the interactions between the component agents with interaction diagrams where solid arrow heads represent synchronous calls, open arrow heads represent asynchronous messages, and dashed lines represent reply messages.

After the manager has given to the worker a task, the worker informs the manager when it has been completed (cf Fig. 1a). In order to give priority to the consumption over the negotiation, the query of the worker for the next task to run takes priority and preempts the manager's interactions with the negotiator. To refine its estimate of the waiting time for the tasks in its bundle, the manager can ask the worker for an estimate of the remaining runtime for the current task (cf Fig. 1a).

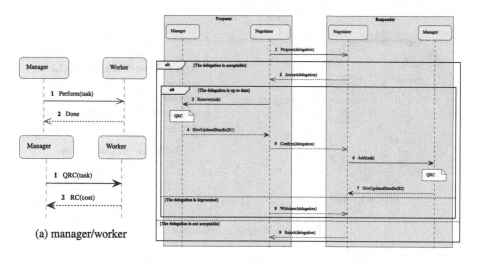

(a) manager/worker

(b) manager/negotiator

Fig. 1. Interactions between the manager, the worker and the negotiator

In a first negotiation stage, the agents negotiate delegations (cf Fig. 1b). To confirm such a bilateral reallocation, the proposer's negotiator synchronously asks the manager to update the task bundle so that it can update its belief base before engaging in new negotiations. After this confirmation, the responder's negotiator does the same. The QRC tag indicates that the manager interacts with the worker according to the protocol in Fig. 1a in order to take into account the remaining runtime for the current task. In a second negotiation stage, the agents bargains task swapping and the interactions are similar.

Despite our modular architecture, the main difficulty lies in the design of the behaviours of the agents, which are specified in [3] by automata[1], and whose complexity is measured in Fig. 2b with the number of states, transitions and lines of code.

The **worker** is either free or busy to run a task and it can therefore estimate the remaining runtime of the current task.

The **manager** handles the task bundle and coordinates the task consumptions of the worker with the reallocations bargained by the negotiator. When the latter informs the manager that there is no more socially rational delegations to propose and that the negotiator is waiting for proposals from peers, the manager informs the supervisor. The manager also continues to distribute tasks to the worker until the bundle is empty. Informed that no node agent detects a reallocation opportunity, the supervisor triggers the next negotiation stage. Finally, the supervisor completes the process when it learns from the managers that all tasks have been consumed.

The **negotiator** responds to the proposals of its peers and updates its belief base, which make it possible to detect reallocation opportunities. After proposing a delega-

---

[1] https://gitlab.univ-lille.fr/maxime.morge/smastaplus/-/tree/worker/doc/specification.

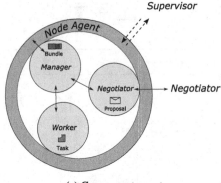

(a) Component agents

Agent	States	Transitions	Lines
worker	2	7	173
manager	5	23	465
negotiator	9	74	1306
supervisor	9	69	626

(b) Behaviour Complexity

Fig. 2. Node Agent Architecture

tion, the negotiator waits for an acceptance, a rejection or a counter-proposal before a deadline. When the negotiator has accepted a proposal or made a counter-proposal, its waits for a confirmation or a withdrawal from its interlocutor (if the task has been consumed). When the negotiator has confirmed its acceptance of a counteroffer, it also waits for a double-confirmation. When the offer strategy does not suggests delegation, the belief base is updated until a new opportunity is found.

7 Experiments

Our experiments aim to validate that the strategy of reallocation, when applied continuously during the consumption: (1) improves the flowtime; (2) does not penalise the consumption; (3) is robust against execution hazards (i.e. node slowdowns). We present here our metrics, our experimental protocol and our results[2].

Instead of the expected execution time (Eq. 1), we consider here $c^S(\tau, \nu)$, the effective cost for the node ν to perform the task:

– with a perfect knowledge of the computing environment, $c^{S_E}(\tau, \nu_i) = c(\tau, \nu_i)$
– with the slowing down of half of the nodes,

$$c^{S_H}(\tau, \nu_i) = \begin{cases} 2 \times c(\tau, \nu_i) & \text{if } i \bmod 2 = 1 \\ c(\tau, \nu_i) & \text{otherwise} \end{cases} \quad (10)$$

Therefore, we distinguish: the **simulated flowtime** $C^S_{mean}(\overrightarrow{A_t})$ according to the effective costs; the **realised flowtime** $C^R_{mean}(\overrightarrow{A_t})$ according to the task completion times which are measured. We define the **rate of performance improvement**: $\Gamma = \frac{C^R_{mean}(\overrightarrow{A_0}) - C^R_{mean}(\overrightarrow{A_e})}{C^R_{mean}(\overrightarrow{A_0})}$ where $\overrightarrow{A_e}$ is the allocation when the tasks are performed and $\overrightarrow{A_0}$ is the initial allocation. The rate of performance improvement is positive if the realised

---

[2] The experiments are reproducible using the following instructions: https://gitlab.univ-lille.fr/ maxime.morge/smastaplus/-/tree/master/doc/experiments.

flowtime obtained by the reallocation process is better (i.e. lower) than that of the initial allocation.

Our prototype [3] is implemented using the Scala programming language and the Akka library [11] which is suitable for highly concurrent, distributed, and resilient message-driven applications. Experiments have been conducted on a blade with 20 CPUs and 512Go RAM. The fact that, in our experiments, the difference between the realised flowtime and the simulated flowtime of the initial allocation ($C^R_{mean}(\overrightarrow{A_0})$ − $C^S_{mean}(\overrightarrow{A_0})$), which measures the cost of the infrastructure, is negligible supports this technological choice.

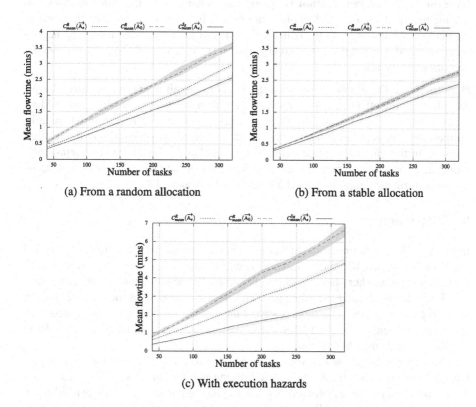

(a) From a random allocation   (b) From a stable allocation

(c) With execution hazards

Fig. 3. The strategy of reallocation improves the flowtime

The experimental protocol consists of randomly generating 25 initial allocations for different $STAP$ problems. We have empirically chosen $\kappa = 2$ as a realistic value to capture the overhead of fetching remote resources in a homogeneous network. We consider $m = 8$ nodes, $l = 4$ jobs, $n \in [40; 320]$ tasks with 10 resources per task. Each resource ρ_i is replicated 3 times and $|\rho_i| \in [0; 500]$. In order to avoid unnecessary negotiations due to the asynchronicity of the consumption operations, we assume in our experiments that a bilateral reallocation is socially rational if it decreases the flowtime by at least one second.

Hypothesis 1: The reallocation strategy improves the flowtime. We assume here that the initial allocations are random and that agents have perfect knowledge of the environment (c^{S_E}). Figure 3a shows the medians and standard deviations of our metrics as functions of the number of tasks. We observe that the realised flowtime of the reallocation is better than the realised flowtime of the initial allocation and it is bounded by the simulated flowtime of the reallocation (if an oracle computes the reallocation in constant time). Our strategy improves the *flowtime* by continuously reallocating the remote tasks whose delegation reduces their costs during the consumption process. The rate of performance improvement (Γ) is between 20% and 37%.

Hypothesis 2: The reallocation strategy does not penalise the consumption. We assume here that the initial allocations are stable. In Fig. 3b, the realised flowtime of the reallocation is similar to the realised flowtime of the initial allocation. The negotiation overhead is negligible since no negotiation is triggered if the agents consider the allocation to be stable.

Hypothesis 3: The reallocation strategy is robust against execution hazards. We consider here the effective cost of the tasks, which simulates the slowing down of half of the nodes, c^{S_H}. In Fig. 3c, the flowtimes have doubled due to execution hazards. Furthermore, the realised flowtime of the reallocation remains better than the realised flowtime of the initial allocation despite imperfect knowledge of the computing environment. Taking into account the effective runtimes of the tasks already executed, the rate of performance improvement (Γ) is between 30% and 37%.

8 Discussion

In order to design autonomous agents that simultaneously perform consumption and reallocation, we have proposed a modular agent architecture composed of three component agents: the worker which performs the tasks; the negotiator which bargains reallocations with peers; and the manager which locally coordinates these operations by managing the task bundle. Without knowing the global state of the system, i.e. the allocation, these agents have local knowledge (e.g. the current task, the task bundle) and beliefs that guide their behaviour.

Our experiments show that the rate of performance improvement due to our reallocation strategy, when used continuously during the consumption process, can reach 37%. Furthermore, the negotiation overhead is negligible since it is suspended when the allocation is stable. Finally, even if some nodes are slowed down, our strategy of reallocation adapts to the execution context by distributing more tasks to the nodes that are not slowed down since it takes into account the effective runtime of the tasks already executed, without requiring a learning phase.

A sensitivity analysis of the influence of the replication factor, of the remote resource fetch overhead (κ) and of the negotiation timeout is beyond the scope of this article, but would deserve a thorough study. We would also like to evaluate the responsiveness of our strategy to the release of jobs over time.

More generally, our future work will focus on integrating task reallocation into a provisioning process that adds or removes computing nodes at runtime according to user needs in order to propose an elastic multi-agent strategy for scalability.

References

1. Baert, Q., Caron, A.C., Morge, M., Routier, J.C., Stathis, K.: An adaptive multi-agent system for task reallocation in a MapReduce job. J. Parallel Distrib. Comput. **153**, 75–88 (2021)
2. Beauprez, E., Caron, A.C., Morge, M., Routier, J.C.: Task bundle delegation for reducing the flowtime. In: Rocha, A.P., Steels, L., van den Herik, J. (eds.) ICAART 2021. LNCS, vol. 13251, pp. 22–45. Springer, Cham (2022). https://doi.org/10.1007/978-3-031-10161-8_2
3. Beauprez, E., Morge, M.: Scala implementation of the Extended Multi-agents Situated Task Allocation (2020). https://gitlab.univ-lille.fr/maxime.morge/smastaplus
4. Chen, Y., Mao, X., Hou, F., Wang, Q., Yang, S.: Combining re-allocating and re-scheduling for dynamic multi-robot task allocation. In: Proceedings of SMC, pp. 395–400 (2016)
5. Choi, H.L., Brunet, L., How, J.P.: Consensus-based decentralized auctions for robust task allocation. IEEE Trans. Rob. **25**(4), 912–926 (2009)
6. Creech, N., Pacheco, N.C., Miles, S.: Resource allocation in dynamic multiagent systems. CoRR abs/2102.08317 (2021)
7. Damamme, A., Beynier, A., Chevaleyre, Y., Maudet, N.: The power of swap deals in distributed resource allocation. In: Proceedings of AAMAS, pp. 625–633 (2015)
8. Dean, J., Ghemawat, S.: MapReduce: simplified data processing on large clusters. In: Proceedings of OSDI, pp. 137–150 (2004)
9. Jiang, Y.: A survey of task allocation and load balancing in distributed systems. IEEE Trans. Parallel Distrib. Syst. **27**(2), 585–599 (2016)
10. Lerman, K., Jones, C., Galstyan, A., Matarić, M.J.: Analysis of dynamic task allocation in multi-robot systems. Int. J. Robot. Res. **25**(3), 225–241 (2006)
11. Lightbend: Akka is the implementation of the actor model on the JVM (2020). http://akka.io
12. Mayya, S., D'antonio, D.S., Saldaña, D., Kumar, V.: Resilient task allocation in heterogeneous multi-robot systems. IEEE Robot. Autom. Lett. **6**(2), 1327–1334 (2021)

When Extrinsic Payoffs Meet Intrinsic Expectations

Janvi Chhabra$^{(\boxtimes)}$, Karthik Sama , Jayati Deshmukh ,
and Srinath Srinivasa

International Institute of Information Technology, Bangalore, Bangalore, India
{janvi.chhabra,sai.karthik,sri}@iiitb.ac.in, jayati.deshmukh@iiitb.org

Abstract. Rational interactions between agents are often confounded due to disparity in their latent, *intrinsic motivations*. We address this problem by modelling interactions between agents with disparate intrinsic motivations in different kinds of social networks. Agents are modelled with a variegated profile over the following kinds of intrinsic motivations: *power*, *achievement*, and *affiliation*. These agents interact with their one-hop neighbours in the network through the game of Iterated Prisoners' Dilemma and evolve their intrinsic profiles. A network is considered settled or stable, when each agent's extrinsic payoff matches its intrinsic expectation. We then address how different network-level parameters affect the network stability. We observe that the distribution of intrinsic profiles in a stable network remains invariant to changes in network-level parameters over networks with the same average degree. Further, a high proportion of affiliation agents, who tend to cooperate, are required for various networks to reach a stable state.

Keywords: multi-agent systems · intrinsic motivation · game theory

1 Introduction

Evolution of cooperation among self-interested agents, has been in research focus over the years [1,16,18,20]. Conventionally, reciprocity, iterated interactions with memory, and ability for agents to evolve their strategies over time, have been found to be conducive for the evolution of cooperation. However, interactions among human rational agents are complicated by the fact that humans may possess different forms of *intrinsic motivations* that affect how they value different extrinsic payoffs.

Intrinsic motivation and its effects have received a lot of research interest in the fields of psychology, organisation theory and behavioural economics [5,7,10,11,22,24,26]. More recently Heckhausen & Heckhausen used motivational psychology, to elaborate motivated behaviour in agents by proposing three fundamental drivers for intrinsic motivation, namely: power, achievement, and affiliation [7]. Another reason for modelling intrinsic motivation is

---

J. Chhabra and K. Sama—These authors contributed equally to this work.

P. Mathieu et al. (Eds.): PAAMS 2023, LNAI 13955, pp. 40–51, 2023.
https://doi.org/10.1007/978-3-031-37616-0_4

to understand and design autonomous agency in highly complex and uncertain environments [9] as in such cases, it is difficult to model preferences of agents in advance.

In this paper, we visit the problem of intrinsic motivation from the context of multi-agent interactions, specifically based on the intrinsic motivation framework of Heckhausen & Heckhausen [7]. An intrinsic motivation of *power* aims to dominate a rational interaction to not only maximise one's payoffs but also increase the disparity between oneself and others. The motivational profile called *achievement* primarily strives to maximise one's own payoff without recourse to how others fare. Finally, the motivational profile of *affiliation* aims to "belong," and values the establishment and maintenance of relationships, over maximising one's payoffs or dominance.

We model a network of agents with these intrinsic profiles in the setting of iterated Prisoners' Dilemma. We propose that an intrinsic profile agent is satisfied when the external payoffs received by the agent lie within its intrinsic expectations. When an agent is not satisfied it evolves its intrinsic profiles. We then study what network-level parameters influence the settled proportions of satisfied agents.

2   Related Work

In this section, we discuss some of the work which has been done in the area of modelling intrinsic motivation in autonomous agents. The relevance of intrinsic motivation in human decision-making process has been discussed by Morse [15] through the concept of extrinsic incentives bias [6]. This bias questions the belief that people are motivated more by extrinsic rewards than intrinsic incentives. People often perform actions that are not always about maximising their extrinsic rewards. For example, actions like volunteering, social welfare, etc. [22] are performed since these have high intrinsic value despite having a low extrinsic reward.

A variety of psychological motivation theories also model intrinsic motivation in humans and animals [2,3,19]. Some of these theories have been used to build computational models for autonomous agents having different intrinsic motivations [17]. The focus of these works has been to design agents having different kinds of profiles, to exhibit diverse and more realistic behaviours.

Intrinsic motivation has also been modelled in robots, agents in Reinforcement Learning (RL) and Multi-Agent Reinforcement Learning (MARL) setups. These frameworks enable the incorporation of diverse behavioural agents in a network. Specifically, intrinsic motivation and curiosity are useful to incorporate exploratory behaviour in agents [8]. Barto [4] argues that it is possible to incorporate intrinsic motivation in autonomous agents using RL-based techniques, specifically using Intrinsically Motivated Reinforcement Learning (IMRL) framework [25] and its extensions [21]. He posits that modelling intrinsic motivation which embodies desirable standards will be useful to build autonomous agents with *competent autonomy*, where the agents can reliably operate in new environments.

The 'Influential trio' proposed by Heckhausen and Heckhausen [7] origins from the attempts to model the motivation of agents from an intrinsic perspective. This trio comprises of three intrinsic motivation profiles– agents motivated by power, achievement, and affiliation. Merrick and Shafi [13,14] have modelled these motivation profiles in game theoretic setting. They also present results of intrinsically motivated agents playing a variety of mixed-motive games like Prisoners' Dilemma, Battle of the sexes, Chicken game, etc. They model how the agents with different motivation profiles perceive the same games differently.

Agents with adaptive behaviour have been modelled in spatial Prisoners' Dilemma scenario where the adaptive behaviour of agents is modelled in terms of expectations [27]. Intrinsic motivation is relevant not just in the case of single agents but also in a multi-agent setup where agents interact with each other [12]. Agents update their intrinsic motivation profiles based on their interactions with other agents in the system and on the type of their neighbourhood profile using genetic algorithms [23]. We study interaction of intrinsically motivated agents in different kinds of networks where they evolve their intrinsic profiles using the process of belief revision.

3   Modelling Intrinsic Motivation

In this section, we elaborate on how we model intrinsic motivation in a network of autonomous agents. We briefly discuss how the Influential Trio [7] perceive the game of Prisoners' Dilemma in a two-player setting. Then we extend these interactions between agents with different intrinsic profiles to the network level. Finally, we discuss the process of belief revision in the context of these intrinsically motivated agents.

3.1   Prisoners' Dilemma with Intrinsic Profiles

Prisoners' Dilemma(PD) models the situation where players can choose to either Cooperate, C or Defect, D. Table 1 represents the payoff matrix of the game. When both players choose to cooperate, they get a payoff R (reward for cooperation). However, as long as one cooperates, it rationally makes sense for the other to defect and get a higher payoff T (temptation to defect). In this case, the other player gets a lower payoff S (suckers payoff). Lastly when both the players defect each other, they get a low payoff of P (punishment for defection). The D(defect) is the dominant strategy and game state DD is the Nash equilibrium for the PD game. In this game, payoff values follow the inequalities, $T > R > P > S$ and $R > (S + T)/2$ [1].

For each of the intrinsically motivated profile from the influential trio, Merrick and Shafi [13] define an optimally motivating incentive, I^*. Each agent tries to minimise the difference between the I^* and received payoff. We extend the I^* range for affiliation agents from $[S, \frac{P+S}{2}]$ defined by Merrick and Shafi [13] to $[S, R)$, this would make the spectrum of expectation ranges continuous, which becomes crucial in the belief revision logic, discussed in Sect. 3.2. For each intrinsic profile, the corresponding ranges of I^*, can be referred from table in the Fig. 1. Based on the values of I^*, agents perceive the payoff differently as T', R', P', S', which is elaborated in work of Merrick and Shafi [13].

3.2 Network of Intrinsically Motivated Agents

We extend these notions of intrinsic profiles in an one-shot PD to a network of interactions with an evolutionary variant. In a network of agents, each agent is initialised with one of the three intrinsic profiles. Every agent plays a Prisoners' Dilemma game with its one-hop neighbours. We now describe the modelling of behaviour of these agents in the network and their belief revision process below.

Modelling Behaviour of Agents. In a network, an intrinsic agent plays the PD with each of its neighbour, accounting to multiple PD games in an epoch. We assume that an agent has no knowledge about the behaviour of its neighbours, and translate its intrinsic profile to a probability with which it defects. This probability of defection for each agent describes the behaviour of the agent. We use the perceived T', R', P', S' values, discussed in Sect. 3.1, to compute the defect probability range of an intrinsic profile. Suppose an intrinsically motivated

Table 1. Payoff Matrix for 2-player Prisoners' Dilemma

Player 1	Player 2	
	C	D
C	$R = 3, R = 3$	$S = 0, T = 5$
D	$T = 5, S = 0$	$P = 1, P = 1$

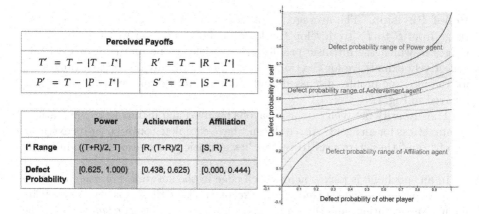

Fig. 1. Table of perceived payoffs in terms of I^*, Table of I^* range and corresponding defect probability and Graph plotting defect probability for different intrinsic profiles

agent a_1 plays the PD game with another agent a_2. Let p be the probability with which a_2 defects. Then we can compute the expected payoffs of each action of a_1 in terms of perceived payoffs of $a_1(T', R', P', S')$, and p.

$$E(C) = pS' + (1-p)R'$$
$$E(D) = pP' + (1-p)T'$$

(1)

Then the probability with which agent a_1 would defect can be computed as follows,

$$defect(a_1) = \frac{E(D)}{E(D)+E(C)} = \frac{pP' + (1-p)T'}{p(P'+S') + (1-p)(T'+R')}$$

(2)

We assume agent a_1 has no knowledge of the nature of agent a_2. Thus, we examine the $defect()$ function of a_1 for all possible p, to determine the behaviour of agent a_1. Across different values of I^* and intrinsic profiles, the function $defect()$ is found to be a monotonically increasing hyperbolic function in terms of $p \in [0,1]$. We then pick specific initialisation of I^* for each intrinsic profile, where the ranges of $defect()$ function overlap minimally. This would allow agents with different intrinsic profiles to exhibit distinct behaviours in terms of their defect probabilities. Different contours of the $defect()$ function have been plotted in Fig. 1, the least overlapping ranges have been obtained when we set $I^* = 5$ for power, $I^* = 3.5$ for achievement and $I^* = 0$ for affiliation, all these initialisation of I^* for the intrinsic profiles fall within their respective optimally motivating ranges. The specific $defect$ functions and their ranges are highlighted in dark. While the other initialisation that have been lightened, show significant intersection with ranges. The final defect probability ranges for each intrinsic profile agent can be referred in Fig. 1. Each instance of an agent with a particular intrinsic profile is assigned a defect probability picked at random from its respective intrinsic profile's defect probability range.

Belief Revision. The average payoff received by an agent in a network can range from S to T. To develop the logic for belief revision we need the payoff ranges in which the intrinsic profiles are satisfied, to be mutually disjoint and collectively exhaustive for the range $[S,T]$. The optimally motivating ranges I^*, for the intrinsic profiles discussed abide to both these requirements, and can be referred in Fig. 1.

The disparity between extrinsic payoffs received and its intrinsic expectations creates stress for an agent. Also it doesn't have complete control over its extrinsic payoffs, and thus it resorts to update its intrinsic expectation to minimise its stress.

In an epoch, PD is played across each edge in the network. For each agent we define a parameter $confidence$ which keeps track of the disparity between its intrinsic expectations and the average payoff it receives. The $confidence$ variable also serves as the memory for an agent to remember this disparity in the previous epochs. A decay factor for $confidence$ ensures that older disparities have a lesser

---

Algorithm 1: Pseudocode of model

---

1   Generate a network N of n agents
2   **for** *agent $a_i \in N$* **do**
3   Assign *Motivation_Type$_{a_i,0}$*
4      $payoff_{a_i,0} \leftarrow 0$
5      $confidence_{a_i} = 0$
6   **end**
7   $t \leftarrow 1$
8   **while** $\exists a_i : Motivation\_Type_{a_i,t} \neq Motivation\_Type_{a_i,t-1}$ **do**
9   **for** *agent $a_j \in N$* **do**
10   **for** *agent $a_k \in neighbourhood(a_j)$* **do**
11            $p_1, p_2 \leftarrow PD(a_j, a_k)$
12            $payoff_{a_j,t} + = p_1$
13            $payoff_{a_k,t} + = p_2$
14   **end**
15   **end**
16   **for** *agent a_j* **do**
17         $confidence_{a_j} = \gamma * confidence_{a_j} +$
           $Cur\_Confidence(payoff_{a_j,t}, Motivation\_Type_{a_j,t-1})$
18         $Motivation\_Type_{a_j,t} =$
           $Update\_Type(confidence_{a_j}, Motivation\_Type_{a_j,t-1})$
19   **end**
20   **end**

Algorithm 2: Functions for belief revision

---

1   **Function** `Cur_Confidence`($payoff, Motivation\_Type$):
2      $[l, r] \leftarrow Range(Motivation\_Type)$
3      $normalize \leftarrow max(T - R, (T + R)/2 - S)$
4   **if** $payoff < l$ **then**
5         $confidence\_change = (payoff - l)/normalize$
6   **else if** $payoff > r$ **then**
7         $confidence\_change = (payoff - r)/normalize$
8   **else**
9         $confidence\_change = 0$
10   **return** $confidence\_change$
11   **End Function**
12   **Function** `Update_Type`($confidence, Motivation\_Type$):
13   **if** $confidence <= $ -$confidence\_threshold$ **then**
14         $Motivation\_Type \mathrel{-}= 1$
15         $confidence = 0$
16   **else if** $confidence >= confidence\_threshold$ **then**
17         $Motivation\_Type \mathrel{+}= 1$
18         $confidence = 0$
19   **return** $Motivation\_Type$
20   **End Function**

weight over the current disparity. We define a threshold $t : t > 0$, to mark when an agent has gained or lost enough confidence to switch its intrinsic profile. The switching of intrinsic profiles of agents, given t has been summarised below.

Case I: *confidence* $> t$. In this scenario an agent switches to the closest profile which has greater intrinsic expectation. Thus, an affiliation agent would switch to achievement while an achievement agent would switch to power.

Case II: *confidence* $< t$. In this scenario an agent switches to the closest profile which has lesser intrinsic expectation. Thus, a power agent would switch to achievement while an achievement agent would switch to affiliation.

Agents use belief revision to minimise stress. In order to reduce the stress, they adapt their intrinsic expectations with respect to the payoffs they receive from their external environment. For instance, if an agent consistently receives more extrinsic payoff than it expects, then it becomes greedy and increases its intrinsic expectations. On the other hand, if an agent consistently receives a lesser extrinsic payoff than it expects, it lowers its expectations. The network is said to be stabilised when no agent in the network updates its *confidence* parameter i.e. every agent receives an expected payoff that lies within the range of its intrinsic expectation. In the stabilised network the overall stress of agents is zero. Algorithm 1 provides the pseudocode for the overall simulation, while Algorithm 2 shows the logic of belief revision and *confidence* update.

4   Experiments and Results

In this section, we describe the experiments performed on the model built in Sects. 3. We generate network using "NetworkX" python package, where nodes of the network represent agents. We initialise agents with certain intrinsic profile, in proportions determined by specific experiment. Each agent then plays iterated version of PD with its neighbours. As discussed earlier, a network stabilises when no agent is stressed and "settled proportion" refers to the proportion of intrinsic profiles in this state. We elaborate the exact initial parameters of the network used for each experiment and study how these parameters affect the settled proportion in stabilised network.

4.1   Varying the Topology of the Network

Interactions among agents in a social network have been described using a variety of models in network science. For instance, in the Barabási-Albert model also called the hub and spoke model, nodes prefer to attach with another node having a high degree. This results in a degree distribution following a power law. While the Watts-Strogatz model incorporates triadic closure which denotes that if a node is connected with two nodes then those two nodes are also connected with a high probability. This phenomenon is observed in many real-world networks. The Erdős-Rényi model simulates a random graph. It would be interesting to

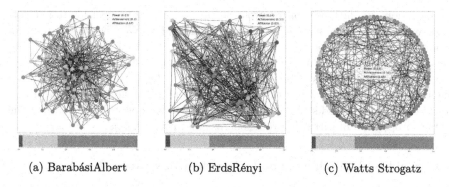

(a) BarabásiAlbert   (b) ErdsRényi   (c) Watts Strogatz

Fig. 2. Settled proportions across different types of networks for (Power, Achievement, Affiliation) agents (100 nodes, average degree 5).

analyse if these network topologies, that model diverse social contexts, influence the settled proportion in a stabilised network of intrinsic agents.

We observe that the trend of settled proportion of intrinsic profiles is invariant across all three network models discussed above. Figure 2 summarises our findings, where the stacked bar charts below represent the proportions of Power, Achievement and Affiliation in the stabilised network. Thus we can conclude that varying the network topologies, having different degree distributions, has no effect on the settled proportion of intrinsic profiles in the stabilised network.

4.2 Varying Initial Proportion of Intrinsic Profiles

Next, we explore the impact of varying initial proportion of intrinsic profiles on settled proportion in the stabilised network. Initial proportion of intrinsic profiles of agents in a network have been varied as follows: a) All power agents b) All achievement agents c) All affiliation agents and d) Agents randomly initialised with power, achievement or affiliation.

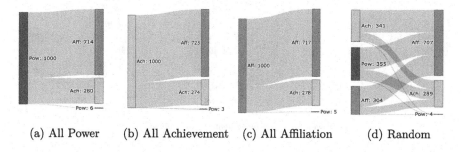

(a) All Power   (b) All Achievement   (c) All Affiliation   (d) Random

Fig. 3. Varying initial proportion of intrinsic profiles (Erdős-Rényi network, 1000 nodes, avg degree 8)

Variations of initialisation of intrinsic profiles is done on Erdős-Rényi network with 1000 nodes having an average degree of 8. We observe that initial proportion of intrinsic profiles does not affect its settled proportion. We varied these initial proportions in Watts-Strogatz and Barabási-Albert network models as well and arrived at the similar observation. Figure 3 presents a Sankey diagram which helps visualise the switch of agents' intrinsic profile from initial states to their stabilised states in the form of flows. We observe invariance in the settled proportion of intrinsic profiles across all initialisations.

4.3   Stabilised Neighbourhood of Intrinsically Motivated Agents

In this section, we study the composition of stabilised neighbourhoods. Figure 4 summarises the average stabilised neighbourhoods of different intrinsic profiles. We interpret these stabilised neighbourhoods as follows:

(a) **Neighbourhood of a power agent:** Power agent expect a high average payoff, thus majority of its interactions must be where it defects while its neighbours cooperate. We observe from the first pie chart of Fig. 4, that the average stabilised neighbourhood of a power agent comprises of all affiliation agents.

(b) **Neighbourhood of an achievement agent:** Achievement agents have a moderate expectation, thus they can sustain a few defects. Hence, their stabilised neighbourhoods have a few other achievement agents and the rest are affiliation agents, as shown in second pie chart of Fig. 4.

(c) **Neighbourhood of an affiliation agent:** Affiliation agents expect minimal payoffs, thus few defects from their neighbourhood are required for them not to increase their expectations. Thus, a significant amount of achievement agents and a few power agents are present in their stabilised neighbourhoods, as shown in third pie chart of Fig. 4.

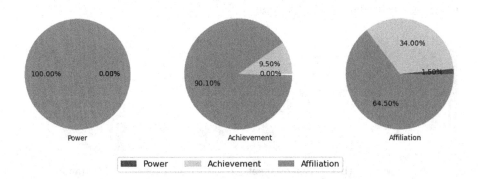

Fig. 4. Average neighbourhood proportions of power, achievement and affiliation agents in stabilised network. (Erdős-Rényi network, 1000 nodes, avg degree 8)

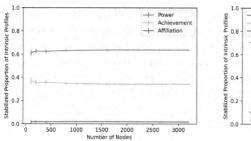
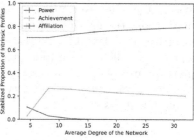

(a) Varying num of nodes (avg degree 14)   (b) Varying avg degree (1500 nodes)

Fig. 5. Varying number of nodes and average degree of Erdős-Rényi network (with Standard Error over 20 runs)

4.4   Varying Number of Nodes in the Network

Next, we study the effect of number of agents in the network on the stabilised proportion. We use Erdős-Rényi model and vary the number of nodes from 100 to 3200 while keeping the average degree ≈14. We observe even with increasing number of agents in a network, the ratio of all three intrinsic profiles remains invariant, as shown in Fig. 5a.

4.5   Varying Average Degree of the Network

Finally we study how varying the average degree of the network influences the settled proportion. We generate an Erdős-Rényi network with 1000 nodes and vary the average degree of the network from 5 to 30. The trend of settled proportions of intrinsic profiles can be observed in Fig. 5b. Similar trends were also observed in other network models as well.

As average degree increases, the proportion of agents with power profile decrease while agents with achievement profile increase (Fig. 5b) before settling to constant configuration. In a network with small average degree, each agent has a small neighbourhood. Hence, it is easier for power agents to have all affiliators in its neighbourhood. However as average degree increases, the size of neighbourhood increases. Then it is unlikely to have all affiliation agents in a large neighbourhood. Hence, it is difficult for power agents to sustain in large neighbourhoods and eventually they vanish when the average degree crosses 12.

5   Discussion

The primary aim of the current work was to model intrinsic motivation in agents and study its effect on network interactions when agents try to reconcile between external rewards and their intrinsic expectations. We observe that across a variety of network configurations, a high stabilised proportion (≈70%) of affiliators always emerges. However, we also observe that by modelling agents with intrinsic motivation, the presence of only affiliators who predominantly cooperate is not sufficient to create a stable system. Achievement and power agents are also present in a stable configuration. This implies that agents with diverse intrinsic motivation profiles are necessary for a stable network. The resultant stable distribution is an emergent property when agents individually try to minimise their internal stress.

6   Conclusions and Future Work

Intrinsic motivation gives a new perspective of modelling interactions between autonomous agents. It accommodates for the fact that agents perceive the same payoffs differently, which in turn affects their behaviour. In this model, agents aim to minimise stress, which happens when the extrinsic payoffs they receive meet their intrinsic expectations. As a part of this work, we studied the proportion of intrinsic profiles in the stabilised network. We observed that irrespective of any variation in network level parameters, ratio of affiliation agents (relationship building agents displaying cooperative behaviour) is high in the settled population.

In future, we plan to build more diverse models for interactions between autonomous agents based on their intrinsic motivation. We plan to experiment with different kinds of interactions in a network, modelled using different mixed-motive games. In more realistic setups, autonomous agents contextually switch their intrinsic profiles. For example, they might have a power profile in a formal competitive setup and an affiliation profile in a friendship network. In future, we also plan to model agents such that they can probabilistically make decisions based on mixed intrinsic motivation profiles. Also, instead of updating their intrinsic profiles, simulation can be designed so that agents can change the edges when they are stressed. It will be interesting to study the network characteristics of these resultant emergent network in future.

References

1. Axelrod, R., Hamilton, W.D.: The evolution of cooperation. Science **211**(4489), 1390–1396 (1981)
2. Baldassarre, G.: What are intrinsic motivations? A biological perspective. In: 2011 IEEE ICDL, vol. 2, pp. 1–8. IEEE (2011)
3. Baldassarre, G., Stafford, T., Mirolli, M., Redgrave, P., Ryan, R.M., Barto, A.: Intrinsic motivations and open-ended development in animals, humans, and robots: an overview. Front. Psychol. **5**, 985 (2014)
4. Barto, A.G.: Intrinsic motivation and reinforcement learning. In: Baldassarre, G., Mirolli, M. (eds.) Intrinsically Motivated Learning in Natural and Artificial Systems, pp. 17–47. Springer, Heidelberg (2013). https://doi.org/10.1007/978-3-642-32375-1_2
5. Frey, B.S.: How intrinsic motivation is crowded out and in. Ration. Soc. **6**(3), 334–352 (1994)

6. Heath, C.: On the social psychology of agency relationships: lay theories of motivation overemphasize extrinsic incentives. Organ. Behav. Hum. Decis. Process. **78**(1), 25–62 (1999)
7. Heckhausen, J.E., Heckhausen, H.E.: Motivation and Action. Cambridge University Press, Cambridge (2008)
8. Hester, T., Stone, P.: Intrinsically motivated model learning for developing curious robots. Artif. Intell. **247**, 170–186 (2017)
9. Hull, C.L.: Principles of behavior: an introduction to behavior theory (1943)
10. James, H.S., Jr.: Why did you do that? An economic examination of the effect of extrinsic compensation on intrinsic motivation and performance. J. Econ. Psychol. **26**(4), 549–566 (2005)
11. Kahneman, D., Tversky, A.: Prospect theory: an analysis of decision under risk. Econometrica **47**(2), 263–291 (1979). http://www.jstor.org/stable/1914185
12. Khan, M.M., Kasmarik, K., Barlow, M.: Toward computational motivation for multi-agent systems and swarms. Front. Robot. AI **5**, 134 (2018)
13. Merrick, K., Shafi, K.: A game theoretic framework for incentive-based models of intrinsic motivation in artificial systems. Front. Psychol. **4** (2013)
14. Merrick, K.E., Shafi, K.: Achievement, affiliation, and power: motive profiles for artificial agents. Adapt. Behav. **19**(1), 40–62 (2011)
15. Morse, G.: Why we misread motives. Harv. Bus. Rev. **81**(1), 18 (2003)
16. Nowak, M.A.: Five rules for the evolution of cooperation. Science **314**(5805), 1560–1563 (2006)
17. Oudeyer, P.Y., Kaplan, F.: What is intrinsic motivation? A typology of computational approaches. Front. Neurorobot. **6** (2009)
18. Riolo, R.L., Cohen, M.D., Axelrod, R.: Evolution of cooperation without reciprocity. Nature **414**(6862), 441–443 (2001)
19. Ryan, R.M., Deci, E.L.: Intrinsic and extrinsic motivations: classic definitions and new directions. Contemp. Educ. Psychol. **25**(1), 54–67 (2000)
20. Santos, F.C., Pacheco, J.M.: A new route to the evolution of cooperation. J. Evol. Biol. **19**(3), 726–733 (2006)
21. Schembri, M., Mirolli, M., Baldassarre, G.: Evolving internal reinforcers for an intrinsically motivated reinforcement-learning robot. In: 2007 IEEE 6th International Conference on Development and Learning, pp. 282–287. IEEE (2007)
22. Sen, A.K.: Rational fools: a critique of the behavioral foundations of economic theory. Philos. Public Affairs **6**(4), 317–344 (1977)
23. Shafi, K., Merrick, K.E., Debie, E.: Evolution of intrinsic motives in multi-agent simulations. In: Bui, L.T., Ong, Y.S., Hoai, N.X., Ishibuchi, H., Suganthan, P.N. (eds.) SEAL 2012. LNCS, vol. 7673, pp. 198–207. Springer, Heidelberg (2012). https://doi.org/10.1007/978-3-642-34859-4_20
24. Srivastava, N., Kapoor, K., Schrater, P.R.: A cognitive basis for theories of intrinsic motivation. In: 2011 IEEE ICDL, vol. 2, pp. 1–6. IEEE (2011)
25. Stout, A., Konidaris, G.D., Barto, A.G.: Intrinsically motivated reinforcement learning: a promising framework for developmental robot learning. Technical report, Massachusetts University, Amherst Department of Computer Science (2005)
26. Sun, R.: Intrinsic motivation for truly autonomous agents. In: Abbass, H.A., Scholz, J., Reid, D.J. (eds.) Foundations of Trusted Autonomy. SSDC, vol. 117, pp. 273–292. Springer, Cham (2018). https://doi.org/10.1007/978-3-319-64816-3_15
27. Xianyu, B.: Prisoner's dilemma game on complex networks with agents' adaptive expectations. J. Artif. Soc. Soc. Simul. **15**(3), 3 (2012)

Multi-agent Reinforcement Learning for Structured Symbolic Music Generation

Shayan Dadman$^{(\boxtimes)}$ and Bernt Arild Bremdal

Department of Computer Science, Arctic University of Tromsø,
Lodve Langesgate 2, 8514 Narvik, Norway
shayan.dadman@uit.no

Abstract. Generating structured music using deep learning methods with symbolic representation is challenging due to the complex relationships between musical elements that define a musical composition. Symbolic representation of music, such as MIDI or sheet music, can help overcome some of these challenges by encoding the music in a format that allows manipulation and analysis. However, the symbolic representation of music still requires interpretation and understanding of musical concepts and theory. In this paper, we propose a method for symbolic music generation using a multi-agent structure built on top of growing hierarchical self-organizing maps and recurrent neural networks. Our model primarily focuses on music structure. It operates at a higher level of abstraction, enabling it to capture longer-term musical structure and dependency. Our approach involves using reinforcement learning as a self-learning method for agents and the human user as a musical expert to facilitate the agents' learning of global dependency and musical characteristics. We show how agents can learn and adapt to the user's preferences and musical style. Furthermore, we present and discuss the potential of our approach for agent communication, learning and adaptation, and distributed problem-solving in music generation.

Keywords: Adaptive learning · distributed problem solving · deep learning (DL) · deep Q-network (DQN) · multi-agent systems (MAS) · reinforcement learning (RL) · music generation

1 Introduction

Music has a clear, well-defined structure that provides the foundation for creating a piece. It can sound disorganized, disjointed, and lacking musical coherence without a clear structure. The structure challenge in symbolic music generation involves generating a musical piece that follows the rules of music theory while maintaining a coherent structure throughout the piece. These rules can include adhering to a consistent key signature, following chord progressions, and maintaining a steady rhythm and tempo. Additionally, the generated piece must have a clear structure that captures the listener's attention. This requires creating a

P. Mathieu et al. (Eds.): PAAMS 2023, LNAI 13955, pp. 52–63, 2023.
https://doi.org/10.1007/978-3-031-37616-0_5

sense of tension and release throughout the piece, as well as varying the melody, harmony, and rhythm to add contrast and variety.

Deep learning models can address the structure challenge in symbolic music generation in various ways, as highlighted by [3]. Models such as MusicVAE [14], Music Transformer [8], and MuseGAN [5] generate music that is musically coherent and stylistically consistent with the input dataset. In some cases, the music generated by these programs can be tedious or repetitive, particularly in longer pieces where there is a lack of variation over time. These note-based models struggle to capture the complexity of musical expressions, such as rhythm, dynamics, and articulation, as they focus primarily on the immediate context of the preceding notes [18]. Furthermore, the optimization objective of these models is often based on minimizing a loss function that measures the discrepancy between the generated music and the training data.

In contrast, reinforcement learning (RL) models learn through an iterative trial and error process, providing flexibility and adaptability to changes in the task or environment. RL-Tuner [9] utilizes two DQN and two RNN models to generate melodies using user-defined constraints. Later, [11] proposed an extension to RL-Tuner that uses the Latent Dirichlet Allocation (LDA) called RE-RLTuner. RL-Chord [10] is a melody harmonization system using RL and conditional LSTM (CLSTM) to generate chord progression. [1] proposed a method using RL and LSTM to compose Guzheng music. They first trained the LSTM model on MIDI examples and optimized it by introducing the Guzheng playing techniques using the DQN algorithm. Nevertheless, despite the RL advantage in music generation, defining a reward function for musical structure remains challenging [3]. Therefore, the generated music by RL models may still lack coherency and structure.

Another potential approach to addressing symbolic music generation is using multi-agent systems (MAS). MAS are systems composed of multiple agents that interact with each other to achieve a common goal autonomously using a learning method [17]. Similar to how musicians in a band collaborate and coordinate, agents in MAS architecture can work together, each focusing on specific aspects of the musical structure. These agents can be equipped with different methods of music generation, ranging from rule-based systems to machine-learning models. Despite its potential, MAS has limitations, including the challenge of coordinating multiple agents, which can lead to high computational complexity and difficulties in balancing agents' autonomy with system coherence. In order to address these challenges, reinforcement learning (RL) can serve as an effective learning method. By employing RL within MAS, agents can engage in a self-learning process where they refine their behaviors through trial and error [3]. This approach allows the agents to adapt to the musical context and each other, resulting in more harmonious and engaging compositions.

Smith and Garnett [15] propose a musical agent with adaptive resonance theory (ART) and reinforcement learning (RL) to generate monophonic melody. ART is similar to Self-Organizing Maps (SOMs), used to classify and categorize the data vectors. Improvagent [2] is a musical agent that utilizes Sarsa reinforcement learning algorithm. Given the inputs, the agent computes a set of features like onset, pitch, and rhythm. It considers the features as the states of the environment and clusters them using the k-nearest neighbors algorithm with Euclidean distance.

Furthermore, MAS provides a platform for integrating human creativity and expertise into the music generation. Communication between agents and a human agent allows for guidance on the overall direction of the music generation, while agents handle the low-level details of generating individual musical elements. Indeed, by orchestrating agents similar to musicians in a band and facilitating communication with a human agent, MAS can capture and model the complex interactions and dependencies between musical elements.

Here, we propose a method for symbolic music generation using MAS built on top of growing hierarchical self-organizing maps and recurrent neural networks. Our model works directly with musical patterns. It operates at a higher level of abstraction than note-based models. The idea is to capture the long-term musical structure and dependency by learning to identify and manipulate patterns to generate more complex and interesting musical pieces. Besides, our model utilizes MAS architecture by incorporating RL deep Q-network (DQN) as a self-learning paradigm and the human agent as a musical expert. Through interaction with the environment, the agents receive input and feedback for the generated music from the music-related reward functions and the human agent. This enables the agents to learn and adapt to the user's preferences and musical style. Furthermore, we introduce a method utilizing the DQN replay buffer as the MAS communication method. This method represents a collaborative learning process, allowing the agents to coordinate their actions more effectively and achieve better results. Our framework offers interactivity, flexibility, and adaptability throughout the generation process.

2   Background

Growing Hierarchical Self-Organizing Maps (GHSOM) is an unsupervised machine learning algorithm that learns to represent high-dimensional input data in a lower-dimensional space [4]. GHSOM is useful for clustering and visualization of data and able to grow a hierarchical structure of self-organizing maps (SOMs). It can capture the input data's local and global structure by recursively splitting a SOM into smaller SOMs. At each level of the hierarchy, GHSOM learns a codebook of prototype vectors representing the input data through a process known as competitive learning.

Recurrent Neural Networks (RNNs) are a class of neural networks that can process sequential data by allowing information to persist over time. Despite their usefulness, RNNs can suffer from the vanishing and exploding gradient problem. This limits their ability to capture long-term dependencies in sequential data. Long Short-Term Memory (LSTM) is a type of RNN that effectively addresses this problem with gating mechanisms, consisting of three sigmoidal units and one hyperbolic tangent unit, that selectively update, forget, and output information. By using a cell state as "memory", LSTMs can effectively capture long-term dependencies in sequential data.

Reinforcement Learning (RL) is a machine learning subfield that teaches agents to make decisions based on rewards and punishments. The agent interacts with an environment, learns from feedback, and adapts its behavior to achieve a specific goal. The agent's objective is to maximize its cumulative reward over time by learning a policy that maps states to actions. RL algorithms can be value-based or policy-based. Value-based methods aim to learn the optimal value function, and policy-based methods aim to learn the optimal policy directly. Additionally, there are hybrid approaches, such as deep Q-networks (DQN) [12], which combine Q-learning with deep neural networks to approximate the Q-value function and handle large and continuous state spaces. RL is useful in developing autonomous agents that can learn from experience, improve their decision-making processes, and optimize their behavior over time.

Dimensionality Reduction is a technique that involves reducing the number of features or variables in a dataset while maintaining as much information as possible. This is typically achieved by projecting high-dimensional data onto a lower-dimensional space. There are two main categories of dimensionality reduction techniques: linear and nonlinear. Linear techniques, such as Principal Component Analysis (PCA) and Linear Discriminant Analysis (LDA), are commonly used for datasets with a linear structure. Nonlinear techniques, such as t-Distributed Stochastic Neighbor Embedding (t-SNE), UMAP (Uniform Manifold Approximation and Projection), and ISOMAP (Isometric Feature Mapping), are used when the underlying structure of the data is nonlinear.

For music, [6] and [13] performed a comparative analysis between PCA, t-SNE, ISOMAP, and SOMs methods using extracted meaningful features from music and textural sound data. They observed that t-SNE performs much better in preserving the local structure of the original data and keeping the distinct sub-groups separated in visualization.

3   System Design

In the following, we explain different aspects of our multi-agent reinforcement learning system for structured symbolic music generation. We first explain the data processing approach and then continue with training and generation processes. Figure 1 illustrates the components of our model and depicts the training and generation processes. Overall, our model involves a perceiving agent, a generative (decision-making) agent, and a human agent (user). The perceiving agent organizes and processes the inputs and passes them to the generative agent. The generative agent carries out the system's output by considering the previous and current state. Indeed, the perceiving agent provides the generative agent with

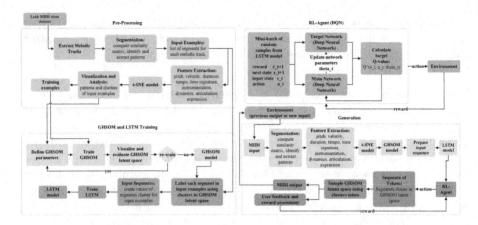

Fig. 1. The architecture of the proposed multi-agent reinforcement learning model.

a better understanding of the environment by encoding the inputs in a higher level of abstraction. In this manner, the generative agent concentrates more on its action improvement. The user evaluates the model's output and provides new inputs to guide the generations. User feedback enables the generative agent to adapt and learn the user's preferences, introduce novelty and creativity, and navigate through complex environments such as music structure. Furthermore, the perceiving agent observes the changes in the environment, such as the human feedback given to the generative agent to provide input according to the related musical context.

3.1 Data Processing

Symbolic representation of music refers to the process of encoding musical information using a set of symbols, typically in the form of a digital score or MIDI file. Each musical event is represented in this format by a combination of symbols that encode its pitch, duration, timing, and other relevant attributes.

Here, we consider Clean MIDI subset of the Lakh MIDI dataset[1]. This subset consists of 45,129 MIDI files that have been filtered and cleaned to remove any duplicates, corrupt files, or files that do not meet specific quality standards. These quality standards include having a minimum number of tracks, a minimum duration, and being free of obvious errors such as missing or extraneous notes. We process each MIDI example to identify and maintain only melodic tracks. We identify the short and long patterns within the melodic tracks using the similarity matrix, similar to [1] approach. We mark and segment the melodic tracks based on identified patterns and extract each segment as a separate MIDI file. We also maintain the order of segments in original melodic tracks. We extract relevant musical features as a feature vector for each extracted segment. The

---

[1] https://colinraffel.com/projects/lmd/.

musical features include pitch, duration, velocity, tempo, time signature, instrumentation, dynamics, articulation, and expression. After creating the feature vectors, we normalize them so that each feature is scaled to the same range. We use t-SNE to reduce the dimensionality of the feature vectors before passing them to GHSOM for training.

3.2 Perceiving Agent - Learning Musical Structure

We follow the instructions given by [4] to implement the model and train it after processing and preparing the training examples as described in Sect. 3.1. Furthermore, to define the model parameter, we utilize the t-SNE algorithm. In particular, we use t-SNE to determine the number of levels in the GHSOM hierarchy, the size of the maps at each level, and the learning rate and neighborhood function parameters.

To determine the number of levels in the GHSOM hierarchy, we use t-SNE to visualize and inspect the resulting clusters or patterns in the data. The number of levels in the GHSOM hierarchy can be chosen to correspond to the level of abstraction suggested by the t-SNE visualization. To determine the size of the maps at each level, we use t-SNE to estimate the local density of the data in the lower-dimensional space. In GHSOM, maps at each level should be large enough to capture the local structure of the data but not so large as to lose the resolution needed to distinguish between neighboring clusters. The size of the maps can be chosen based on the local density estimated from the t-SNE visualization. We choose the learning rate and neighborhood function parameters using the identified clusters or patterns in the data by t-SNE. These parameters maintain balance in the exploration of the high-dimensional space with the exploitation of the clusters or patterns suggested by the t-SNE visualization.

Note that we use t-SNE as a tool for exploration and interpretation rather than as a definitive guide to the GHSOM parameter selection.

Following the same order of the segments in the original melodic track, we use the trained GHSOM to label each segment with the corresponding cluster number. In this manner, we create a vector of numbers and prepare the training examples for the LSTM model. Essentially, we train the LSTM model to capture the temporal dependencies to predict the next token. The model architecture includes an LSTM layer with 128 units with a 0.2 drop-out rate followed by a densely connected layer to carry out the predictions. We used ELU (Exponential Linear Unit) as an activation function for the LSTM layer and softmax for the dense layer, and Adam as an optimizer to minimize the cross-entropy function.

3.3 Generative Agent - Optimization with RL

Model Architecture. While the GHSOM captures the topological structure and the LSTM model learns the dependency among segments from the original melodic tracks, the model may get stuck with a specific order of segments and need help to explore new variations. We use Reinforcement Learning DQN algorithm to further optimize the model's performance. DQN [12] is a model-free RL algorithm that uses Q-learning to learn optimal policies. It maximizes the total reward at the end of each epoch by selecting policies based on a minibatch of random samples from the LSTM model. The main network generates actions, and the target network produces a stable target to compute the loss of the selected action. At each time step, the agent generates an action, a_t, following a policy, π, and based on the current state, s_t. The environment then generates a reward, r_{t+1}, and a new state, s_{t+1}. This process continues until a satisfactory result is achieved.

We train the main network, to approximate the optimal action-value function $Q(st, at)$. $Q(st, at)$ represents the expected cumulative reward for taking action, a_t, in state, s_t, and following the optimal policy after that. The input to the network is the current state, s_t, and the output is a vector of Q-values for each possible action, a_t, in that state. During training, the network is updated using a variant of the Q-learning algorithm that minimizes the difference between the predicted Q-values and the true Q-values obtained from the Bellman equation. The target network is a separate copy of the main network that is used to generate the target Q-values used in the Q-learning update. The target network is not updated during the Q-learning update step but is periodically updated to match the weights of the main network. This helps to stabilize the training process by preventing the Q-values from oscillating or diverging during training. During the training process, the agent predict a sequence of tokens, where it learns the structure and capture the transitions between the segments. Therefore, the model parameters are updated after generating a complete sequence rather than a single token.

Moreover, to encourage the model to explore action space, we use NoisyNet [7]. NoisyNet addresses the exploration-exploitation tradeoff by adding noise to the weights of the neural network used to estimate the Q-values or policy. The noise is added in a way that preserves the differentiability of the network. In this manner, it can still be trained using gradient descent. The main advantage of NoisyNet is that it provides a principled way of balancing exploration and exploitation without requiring additional exploration noise to be added to the actions. We use Python and Tensorflow library with Keras to implement functionalities and agents.

Reward Definition. We define the reward policy based on three criteria:

- r_{ground_truth}: Ground truth reward based on the original melodic tracks
- $r_{structure}$: Sequence structure reward based on manual rules
- r_{hil}: Human feedback reward

The ground truth reward, r_{ground_truth}, evaluates the generated sequence based on the original melodic tracks. As described in Sect. 3.1, each melodic track in the dataset are segmented based on the variation of patterns. We measure the gap between the model's output and the ground truth using the negative log-likelihood (NLL) loss. NLL penalizes the model for assigning a low probability to the observed data and rewards it for assigning a high probability to the observed data. The objective is to decrease the loss as the agent continues learning.

The sequence structure reward, $r_{structure}$, is proposed to evaluate the transition between the segments within the generated sequence. The main objective is to prevent the model from sudden transitions that are relatively quick or completely irrelevant. To do so, we train a smaller GHSOM model using only the vector of segments within each melodic track. Then we use the topological latent space of GHSOM to assess the transitions based on the closeness of the segment at step t to the t-1 segment within the predicted sequence. To measure the closeness, we use Euclidean (L2) distance. Given the calculated distance, the definition of the reward is

$$r_{structure}(d) = \begin{cases} -1, & \text{if } d > threshold \\ 1, & \text{if } d < threshold \end{cases} \tag{1}$$

where the *threshold* is an experimental value calculated by taking a percentage of the average distance between all of the data points.

The human feedback reward, r_{hil}, incorporates the human-in-the-loop (HIL). The basic idea behind HIL is to use feedback from a human expert to shape the reward function of the reinforcement learning agent. The user provides feedback in the form of evaluations of the agent's actions, which are then used to adjust the reward function to better align with the user's preferences. Specifically, the reward function is augmented with a term that captures the feedback from the user. The user provides explicit evaluations of the generation with +1 as positive reward and −1 as negative reward. The human feedback reward is as follows:

$$r_{hill}(s_t, a_t) = w * e(s_t, a_t) \tag{2}$$

where w is a weight that controls the influence of the expert evaluations on the reward function, and $e(s_t, a_t)$ is the expert evaluation of the agent's action in state s_t and action a_t.

The instant reward r_t for the action to be taken at time t is

$$r_t = \alpha * r_t^{ground\_truth} + \beta * r_t^{structure} + \gamma * r_t^{hil} \tag{3}$$

where α, β, and γ are the weight factors that are experimental values. They controls the impact of each reward function in guiding the agents behavior and can be adjusted during training.

3.4   Agents Communication

Communication is an essential aspect of MAS, as agents need to exchange information and coordinate their actions. Various communication methods have been proposed and implemented in MAS, ranging from message-passing and negotiation protocols to the use of shared memory spaces [17]. Our communication method uses the DQN replay buffer that stores the agent's experiences as tuples (state, action, reward, next state) that stabilizes and improves the learning process. By extending the replay buffer to serve as a communication repository, agents can access a shared replay buffer to not only learn from their experiences but also benefit from the experiences of other agents. This collaborative learning process allows the agents to coordinate their actions more effectively and achieve better results in complex environments.

3.5 Generation

During the generation process, the model's input consists of the outputs in the previous step and the human inputs. In the first step, the perceiving agent processes the given input as described in Sect. 3.1. Then it uses GHSOM to identify the input cluster within the GHSOM latent space. Using the output of GHSOM, it creates the input vector for the generative agent to generate the next sequence of tokens. At this stage, the system provides the human user with the generated sequence for evaluation. The system incorporates the evaluations obtained from the human user and other reward functions using Eq. 3 to guide the agents. To generate content, the system takes the tokens in the generated sequence and uses the GHSOM latent space to sample the corresponding cluster of segments randomly. Figure 1 illustrates the generation process of the system.

The generative agent incorporates the given feedback to adjust its behavior and improve its actions in the next step. Simultaneously, using the communication method, the perceiving agent assesses whether its input to the generative agent was optimal. To achieve this, it groups and selects specific tuples from the replay buffer using t-SNE algorithm. This selection process is influenced by the action and reward values associated with each tuple, where the action corresponds to the corresponding GHSOM cluster. This allows the perceiving agent to identify which actions yielded the highest rewards and, therefore, which input would be more optimal in the future.

4 Discussion

Each agent in the multi-agent system can focus on specific elements of the music composition, such as melody, harmony, or rhythm, and learn to create these components autonomously [3]. However, certain challenges exist, including the complexity of coordinating numerous agents, the high computational demand of the system, and the difficulty in achieving a balance between the autonomy of individual agents and the overall coherence of the music produced [16]. Here, we proposed a multi-agent reinforcement learning approach that works directly with musical patterns to mitigate these challenges. In the proposed system, the agents refine their behaviors iteratively through interaction with each other and the human user as an agent to generate new pieces of music by combining, manipulating, and rearranging the patterns creatively.

In our approach, the agents can also learn from the human user's feedback to generate music. In this way, the generated music is more aligned with the user's preferences. As an expert, the human user can provide valuable feedback on the quality and guide the desired structure, style, and emotional content of the music. The human user also provides input throughout the interaction. The given input can include examples of music in a particular structure or style. The agent uses the input to improve the quality of generated music and adjusts its behavior regarding musical style and structure. Similarly, it can generate a complete piece based on that input.

MAS architecture allows modularity and the use of various computational methods. It promotes distributed problem solving, which is solving complex problems by breaking them down into smaller, more manageable sub-problems that can be solved by multiple agents working together. Our system consists of three agents: perceiving, generative, and human agents. The perceiving and generative agents use the replay buffer as a communication repository to coordinate their actions collaboratively. During their interaction, both agents carefully observe the feedback from the human and use it to improve their performance. The generative agent learns and adapts to the user's preferences based on the feedback received, while the perceiving agent uses the feedback to provide relevant input to the generative agent. The perceiving agent interacts with the replay buffer by grouping and selecting the experiences based on their similarity to human feedback. In essence, this process ensures the system continually learns and adapts, enhancing its capability to deliver user-tailored content.

Additionally, we can incorporate human expertise and preferences into the communication process by observing and providing feedback on the experiences stored in the shared replay buffer. We can add human feedback as metadata in the replay buffer. This input could be suggestions for alternative actions, additional context information, or other guidance based on human feedback. In this manner, the human agent can guide the agents to focus on specific experiences or suggest alternative actions. Additionally, we can access the agents' evaluations and suggestions in the shared replay buffer to better understand the MAS's current state, decision process, and performance.

One approach to creating an interactive interface for human agents to interact with MAS is the use of PureData (PD) and Open Sound Control (OSC). PD's visual programming environment ensures that interaction is intuitive and user-friendly, while OSC facilitates efficient communication between the PD interface and the Python-based MAS. This approach enables real-time adjustments and feedback integration. Additionally, we can integrate PD with a Digital Audio Workstation (DAW) to enhance the user experience further.

We can expand the system by introducing several RL agents with diverse behaviors, each assigned to a specific task, such as melody, harmony, and rhythm generation. Nonetheless, adding more RL agents introduces challenges in effectively coordinating them as system complexity rises. Indeed, maintaining a shared replay buffer for many agents can lead to increased memory and computational requirements. We can explore techniques such as data compression, prioritized experience replay, and hierarchical organization of agents to optimize the system for several agents. Data compression techniques can help reduce the replay buffer's memory footprint, while prioritized experience replay can enhance the learning process by focusing on the most informative experiences. Hierarchical organization of agents, where a group of specialized agents works under a higher-level coordinating agent, can simplify the complexity of managing multiple agents and their interactions. However, these optimizations might introduce trade-offs in system performance, learning speed, and resource consumption. The replay buffer communication is also limited in its applicability in heterogeneous MAS. This poses a challenge to managing possible conflicts and the agent's ability to negotiate or compromise to find a mutually acceptable solution.

One strategy is to train agents to learn from the actions of other agents in their local environment using decentralized training. It can lead to robust and adaptive agents, as each agent can learn from its own experiences and adapt to environmental changes. We can integrate decentralized learning with a shared replay buffer to form a hybrid approach for MAS. This approach combines decentralized learning's scalability, robustness, and flexibility with shared replay buffer's enhanced coordination, knowledge transfer, and human-agent interaction, resulting in more effective learning and collaboration among diverse agents. Consequently, the integrated approach can lead to improved overall performance, alignment with human preferences, and efficient achievement of shared goals in complex multi-agent environments.

5   Conclusion

In this study, we discussed the current approaches in symbolic music generation and their shortcomings. Notably, we emphasized the challenges involved with these models to address musical structure. Mainly, these models struggle to generate innovative and expressive music with long-term structure. In a way, the note-based approach of these models limits their ability to capture the complexity of musical expressions, such as rhythm, dynamics, and articulation. On the other hand, reinforcement learning models offer more flexibility and adaptability but face challenges in navigating complex environments and definition of music related reward functions.

To alleviate these challenges, we proposed an approach based on multi-agent systems and reinforcement learning algorithms that works directly with musical patterns. The proposed approach particularly improves the agent's adaptability to human preferences and learning of musical elements dependency to capture the structure and overall flow of the music. Additionally, we discussed that the modularity of MAS architecture allows for distributed problem-solving by utilizing multiple agents, each specializing in specific musical tasks. However, challenges exist in programming agents to coordinate effectively, particularly when introducing a diverse range of agents. Therefore, we discussed how combination of decentralized training and replay buffer could be a suitable strategy to alleviate this challenge. Overall, the proposed model represents an interactive, adaptable, and flexible framework for music generation.

References

1. Chen, S., Zhong, Y., Du, R.: Automatic composition of guzheng (Chinese zither) music using long short-term memory network (LSTM) and reinforcement learning (RL). Sci. Rep. **12**(1), 15829 (2022)
2. Collins, N.: Reinforcement learning for live musical agents. In: ICMC (2008)
3. Dadman, S., Bremdal, B.A., Bang, B., Dalmo, R.: Toward interactive music generation: a position paper. IEEE Access **10**, 125679–125695 (2022)
4. Dittenbach, M., Merkl, D., Rauber, A.: The growing hierarchical self-organizing map. In: Proceedings of the IEEE-INNS-ENNS International Joint Conference on Neural Networks, IJCNN 2000, Neural Computing: New Challenges and Perspectives for the New Millennium, vol. 6, pp. 15–19. IEEE (2000)
5. Dong, H.W., Hsiao, W.Y., Yang, L.C., Yang, Y.H.: MuseGAN: multi-track sequential generative adversarial networks for symbolic music generation and accompaniment. In: Proceedings of the AAAI Conference on Artificial Intelligence, vol. 32 (2018)
6. Dupont, S., Ravet, T., Picard-Limpens, C., Frisson, C.: Nonlinear dimensionality reduction approaches applied to music and textural sounds. In: 2013 IEEE International Conference on Multimedia and Expo (ICME), pp. 1–6. IEEE (2013)
7. Fortunato, M., et al.: Noisy networks for exploration. arXiv preprint arXiv:1706.10295 (2017)
8. Huang, C.Z.A., et al.: Music transformer. arXiv preprint arXiv:1809.04281 (2018)
9. Jaques, N., Gu, S., Turner, R.E., Eck, D.: Tuning recurrent neural networks with reinforcement learning (2017)
10. Ji, S., Yang, X., Luo, J., Li, J.: RL-chord: CLSTM-based melody harmonization using deep reinforcement learning. IEEE Trans. Neural Netw. Learn. Syst. (2023)
11. Liu, H., Xie, X., Ruzi, R., Wang, L., Yan, N.: RE-RLtuner: a topic-based music generation method. In: 2021 IEEE International Conference on Real-time Computing and Robotics (RCAR), pp. 1139–1142. IEEE (2021)
12. Mnih, V., et al.: Playing Atari with deep reinforcement learning. arXiv preprint arXiv:1312.5602 (2013)
13. Pál, T., Várkonyi, D.T.: Comparison of dimensionality reduction techniques on audio signals. In: ITAT, pp. 161–168 (2020)
14. Roberts, A., Engel, J., Raffel, C., Hawthorne, C., Eck, D.: A hierarchical latent vector model for learning long-term structure in music. In: International Conference on Machine Learning, pp. 4364–4373. PMLR (2018)
15. Smith, B.D., Garnett, G.E.: Reinforcement learning and the creative, automated music improviser. In: Machado, P., Romero, J., Carballal, A. (eds.) EvoMUSART 2012. LNCS, vol. 7247, pp. 223–234. Springer, Heidelberg (2012). https://doi.org/10.1007/978-3-642-29142-5_20
16. Veale, T., Cardoso, F.A.: Computational Creativity: The Philosophy and Engineering of Autonomously Creative Systems. Springer, Heidelberg (2019). https://doi.org/10.1007/978-3-319-43610-4
17. Wooldridge, M.J.: An Introduction to Multiagent Systems, 2nd edn. Wiley, Chichester (2009)
18. Wu, S.L., Yang, Y.H.: MuseMorphose: full-song and fine-grained music style transfer with one transformer VAE. arXiv preprint arXiv:2105.04090 (2021)

A Multi-level Density-Based Crowd Simulation Architecture

Huu-Tu Dang$^{(\boxtimes)}$, Benoit Gaudou, and Nicolas Verstaevel

UMR 5505 IRIT, University Toulouse 1 Capitole, Toulouse, France
{huu-tu.dang,benoit.gaudou,nicolas.verstaevel}@ut-capitole.fr

Abstract. Large-scale crowd phenomena are complex to model as the behaviour of pedestrians needs to be described at both strategic, tactical, and operational levels and is impacted by the density of the crowd. Microscopic models manage to mimic the dynamics at low densities, whereas mesoscopic models achieve better performances in dense situations. This paper proposes and evaluates a novel agent-based architecture to enable agents to dynamically change their operational model based on local density. The ability to combine microscopic and mesoscopic models for multi-scale simulation is studied through a use case of pedestrians at the Festival of Lights, Lyon, France. Simulation results are compared to different models in terms of density map, pedestrian outflow, and computation time. The results demonstrate that our agent-based architecture can effectively simulate pedestrians in diverse-density situations, providing flexibility for incorporating various models, and enhancing runtime performance while achieving comparable pedestrian outflow results to alternative models.

Keywords: Agent-based architecture · Multi-level behaviour · Pedestrian modeling · Multi-scale simulation

1 Introduction

Pedestrian simulation is an effective tool to model and study the behaviour of pedestrian in various contexts, from optimisation of pedestrian flows to safety issues [1]. Pedestrian behaviour can be modelled into three-layer level architecture [2]:

- **Strategic level:** pedestrians determine a list of activities (or targets) and when they want to perform these activities.
- **Tactical level:** pedestrians choose a path to the predefined destinations based on information about the environment.
- **Operational level:** pedestrians adjust their local movements such as collision avoidance to adapt to the surrounding area.

In order to build a pedestrian simulation, a modeller has to effectively instantiate one model for each of the three layers, that is to say at least one strategic

© The Author(s), under exclusive license to Springer Nature Switzerland AG 2023
P. Mathieu et al. (Eds.): PAAMS 2023, LNAI 13955, pp. 64–75, 2023.
https://doi.org/10.1007/978-3-031-37616-0_6

model (also referred to as *goal selection* model) [3,4], one tactical level model (also known as *path planning* model) [5,6], and one operational level model [7,8]. In this paper, we focus on selecting the proper algorithm for the operational level. Those models are used to compute the velocities and speed of each pedestrian based on local information.

Many types of operational models exist in the literature, each model being built to capture and mimic a specific phenomenon [9]. Therefore, their performance differs if they are put into context for which they have not been designed. Microscopic models are usually suited to simulate pedestrians in low- and medium-density situations, where the density level is less than 2 ped/m² [1]. These models encounter specific problems when applied to high-density situations, such as abnormal vibrations with the Social Force Model [10], congestion in dense bidirectional flow with the Velocity Obstacle model [11], unrealistic results in terms of collision metrics with the data-driven models [12]. On the other hand, pedestrian dynamics in high-density situations are similar to fluid flow [13], and fluid-like equation models [13,14] are particularly appropriate for these scenarios due to their assumption of the continuous of pedestrian flow.

Given that we observe varying performance of pedestrian models in different crowd densities, this contribution proposes and evaluates an agent-based architecture to enable agents to dynamically change their operational model based on local density to adapt to their dynamic environments. Local density estimation is achieved through predefined regions in the environment, which enables contextual and structured adaptation to various environments. Additionally, the use of predefined areas can facilitate the implementation of the model by providing a more intuitive and manageable approach to estimating density.

The paper is organized as follows: In Sect. 2, a summary of related works is provided. Section 3 describes our proposed agent-based architecture for the multi-level behaviour of pedestrians. Next, Sect. 4 illustrates the experimental design and presents our simulation results. Finally, the paper ends with a conclusion and discussion in Sect. 5.

2 Related Work

Helbing et al. introduced the Social Force Model (SFM) [7], which describes pedestrian motion as driven by social forces. These forces result from both internal factors, such as an individual's attraction towards a personal goal, and external factors, like repulsion from neighboring pedestrians and walls. The SFM is formulated based on Newton's second law:

$$m_i\frac{dv_i}{dt} = m_i\frac{v_i^0(t)e_i^0(t) - v_i(t)}{\tau_i} + \sum_{j\neq i} f_{ij} + \sum_W f_{iW} \tag{1}$$

where m_i, v_i, v_i^0, and e_i^0 represent the mass, current velocity, preferred speed, and desired direction of pedestrian i, respectively. The first term of Eq. 1 accounts for the acceleration from current velocity to the preferred velocity within the reaction time τ_i, while f_{ij} and f_{iW} describe interaction forces with other pedestrians and walls, respectively. The SFM has been demonstrated to realistically reproduce self-organization phenomena in low-density situations such as lane formation and arc-shaped clogging at bottlenecks [7].

On the other hand, Treuille et al. [14] proposed the Continuum Crowds (CC) model which treats pedestrian flow similarly as a continuum without taking into account individual differences. Global navigation is managed by dynamic potential field using the eikonal equation (Eq. 2):

$$||\nabla\phi(x)|| = C \tag{2}$$

$$v = -f(x,\theta)\frac{\nabla\phi(x)}{||\nabla\phi(x)||} \tag{3}$$

where ϕ, C are potential function and unit cost in the direction $\nabla\phi$, respectively. The cost value to the goals is based on distance, time and discomfort factor. Pedestrian velocity is determined by the direction opposite the gradient of function in Eq. 2, with the magnitude dependent on the local area's density field and velocity field. The CC model is suitable for simulating large crowds in extreme-density situations with computational efficiency.

The aforementioned models are only suitable for simulating pedestrians in either low-density or high-density scenarios [10,14]. To simulate pedestrians in both low-density and high-density situations simultaneously, hybrid modeling is often employed, typically combining macroscopic and microscopic models. Auto-switch models [15,16] move from a macroscopic model to a microscopic model and vice versa on a trigger condition, while region-based model [17] specifies certain areas for each model. A mechanism for the aggregation and disaggregation of crowds is required for these models to have a consistent transition between the macroscopic and microscopic levels. However, these models normally ignore a higher level of pedestrian behaviour modeling and are therefore only applied in a simple environment with a single infrastructure. Recently, Curtis et al. [18] proposed the Menge framework, a crowd simulator that aggregates different modeling algorithms for each level of pedestrian behaviour. Despite its advancements, this framework only allows for one modeling technique to be implemented at the operational level in the whole simulation.

Currently, there is a lack of a general framework for modeling multi-level pedestrian behaviour that allows agents to dynamically change their operational model. To tackle this challenge, our work focuses on developing an agent-based architecture that models multi-level pedestrian behaviour and is compatible with a variety of modeling algorithms at each level. Moreover, this architecture enables pedestrian agents to switch their operational model in response to changes in local density. A detailed description is provided in the following section.

3   Proposed Model

3.1   General Overview

In dynamic environments where the density state of each area changes over time, the environment is divided into several zones either based on expert knowledge or dynamic segmentation according to crowd density. These zones are classified as *high-density zones* (as shown by the red dashed area in Fig. 1) and low-density regions (the region outside of the dashed area in Fig. 1). Each zone is associated with specific triggering rules and transition functions.

The triggering rules evaluate pedestrian and environmental characteristics within the respective zone to select suitable models for pedestrian simulation. Due to the varying performance of pedestrian models across different crowd densities, these rules identify appropriate models to accurately capture the dynamics within each area. When new individuals enter a zone, the transition functions are activated to adapt their information, facilitating a smooth transition from their previous zone to the current one.

When entering a new zone, pedestrians adjust their tactical and operational models to align with the requirements of the corresponding zone. To ensure a generic and extensible approach for various models, an agent-based architecture is proposed in Sect. 3.2 to model the multi-level behaviour of pedestrians. This agent-based architecture enables pedestrians to dynamically select the appropriate modeling algorithm at each level of behaviour.

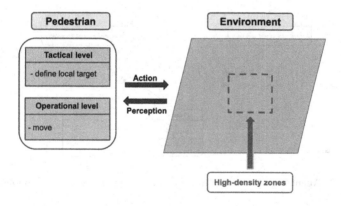

Fig. 1. General overview.

3.2   Agent-Based Architecture for Multi-level Behaviour

To develop an agent-based architecture for multi-level pedestrian behaviour, an abstraction is first introduced to describe the problem of pedestrian modeling.

The problem is divided into two subproblems: *tactical* and *operational subproblem*[1]. Suppose that $S = \{E, A\}$, where E and A are the environment and the set of agents in simulation respectively. The *tactical subproblem* can be formalized by the function T, $T : S \times t \times \mathbb{R}^2 \to \mathbb{R}^2$, which maps the simulation state, time, and the agents' destination to the local target which is in $\mathbb{R}^2$. The *operational subproblem* can be formalized as follows: $O : S \times t \times \mathbb{R}^2 \times [0,1] \to \mathbb{R}^2$. The function O maps the local simulation state S, time, local target, and check if agents in *high-density zones* to a feasible velocity, which is then used to update agents' locations in the next simulation step. In general, the problem of pedestrian modeling can be stated by the following mathematical formulation:

$$v_i(t) = O_i(T_i(t)) \tag{4}$$
$$p_i(t+1) = p_i(t) + v_i(t)\Delta t \tag{5}$$

where $v_i(t)$ and $p_i(t)$ are the velocity and the location of agent i in the xy-coordinate system at time t respectively and Δt is the duration of a simulation step.

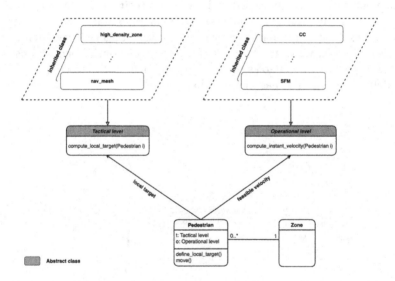

Fig. 2. Agent-based architecture for multi-level pedestrian behaviour.

Given the description above, an agent-based architecture is designed as shown in Fig. 2. To include different modeling algorithms, each subproblem is represented by an abstract class. The *tactical subproblem* is presented by the *Tactical level* while the *Operational level* class presents the *operational subproblem*. Each abstract class can contain different inheritance subclasses, where each subclass represents a specific model to simulate various behaviour depending on the situations (strategy pattern). The pedestrian agents are only allowed to present one

---

[1] The integration of *strategic subproblem* is not in the scope of this paper.

model for each level of behaviour at a time, but that model may be changed based on the state of the environment in which the pedestrian agents are operating.

Each modeling algorithm for each level needs to inherit the corresponding abstract class. The *Tactical Level* and *Operational Level* classes return the local target and feasible velocity for pedestrians, respectively. What should be noted here is that in the simulation environment, excluding *Pedestrian* class, only one single instance of each class is created (singleton pattern). Therefore, our architecture does not increase complexity but improves the flexibility of simulation. Furthermore, it is possible to change the modeling algorithm at each level of behaviour by simply updating the variables t and o in *Pedestrian* class.

3.3   Pedestrian Activity Diagram

Figure 3 illustrates the activity diagram of pedestrian agents at each simulation step. Initially, the agents perceive their surrounding environment to identify neighboring agents. Subsequently, if the agents have either reached their current local target or do not have a local target, they execute *define local target* behaviour which invokes their corresponding inheritance model from the *Tactical level* class to assign a new local target. Afterward, pedestrian agents perform the *move* behaviour using the returned velocity from their respective inheritance model in the *Operational level*.

After moving to new locations, pedestrians check whether they have arrived at their destination. If yes, their movement is completed. Otherwise, they determine if they have transitioned into a new zone. In such cases, pedestrian agents need to update their states by sending a request to the Zone entity to obtain information about the tactical and operational models employed in this new zone. This query returns the results o_{new} and t_{new}, which represent the operational and tactical in use within the zone, respectively. Pedestrians then update their attributes by setting their operational variable o to o_{new} and their tactical variable t to t_{new}.

This continuous process of perceiving the environment, defining local targets, moving, and updating states based on zone transitions enables pedestrian agents to navigate through the simulation space effectively. This dynamic approach allows for the modeling of complex scenarios and interactions between agents, accounting for varying tactical and operational models across different zones.

4   Experiments and Results

This section presents a set of simulations to demonstrate the capabilities of our proposed architecture. More precisely, the ability to dynamically change the operational model is studied through simulations of crowd exit during the Festival of Lights [19] at the Place des Terreaux, Lyon, France. Simulation results are compared between our model and different other models in terms of density map, pedestrian outflow, and performance.

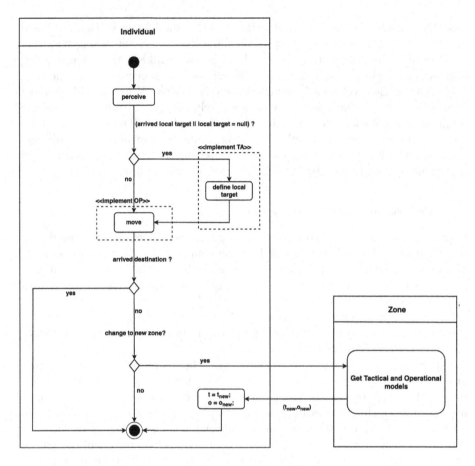

Fig. 3. Pedestrian's activity diagram at each simulation step.

4.1 Experiment Design

The simulation area is the Place des Terreaux, a large plaza located in Lyon, France (highlighted by the red dashed rectangle in Fig. 4a) with an area of 7000 m². During the Festival of Lights [19], pedestrians gather at the plaza to watch the show, which is projected onto the walls of the surrounding buildings (see Fig. 4b). After the show ends, pedestrians head towards the two pre-configured exits (as illustrated by the bottom-left blue arrows in Fig. 4a) to explore new attractions. To accommodate these movements, the environment is discretized into three distinct zones (illustrated by the three dashed rectangles in Fig. 4a).

During the pedestrian exit process, the plaza experiences high density, while the two exits exhibit lower density. Our proposed architecture can effectively handle such multi-density situations. The experiment configuration is as follows:

– The simulation is conducted with a time step $\Delta t = 0.1$ s, with 6000 agents.

(a) Main circulation of the exiting crowd.

(b) Pedestrians watching the show at the Place des Terreaux.

Fig. 4. Information of the Festival of Lights [19]. (https://www.fetedeslumieres.lyon. fr/fr/oeuvre/grand-mix-au-musee-des-beaux-arts-de-lyon.)

- The CC model [14] for a single target cell is used to simulate pedestrians in the plaza (*high-density zones*) due to its effectiveness in dense scenarios. This approach leads to further discretization into cells, each storing information about the environment and the pedestrians, such as average velocity and local density.
- The SFM [7] is applied for those who have exited the plaza as it can realistically simulate pedestrians in low-density situations.
- In the CC model, the minimum and maximum speeds are set to 0.05 m/s and 1.4 m/s respectively.
- The parameters for the SFM are chosen to be consistent with those in [20], where the distribution of the preferred speed is Gaussian with the mean of 1.34 m/s and the standard deviation of 0.26 m/s, with a maximum preferred speed of 1.74 m/s.

The proposed model is compared to three others: SFM-only (which applies the SFM in all three zones), 3-CC-1 model (consisting of three separate CC models, each with one target cell for simulating a single zone), and 1-CC-2 model (using one CC model for simulating the entire environment, with two target cells for two exits in two blue dashed areas in Fig. 4a). These comparisons are based on simulations of crowd exits with 6000 agents. For each simulation, three indicators are computed, and an average is determined from a total of 15 simulations for each model:

- Density map (in ped/m^2) of pedestrian density distribution across the simulation area.
- Outflow (in $ped/simulation\ step$) of pedestrians exiting the plaza to the two exits.
- Computation time (in s) required to calculate one simulation step.

All simulations are conducted using the GAMA platform [21] on a M1 MacBook Pro with 32 GB of memory.

4.2   Results

Figure 5a displays the simulation of 6000 agents at Place des Terreaux, with pedestrians in *high-density zones* represented in red and pedestrians in low-density regions shown in blue. In comparison, Fig. 5b presents the histogram of pedestrian speeds for both low-density regions and *high-density zones*. As expected, the speed distribution in the *high-density zones* differs from that in the low-density regions. The mean speed of pedestrians in the *high-density zones* is 0.39 m/s, which is substantially lower than the mean speed of 1.37 m/s in the low-density regions. The observed differences in speed distributions between the two areas suggest that the characteristics of pedestrians in low- and high-density situations can be mimicked by incorporating suitable models at the operational level in our architecture.

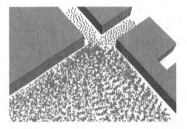

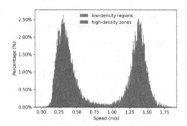

(a) Simulation of 6000 agents at the Place des Terreaux.

(b) Comparison of speed histogram of two regions.

Fig. 5. Simulation results.

Next, comparisons of different models are evaluated in terms of the density map and pedestrian outflow. Figure 6 presents the density maps of various models over different time steps ($t = 60$ s, 150 s, 240 s). In the SFM-only model, the highest density area, with a maximum density of 3.5 ped/m^2, is observed in both the plaza and the two exits. Similarly, the 3-CC-1 model and 1-CC-2 model can simulate extremely high densities of 6–8 ped/m^2, but these extremely high-density areas also appear in both the plaza and the two exits. In contrast, our model exhibits a clear difference in density levels between the plaza and the two exits. Moreover, Fig. 7a, which shows the outflow of pedestrians exiting the plaza for each model over the simulation time, shows that our model's pedestrian outflow results are similar to those of the other models, with a maximum outflow of approximately 1.4 pedestrians per simulation step and a total of approximately 6800 simulation steps. These results indicate that our model can effectively simulate pedestrians in environments with a mix of low- and high-density situations while having similar results of the pedestrian outflow with the other models. Furthermore, a key advantage of this architecture is its generic nature and flexibility, as it can accommodate any combination of zones and models, enabling the modeling of various scenarios and crowd dynamics.

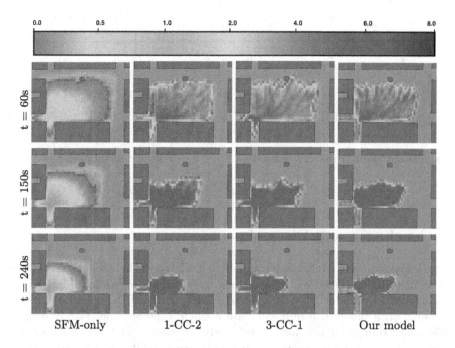

Fig. 6. Density maps among different models with 6000 simulated agents.

Finally, various numbers of pedestrian agents ($3K$ to $15K$) are used to evaluate the simulation time of different models. The results, shown in Fig. 7b, indicate that the SFM-only and 3-CC-1 models have the longest simulation times,
which increase significantly as the number of pedestrians grows, while the 1-CC-
2 model has a similar simulation time to them at first but drops as the number
of agents increases. In contrast, our model demonstrates superior performance in
terms of simulation time, with a large difference from the other models observed
as the number of pedestrians grows. This finding indicates that using mesoscopic models for low-density regions is unnecessary, and they can be replaced
with microscopic models. These results suggest that having different modeling
algorithms at each level not only improves the variety of behaviour observed in
various scenarios but also enhances overall performance compared to using only
microscopic models or multiple mesoscopic models.

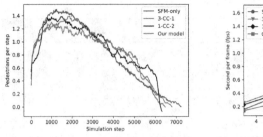 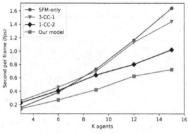

(a) The outflow over the simulation time.   (b) Model performance.

Fig. 7. Comparison results of different models.

5   Conclusion and Discussion

Large-scale crowd phenomena are complex to model as the behaviour of pedestrians needs to be described at both strategic, tactical, and operational levels and it is impacted by the density of the crowd. Particularly in the operational level modeling, each model can only simulate a single type of pedestrian dynamic, while pedestrian dynamics vary significantly depending on the density of the environment. This paper proposes an agent-based architecture for simulating the multi-level behaviour of pedestrians, where agents are able to dynamically change their operational model based on local density. Our architecture is evaluated through a use case of pedestrians at the Festival of Lights, Lyon, France with simulation results compared to different models in terms of density map, pedestrian outflow, and computation time. The results demonstrate that our agent-based architecture can effectively simulate pedestrians in diverse-density situations, providing flexibility for incorporating various models, and enhancing runtime performance while achieving comparable pedestrian outflow results to alternative models. Our architecture is not only generic in the domain of pedestrian modeling but also extensible to other domains such as traffic simulation and social simulation.

Our future work aims to incorporate a greater variety of modeling algorithms for each level of behaviour, particularly at the operational level. Then, the selection of an optimal algorithm at each level of behaviour and the criteria for switching these algorithms need to be defined based on the density of each region. Another promising direction involves applying density-based clustering algorithms to pedestrian coordinates in order to dynamically estimate the local density of environments.

Acknowledgements. The authors acknowledge the Franco-German research project MADRAS funded in France by the Agence Nationale de la Recherche (ANR, French National Research Agency), grant number ANR-20-CE92-0033, and in Germany by the Deutsche Forschungsgemeinschaft (DFG, German Research Foundation), grant number 446168800.

References

1. Duives, D., Daamen, W., Hoogendoorn, S.: State-of-the-art crowd motion simulation models. Transp. Res. Part C: Emerg. Technol. **37**, 193–209 (2013)
2. Hoogendoorn, S., Bovy, P.: Pedestrian route-choice and activity scheduling theory and models. Transp. Res. Part B: Methodol. **38**, 169–190 (2004)
3. Haghani, M., Sarvi, M.: Human exit choice in crowded built environments: investigating underlying behavioural differences between normal egress and emergency evacuations. Fire Saf. J. **85**, 1–9 (2016)
4. Kielar, P., Borrmann, A.: Modeling pedestrians' interest in locations: a concept to improve simulations of pedestrian destination choice. Simul. Modell. Pract. Theory **61**, 47–62 (2016)
5. Van Toll, W., Cook, A., IV., Geraerts, R.: Real-time density-based crowd simulation. Comput. Anim. Virtual Worlds **23**, 59–69 (2012)
6. Jiang, Y., Chen, B., Li, X., Ding, Z.: Dynamic navigation field in the social force model for pedestrian evacuation. Appl. Math. Model. **80**, 815–826 (2020)
7. Helbing, D., Farkas, I., Vicsek, T.: Simulating dynamical features of escape panic. Nature **407**, 487–490 (2000)
8. Berg, J., Guy, S., Lin, M., Manocha, D.: Reciprocal n-body collision avoidance. Robot. Res. 3–19 (2011)
9. Papadimitriou, E., Yannis, G., Golias, J.: A critical assessment of pedestrian behaviour models. Transp. Res. Part F: Traffic Psychol. Behav. **12**, 242–255 (2009)
10. Pelechano, N., Allbeck, J., Badler, N.: Controlling individual agents in high-density crowd simulation. In: 2007 Eurographics/SIGGRAPH Symposium on Computer Animation, pp. 99–108 (2007)
11. Zhao, M., Zhong, J., Cai, W.: A role-dependent data-driven approach for high-density crowd behaviour modeling. ACM Trans. Model. Comput. Simul. (TOMACS) **28**, 1–25 (2018)
12. Korbmacher, R., Dang-Huu, T., Tordeux, A., Verstaevel, N., Gaudou, B.: Differences in pedestrian trajectory predictions for high-and low-density situations. In: 14th International Conference on Traffic And Granular Flow (TGF) 2022 (2022)
13. Helbing, D.: A fluid dynamic model for the movement of pedestrians. Complex Syst. **6** (1998)
14. Treuille, A., Cooper, S., Popović, Z.: Continuum crowds. ACM Trans. Graph. (TOG) **25**, 1160–1168 (2006)
15. Xiong, M., et al.: A case study of multi-resolution modeling for crowd simulation. In: Proceedings of the 2009 Spring Simulation Multiconference, pp. 1–8 (2009)
16. Xiong, M., Tang, S., Zhao, D.: A hybrid model for simulating crowd evacuation. N. Gener. Comput. **31**, 211–235 (2013)
17. Xiong, M., Lees, M., Cai, W., Zhou, S., Low, M.: Hybrid modelling of crowd simulation. Procedia Comput. Sci. **1**, 57–65 (2010)
18. Curtis, S., Best, A., Manocha, D.: Menge: a modular framework for simulating crowd movement. Collect. Dyn. **1**, 1–40 (2016)
19. Festival of Lights. https://www.fetedeslumieres.lyon.fr
20. Helbing, D., Molnar, P.: Social force model for pedestrian dynamics. Phys. Rev. E **51**, 4282 (1995)
21. Taillandier, P., et al.: Building, composing and experimenting complex spatial models with the GAMA platform. GeoInformatica **23**, 299–322 (2019)

Resolving the Dilemma of Responsibility in Multi-agent Flow Networks

Jayati Deshmukh$^{(\boxtimes)}$ (ID), Nikitha Adivi (ID), and Srinath Srinivasa (ID)

International Institute of Information Technology, Bangalore, Bangalore, India
jayati.deshmukh@iiitb.org, {nikitha.adivi,sri}@iiitb.ac.in

Abstract. Multi-agent networks often face the "dilemma of responsibility" where optimising for individual utility may result in sub-optimal network-level outcomes. But, imposing constraints on individual agents for obtaining better network-level indicators, may severely impede their utilities and rationale for participating in the network. We address this problem of the conflict between individual utility and collective outcomes, using a decentralised approach called *Computational Transcendence* (CT) which is based on modelling agents with an *elastic sense of self*. We discuss how this model can be applied to realistic multi-agent application scenarios. The first scenario is on decision-making in multi-agent supply chains, and the second is on adaptive signalling in a road network. In both these applications, we compare CT with several baseline models and find improvements across multiple application-specific metrics. CT is shown to outperform strategies for individual utility maximisation, by improving network-level indicators in an emergent manner, without posing a high burden of responsibility on individual agents.

Keywords: multi agent systems · responsible AI · identity

1 Introduction

Autonomous agents are gaining prevalence across a variety of applications like customer service, healthcare, automobile, agriculture, military etc [19,20]. The increasing prevalence of autonomous agents has raised the urgency of designing for *responsible autonomy* in multi-agent interactions. Responsible autonomy in multi-agent flow networks can be viewed as a subset of a larger set of ethical issues that are particularly concerned with protecting common welfare while pursuing self-interest.

Different approaches have been used to address responsible behaviour in autonomous agents [1,24]. Top-down approaches add an additional ethical layer and expected behaviours are translated into norms and constraints that the agents must uphold [4]. On the other hand, in case of bottom-up approaches, agents learn expected behaviours based on their interactions with other agents and the environment using techniques like reinforcement learning and evolutionary computing. Finally, hybrid approaches combine both these approaches bringing in learning of agents and expertise of the system designer.

© The Author(s), under exclusive license to Springer Nature Switzerland AG 2023
P. Mathieu et al. (Eds.): PAAMS 2023, LNAI 13955, pp. 76–87, 2023.
https://doi.org/10.1007/978-3-031-37616-0_7

In addition, the concept of responsibility in autonomous decision making is itself pursued from multiple paradigmatic viewpoints [8,9,24]. In this paper, we develop on an approach called *computational transcendence* [8], where responsibility is modelled as an emergent characteristic of an *elastic sense of self* of individual agents. Such "transcended" autonomous agents are said to have *identified* to different extents, with other agents and stakeholders of the system. However, this model has been demonstrated only on abstract theoretical frameworks so far. In this paper, we extend the core concept of transcendence to realistic application scenarios like supply chains and vehicular traffic management where agents optimise flows in the respective networks using a continuous utility function leading to emergent responsible behaviour.

A supply chain comprises of producers, consumers, and several intermediaries who aggregate and ship orders in order to obtain economies of scale. Autonomous decision-making by intermediaries on when to ship orders, is primarily based on maximising their returns, but it also has an impact on the prospects of the buyers and sellers. Responsible autonomy requires agents to operate such that not just their individual prospects improve, but their actions also lead to efficient flow of orders in the the supply chain as a whole.

Another application is of adaptive traffic lights, which make traffic flows smoother and efficient [16]. These traffic lights change phase dynamically depending on the traffic flows on different incoming lanes of an intersection. However, most existing models of adaptive traffic lights optimise to regulate traffic only at its own intersection, which may often conflict with the prospects of other traffic lights in the vicinity. We apply computational transcendence for this application scenario to manage traffic flows based on traffic at neighbourhood level.

Major contributions presented in this paper are as follows: 1. We reintroduce an intrinsic model of building responsible AI called Computational Transcendence (CT). 2. We model transcended agents in a supply chain scenario and present its impact in comparison to baseline models of virtuous agents which minimise delay and selfish agents which optimise for their metrics. 3. We present results of using transcended traffic lights and compare it with other kinds of existing strategies for adaptive traffic lights.

2   Related Work

In this section, first the broad area of responsible AI and its significance and practical implementations are discussed. Then we discuss some of the existing computational models of autonomous agents in the field of supply chains and traffic lights, specifically focusing on the responsibility aspect of agents.

As systems of autonomous agents gain prevalence, it is crucial to design agents that can be guaranteed to act responsibly. Broadly machine ethics looks at designing systems where agents act ethically [2,18]. Three key paradigmatic approaches to ethics have received a lot of research interest– consequentialism, deontological ethics, and virtue ethics [24]. Consequentialism is focused on acting so as to lead to certain desired consequences– like collective welfare; while deontological ethics is based on learning "expected" behaviour, based on how other agents interact, in order to ascertain what is considered ethical; and finally, virtue ethics is based on upholding a pre-programmed virtue (like courage, loyalty, etc.) irrespective of consequences or acceptability of behaviour.

Ethics is a broad field, with several open philosophical questions. However, a subset of machine ethics, called 'responsible AI' focuses on tractable concerns like upholding safety, accountability, explainability within an overarching framework of ethics [6,7,9,10,22]. Frameworks for responsible AI have been developed for applications like conservation, healthcare, education [11,25,28]. In the case of computational transcendence [8], responsible behaviour is defined as upholding collective welfare in the presence of individually beneficial actions for an agent.

Supply Chain modelling (SCM) is useful to design efficient systems of procurement and distribution that transfer goods and information [17]. A variety of computational models of supply chains are used to simulate different kinds of scenarios and evaluate the system [26]. Simulation techniques are useful to understand how different components interact with each other and to evaluate the systems, on metrics like quality, cost, delays etc [21]. For decentralised control in supply chains, multi-agent and game-theoretic modelling becomes attractive [5].

Managing traffic in a network is an adaptation instead of an optimisation problem [14]. Traffic flow can be modelled on a network with intersections (controlled by traffic lights) as nodes and roads as edges. A variety of techniques have been used to design and model intelligent traffic lights [27,29].

3   Computational Transcendence

Computational transcendence [8] models an elastic sense of self in agents such that they can *identify* with other agents, collectives and concepts in the system. Formally, the sense of self of an agent a is modelled as follows: $S(a) = (I_a, d_a, \gamma_a)$

Here, I_a represents the identity set which consists of aspects (agents, collectives and concepts) which agent a identifies with. d_a represents semantic distance of agent a to every aspect in its identity set. And γ_a represents the level of elasticity or transcendence of the agent. Agent a, with elasticity γ_a identifies with an aspect at o distance $d_a(o)$ with an attenuation factor of $\gamma_a^{d_a(o)}$.

Depending on the elastic identity of an agent, the utility it derives is a combination of its own payoffs as well as scaled payoffs derived by aspects in its identity set. Let $\pi_i(o)$ denote the payoff of aspect o, then the utility u of agent a when the system is in state i is computed as follows:

$$u_i(a) = \frac{1}{\sum\limits_{\forall o \in I_a} \gamma_a^{d_a(o)}} \sum_{\forall o \in I_a} \gamma_a^{d_a(o)} \pi_i(o) \tag{1}$$

Transcendence in game theoretic scenarios like prisoners' dilemma, 3−player games with collusion, effect of adversarial agents, evolutionary variant of transcendence etc. has been discussed in detail [8]. In this paper, we look at some practical, real-world applications of transcendence.

4   Applications of Computational Transcendence

In game-theoretic contexts like prisoners' dilemma and collusion, computational transcendence leads to collective good even when there is an incentive to act selfishly [8]. Computational Transcendence is therefore applicable in all cases where agents face the dilemma of responsibility with the following conflicting choices– a *responsible* choice that may incur a cost, but brings overall benefit vs a *selfish* or an *irresponsible* choice that minimises cost for the agent, but may negatively affect the overall system. The core model can thus be potentially adapted to applications in areas where autonomous agents are expected to act responsibly. In this section, we demonstrate how this paradigm can be incorporated in autonomous agents in supply chains and traffic management.

4.1   Supply Chain Management

Multi-agent systems provide tools for decentralised supply chain management [13], by representing its components, behaviours and interactions using autonomous entities which makes decisions autonomously in known and unknown scenarios [23]. Self-organisation based evolutionary techniques have also been used for manufacturing systems [3]. Autonomous entities like material vendors, suppliers, distributors, retailers etc. work towards a common goal of the supply chain while trying to minimise their own cost, thus creating a prisoners' dilemma like situation. Supply chains should operate such that overall system level goals are met and individual agents in the supply chain are also able to fulfil their individual objectives. Thus computational transcendence is useful in this context to design a responsible supply chain management system. We discuss the modelling of a supply chain with transcended agents and conduct experiments and analysis on this model.

Methodology. We consider a community of autonomous agents forming a supply chain network represented by a simple, undirected graph, with nodes representing agents and edges representing pair-wise interactions between agents.

In this network, each node can perform following activities: (a) Initiating the order and (b) Forwarding orders from others. This supply chain is a $1-tier$ supply chain of a seller, wholesaler and buyer, i.e. the order starts from the source (seller) and passes through one intermediary (wholesaler) before reaching the destination (buyer). Orders O in the supply chain are generated at random and represented as follows: $O = <s, i, d, ts>$ Here, s represents the seller, i represents the intermediary, d represents the buyer and ts is the timestamp at which the order is generated. Agent that initiates an order gets a payoff (μ) when the order successfully reaches its destination and incurs a cost based on delay (Δ) by the intermediary in shipping the order ($C_{total} = c \times \Delta$) where c is the cost per unit of delay. Intermediaries have following two choices:

1. *Wait, w*: Every agent has a wait queue (Q) that represents the warehouse of a supply chain entity. When the agent chooses to wait, orders are pushed into

the wait queue. For each order in the wait queue, the agent incurs a small bookkeeping cost that is a function of the delay since when the order has been pushed into the wait queue. ($bk_{total} = \Delta \times bk$.)

2. *Forward, f*: When the agent chooses to forward, the wait queue or the warehouse is emptied and the agent incurs a van cost (vc) that represents the transportation costs in a supply chain. The agent however does not obtain any payoff for successfully delivering the order.

As the bookkeeping cost is relatively less than the van cost, there is no rational incentive for an agent to forward orders sent by others. However, agents initiating the orders, need the cooperation of intermediaries to successfully complete their orders. The intermediaries can thus follow different strategies to make this choice and it impacts both the intermediary as well as the seller.

Types of Agents: We introduce the following three types of intermediary agents and their strategies of forwarding orders in the supply chain network:

1. *Selfish Agent*: This agent acts selfishly and minimises its total cost at the node level. When the bookkeeping cost of all the orders in the wait queue becomes higher than the van cost, the agent forwards. The forward logic is as follows:
$$prob(f) = 1 \text{ if } bk_{total} > vc$$

2. *Virtue Agent - Delay*: This agent acts virtuously by minimising the average delay per order. Minimising delays leads to lower cost for the seller and in turn for the buyer. It is modelled such that as its delay increases, its forward probability exponentially increases as follows:
$$prob(f) = 1 - e^{-\frac{\Delta}{total waiting}}$$

3. *Transcended Agent*: A transcended agent decides based on its own cost and utility as well as the impact of its action on the source (seller) agent. The payoff matrix for the intermediary agent i and source agent s is shown in Table 1. When i forwards, it incurs a van cost vc while the source agent gets a payoff depending on the utility and delay for its orders. On the other hand when i waits, it incurs a bookkeeping cost bk while the source incurs a cost proportional to the delay of its orders. Here sellers are the aspects which a transcended agent accounts for by having transcendence level γ and a semantic distance d to each of its sellers. Expected utility of the two choices of forward or wait is computed and based on it the intermediary decides the probability to forward the orders as follows:
$$u_f = \frac{1}{1+\gamma^d}[-vc + \gamma^d(\mu_{total} - C_{total})] \quad and \quad u_w = \frac{1}{1+\gamma^d}[-bk_{total} + \gamma^d(-C_{total})]$$
$$prob(f) = \frac{u_f}{u_f + u_w}$$

Supply Chain Efficiency Indicators: We account following three criteria that reflect the effectiveness of a supply chain. Also, an efficient supply chain minimises total cost, maximises total utility and minimises average delay per order.

Table 1. Payoffs for intermediary (i) and source (s) for intermediary's decision

		Agent i	Agent s
Agent i	forward	$-vc$	$\mu_{total} - C_{total}$
	wait	$-bk_{total}$	$-C_{total}$

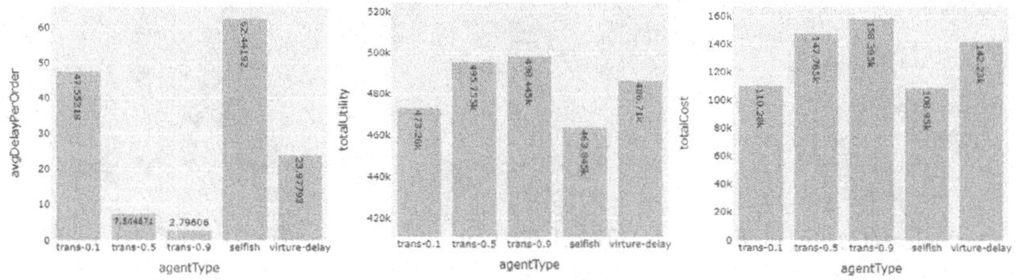

(a) Avg Delay per Order   (b) Total Utility   (c) Total Cost

Fig. 1. Supply chain metrics of different types of agents

1. *Total Cost:* It represents the total logistic cost of the supply chain, sum total of the van cost and the bookkeeping cost of all the nodes in the network.
2. *Total Utility:* It represents the net utility gained due to the successful shipping of the orders. It also accounts for the cost due to the delay.
3. *Average delay per order:* It represents the latency of the supply chain. It shows the typical time it takes for a consumer to get the order.

Experiments and Results. The supply chain setup represents a 1−tier supply chain modelled using an Erdős-Rényi network of 100 nodes and 10,000 orders. Following are the key parameters with their default values– order utility ($\mu = 50$), van cost ($vc = 60$), bookkeeping cost ($bk = 5$) and order cost ($c = 5$) which are used for the simulation. However, these can be tweaked based on a specific supply chain use case.

Efficiency of supply chains for different industries is determined by a variety of indicators. For some industries like fast fashion and perishable goods industry, time is an extremely important factor. For other industries, transportation costs and warehouse capacity might have to be considered. For industries that are just starting out, minimising average delay per order is extremely important for customer attraction and gaining a hold of the market. Amongst the diverse factors that affect decision making in a supply chain, we experiment with a few of them and discuss corresponding results as follows.

Across Different Transcendence Levels
We perform the simulation for three transcendence levels $\gamma = \{0.1, 0.5, 0.9\}$ as shown in Fig. 1. We observe that as transcendence level γ increases, total cost increases and total utility also increases. At the same time, average delay per order reduces leading to higher customer satisfaction. Varying transcendence level γ generates agents displaying a broad variety of responsible behaviour.

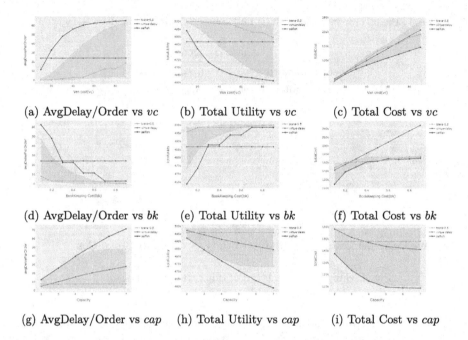

(a) AvgDelay/Order vs *vc*   (b) Total Utility vs *vc*   (c) Total Cost vs *vc*

(d) AvgDelay/Order vs *bk*   (e) Total Utility vs *bk*   (f) Total Cost vs *bk*

(g) AvgDelay/Order vs *cap*   (h) Total Utility vs *cap*   (i) Total Cost vs *cap*

Fig. 2. Supply chain metrics on varying van cost *vc*, storage cost *bk* and warehouse capacity *cap* for different supply chains (Color figure online)

We observed that transcended agents with different transcendence levels γ represent different behaviours. Therefore for further analysis as shown in Fig. 2, we vary γ in the range [0.1, 0.9] which is represented by the yellow shaded region and yellow line represents transcended agent with $\gamma = 0.5$. This is useful to present the complete extent of cost, utility and average delay of transcended agents and compare it with selfish agents represented by blue line and virtue-delay agent represented by pink line.

Effect of Transportation Cost *vc*

Figures 2a, 2b and 2c show the supply chain efficiency indicators for different kinds of agents as transportation cost indicated by van cost *vc* is varied on the x−axis. Transportation cost denotes the cost incurred by intermediary in shipping the order. Shipping cost varies depending on the type of product being shipped like pharmaceuticals, automobile etc. As transportation cost increases, for all types of agents total cost increases. A selfish agent has the lowest cost since it optimises to reduce its node level cost. On the other hand, total utility reduces and average delay increases as van cost is increased for transcended and selfish agents. Utility and average delay of virtue-delay agent is unaffected by varying van costs.

We observe that at higher transcendence levels ($\gamma > 0.5$), transcended agents incur moderate costs and get high utility. Average delay per order is reduced for higher transcended agents despite increase in van cost since it ships orders sooner. The impact of transcendence is significant in case of high transportation cost ($vc > 50$).

Effect of Inventory Cost bk

Figures 2d, 2e and 2f show the efficiency indicators for different agents as storage costs indicated by book keeping cost bk is varied on the x−axis. For time sensitive products like perishable goods, fast fashion etc., delay has to be minimised and it needs to reach the end-user as soon as possible [30]. We have modelled bookkeeping cost as a function of the delay in our simulation. Bookkeeping cost is high for time sensitive products. We note that transcended agent performs best along all the efficiency indicators as compared to selfish and virtue-delay agents, when fulfilling time sensitive orders having high bookkeeping cost.

Effect of Warehouse Capacity cap

Supply chains are often constrained by warehouse capacity and this affects the way it operates [15]. If the supply chain entity does not have enough warehouse capacity, it is forced to forward the orders, thus incurring van cost. Figures 2g, 2h and 2i show the metrics for varying warehouse capacity. For lower capacity, the agent is forced to ship the orders, so transcending marginally reduces total utility and increases average delay per order. An agent with low transcendence level ($\gamma = 0.1$), shows similar trends across all metrics like a selfish agent. In case of low capacity, virtue-delay agent minimising delays has the lowest delays, highest utility but also highest costs. On the other hand, for supply chains having moderate/high capacity ($cap > 5$), even moderately transcended agents ($\gamma = 0.5$) are able to minimise delays, incur moderate cost and get a high utility.

4.2 Traffic Management

Adaptive traffic lights are gaining prominence with the advances in technology. An adaptive traffic light, which dynamically adapts to the traffic flow is better than a traditional fixed-cyclic traffic light. Most adaptive traffic lights in literature adapt based on traffic parameters like waiting time, queue length etc. at its own intersection. However, each traffic light optimising for itself is not necessarily optimal for the traffic flows at the network level [12]. In this paper, we propose transcended traffic lights which factor neighbouring traffic lights.

Methodology. Transcended traffic lights care about the waiting time of the vehicles they sent at the neighbouring intersections. This promotes smooth traffic flows in the network as a whole. A traffic light turns green for one of the incoming lanes and red for the rest. If a transcended traffic light I turns green for lane k and is red for all other lanes k', then other neighbouring traffic lights incur a cost, since the vehicles they sent have to wait at traffic light I where waiting time is denoted by wtk'. And the traffic light S which sent traffic in direction k gets a utility based on the number of cars which were cleared, qlk and the value it assigns to each car, $carU$. It gets a utility $qlk * carU$. The payoff matrix of traffic lights is shown in Table 2. Thus a transcended traffic light I, which values its neighbours $N(I)$ by γ and has a semantic distance d_n to each of its n neighbours, receives a utility for turning green for lane k as follows:

Table 2. Payoff matrix of traffic lights

		TL S_N	TL S_S	TL S_E	TL S_W
TL I	N	qlN * carU	-wtS	-wtE	-wtW
	S	-wtN	qlS * carU	-wtE	-wtW
	E	-wtN	-wtS	qlE * carU	-wtW
	W	-wtN	-wtS	-wtE	qlW * carU

$$u(I_k) = \frac{1}{1 + \sum\limits_{n \in N(I)} \gamma^{d_n}} \left(-\left(\sum_{n \in N(I)-\{I_k\}} \gamma^{d_n} * wtn \right) + \gamma^{d_k} (qlk * carU) \right) \quad (2)$$

Here, a transcended traffic light gets a scaled utility and cost of its neighbours. Next, it computes the utility for turning green for each of the incoming lanes. And then it probabilistically decides to turn green for one of the lanes.

Types of Traffic Lights: We have modelled following kinds of traffic lights:

1. *Maximum Waiting Time TL*: Find the waiting time of vehicles in each lane and turn green for the lane which has the most waiting time.
2. *Maximum Queue Length TL*: Find the queue length of vehicles in each lane and turn green for the lane which has the most queue length.
3. *Transcended TL*: It takes into account the traffic being sent by its neighbours. It periodically updates the semantic distance d_n to each of its n neighbouring traffic lights depending on the change in traffic flows since the previous update.

Traffic Related Metrics: We have used following traffic metrics to quantify traffic related parameters in the system as a whole:

1. *Average waiting time*: Waiting time is the time a vehicle spends below speed $0.1 m/s$ since the last time it was faster than that. Average waiting time is the average of waiting time of all the vehicles during the duration of the simulation.
2. *Average speed*: Average speed is the mean of average speed of each vehicle over the duration of the simulation.

Experiments and Results. Traffic simulation is done in a grid of 4 intersections as shown in Fig. 3a. Every intersection has 4 neighbours in four directions, $\{N, S, E, W\}$ as shown in Fig. 3b. Every edge is a single lane road. Every traffic light turns green for one edge and red for the rest of the edges. This duration denotes a phase of the traffic light. If two consecutive phases of a traffic light are different then a short yellow phase is inserted. The duration of green and yellow phases is fixed during the simulation. Traffic simulation is done using Simulation of Urban MObility (SUMO) and Traffic Control Interface (TraCI).

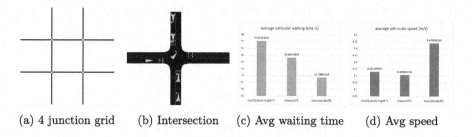

(a) 4 junction grid   (b) Intersection   (c) Avg waiting time   (d) Avg speed

Fig. 3. Traffic simulation in a grid and average resultant metrics

Traffic in the 4 intersection grid is randomly generated with around 2800 vehicles over the duration of 5400 time-steps with each vehicle having a random route in the grid. All four traffic lights are initialised to a fixed type and then we simulate traffic for 100 episodes. Average results of the traffic simulation are presented in Fig. 3c and 3d. Figure 3c shows the average vehicular waiting time where we note that max queue length traffic lights have the highest waiting time and transcended traffic lights have lowest waiting time. Similarly, Fig. 3d shows the average vehicular speed and we observe that speed is highest in case of a network with transcended traffic lights. Thus, we note that network-level traffic is smoothest with transcended traffic lights which factors its neighbours.

5   Discussion

Incorporating Transcendence in Applications. The model of computational transcendence is relevant in any scenario where there is a dilemma of responsibility, i.e. individual utility vs collective good. Computational transcendence can be incorporated in an application area by first identifying choices available to autonomous agents. For each choice, agents and entities in its identity set get a payoff as shown in Table 3.

Let t be a transcended agent with identity set consisting of agents denoted by $I = \{s_1, ..., s_n\}$ with semantic distances $\{d_1, ..., d_n\}$. For a choice k, it gets a payoff of a_k while all i agents in its identity set get a payoff of b_{ki}. Utility of choice k for agent t is represented by $u_k(t)$ which can be computed as follows:

$$u_k(t) = \frac{1}{1 + \gamma^{d_1} + ... + \gamma^{d_n}} [a_k + \gamma^{d_1} b_{k1} + ... + \gamma^{d_n} b_{kn}] \tag{3}$$

Using Eq. 3 and Table 3, agents can compute expected utility for each choice. Transcended agents account for their utilities as well as utilities of other aspects in their identity set leading to emergent responsible behaviour.

Adaptive Behaviour Using Transcendence. Responsible behaviour is not binary such that agents can be either responsible or irresponsible but rather it is a continuum. Transcendence can be used to model agents demonstrating varying levels of responsibility. Also, as discussed in [8], adaptive transcended

Table 3. Payoff matrix for transcendence agent t and identity set agents $\{s_1, ..., s_n\}$ as a result of decisions taken by agent t.

		Agent t	Agent s_1	...	Agent s_n
Agent t	$choice_1$	a_1	b_{11}	...	b_{1n}
	$choice_2$	a_2	b_{21}	...	b_{2n}
	$choice_k$	a_k	b_{k1}	...	b_{kn}

agents modify their behaviour based on dynamically changing environment. For example, in supply chain management, companies can use transcended agents which can adapt to ever changing markets, transportation costs, storage costs, etc.

6   Conclusions

Transcended agents have an elastic identity and thus they account for not just their payoffs but also the payoffs of others agents or aspects they identify with and thus they are able to resolve the dilemma of responsibility. We demonstrated that transcended agents can be modelled across a variety of realistic scenarios like supply chains, traffic management etc. These agents optimise network flows using continuous utility function and demonstrate intrinsically emergent responsible behaviour which upholds collective welfare. We hope that this work motivates and builds a case for designing responsible autonomous agents using computational transcendence across a diverse set of real-world applications.

References

1. Allen, C., Smit, I., Wallach, W.: Artificial morality: top-down, bottom-up, and hybrid approaches. Ethics Inf. Technol. **7**(3), 149–155 (2005)
2. Anderson, M., Anderson, S.L.: Machine ethics: creating an ethical intelligent agent. AI Mag. **28**(4), 15–15 (2007)
3. Barbosa, J., Leitão, P., Adam, E., Trentesaux, D.: Dynamic self-organization in holonic multi-agent manufacturing systems: the ADACOR evolution. Comput. Ind. **66**, 99–111 (2015)
4. Bremner, P., Dennis, L.A., Fisher, M., Winfield, A.F.: On proactive, transparent, and verifiable ethical reasoning for robots. Proc. IEEE **107**(3), 541–561 (2019)
5. Cachon, G.P., Netessine, S.: Game theory in supply chain analysis. Models, methods, and applications for innovative decision making, pp. 200–233 (2006)
6. Clarke, R.: Principles and business processes for responsible AI. Comput. Law Secur. Rev. **35**(4), 410–422 (2019)
7. Dastani, M., Yazdanpanah, V.: Responsibility of AI systems. AI Soc. (2022). https://doi.org/10.1007/s00146-022-01481-4
8. Deshmukh, J., Srinivasa, S.: Computational transcendence: responsibility and agency. Front. Robot. AI **9** (2022). https://doi.org/10.3389/frobt.2022.977303

9. Dignum, V.: Responsible autonomy. In: Proceedings of the Twenty-Sixth International Joint Conference on Artificial Intelligence, IJCAI-17, pp. 4698–4704 (2017)
10. Dignum, V.: Responsibility and artificial intelligence. Oxford Handb. Ethics AI **4698**, 215 (2020)
11. Dignum, V.: The role and challenges of education for responsible AI. Lond. Rev. Educ. **19**(1), 1–11 (2021)
12. France, J., Ghorbani, A.A.: A multiagent system for optimizing urban traffic. In: 2003 IEEE/WIC International Conference on Intelligent Agent Technology, IAT 2003, pp. 411–414. IEEE (2003)
13. Frey, D., Woelk, P.O., Stockheim, T., Zimmermann, R.: Integrated multi-agent-based supply chain management. In: 2003 Twelfth IEEE International Workshops on Enabling Technologies, pp. 24–29. IEEE (2003)
14. Gershenson, C.: Self-organizing traffic lights. arXiv preprint nlin/0411066 (2004)
15. Lee, W., Wang, S.P.: Managing level of consigned inventory with buyer's warehouse capacity constraint. Prod. Plann. Control **19**(7), 677–685 (2008)
16. McKenney, D., White, T.: Distributed and adaptive traffic signal control within a realistic traffic simulation. Eng. Appl. AI **26**(1), 574–583 (2013)
17. Min, H., Zhou, G.: Supply chain modeling: past, present and future. Comput. Industr. Eng. **43**(1–2), 231–249 (2002)
18. Moor, J.H.: The nature, importance, and difficulty of machine ethics. IEEE Intell. Syst. **21**(4), 18–21 (2006)
19. Pěchouček, M., Mařík, V.: Industrial deployment of multi-agent technologies: review and selected case studies. Auton. Agent. Multi-Agent Syst. **17**(3), 397–431 (2008)
20. Pechoucek, M., Thompson, S.G., Voos, H.: Defence Industry Applications of Autonomous Agents and Multi-agent Systems. Springer, Heidelberg (2008). https://doi.org/10.1007/978-3-7643-8571-2
21. Persson, F., Olhager, J.: Performance simulation of supply chain designs. Int. J. Prod. Econ. **77**(3), 231–245 (2002)
22. Peters, D., Vold, K., Robinson, D., Calvo, R.A.: Responsible AI-two frameworks for ethical design practice. IEEE Trans. Technol. Soc. **1**(1), 34–47 (2020)
23. Terrada, L., El Khaïli, M., Ouajji, H.: Multi-agents system implementation for supply chain management making-decision. Procedia Comput. Sci. **177**, 624–630 (2020)
24. Tolmeijer, S., Kneer, M., Sarasua, C., Christen, M., Bernstein, A.: Implementations in machine ethics: a survey. ACM Comput. Surv. (CSUR) **53**(6), 1–38 (2020)
25. Trocin, C., Mikalef, P., Papamitsiou, Z., Conboy, K.: Responsible AI for digital health: a synthesis and a research agenda. Inf. Syst. Front. 1–19 (2021)
26. Voß, S., Woodruff, D.L.: Introduction to Computational Optimization Models for Production Planning in a Supply Chain, vol. 240. Springer, Cham (2006). https://doi.org/10.1007/3-540-29879-7
27. Wang, Y., Yang, X., Liang, H., Liu, Y.: A review of the self-adaptive traffic signal control system based on future traffic environment. J. Adv. Transp. **2018** (2018)
28. Wearn, O.R., Freeman, R., Jacoby, D.M.: Responsible AI for conservation. Nat. Mach. Intell. **1**(2), 72–73 (2019)
29. Wiering, M., Veenen, J.V., Vreeken, J., Koopman, A., et al.: Intelligent traffic light control (2004)
30. Yu, M.: Analysis, design, and management of supply chain networks with applications to time-sensitive products. University of Massachusetts Amherst (2012)

Lessons Learned on the Design of a Predictive Agent for LoRaWAN Network Planning

Celia Garrido-Hidalgo[1,2(✉)], Jonathan Fürst[3], Luis Roda-Sanchez[2,4],
Teresa Olivares[1,2], and Antonio Fernández-Caballero[1,2]

[1] Departamento de Sistemas Informáticos, Universidad de Castilla-La Mancha,
Albacete, Spain
Celia.Garrido@uclm.es

[2] Instituto de Investigación en Informática de Albacete, Albacete, Spain

[3] Zürich University of Applied Sciences, Zürich, Switzerland

[4] NEC Ibérica, Madrid, Spain

Abstract. LoRaWAN is a low-power wide-area network standard widely used for long-range machine-to-machine communications in the Internet of Things ecosystem. While enabling ultra-low-power communication links, its open nature impulsed exponential market growth in the last years. Given its Aloha-like medium access nature, several scalability-oriented improvements were proposed in the last years, with time-slotted communications having raised special interest. However, how to efficiently allocate resources in a network where the cost of downlink communication is significantly higher than that of the uplink represents a significant challenge. To shed light on this matter, this work proposes the use of multi-agent systems for network planning in time-slotted communications. To do so, a predictive network planning agent is designed and validated as part of an end-to-end multi-agent network management system, which is based on multi-output regression that predicts the resulting network scalability for a given set of joining devices and setup scenarios being considered. A preliminary evaluation of network-status predictions showed a mean absolute error lower than 3% and pointed out different lessons learned, in turn validating the feasibility of the proposed agent for LoRaWAN-oriented network planning.

Keywords: MAS · LoRaWAN · Network Prediction · Scheduling

1 Introduction

LoRaWAN [11] is one of the dominant Low-Power Wide-Area Networks (LPWANs) for machine-type communication. While providing multiple benefits in terms of long-range and ultra-low power in the Internet of Things (IoT) domain, several scalability limitations were identified in recent years due to its Aloha-like medium access protocol nature [1]. While relevant resource-allocation strategies [10,12] have been recently proposed, the half-duplex nature of most

© The Author(s), under exclusive license to Springer Nature Switzerland AG 2023
P. Mathieu et al. (Eds.): PAAMS 2023, LNAI 13955, pp. 88–99, 2023.
https://doi.org/10.1007/978-3-031-37616-0_8

LoRaWAN gateways continues to be a key constraint limiting the use of down-link resources to a great extent [15]. Hence, an online trial-and-error allocation of resources is not typically possible, which highlights the importance of efficient decision-making based on the available network information.

This paper extends a recent work [5], where a multi-agent network resource allocation manager was presented and bench-marked according to different channel utilization performance metrics. At this point, we propose a *predictive network planning agent* responsible for rating suitable schedule-deployment setups based on a series of scalability-oriented predictions built on top of the available ground truth collected. This proposal is in line with recent literature, where the use of multi-agent systems (MAS) has been proposed for improving LoRaWAN energy efficiency [14] and reliability [7,9] based on reinforcement learning approaches. In this work, nevertheless, a lightweight network planning agent is proposed, which aims at predicting the impact of different slot design criteria on the maximum-achievable network size based on limited network knowledge.

2 Multi-agent System for Predictive Network Planning

2.1 Fundamentals

This section presents the fundamentals of LoRaWAN technology the main network metrics and the nomenclature used in this work.

LoRa(WAN) Technology. The LoRaWAN standard is a Medium Access Control (MAC) layer provided by the LoRa Alliance [11] and built on top of LoRa's physical layer (PHY) for long-range and low-power communication.

LoRa is based on Chirp-Spread Spectrum (CSS) modulation and defines six different spreading factors, SF7 to SF12, over which transmissions can take place: the higher the SF, the longest the communication range at the expense of lower data rates (DRs) and, therefore, longer transmission air times (T_{tx}). The latter, in turn, are also influenced by additional PHY configurations such as the selected coding rate (CR) or bandwidth (BW), among others. LoRa transmissions using the same BW but different SF are known to be quasi-orthogonal, which opens the possibility of extending the network's scalability through the allocation of simultaneous cross-SF transmissions as long as these using the same SF are properly scheduled not to overlap in time with one another [2,4].

LoRaWAN packets sent by end-nodes are received at central gateways which, following a star-of-stars topology, forward them to network and application servers via a backhaul (e.g., Ethernet, 4G/5G) for de-duplication, decryption, and processing tasks. While this is referred to as *uplink* traffic, it is encouraged over *downlink* given the half-duplex nature of gateways. In addition, multi-channel gateways are able to listen to eight simultaneous uplink channels—each enabling the possibility of orthogonal SF decoding—so that thousands of end nodes can be served with a single gateway, as long as they adhere to downlink usage policies. Specifically, it is the European Telecommunications and Standards Institute (ETSI) which regulates the maximum duty cycle per device and band in the European space to, typically, 1% for end nodes and 10% for gateways (please, see EN300.220 standard [3] for further detail).

Performance Metrics. Let T_{sk} be the *clock skew* of a specific microcontroller unit (MCU) which, as specified in the manufacturer's datasheet, will cause the deviation of end-node's oscillator over time in either a positive or negative direction. In time-slotted communications—more specifically Time Division Multiple Access (TDMA [8])—, the *guard time* (T_g) is defined as the time window to be added at the beginning and end of each time slot so that device's desynchronization does not cause the overlap of neighbor transmissions (see Eq. 1). The slot length, in turn, is defined as the sum of T_g and T_{tx}.

$$T_g = \left\lceil \frac{2 \times T_{sk} \times T_{syn}}{10^6} \right\rceil \tag{1}$$

Based on the formulation, let us define the two channel-utilization metrics used in this work from [5]. The following definitions consider LoRaWAN Class A —as mandatory supported by any end node—, and a unique gateway listening to a single uplink-downlink channel (computations can be extrapolated for multi-channel gateways).

On the one hand, the *uplink channel occupancy* (T_{UL}) is defined as the time window during which a specific SF-based schedule is reserved due to either direct uplink communication or indirect channel reservation due to on-going downlink replies in any of the parallel schedules (see Eq. 2). Once any of the schedules reaches congestion, no additional end nodes will be able to be assigned regardless of the SF being used, since every new end node allocation involves the reservation of a certain time in all simultaneous schedules.

$$T_0 = \left(\frac{S_{len}}{T_{UL}} + \sum_{i=SF7}^{SF12} \frac{\left\lceil \frac{S_{len}^*}{S_{len_i}} \right\rceil S_{len_i}}{T_{syn}} \right) \times 100 \tag{2}$$

where T_{syn} is the synchronization period at a specific SF, T_{UL} is the uplink period required by the end device, S_{len}^* is the slot length at a specific SF-based schedule, and S_{len_i} is the slot length at SF equal to i.

On the other hand, the *downlink usage* (U_{DL}) is defined as the time percentage that downlink will be unavailable due to an ongoing transmission of a specific node or the associated black-put period (BP) required for duty cycle compliance, as shown in Eq. 3.

$$U_{DL} = \sum_{n=0}^{N} \frac{T_{tx_n} + BP_n}{T_{syn_n}} \times 100 \tag{3}$$

where T_{tx_n} is the time on air of node n required for transmission at the scheduled SF, BP_n is the blackout period of node n using such SF, and T_{syn_n} is its synchronization period.

Table 1. Nomenclature and definitions.

Symbol	Definition
N_{dev}	Maximum number of devices served
T_{tx}	Transmission time, also known as time on air (T_{OA})
T_g	Guard time reserved to prevent transmission overlapping in time
S_{len}	Time slot length that accommodates T_{tx} and T_g
T_{sk}	Clock skew as given in the device manufacturer's datasheet
T_{syn}	Synchronization period between a given node and the global time reference
T_{UL}	Transmission period of a given device as given by application requirements
T_0	Uplink channel occupancy at a specific SF-based schedule
U_{DL}	Downlink channel usage at the gateway level
BP	Black-out period required for ETSI compliance
PL	LoRaWAN payload length

Nomenclature. Table 1 provides a summary of the nomenclature and main definitions used throughout this work in the context of LoRaWAN time-slotted resource allocation.

2.2 Predictive Network Planning

The purpose of this section is twofold: first, briefly introducing the architecture and logic behind the reference LoRaWAN resource-allocation MAS and, second, providing a comprehensive description of the newly-integrated predictive network planning agent according to physical network constraints.

Network Management System Architecture. This work presents a predictive network planning agent for improving the scalability of LoRaWAN time-slotted communications. This agent represents an extension of a previous work [5], where a MAS for efficient online resource allocation at the gateway level was presented and validated through the emulation of thousands of joining LoRaWAN end-nodes. In this section, the architecture and logic of the baseline MAS is briefly described as a means of highlighting the role of the proposed predictive agent in terms of increasing the flexibility and scalability of the local network.

Following a time-slotted scheduling approach [6], let a series of LoRaWAN end nodes join a single-gateway network by providing individual constraints (e.g., clock skew, transmission payload size, uplink periodicity, etc.) and metadata (e.g., minimum-possible SF). In order to be processed by the multi-agent network management system shown in Fig. 1 for the allocation of specific transmission slots in any of the available SF-based schedules, three stages are undergone:

(i) *Warm-up.* Context information collection during low traffic loads, including the registration of joining end nodes. No scheduling is required at this stage.
(ii) *Schedule launching.* Collected information is processed by agents to select the most appropriate slot lengths and deploy their associated SF-based schedules at gateway level (this is done by network scheduling entities in Fig. 1).

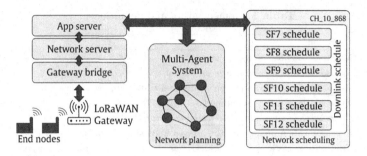

Fig. 1. End-to-end system architecture.

(iii) *End-node joining.* Once schedules are deployed, agents will decide on which is the most suitable SF and synchronization period for joining end nodes, based on their individual and physical constraints.

Having described the system architecture, let us focus on the new aspects introduced in this work. The design criteria of slot lengths across different simultaneous SF-based schedules—*schedule launching*—has different implications. First, the higher the required SF (given the physical constraints), the highest the proportional channel utilization for the same payload size to be transmitted. Second, since the downlink channel is shared by all end-nodes at the gateway level, regardless of the SF being used, synchronization replies from the network served to end nodes need to be accordingly accommodated. Moreover, the fact that downlink resources are more constrained than uplink ones, once a specific *schedule launching* strategy is adopted by the network management system, a compelling reason is required to re-schedule the entire network based on a different slot design strategy.

Predictive Planning Agent Design. We propose the extension of the system through a new *predictive network planning agent* responsible for selecting the most suitable *schedule launching* setup that will be followed by the MAS during the *device joining* stage. For this, this agent is aimed at predicting the LoRaWAN cell capacity for the given context information and a series of guard-time-based setups during *schedule launching* and *end-node joining* stages.

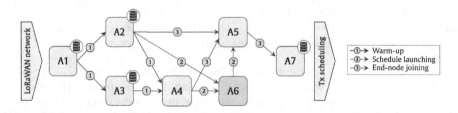

Fig. 2. Precedence diagram of the multi-agent network management system for operational stages 1 (*warm-up*) to 3 (*end-node joining*).

Table 2. Precedence relationships and data exchange detail.

ID	Agent	Input parameters	Output parameters
A1[1,2,3]	Device registration	LoRaWAN packet	A2: payload, A3: metadata
A2[1,2,3]	Payload formatting	A1: payload	A4: PL, A5, A6: T_{sk}, T_{UL}
A3[1,2,3]	Data rate discarding	A1: metadata	A4: SF list
A4[1,2,3]	Air-time calculation	A2: PL, A3: SF list	A5, A6: T_{tx} list
A5[2,3]	Resource allocation	A2: T_{sk}, T_{UL}, A4: T_{tx} list, A6: S_{len}	A7: node, SF
A6[2]	Network planning	A2: T_{sk}, T_{UL}, A4: T_{tx} list	A5: S_{len}
A7[3]	Instance deployment	A5, A6: S_{len}	Launch schedules

Agent involved in: [a] *warm-up* stage; [b] *schedule launching* stage; and [c] *end-node joining* stage.

This agent integrates with the MAS as shown in the precedence diagram from Fig. 2 (see A6), while Table 2 shows the role of each of the agents in the system (A1 to A7) including their precedence relationship as well as the input/output parameters at the agent level.

In order to predict the impact of certain device-joining conditions on the overall uplink channel occupancy T_0 and downlink usage U_{DL}, the dataset obtained in [5] was used to train a multi-output regression model. To do so, two groups of input features were considered:

(a) *Known features.* These include the known number of devices and their clock skew (T_{sk}), joining SF (SF_0), payload length (PL), and uplink periodicity (T_{UL}), schedule-launching setup (SE), and end-node joining strategy (ST).
(b) *Heuristic-based features.* These are individually predicted for each joining device based on the previous features. They include the selected SF (SF_i), synchronization period (T_{syn}), time on air (T_{tx}), and slot length (S_{len}).
(c) *Predicted features.* These refer to the previous known uplink network status (T_0) per SF-based schedule which, in turn, are obtained from the model's prediction given the entire set of features.

Based on the previous features, a multi-output regression model is proposed to predict the impact of a given set of joining nodes on each of the six: (i) simultaneous uplink channels (SF schedules), and (ii) SF-based downlink usages. The intuitive idea behind this is that, based on a known subset of joining nodes, this agent can predict which setup (SE) and strategy (ST) will reach the highest scalability. Hence, the MAS can leverage long-term predictions for decision-making at the expense of lower accuracies in channel occupancy computations. Instead, multiple heuristics are compressed into a simpler representation that avoids numerous agent-to-agent communication and database-access events while still being able to provide valuable closed-loop feedback for decision-making.

The machine learning algorithm used in this work is a Random-Forest (RF) model. The RF algorithm can be used for both classification and regression. It is an ensemble learning method that combines multiple decision trees for more accurate and robust predictions. It is chosen due to its wide applicability in similar cases, where it can deliver good predictions with small datasets. RF can only handle a single output target. As there exist multiple targets that need to be predicted for the MAS by the model, one RF regressor per target variable is trained. To facilitate the training and prediction, the scikit-learn's MultiOutputRegressor model is used [13]. Different hyperparameter combinations were evaluated and the best results were achieved with max_depth = 16 and n_estimators = 5. These parameters will create only few decision trees that however can grow in depth to better fit the relatively small number of samples available.

3   Results and Discussion

This work focuses on the evaluation of *schedule-launching* decision-making, that is, on the most suitable setup to select according to a given subset of joining nodes. The following setups are considered (please, refer to [5] for further detail):

- *Setup 0 (baseline).* All SF schedules share the same guard time, based on a nominal clock skew of 20 ppm. Additionally, standard LoraWAN heuristics are used for SF allocation, that is, assigning the minimum-possible SF regardless of current uplink occupancy.
- *Setup 1 (balanced).* All SF schedules share the same guard time, based on the maximum known clock skew in the network.
- *Setup 2 (exponentially falling).* Guard times assigned follow an exponentially falling distribution (the higher the SF, the shorter the guard time), with their sum being equal to that of guard times in Setup 1.
- *Setup 3 (exponentially rising).* Guard times assigned follow an exponentially rising distribution (the higher the SF, the longer the guard time), with their sum being equal to that of guard times in Setup 1.

3.1   Data Collection and Preparation

The dataset used consisted of 5366 rows and was obtained from the results presented in [5], each of them representing a device joining under variable conditions (*known features*) and resulting in different *heuristic-based* and *predicted* features. 76.66% of this dataset was used for training the model, while the remaining 33.33% was used for testing its performance. To do so, the Root Mean Square Error (RMSE) and the Mean Absolute Error (MAE) were computed. RMSE and MAE are both commonly used evaluation metrics for regression models. RMSE measures the average deviation of the predicted values from the actual values, taking into account the square of the differences between the predicted and actual values. MAE measures the average absolute deviation of the predicted values from the actual values. As RMSE squares the magnitude of prediction errors, it is more sensitive to outliers, while MAE treats all errors equally with their absolute value.

In order to find a trade-off between the model's execution complexity (based on the number of iterations required on top of the *previous network state* prediction) and its accuracy, different sampling intervals were tested. These consisted of grouping the available data in intervals of 50, 100, and 150 devices.

Table 3 shows the resulting model evaluation for these input intervals using different testing data. The *overall* column provides the combined uplink and downlink evaluation on the reserved test data. Conversely, UL^{SE} columns focus on uplink performance and extend this evaluation to the entire dataset (in order to enable application-oriented validation) for different inputs being considered as the *predicted features*: in *w/ GT* these features are directly collected from the ground truth itself while, in *w/o GT*, the model bases its output on the predicted current network status. RMSE was, in all cases, higher than MAE given its higher sensitivity to outliers.

Table 3. MAE and RMSE metrics for channel utilization predictions on top of different subsets of data.

Interval	Metric	Overall^{TT}	UL^{SE} [w/ GT]	UL^{SE} [w/o GT]
50	MAE [%]	1.4577	1.3065	9.0833
	RMSE [%]	2.0561	1.9110	11.1527
100	MAE [%]	2.8030	2.1039	8.2151
	RMSE [%]	3.5896	3.0371	10.1492
150	MAE [%]	4.0636	3.6500	7.4991
	RMSE [%]	5.7413	5.1789	9.8456

^{TT}Uplink and downlink evaluation, test data subset.
^{SE}Uplink evaluation, dataset including all network setups.

As a result, the original dataset was split into blocks of 100 devices as a trade-off between the number of model iterations and its performance. To do so, all features except for the number of devices and the uplink occupancy were transformed into the average of the previous 100 elements for training.

3.2   Setup-Oriented Evaluation Results

The evaluation focus was first put on uplink occupancy. To do so, both *known features* and *heuristic-based features* were assumed as available to the network planning agent. The prediction model was executed for the four setups being considered, each of them resulting in turn into six different uplink occupancy predictions. Some representative cases are displayed in Fig. 3, where the ground truth time series (GT) is shown with two predictions (P): first using as a feature the available occupation ground truth (w/ GT), and second using as a feature the previous prediction (w/o ground truth). The latter represents a more realistic application scenario, where no ground truth from the network is available.

Even in case of no available ground truth as *predicted features*, the agent was able to determine which SF schedules were first reaching congestion. The worst model performance was observed for the highest and lowest SFs (SF12 and SF7), especially when high uplink occupancies were reached. This can be observed, for instance, in Fig. 3d. In these cases, by design, the MAS reserves highly-congested SF schedules (e.g. those where T_0 is higher than 80%, like SF7 in Setup 2) and start assigning higher available ones. This might be due to the

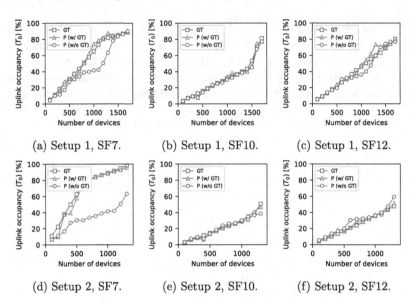

(a) Setup 1, SF7.   (b) Setup 1, SF10.   (c) Setup 1, SF12.

(d) Setup 2, SF7.   (e) Setup 2, SF10.   (f) Setup 2, SF12.

Fig. 3. Predicted uplink channel occupancy with ground truth (P (w/ GT)), and without ground truth (P (w/o GT)) for different network setups and SFs.

limited availability of training data showing this behavior, since this situation is only expected to take place in fast-growing uplink occupancy scenarios such as longer-than-expected slot lengths (e.g. SF7 in Setup 2 or SF12 in Setup 3).

In order to overview the model performance for each of the setups (*P (w/o GT)* case), Fig. 4 shows the uplink occupancy's MAE from a model- and an application-oriented perspective. Figure 4a shows the MAE considering all prediction states, and Fig. 4b considers only the last prediction state, which is the one that agents use for deciding the best-possible setup. Again, in both cases, it is clear how the influence of longer-than-expected slots at SF7 (Setup 2) and SF12 (Setup 3) results in a higher error. In the case of Setup 0, the error might be due to the unbalanced nature of the dataset used, in which data from Setup 0 are based on baseline LoRaWAN standard heuristics while data from Setups 1 to 3 are based on the proposed MAS-oriented heuristics.

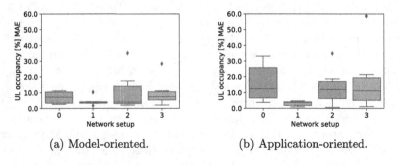

(a) Model-oriented.   (b) Application-oriented.

Fig. 4. Uplink occupancy MAE per network setup.

Finally, Table 4 shows an overview of effective uplink and downlink predictions (P rows) and ground truth (GT rows) where, for each of the setups, the channel with the highest influence on network congestion is highlighted. From all scenarios considered in Table 4), only the ground-truth Setup 0 scenario reached congestion due to downlink channel congestion. In the remaining scenarios, the cause of network congestion was identified in uplink channels.

In order to define setup-selection priorities for the MAS, a cost function to be minimized is proposed in Eq. 4 and 5. Specifically, Eq. 4 considers the maximum uplink channel occupancy ($T_{0_{max}}$) as minimization target, while Eq. 5 focuses on minimizing downlink channel usage (U_{DL}). This cost function was validated using the ground truth data available, the rating results of which are presented in Table 5. To do so, a normalized cost value was obtained by dividing each cost by the maximum into each of the categories (either GT or P).

Table 4. Application-oriented uplink occupancy and downlink usage per Setup.

			T_0 [%]						U_{DL} [%]
			SF7	SF8	SF9	SF10	SF11	SF12	All SFs
Setup	0	GT	49.34	4.11	45.69	39.57	55.04	81.79	**97.49**
		P	62.44	69.98	**78.86**	43.32	50.20	69.90	60.24
	1	GT	**88.71**	85.38	84.75	81.11	72.36	80.34	36.00
		P	**89.98**	80.64	83.78	76.99	68.23	76.80	35.33
	2	GT	**98.36**	88.42	82.33	50.99	44.70	47.76	51.78
		P	63.40	69.77	**77.85**	38.52	44.08	59.56	28.69
	3	GT	33.64	30.09	39.84	34.08	57.58	**94.95**	17.73
		P	32.52	43.13	**49.38**	30.28	36.10	36.30	16.14

$$C = \begin{cases} \dfrac{T_{0_{max}}}{N_{dev}} & T_{0_{max}} \geq \sum_{i=SF7}^{SF12} U_{DL,i} \qquad (4) \\[3mm] \dfrac{\sum_{i=SF7}^{SF12} U_{DL,i}}{N_{dev}} & otherwise \qquad (5) \end{cases}$$

From Table 5, the maximum number of devices served by the MAS in each Setup (as taken from ground truth datasets) validates the ratings obtained by minimizing the proposed cost function. Specifically, Setup 1 is rated as the most scalable one, followed by Setups 0, 2 and 3. However, in the case of predicted setups (P rows), the model was able to identify the sequence of setups 1, 0 and 2, but failed to rate Setup 3 as the least scalable one. This aligns with the results shown in Fig. 4b, where an outlier of nearly 60% MAE was identified for Setup 3. Nevertheless, the obtained results helped us validate the potential usefulness of the proposed network planning agent, the performance of which can be further improved based on learned lessons. To do so, the following improvements are proposed:

Table 5. Setup rating obtained minimizing cost normalized function $\hat{C}$.

			N_{dev}	Target	C	$\hat{C}$	Rating
Setup	0	GT	1300	DL[a]	0.0750	0.7898	2
		P		UL^2	0.0607	1.0000	3
	1	GT	1700	UL[b]	0.0522	0.5496	1
		P		UL[b]	0.0529	0.8726	2
	2	GT	1400	UL[b]	0.0703	0.7400	3
		P		UL[b]	0.0556	0.9167	4
	3	GT	1000	UL[b]	0.0949	1.0000	4
		P		UL[b]	0.0494	0.8140	1

[a]Minimize downlink usage; [b]Minimize uplink occupancy.

– *Dataset augmentation.* Extension of the number of dataset training samples through the simulation of additional network setups for varying *known features*.
– *Model comparison.* Performance comparison of the current model with neural-network-based models trained on top of the extended dataset.
– *Model split.* Given the high differences identified in the MAE variance across setups, it might be interesting to train a different model for each of the setups and evaluate whether a trade-off between the network planning agent's complexity and prediction accuracy is reached.

4 Conclusions

This work is built upon a multi-agent network management system architecture for large-scale LoRaWAN deployments, which addresses the design of a novel network planning agent. The MAS is part of an end-to-end system architecture for LoRaWAN time-slotted communications. The proposed agent is responsible for carrying out predictions based on the constraints of nodes and on the available network information such as uplink channel occupancy or downlink usage.

To do so, three categories of input features were identified and a multi-output regressor model based on RF was trained and tested for different network setups. These refer to different time-slotted design approaches which, according to the used dataset, resulted in different long-term network scalability results. The agent implementing the proposed model achieved an MAE and RMSE lower than 3% and 4% respectively in overall channel utilization predictions including uplink and downlink. Additionally, when the trained model was applied to each of the real setup-based scenarios with no ground truth being available, these remained approximately below 9% and 11%, respectively.

The model's performance was also analyzed from an application-oriented perspective for each of the setups, that is, considering the effective channel utilization for the highest-possible number of devices as provided in the set of input features. In this case, although some outliers prevented the model from accurately rating the setups to be prioritized, it was still able to successfully identify a sequence of three consecutive setup scenarios out of four. Based on the obtained results, a set of learned lessons are provided.

In future work, the learned lessons from this work will be used to improve the model's performance and enable predictive planning in more specific scenarios. These include decision-making based on a reduced set of known end nodes and SF allocation strategies based on the known network status.

Acknowledgments. Grant 2023-GRIN-34056 funded by Universidad de Castilla-La Mancha. Grant 2019-PREDUCLM-10703 funded by Universidad de Castilla-La Mancha and by "ESF Investing in your future". Grant DIN2018-010177 funded by MCIN/AEI/ 10.13039/501100011033. Grant PID2021-123627OB-C52 funded by MCIN/AEI/ 10.13039/501100011033 and by "ERDF A way to make Europe".

References

1. Van den Abeele, F., Haxhibeqiri, J., Moerman, I., Hoebeke, J.: Scalability analysis of large-scale LoRaWAN networks in NS-3. IEEE Internet Things J. **4**(6), 2186–2198 (2017)
2. Caillouet, C., Heusse, M., Rousseau, F.: Optimal SF allocation in LoRaWAN considering physical capture and imperfect orthogonality. In: 2019 IEEE Global Communications Conference, pp. 1–6. IEEE (2019)
3. European Telecommunications Standards Institute (ETSI): Short Range Devices (SRD) operating in the frequency range 25 MHz to 1 000 MHz (2017). Rev. 3.1.1
4. Garrido-Hidalgo, C., et al.: LoRaWAN scheduling: from concept to implementation. IEEE Internet Things J. **8**(16), 12919–12933 (2021)
5. Garrido-Hidalgo, C., Roda-Sanchez, L., Ramírez, F.J., Fernández-Caballero, A., Olivares, T.: Efficient online resource allocation in large-scale LoRaWAN networks: A multi-agent approach. Comput. Netw. **221**, 109525 (2023)
6. Haxhibeqiri, J., Moerman, I., Hoebeke, J.: Low overhead scheduling of LoRa transmissions for improved scalability. IEEE Internet Things J. **6**(2), 3097–3109 (2018)
7. Huang, X., Jiang, J., Yang, S.H., Ding, Y.: A reinforcement learning based medium access control method for LoRa networks. In: 2020 IEEE International Conference on Networking, Sensing and Control (ICNSC), pp. 1–6. IEEE (2020)
8. ITU: Spectrum occupancy measurements and evaluation (2018). Rev. 1
9. Ivoghlian, A., Salcic, Z., Wang, K.I.K.: Adaptive wireless network management with multi-agent reinforcement learning. Sensors **22**(3), 1019 (2022)
10. Lima, E., Moraes, J., Oliveira, H., Cerqueira, E., Zeadally, S., Rosário, D.: Adaptive priority-aware LoRaWAN resource allocation for Internet of Things applications. Ad Hoc Netw. **122**, 102598 (2021)
11. LoRa Alliance: LoRaWAN^TM 1.0.3 Specification (2018). Rev. 1.0.3
12. Minhaj, S.U., et al.: Intelligent resource allocation in LoRaWAN using machine learning techniques. IEEE Access **11**, 10092–10106 (2023)
13. Scikit-learn: scikit-learn machine learning in python (2023). https://scikit-learn.org
14. Zhao, G., Lin, K., Chapman, D., Metje, N., Hao, T.: Optimizing energy efficiency of LoRaWAN-based wireless underground sensor networks: a multi-agent reinforcement learning approach. Internet Things **22**, 100776 (2023)
15. Zorbas, D.: Improving LoRaWAN downlink performance in the EU868 spectrum. Comput. Commun. **195**, 303–314 (2022)

A Solution Concept with an Exploration Bias for Repeated Stochastic Coalitional Games

Josselin Guéneron[(✉)] and Grégory Bonnet

Normandie Univ, UNICAEN, ENSICAEN, CNRS, GREYC, Caen, France
{josselin.gueneron,gregory.bonnet}@unicaen.fr

Abstract. Classically, in coalition formation, agents know in advance the deterministic utilities they will obtain from coalitions. Relaxing these two assumptions (determinism and *a priori* knowledge) is important to deal with real-world applications. A way to do that is to consider the framework of repeated stochastic coalitional games. Here, agents decide at each time step which coalition to form on the basis of limited information. Then, their observations allow them to update their knowledge. We propose a solution concept that explicitly integrates an exploration bias to allow agents to sometimes form coalitions that have a low utility but that would be interesting to form to obtain more information. We compare this concept to a greedy approach and highlight its efficiency with respect to the structure of the real utilities, unknown to the agents.

Keywords: Coalition Formation · Cooperative Game Theory · Sequential Decision

1 Introduction

In MAS, individual agents are not always able to perform certain tasks alone. When the system is composed of selfish and rational agents, the agents may form groups, called coalitions, in order to jointly perform tasks that cannot be handled individually. However, the majority of work on coalition formation makes two strong assumptions. The first is that agents have perfect *a priori* knowledge of the payoff they obtain when forming a coalition. The second one is that this payoff is deterministic. Both assumptions do not seem adequate for real-world problems where the exact payoff obtained by a coalition is only known a posteriori. Moreover, if the same coalition is subsequently reformed, its payoff has no reason to be strictly the same, due to internal or external factors. For example, consider legal entities that have to repeatedly form consortia to work temporarily on projects. These consortia formations are repeated by the same agents. However, the quality of the results produced by each consortium may vary. For instance an internal factor may be the agents' individual skills, whose effects may be stochastic, coupled with their ability to interact better with some agents than with others. An external factor could be an environmental effect

P. Mathieu et al. (Eds.): PAAMS 2023, LNAI 13955, pp. 100–112, 2023.
https://doi.org/10.1007/978-3-031-37616-0_9

independent of the agents, such as a disaster in the office of one of them. Thus, it seems interesting to relax assumptions of determinism and *a priori* knowledge.

However, it raises new questions. If agents no longer have knowledge about coalitions, how can they obtain it? If the payoff from coalitions is stochastic, how can they estimate it? The literature then proposes to consider repeated games, which allow the outcome of the same game to be observed sequentially. Thus, agents can observe the state of the game at different times and are able to extract information from it. Nevertheless, the main objective of coalition formation is to partition the agents into coalitions. In this new context, where the utilities of coalitions are stochastic and unknown to the agents, how do we decide which coalitions to form? This choice can be broken down into several questions. How can agents favour the formation of one coalition over another based on what they know about them? At what point do they consider that they know enough about a coalition to properly assess its usefulness? How can agents collectively decide which interactions could be accepted by all?

In this article, we propose a new solution concept for repeated stochastic coalition formation, based on an exploration-exploitation trade-off, well-known in reinforcement learning. To do so, we redefine an existing solution concept, integrating a notion of interest in exploration in order to allow agents to form stable coalitions while accepting to form them to obtain more information. This consists in introducing a new notion of stability for repeated stochastic coalitional games, to allow a trade-off between exploiting a rather known payoff and exploring coalitions with unknown or very uncertain payoffs (taking into account mean and variance of the characteristic function known at a given time step). We show that our solution concept is very efficient on unstructured characteristic functions, and is better than an ϵ-greedy strategy except in the case of a highly structured characteristic function. These results extend previous results [11] which did not considered some informations (i.e. variance) and unstructured characteristic functions.

Section 2 presents coalitional games and their stochastic and repeated extensions. Section 3 describes our solution concept which explicitly integrates a notion of exploration, as well as an instantiation of such notion. Finally, Sect. 4 presents experimental results, highligthing the interest of our solution concept.

2 State of the Art

In cooperative game theory, agents cooperate by forming *coalitions* which produce some *utilities*.

Definition 1 (Coalitional game). *A coalitional game is a tuple $\mathcal{G} = \langle N, v \rangle$ where $N = \{a_1, \ldots, a_n\}$ is a set of agents and $v : 2^N \to \mathbb{R}$ is the characteristic function that associates a utility $v(C)$ to each coalition $C \subseteq N$.*

A partition of agents into coalitions is called a *coalition structure* and a *solution* to a coalitional game is defined as follows.

Definition 2 (Solution). *A solution to a coalitional game $\mathcal{G}$ is a tuple $S_{\mathcal{G}} = \langle \mathcal{CS}, \vec{x} \rangle$ where $\mathcal{CS}$ is a coalition structure of N, $\vec{x} = \{x_1, \ldots, x_n\}$ is a payoff vector for agents where $x_i \geq 0$ is the payoff of agent a_i.*

As agents are selfish, a solution must be accepted by all of them. This is why a solution must belong to a *solution concept*. A solution concept is the set of solutions that respect a certain notion of stability, e.g. the agents do not wish to form or join another coalition where they could earn more. We focus in this article on the concept of the core and its generalization, the ϵ-*core* [15,17].

Definition 3 (ϵ-core). *A solution $\langle \mathcal{C}, \vec{x} \rangle$ belongs to the ϵ-core if and only if:*

$$\forall C \subseteq N, x(C) \geq v(C) - \epsilon \text{ with } x(C) = \sum_{a_i \in C} x_i$$

The ϵ-core allows to define the *least core*, which contains all ϵ-core solutions for the smallest value of ϵ for which the solution concept is non-empty [7]. On the first hand, the determinism of the characteristic function can be relaxed in the literature with stochastic coalitional games [6,8,12]. The nature of uncertainty in these models differs, from probabilitic distribution on deterministic characteristic functions [12] to agents having beliefs about capabilities of others [6]. The most general and abstract model we can consider was proposed by Charnes and Granot [9]. Here, the characteristic function $v : 2^N \to \mathcal{X}_{2^N}$ is simply defined by random variables, and the payoff vectors of the solutions are calculated on the expectation of those variables. In the sequel, we consider such kind of model.

On the other hand, relaxing the *a priori* knowledge of the characteristic function leads to repeated games [4]. Such games consists in repeating the following process at each time step: (1) the agents form coalitions based on their current knowledge; (2) the coalitions are formed and produce payoffs; (3) the agents update their knowledge based on the previous observed payoffs. Here again, models in the literature essentially differ on the nature of what the agents learn and how they estimate the coalitions. Generally, they learn a reliability value or skill expertise for each agent, which impacts in turn the characteristic function [5,6,13]. However from the most abstract point of view, they can simply learn the characteristic function [11]. In the sequel, we consider such an abstract model for shake of generality.

Definition 4 (Repeated stochastic coalitional game). *Let $\mathcal{G} = \langle N, \mathbb{T}, v, \hat{v} \rangle$ be a repeated stochastic coalitional game (RSCG) where: $N = \{a_1, \ldots, a_n\}$ is a set of agents, $\mathbb{T} \subset \mathbb{N}^+$ is a set of distinct time steps, $v : 2^N \to \mathcal{X}^{2^N}$ a stochastic characteristic function – unknown to the agents – that associates a random variable to each coalition, and $\hat{v} : 2^N \times \mathbb{T} \to \hat{\mathcal{X}}^{2^N}$ a characteristic function that associates an estimated utility to each coalition at each time step.*

At each time step, agents have to decide on a solution to the game, despite the fact that they do not know the characteristic function v *a priori*. A solution is, like in a deterministic context, a tuple made of a coalition structure and an *ex ante* payoff vector, i.e. an estimated payoff vector based on what the agents know about v.

Definition 5 (Solution to a RSCG). *A solution S^t at the time step $t \in \mathbb{T}$ to a RSCG $\mathcal{G}$ is a tuple $S^t = \langle \mathcal{CS}^t, \vec{x}^t \rangle$ where $\mathcal{CS}^t$ is a coalition structure (disjointed partition) of N, and $\vec{x}^t = \{x_1^t, \ldots, x_n^t\}$ is a payoff vector such that $x_i^t \geq 0$ is the payoff of the agent a_i based on $\hat{v}$ and the coalition a_i belongs to in $\mathcal{CS}^t$.*

It has been shown that repeated coalition formation processes converge towards equilibria if agents sequentially form Pareto-efficient coalition structures [13]. However, forming Pareto-efficient coalition structures allows agents to form irrational solutions, i.e. at least one agent receive a payoff lesser than the utility he would receive while being alone. Interestingly, the processes still converge experimentally with greedy strategies [5,6,11] based on the expected values of coalitions. However, RSCG may allow to have more information than just the expected value of the characteristic function, for instance all standardized moments (mean, variance, skewness, kurtosis). As in other sequential decision-making problems it has been demonstrated that exploring can help on the long-term, i.e. making *a priori* sub-optimal decision in order to acquire knowledge [10,14], we propose to extend RSCG with an explicit notion of information, and with a new solution concept which takes into account the collective interest to make such sub-optimal choices.

3   An Exploration-Based ϵ-Core

We propose to adapt the RSCG framework and the associated ϵ-core solution concept by considering that the value of a coalition, i.e. its interest to be formed at a given time step, depends on two elements: an estimation of its utility from which the payoffs are directly derived, and an interest that the agents have in forming it in order to obtain more information on its real utility. Notice that unlike what was done in [11], the interest is intrinsic to the game definition.

Definition 6 (Interest-biased repeated stochastic coalitional game).
Let $\mathcal{G} = \langle \mathcal{G}, i \rangle$ be an interest-biased repeated stochastic coalitional game (IRSCG) where $\mathcal{G}$ is a RSCG and $i : 2^N \times \mathbb{T} \to \mathbb{R}$ an interest function that associates a quantitative interest to each coalition at each time step. We denote $i(C, t)$ the interest of the coalition C at time step t.

As mentioned in Sect. 2, the agents' payoff for a given solution is an estimate. Once the solution is found and coalitions are formed, the actual utilities they produced are the result of stochastic processes parameterised by the characteristic function. We assume that these utilities are observed by all agents. We denote X_t^C the observation of the utility produced by C at time step t.

Definition 7 (Observations). *Let $\mathcal{O}_t = \{(C, t', X_{t'}^C) : C \subseteq 2^N, t' \in \mathbb{T}, t' < t\}$ be a set of observations at time step t corresponding to the set of the coalitions formed at each time step before t and their ex-post payoffs.*

Thereafter, let us note $\mathcal{O}_t(C)$ the set of observations at time step t associated with the coalition $C \subseteq 2^N$. This set of observations allows to update the knowledge of agents about the characteristic function. In the following, we assume that agents estimate the utility of coalitions as normal distributions. Thus, for a given coalition $C \subseteq 2^N$, $\hat{v}(C,t)$ is characterised by the expectation and variance of a normal distribution over all observations.

Definition 8 (Utility estimation). *At time step $t \in \mathbb{T}$ and for the coalition $C \subseteq 2^N$, the estimated value of C, $\hat{v}(C,t)$, is given by $\hat{\mu}^2(C,t)$ its expectation and $\hat{\sigma}^2(C,t)$ its variance, which are computed from the observations of $\mathcal{O}_t(C)$.*

Thus, the learning method we used is tabular and is similar to what is used for multi-armed bandits. Since there is uncertainty about the utility produced by the coalitions once formed, a solution must take this uncertainty into account to be stable.

3.1   Interest of Coalitions

The exact nature of the interest that agents have in a coalition may depend on the problem. However, the purpose of this interest is to make it possible to explore other solutions that are potentially interesting for the agents but that might be considered unstable in the sense of a classical solution concept. However, it is important to note that in coalition formation we need to compare coalition structures, which therefore involves comparing different coalitions. For example, in the case of the core solution concept, checking the stability of a solution involves comparing the utility of a coalition to the sum of the individual gains of the agents in that same coalition wherever they are in the solution. We need to consider a form of interest that allows us to make such comparisons, i.e. to calculate from the interest of a coalition the individual interest of the agents that compose it.

Definition 9 (Individual interest). *The* individual interest *$i_j(C_j,t)$ of a agent a_j for a coalition C_j to which he belongs at a time step t is:*

$$i_j(C_j,t) = \frac{i(C_j,t)}{|C_j|}$$

This egalitarian distribution is one of many ways of distributing interest, and it represents the fact that each agent in a coalition has the same interest in that coalition, regardless of the other coalitions to which they may belong. However, it should be noted that the more agents a coalition contains, the lower their individual interest will be. This distribution therefore tends to favour coalitions of low cardinality, as several distinct observations can yield more information than a single one. This individual interest allows us to define the interest of a coalition with respect to a given coalition structure, regardless of whether or not the coalition agents are together in the structure.

Definition 10 (Collective interest). *The* collective interest *$i^{CS}(C,t)$ of the agents of the coalition C w.r.t. of a coalition structure CS at a time step t is:*

$$i^{CS}(C,t) = \sum_{a_j \in C} i_j(C_j^{CS},t)$$

where C_j^{CS} is the coalition of the agent a_j in the structure CS.

3.2 λ-Core

In order to integrate this interest in coalitions into the solution concept, we must aggregate it with utility. In order to remain generic at first, we consider in an abstract way an aggregation operator noted $\oplus$. Depending on the exact nature of the interest, this operator can take different forms, for example an *addition*, a *multiplication* or even a *maximum*. The various elements describing the interest of the agents being defined, we can now build our solution concept, the λ-core, based on an exploration-exploitation trade-off. To do this, we adapt the concept of the ϵ-core by integrating the aggregation operator and the interest function. We therefore add, on one side of the inequation, the interest of a coalition to the expected utility of the coalition, and on the other side the collective interest to the sum of the agents' gains with respect to the solution considered.

Definition 11 (λ-core). *A solution $\langle CS^t, \vec{x}^t \rangle$ belongs to the λ-core if and only if $\forall\, C \subseteq N$:*

$$\vec{x}^t(C) \oplus i^{CS^t}(C,t) \geq \hat{\mu}(C,t) \oplus i(C,t) - \lambda \text{ with } \vec{x}^t(C) = \sum_{a_i \in C} \vec{x}_i^t$$

In a similar way to the ϵ-core, the least core for this concept of the λ-core is defined as the one with the smallest λ for which a solution exists. We can now propose an example of instantiation of this solution concept by defining the interest as an exploration bias, and the aggregation operator as an *addition*.

3.3   Example of Interest: Exploration Bias

A relevant notion of interest is that of exploration, which we find in the multi-armed bandit problem. For this problem, many strategies have been proposed, and in particular strategies based on a *Upper Confidence Bound* called *UCB* [1]. Among the strategies based on this principle, there is *UCB-V*, which was proposed for the multi-armed bandit problem by Audibert *et al.* [2]. This describes an exploration bias taking into account the variance of the underlying probability distributions of the multi-armed bandit's arms and has been shown to be more efficient than the strategy *UCB-1* [3]. We therefore adapt *UCB-V* to apply it to interest-biased repeated stochastic coalitional games.

Definition 12 (UCB-V exploration bias). *The UCB-V exploration bias for a given coalition C at a time step t is defined as follows:*

$$i(C,t) = \sqrt{\frac{2\hat{\sigma}^2(C,t)\eta}{|O_t(C)| + 1}} + c\frac{3b\eta}{|O_t(C)| + 1} \text{ with } \eta = \zeta.log(|O_t| + 1)$$

Some constants must be defined. The constant b defines the upper bound of the problem's payoffs, so this is dependent on the latter. However, we can assume that the utilities are normalized over the interval $[0,1]$ as in multi-armed bandit problem, and thus define $b = 1$. The constants ζ and c are control parameters of the exploration (in particular ζ). We take here the values of the original article, in which Audibert *et al.* show the efficiency of these constants when they are defined as $\zeta = 1.2$ and $c = 1$.

4 Experiments

In order to evaluate the performance of our solution concept, we proceed empirically. We generate random sets with different characteristic functions, constructed in structured and random ways. We then apply our solution concept to these games, as well as to mixtures of these games, in order to test our concept on different degrees of structuring, from fully structured to fully random games. The performance is measured with the instant regret of the stable solutions found at each time step, in order to calculate the cumulative regret over all time steps.

4.1 Experimental Protocol

In a first step, we construct 200 different pairs of games with unique characteristic functions, for 6 agents. Each pair of games is constructed with two different characteristic function structures. The first characteristic function is drawn according to the NDCS (*Normally Distributed Coalition Structures*) [16] model. This model makes it possible to construct structured characteristic functions, but without strongly constraining the model as with monotonic or superadditive structures [7]. Thus, the utility expectation μ_C of each coalition $C \subseteq N$ is drawn according to a normal distribution $\mathcal{N}(|C|, \sqrt{|C|})$. The second characteristic function is unstructured, as it is drawn randomly and uniformly for each coalition. Thus, the utility expectation μ_C of each coalition $C \subseteq N$ is drawn according to a uniform distribution $\mathcal{U}(0,1)$. In both structuring models, the variances σ_C^2 of each coalition C are drawn according to a uniform distribution $\mathcal{U}(0, \frac{\mu_C}{2})$. Each characteristic function is then normalized on the interval $[0,1]$.

In a second step, in order to create a series of games from the most to the least structured, for each pair of games, we create intermediate games using a linear transformation by applying a transformation factor $w \in [0,1]$. Thus, a transformation factor of 0 corresponds to the NDCS structured game, while the factor 1 corresponds to the randomly structured game. A game is created in 0.05 steps for w between the two games of the pair, which corresponds to 19 additional intermediate games. Our solution concept is thus evaluated over 4200 games and 100 time steps each.

Example 1. Let C and C' be two coalitions, and v_1 and v_2 be two characteristic functions, respectively randomly and NDCS structured:

$$v_1 = \{C = \mathcal{N}(0.6, 0.2), C' = \mathcal{N}(0.1, 0.4)\}$$
$$v_2 = \{C = \mathcal{N}(0.2, 0.4), C' = \mathcal{N}(0.5, 0.1)\}$$

For a transformation factor of 0.4, the utilities of C and C' are such that:

$$v^{0.4}_{(1,2)} = \{C = \mathcal{N}(0.36, 0.32), C' = \mathcal{N}(0.34, 0.22)\}$$

For a transformation factor of 1, the resulting characteristic function is v_1:

$$v^1_{(1,2)} = \{C = \mathcal{N}(0.6, 0.2), C' = \mathcal{N}(0.1, 0.4)\}$$

For a transformation factor of 0, the resulting characteristic function is v_2:

$$v^0_{(1,2)} = \{C = \mathcal{N}(0.2, 0.4), C' = \mathcal{N}(0.5, 0.1)\}$$

These games are also played with the ϵ-greedy strategy, which will be our reference strategy. It also describes an exploration-exploitation trade-off, exploring randomly with probability ϵ, and exploiting with probability $1 - \epsilon$. In our implementation, the exploitation consists in using the concept of the least core with an ϵ (for ϵ-greedy) value of 0.05.

4.2 Performance Measures

The first measure is the *instant regret*, which is the difference between the maximum social welfare – i.e. the maximum sum of payoffs produced by a coalition structure – of the game and the sum of the actual expected utilities of the coalitions of the structure formed at time step t. Formally:

Definition 13 (Instant regret). *Given the optimal solution* $S^* = \langle CS^*, \vec{x}^* \rangle$ *in the sense of social welfare, the instant regret at time step t, noted R^t, is defined such that:*

$$R^t = \sum_{C^* \in CS^*} \mu_{C^*} - \sum_{C \in CS^t} \mu_C$$

Due to stochasticity, instant regret can oscillate (sometimes with a large amplitude), which is why the second measure is the *cumulative regret*. This measures the evolution of instant regret over time and highlights the convergence of regret, i.e. the time step at which the strategies have reached their exploration-exploitation equilibrium and therefore produce constant instant regret. At a time step t, the cumulative regret is the sum of the instant regrets of each time step $t' \leq t$. Formally:

Definition 14 (Cumulative regret). *Given the optimal solution $S^* = (CS^*, \vec{x}^*)$ in the sense of social welfare, the cumulative regret at time step t, noted R^t_c, is defined such that:*

$$R^t_c = \sum_{t'=0}^{t} R^{t'}$$

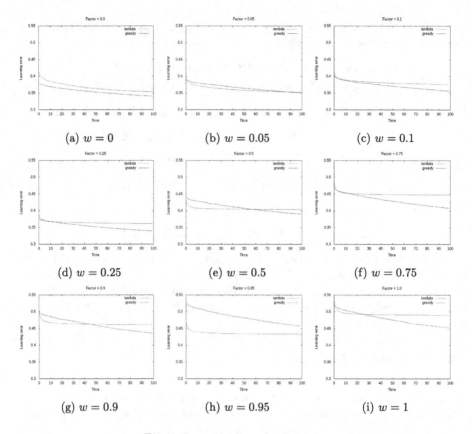

Fig. 1. Learning error for 6 agents

Finally, in order to evaluate the learning that the agents do of the real characteristic function over time, we use the *mean absolute error* (MAE) on the estimated and real utilities of the coalitions. The closer the MAE is to 0, the more accurate the estimated characteristic function is. The MAE is defined as:

Definition 15 (Mean absolute error). *Let v and $\hat{v}$ be two characteristic functions, the* mean absolute error D_{MAE}^t *between v and $\hat{v}$ at time step t is defined as:*

$$D_{MAE}^t = \frac{\sum_{C \in 2^N} |\hat{\mu}(C, t) - \mu_C|}{|2^N|}$$

4.3 Results

Figures 1 and 2 show respectively the evolution of the means of the learning error and the cumulative regret of the set of games for a given configuration (i.e. a linear transformation factor w) over the 100 time steps. Figure 3 summarizes the

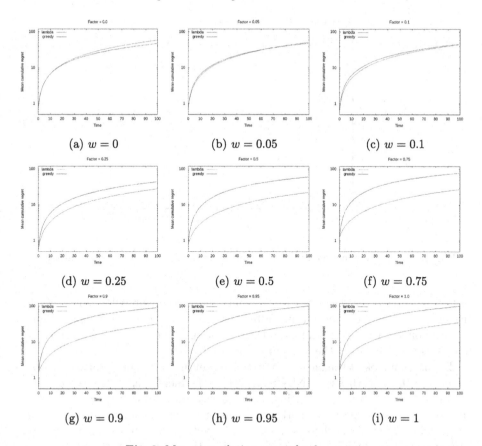

Fig. 2. Mean cumulative regret for 6 agents

results with the relative percentage of efficiency of the λ-core versus ϵ-greedy for the different transformation factors.

Concerning the learning error in Fig. 1, a first point to underline is that the more the characteristic function is structured (thus the closer the transformation factor w is to 0), the less the learning error is. In general, the ϵ-greedy strategy is the one that learns best, with a few exceptions such as for $w = 0.95$ where the λ-core allows better learning, or $w = 0.05$ where the results of the two methods are very close. However, we can see graphically a difference in behaviour between them according to the structuring of the characteristic functions. Indeed, the more structured the characteristic functions are, the more the ϵ-greedy strategy learns between the beginning and the end of the experiments. For example, its learning error decreases respectively by 10.59%, 11.45% and 13.20% for $w = 0$, $w = 0.5$ and $w = 1$. Let us note that this decrease is quasi-linear with the variation of the factor w. Concerning the λ-core, we can see that the learning converges quickly, due to the *UCB-V* exploration bias, and this more and more quickly as the characteristic functions are destructured. For example, for $w =$

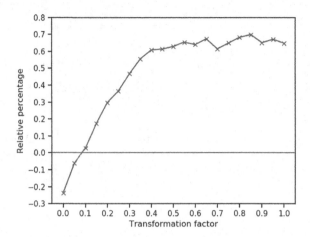

Fig. 3. Relative percentage of efficiency of λ-core against the ϵ-greedy strategy

0, the learning error decreases throughout the experiment, while for $w = 1$, the error almost stops decreasing after the time step $t = 20$. From a more general point of view for both methods, the more unstructured the characteristic functions are, the larger the learning error is initially.

Let us then look at the mean cumulative regret in Fig. 2. For a transformation factor $w = 0$, i.e. with a pure NDCS structure, the mean cumulative regret is in favour of the ϵ-greedy strategy, just as for a $w = 0.05$. However, from $w = 0.1$ onwards, the λ-core performs better in terms of regret, and the gap is larger for larger values of w. From these results, we can deduce that the ϵ-greedy strategy performs well on highly structured characteristic functions but that the less structuring there is, the less well it performs. However, it should be noted that when the ϵ-greedy strategy is outperformed by the λ-core, it is mainly the latter that gains in performance more than the ϵ-greedy strategy loses. Indeed, the latter obtains a mean cumulative regret of 45.91 for $w = 0$ and 47.13 for $w = 0.1$, i.e. a difference of 1.22. For its part, the λ-core obtains a mean cumulative regret of 58.28 for $w = 0$ and 44.58 for $w = 0.1$, i.e. a difference of 13.70. This difference is 16.07 for $w = 0.25$, 37.91 for $w = 0.5$, 35.11 for $w = 0.75$, up to a difference of 64.39 for $w = 1$. In the latter case, the mean cumulative regret for the λ-core is 34.98 while it is 99.37 for the ϵ-greedy strategy. The relative efficiency of λ-core against the ϵ-greedy strategy is highlighted in Fig. 3. On the latter, we can see that the gap in favour of the λ-core only increases until $w = 0.4$ and then stabilises. For $w = 0$, λ-core is $23,66\%$ less efficient than ϵ-greedy. It becomes $2,9\%$ more efficient from $w = 0.1$, until $60,87\%$ for $w = 0.4$. Then, for $w \geq 0.4$, the relative efficiency in favour of λ-core stabilises around 65%, with a maximum of 69.90% for $w = 0.85$. Thus, the λ-core solution concept performs very well on unstructured characteristic functions, and remains more efficient than the ϵ-greedy strategy as long as the structuring is not very important. It is however necessary to note that the λ-core is more efficient on slightly structured characteristic functions. For example, it obtains a mean cumulative regret of 22.39 with $w = 0.5$, while for $w = 1$ it is 34.98 (with a minimum for $w = 0.45$ with 21.94 of mean cumulative regret).

5 Conclusion

In this paper, we proposed the interest-biased repeated stochastic coalitional games. This model allows a new solution concept, the λ-core, based on an exploration-exploitation trade-off by integrating a notion of interest for the agents. By setting this interest to an exploration bias and defining the aggregation as an addition, we have shown that this solution concept is efficient on repeated stochastic coalitional games, especially when the characteristic functions are not very strongly structured. However, the computation of the λ-core is time consuming due to exploration bias. Indeed, this bias leads the least core to have a high value of λ, and thus to traverse more the space of the solutions because a naive approach of this calculation consists in seeking λ-core by iteratively incrementing the value of λ. Thus, it would be relevant to work on a distributed or decentralised approach of the calculation.

References

1. Agrawal, R.: Sample mean based index policies by $\mathcal{O}(\log n)$ regret for the multi-armed bandit problem. Adv. Appl. Probab. **27**(4), 1054–1078 (1995)
2. Audibert, J., Munos, R., Szepesvári, C.: Exploration-exploitation tradeoff using variance estimates in multi-armed bandits. Theor. Comput. Sci. **410**(19), 1876–1902 (2009)
3. Auer, P., Cesa-Bianchi, N., Fischer, P.: Finite-time analysis of the multiarmed bandit problem. Mach. Learn. **47**(2), 235–256 (2002)
4. Benoit, J.P., Krishna, V.: Finitely repeated games. In: Foundations in Microeconomic Theory, pp. 195–212 (1984)
5. Blankenburg, B., Dash, R.K., Ramchurn, S.D., Klusch, M., Jennings, N.R.: Trusted kernel-based coalition formation. In: 4th AAMAS, pp. 989–996 (2005)
6. Chalkiadakis, G., Boutilier, C.: Sequential decision making in repeated coalition formation under uncertainty. In: 7th AAMAS, pp. 347–354 (2008)
7. Chalkiadakis, G., Elkind, E., Wooldridge, M.: Computational aspects of cooperative game theory. Synthesis Lect. Artif. Intell. Mach. Learn. **5**(6), 1–168 (2011)
8. Charnes, A., Granot, D.: Prior solutions: Extensions of convex nucleus solutions to chance-constrained games. Technical report, Texas Univ. (1973)
9. Charnes, A., Granot, D.: Coalitional and chance-constrained solutions to n-person games. I: the prior satisficing nucleolus. SIAM J. Appl. Math. **31**(2), 358–367 (1976)
10. Gittins, J.C.: Bandit processes and dynamic allocation indices. J. R. Stat. Soc. Ser. B Stat. Methodol. **41**(2), 148–164 (1979)
11. Guéneron, J., Bonnet, G.: Are exploration-based strategies of interest for repeated stochastic coalitional games? In: Dignum, F., Corchado, J.M., De La Prieta, F. (eds.) PAAMS 2021. LNCS (LNAI), vol. 12946, pp. 89–100. Springer, Cham (2021). https://doi.org/10.1007/978-3-030-85739-4_8

12. Ieong, S., Shoham, Y.: Bayesian coalitional games. In: 23rd AAAI Conference on Artificial Intelligence, pp. 95–100 (2008)
13. Konishi, H., Ray, D.: Coalition formation as a dynamic process. J. Econ. Theory **110**(1), 1–41 (2003)
14. Mahajan, A., Teneketzis, D.: Multi-armed bandit problems. In: Hero, A.O., Castañón, D.A., Cochran, D., Kastella, K. (eds.) Foundations and Applications of Sensor Management, pp. 121–151. Springer, Boston (2008). https://doi.org/10.1007/978-0-387-49819-5_6
15. Mochaourab, R., Jorswieck, E.A.: Coalitional games in MISO interference channels: epsilon-core and coalition structure stable set. IEEE Trans. Signal Process. **62**(24), 6507–6520 (2014)
16. Rahwan, T., Ramchurn, S.D., Jennings, N.R., Giovannucci, A.: An anytime algorithm for optimal coalition structure generation. J. Artif. Intell. Res. **34**, 521–567 (2009)
17. Shapley, L.S., Shubik, M.: Quasi-cores in a monetary economy with nonconvex preferences. Economet.: J. Economet. Soc. 805–827 (1966)

Governing Online Forum Interactions with Multi-agent System: A Reddit Use Case with the JaCaMo Platform

Nesrine Hafiene[(✉)] [iD], Luis G. Nardin[iD], Antoine Zimmermann[iD],
and Olivier Boissier[iD]

Mines Saint-Etienne, Univ Clermont Auvergne, INP Clermont Auvergne, CNRS,
UMR 6158 LIMOS, 42023 Saint-Etienne, France
`nesrine.hafiene@emse.fr`

Abstract. Autonomous agents are intelligent software systems that can carry out tasks on behalf of users without their intervention. On online forums, autonomous agents can operate to read and post messages on behalf of users. The proper regulation of agents' interactions are required for achieving the expected results on online forums. One way to govern these interactions is using multi-agent oriented programming platforms. Here we introduce the use of JaCaMo, a multi-agent oriented programming platform, for governing agents' interactions within online forums. We show its feasibility for regulating agents' interactions within a popular online forum, Reddit.

Keywords: Multi-agent systems · JaCaMo · Online forum · Reddit

1 Introduction

Online forums create opportunities for information sharing and collaboration. Yet they pose significant challenges in terms of information trust and reliability. Users often encounter inaccurate or misleading information, thus they may be hesitant to trust the advice and guidance provided by anonymous online sources. Multi-agent systems can support addressing the information credibility and reliability problem based on factors such as the source of information. For example, agents can analyze news articles' sources and claims by referencing them with other reliable sources of information. This analysis may allow agents to provide a trust score for the information, which could be used to filter out unreliable or false information, ultimately creating more trustworthy online communities.

A first step for tackling this complex issue, however, is the regulation of users' activities on online forums. Because human users and autonomous agents acting on behalf of human users can operate on these forums, any regulation approach has to take into account activities performed directly by both types of users. Multi-agent system (MAS) is a suitable approach for dealing with the regulation of online forums as MAS can abstract both types of users as agents and enables the regulation and enforcement of their interactions through norms.

P. Mathieu et al. (Eds.): PAAMS 2023, LNAI 13955, pp. 113–124, 2023.
https://doi.org/10.1007/978-3-031-37616-0_10

This paper presents an application scenario exploiting JaCaMo [3][1], a multi-agent oriented programming platform, for governing agents' interactions on a popular online forum, Reddit[2].

JaCaMo is a powerful platform for the development of complex multi-agent systems that has been used in a wide range of domain applications, including smart home [12], finance [1] and accountability [2]. JaCaMo allows to build intelligent agents with sophisticated reasoning capabilities and to regulate their interactions within a shared environment. The JaCaMo meta-model [3] combines four MAS dimensions: Agent [5], Environment [13], Interaction [14] and Organization [11]. Each dimension is seamlessly connected with each other making possible for agents to interact with the environment and to participate in organizations situated on that environment. The situatedness of organizations is achieved through constitutive norms that extend the concept of artificial institutions. These constitutive norms connect the environment within which the agents interact with regulative norms used for regulating agents' interactions in the context of the organization [10]. Constitutive norms express which environmental facts count as organizational facts used in regulative norms. Regulative norms are rules and guidelines that establish expected agents' behaviors within a community. Regulative norms are essential for establishing trust, building relationships and promoting positive social interactions.

The remaining of the paper is organized as follows. First, we present a motivating scenario in which agents have to interact in the context of an online forum, Reddit (Sect. 2). We then introduce the JaCaMo platform and explain how it can be used to govern interactions on online forums (Sect. 3). We describe the implementation of agents' interactions on Reddit using JaCaMo and provide a detailed explanation of the agents, organization, environment and normative and constitutive norms (Sect. 4). Next, we present a proof-of-concept based on the Reddit use case in which agents participate in an online forum discussion by retrieving and submitting posts under explicit regulative and constitutive norms (Sect. 5). Finally, we conclude the paper (Sect. 6).

2   Reddit Motivating Scenario

Reddit is a social network with individual communities (i.e., online forums) called *subreddits*. Subreddits are created and moderated by users and dedicated to specific topics from news and politics to hobbies and entertainment (e.g., Fig. 1). Reddit provides two main roles that users can adopt per subreddit: *subscriber* and *contributor*. A subscriber is a user who follows a particular subreddit, i.e., the user receives updates of new posts and can upvote or downvote them. A contributor is a user who can submit posts (i.e., links, images, videos, or text).

In this scenario, *Alice* and *Bob* are two Reddit users interacting with the "Movies" subreddit. *Alice* is a subscriber to this subreddit, i.e., she can access the "Movies" subreddit and view movie-related content; *Bob* is a contributor to

---

[1] https://github.com/jacamo-lang/jacamo.
[2] https://www.reddit.com/.

Fig. 1. Structure of the "Movies" subreddit in Reddit

this same subreddit, i.e., he can share interesting movie-related content with the subreddit community. One day, *Bob* posts a new movie trailer that has just been released. *Alice* sees the post and finds it interesting. She clicks on the post to know more about the movie and decides to upvote it, helping the post to gain visibility and popularity within the community. Through this interaction, *Alice* and *Bob* are able to engage with each other and the community, sharing their knowledge and opinions about the world of movies. This type of social interaction and collaboration is made possible by the structure of Reddit and the specific roles and functions assigned to users within their communities.

In online forums like Reddit, users often interact with others who they do not know, which can lead to trust issues. There is a risk that people may post false information, engage in trolling or even use the online forum to spread malicious content. The lack of trust in online forums is a significant issue. On Reddit, norms are used to enforce behavior in order to overcome this issue. Firstly, norms can be established by the community itself through discussion, voting and consensus building. For instance, users can agree on what constitutes acceptable behavior in a particular subreddit, such as keeping discussions on-topic or refraining from personal attacks. These norms can be communicated through subreddit rules, guidelines and community standards, which moderators can enforce. Secondly, norms can be reinforced by moderators or through social pressure and community expectations. For instance, users who consistently violates community norms may face negative feedback from other users in the form of comments, downvotes or reports. This social pressure can discourage rule-breaking behavior and encourage users to conform to community norms.

Norms in online forums are usually expressed in a human-readable format. A challenge is to express them into a machine-readable format that autonomous agents can handle and to relate instances of these norms with actions being performed in the online forum. This requires to identify the actions in the online forum that hold regulatory significance for the community and to situate these norms on the web due to the nature of online forums. By effectively addressing these challenges, online forums can be an environment for human users and autonomous agents to engage in meaningful discussions and share information.

Here we propose using multi-agent systems, in particular the JaCaMo platform, to enforce these community norms through automated processes tackling the regulation of users' activities. In JaCaMo, we can establish clear and agent-readable norms and explicitly relate them to users' behaviors in the context of an organization. This automate regulation enables agents regulation more precise and consistent than humans would be able to achieve manually.

3   Background

JaCaMo is a multi-agent oriented programming platform particularly relevant for the development of complex systems. By allowing agents to interact with each other through communication and coordination, the JaCaMo platform enables effective decision-making and efficient resource allocation in complex systems. The JaCaMo meta-model [3] provides a comprehensive view of multi-agent systems by defining four dimensions: Agent, Environment, Interaction, and Organization. Concepts and primitives of the agent dimension defines the agents involved in the system, their beliefs, goals and their behaviors. The environment dimension defines the artifacts (i.e., encapsulation of operations and observable properties) used by agents to achieve their goals. The interaction dimension deals with the means by which agents communicate with each other to coordinate their actions. The organization dimension focuses on the rules and norms that govern the behavior of agents within the system.

Several extensions enable connecting JaCaMo platform with the web [7]. For instance, Charpenay et al. [6] propose Hypermedea, a framework that extends JaCaMo by enabling agents to operate on the web. In Hypermedea, agents can interact with physical devices and access data on the web, allowing for more sophisticated and diverse applications. However, bringing agents onto the web introduces new challenges related to regulation and control. In order to address these challenges, it is necessary to ensure that actions taken on the web are properly accounted for in the regulation of the system. Ciortea et al. [4,8] provide valuable insights into some of these challenges.

Although used to enable agents to interact on the web, JaCaMo has not yet been explored in regulating online forum interactions. Online forums are intricate systems that involve multiple agents with different objectives, preferences and behaviors. Investigating the potential of JaCaMo to regulate online forum interactions could have significant implications for improving user experience and engagement in these virtual environments. Further research is necessary to explore the feasibility, identify challenges and uncover opportunities of JaCaMo platform in this domain application. Here we provide insights into how the JaCaMo platform can be used to regulate agents' interactions in online forums.

One interesting JaCaMo's feature is enabling the direct connection between the organization and the environment, thus eliminating the need for agents to explicitly update the organization status. This feature is facilitated by the use of constitutive and regulative norms. Constitutive norms are rules that define what counts-as institutional facts. These institutional facts are used in regulative norms that define what is considered valid, acceptable and appropriate within the organization. For example, the commitment of an agent to an organizational goal is represented in the organization as a regulative norm obliging the agent to achieve such goal. Constitutive norms are used to inform the organization that a goal has been achieved once an action leading to the achievement of that goal is performed in the environment. Thus, signaling that the agent has fulfilled its obligation without requiring the agent to inform the organization about the achievement of the goal. Together constitutive and regulative norms create a set of rules that enables the automated regulation of agents' interactions and behavior. In the next section, we offer a novel perspective on how JaCaMo can help on this task.

4   JaCaMo-Based Reddit Specification

In this section, we provide a description of the various elements that constitute the JaCaMo-based Reddit specification used in Sect. 5 to implement a use case. We describe the agents (Sect. 4.1), the organization with the regulative norms stating their expected behavior (Sect. 4.2), the environment in which they operate (Sect. 4.3), and the connection between the organization and actions performed in the environment with a focus on constitutive norms (Sect. 4.4).

4.1   Agents

Agents aim to successfully achieve their respective goals. They may work together and collaborate, each contributing with their skills and perspectives to the group.

On the JaCaMo-based Reddit specification, agents are responsible for performing tasks on behalf of users, i.e., submitting posts to and retrieving posts from subreddits. These agents have beliefs about the tasks they have to perform. Specifically, agents have beliefs about the subreddit where to post, the post's title and content when posting on Reddit; and they have beliefs about the subreddit from where to retrieve the post and the post ID when retrieving a post from Reddit.

Listing 1 shows the plan in AgentSpeak(L) allowing agents to submit a post to a subreddit on Reddit using JaCaMo.

```
+!submit_post: subreddit_post(SP) & title(T) & content(C)
    <- submitPost(SP, T, C);
       .wait(700).
```

Listing 1. Submit post plan

The `+!submit_post` defines a plan to submit a post whenever the agent has such goal and also has in its belief base the post's title (`title(T)`) and content (`content(C)`) to be submitted to a specific subreddit (`subreddit_post(SP)`). The plan uses the subreddit, the title and the content of the post to call the `submitPost` operation (see Sect. 4.3 for further details) that actually submits the post to Reddit.

Listing 2 shows the plan in AgentSpeak(L) language allowing agents to retrieve a post from a subreddit on Reddit using JaCaMo.

```
+!retrieve_post: subreddit_get(SG) & post_id(ID)
    <- retrievePost(SG, ID);
       .wait(700).
```

Listing 2. Retrieve post plan

The `+!retrieve_post` defines a plan to retrieve a post whenever the agent has such goal and also has in its belief base the post ID (`post_id(ID)`) to be retrieved from a specific subreddit (`subreddit_get(SG)`). The plan uses the subreddit and post ID to call the `retrievePost` operation (see Sect. 4.3 for further details) that actually retrieves the post from Reddit.

4.2   Organization

JaCaMo provides a comprehensive framework for modeling Reddit in an organizational context. The JaCaMo-based Reddit organization reflects the structure and functions of Reddit as an organization within JaCaMo. This mapping enables autonomous agents to effectively understand Reddit's functionalities through JaCaMo representation and to achieve the goals of submitting and retrieving posts on subreddits. The `reddit_organization` organization in JaCaMo defines the roles, group structure, missions and goals that align with Reddit's functionalities, and the norms that outline the expected behavior of agents within subreddits.

The Reddit organization specification is structured around the (`reddit_group`) group that represents a subreddit. Groups are composed of agents playing the subscriber (`reddit_subscriber`) and the contributor (`reddit_contributor`) roles. Agents may adopt multiple roles in a group or participate in various groups. Different groups may have a different sets of agents that adopt different roles. The social scheme `reddit_scheme` defines the organizational goals (Fig. 2).

Figure 3 details how the `reddit_scheme` is structured. The main organizational goal (`interact_reddit`) is composed of two sub-goals that can be performed in parallel (i.e., `submit_post` and `retrieve_post`). Goals are achieved through missions that agents can commit to. The `submit` mission is associated to the `submit_post` goal for submitting a post to Reddit and the `retrieve` mission is associated to the `retrieve_post` goal for retrieving a post from Reddit.

Norms are defined specifying that only agents playing the `reddit_subscriber` role are allowed to commit to the `retrieve` mission and achieve the

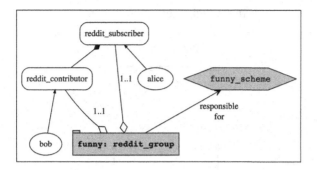

Fig. 2. Instance of the `reddit_organization` composed of a `reddit_group` group called `funny`, which is responsible for the instance of the `reddit_scheme` social scheme called `funny_scheme`, and composed of the `reddit_subscriber` and `reddit_contributor` roles played by the *Alice* and *Bob* agents

goal of retrieving posts from a subreddit (i.e., `retrieve_post`); and only those playing the `reddit_contributor` role are allowed to commit to the submit mission and achieve the goal of submitting posts to a subreddit (i.e., `submit_post`).

4.3 Environment

To enable agents to interact with Reddit, we developed an artifact called `RedditMgmt`. The `RedditMgmt` provides a set of primitives that enables agents to interact with the Reddit API and collect data on user's interactions on Reddit. This artifact provides a range of methods for accessing Reddit's REST API, enabling agents to retrieve posts from and submit posts to subreddits.

In particular, the `RedditMgmt` artifact provides the retrieve (`retrievePost`) and submit (`submitPost`) operations. The retrieve operation retrieves a post from a particular subreddit, while the submit operation submit a post to a subreddit. The retrieve operation takes two input parameters, the subreddit and the post ID, and returns a JSON string of the post retrieved from the subreddit. The submit operation takes five input parameters, subreddit, title, content, url and topic. But before submitting, the submit operation checks if the topic of the post is related to the subreddit. If so, it submits the post to the subreddit. Otherwise, the artifact generates an error message to signal to the agent that there was a problem with the post submission.

4.4 Organization and Environment

Here we describe how to monitor and control the regulation based on the operations performed in the environment. For such, we define a set of constitutive norms that state that events created in the environment count-as states in the organization (i.e., status functions).

For example, when an agent on a subreddit adopts a role as a `reddit_subscriber` or `reddit_contributor`, this can be considered as a state

funny_scheme: reddit_scheme

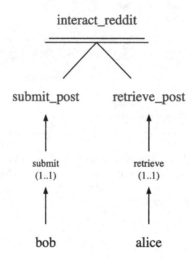

Fig. 3. Organization scheme with goal decomposition

change in the organization that reflects the agent's role as a member of a group; if an agent subscribes to a specific subreddit, this can be considered as a state in the organization that reflects their interest in a particular topic; if an agent commits to contributing to a particular discussion thread or subreddit, this can be considered as a state in the organization that reflects their commitment to contributing to the community. By defining these state changes through constitutive norms, we can establish a clear connection between agent's actions in Reddit and the organization's status functions. This connection can be used to monitor and control the agents' behavior while pursuing their goals within the context of the organization.

Constitutive norms are used to assign status-functions to concrete elements, following the formula: X count-as Y in C [9]. A constitutive norm can be defined to state that an agent (X) count-as playing the role of a `reddit_contributor` (Y) in the context of the `funny` group (C), where the agent can participate in discussions and contribute to the community's content. JaCaMo provides other status-functions in addition to "play" including "responsible" (i.e., assigns responsibility to a group or individual for certain tasks), "committed" (i.e., establishes a commitment to a specific mission or goal), "achieved" (i.e., denotes the successful completion of a task), "mission_role" (i.e., defines the role of an individual within a mission), "done" (i.e., indicates the successful completion of a task), and "well_formed" (i.e., implies that the group is functioning effectively). The constitutive norms we define to establish the relationship between the status-functions and concrete elements within the context of Reddit are shown in Fig. 4.

Rule 1 and 2 use the status-function of "play" to define that agents *Bob* and *Alice* adopt respectively the `reddit_contributor` and `reddit_subscriber`

```
status_functions:
states: play(A,R,G), responsible(G,S), committed(A,Mission,S), achieved(S,G,A),
mission_role(M,R), done(S,G,A), well_formed(Group).

constitutive_rules:
1: count-as play(bob,reddit_contributor,"funny") .
2: count-as play(alice,reddit_subscriber,"funny").
3: count-as responsible("funny","funny_scheme")
   while play(A,reddit_contributor,"funny") | play(A,reddit_subscriber,"funny").
4: play(A,reddit_contributor,"funny")
   count-as committed(A,submit,"funny_scheme")
   while responsible("funny","funny_scheme").
5: play(A,reddit_subscriber,"funny")
   count-as committed(A,retrieve,"funny_scheme")
      while responsible("funny","funny_scheme").
6: count-as done(funny_scheme,submit_post,A)
      when submit(funny, test, test, "https://i.imgur.com/Hyo0tWD.jpeg",
      fun)[sai__agent(A)].
7: count-as done(funny_scheme,retrieve_post,A)
      when retrieve(funny)[sai__agent(A)].
```

Fig. 4. Constitutive norms

roles in the **funny** group. Rule 3 defines that the **funny** group is responsible for the **funny_scheme** scheme as long as there is an agent playing the **reddit_contributor** or **reddit_subscriber** role. Rule 4 and 5 define that agents playing the **reddit_subscriber** or the **reddit_contributor** are committed respectively to the **retrieve_post** or **submit_post** mission in the **funny** group. Rule 6 defines that using the submit operation on the *funny* subreddit count-as achieving the goal of submitting a post. Rule 7 defines that using the retrieve operation from the *funny* subreddit count-as achieving the goal of retrieving.

5   JaCaMo-Based Reddit Use Case

In the previous section, we presented a JaCaMo-based Reddit specification, that outlined the roles, goals and actions of the agents in Reddit. In this section, we will instantiate a use case by defining the agents and their interactions using JaCaMo[3].

The use case involves two agents, *Alice* and *Bob* who are assigned to the **funny** group. *Alice* adopts the **reddit_subscriber** role and can read and engage with other people's posts, while *Bob* adopts the **reddit_contributor** role in this group and can submit posts to Reddit. Below we show a proof-of-concept of how *Alice* and *Bob* can interact with each other using JaCaMo and achieve their goals in the scenario. First, we tasked *Bob* with the goal of submitting a post related

---

[3] Source-code available at https://github.com/Nesrine-Hafiene/JaCaMo_Reddit.

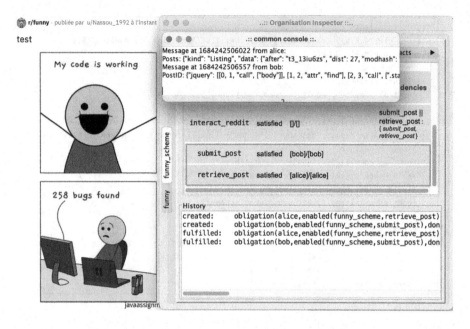

Fig. 5. Alice and Bob achieved their goals

to the topic "fun" to the *funny* subreddit and *Alice* with the goal of retrieving a post from the same subreddit. Figure 5 illustrates that both agents are able to fulfill their goals successfully.

In the second situation, however, we deliberately tasked *Bob* with the goal of submitting a post not related to the topic "fun" to the *funny* subreddit. Figure 6 illustrates that *Bob* failed to achieve his goal as the topic of the post was not one of the main topics of the subreddit.

The agent's successful submission and retrieval of posts from Reddit demonstrates its ability to operate effectively within the organization without requiring knowledge of the organization's content or objectives. The constitutive norms make possible to monitor the progress of the regulation based on the action performed in the environment. This proof-of-concept shows the usefulness of JaCaMo in facilitating goal achievement in the Reddit context, but also highlight the importance of carefully selecting relevant topics for successful agent performance. Overall, these findings suggest that JaCaMo holds potential for use in facilitating efficient and effective human–agent collaboration in online communities.

6   Conclusions

The compatible characteristics of multi-agent systems and the web, such as distributed, adaptable and flexible, provide several advantages for using the former to develop governance systems for the latter. By distributing decision-making

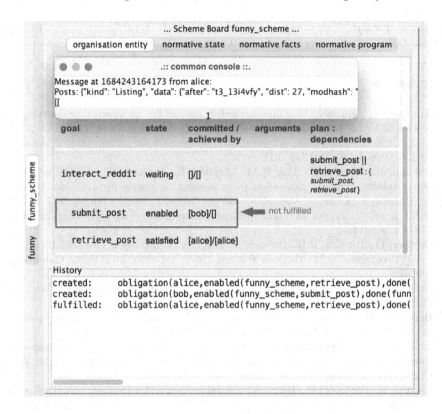

Fig. 6. Bob failed in achieving his goal

and enabling agents to autonomously learn and adapt, multi-agent systems provide a resilient and context-specific governance solution. Here, we showed the use of JaCaMo in combination with Reddit's API as a powerful tool for developing and governing autonomous agents interacting within Reddit. Our case study showed the feasibility of using JaCaMo to effectively regulate the agents' actions to submit and retrieve posts in Reddit with the purpose of achieving their goals. Moreover, the separation of concerns between regulative and constitutive norms in JaCaMo offers a promising approach to develop more sophisticated and nuanced regulations for online forums. By developing constitutive norms that analyze the content of a post and determine whether it meets certain standards, we can create a more targeted regulation to online forums. Future works should be conducted to highlight the advantages and explore the potentials offered by multi-agent systems for governing web components. Additionally, more extensive experimental validation, including a broader range of scenarios and larger-scale experiments, is required to fully evaluate and demonstrate such advantages and potentials. Besides contributing to the advancement of the field, such experimental validations will contribute to the development of more effective and trustworthy social network systems.

Acknowledgment. This work was funded by the ANR HyperAgents project (ANR-19-CE23-0030).

References

1. Amaral, C.J., Hübner, J.F.: Jacamo-web is on the fly: an interactive multi-agent system IDE. In: Dennis, L.A., Bordini, R.H., Lespérance, Y. (eds.) EMAS 2019. LNCS (LNAI), vol. 12058, pp. 246–255. Springer, Cham (2020). https://doi.org/10.1007/978-3-030-51417-4_13
2. Baldoni, M., Baroglio, C., May, K.M., Micalizio, R., Tedeschi, S.: ADOPT JaCaMo: accountability-driven organization programming technique for JaCaMo. In: An, B., Bazzan, A., Leite, J., Villata, S., van der Torre, L. (eds.) PRIMA 2017. LNCS (LNAI), vol. 10621, pp. 295–312. Springer, Cham (2017). https://doi.org/10.1007/978-3-319-69131-2_18
3. Boissier, O., Bordini, R.H., Hubner, J., Ricci, A.: Multi-agent Oriented Programming: Programming Multi-agent Systems Using JaCaMo. MIT Press, Cambridge (2020)
4. Boissier, O., Ciortea, A., Harth, A., Ricci, A.: Autonomous agents on the Web. In: Dagstuhl-Seminar 21072: Autonomous Agents on the Web, p. 100p. (2021)
5. Bordini, R.H., Hübner, J.F., Wooldridge, M.: Programming Multi-agent Systems in AgentSpeak Using Jason. Wiley, Hoboken (2007)
6. Charpenay, V., Zimmermann, A., Lefrançois, M., Boissier, O.: Hypermedea: a framework for web (of things) agents. In: Companion Proceedings of the Web Conference 2022, pp. 176–179 (2022)
7. Ciortea, A., Boissier, O., Ricci, A.: Engineering world-wide multi-agent systems with hypermedia. In: Weyns, D., Mascardi, V., Ricci, A. (eds.) EMAS 2018. LNCS (LNAI), vol. 11375, pp. 285–301. Springer, Cham (2019). https://doi.org/10.1007/978-3-030-25693-7_15
8. Ciortea, A., Mayer, S., Gandon, F., Boissier, O., Ricci, A., Zimmermann, A.: A decade in hindsight: The missing bridge between multi-agent systems and the world wide web. In: Proceedings of the International Conference on Autonomous Agents and Multiagent Systems (2019)
9. Cunha, R.R., Hübner, J.F., de Brito, M.: A conceptual model for situating purposes in artificial institutions. Rev. Inform. Teórica e Aplicada **29**(1), 68–80 (2022)
10. De Brito, M., Hübner, J.F., Boissier, O.: Situated artificial institutions: stability, consistency, and flexibility in the regulation of agent societies. Auton. Agent. Multi-Agent Syst. **32**, 219–251 (2018)
11. Hubner, J.F., Sichman, J.S., Boissier, O.: Developing organised multiagent systems using the MOISE+ model: Programming issues at the system and agent levels. Int. J. Agent-Oriented Softw. Eng. **1**(3–4), 370–395 (2007)
12. Martins, R., Meneguzzi, F.: A smart home model using JaCaMo framework. In: 2014 12th IEEE International Conference on Industrial Informatics, pp. 94–99. IEEE (2014)
13. Ricci, A., Piunti, M., Viroli, M., Omicini, A.: Environment programming in CArtAgO. Multi-agent Program.: Lang. Tools Appl. 259–288 (2009)
14. Zatelli, M.R., Hübner, J.F.: The interaction as an integration component for the JaCaMo platform. In: Dalpiaz, F., Dix, J., van Riemsdijk, M.B. (eds.) EMAS 2014. LNCS (LNAI), vol. 8758, pp. 431–450. Springer, Cham (2014). https://doi.org/10.1007/978-3-319-14484-9_22

Fuzzy Hyperplane Based Twin-KSVC and Its Applications to Stock Price Movement Direction Prediction Based on News Articles

Pei-Yi Hao[✉]

National Kaohsiung University of Science and Technology, Kaohsiung, Taiwan, R.O.C.
haupy@nkust.edu.tw

Abstract. With the extensive development of the social economic, different kinds of financial investment products has been emerged. Stock is one of the most active financial products. Successful prediction of behavior of stock market can promise high profits. Moreover, for policymakers, the rationality of policies can be assessed through market trends, so a better development of the stock market can be promoted. However, successfully prediction the trend of stock market is a very difficult problem due to the stock market's behavior are influenced by various reasons. Financial news offers useful information that can help the investor to make better stock investment decisions. This study incorporates fuzzy set theory into Twin-KSVC (twin support vector classification machine for K-class classification) and develops a new fuzzy hyperplane-based twin support vector machine for K-class classification (FH-Twin-KSVC) to predict the trend of stock market based on financial news. The distinguishing feature of the proposed FH-TWIN-KSVC are that every data sample is assigned a membership degree based on the important level of the corresponding training sample in the training process, and the components for determining the optimal separating hyperplane are fuzzy numbers. The fuzzy hyperplane is useful for capturing the imprecise natures existing in real-world environment by describing inexact characteristics in the training samples using fuzzy sets. The fuzzy hyperplane of our FH-TWIN-KSVC is able to significantly reduce the influence of noise. The experimental results on the real-world stock prediction application show that the proposed FH-TWIN-KSVC model combines the advantage of Twin-KSVC in improving classification performance in multi-classes classification problem and the advantage of a FH-SVM in increasing robustness and decreasing the influences of noises.

Keywords: Support Vector Machine · Twin Support Vector Machine · Fuzzy Set Theory · Stock Prediction · Multi-class classification

1 Introduction

The stock market is a capitalistic haven for the trading, transfer and circulation of issued stocks. Financial markets play a pivotal role in modern economies. None are independent of the financial environment. Accurately forecasting price trends in financial products (i.e., stocks, derivatives, and debt obligations,) are able to potentially avert the harmful

P. Mathieu et al. (Eds.): PAAMS 2023, LNAI 13955, pp. 125–136, 2023.
https://doi.org/10.1007/978-3-031-37616-0_11

influences that impending financial crises could happen on everyday. Moreover, the desire of every investor is to accurately forecast the stock price movement direction and seek to maximize profits and reduce the risk of surprises. This is a difficult problem due to stock market's behavior is noncertain, stochastic, and effected by a variety of reasons including politics, the microeconomics, anticipation psychology of investor, and more. Fuzzy set theory helps to solve the stock trend forecasting problem due to the boundaries separating the rising, falling and sideways categories are fuzzy. A sample that corresponds to stocks price change ratio -2% is more representative for the falling class than a sample that corresponds to stocks price change ratio -0.2%. Moreover, a sample that corresponds to stock price change ratio $+0.25\%$ may have 75% of belonging to the {flat} class and 25% of belonging to the {rising} class.

Support Vector Machine (SVM) is a powerful algorithm developed by Vapnik [1] for binary classification problems. Unlike other classification algorithms (such as multilayer perceptron) that aim to minimize empirical risk, support vector machines aim to minimize an upper bound on true risk by using the principle of structural risk minimization (SRM). SVMs have been successfully used in a wide-ranging of practical applications, such as image recognition, face classification, and text classification [2]. SVMs are useful for binary classification task. To extend SVMs for solving multi-class classification problem, we can use the "one-vs-one" strategy or "one-vs-rest" strategy. The "one-vs-one" strategy [3] constructs $K(K-1)/2$ binary SVMs classifiers. Every classifier separates two given categories, and the classification model is constructed based on the training samples from the two given classes. The "one-vs-one" strategy may obtain unfavorable classification performance because the information of the training samples from rest category is ignored in the learning procedure of every classification model. The "one-vs-rest" strategy [4] constructs K binary classifiers. Every binary classifier divides one category from the rest categories, and the classification model is constructed based on all of the training samples. The "one-vs-rest" strategy may have class imbalance problem because the number of training data points in one category is much fewer than the number of training data points in the rest categories. Angulo et al. [5] developed a new approach that is called K-SVCR for multi-class classification problem. K-SVCR employed "one-vs-one-vs-rest" strategy and have a ternary output structure $\{-1, 0, +1\}$. The K-SVCR constructs $K(K-1)/2$ classifiers such that every classification model is constructed based on all of the training samples, which solve the problem of class imbalance and risk of information loss.

Xu et al. [6] developed a new Twin-KSVC approach that combines the advantages of high accuracy rate of K-SVCR in multi-class classification problem and advantages of less computational time of the twin SVM. Nasiri et al. [7] developed a least squares-based Twin-KSVC which is called LSTKSVC. Tanveer et al. [8] proposed a least squares based-K-nearest neighbor weighted Twin-KSVC. Moreover, in many practical applications, the training data samples often have some outliers. However, original K-SVCR is significantly sensitive to noises. Bamakan et al. proposed the Ramp-KSVCR [9] that partially reduce the effect of noises on the classifiers by employing the ε-insensitive ramp loss function. Inspired by the research of K-SVCR and LS-SVM, Ma et al. [10] developed a robust least squares-based K-SVCR (K-RLSSVCR) that employ a squares ε-insensitive ramp loss rather than the hinge loss in K-SVCR.

However, for many practical tasks, observed samples are often of bad quality or pollute by outlier or noise. Traditional Twin-KSVC regards all training samples as the same important, so it is particularly sensitive to outliers or noise. Lin and Wang [11] developed a fuzzy support vector machine (FSVM), where every training sample is assigned a fuzzy member degree based on the contributions of the corresponding training sample to the learning process of the classification model. Fuzzy member degree reduces the influence of outliers or noise. Hao [12] developed a fuzzy hyperplane version of support vector machine (FH-SVM), where the components for determining the optimal separating hyperplane are fuzzy numbers. Chen et al. [13] developed an entropy-based least squares twin fuzzy support vector machine that evaluates the fuzzy member degree of training samples based on the entropy function. Hao et al. [14] developed a twin version of support vector machine using a fuzzy hyperplane for stock forecasting.

According to the research ideas of Twin-KSVC [6] and FH-SVM [12], this paper developed a fuzzy hyperplane based Twin-KSVC, called fuzzy hyperplane-based K-type twin support vector machine classification (FH-TWIN-KSVC). Our FH-TWIN-KSVC replaces the crisp hyperplane in Twin-KSVC with a fuzzy hyperplane when defining the one-vs-one decision function in multi-class classification problems. Our FH-TWIN-KSVC leverages both the benefits of Twin-KSVC in improving classification performance for multi-class classification tasks and the benefits of FH-SVM in improving the performance to against noise or outlier. The fuzzy hyperplane of our FH-TWIN-KSVC resolves the fuzziness in the set of training samples and reduces the impact of outlier or noise. Therefore, our FH-TWIN-KSVC has better ability to against noise than the traditional Twin-KSVCR classifier if the training samples are noisy. Experimental results using a real stock forecasting application validate that our FH-TWIN-KSVC has statistically comparable classification performance to state-of-the-art stock forecasting models.

2 Review of Previous Studies

2.1 *K*-Class Twin Support Vector Classification Machine (Twin-KSVC)

Xu et al. [6] developed a new Twin-KSVC method, which integrates the benefits of twin SVMs in decreasing the training time complexity and the benefits of K-SVCR in improving the classification accuracy in multi-class classification problem. Like K-SVCR [5], Twin-KSVC employed a "1-versus-1-versus-rest" strategy to evaluates all training samples, that is, two classes of data points choosen from k categories are regarded as key partitions, and it seeks a pair of non-parallel hyperplanes instead of two parallel hyperplanes. The remaining samples are located at the area between a pair of non-parallel planes. Namely, Twin-KSVC uses a ternary output structure $\{-1, 0, +1\}$. Also, it finds the solution for a pair of smaller QPPs rather than one large QPP. Let A and B represent the positive and negative categories, labeled "+1" and "−1", respectively. Let C represents the rest class whose class labels are "0", where $A_{l_1 \times n} = \{x_1; x_2; \ldots; x_{l_1}\}$, $B_{l_2 \times n} = \{x_{l_1+1}; x_{l_1+2}; \ldots; x_{l_1+l_2}\}$, $C_{l_3 \times n} = \{x_{l_1+l_2+1}; x_{l_1+l_2+2}; \ldots; x_{l_1+l_2+l_3}\}$, and $x_i \in R^n$. Similar to Twin-SVM, Twin-KSVC seeks a pair of non-parallel hyperplanes for positive and negative category so that every hyperplane is closer to one category and as far away from the other as possible. The following constraints holds for the data points from the remaining category:

$$-(Cw_1 + e_3b_1) \geq e_3(1 - \epsilon) \text{ and } Cw_2 + e_3b_2 \geq e_3(1 - \epsilon); \qquad (1)$$

where ϵ is a positive parameter chosen a priori. The pair of nonparallel hyperplanes $w_1^T x + b_1 = 0$ and $w_2^T x + b_2 = 0$ can be yielded by seeking the solution of the following two QPPs

$$\min_{w_1, b_1, \xi, \eta} \frac{1}{2} \|Aw_1 + e_1b_1\|^2 + c_1 e_2^T \xi + c_2 e_3^T \eta$$

$$\text{s.t. } -(Bw_1 + e_2b_1) + \xi \geq e_2 \qquad (2)$$

$$-(Cw_1 + e_3b_1) + \eta \geq e_3(1 - \epsilon)$$

$$\xi \geq 0e_2, \eta \geq 0e_3$$

and

$$\min_{w_2, b_2, \xi^*, \eta^*} \frac{1}{2} \|Bw_2 + e_2b_2\|^2 + c_3 e_1^T \xi^* + c_4 e_3^T \eta^*$$

$$\text{s.t. } (Aw_2 + e_1b_2) + \xi^* \geq e_1 \qquad (3)$$

$$(Cw_2 + e_3b_2) + \eta^* \geq e_3(1 - \epsilon)$$

$$\xi^* \geq 0e_1, \eta^* \geq 0e_3$$

Let $H = [A \ e_1]$, $G = [B \ e_2]$, $M = [C \ e_3]$, and using the Langrange multipliers technique, we obtain the dual problem of (2) and (3) as follows:

$$\max_{\gamma} \frac{-1}{2} \gamma^T N (H^T H)^{-1} N^T \gamma + h^T \gamma$$

$$\text{s.t. } 0 \leq \gamma \leq F \qquad (4)$$

where $N = [G; M]$, $h = [e_2; e_3(1 - \epsilon)]F = [c_1e_2; c_2e_3]$, and

$$\max_{\rho} \frac{-1}{2} \rho^T P (G^T G)^{-1} P^T \rho + k^T \rho$$

$$\text{s.t. } 0 \leq \rho \leq S \qquad (5)$$

where $P = [H; M]$, $k = [e_1; e_3(1 - \epsilon)]F = [c_3e_1; c_4e_3]$. The bias term and normal vector for the pair of nonparallel hyper-planes can been calculated by using the following equations:

$$[w_1; b_1] = (H^T H)^{-1} N^T \gamma \qquad (6)$$

$$[w_2; b_2] = (G^T G)^{-1} P^T \rho \qquad (7)$$

The Twin-KSVC uses a "1-verious-1-verious-rest" strategy to evaluate all data vectors, and the outputs of Twin-KSVC is a ternary vector $\{+1, 0, -1\}$. Given a new test sample x_i, its class label is calculated by the following decision function:

$$f(x_i) = \begin{cases} 1 \ if \ w_1^T x_i + b_1 > -1 + \epsilon \\ -1 \ if \ w_2^T x_i + b_2 < 1 - \epsilon \\ 0 \ otherwise \end{cases} \qquad (8)$$

2.2 Fuzzy Hyperplane Version of Support Vector Machine (FH-SVM)

Fuzzy hyperplane version of support vector machines (FH-SVM) seeks a fuzzy separating hyperplane that distinguish negative and positive categories. All components for determining the optimal hyperplane, such as the elements in the wight vector **w** the bias term b, are fuzzy numbers [12]. To find the optimal separating fuzzy hyperplane that distinguishes the negative and positive categories using the largest margin, FH-SVM employs the following preliminaries.

Preliminary 1 [12]: For arbitrary triangular symmetric fuzzy numbers $A = (m_A, c_A)$ and $B = (m_B, c_B)$, where c denotes the spread and m denotes the center, the partial ordering of fuzzy set A and B is determine as follows:

$$A \underset{f}{\geq} B \ iff \ m_A + c_A \geq m_B + c_B \ and \ m_A - c_A \geq m_B - c_B. \qquad (9)$$

where "$\underset{f}{\geq}$" represents the *fuzzy* larger than relation

Preliminary 2 [12]: For the fuzzy hyperplane.

$$Y = \tilde{W}_1 x_1 + \cdots + \tilde{W}_n x_n + \tilde{B} = \tilde{W}^t x + \tilde{B}, \qquad (10)$$

where $\tilde{B} = (b, d)$ denotes the fuzzy bias term $\tilde{W} = (w, c)$ denotes the fuzzy weight vector. The membership function of the fuzzy version of separating hyperplane $Y = \tilde{W}^t x + \tilde{B}$ is as follows:

$$mem_Y(y) = \begin{cases} 1 - \frac{|y - (w^t x + b)|}{c^t |x| + d} x \neq 0 \\ 1 x = 0, y = 0 \\ 0 x = 0, y \neq 0 \end{cases} \qquad (11)$$

where $\mu_Y(y) = 0$ if $c^t|x| + d \leq |y - (w^t x + b)|$. The set of training data vectors is "fuzzy linearly separable" if

$$y_i(W^t x_i + B) \underset{f}{\geq} I_F \qquad (12)$$

is hold for every data vector x_i in the set of training sample. Here, I_F denotes a triangular symmetric fuzzy number with center equaling to one and spread is I_w. Employing the above preliminaries, the FH-SVM seeks a best fuzzy separating hyperplane by finding the solution of the optimization problem as follows:

$$\underset{w,c,b,d,\xi_{1i},\xi_{2i}}{\text{minimize}} \ \frac{1}{2} w^t w + C \left(v \left(\frac{1}{2} c^t c + d \right) + \frac{1}{N} \sum_{i=1}^{N} \mu_i (\xi_{1i} + \xi_{2i}) \right) \qquad (13)$$

subject to

$$y_i(w^t x_i + b) + (c^t |x_i| + d) \geq 1 + I_w - \xi_{1i}$$
$$y_i(w^t x_i + b) - (c^t |x_i| + d) \geq 1 - I_w - \xi_{2i}, \ d \geq 0, \xi_{1i}, \xi_{2i} \geq 0, i = 1, \ldots, N,$$

3 Fuzzy Hyperplane-Based Twin-KSVC for K-Class Classification (FH-K-SVCR)

According to the research ideas of Twin-KSVC [6] and FH-SVM [12], this paper develops a fuzzy hyperplane based Twin-KSVC, called fuzzy hyperplane-based K-type twin support vector machine classification (FH-Twin-KSVC). Our FH-Twin-KSVC replaces the crisp hyperplane in Twin-KSVC with a fuzzy hyperplane when defining the one-vs-one decision function for multi-categories classification problems. Our FH-Twin-KSVC leverages both the benefits of Twin-KSVC in improving classification performance for multi-categories classification problems and the benefits of FH-SVM in improving the ability to against noises or outliers. Let A and B represents the positive and negative category, labeled "+1" and "−1", respectively. Let D represent the rest class, whose class labels are "0", where $A_{l_1 \times n} = \{x_1; x_2; \ldots; x_{l_1}\}$, $B_{l_2 \times n} = \{x_{l_1+1}; x_{l_1+2}; \ldots; x_{l_1+l_2}\}$, $D_{l_3 \times n} = \{x_{l_1+l_2+1}; x_{l_1+l_2+2}; \ldots; x_{l_1+l_2+l_3}\}$, and $x_i \in R^n$. The proposed FH-Twin-KSVC separates class i and j in "one-vs-one-vs-rest" manner. In other words, the pair of non-parallel fuzzy hyperplane $\tilde{W}_1 x + \tilde{B}_1$ and $\tilde{W}_2 x + \tilde{B}_2$ satisfies the following fuzzy conditions:

$$\tilde{W}_2 x_i + \tilde{B}_2 \underset{f}{\geq} \tilde{I}_F, i = 1, \ldots, l_1 \tag{14}$$

$$\tilde{W}_2 x_i + \tilde{B}_2 \underset{f}{\geq} \tilde{I}_F - \epsilon, i = l_1 + l_2 + 1, \ldots, l_1 + l_2 + l_3 \tag{15}$$

$$-\left(\tilde{W}_1 x_i + \tilde{B}_1\right) \underset{f}{\geq} \tilde{I}_F, i = l_1 + 1, \ldots, l_1 + l_2 \tag{16}$$

$$-\left(\tilde{W}_1 x_i + \tilde{B}_1\right) \underset{f}{\geq} \tilde{I}_F - \epsilon . i = l_1 + l_2 + 1, \ldots, l_1 + l_2 + l_3 \tag{17}$$

Here, the nation "$\underset{f}{\geq}$" indicates the condition for *fuzzy* larger than. Besides, $\tilde{I}_F$ is a triangular symmetric fuzzy number with spread equaling to I_w and center is 1. Moreover, $0 < \epsilon < 1$ is a constant chosen by user. According to Preliminaries 1 and 2 given in Eqs. (9) and (11), the fuzzy normal vector $\tilde{W}_1 = (w_1, c_1)$ and $\tilde{W}_2 = (w_2, c_2)$ and the fuzzy bias term $\tilde{B}_1 = (b_1, d_1)$ and $\tilde{B}_2 = (b_2, d_2)$ for the two non-parallel fuzzy hyperplane can be yielded by finding the solution of the following constrained optimization problem:

$$\min_{w_1,c_1,b_1,d_1,\xi_{11},\xi_{12},\eta_{11},\eta_{12}} \frac{1}{2}\|Aw_1 + e_1b_1\|^2 + \frac{1}{2}\left(\|w_1\|^2 + \|c_1\|^2 + b_1^2 + d_1^2\right)$$

$$+c_1s_2^T(\xi_{11} + \xi_{12}) + c_2s_3^T(\eta_{11} + \eta_{12})$$

$$\text{s.t.} \quad -[(Bw_1 + e_2b_1) + (Bc_1 + e_2d_1)] + \xi_{11} \geq e_2(1 + I_w)$$

$$-[(Bw_1 + e_2b_1) - (Bc_1 + e_2d_1)] + \xi_{12} \geq e_2(1 - I_w) \qquad (18)$$

$$-[(Dw_1 + e_3b_1) + (Dc_1 + e_3d_1)] + \eta_{11} \geq e_3(1 - \epsilon + I_w)$$

$$-[(Dw_1 + e_3b_1) - (Dc_1 + e_3d_1)] + \eta_{12} \geq e_3(1 - \epsilon - I_w)$$

$$\xi_{11}, \xi_{12}, \eta_{11}, \eta_{12} \geq 0$$

and

$$\min_{w_2,c_2,b_2,d_2,\xi_{21},\xi_{22},\eta_{21},\eta_{22}} \frac{1}{2}\|Bw_2 + e_2b_2\|^2 + \frac{1}{2}\left(\|w_2\|^2 + \|c_2\|^2 + b_2^2 + d_2^2\right)$$

$$+c_3s_1^T(\xi_{21} + \xi_{22}) + c_4s_3^T(\eta_{21} + \eta_{22})$$

$$\text{s.t.} \quad [(Aw_2 + e_1b_2) + (Ac_2 + e_1d_2)] + \xi_{21} \geq e_1(1 + I_w)$$

$$[(Aw_2 + e_1b_2) - (Ac_2 + e_1d_2)] + \xi_{22} \geq e_1(1 - I_w) \qquad (19)$$

$$[(Dw_2 + e_3b_2) + (Dc_2 + e_3d_2)] + \eta_{21} \geq e_3(1 - \epsilon + I_w)$$

$$[(Dw_2 + e_3b_2) - (Dc_2 + e_3d_2)] + \eta_{21} \geq e_3(1 - \epsilon - I_w)$$

$$\xi_{21}, \xi_{22}, \eta_{21}, \eta_{22} \geq 0$$

Minimizing $\|w_2\|^2$ will increases the hyperplane's margin and minizing $\|c_2\|^2 + d_2^2$ will reduce the hyperplane's fuzziness. More ambiguity gives more ambiguous class boundaries, less fuzziness gives more crisp class boundaries. Moreover, $C > 0$ is a constant chosen a prior. The fuzzy member degree s represents the important level of the training data point for constructing the classification model and ξ and η are the degree that fuzzy separable constraint doesn't hold. A larger s_i fpr data point i means the training mistake for training data point $\mathbf{x}_i$ cannot be accepted. To solve the above optimization problem in Eq. (18), we employ the following Lagrangian multipliers technique:

$$L = \frac{1}{2}\|Aw_1 + e_1b_1\|^2 + \frac{M_1}{2}\left(\|w_1\|^2 + \|c_1\|^2 + b_1^2 + d_1^2\right) + c_1s_2^T(\xi_{11} + \xi_{12})$$

$$+c_2s_3^T(\eta_{11} + \eta_{12})$$

$$-\alpha_{11}^T(-[(Bw_1 + e_2b_1) + (Bc_1 + e_2d_1)] + \xi_{11} - e_2(1 + I_w))$$

$$-\alpha_{12}^T(-[(Bw_1 + e_2b_1) - (Bc_1 + e_2d_1)] + \xi_{12} - e_2(1 - I_w)) \qquad (20)$$

$$-\beta_{11}^T(-[(Dw_1 + e_3b_1) + (Dc_1 + e_3d_1)] + \eta_{11} - e_3(1 - \epsilon + I_w))$$

$$-\beta_{12}^T(-[(Dw_1 + e_3b_1) - (Dc_1 + e_3d_1)] + \eta_{12} - e_3(1 - \epsilon - I_w))$$

$$-\gamma_{11}^T\xi_{11} - \gamma_{12}^T\xi_{12} -_{11}^T \eta_{11} -_{12}^T \eta_{12}$$

where $\alpha_{11}, \alpha_{12}, \beta_{11}, \beta_{12}, \gamma_{11}, \gamma_{12}, \lambda_{11}$, and λ_{12} are Lagrange multipliers. Differentiating L with respect to $\mathbf{w}_1, \mathbf{c}_1, b_1, d_2, \xi_{11}, \xi_{12}, \eta_{11}$ and η_{12} and setting the outputs to be zero, we obtain the Kuhn-Tucker conditions (KKT) for optimality. Employing the KKT conditions gives the following dual problem for QPP (18):

$$
\max_{\alpha_{11},\alpha_{12},\beta_{11},\beta_{12}} \frac{-1}{2}[\left(\alpha_{11}^T + \alpha_{12}^T\right)G + \left(\beta_{11}^T + \beta_{12}^T\right)P](H^T H
$$

$$
+M_1 I_1)^{-1}\left[G^T(\alpha_{11} + \alpha_{12}) + P^T(\beta_{11} + \beta_{12})\right]
$$

$$
-\frac{1}{2M_1}\left[\left(\alpha_{11}^T - \alpha_{12}^T\right)G + \left(\beta_{11}^T - \beta_{12}^T\right)P\right]\left[G^T(\alpha_{11} - \alpha_{12}) + P^T(\beta_{11} - \beta_{12})\right] \quad (21)
$$

$$
+(1 + I_w)\alpha_{11}^T e_2 + (1 - I_w)\alpha_{12}^T e_2
$$

$$
+(1 - \epsilon + I_w)\beta_{11}^T e_3 + (1 - \epsilon - I_w)\beta_{12}^T e_3
$$

$$
\text{s.t. } 0e_2 \le \alpha_{11}, \alpha_{12} \le c_1 s_2, \ 0e_3 \le \beta_{11}, \beta_{12} \le c_2 s_3
$$

where $H = [A\ e_1]$, $G = [B\ e_2]$, $P = [D\ e_3]$. After solving the QPP in Eq. (21), the fuzzy bias term $\tilde{B}_1 = (b_1, d_1)$ and the fuzzy weight vector $\tilde{W}_1 = (w_1, c_1)$ can be obtained by the following equations:

$$
[w_1; b_1] = -(H^T H + M_1 I_1)^{-1}\left[G^T(\alpha_{11} + \alpha_{12}) + P^T(\beta_{11} + \beta_{12})\right] \quad (22)
$$

$$
[c_1; d_1] = \frac{-1}{M_1}\left[G^T(\alpha_{11} - \alpha_{12}) + P^T(\beta_{11} - \beta_{12})\right] \quad (23)
$$

Similarly, by using the Lagrangian multipliers technique and calculating the Kuhn-Tucker conditions for optimality, we obtain the dual problem for QPP (19) as follows:

$$
\max_{\alpha_{21},\alpha_{22},\beta_{21},\beta_{22}} \frac{-1}{2}[\left(\alpha_{21}^T + \alpha_{22}^T\right)H + \left(\beta_{21}^T + \beta_{22}^T\right)P](G^T G
$$

$$
+M_2 I_2)^{-1}\left[H^T(\alpha_{21} + \alpha_{22}) + P^T(\beta_{21} + \beta_{22})\right]
$$

$$
-\frac{1}{2M_2}\left[\left(\alpha_{21}^T - \alpha_{22}^T\right)H + \left(\beta_{21}^T - \beta_{22}^T\right)P\right]\left[H^T(\alpha_{21} - \alpha_{22}) + P^T(\beta_{21} - \beta_{22})\right] \quad (24)
$$

$$
+(1 + I_w)\alpha_{21}^T e_1 + (1 - I_w)\alpha_{22}^T e_1
$$

$$
+(1 - \epsilon + I_w)\beta_{21}^T e_3 + (1 - \epsilon - I_w)\beta_{22}^T e_3
$$

$$
\text{s.t. } 0e_1 \le \alpha_{21}, \alpha_{22} \le c_3 s_1, \ 0e_3 \le \beta_{21}, \beta_{22} \le c_4 s_3
$$

where $\alpha_{21}, \alpha_{22}, \beta_{21}$ and β_{22} are Lagrange multipliers. After solving the QPP in Eq. (24), the fuzzy bias term $\tilde{B}_2 = (b_2, d_2)$ and the fuzzy weight vector $\tilde{W}_2 = (w_2, c_2)$ can be obtained by the following equations:

$$
[w_2; b_2] = (G^T G + M_2 I_2)^{-1}\left[H^T(\alpha_{21} + \alpha_{22}) + P^T(\beta_{21} + \beta_{22})\right] \quad (25)
$$

$$
[c_2; d_2] = \frac{1}{M_2}\left[H^T(\alpha_{21} - \alpha_{22}) + P^T(\beta_{21} - \beta_{22})\right] \quad (26)
$$

For any data point x_i, the output of the two non-parallel fuzzy hyperplane $\tilde{Y}_1 = \tilde{W}_1 x + \tilde{B}_1$ and $\tilde{Y}_2 = \tilde{W}_2 x + \tilde{B}_2$ are two triangular symmetric fuzzy number whose centers are

$w_1 x_i + b_1$ and $w_2 x_i + b_2$, respectively, and whose widths are $c_1 x_i + d_1$ and $c_2 x_i + d_2$, respectively. Our FH-Twin-KSVC employs the partial ordering relation for fuzzy numbers to evaluate the fuzzy member degree for data vector x_i belonging to the positive category. Let $A = (m_A, c_A)$ and $B = (m_B, c_B)$ respectively represent two triangular symmetric fuzzy numbers, the fuzzy member level A greater than B is determined by the following formulation:

$$R_{\geq B}(A) = R(A, B) = \begin{cases} 1 \text{ if } \alpha > 0 \text{ and } \beta > 0 \\ 0 \text{ if } \alpha < 0 \text{ and } \beta < 0 \\ 0.5\left(1 + \frac{\alpha+\beta}{\max(|\alpha|,|\beta|)}\right) \text{ o.w.} \end{cases}, \tag{27}$$

where $\alpha = (m_A + c_A) - (m_B + c_B)$ and $\beta = (m_A - c_A) - (m_B - c_B)$. For class i and j, the fuzzy decision function of the proposed FH-TWIN-KSVC is defined as follows:

$$f(x_i) = \begin{cases} R_{\geq \tilde{I}_F - \epsilon}\left(\tilde{Y}_1\right) \text{ if } w_1 x_i + b_1 > -1 + \epsilon \\ -R_{\geq \tilde{Y}_2}\left(-\tilde{I}_F + \epsilon\right) \text{ if } w_2 x_i + b_2 < 1 - \epsilon \\ \min\left(R_{\geq -\tilde{I}_F + \epsilon}\left(\tilde{Y}_1\right), -R_{\geq \tilde{Y}_2}\left(-\tilde{I}_F + \epsilon\right)\right) \text{ otherwise} \end{cases} \tag{28}$$

The returned value of the above decision function in our FH-Twin-KSVC in the region $[-1, 1]$ rather than a ternary output structure $\{-1, 0, +1\}$. The return value of the above decision function indicates the fuzzy member degree of a given data vector belonging to the positive, negative or rest categories. If the returned value of the above decision function is 1, the given data vector is 100 percentage belonging to positive category. If the returned value of the above decision function is -1, the given data vector is 100 percentage belonging to negative category. If the returned value if between -1 and 1, the given data vector is an ambiguous member and partially belongs to the negative, positive, and rest categories at the same time.

4 Experiments

The desires of every investor is to accurately forecast stock price's trends. However, it is very difficult due to the stock market's behavior is noncertain, stochastic and varies by various reasons. Financial news provides a sentiment score for breaking news events and exposes the clues about the trend of stock market's behavior. There are several successful researches that forecasts stock price moving trend at next based on daily financial news. In this paper, a released news article is assigned to a certain stock if the company name of the selected stock is in the content or title of that news. The news article that doesn't belong to any stock is removed. All news articles that collect from the http://www. cnyes.com and corresponding to the same stock and have the same release timestamp are combined into the daily news corpus. The stock price series collecting from Yahoo Taiwan Finance website are aligned to a daily news corpus based on news release dates. Any transaction dates that don't have any released news will be removed. The stock samples with price change percentage $\frac{p_d - p_{d-1}}{p_{d-1}} \geq 0.5\%$ are labeled as {rising} class and price change percentage $\frac{p_d - p_{d-1}}{p_{d-1}} \leq -0.5\%$ are labeled as {falling} class, where p_d

denotes the closing price at dth day for the target stock. The stock samples with price movement percentage between 0.55% and −0.55% are labeled as {flat} class. Sixteen stocks of food companies and semiconductor companies are collected to evaluate the performance of our FH-Twin-KSVC for the period of 1/1/2019 to 122/31/2020. In the feature extraction procedure, we employ the Chinese Linguistic Inquiry and Word Count (Chinese LIWC) dictionary [15] to discovery the semantic attributes and apply the latent Dirichlet allocation [16] (LDA) procedure to identify the hidden topics attributes in the news article.

Fuzzy set theory helps to solve the stock trend forecasting problem due to the boundaries separating the rising, falling and sideways categories are fuzzy. A sample that corresponds to stocks price change ratio −2% is more representative for the falling class than a sample that corresponds to stocks price change ratio −0.2%. Moreover, a sample that corresponds to stock price change ratio +0.25% may have 75% of belonging to the {flat} class and 25% of belonging to the {rising} class. The fuzzy member degree for each stock sample is determined using the membership function depicted in Fig. 1.

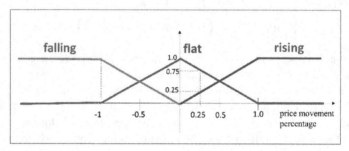

Fig. 1. The fuzzy membership functions that define the fuzzy set for {rising}, {falling}, and {flat} categories.

This experiment compares our FH-TWIN-KSVC with several novel multi-class classification SVM models, including K-SVCR [5], Twin-KSVC [6], LSTKSVC [7], KNN-Twin-KSVC [8], Ramp-KSVCR [9], K-RLSSVCR [10]. The setting for the regularization parameter C and kernel parameter is determined based on grid search procedure for each SVM model. The standard ten-fold cross-validation procedure is employed to evaluate the metric of classified accuracy ratio. Table 1 compares classified accuracy ratio of each multi-class SVM classification model. As shown in Table 1, our FH-TWIN-KSVC yields satisfactory when comparing with other novel multi-class SVM classification model. This shows that our FH-Twin-KSVC can better capture the fuzziness and imprecision nature in the practical stock movement trend recognition application by applying fuzzy set theory and fuzzy classification boundary.

Table 2 gives the comparison of our FH-TWIN-KSVC with several novel deep neural network models, including Yun's CNN-based stock forecasting approach [17], Pinheiro's RNN-based stock forecasting approach [18] and Day's DNN-based stock forecasting approach [19]. As shown in Table 2, our FH-TWIN-KSVC has better classified accuracy ratio than other (non-fuzzy) deep neural network model, which is mainly due to our FH-TWIN-KSVC allows different training sample to has different important degree when

Table 1. Comparison of the proposed FH-TWIN-KSVC with other multi-class SVM models.

Dataset	K-SVCR	Twin-KSVC	LST-KSVC	KNN-Twin-KSVC	Ramp-KSVCR	K-RL-SSVCR	Our approach
Food stocks	68.46	71.32	69.67	72.85	71.59	72.17	**72.76**
Semiconductor stocks	61.25	64.39	59.98	64.48	63.65	64.23	**65.19**
Average acc ratio	64.855	67.855	64.825	68.665	67.62	68.20	**68.975**

training the classification model. Moreover, the effects of nois or outlier is reduced by applying the fuzzy set theory and fuzzy decision boundary.

Table 2. Comparison of the proposed FH-TWIN-KSVCwith other deep learning models.

Dataset	Yun's CNN model	Pinheiro's RNN model	Day's DNN model	Our approach
Food stocks	71.18	68.57	65.34	**72.76**
Semiconductor stocks	62.79	59.72	57.63	**65.19**
Average acc ratio	66.985	64.145	61.485	**68.975**

5 Conclusion

This paper develops a new fuzzy hyperplane based Twin-KSVC, called Fuzzy Hyperplane-based twin support vector machines for K-categories classification (FH-Twin-KSVC). Our FH-TWIN-KSVC replaces the crisp hyperplane in Twin-KSVC with a fuzzy hyperplane and solve the multi-categories classification problem by using the "one-vs-one-vs-rest" strategy. Our FH-TWIN-KSVC leverages both the benefits of Twin-KSVC in improving classification performance for multi-class classification tasks and the benefits of FH-SVM in improving the ability to against the noise and outlier. Experimental results verify that our FH-TWIN-KSVC has satisfactory results on stock price trend forecast problem. Furthermore, decision making must take the risk and confidence in to account. Usually, the larger the risk involved in a decision, we require larger confidence to support the decision-making to prevent increased risk. Our FH-TWIN-KSVC evaluates the fuzzy member degree of an unseen stock samples to rising, falling and flat categories. This level of membership gives an indicator to quantify the confidence of the forecasting result. Therefore, our FH-TWIN-KSVC is very suitable for decision-making tasks. In the future, we intend to compare the classification performance of the proposed FH-TWIN-KSVC with more deep learning models on different stock markets.

References

1. Cortes, C., Vapnik, V.: Support-vector networks. Mach. Learn. **20**(3), 273–297 (1995)
2. Khan, N.M., Ksantini, R., Ahmad, I.S., Boufama, B.: A novel SVM+ NDA model for classification with an application to face recognition. Pattern Recognit. **45**(1), 66–79 (2012)
3. Kressel, U.: Pairwise classification and support vector machines. In: Scholkopf, B., et al. (eds.) Advances in Kernel Methods: Support Vector Learning, pp. 255–268 (1998)
4. Hsu, C.-W., Lin, C.-J.: A comparison of methods for multiclass support vector machines. IEEE Trans. Neural Netw. **13**(2), 415–425 (2002)
5. Angulo, C., Català, A.: K-SVCR. A multi-class support vector machine. In: López de Mántaras, R., Plaza, E. (eds.) ECML 2000. LNCS (LNAI), vol. 1810, pp. 31–38. Springer, Heidelberg (2000). https://doi.org/10.1007/3-540-45164-1_4
6. Xu, Y., Guo, R., Wang, L.: A twin multi-class classification support vector machine. Cogn. Comput. **5**(4), 580–588 (2013)
7. Nasiri, J.A., Charkari, N.M., Jalili, S.: Least squares twin multi-class classification support vector machine. Pattern Recogn. **48**(3), 984–992 (2015)
8. Tanveer, M., Sharma, A., Suganthan, P.N.: Least squares KNN-based weighted multiclass twin SVM. Neurocomputing **459**, 454–464 (2021)
9. Bamakan, S.M.H., Wang, H., Shi, Y.: Ramp loss K-support vector classification-regression; a robust and sparse multi-class approach to the intrusion detection problem. Knowl. Based Syst. **126**, 113–126 (2017)
10. Ma, J., Zhou, S., Chen, L., Wang, W., Zhang, Z.: A sparse robust model for large scale multi-class classification based on K-SVCR. Pattern Recognit. Lett. **117**, 16–23 (2019)
11. Lin, C.-F., Wang, S.-D.: Fuzzy support vector machines. IEEE Trans. Neural Netw. **13**(2), 464–471 (2002)
12. Hao, P.-Y.: Support vector classification with fuzzy hyperplane. J. Intell. Fuzzy Syst. **30**(3), 1431–1443 (2016)
13. Chen, S., Cao, J., Chen, F., Liu, B.: Entropy-based fuzzy least squares twin support vector machine for pattern classification. Neural Process. Lett. **51**, 41–66 (2020)
14. Hao, P.-Y., Kung, C.-F., Chang, C.-Y., Ou, J.-B.: Predicting stock price trends based on financial news articles and using a novel twin support vector machine with fuzzy hyperplane. Appl. Soft Comput. **98**, 106806 (2021)
15. Huang, J.-L., et al.: Establishment of a Chinese dictionary of language exploration and word counting. Chinese J. Psychol. **54**(2), 185–201 (2012)
16. Blei, D.M., Ng, A.Y., Jordan, M.I.: Latent Dirichlet allocation. J. Mach. Learn. Res. **3**, 993–1022 (2003)
17. Yun, H., Sim, G., Seok, J.: Stock prices prediction using the title of newspaper articles with Korean natural language processing. In: International Conference on Artificial Intelligence in Information and Communication (ICAIIC), pp. 019–021. IEEE (2019)
18. Pinheiro, L.D.S., Dras, M.: Stock market prediction with deep learning: a character-based neural language model for event-based trading. In: Proceedings of Australasian Language Technology Association Workshop, pp. 6–15 (2017)
19. Day, M.-Y., Lee, C.-C.: Deep learning for financial sentiment analysis on finance news providers. In: 2016 IEEE/ACM International Conference on Advances in Social Networks Analysis and Mining (ASONAM), pp. 1127–1134 (2016)

Enhancing Safety Checking Coverage with Multi-swarm Particle Swarm Optimization

Tsutomu Kumazawa[1,2]([⊠]) [iD], Munehiro Takimoto[3], Yasushi Kodama[4],
and Yasushi Kambayashi[1]

[1] Sanyo-Onoda City University, 1-1-1 Daigakudori, Sanyo-Onoda, Yamaguchi, Japan
`{kumazawa,yasushi}@rs.socu.ac.jp`
[2] Software Research Associates, Inc., 2-32-8 Minami-Ikebukuro,
Toshima-ku, Tokyo, Japan
[3] Tokyo University of Science, 2641 Yamazaki, Noda-shi, Chiba, Japan
`mune@rs.tus.ac.jp`
[4] Hosei University, 2-17-1 Fujimi, Chiyoda-ku, Tokyo, Japan
`yass@hosei.ac.jp`

Abstract. Model checking analyzes behaviors of software systems for verifying the absence of errors formally. Traditionally, such errors are detected with exhaustive search algorithms. As an alternative approach, metaheuristics and Swarm Intelligence have been applied to model checking. However, because of their non-exhaustiveness and locality, it is difficult to cover a wide region of the entire search space to users' satisfaction. In order to mitigate this incomplete coverage problem, we propose an incremental model checking approach that uses Multi-swarm Particle Swarm Optimization for error detection. The proposed approach conducts the optimization repeatedly while updating knowledge about the problem domain. The update guides the optimization to explore the search space more intensively as the repetition proceeds. Furthermore, we propose novel coverage metrics to measure diversity and intensity of the search by Swarm Intelligence. The proposed metrics make it easy for users to grasp how much model checking progresses. They can be used for large systems that tend to cause state space explosion, which is a major obstacle in model checking. Our experimental results show that the proposed incremental approach is effective as compared to simple random re-initialization approach in terms of diversity and intensity.

Keywords: Model Checking · Safety Property · Multi-swarm Particle Swarm Optimization · Coverage Metrics

1 Introduction

Model checking [7,8] has successfully been used in both academia and industry as a rigorous yet practical member of formal verification techniques in software engineering. The inputs to model checking are a *finite state model* and its logically described *specification*. The model describes the system's behavior, whereas

P. Mathieu et al. (Eds.): PAAMS 2023, LNAI 13955, pp. 137–148, 2023.
https://doi.org/10.1007/978-3-031-37616-0_12

the specification is a description of the system's desired property. Model checking decides whether the model conforms to the specification. Roughly speaking, model checking tries to find errors in the model. It constructs a state space using the model and specification, and explores the space exhaustively to find a *counterexample*. A counterexample is an erroneous execution path that does not conform to the specification. Such a counterexample is reported to the user as an output. A main research challenge of model checking has been to balance the trade-off between *comprehensibility* and *efficiency* [15,16]. We want counterexamples as short as possible since lengthy ones arise difficulties in manual analysis. Although finding a short one requires an exhaustive shortest path search, most real-world verification problems demand huge state spaces and cause either performance deterioration or failure of exhaustive search. This is called *State Space Explosion Problem*. This problem has motivated researchers to apply the approaches of Search-Based Software Engineering [12] to formal verification. Recent research has developed non-exhaustive and localized model checking techniques with metaheuristic and Swarm Intelligence algorithms [10,14,15]. A comparative study [6] reveals that metaheuristic verification methods are more efficient than exhaustive formal verification methods. One of the state-of-the-art model checking methods is msPSO-safe [16], which adopts a multi-swarm variant of Particle Swarm Optimization (PSO) [13]. The preliminary experiments reveal that msPSO-safe achieves a good balance in comprehensibility and efficiency.

Unfortunately, non-exhaustiveness of Swarm Intelligence including msPSO-safe has a weak point. Its search locality causes some unexplored subspaces in the search space. Thus, even when a non-exhaustive model checker finds a counterexample, it may overlook much shorter ones. This is the problem of incomplete state space coverage by the model checker and makes it difficult to attain comprehensibility to users' satisfaction. In order to mitigate this problem without requiring parameters' fine-tuning of msPSO-safe, we propose msPSO-safe-inc, i.e., an incremental model checking using msPSO-safe. Encouraged by the observation that msPSO-safe completes within a reasonable running time [16], msPSO-safe-inc runs msPSO-safe repeatedly by updating acquired knowledge in an attempt to cover sufficiently large subspaces. In addition, we propose effective coverage metrics to support the user to understand the outline of model checking progress. The experimental results show that the multiple updates of the proposed regularization effectively accelerates the exploration coverage.

The rest of this paper is organized as follows. Section 2 introduces an automata-theoretic approach for model checking and msPSO-safe. Section 3 discusses our incremental model checking method called msPSO-safe-inc and our coverage metrics. Section 4 reports the results of our experiments. Section 5 is the literature review. Section 6 concludes our discussion.

2   Background

This section briefly introduces automata-theoretic model checking and an application of Multi-swarm Particle Swarm Optimization to this model checking.

2.1   Model Checking

Model checking [7,8] rigorously verifies that software systems are error-free and conform to their specifications. This paper focuses on an automata-theoretic approach for model checking [8,11,21]. This approach is based on the finite state machine formalism. Typically, the target system and specification is described by a Kripke structure (called a *model*) and a Büchi automaton respectively [8]. The Büchi automaton accepts the words contradicting the specification (called the *specification automaton* in the following). A specification automaton is depicted as a directed graph with a set of states including accepting states and one or more initial states. It accepts the paths of infinite length passing through some accepting state infinitely many times. Model checking tries to refute the claim that the model contains no path that violates the specification. First, the system computes the state space, i.e., the intersection of the model and specification automaton. The intersection is a Büchi automaton that accepts the words conforming to the model but contrary to the specification. This is constructed by applying the product operation to the model and specification automaton. The operation is defined on some state machine formalism [8,11]. We then test the emptiness of the intersection. If the intersection is not empty, the user receives a report that states the model violates the specification and describes an accepting path called a *counterexample*. The class of specifications considered in this paper is the *safety* property [17]. It says that no path on the model reaches any error states. It is known that we can construct a specification automaton contradicting the property and an intersection such that they contain a single accepting state [11]. The accepting state is viewed as the deadlocked error state, which has no outgoing transitions. Checking a safety property is reduced to reachability analysis to an error state over the intersection typically via exhaustive algorithms, e.g., Depth-First Search.

2.2   Multi-swarm Particle Swarm Optimization for Model Checking

Particle Swarm Optimization (PSO) [13] is a Swarm Intelligence optimization known for its performance superiority. PSO simulates cooperative behavior of a *swarm*, which is a flock of agents called *particles*. A particle p_i traverses over the search space by updating its position vector x_i, velocity vector v_i, and personally best position x_i^{pb} iteratively in accordance with the following equations:

$$v_i = wv_i + c_1 r_1(x^{gb} - x_i) + c_2 r_2(x_i^{pb} - x_i), \tag{1}$$
$$x_i = x_i + v_i \tag{2}$$

where w, c_1 and c_2 are parameters whose values are determined by the user. Also, r_1 and r_2 are random values within the range $[0, 1]$. The position x^{gb} is the globally best position and represents knowledge shared between particles. The vectors x_i^{pb} and x^{gb} are determined by the given objective function to optimize. Ferreira *et al.* [10] put PSO to use in model checking of safety properties.

We proposed PSO with multiple dynamically created swarms for solving safety checking problems [16]. The proposed method is called msPSO-safe. The core idea of `msPSO-safe` is an effective state space decomposition by *state abstraction*. Recall that the state space is an intersection of the model and specification automaton. From its construction [8,11], each state in the state space is formalized as a tuple $s = (s_m, s_{sp})$ where s_m and s_{sp} are the states of the model and specification automaton respectively. Thus, we can view s_{sp} as a representative of a state group whose members have state tuples containing s_{sp}. We say that s_{sp} is an *abstract state* of s and that s *belongs to* s_{sp}. The specification automaton is called an *abstraction* or *abstract state space* of the intersection. Our decomposition strategy is to divide the entire state space into the disjoint abstract state groups and to assign swarms to them. We could achieve a good balance between efficiency and comprehensibility since our decomposition strategy allows each swarm to explore only one of the divided subspaces. Each swarm conducts an extension of PSO [10] whose objective function to maximize is formulated as follows:

$$f(x) = DL \cdot deadlock(x) + numblocked(x) +$$
$$\frac{1}{1 + pathlen(x) + rdistance(x)} + pathlen(x) \cdot firstvisit(x) \quad (3)$$

where a particle's position x encodes a path on the state space, which is denoted by $path(x)$. The dimension of the vectors $maxlen$ is given by the user. We denote the length of $path(x)$ by $pathlen(x)$. In the formula, DL is a user-defined parameter; $deadlock(x)$ is an indicator function to detect whether $path(x)$ reaches an accepting state; $numblocked(x)$ evaluates the degree of deadlocking after the traversal of $path(x)$. The other functions $rdistance$ and $firstvisit$ are heuristics. The former estimates the remaining distance from the last state of $path(x)$ to the accepting state. The estimation is computed beforehand with the shortest path search on the inversely directed graph of the specification automaton. This heuristic comes from the idea that, from the construction of the intersection, when t step is expected to arrive at the accepting state from the current state on the specification automaton, the number of the remaining steps on the intersection is at least t. On the other hand, the latter penalizes the multiple times arrivals of an abstract state. Finally, `msPSO-safe` terminates when no swarm can find better solutions after consecutive search trials. This situation is controlled by the parameter *stag_rounds*.

3   Incremental Model Checking Inducing High Coverage

One of the notable features of metaheuristics and Swarm Intelligence including `msPSO-safe` is that it is a non-exhaustive and "best-effort" approach. Such an approach covers only a part of the state space to enhance performance at the expense of always finding the shortest counterexamples. In other words, even when the approach finds a counterexample, there is a possibility that shorter and more comprehensible ones may exist in the uncovered part. This coverage problem is rooted in poor population diversity of Swarm Intelligence [5,19,20]. In this section, we propose the following two mitigation techniques to this problem: 1) to induce a model checker to cover the state space incrementally without a tangled fine-tuning process, and 2) to provide the effective metrics to measure the state space coverage.

3.1 Incremental Model Checking

In order to cover a large portion of a given state space, we propose an incremental exploration using msPSO-safe, called msPSO-safe-inc. As summarized in Algorithm 1, msPSO-safe-inc runs msPSO-safe repeatedly and records a counterexample that has been the most qualified in terms of the length. When the predefined termination condition holds, the system reports the user the shortest one. The termination condition can be tailored to specific model checking problems or the user's confidence level. A candidate termination condition is to test the coverage of the traversed states over the state space. We discuss the coverage metrics appropriate for model checking in the next subsection.

Algorithm 1. msPSO-safe-inc

1: $shortest\_path \leftarrow \emptyset$
2: **while** Termination condition does not hold **do**
3:    Run msPSO-safe
4:    $path \leftarrow$ best counterexample path found by msPSO-safe
      {Update shortest path}
5:    **if** $(path \neq \emptyset) \wedge ((shortest\_path = \emptyset) \vee (length(path) < length(shortest\_path)))$ **then**
6:        $shortest\_path \leftarrow path$
7:    **end if**
8:    Update heuristics or objective function
9: **end while**
10: **if** $shortest\_path \neq \emptyset$ **then**
11:    **return** "Not Conformed", $shortest\_path$
12: **else**
13:    **return** "Likely Conformed"
14: **end if**

At line 8 of Algorithm 1, msPSO-safe-inc cumulatively adjusts an influential regularization term in the objective function using counterexamples that have detected in the past iterations. This procedure aims to prevent the rediscovery of such counterexamples and to make the subsequent runs of msPSO-safe explore as wide distinct part of the state space as possible. For simplicity, msPSO-safe-inc employs a greedy approach, i.e., we restore none of the previously used regularization. We can view msPSO-safe-inc as one of the re-initialization techniques of PSO, which is known to be effective to promote diversity [5]. Rather than introducing some complicated mechanisms such as monitoring swarms' dynamics [5], we simply use the previously detected counterexamples. The success of `msPSO-safe-inc` depends on the assumption that we can run `msPSO-safe` many times without depleting computational resources. This assumption is acceptable when we can take advantages of a garbage collection mechanism. A garbage collection releases the memory resources consumed by `msPSO-safe` appropriately as the one built in Python. The rest of this subsection investigates the following two update strategies of the regularization terms that are suitable with Formula (3). The difference between these strategies is the manner of adding regularization to the objective function.

Updating rdistance. The role of the heuristic *rdistance* is to entice particles into accepting states apace. The first update strategy is rewriting *rdistance* so that the previous counterexamples can adversely affect its distance estimation. Consider each abstract state that appears in a counterexample returned by `msPSO-safe` at line 4 of Algorithm 1. We increase the estimated distance from this abstract state to the accepting state of the specification automaton by the number of the abstract states. In case that the previous `msPSO-safe` fails to find accepting paths, we choose an abstract state at random and increase the estimated distance in the same manner. The modified *rdistance* is applied to the next `msPSO-safe`. We call this update strategy *APUP (Accepting Path UPdate)*.

Adding Regularization to Objective Function. The other update strategy is to add a regularization term $penalty(\boldsymbol{x})$ to Formula (3), where $\boldsymbol{x}$ is a position vector. The term $penalty(\boldsymbol{x})$ imposes the path $path(\boldsymbol{x})$ on a penalty when $path(\boldsymbol{x})$ reaches some abstract state appearing in the counterexamples that have been detected previously. The penalty assigned to each abstract state is updated in the following manner. At the initialization of Algorithm 1, a penalty for each abstract state is initialized to 0. At line 8, the penalty for each abstract state in the counterexample obtained in this iteration increases just the same manner as APUP strategy. When `msPSO-safe` does not detect a counterexample, we choose an abstract state randomly and increase its penalty like APUP strategy. Note that $penalty(\boldsymbol{x})$ returns a negative value since Formula (3) is to be maximized. In the following, we call this strategy *APP (Abstract Path Penalty update)*.

3.2 Abstract Coverage Metrics

Although `msPSO-safe-inc` helps the user to have confidence in the check result, we have to develop an effective manner to offer the user how much a check progresses. To put it simply, the user wants to know the rate of the explored state space such as "My model checker has completed roughly 80% of the entire state space." In line with [4], we propose two novel coverage metrics for model checking. The proposed metrics aim to capture well-known diversification (exploration) and intensification (exploitation) capabilities in Swarm Intelligence. They offer the user a helpful clue to decide whether a model checker has explored a sufficiently large subspace in an appropriate manner. The computation of such coverage metrics on the state space is not an easy task since the notion of "coverage" depends on the unrealistic assumption that we know the entire state space with no regard for the state space explosion problem. Instead of considering the state space coverage on the entire state space, we compute coverage criteria based on the corresponding abstract state space. Such *abstract coverage metrics* are estimations of the coverage metrics on the entire state space. As we have the specification automaton beforehand as discussed in Sect. 2.1, it is acceptable to use this automaton for computing the proposed coverage metrics.

The first metric evaluates the diversification capability. It counts abstract states to estimate the rate of the visited states by a model checker. Let S_{sp}^e and S_{sp} be the set of visited states of the specification automaton and the set of states of the specification automaton, respectively. The diversification metric AC_{div} is defined as below.

$$AC_{div} = \frac{|S_{sp}^e|}{|S_{sp}|} \tag{4}$$

The second metric measures the intensification capability for an abstract state s_{sp}. A simple quantification is the rate of states that belongs to s_{sp} and that have been unfolded with msPSO-safe. In order to avoid the state space explosion problem, we simply count the number of unfolded states whose abstract state is s_{sp} instead of computing the rate strictly. The metric $AC_{int}(s_{sp})$ is defined as *the number of visited states that belongs to s_{sp}, which is counted on the entire state space*. We believe that it helps the user to see the picture of which abstract states are intensified.

4 Experiments

We have conducted numerical experiments on msPSO-safe-inc. This section reports the results of our experiments.

4.1 Experimental Setting

We implemented msPSO-safe-inc with Python 3. The termination condition of msPSO-safe-inc is stopping after two hundred iterations. Our implementation invokes a re-implementation of msPSO-safe that is used for the experiments in the previous work [15]. We solved several implementation problems and limitations which we discovered after the publication of [15]. Considering performance enhancement, we added another msPSO-safe's termination condition, i.e., msPSO-safe terminates as soon as it reaches an accepting state. We list the parameter setting for the initial msPSO-safe in Table 1. It was based on the preliminary experiments [16] except that the value of *stag_rounds* was determined aiming at favorable performance.

A benchmark systems in each of our experiments consists of p interactive processes ($p = 2, 3, 4, 5, 6$). Each process and a specification automaton are independent Erdős-Rényi graphs [9] with the number of states to be 100 and the probability for edge creation to be 0.05. Edge directions and system actions are added to them at random. We added an accepting state to the specification automaton and randomly generated edges to this state. We selected this benchmark problem because we did not want to inject biases that depend on specific

Table 1. Parameter Setting of `msPSO-safe`

Parameter	Value	Parameter	Value
w	Linearly changing from 1.2 down to 0.6	Number of Iterations	30
c_1	2	Particle size	20
c_2	2	$maxlen$	5
DL	10000	$stag\_rounds$	1
$itupert$	5		

problems. For each p processes, we used three models; we call them case1, case2 and case3 respectively.

4.2   Experimental Results

Figures 1, 2 and 3 show the experimental results. In the figures, "none" indicates the baseline, which simply repeats `msPSO-safe` with no update strategies. First of all, our results show that `msPSO-safe-inc` promotes diversification as the number of `msPSO-safe`'s executions increases. We observe the upsurge in diversity AC_{div} only at the early iterations, although intensity AC_{int} increases monotonically for all iterations. In `msPSO-safe-inc`, diversification dominates intensification at an early stage, while the converse is true at a later stage. For only one model, i.e., the case2 of $p = 5$, the baseline presents the fastest increase in terms of diversity (the number of visited states and AC_{div}) and intensity (AC_{int}). For other models, either of the proposed update strategies achieves the comparable or faster increase. The comparable results are seen in several small-sized cases of $p = 2$ and 3. The comparison of APP and APUP strategies is difficult. Because the effect of each strategy on the efficient increase of coverage depends on a specific model, it is hard to conclude which strategy presents more efficient coverage in general. We have to investigate the strategies with other benchmarks for future. For the lengths of counterexamples, owing to efficient increase in coverage, `msPSO-safe-inc` successfully detects the shorter counterexamples as compared to `msPSO-safe`'s first single run does. The baseline and our update strategies achieve approximately comparable effectiveness for detecting short counterexamples. An interesting observation is that the search intensity AC_{int} is approximately proportional to the number of visited states. This finding suggests that `msPSO-safe` unfolds each abstract state with fair intensity for each iteration. Finally, the above discussion on diversification and intensification owes the proposed metrics AC_{div} and AC_{int}. That retrospectively demonstrates their appropriateness as coverage metrics for model checking.

5   Related Work

Our incremental model checking is inspired by literature on incomplete model checking explorations discussed in the following. This kind of research generate

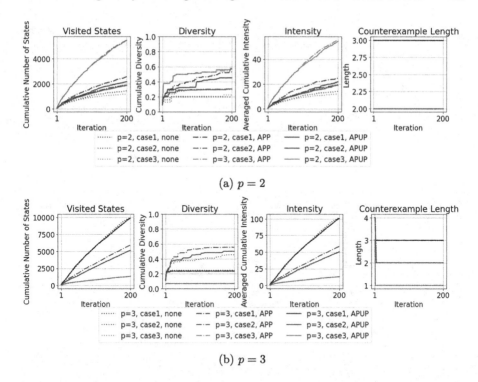

Fig. 1. Experimental Results for Random Graph Benchmark ($p = 2, 3$). The followings are plotted from left to right: the number of visited states cumulatively, the cumulative value of AC_{div}, the average of the accumulated AC_{int} over every abstract state, and the length of counterexamples.

helpful information when model checking fails because of depletion of computational resources. Our research aims to overcome incomplete checks due to non-exhaustiveness of Swarm Intelligence rather than failure. Beyer et al. [1] collect the relevant information for the further verification. Pavese et al. [18] advocate a probabilistic quantification of partial exploration. Castaño et al. [3] present information about analyzing software execution traces. Because all the above work are assumed to check source codes or programs having rich heuristic information, it is difficult to generalize them to standard model checking directly. Other than model checking, Busse et al. [2] propose a memoization technique to avoid execution failure in symbolic execution.

The aim of our coverage metrics is similar to that of Verification Coverage [4], which assumes the presence of source codes. Our metrics are applicable in broad phases of a software development process without source codes, e.g., software design. In pioneering work [19,20], PSO's population diversity is proposed to analyze dynamics of swarms. It is measured by position diversity, velocity diversity and cognitive diversity. We do not take this approach since the population diversity does not evaluate the state space coverage. The position diversity and

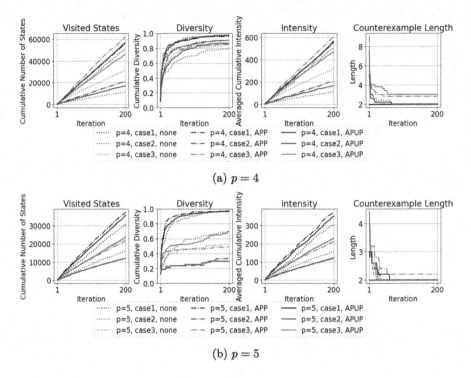

(a) $p = 4$

(b) $p = 5$

Fig. 2. Experimental Results for Random Graph Benchmark ($p = 4, 5$).

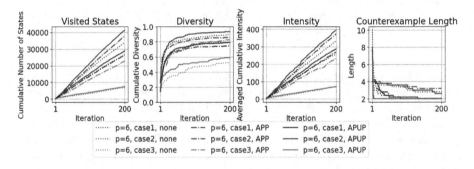

Fig. 3. Experimental Results for Random Graph Benchmark ($p = 6$).

cognitive diversity are the metrics in terms of particles' positions, whereas the velocity diversity measures the variation of their velocities. Following Ferreira *et al.* [10], `msPSO-safe` represents a position vector as a path on a directed graph. The diversity of paths does not offer coverage information directly since distinct paths can share several states. For velocity diversity, it is hard to naturally interpret a velocity in Formula (1) from the model checking viewpoint.

6   Conclusion

Applying non-exhaustive Swarm Intelligence to model checking has achieved a great success in the world of model checking. Meanwhile, the state space coverage problem has to be addressed. In this paper, we have proposed a novel incremental model checking approach called msPSO-safe-inc, which covers the state space using a Swarm Intelligence model checking method msPSO-safe gradually and effectively. Our approach greedily repeats the process of running msPSO-safe and updating a selected regularization term in its objective function. We have also proposed two coverage metrics for model checking to quantify search diversity and intensity. Our experiments have revealed that msPSO-safe-inc with an appropriate update strategy covers state spaces more efficiently than the simple re-initialization method does. For future work, it is interesting to apply the idea of incremental approach to metaheuristic model checking methods other than msPSO-safe. To this aim, we plan to study effective strategies that update some configurations of the metaheuristics.

Acknowledgements. This work was supported by JSPS KAKENHI Grant Number JP22K11988.

References

1. Beyer, D., Henzinger, T.A., Keremoglu, M.E., Wendler, P.: Conditional model checking: a technique to pass information between verifiers. In: ACM SIGSOFT 20th International Symposium on the Foundations of Software Engineering (FSE 2012) (2012). https://doi.org/10.1145/2393596.2393664
2. Busse, F., Nowack, M., Cadar, C.: Running symbolic execution forever. In: 29th ACM SIGSOFT International Symposium on Software Testing and Analysis (ISSTA 2020), pp. 63–74 (2020). https://doi.org/10.1145/3395363.3397360
3. Castaño, R., Braberman, V., Garbervetsky, D., Uchitel, S.: Model checker execution reports. In: 32nd IEEE/ACM International Conference on Automated Software Engineering, pp. 200–205. IEEE (2017). https://doi.org/10.1109/ASE.2017.8115633
4. Castaño, R., Braberman, V.A., Garbervetsky, D., Uchitel, S.: Verification coverage. arXiv preprint arXiv:1706.03796 (2017)
5. Cheng, S., Shi, Y., Qin, Q.: Promoting diversity in particle swarm optimization to solve multimodal problems. In: Lu, B.-L., Zhang, L., Kwok, J. (eds.) ICONIP 2011. LNCS, vol. 7063, pp. 228–237. Springer, Heidelberg (2011). https://doi.org/10.1007/978-3-642-24958-7_27
6. Chicano, F., Ferreira, M., Alba, E.: Comparing metaheuristic algorithms for error detection in Java programs. In: 3rd International Conference on Search Based Software Engineering, pp. 82–96 (2011). https://doi.org/10.1007/978-3-642-23716-4_11
7. Clarke, E.M., Emerson, E.A.: Design and synthesis of synchronization skeletons using branching time temporal logic. In: Kozen, D. (ed.) Logic of Programs 1981. LNCS, vol. 131, pp. 52–71. Springer, Heidelberg (1982). https://doi.org/10.1007/BFb0025774

8. Clarke, E.M., Jr., Grumberg, O., Kroening, D., Peled, D., Veith, H.: Model Checking, 2nd edn. MIT Press, Cambridge (2018)
9. Erdős, P., Rényi, A.: On random graphs I. Publicationes Mathematicae Debrecen **6**, 290–297 (1959)
10. Ferreira, M., Chicano, F., Alba, E., Gómez-Pulido, J.A.: Detecting protocol errors using particle swarm optimization with Java pathfinder. In: High Performance Computing and Simulation Conference, pp. 319–325 (2008)
11. Giannakopoulou, D., Magee, J.: Fluent model checking for event-based systems. In: 9th European Software Engineering Conference Held Jointly with 11th ACM SIGSOFT International Symposium on Foundations of Software Engineering, pp. 257–266 (2003). https://doi.org/10.1145/940071.940106
12. Harman, M., Mansouri, S.A., Zhang, Y.: Search-based software engineering: trends, techniques and applications. ACM Comput. Surv. **45**(1), 1–61 (2012). https://doi.org/10.1145/2379776.2379787
13. Kennedy, J., Eberhart, R.: Particle swarm optimization. In: International Conference on Neural Networks, pp. 1942–1948 (1995)
14. Kumazawa, T., Takimoto, M., Kambayashi, Y.: A survey on the applications of swarm intelligence to software verification. In: Handbook of Research on Fireworks Algorithms and Swarm Intelligence, pp. 376–398 (2020). https://doi.org/10.4018/978-1-7998-1659-1.ch017
15. Kumazawa, T., Takimoto, M., Kambayashi, Y.: Exploration strategies for balancing efficiency and comprehensibility in model checking with ant colony optimization. J. Inf. Telecommun. **6**(3), 341–359 (2022). https://doi.org/10.1080/24751839.2022.2047470
16. Kumazawa, T., Takimoto, M., Kambayashi, Y.: A safety checking algorithm with multi-swarm particle swarm optimization. In: Proceedings of the Genetic and Evolutionary Computation Conference Companion (GECCO 2022), pp. 786–789 (2022). https://doi.org/10.1145/3520304.3528918
17. Lamport, L.: Proving the correctness of multiprocess programs. IEEE Trans. Softw. Eng. **SE-3**(2), 125–143 (1977). https://doi.org/10.1109/TSE.1977.229904
18. Pavese, E., Braberman, V., Uchitel, S.: My model checker died! How well did it do? In: 2010 ICSE Workshop on Quantitative Stochastic Models in the Verification and Design of Software Systems (QUOVADIS 2010), pp. 33–40 (2010). https://doi.org/10.1145/1808877.1808884
19. Shi, Y., Eberhart, R.: Monitoring of particle swarm optimization. Front. Comp. Sci. **3**(1), 31 (2009). https://doi.org/10.1007/s11704-009-0008-4
20. Shi, Y., Eberhart, R.C.: Population diversity of particle swarms. In: 2008 IEEE Congress on Evolutionary Computation (IEEE World Congress on Computational Intelligence), pp. 1063–1067 (2008). https://doi.org/10.1109/CEC.2008.4630928
21. Vardi, M.Y., Wolper, P.: An automata-theoretic approach to automatic program verification. In: First Symposium on Logic in Computer Science, pp. 322–331 (1986)

A Decentralized Resource Allocation Protocol in Social Networks

Mojtaba Malek-Akhlagh$^{(\boxtimes)}$ and Jens H. Weber

Department of Computer Science, University of Victoria, Victoria, Canada
{mojmalek,jens}@uvic.ca

Abstract. In this paper, we study a variant of the dynamic resource allocation problem, where agents are connected in a social network and perform tasks which require multiple items of different resource types. Each individual agent can only interact with its direct neighbors in the network and only has knowledge about its own tasks and resources, which arrive over time. We present a decentralized negotiation-based protocol, which allows a multi-agent system in a dynamic environment to adjust its resource allocation in order to maximize the welfare of the overall system. The proposed protocol allows the agents to cascade requests and combine offered resources along the network by incorporating timeouts in their interactions. It allows the multi-agent system to be self-organized, as all decisions are made by individual agents and there is no central controller either internal or external. We evaluate our protocol by conducting simulation experiments in different types of social networks, namely small-world, scale-free, and random networks. The results demonstrate that our protocol performs well compared to a centralized approach with complete knowledge of all tasks and resources, and outperforms a decentralized approach with no cascading behavior.

Keywords: Resource allocation · Social networks · Self-organization

1 Introduction

Resource allocation among multiple agents in a dynamic environment can be observed in many real-world applications. In this study, we consider environments in which supply and demand of resources may change over time. In our model, the individual agents have a domain specific motivation to collaborate, and share a common goal to maximize the total utilities gained by all agents over time. In particular, we consider agents to be connected in a social network, which constrains their interactive behavior, inspired by business relations among organizations in real-world scenarios. An instance of such problems can be found in the allocation of required resources to hospitals distributed in a region, where the dynamism comes from sudden changes in demand such as an increase in the number of patients appearing, and hence a shortage of resources e.g. healthcare products. In particular, a pandemic scenario exhibits such an unforeseen demand, which could not be estimated by current prediction models.

P. Mathieu et al. (Eds.): PAAMS 2023, LNAI 13955, pp. 149–162, 2023.
https://doi.org/10.1007/978-3-031-37616-0_13

Existing resource allocation mechanisms often fail to address the requirements related to the social network, which restricts interaction among the agents. In this paper, we present a decentralized, self-organized protocol [14,20] which allows agents in a social network to negotiate resources in a dynamic environment. Self-organisation is a localized and decentralized operation, which allows a multi-agent system to be more scalable and highly adaptive to dynamic requirements [7]. Hence, the system avoids a single point of failure since it does not rely on any central entity neither internal nor external.

The protocol presented in this paper extends upon earlier work by the same authors [12]. We have extended our protocol design to address the dynamic resource allocation problem when the connectivity among agents is determined by a social network. The new design allows agents to cascade requests, and combine contributions from multiple offers along the network. Moreover, agents incorporate timeouts in their messages, and apply them in their deliberations, when sending and receiving the messages. Applying timeouts allows the agents' communications to be asynchronous, while maintaining the reliability of their interactive behavior [4,5].

We evaluate the efficiency of the proposed protocol by performing simulation experiments using different types of social networks. We compare its performance with a centralized approach, in which one agent has complete knowledge of all agent tasks and resources, and with a decentralized protocol with no cascading behavior. The simulation results illustrate the impact of cascading behavior on the social welfare for different values of resource quantities, types, and network degrees. The remainder of the paper is organized as follows. Section 2 reviews the related work. Section 3 formally defines the dynamic resource allocation problem in a social network. Section 4 presents the proposed protocol. Section 5 presents our simulation models and experiment results. Finally, Sect. 6 gives concluding remarks and outlines our future directions.

2   Related Work

Kash et al. [10] proposed a centralized resource allocation mechanism based on fair division theory in dynamic settings where agents arrive over time. Their objective is to find an equilibrium among all agents such that no one has an incentive to change the resource allocations. Their method requires a central controller and global information. However, centralized mechanisms have a single point of failure and contrast to our decentralized protocol which allows a multi-agent system to be self-organized.

Fatima and Wooldridge [8] developed a system called TRACE, which includes a resource allocation protocol (RAP). In a dynamic environment, each organization receives requests for different tasks, so that one organization could have a shortage of resources, while another one could have extra resources. RAP allows organizations to reallocate resources between themselves in accordance with their demands. RAP uses ideas from computational market systems, by calculating the total supply and demand for resources in the system and determining the equilibrium price. Our work contrasts with theirs as we study the resource allocation problem when tasks require multiple types of resources and also agent behavior is constrained by a social network. Moreover, TRACE requires both local and global information; while in our protocol, all the decisions are made through local interactions based on local information.

An et al. [1] proposed a negotiation-based resource allocation mechanism for self-interested agents in electronic commerce markets. In their model, multiple buyer and seller agents are allowed to negotiate with each other concurrently for trading multiple resources. Agents make tentative agreements for each resource before committing to final agreements. They determine a reserve price for each resource and adjust tentative agreements dynamically based on a time-dependent strategy in response to the market situation. Their model contrasts with ours as we consider collaborative agents connected in social networks, while the agents aim to maximize their total utilities.

Delgado-Roman et al. [6] proposed the Coalition Oriented Sensing Algorithm (COSA) for coordination among nodes in wireless sensor networks. COSA allows a network to save energy and extend its useful battery life by avoiding redundant sensing in dynamic environments. It is fully decentralized by making the nodes autonomous and relies on peer to peer negotiation among neighboring nodes in order to reallocate sensing tasks over time. Our work differs with theirs as we consider tasks which require multiple resource types and also our protocol allows cascading requests in order to find resources further away in the network.

Macarthur et al. [11] proposed a decentralized anytime algorithm for task allocation in dynamic environments, where the set of agents and tasks may change over time. They improved the efficiency and scalability of an existing fast-max-sum algorithm by introducing an online pruning procedure that simplifies the problem, and a branch-and-bound technique that reduces the search space. However, they do not address the task allocation problem in a social network, which restricts the agents' interactions to their direct neighbors.

Georgara et al. [9] studied the problem of allocating teams of agents to a collection of tasks, where each team is in charge of a specific task. They proposed an anytime heuristic algorithm, which first finds an initial feasible allocation, then improves it by swapping agents among teams. It contrasts with our model as we consider resources of each agent to be used by multiple tasks in a social network, and we propose a negotiation-based approach.

De Weerdt et al. [18,19] studied the task allocation problem in social networks. In their model, each agent is given a set of tasks to perform, and has a set of resources of different types. The agents are only allowed to interact with their direct neighbors, and only allowed to use resources provided by them. The authors proposed a greedy distributed protocol based on the Contract Net protocol [16], in which an agent in charge of a task acts like a manager and its neighbors act like participants. Our protocol extends their work by allowing requests to be cascaded along the network. Moreover, we investigate the resource allocation problem in dynamic environments, where both tasks and resources may change over time.

3   Social Resource Allocation Problem

We consider a multi-agent system comprising of n agents, $A = \{a_1, \ldots, a_n\}$. Each agent $a \in A$ receives tasks over time from a domain, $T = \{t_1, \ldots, t_m\}$. Each task $t \in T$ requires resources defined by a function: $rqr\colon T \times R \to \mathbb{N}$, where $R = \{r_1, \ldots, r_l\}$ is set of resource types. Each task has a *utility* indicating its importance; and it has a *deadline*, which indicates the latest time at which the task could be carried out. The set of tasks assigned to an agent at any given time considering their deadlines is defined by a function: $tsk\colon A \times Time \to P(T)$, where $P(T)$ denotes the power set of the task domain. Each agent $a \in A$ also receives resources over time. Each resource item has a *lifetime*, which indicates its expiry time. The number of available resources to an agent at any given time considering their lifetimes is defined by a function: $rsc\colon A \times R \times Time \to \mathbb{N}$. Moreover, we assume agents are connected by a social network defined as follows.

Definition 1. (*Agent Social Network*): An agent social network $ASN = (A, E)$ is an undirected graph, where vertices A are set of agents, and each edge $e_{i,j} \in E$ indicates a social connection between agents a_i and a_j.

The agent social network constrains the agents' interactions so that they can only communicate and share information with their direct neighbors. Resource items can be allocated by an agent to any other agent in the network even if they are not neighbors. A resource item can be reallocated multiple times along the network until it is consumed in performing a task or it is expired. The environment in which the agents are operating is considered to be dynamic in two ways: the tasks may arrive at different rates over time; also, the resources may be procured at different rates over time. The knowledge regarding tasks and resources is local, i.e. an agent only knows its own tasks and resources; hence each agent individually decides on which tasks to perform given its own resources at a time.

Each agent gains utilities by performing tasks over time. We define *social welfare* of the multi-agent system as sum of utilities gained by all agents, $\sum_{a \in A} util_a^t$, where $util_a^t$ is sum of utilities gained by agent a up to time t. Now, given a set of agents A connected by a social network $ASN = (A, E)$, and sets of all tasks and resources assigned to them at time t, the problem is to find out which tasks of which agents to perform, and which resources of which agents to use for these tasks, in order to maximize the social welfare. The complexity of finding the optimal solution for the resource allocation problem without the condition of the social network is NP-hard [15], which comes from the exponential number of subsets of the set of tasks assigned to the agents. De Weerdt et al. [18,19] showed that this problem with an arbitrary social network is also NP-complete, even when the utility of each task is 1, and the quantity of all required and available resources is 1.

4   A Decentralized Protocol

We propose a decentralized negotiation-based protocol for the social resource allocation problem. The protocol is self-organizing as all the decisions are made by individual agents and there is no central controller. It allows real-time concurrent negotiations in which an agent in need of resources is allowed to select multiple providers and combine their resource contributions. It also allows the agents to collaborate in a social network by cascading information along the network. A high-level description of the protocol is as follows.

When an agent a_i has a set of tasks to do, it checks if it can locally allocate the required resources to fully accomplish them, otherwise it considers creating a request based on the missing quantity for each resource type and sends them to its neighbors in the social network. A neighboring agent a_j who receives a request decides whether it can fully provide the requested quantity. In that case, it considers sending an offer to a_i; otherwise, it considers creating a new request based on the new missing quantity and sends it to its own neighboring agents. In such case, a_j waits for offers from its neighbors before sending an offer to a_i. If a_j receives offers to its new request, it combines them with its own offer and sends it to a_i. Since multiple neighboring agents can offer to a request, a_i may receive multiple offers. In such case, it confirms a combination of them which maximizes the social welfare. The corresponding partial confirmations are sent by a_j to the original offerers. In the following, we present specifications of the six protocol phases: requesting, cascading requests, offering, cascading offers, confirming, and cascading confirmations.

4.1   Requesting

Agent a_i evaluates its current set of tasks using a greedy approach. It sorts the tasks based on a heuristic called *task efficiency*, defined as the ratio between task utility and its total number of required resources. Then it determines if it has shortage of resources by the task deadlines, and creates a request based on missing quantity for each resource type. For each request, a_i computes a utility function: $utl : \mathbb{N} \longrightarrow \mathbb{N}$ computed as utility gains for partial quantities in

---

Algorithm 1: Requesting process

Input   : agent: a_i, resource types: R
Output : requests sent by a_i: $sentReqs$
1 $sentReqs \leftarrow \emptyset$
2 $T_{a_i} \leftarrow tsk(a_i, currentTime)$
3 $t_{req} \leftarrow$ compute from task deadlines in T_{a_i}
4 **foreach** r *in* R **do**
5 $\qquad reqQ \leftarrow \sum_{t \in T_{a_i}} rqr(t, r)$
6 $\qquad availQ \leftarrow rsc(a_i, r, t_{req})$
7 $\qquad$ **if** $availQ < reqQ$ **then**
8 $\qquad\qquad A_{req} \leftarrow a_i$'s neighbors
9 $\qquad\qquad q_{req} \leftarrow reqQ$ - $availQ$
10 $\qquad\qquad utl \leftarrow$ compute utility function for $\{q : 0 < q \leq q_{req}\}$
11 $\qquad\qquad t^o_{req} \leftarrow t_{req}$
12 $\qquad\qquad$ send $request(r, q_{req}, utl, A_{req}, t_{req}, t^o_{req})$ to A_{req}; add to $sentReqs$

$\{q : 0 < q \leq q_{req}\}$, where q_{req} is the missing quantity. utl indicates benefit of partial contributions, and allows the other agents to offer a partial amount, q. a_i sends each request to all of its neighbors and includes their ids in the request message, considering each agent in the social network has a unique id. A request message sent by a_i has the following format:

$$Request(r, q_{req}, utl, A_{req}, t_{req}, t^o_{req})$$

where q_{req} indicates quantity requested for resource type r, utl is the request utility function, A_{req} is the set of all agent ids that receive this request, t_{req} is the request timeout, i.e. a_i waits for potential offers to its request until t_{req} and then the request is expired; and t^o_{req} is the original request timeout which initially is the same as t_{req}, but it is different when the request is cascaded as described in the next section. Algorithm 1 formalizes the requesting process of a_i.

4.2 Cascading Requests

An agent a_j may receive multiple requests from different agents for a resource type r. In a greedy approach, a_j sorts the requests based on their efficiency. The *request efficiency* is defined as the ratio between its utility and requested quantity. Then, for each received request, a_j considers cascading it to its own neighbors, who are not given in the set of request recipients A_{req}. a_j may decide

---

Algorithm 2: Cascading requests process

Input : requests received by a_j: *receivedReqs*, resource types: R
Output : requests cascaded by a_j: *cascadedReqs*

1 $cascadedReqs \leftarrow \emptyset$
2 **foreach** r *in* R **do**
3       $requestsForType \leftarrow$ requests in *receivedReqs* for r
4   sort $requestsForType$ by efficiency in descending order
5   **foreach** $request(r, q_{req}, utl, A_{req}, t_{req}, t^o_{req})$ *in* $requestsForType$ **do**
6   **if** $currentTime < t_{req}$ & a_j has neighbor(s) $\notin A_{req}$ **then**
7               $availQ \leftarrow rsc(a_j, r, t^o_{req})$
8               $A'_{req} \leftarrow A_{req} \cup a_j$'s neighbor(s)
9               $t'_{req} \leftarrow t_{req}$ - $timeoutReduction$
10   **if** $availQ < q_{req}$ **then**
11                  $q'_{req} \leftarrow q_{req}$ - $availQ$
12                  $utl' \leftarrow$ compute utility function for $\{q : 0 < q \leq q'_{req}\}$
13   reserve $availQ$ of type r
14   update $rsc(a_j, r, t^o_{req})$
15   send $request(r, q'_{req}, utl', A'_{req}, t'_{req}, t^o_{req})$ to $A'_{req} - A_{req}$; add to $cascadedReqs$
16   **else if** $utl(availQ) < cost$ of providing $availQ$ **then**
17   send $request(r, q_{req}, utl, A'_{req}, t'_{req}, t^o_{req})$ to $A'_{req} - A_{req}$; add to $cascadedReqs$

---

to cascade a request if it does not have enough resources to fully provide the requested quantity q_{req}, or if cost of providing is more that the benefit given in the utility function utl. When cascading a request, a_j reserves an available amount of resources it can provide, and updates q_{req} and utl, accordingly. It also adds its own neighbors to A_{req}. Moreover, the cascaded request timeout must be sooner than the request timeout t_{req}, in order for a_j to have enough time to receive potential offers from its neighbors and process them. Hence, t_{req} is reduced by a parameter called *timeoutReduction*, which its value depends on the communication channel. The original request timeout t_{req}^o is also included in the message and is used in the offering process described in the next section. Note that a_j reserves only resource items that are not expired until t_{req}^o. Algorithm 2 formalizes the cascading requests process of a_j.

4.3   Offering

In a greedy approach, similar to cascading requests, while there are available resources, a_j considers offering to received requests sorted by efficiency. The offerer a_j is allowed to offer partially, and determines an amount of resources it can provide q_{off}, up to the requested amount q_{req}. It deliberates about offering to each request by computing the cost of offering, defined as a function: $cst : \mathbb{N} \longrightarrow \mathbb{N}$. The offer cost function is computed as utility losses for partial quantities in $\{q : 0 < q \leq q_{off}\}$. It indicates cost of partial contributions by the offerer.

The offerer a_j compares its offering cost for quantity q_{off}, $cst(q_{off})$, with the request utility for the same quantity, $utl(q_{off})$. Eventually, a_j sends an offer if $cst(q_{off}) < utl(q_{off})$. An offer has a timeout which is later than the original request timeout in order for a_j to have enough time to receive potential

---

Algorithm 3: Offering process

    Input   : requests received by a_j: *receivedReqs*, resource types: R
    Output : offers sent by a_j: *sentOffs*
1 *sentOffs* $\leftarrow \emptyset$
2 **foreach** r *in* R **do**
3   *requestsForType* $\leftarrow$ requests in *receivedReqs* for r
4   sort *requestsForType* by efficiency in descending order
5   **foreach** $request(r, q_{req}, utl, A_{req}, t_{req}, t_{req}^o)$ *in* *requestsForType* **do**
6           $availQ \leftarrow rsc(a_j, r, t_{req}^o)$
7   **if** $currentTime < t_{req}$ & $availQ > 0$ **then**
8               $q_{off} \leftarrow \min(q_{req}, availQ)$
9               $cst \leftarrow$ compute cost function for $\{q : 0 < q \leq q_{off}\}$
10   **if** $cst(q_{off}) < utl(q_{off})$ **then**
11                   $itm_{off} \leftarrow$ reserve q_{off} resource items of type r
12   update $rsc(a_j, r, t_{req}^o)$
13                   $t_{off} \leftarrow t_{req}^o + timeoutExtension$
14   send $offer(r, q_{off}, cst, itm_{off}, t_{off})$ to the requester; add to *sentOffs*

confirmation from the original requester. Hence, the offer timeout is set by extending t^o_{req} by a parameter called *timeoutExtension*, which its value depends on the communication channel. An offer message sent by a_j has the following format:

$$Offer(r, q_{off}, cst, itm_{off}, t_{off})$$

where q_{off} indicates maximum quantity offered for resource type r, $cst : \mathbb{N} \to \mathbb{N}$ is the offer cost function, $itm_{off} : \mathbb{N} \to \mathbb{N}$ shares information regarding lifetimes of offered resources by mapping each item id to its lifetime, and t_{off} is the offer timeout; i.e. a_j waits for potential confirmation until t_{off} and then the offer is expired. Note that a_j offers only resource items that are not expired until t^o_{req}. The offering process is formalized in Algorithm 3.

4.4   Cascading Offers

For each cascaded request, the agent a_j waits for potential offers from its neighbors before sending an offer to the original requester. The rationale for waiting is to receive as many offers as possible. Eventually, a_j creates an offer, called cascaded offer, with a quantity up to the original requested quantity. a_j computes a cost function by selecting resource items which minimizes the total cost. The selected items may include any item that has been reserved when cascading the original request, combined with any other item offered by a_j's neighbors. The cascaded offer timeout is set by extending the original request timeout t^o_{req} by *timeoutExtension*. The waiting period before cascading offers is determined by a parameter called *waitToCascadeOffers*, which its value depends on the application domain. Algorithm 4 formalizes the cascading offers process of a_j.

4.5   Confirming

The requester a_i waits for potential offers to its request for a resource type r. Similar to waiting before cascading offers, the rationale here is to receive as many offers as possible. Hence, a_i may receive multiple offers from multiple providers. In that case, it selects a combination of offers that maximizes the difference between utility of the request and total cost of all the selected offers. Note that a_i is allowed to take partial amounts of offered resources in multiple offers up to the requested amount. Formally, suppose there are n offers for a request with requested quantity q_{req} and utility function utl; then a_i selects a quantity q^k_{cnf} from each offer $k \in \{1, ..., n\}$ with offered quantity q^k_{off} and cost function cst_k; in order to solve the integer linear program P_{cnf} given below:

$$\max_{q^1_{cnf}, ..., q^n_{cnf}} \quad utl\left(\sum_{k=1}^{n} q^k_{cnf}\right) - \sum_{k=1}^{n} cst_k(q^k_{cnf}) \tag{1}$$

$$\text{s.t.} \quad 0 \le q^k_{cnf} \le q^k_{off} \tag{2}$$

$$\sum_{k=1}^{n} q^k_{cnf} \le q_{req} \tag{3}$$

Algorithm 4: Cascading offers process

Input	: requests cascaded by a_j: *cascadedReqs*, offers received by a_j: *receivedOffs*
Output	: offers cascaded by a_j: *cascadedOffs*

1 $cascadedOffs \leftarrow \emptyset$
2 **foreach** $request(r, q_{req}, utl, A_{req}, t_{req}, t^o_{req})$ *in* cascadedReqs **do**
3   **if** $0 < t_{req}$ - *currentTime* $<$ *waitToCascadeOffers* **then**
4          $resItems \leftarrow$ resource items reserved for *request* in Algorithm 2
5          $offeredItems \leftarrow resItems$
6          $offersForReq \leftarrow$ offers in *receivedOffs* for *request*
7   **foreach** $offer(r, q_{off}, cst, itm_{off}, t_{off})$ *in* offersForReq **do**
8   add itm_{off} to *offeredItems*
9   **if** $|offeredItems| > 0$ **then**
10             $q'_{off} \leftarrow \min(|offeredItems|, q_{req} + |resItems|)$
11             $itm'_{off} \leftarrow$ select q'_{off} from *offeredItems* with min total cost
12             $cst' \leftarrow$ compute cost function for $\{q : 0 < q \leq q'_{off}\}$
13             $t'_{off} \leftarrow t^o_{req} +$ *timeoutExtension*
14   send $offer(r, q'_{off}, cst', itm'_{off}, t'_{off})$ to the requester; add to *cascadedOffs*

The waiting period before confirming offers is determined by a parameter called *waitToConfirmOffers*, which its value depends on the application domain. A confirmation message sent by a_i for each selected offer has the following format:

$$Confirm(r, q_{cnf}, itm_{cnf})$$

where q_{cnf} indicates partial amount confirmed for resource type r, and itm_{cnf} : $\mathbb{N} \rightarrow \mathbb{N}$ maps each confirmed resource item id to its lifetime. A confirmation message with $q_{cnf} = 0$ and $itm_{cnf} = \emptyset$ implies a rejection. We formalize the confirming process in Algorithm 5.

Algorithm 5: Confirming process

Input	: requests sent by a_i: *sentReqs*, offers received by a_i: *receivedOffs*
Output	: confirmations sent by a_i: *sentConfs*

1 $sentConfs \leftarrow \emptyset$
2 **foreach** $request(r, q_{req}, utl, A_{req}, t_{req}, t^o_{req})$ *in* sentReqs **do**
3   **if** $0 < t_{req}$ - *currentTime* $<$ *waitToConfirmOffers* **then**
4          $offersForReq \leftarrow$ offers in *receivedOffs* for *request*
5   **if** $offersForReq \neq \emptyset$ **then**
6              $confQuantities \leftarrow$ solve P_{cnf} for *offersForReq*
7   **foreach** $(offer, q_{cnf})$ *in* confQuantities **do**
8                  $itm_{cnf} \leftarrow$ select q_{cnf} from itm_{off} in *offer*
9   send $confirm(r, q_{cnf}, itm_{cnf})$ to the offerer; add to *sentConfs*

Algorithm 6: Cascading confirmations process

    Input   : confirmations received by a_j: $receivedConfs$, offers sent by a_j: $sentOffs$
    Output : confirmations cascaded by a_j: $cascadedConfs$

1 $cascadedConfs \leftarrow \emptyset$
2 **foreach** $receivedConf(r, q_{cnf}, itm_{cnf})$ in $receivedConfs$ **do**
3      $sentOff(r, q_{off}, cst, itm_{off}, t_{off}) \leftarrow$ offer in $sentOffs$ for $receivedConf$
4      $neighborsOffs \leftarrow$ offers from neighbors included in $sentOff$
5   **foreach** $offer(r, q'_{off}, cst', itm'_{off}, t'_{off})$ in $neighborsOffers$ **do**
6         $itm'_{cnf} \leftarrow itm'_{off} \cap itm_{cnf}$
7         $q'_{cnf} \leftarrow |itm'_{cnf}|$
8   send $confirm(r, q'_{cnf}, itm'_{cnf})$ to the offerer; add to $cascadedConfs$
9   **if** $q_{cnf} < q_{off}$ **then**
10   restore local reserved items in $itm_{off} - itm_{cnf}$

4.6 Cascading Confirmations

When an offerer agent a_j receives a confirmation for its offer, it checks if the offer includes partial offers from its neighbors; i.e. it is a cascaded offer combining multiple offers. In that case, a_j cascades partial confirmations to the corresponding offerers. Since a confirmation message contains item ids, a_j is able to distinguish its local offered items from the items offered by its neighbors. Hence, a_j is able to restore any of its local offered items that has not been confirmed. Note that this process is repeated by the corresponding neighbors as long as there are partial offers along the network. We formalize the cascading confirmations process in Algorithm 6.

5 Evaluation

We have developed an abstract simulator in Java using the JADE framework [3], which allows us to evaluate the performance of our decentralized protocol. We perform experiments using three different social networks as follows. We use the JGraphT library [13] in order to generate these networks. *Small-world networks* are networks in which most neighbors of an agent are also connected. We generate small-world graphs based on the Watts-Strogatz model [17] with a fixed rewiring probability of 0.05. *Scale-free networks* are networks in which a small amount of nodes have many connections, while many nodes have a small number of connections [2]. We also generate *Random networks* by first connecting each agent to another agent, and then randomly add more connections until an average degree has been reached [18,19].

In our experiments, we investigate the efficiency of our decentralized protocol (DEC) by comparing it with a centralized approach (CEN) and also with a decentralized protocol with no cascading behavior (DEC-NoCas). In CEN, a master agent receives over time all the tasks and resources information from all agents and knows the social network connections. It uses the same greedy method in selecting tasks based on the task efficiency heuristic. To allocate required resources to each task, the master agent first uses the resources of the agent owning the task and then its direct neighbors and then their neighbors and so on until all the required resources are allocated for each resource type. In DEC-NoCas, agents use the same greedy method in selecting tasks, however, they do not cascade received requests, which is similar to the work by De Weerdt et al. [18,19]. In our experiments, we measure the social welfare result computed by different approaches.

In our simulation model, the agents interact in real time and the communication model is asynchronous; i.e. messages can be sent and received at any time, and the communication does not block other activities. Moreover, the communication channel is considered to be reliable; therefore, the messages are received after a known transmission delay. Each agent is always responsive and executes the six processes specified in Sect. 4 consecutively. We use the following settings in our simulations. There are 10 agents, which receive tasks and resources in every second. Two of them receive more tasks than the other agents, while another two of them receive more resources than the others. The task deadline is two seconds and the resource item lifetime is 10 s. The request timeout is 500 milliseconds after it has been sent. The offer *timeoutExtension, waitToCascadeOffers*, and *waitToConfirmOffers* are 200, 100, and 50 milliseconds, respectively. Each task requires four items per resource type, and has a utility of 10. An agent performs a task 200 milliseconds before its deadline by allocating its required resources, and gains its utility. We run each experiment for 60 s; and our results are the average over 20 random runs.

In our first experiment, we observe how DEC behaves in small-world and scale-free networks when the available resource quantity is changing. By default, each agent receives one task and two resource items per each resource type; while two of them receive four tasks, and another two receive more resources varying from 4 to 16. There are two resource types. The small-world network has an average degree of two. The request *timeoutReduction* is 30 ms, which allows a request to be cascaded more than 10 times. Figure 1 illustrates

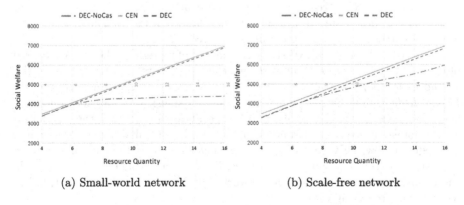

(a) Small-world network   (b) Scale-free network

Fig. 1. Results for varying the available resource quantity

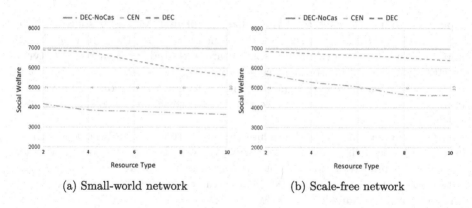

(a) Small-world network   (b) Scale-free network

Fig. 2. Results for varying the number of resource types

simulation results for comparing DEC with DEC-NoCas and CEN. We can observe that DEC outperforms DEC-NoCas when there are more available resources, and it achieves social welfare results which are close to those of CEN in all the resource quantity range in both networks, while the results are better for the small-world network. The results of this experiment suggests that when the number of resource types is low, and requests can be cascaded at least as many times as the number of agents in the network, DEC performs almost as good as CEN.

In our second experiment, we study the impact of increasing the number of resource types. All the parameters are the same as in the first experiment, except that the two agents with more available resources receive 16 items per resource type in every second; and we vary the number of resource types from 2 to 10. Figure 2 illustrates the simulation results for small-world and scale-free networks. As can be seen, DEC achieves less social welfare compared to CEN when there are more resource types, but outperforms DEC-NoCas in the entire resource type range. Also, DEC achieves better results for higher number of resource types in scale-free compared to small-world network. This is because in scale-free network there are few agents with high number of connections, who are more capable of procuring required resources of all types.

In our third experiment, we study the impact of increasing the average degree of connectivity in the social network. All the parameters are the same as in the second experiment, expect that there are two resource types, and the request *timeoutReduction* is 300 ms, which only allows a request to be cascaded once. We vary the network average degree from 2 to 8. Figure 3 illustrates the simulation results for small-world and random networks. The results suggest that when the degree is low, DEC and DEC-NoCas converge since DEC can only cascade requests once, but as the degree increases, DEC outperforms DEC-NoCas, while the results are better for random network; and they both converge with CEN when the degree is high.

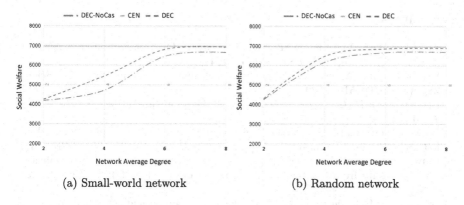

(a) Small-world network   (b) Random network

Fig. 3. Results for varying the network average degree

6   Conclusions and Ongoing Work

In this paper, we have presented a decentralized protocol, which allows agents
in a social network to negotiate with each other on allocating resources to their
tasks at execution time. The protocol allows the agents to cascade requests and
combine offered resource contributions along the network. It allows a multi-
agent system to be self-organized, since all the decisions are made through local
interactions, without a central controller either internal or external. Hence, the
system can avoid a single point of failure and is robust to failures in communication. Its adaptive behavior allows it to be efficient in dynamic environments,
where the set of tasks and resources may frequently change over time. We have
evaluated our protocol in small-world, scale-free, and random social networks;
and compared its performance with a centralized approach, and a decentralized
protocol with no cascading behavior. The simulation results illustrate the impact
of cascading behavior on the social welfare for different values of resource quantities, types, and network degrees. We have observed that when the available
resource quantity is high, the number of resource types is low, and requests can
be cascaded to any potential offerer further away in the network, our protocol
achieves nearly the same social welfare as the centralized approach.

In our protocol, we assume that an agent interacts with all of its neighbors in
its social network. An interesting extension may be addition of reputation information, which can be acquired by reinforcement learning techniques. Hence,
each agent learns its own policy for deciding which neighbors to interact based
on personal experience. This enhancement can potentially reduce the message
complexity while maintaining the efficiency of the protocol, in particular when
the network degree is high. Furthermore, it would be interesting to target one
or more specific real-world instances of the social task allocation problem. In
particular, we plan to explore the sensitivity of performance to other parameters of the protocol such as $waitToCascadeOffers$ and $waitToConfirmOffers$, and
investigate whether our protocol is effective in real-world social networks.

References

1. An, B., Lesser, V., Sim, K.M.: Strategic agents for multi-resource negotiation. Auton. Agent. Multi-Agent Syst. **23**(1), 114–153 (2011)
2. Barabási, A.L., Albert, R.: Emergence of scaling in random networks. Science **286**(5439), 509–512 (1999)
3. Bellifemine, F.L., Caire, G., Greenwood, D.: Developing multi-agent systems with JADE, vol. 7. Wiley (2007)
4. Calvaresi, D., et al.: The challenge of real-time multi-agent systems for enabling IoT and CPS. In: Proc. of Int. Conf. on Web Intelligence, pp. 356–364. ACM (2017)
5. Calvaresi, D., et al.: Multi-agent systems' negotiation protocols for cyber-physical systems: results from a systematic literature review. In: ICAART no. 1, pp. 224–235 (2018)
6. del Carmen Delgado-Roman, M., Sierra, C.: A multi-agent approach to energy-aware wireless sensor networks organization. In: Chesñevar, C.I., Onaindia, E., Ossowski, S., Vouros, G. (eds.) AT 2013. LNCS (LNAI), vol. 8068, pp. 32–47. Springer, Heidelberg (2013). https://doi.org/10.1007/978-3-642-39860-5_4
7. Elmenreich, W., D'Souza, R., Bettstetter, C., de Meer, H.: A survey of models and design methods for self-organizing networked systems. In: Spyropoulos, T., Hummel, K.A. (eds.) IWSOS 2009. LNCS, vol. 5918, pp. 37–49. Springer, Heidelberg (2009). https://doi.org/10.1007/978-3-642-10865-5_4
8. Fatima, S.S., Wooldridge, M.: Adaptive task and resource allocation in multi-agent systems. In: Int. Conf. on Autonomous Agents, pp. 537–544 (2001)
9. Georgara, A., Rodríguez-Aguilar, J.A., Sierra, C.: Allocating teams to tasks: an anytime heuristic competence-based approach. In: Baumeister, D., Rothe, J. (eds.) Multi-Agent Systems (EUMAS 2022). LNCS, vol. 13442, pp. 152–170. Springer, Cham (2022). https://doi.org/10.1007/978-3-031-20614-6_9
10. Kash, I., Procaccia, A.D., Shah, N.: No agent left behind: dynamic fair division of multiple resources. J. Artif. Intell. Res. **51**, 579–603 (2014)
11. Macarthur, K., et al.: A distributed anytime algorithm for dynamic task allocation in multi-agent systems. AAAI Conf. Artif. Intell. **25**(1), 701–706 (2011)
12. Malek-Akhlagh, M., Weber, J.H.: An adaptive resource allocation protocol for dynamic environments. In: Barolli, L. (ed.) Complex, Intelligent and Software Intensive Systems (CISIS 2022). LNNS, vol. 497, pp. 211–222. Springer, Cham (2022). https://doi.org/10.1007/978-3-031-08812-4_21
13. Michail, D., Kinable, J., Naveh, B., Sichi, J.V.: JGraphT–a Java library for graph data structures and algorithms. ACM Trans. Math. Softw. **46**(2), 1–29 (2020)
14. Serugendo, G.D.M., Gleizes, M.P., Karageorgos, A.: Self-organization in multi-agent systems. Knowl. Eng. Rev. **20**(2), 165–189 (2005)
15. Shehory, O., Kraus, S.: Methods for task allocation via agent coalition formation. Artif. Intell. **101**(1–2), 165–200 (1998)
16. Smith, R.G.: The contract net protocol: high-level communication and control in a distributed problem solver. IEEE Trans. Comput. **29**, 1104–1113 (1980)
17. Watts, D., Strogatz, S.: Collective dynamics of 'small-world' networks. Nature **393**(6684), 440–442 (1998)
18. de Weerdt, M., et al.: Distributed task allocation in social networks. In: Int. Joint Conf. on Autonomous Agents and Multiagent Systems, pp. 1–8 (2007)
19. de Weerdt, M., et al.: Multiagent task allocation in social networks. Auton. Agent. Multi-Agent Syst. **25**(1), 46–86 (2012)
20. Ye, D., et al.: A survey of self-organization mechanisms in multiagent systems. IEEE Trans. Syst. Man Cybern. Syst. **47**(3), 441–461 (2016)

Multi-agent Learning of Causal Networks in the Internet of Things

Stefano Mariani$^{(\boxtimes)}$, Pasquale Roseti , and Franco Zambonelli

University of Modena and Reggio Emilia, 42122 Reggio Emilia, Italy
{stefano.mariani,pasquale.roseti,franco.zambonelli}@unimore.it

Abstract. In Internet of Things deployments, such as a smart home, building, or city, it is of paramount importance for software agents to be aware of the *causal model* of the environment in which they operate (i.e. of the causal network relating actions to their effects and observed variables to each other). Yet, the complexity and dynamics of the environment can prevent to specify such model at design time, thus requiring agents to *learn* its structure at run-time. Accordingly, we introduce a distributed *multi-agent protocol* in which a set of agents, each with partial observability, cooperate to learn a coherent and accurate personal view of the causal network. We evaluate such protocol in the context of a smart home scenario and for a two-agents case, showing that it has superior accuracy in recovering the ground truth network.

Keywords: Multi-agent systems · Causal learning · Causal networks · Internet of Things · Smart home

1 Introduction

In Internet of Things (IoT) scenarios, where multiple sensor and actuator devices have many inter-dependencies, it is impractical (if not impossible) for the system designer to foresee (i) all the possible relations between the environmental variables, and (ii) all the possible effects of acting on them. Yet, for software agents, to have explicit knowledge of the network of cause-effects relations (aka of the causal model of the agents-environment system [14]) is of fundamental importance to make sense of their operational environment, properly decide plans of actions, and being able to explain such decisions [2,11]. Thus, in many cases, the only solution is to have agents autonomously *learn* such causal model once deployed in the target (simulated) environment, with minimal apriori knowledge.

Causal learning techniques [6] enable distinguishing causal relations from mere associations. For instance, recognizing that the states of the air conditioning system and of the temperature in a room are not simply correlated, but that the first causes the second to change. The result of such causal learning process is thus a *causal network* relating causes and effects with directed edges.

Work supported by the MIUR PRIN 2017 Project "Fluidware" (N. 2017KRC7KT).

P. Mathieu et al. (Eds.): PAAMS 2023, LNAI 13955, pp. 163–174, 2023.
https://doi.org/10.1007/978-3-031-37616-0_14

In most existing proposals, such process assumes a *centralized* setting, with a single learner/agent having full observability and control over the environment variables, or with a central site aggregating distributed observations or merging local models [6,8,19]. However, the centralized assumption can rarely hold for IoT deployments, where multiple agents are typically deployed in different regions of an environment. There, each agent only has partial observability of the environmental variables, and the capability of affecting only a limited portion of the overall environmental variables through its own actuators.

Against this background, we propose a *multi-agent protocol for distributed learning of causal networks*, aimed at letting agents in a MAS cooperate in unveiling causal relationships that individuals could not reveal by themselves, due to partial observability. In particular, the key contributions of the paper are to: *(i)* formulate the problem of multi-agent learning of causal networks; *(ii)* introduce a coordination protocol to let agents collaborate in refining their locally learnt causal networks; *(iii)* experimentally evaluate the effectiveness of the protocol in the context of a two-agents smart home scenario, chosen as it represents well the essence of more complex IoT deployments (e.g. smart buildings or cities). The experiments show that our multi-agent protocol enables achieving higher accuracy than centralized counterparts.

2   Background

Causal networks capture and quantify cause-effect relationships between variables of a domain of interest, a task that has been shown to be out of reach for statistical machine learning models [17], which rely on purely *observational* data to learn *associations*, but ignore the notion of *interventions*. As a formal definition of causality is known to be elusive and prone to debate [7], in the following, we assume an informal definition of causality based on commonsense interpretation, and in line with Pearl's book informal definition [15].

2.1   Interventions and Causal Learning

Interventions are the fundamental mechanisms to check whether two variables are linked in a cause-effect relationship and not by a mere correlation [15]. Intuitively, an intervention deliberately changes the value of a variable, *all others being untouched*, to see whether it affects others. Such as operating on an actuator and then observing possible changes in sensors' readings. As such, interventions require the ability to *control* variables, as is the case of the variables expressing the status of actuators in agent systems.

The intervention operation has been formalized with the introduction of the do-calculus [13]: $\mathbf{do}(C = c)$ means that the controlled variable C is forced to take value c by an environment action. As an example, by assuming to be able to control (i.e., intervene on) the air conditioning systems (A/C) the following simple causal network can be learnt: A/C $\rightarrow$ Temperature. Calling $\mathcal{P}(X)$ the probability distribution of variable X, in fact, we would have:

$$\mathcal{P}(\text{Temperature}) \neq \mathcal{P}(\text{Temperature} \mid \mathbf{do}(\text{A/C=on})) \qquad (1)$$

$$\mathcal{P}(\text{A/C}) = \mathcal{P}(\text{A/C} \mid \mathbf{do}(\text{Temperature=t})) \qquad (2)$$

where t is any temperature value. That is, the temperature does not affect the A/C, but the other way around (as the causal network expresses). This is of course just an example: the temperature can affect the A/C in general, for instance if a feedback loop is installed so that the temperature sensor automatically triggers the A/C actuator—as in most modern homes.

Intervention clearly cannot apply to *uncontrolled* variables, yet techniques exist to be able to learn causal relationships from observational data alone [6]. For instance, in the following causal network A/C $\rightarrow$ Temperature $\leftarrow$ Season we can learn that the season is the cause for the temperature, while being unable to intervene on either variable, provided that specific *identifiability* conditions hold [16], such as that the causal network is a Directed Acyclic Graph (DAG, i.e. no cycles amongst variables), and that there are no unknown confounders (i.e. all the causes of effects are known).

Both to describe techniques for causal learning (with and without interventions) and such conditions is out of the scope of this paper, since we only care that such techniques do exist, exploiting them as pluggable "black-boxes" within our proposed multi-agent protocol, and assume the conditions do hold (as most of the literature on learning causal networks does).

2.2   The Multi-agent Causal Learning Problem

In the exemplary situation in Fig. 1, multiple agents have partial observability and control over the variables of a shared environment. The need for collaboration during learning is apparent: agent i cannot fully explain the values it sees for variable U_2, as it is influenced (also) by variable U_3 that agent i is not even aware of. Or, agent k is not fully aware of the implications of its operations on variable C_5, as it influences variable C_4 that agent k is not aware of.

Accordingly, we consider N agents $\mathcal{A} = \{\mathcal{A}_i\}$, $i = 1, \dots, N$ willing to learn a causal network M_i of the relationships between V environment variables. We focus on *causal discovery*, namely the *structure* of the causal network, that is, the existence and direction of the arrows connecting the variables, as it is an enabler for causal *inference* (i.e. estimating the effects of one variable on others). The set V is partitioned into two (possibly, empty) sets, one of *controlled* variables $\mathcal{C}$ (i.e. corresponding to actuators, where interventions are possible) and one of *uncontrolled* variables U (i.e. sensors, where agents cannot intervene), such that $V = \mathcal{C} \cup U$. Each agent knows an algorithm for *independently* learning its own local causal network $\mathcal{L}_i$, that is, the causal network learnt by relying solely on its own known variables P_i (i.e. without running our multi-agent protocol). We do not care which one, as already discussed in Subsect. 2.1, but for our implementation, we choose one already adopted in an agent-oriented scenario [3]. Each agent also has *partial observability of the environment*, that is, is aware of only P_i out of the V variables. Formally: $P_i = \mathcal{C}_i \cup U_i$, $P_i \subset V \Rightarrow \mathcal{C}_i \subset \mathcal{C}, U_i \subset U$.

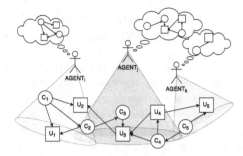

Fig. 1. Problem setting: multiple agents with partial observability over a shared environment want to learn each their own causal model.

However, no variable in V can be unknown to every agent, that is: $V = \bigcup_{i=1}^{N} P_i$—note that an overlap between the different P_i is admitted. This assumption is linked to the aforementioned identifiability conditions: if it does not hold, we would need to select another learning algorithm, and tolerate fewer guarantees that the learnt DAG will be the ground truth.

We assume that there exists a criterion, known to agents $\mathcal{A}_i$, to recognize when their own network $\mathcal{L}_i$ is not correct and complete. For instance, agents could monitor their uncontrolled variables to detect anomalies, such as actuators not causing changes when they should, sensors not changing their readings when expected, or that report a change when they should not (e.g. the agent did not operate the actuator known to causally affect such sensor). When this happens, the multi-agent causal learning protocol described in the next section is triggered. This is just an example of a reasonable triggering criterion working in stationary environments, i.e. where the probability distributions of variables do not change over time. In more complex environments more sophisticated detection techniques could be employed. However, one admissible criterion to trigger our protocol is also the trivial one of doing so periodically, by default.

It is worth emphasizing that M_i is not necessarily the *global* causal network G, that is, the one including every variable in V and every link amongst them. Rather, it is the "minimal" causal network that each agent "needs" to correctly understand situations and plan actions. That is, M_i contains all the variables in P_i and their links, plus the subset of variables in $V \setminus P_i$ that have links with variables in P_i. Learning the global causal model G is trivial once all the M_i have been learnt, as it is simply the set union of all the M_i.

3   Multi-agent Learning Protocol

The protocol unfolds as follows, where agents are assumed to exploit multiple threads to carry out interactions with others in parallel.

Thread 1 whenever an agent, let's say $\mathcal{A}_i$, recognizes that its own locally learnt causal network $\mathcal{L}_i$ is not correct and complete—e.g. by assuming so, or periodically monitoring anomalies in sensors' readings or actuators' effects

1. it asks for help by communicating to others, let's say $\mathcal{A}_j, j \neq i$, the set of variables it suspects to have missing links—its "frontier" (F_i);
2. then collects replies as they come in, and re-starts the single-agent learning algorithm (executed locally to the agent) with the newly acquired information (simply appended to the local data store tracking variables values), described below;

Thread 2 in parallel, agent $\mathcal{A}_i$ replies to incoming help requests, if any, by considering each received variable $f \in F_j$ and distinguishing two cases
1. if the variable is known to $\mathcal{A}_i$ (i.e. $f \in P_i$), it replies with what it knows about f, that is, the sub-network $\mathcal{L}_f \subseteq \mathcal{L}_i$ with its links to variables in P_i—so that the requesting agent can merge the causal (sub)nets;
2. if the variable is not known to $\mathcal{A}_i$ (i.e. $f \notin P_i$), the intervention-observation sub-protocol described next starts.

In step (1) of Thread 1 the agent A_i communicates: *(i)* the IDs of variables in F_i, assumed to be unique in the whole environment; *(ii)* for each $f \in F_i$, whether it is controlled $(f \in \mathcal{C}_i)$ or not $(f \in U_i)$—necessary to decide whether $\mathcal{A}_i$ or $\mathcal{A}_j$ will carry out interventions, or none of them (in the case where f is uncontrolled by both); *(iii)* for each f, whether $\mathcal{A}_i$ is looking for causes or effects—same reason above; *(iv)* for each f, a batch $\mathcal{B}_i$ of its past data, that is, observed values if $f \in U_i$ and issued commands if $f \in \mathcal{C}_i$—to unveil causal relationships amongst uncontrolled variables, by testing changes in probability distributions. In step (1) of Thread 2 it communicates, similarly: *(i)* the IDs of its known variables linked to f (that is: $v \in P_i \mid (v, f) \in \mathcal{L}_i$); *(ii)* whether such variables are controlled $(v \in \mathcal{C}_i)$ or not $(v \in U_i)$; *(iii)* whether such variables are causes or effects of f; *(iv)* a batch of past data regarding such variables.

The intervention-observation sub-protocol unfolds as follows (recall that we stick to the perspective of agent $\mathcal{A}_i$):

1. if the unknown variable f, received by $\mathcal{A}_i$ as part of a help request by, let's say, $\mathcal{A}_j$, is controlled by $\mathcal{A}_j$, then $\mathcal{A}_j$ does the interventions on f while $\mathcal{A}_i$ observes its $\mathcal{P}(P_i)$;
2. if, instead, f is not controlled by $\mathcal{A}_j$, then
   (a) for each $c \in \mathcal{C}_i$, it is $\mathcal{A}_i$ that does the interventions on c while $\mathcal{A}_j$ observes changes in its $\mathcal{P}(P_j)$;
   (b) for each $u \in U_i$, $\mathcal{A}_i$ sends a batch $\mathcal{B}_i$ of its past data, that is, its observed values for that variable u, to $\mathcal{A}_j$.

In either case, when interventions are concluded, both agents can correct/complete their own local model $\mathcal{L}$ with the data and metadata exchanged with the other, that is: *(i)* the IDs of variables $v \in \mathcal{P}(P)$ for which unexpected changes have been detected; *(ii)* for each of them, the batch $\mathcal{B}_v$ of the data (about both interventions and observations) collected during interventions—to unveil causal relationships by testing changes in probability distributions; *(iii)* for each of them, whether it is controlled or not—from the perspective of who is sending the data. In our experiments, interventions are actually carried out by agents by changing the values of their controlled variables through the simulation software that provides access to virtual devices (described in Sect. 4). For instance, an agent may repeatedly (at a given time interval, during a given time period) activate and de-activate the A/C to check (or let other agents check) whether the temperature changes as a consequence.

It is worth emphasizing here that, since in the real world operating on actuators may require time, and observing the results of actions on sensors' readings may incur delays, to correctly carry out the intervention-observation sub-protocol the agents need to agree on an "intervention time window". During such time, agents need to monitor both controlled and uncontrolled variables, *while a single agent in the whole MAS carries out a single intervention*. In other words, it must be guaranteed that only one variable in the whole system gets intervened upon at any one time. In fact, since agents do not know the ground truth causal model, they have no heuristic available to possibly operate multiple interventions in parallel. This bottleneck is intrinsic to the causal discovery problem.

4   Evaluation

We evaluate our multi-agent protocol for causal network learning in a smart home scenario, simulated with the iCasa platform [10]. iCasa allows the simulation of a wide range of devices (and the creation of custom ones) that can be displaced in the various zones of a customizable smart home map. We exploited iCasa to generate observational data and perform run-time interventions. The codebase for the learning algorithms, both the single-agent and the multi-agent protocol, is available at https://github.com/smarianimore/multiagent_algorithm, whereas the source code for the iCasa simulation environment is available at https://github.com/smarianimore/iCasa.

4.1   Scenario

To illustrate what the multi-agent learning protocol achieves in terms of accuracy, the following subsections report the learnt causal networks in the smart home scenario depicted in Fig. 2a. Such a scenario is simple yet representative of common smart home installations. Its ground truth causal model is depicted as a causal network in Fig. 2b. Such ground truth has been arbitrarily defined, and is not meant to faithfully represent any specific real scenario (although realistic): any ground truth would be fine, as long as there are causal links amongst variables not shared by agents. The learnt causal networks are shown with respect to such ground truth: green arrows denote correctly discovered causal relations, red arrows denote undiscovered causal relations (false negatives), and blue ones denote wrongly discovered causal relations (false positives).

In such a scenario, we partitioned the graph by imagining agent $\mathcal{A}_1$ to be aware of variables Pr, L, S, Pow, H, and C, that is, $\{Pr, L, S, Pow, H, C\} \in P_1$, and agent $\mathcal{A}_2$ to know the remaining ones, that is, $\{O, T, W, B, A, CO, CO_2\} \in P_2$. Thus, there is no overlap between P_1 and P_2, that is, $P_1 \cap P_2 = \emptyset$. The exact

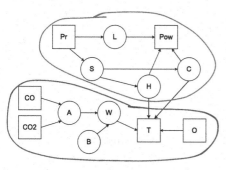

(a) Causal network partitions.

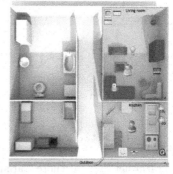

(b) Smart home's sensors and actuators.

Fig. 2. Ground truth causal network of the smart home scenario, partitioned between "agent red" ($\mathcal{A}_1$) and "agent blue" ($\mathcal{A}_2$). Square nodes denote uncontrolled variables (sensors), whereas round nodes are the controlled ones (actuators). Pr = presence, L = lights, S = A/C switch, Pow = power meter, H = heater, C = cooler, O = outdoor temp., T = indoor temp., W = window, B = window button, A = alarm, CO = CO meter, $CO2$ = CO_2 meter. (Color figure online)

nature of the partitioning is not important, actually: we could have partitioned the network differently. What does matter, instead, is that in this setting, it is impossible for agent $\mathcal{A}_2$ to independently learn a causal network M_2 that completely explains its own variables. In fact, $\mathcal{A}_2$ is unable to explain (find the cause of) a change in indoor temperature T while observing the outdoor temperature O and window W (its known effects). This is because T is the effect of two causes unknown to agent $\mathcal{A}_2$: heater H and cooler C. On the other hand, also agent $\mathcal{A}_1$ cannot learn a "complete" causal network M_1 of its known variables: it does not know all the effects of variables H and C. It knows that they cause power consumption Pow, but ignores their effect on T.

The following section discusses the results of *single-agent learning*, as a baseline to compare with, and the improvement brought by our proposed multi-agent learning protocol. The metrics tracked to assess the performance are—Table 5:

- *false positives* (FP), as the learnt causal edges that are not in the ground truth network (the lower the better, 0 is optimal);
- *false negatives* (FN), that is, causal connections in the ground truth that are not found by learning (the lower the better, 0 is optimal);
- *recover rate* (RR), as the percentage of causal connections in the ground truth network also present in the learnt network (the higher the better, 100% is optimal);
- a variation of *structural Hamming distance* (SHD) [20], as an accuracy measure accounting for "unknown edges", that is, edges missing from the network because they involve variables not known by the learning agent, given by: SHD = unknown edges + FP + FN (the lower the better, 0 is optimal).

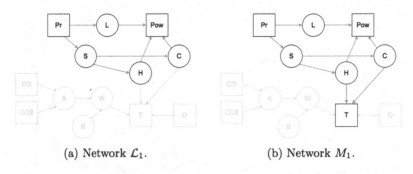

(a) Network $\mathcal{L}_1$.   (b) Network $\mathcal{M}_1$.

Fig. 3. Learnt network $\mathcal{L}_1$ ignores variable T on which H and C have effect. Its refined version $\mathcal{M}_1$, instead, correctly identifies T as effect of both H and C.

4.2   Multi-agent Accuracy vs Single-Agent Baseline

Figure 3a shows the causal network $\mathcal{L}_1$ *independently* learnt by agent $\mathcal{A}_1$ using its single-agent learning algorithm [3]. Its performance metrics are in Table 5, column $\mathcal{L}_1$, with sub-optimal values in bold. The network is *correct* (green arrows indicate true positives), as all the causal relations learnt are in the ground truth (compare with Fig. 2a), but *incomplete*, as not all the causal relations of $v \in P_1$ have been discovered: both C and H, in fact, have an effect on T, that cannot be learnt by $\mathcal{A}_1$ in isolation as $T \notin P_1$. It is worth noting that traditional performance metrics on causal networks, such as FP, FN, and RR, all mask the problem here: they have all optimal values, but are unable to capture the incompleteness of the learnt model. Our modified version of SHD, instead, does so. Figure 3b shows the refined model M_1 learnt by agent $\mathcal{A}_1$ after the application of our multi-agent protocol: the model is now both correct and complete, as variable T has been correctly identified as an effect of both H and C, and no false positives have been found (compare $\mathcal{M}_1$ with $\mathcal{L}_1$ metrics in Table 5).

Figure 4a shows the causal network $\mathcal{L}_2$ independently and locally learnt by agent $\mathcal{A}_2$. It is both incorrect (blue arrows indicate FP) and incomplete (red arrows indicate FN): O and W should not be causally connected, O and T should be, instead, and the connections that T has with C and H have not being learnt as $C, H \notin P_2$. Figure 4b shows instead the refined causal network M_2 learnt by agent $\mathcal{A}_2$. The model is now complete, but still slightly incorrect: an erroneous causal relation has been found between temperature T and switch S. Nevertheless, the improvement with respect to model $\mathcal{L}_2$ is substantial: 2 more causal connections have been learnt (involving variables H, C, and O), and accuracy improved, as $SHD(M_2) = 1 < SHD(\mathcal{L}_2) = 4$ (compare $\mathcal{M}_2$ with $\mathcal{L}_2$ metrics in Table 5).

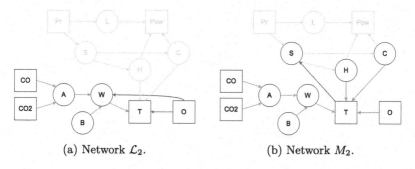

(a) Network $\mathcal{L}_2$.   (b) Network $\mathcal{M}_2$.

Fig. 4. Learnt network $\mathcal{L}_2$ ignores variables H and C as causes of T, misses O as cause of T, and misinterprets O as cause of W. Its refined version $\mathcal{M}_2$, instead, correctly identifies T as effect of both H and C. However, T is now misinterpreted to be a cause for S.

Metric	$\mathcal{L}_1$	$\mathcal{M}_1$	$\mathcal{L}_2$	$\mathcal{M}_2$
FP	0	0	1	1
FN	0	0	1	0
RR	100%	100%	83%	100%
SHD	2	0	4	1

Fig. 5. Both $\mathcal{M}_1$ and $\mathcal{M}_2$ improve performance with respect to both $\mathcal{L}_1$ and $\mathcal{L}_2$.

4.3   Time Performance, False Positives Rate

Figure 6 compares the time taken by multi-agent learning vs. single-agent learning. Comparison is across four networks of increasing size extracted from the ground truth depicted in Fig. 2a: network 1 has 7 variables and 6 edges, network 2 has 9 variables and 9 edges, network 3 has 10 variables and 12 edges, network 4 is the full network (13 variables and 15 edges). In the multi-agent case, each causal network is split among two agents in a balanced way, that is, agents have roughly the same amount of variables and edges to learn. In the single-agent case, such agent is assumed to have *full observability* of all the environment variables, so that it can learn in isolation.

Multi-agent learning has the best performance across all network sizes, with gains increasing with network size. Most of the computation time is spent on single-agent learning, especially for the conditional independence tests required by edges amongst uncontrolled variables (where no intervention is possible), and only a little for actually doing interventions through iCasa and inter-agent communication. Therefore, multi-agent learning achieves superior performance mostly by enabling each agent to deal with smaller sub-networks.

Figure 7 is a zoom-in on false positives, that is by far the most frequent error we found throughout experiments. The improvement with multi-agent learning is substantial. We speculate it is again due to the computational complexity of testing conditional independence in large networks, especially when variables are uncontrolled, and when the causal directed edge to learn connects two uncon-

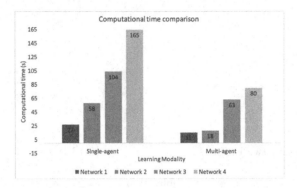

Fig. 6. Learning time in seconds for single-agent and multi-agent learning. The larger the network, the higher the performance gain by going distributed.

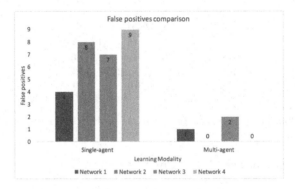

Fig. 7. False positive (FP) edges learnt for single-agent and multi-agent learning. The latter notably reduces the chances of FPs across all network sizes.

trolled variables. In all these cases, the partitioning that the multi-agent protocol offers enables agents to deal with smaller sub-networks.

5   Related Works

The MAS literature is quite scarce of discussions about causal modeling [9], in fact, the role and importance of (multi-agent) causal learning are only recently being recognized [5]. The preliminary work by [12] is the only attempt at multi-agent causal learning to the best of our knowledge: the authors focus on learning a global causal network within a MAS where each agent has partial knowledge of all the variables. Despite the similar goal pursued, their approach differs from our contribution in a few crucial aspects: (i) they assume that agents share at least one variable to cooperate, whereas we allow $P_i \cap P_j = \emptyset$; (ii) they settle for the mere existence of links, whereas we also seek to learn the direction of the causal link (i.e. who is the cause, and who is the effect); (iii) they only consider controlled variables, that is, those upon which agents can intervene at will, whereas we also account for uncontrolled ones; (iv) they aim for a global causal network, we aim for "complete local networks" (from which a global one is trivial to be obtained, nevertheless).

Another agent-based causal learning effort [18] does not aim at learning causal links (a task called *causal discovery*), that are taken for granted as specified by domain experts, but at learning the probabilistic weights attached to such causal links that enable to quantitatively estimate the effects of manipulating causes (a task called *causal inference*). Also [1] is not focussed on causal links and aims at assembling a global model at a central site. However, it proposes a method to detect cross-links, that is, relationships amongst variables at different sites, that is similar to our usage of the notion of frontier variables. The overall protocol proposed partly shares our design, too, although with the obvious differences of not being decentralised and not focussed on strictly causal links.

More approaches can be found outside of MAS. For instance, a common approach is having distributed machines storing *purely observational data* and participating in multiple communication rounds with a *centralized* elaboration site. This constructs a *global* estimate of the causal DAG given such data and local estimates. Similar efforts feature federated learning algorithms [4] where N local models are trained over N data partitions, while a *global* model is approximated at a *central* site by exchanging the local models' parameters—not the original data. However, all of these have profound differences with our proposed approach, both in goal pursued (building globals models) and in assumptions made (observational data solely, centralized coordinator).

6   Conclusion

We formulated the problem of multi-agent learning of causal networks under partial observability constraints, proposed a protocol enabling agents to collaborate in learning such causal networks, and experimentally evaluated such protocol in a smart home simulation featuring two agents. We have shown improved accuracy with respect to single-agent learning.

Our ongoing and future work includes: dealing with the coordination issues arising when multiple agents need to perform interventions on controlled variables, that by definition must be carried out all other conditions being equal (hence in mutual exclusion), adding a comparative evaluation of different single-agent algorithms plugged into our multi-agent protocol, and expanding evaluation of performances (accuracy and scalability) to scenarios of increasing the complexity (e.g. number of inter-agent causal dependencies).

References

1. Chen, R., Sivakumar, K., Khargupta, H.: Learning Bayesian network structure from distributed data. In: Proceedings of the Third SIAM International Conference on Data Mining (2003)

2. Chou, Y., Moreira, C., Bruza, P., Ouyang, C., Jorge, J.A.: Counterfactuals and causability in explainable artificial intelligence: theory, algorithms, and applications. Inf. Fusion **81**, 59–83 (2022)
3. Fadiga, K., Houzé, É., Diaconescu, A., Dessalles, J.: To do or not to do: finding causal relations in smart homes. In: IEEE International Conference on Autonomic Computing and Self-Organizing Systems (2021)
4. Gao, E., Chen, J., Shen, L., Liu, T., Gong, M., Bondell, H.: Federated causal discovery. CoRR abs/2112.03555 (2021). https://arxiv.org/abs/2112.03555
5. Grimbly, S.J., Shock, J.P., Pretorius, A.: Causal multi-agent reinforcement learning: review and open problems. CoRR abs/2111.06721 (2021). https://arxiv.org/abs/2111.06721
6. Guo, R., Cheng, L., Li, J., Hahn, P.R., Liu, H.: A survey of learning causality with data: problems and methods. ACM Comput. Surv. **53**(4), 1–37 (2020)
7. Halpern, J.Y.: A modification of the Halpern-Pearl definition of causality. In: Proceedings of the Twenty-Fourth International Joint Conference on Artificial Intelligence. AAAI Press (2015)
8. Heinze-Deml, C., Maathuis, M.H., Meinshausen, N.: Causal structure learning. Annu. Rev. Stat. Appl. **5**(1), 371–391 (2018)
9. Istrate, G.: Models we can trust: toward a systematic discipline of (agent-based) model interpretation and validation. In: Proceedings of the 20th International Conference on Autonomous Agents and MultiAgent Systems (2021)
10. Lalanda, P., Hamon, C., Escoffier, C., Lévèque, T.: iCasa, a development and simulation environment for pervasive home applications. In: IEEE 11th Consumer Communications and Networking Conference (2014)
11. Lippi, M., Mariani, S., Zambonelli, F.: Developing a "sense of agency" in IoT systems: preliminary experiments in a smart home scenario. In: 19th IEEE International Conference on Pervasive Computing and Communications Workshops (2021)
12. Meganck, S., Maes, S., Manderick, B., Leray, P.: Distributed learning of multi-agent causal models. In: Proceedings of the IEEE/WIC/ACM International Conference on Intelligent Agent Technology (2005)
13. Pearl, J.: Causality, 2nd edn. Cambridge University Press, Cambridge (2009)
14. Pearl, J.: The seven tools of causal inference, with reflections on machine learning. Commun. ACM **62**(3), 54–60 (2019)
15. Pearl, J., Mackenzie, D.: The Book of Why. Basic Books, New York (2018)
16. Peters, J., Mooij, J.M., Janzing, D., Schölkopf, B.: Identifiability of causal graphs using functional models. In: Proceedings of the Twenty-Seventh Conference on Uncertainty in Artificial Intelligence (2011)
17. Schölkopf, B., et al.: Toward causal representation learning. Proc. IEEE **109**(5), 612–634 (2021)
18. Valogianni, K., Padmanabhan, B.: Causal ABMs: learning plausible causal models using agent-based modeling. In: Proceedings of the KDD 2022 Workshop on Causal Discovery, vol. 185 (2022)
19. Vowels, M.J., Camgöz, N.C., Bowden, R.: D'ya like DAGs? A survey on structure learning and causal discovery. CoRR abs/2103.02582 (2021). https://arxiv.org/abs/2103.02582
20. Ye, Q., Amini, A.A., Zhou, Q.: Distributed learning of generalized linear causal networks. CoRR abs/2201.09194 (2022). https://arxiv.org/abs/2201.09194

Investigation of Integrating Solution Techniques for Lifelong MAPD Problem Considering Endpoints

Toshihiro Matsui[⊠][iD]

Nagoya Institute of Technology, Gokiso-cho, Showa-ku, Nagoya 466-8555, Japan
matsui.t@nitech.ac.jp

Abstract. The lifelong multiagent pickup-and-delivery problem has been studied for autonomous carrier robots that perform tasks continuously generated on demand in warehouses. It is an extension of continuous multiagent pathfinding problems, and a set of move paths along which agents simultaneously travel without collision is continuously solved for dynamically updated source and destination locations. Fundamental solution methods employ endpoints (EPs) that can be either beginning or end locations of agents' move paths. EPs are used to consider the situations where some paths are locked by reservation, and deadlocks among reserved paths need to be avoided. While several heuristic techniques have been proposed to improve the solution method, there have been opportunities to investigate their effect and influence in order to integrate these techniques. As an analysis of solution techniques with endpoints for lifelong MAPD problems, we integrated several solution techniques in stages and experimentally investigated their effects and influence. Here, we experimentally present the effect of the proposed approach and generally consider the possibilities of integrated efficient methods. Our results show how the redundancies of problems and move paths can be reduced by the integrated techniques. On the other hand, there are several trade-offs among the heuristics combined for the concurrency of tasks.

Keywords: Multiagent Pickup-and-Delivery · Multiagent Pathfinding · Lifelong Problem · Endpoints

1 Introduction

Multiagent pathfinding (MAPF) problems have been studied with a view to improve various applications such as the navigation of mobile robots, autonomous taxiing of airplanes, autonomous car operation, and video games. A solution to the problem is a set of agents' move paths where the agents simultaneously travel without collision. Multiagent pickup-and-delivery (MAPD) problems have been pursued as an extension of MAPFs for autonomous carrier robots that perform pickup and delivery tasks in warehouses, where a task's path contains a

P. Mathieu et al. (Eds.): PAAMS 2023, LNAI 13955, pp. 175–187, 2023.
https://doi.org/10.1007/978-3-031-37616-0_15

subgoal of a pickup location. The lifelong MAPD, as an extension of MAPDs and continuous MAPFs, formalizes a more practical case in where tasks are continuously generated on demand and allocated to agents. A MAPD problem basically consists of two parts; task allocation and MAPF problems.

There are several approaches to MAPF problems. The CA* [13] algorithm performs the A* algorithm [3,4] to find collision free paths of agents in an order of the agents' decision making. Here, a field/map is searched for each agent's path in a time sequence, and the found path is reserved. Then these reserved paths are avoided in new searches for paths.

The CBS and MA-CBS [11] algorithms employ two layers of search processes. In the high-level layer, a tree-search is performed to resolve collisions of paths, and constraints are added to inhibit the collisions. A constraint inhibits a time-space location of one of the agents with their conflicting paths. In the low-level layer, the A* algorithm in a corresponding time-space is performed under the added constraints. Since the CBS algorithm requires relatively high computational cost, several extensions such as the PBS [7] and ECBS [1] algorithms have been proposed.

PIBT employs a technique to manage the priorities of agents' moves [9,10]. In this method, priority inheritance and backtracking methods are combined to efficiently find agent moves while avoiding stuck situations.

When the sets of all tasks is given at the initial step, the task allocation to agents is a static combinatorial optimization problem that can be formalized with several existing optimization problems [6]. On the other hand, if the tasks are generated on demand, the task allocation is reactive, and (partially) greedy allocation methods are practical [8]. The token passing (TP) algorithm [8] has been adopted to solve lifelong MAPD problems, where tasks are generated on demand, and it employs a greedy task allocation method and the CA* algorithm. Several methods have been proposed to improve the efficiency of this class of algorithms. MLA* [2], as a replacement of CA*, employs pruning and relaxation techniques that consider agents' pickup locations/times in the pathfinding of a pickup-and-delivery path. It also employs an ordering of agents based on the heuristic path lengths of tasks to efficiently allocate the tasks to agents [5]. While TP solves well-formed problems that satisfy the conditions for feasible solutions, the conditions can be partially relaxed. SBDA [15] addresses a special case of maze-like maps with a small number of parking, pickup and delivery locations by employing dynamically prepared standby locations of agents.

Several solution methods including TP for continuous MAPF problems employ endpoints (EPs) that can be the beginning or end locations of agents' move paths. Here, EPs are taken into consideration in the situations where some of the paths are locked by reserved paths, and thus deadlocks among reserved paths are avoided. Since the solutions found by basic approaches with EPs contain relatively large redundancy in their paths, several techniques have been proposed to reduce such redundancy. In addition, several solution methods for continuous MAPF problems of more general/special cases have been recently developed as mentioned above. On the other hand, there should be opportunities to investigate various combinations of efficient techniques based on EPs in

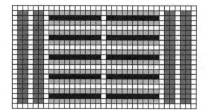

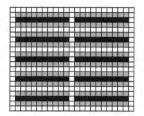

Fig. 1. Env. 1: Well-formed MAPD [8] (White: passageway, black: shelf (obstacle), thin/thick color: task/non-task EP)

Fig. 2. Env. 2: MAPD w/o non-task EPs (White: passageway, black: shelf (obstacle), thin/thick color: task/non-task EP)

the case of MAPD problems as a tool to analyze the relationship among key factors, including the trade-offs between the techniques employed and possible modes in agents' moves.

As an analysis of solution techniques with endpoints for lifelong MAPD problems, we integrated the solution techniques in stages in order to experimentally investigate their effects and influence. We employed several techniques, 1) Prioritizing task allocation, 2) Generalization of EP types, 3) Relaxation of constraints to passing EPs, 4) Dummy retreat paths, and 5) Subgoal divisions of pickup-and-delivery tasks, using tp as the basis of analysis. Our results show how the redundancies of the problems and move paths can be reduced by the integrated techniques, while there are several trade-offs among the heuristics combined for the concurrency of tasks.

2 Preliminary

2.1 Lifelong MAPD

The lifelong MAPD problem is an extended class of multiagent pickup-and-delivery (MAPD) problems and continuous multiagent pathfinding (MAPF) problems, where multiple pickup-and-delivery tasks are allocated to agents and their move paths are determined in such a way to avoid collision. The tasks are generated on demand during a certain period and repeatedly allocated to the agents. A problem consists of an undirected graph $G = (V, E)$ representing the map of a warehouse, a set of agents $\mathcal{A}$, and a set of currently generated pickup-and-delivery tasks $\mathcal{T}$. Each task $\tau_i \in \mathcal{T}$ has the information of its pickup and delivery locations (s_i, g_i), where $s_i, g_i \in V$. An agent that has an allocated task moves from its current location to a delivery location through a pickup location. There are two cases of colliding paths. First, two agents cannot stay at the same location at the same time; second, they cannot move on the same edge at the same time from both ends of the edge.

Well-formed MAPD problems that assure feasible solutions of task allocation and multiple paths have been presented [8,14]. Vertices representing the first and last locations of a path and a pickup location are called endpoints (EPs).

1 Initialize *token* with path $[loc(a_i)]$ for each agent a_i.
2 **until** a termination condition **do** // *All generated tasks in a period are completed.*
3   Add new tasks generated on demand to task set $\mathcal{T}$.
4   **foreach** agent a_i that determines its next path in *token* **do**
5         $\mathcal{T}' \leftarrow \{\tau_j \in \mathcal{T}$ no other agents' paths in *token* ends in s_j or $g_j\}$.
6   **if** $\mathcal{T}' \neq \emptyset$ **then do**
7             $\tau \leftarrow$ arg min $_{\tau_j \in \mathcal{T}'} h(loc(a_i), s_j)$.
8   Assign a_i to τ.
9   Remove τ from $\mathcal{T}$.
10   Update a_i's pickup-and-delivery path in token with $Path1(a_i, \tau, token)$.
11   **done**
12   **else if** no task $\tau_j \in \mathcal{T}$ s.t. $g_j = loc(a_i)$ exists **then**
13   Update a_i's stay path in *token* with path $[loc(a_i)]$.
14   **else**
15   Update a_i's retreat path in *token* with $Path2(a_i, token)$.
16   **done**
17   All agents move along their paths in *token* for one time step.
18 **done**

$loc(a)$: Agent a's location. s_j and g_j: Pickup and delivery locations of task τ_j. $Path1(a_i, \tau, token)$ and $Path2(a_i, token)$: Pathfinding and reservation methods for a pickup-and-delivery path of task τ and a retreat path.

Fig. 3. TP [8]

In fundamental problems, EPs are categorized into non-task EPs, which are initial/parking locations of agents and task EPs of pickup and delivery locations (Fig. 1). With these EPs, the conditions of a well-formed problem are defined as follows (Def. 1 in [8]): A MAPD is well-formed iff a) the number of tasks is finite, b) non-task endpoints are no fewer than the number of agents, and c) for any two endpoints, there exists a path between them that traverses no other endpoints. Multiple tasks' paths can be allocated without deadlocks when the task allocation is sequentially performed while satisfying the following conditions: 1) Each path only contains EPs for the first and last locations and a pickup location, and 2) The last location of each path is not included in any other paths.

2.2 Endpoint Based Methods

The token passing (TP) algorithm [8] is one solution method for well-formed MAPD problems (Fig. 3). Here, the system consists of pickup and delivery agents in a warehouse and a centralized process. With a shared memory called the token, agents sequentially allocate their tasks and reserve corresponding move paths in a greedy order. The token contains the information of a list of pickup-and-delivery tasks waiting to be allocated and paths reserved by agents. The agent without its own allocated tasks allocates a new task that does not form a deadlock with reserved paths and reserves a corresponding path without collision that is found by the A* algorithm performed on a time-space graph. Here, the tasks are prioritized by the distance from the current location of an agent to the pickup location of a task. When no task can be allocated to an agent, the agent retreats to a free EP that does not conflict with delivery locations of tasks in the task list and reserved paths if its current location is the delivery location of a task in the task list. Otherwise, the agent temporarily stays at its current location. Each agent also reserves a retreat/stay path if necessary. At the end of each time step, agents move/stay according to their reserved paths.

Since there is some redundancy in basic solution methods, several techniques have been proposed to deal with this problem. We describe these additional techniques below.

2.3 Prioritizing Task Allocation by Pickup Time

In the task allocation process, several ordering criteria can be employed to select the task for allocation to each agent that currently requires a new task. Although there are a number of possible criteria, there should be some trade-offs in different problem instances as long as such approaches are heuristics [2]. Therefore, we focus on an example heuristic [12] to be compared with a basic one used in TP.

This heuristic is based on the estimated pickup time of tasks. Since each agent knows the time at the last location of its reserved path, the heuristic distance from the last location to a pickup location is added to the last time. When each agent selects its new task to be allocated, it compares its estimated pickup time of the task with those of other agents. If one of the other agents' pickup times is earlier than this agent's own time, such a task is not immediately allocated to this agent.

2.4 Generalization of Paths Having Arbitrary EPs

To reduce the redundancy of paths, an extended solution method that allows the paths containing EPs has been presented [12]. Although, paths may contain arbitrary EPs, deadlocked paths are avoided by considering the conflicting EPs in the task allocation. All EPs in paths are locked, and conflicts with delivery locations of new tasks in the task list are evaluated. Each agent temporarily reserves an additional path, where the agent stays at its last location until it cancels the reservation. This information is used as reference in the path finding process for newly allocated tasks, and the agent's staying location is avoided in the new paths. This approach has an effect similar to the pruning/relaxation in pathfinding improved by MLA* [2]. Although this extension can reduce path lengths, such paths also block more endpoints and thus might reduce the number of tasks that can be allocated.

2.5 Dummy Path to Retreat

The task allocation is affected by locked task endpoints at the last locations of reserved paths. If pickup and delivery locations are locked, such tasks are not allocated to avoid deadlocks of paths. To reduce locked task endpoints, additional dummy paths are employed [5]. With this technique, each agent's path is extended to retreat to a free non-task endpoint. Such a dummy path can be canceled if necessary. The additional staying path of an agent in Sect. 2.4 is a special case of the dummy path. Although a dummy path reduces the locked task endpoints, relatively long retreat paths might be reserved if non-task endpoints are located in separate areas of a warehouse.

2.6   Subgoals of a Task's Path

In lifelong MAPD, tasks are generated on demand and continuously allocated to multiple agents based on the current situation. Therefore, situations might change before long paths are traversed, and this might affect new tasks. Several approaches divide the paths of tasks to postpone/re-plan future paths [5].

   While there are several dedicated approaches that employ sub-paths in time windows, we focus on a simple division by sub-goals of paths for pickup-and-delivery tasks.

3   Integration of Efficient Techniques

To investigate the effects and trade-offs of integrating the techniques described in the previous section, we combine them in stages by modifying several details of each solution method. In particular, we also address the generalized cases without non-task endpoints.

3.1   Generalization of Task/Non-Task EPs

To reduce the redundancy of space utilization in a warehouse, we address the case where the initial and retreat locations of agents can be arbitrary EPs, and settings without non-task EPs are also allowed (Fig. 2). In the modified rules, each agent basically retreats to its nearest EP, excluding the EPs on reserved paths and the delivery locations of unallocated pickup-and-delivery tasks. If there is no available EP in an environment without non-task EPs, agents stay at their current EPs. This modification does not cause deadlocks of paths, and all tasks are completed if a finite number of tasks are generated on demand. In the limited cases based on well-formed MAPD problems, there are feasible solutions when the number of agents is less than the number of EPs.

3.2   Integration with EP Passing

We integrate the generalization of EPs shown in the previous subsection and the technique that allows paths containing arbitrary EPs (Sect. 2.4). The selection rule of the EP to retreat is modified so that EPs locked by reserved paths are excluded. With both approaches, the length of pickup-and-delivery and retreat paths can be reduced.

   However, paths having EPs block the allocation of new tasks whose delivery locations are locked by the paths. We improve the pathfinding algorithm to avoid EPs of new tasks' delivery locations, although other EPs can be included. Since we found that a hard condition to completely avoid such EPs generates relatively long paths, we employ a heuristic weight value for the distance to the EPs. With this modification, the degree of avoidance is adjusted.

To manage the information of locked EPs, we employ an additional two-dimensional map corresponding the floor plan of a warehouse. The additional map is shared as a part of the token, and each vertex/cell in the map has the following data: 1) A counter representing the number of paths locking this location; 2) Start time of an additional staying path of an agent in this location if one exists; and 3) Number of new tasks waiting to be allocated whose delivery locations are this location. The first and second types of data are related to reserved paths and updated when a new path is reserved and when an agent traverses its reserved path at each time step. The last type of data is updated when a new task is generated on demand and when a task is allocated to an agent. Those data are referenced in the operations shown above.

3.3   Integrating Dummy Path Reservation

We then integrate the solutions with a technique for additional dummy path reservation (Sect. 2.5). In the basic case, each dummy path starts from an end of a path to a non-task EP that is a retreat location. We also address the case where any EP can be used as parking locations and the case where there are fewer non-task EPs than the number of agents. Therefore, this technique requires some dynamic management of dummy paths.

For each agent, we introduce a representation of the allocated task sequence consisting of 1) A pickup-and-delivery/retreat task if possible; 2) Optional retreat tasks; and 3) A stay task if there is no other allocated task. Here, any type of move path is generalized as a corresponding type of tasks. The information of task sequence is managed by its owner agents. We limit the total length of task sequence with a parameter T so that the length is within $[1, T]$.

Each agent is basically allocated one of the pickup-and-delivery/retreat/stay tasks and reserves its move path. The dummy paths are added in the following two cases. 1) If an agent has an allocated pickup-and-delivery/retreat task and the end of its move path blocks new tasks waiting to be allocated, an additional retreat task toward one of the other available EPs is allocated if possible. This operation is performed for each agent at every time step.

2) When an agent selects its new pickup-and-delivery task, the task's path is conditionally extended with an additional dummy path. If the delivery location of a new task overlaps other agents' reserved paths (excluding their end locations), and if there is an available EP to which the agent can retreat, then an additional task of the dummy path is combined with the new task. Next, a path including pickup, delivery, and retreat locations is found and reserved. To avoid deadlocks in the environment with a smaller number of non-task EPs, a pickup-and-delivery task without an additional dummy path is prioritized.

After each agent completes the traverse for its pickup-and-delivery task or its first retreat task, the agent cancels subsequent retreat tasks of dummy paths to select its new task. However, such a new selected task might be infeasible, since the agent must move from its current location so that it avoids other agents' paths that get newly reserved after the reservations of its own dummy path. In such cases, the canceled tasks and paths are restored to maintain the consistent reservations. To restrict the total length of paths, we limit the maximum number of additional retreat tasks and the maximum length of each additional retreat path, that are denoted by parameters T and P. If there is no EPs to retreat within range of P from the current path end of an agent, such a dummy path is not added, and preceding tasks are not also allocated.

3.4   Employing Subgoal Division

Finally, we also integrate the techniques with subgoal division of tasks' paths. For our investigation, we simply decompose the path into two parts that starts/ends a pickup location. Namely, a MAPD problem is modified to a MAPF one, so that each original task is decomposed to a pickup task and a delivery task, along with the constraint that the decomposed tasks must be allocated to the same agent.

Because this modification causes new deadlock situations among pickup tasks and delivery tasks, we adjust several conditions to avoid deadlocks: 1) The decomposed tasks are related as an originally single task in the list of tasks to be allocated. 2) Agents recognize their modes of pickup or delivery, and only consistent tasks can be allocated. 3) Agents are prioritized so that delivery agents basically have higher priority. According to the priorities set, agents access the token in order and try to allocate new tasks if necessary. If an agent cannot be allocated any task blocked by other agents, the agent asks one of the blocking agents having lower priorities to retreat to one of the free EPs. An agent that is requested to retreat follows the request if it possible at that time step. Otherwise, the blocked agent tries to request to one of remaining blocking agents. Here, the priorities of the requested agents are increased to immediately perform their decision making. If a request succeeds, the asking agent is prioritized in the next time step to assign the task of the corresponding unblocked subgoal. Although this extension basically resembles PIBT [9,10] that is a well-designed method for continuous MAPF problems, we address a simple extension of TP to investigate the issues in this case. Since we partially employ the technique of priority inheritance, our investigated method optimistically tries to solve the locks. To avoid complicated situations with this approach, we do not employ the techniques of other types of priorities and dummy paths in this case.

4   Evaluation

We experimentally investigated the effects and influence of the integrated techniques. We employed a well-formed problem similar to that shown in a previous study [8]. We performed experiments on the problem instances Env. 1 and 2 shown in Figs. 1 and 2. We set the maximum numbers of agents 152 (number of non-task EPs) and 199 ((number of EPs)−1) for Env. 1 and 2. We varied the number of agents and the settings of tasks. At every time step, NpT tasks were generated, up to 500 tasks in total.

Table 1. Env. 1 (with non-Task EP, $NpT = 1$)

#Agent	10			30			60			152		
Alg.	MS	ST	CT	MS	ST	CT	MS	ST	CT	MS	ST	CT
TP	1192.9	324.0	**0.026**	612.6	62.5	**0.059**	622.4	74.9	**0.114**	624.1	73.9	**0.187**
Pt	1200.4	328.0	0.046	607.6	64.6	0.077	566.6	43.8	0.135	554.2	37.0	0.654
PtTe3	1101.3	281.2	0.056	564.5	42.4	0.094	551.6	34.5	0.154	549.5	30.5	0.606
PtGe	1200.4	328.0	0.045	607.6	64.6	0.077	566.6	43.8	0.133	554.2	37.0	0.653
PtTe3Ge	1101.3	281.2	0.055	564.5	42.4	0.093	551.6	34.5	0.153	549.5	30.5	0.599
+Dp5-3	1117.8	295.9	0.071	558.1	39.9	0.109	**538.5**	**28.1**	0.207	**535.6**	**25.6**	1.002
+Dpc5-3	**1084.8**	**274.7**	0.082	**548.3**	**34.3**	0.139	539.7	28.3	0.242	537.9	25.8	0.910
Te3GeSg	1145.3	304.0	0.051	572.2	43.8	0.122	570.9	50.0	0.231	577.6	52.4	0.828

Table 2. Env. 1 (with non-Task EP, $NpT = 10$)

#Agent	10			30			60			152		
Alg.	MS	ST	CT	MS	ST	CT	MS	ST	CT	MS	ST	CT
TP	1163.4	521.7	**0.029**	533.0	219.8	**0.086**	432.5	159.6	**0.147**	490.6	195.1	**0.376**
Pt	1184.7	526.3	0.063	527.6	226.2	0.265	397.1	159.5	0.380	380.3	154.5	0.871
PtTe3	1074.8	482.6	0.078	436.5	180.3	0.345	304.6	112.4	0.491	285.6	99.2	1.142
PtGe	1184.7	526.3	0.062	527.6	226.2	0.267	397.1	159.5	0.381	380.3	154.5	0.879
PtTe3Ge	1074.8	482.6	0.076	436.5	180.3	0.328	304.6	112.4	0.475	285.6	99.2	1.150
+Dp5-3	1101.4	503.5	0.105	443.2	189.6	0.409	282	116.5	0.710	**256.1**	**97.4**	7.734
+Dpc5-3	**1067.3**	**480.1**	0.119	**425.9**	**178.7**	0.509	275	108.9	1.192	259.3	**97.4**	18.193
Te3GeSg	1126.1	512.1	0.058	504.9	203.1	0.186	362	132.3	0.387	363.1	129.9	1.427

We evaluated the following solution methods that were incrementally extended with techniques represented by the suffixes below.

1) TP: Our baseline implementation based on prior literature of TP [8]. We adjusted several settings for our investigation, while it causes relatively small biases in results. 2) Pt: A method that considers the estimated pickup time when an agent selects the new task to be allocated. 3) TeW: A method that allows an agent to move through EPs. Here, a move to the EPs that are pickup/delivery locations of the tasks to be allocated is weighted by a penalty coefficient value W for heuristic distances to avoid the EPs. 4) Ge: A method that permits generalization of non-task/task EPs. 5) DpT-P: A method that adds at most T dummy retreat tasks of at most P length of each path. 6) Dpc$T$-P: DpT-P with canceling dummy paths at each time step. 7) Sg: A method that decomposes a pickup-and-delivery task into two related tasks.

The results over ten executions with random initial locations of agents were averaged for each problem instance. The experiments were performed on a computer with g++ (GCC) 8.5.0 -O3, Linux 4.18, Intel(R) Core(TM) i7-9700K CPU @ 3.60 GHz and 64 GB memory.

Tables 1 and 2 show the result of Env. 1. We evaluated the makespan (MS) to complete all tasks, service time (ST) to complete each task, and computation time per time step (CT). The unit of MS and ST is logical time step, and that of CT is millisecond. We briefly mention each additional technique from the

Table 3. Env. 1 (with non-Task EP)

NpT	1						10					
#Agent	10		30		60		10		30		60	
Alg.	MS	ST	MS	ST	MS	ST	MS	ST	MS	ST	MS	ST
PtTe1	**1042.9**	**254.7**	590.8	52.5	564.3	40.6	**1010.7**	**445.4**	485.2	180.6	419.8	140.9
PtTe3	1101.3	281.2	564.5	42.4	551.6	34.5	1074.8	482.6	**436.5**	**180.3**	304.6	**112.4**
PtTe5	1118.1	293.7	**561.7**	**42.0**	**549.6**	**34.4**	1098.1	496.2	448.7	188.5	308.1	118.2
PtTe10	1129.8	298.4	563.4	43.5	551.5	34.6	1119.4	508.1	469	196.8	320.8	125.6

Table 4. Env. 1 (with non-Task EP)

NpT	1						10					
#Agent	10		30		60		10		30		60	
Alg. PtTe3Ge	MS	ST	MS	ST	MS	ST	MS	ST	MS	ST	MS	ST
+Dpc1-100	1101.3	281.2	564.5	42.4	551.6	34.5	1074.8	482.6	436.5	180.3	304.6	112.4
+Dpc2-1	**1084.2**	275.5	561.1	39.8	552.4	33.4	**1064.7**	481.8	433.7	180.4	299.4	111.8
+Dpc5-3	1084.8	**274.7**	**548.3**	**34.3**	**539.7**	**28.3**	1067.3	**480.1**	**425.9**	**178.7**	**275**	**108.9**

Table 5. Env. 2 (without non-Task EP, $NpT = 1$)

#Agent	10			30			60			199		
Alg.	MS	ST	CT	MS	ST	CT	MS	ST	CT	MS	ST	CT
PtGe	1196.4	319.9	**0.035**	607.6	60.6	**0.056**	555.5	34.6	**0.091**	1601.6	521.1	**3.911**
PtTe3Ge	1088.6	275.9	0.046	570.3	40.0	0.076	549	29.0	0.113	**1596**	**520.2**	4.157
+Dp5-3	1111.4	288.3	0.057	**556.2**	37.8	0.090	540.1	**25.5**	0.152	**1596**	**520.2**	23.668
+Dpc5-3	**1079.9**	**271.5**	0.064	558.1	**33.4**	0.103	**539.2**	**25.5**	0.168	**1596**	**520.2**	23.489
Te3GeSg	1138.7	298.7	0.039	575.4	44.5	0.096	571.2	52.0	0.211	2498.9	998.4	309.821

Table 6. Env. 2 (without non-Task EP, $NpT = 10$)

#Agent	10			30			60			199		
Alg.	MS	ST	CT	MS	ST	CT	MS	ST	CT	MS	ST	CT
PtGe	1170.3	515.4	**0.051**	516.3	211.8	**0.218**	396.9	147.4	**0.300**	1488.3	643.9	**5.647**
PtTe3Ge	1071.5	478.6	0.065	431.7	175.0	0.288	316.2	108.7	0.408	1474.6	639.6	6.016
+Dp5-3	1091.8	493.8	0.087	437.6	180.5	0.343	289	111.3	0.583	**1471.8**	**639.2**	31.300
+Dpc5-3	**1063.2**	**475.8**	0.096	**420**	**171.3**	0.427	**278.8**	**103.0**	0.833	**1471.8**	**639.2**	31.349
Te3GeSg	1122.7	510.5	0.045	505.5	202.3	0.151	387.7	138.5	0.326	2412.1	1155.1	398.404

results. Pt relatively reduced the pickup time as a result of the heuristic based on a smaller estimated pickup time. It reduced the makespan and service time in the cases where a sufficient number of agents that cover whole areas without congestion were available ($NpT = 1$, 60 agents). Te reduced the makespan and service time because it allows shorter paths that contain EPs in exchange for increaseing the number of temporarily locked EPs. The results with and without Ge were identical in these settings, since there were a sufficient number of EPs to which an agent could retreat. Dp and Dpc were relatively effective in the situations where a relatively large number of agents were continuously processing remaining tasks because those methods improved the concurrency of allocated tasks ($NpT = 10$, 60 and 152 agents). We mention that the results of Dp and Dpc were relatively competitive with that of PIBT for this classes of problems (Table 2 in [9]). Although Sg well worked to complete all tasks in these settings, the overhead of simple rule of dynamic priority increased the wait times of agents when the number of agents increased. Tables 3 and 4 show the influence of several parameters. Regarding the weight parameter W for the distance to EPs, relatively smaller values were better to balance the avoidance of EPs and the total length of detour paths. For the maximum number of dummy retreat tasks T and the maximum length of dummy retreat paths P, there seems to be opportunities to adjust them to avoid excessive locks of EPs due to the dummy paths.

Tables 5 and 6 show the result of Env. 2. Since there was no non-task EP in this problem, the density of agents was relatively high, and trade-offs among additional methods increased in the cases of relatively many agents. When the density of agents is not excessive, the performance of these solution methods based on Ge was competitive with that for the problems having non-task EPs. With appropriate parameters, Dp and Dpc slightly improved the makespan and service time. However, with the density of agents, the overhead of the heuristics also increased. Regarding Sg, its relatively naive deadlock avoidance rules needed more time to resolve the locks among agents. We also note that Sg failed to complete all tasks in a few cases of other settings. It revealed the necessity of a more sophisticated approach to solving such situations.

Taken together, the results show that is possible to reduce the redundancies of problems and solution methods by setting appropriate combinations of efficient methods. 1) Pt is effective in the situations with waiting tasks to be allocated and an appropriate density of agents. 2) TeW is effective in most situations. 3) Ge is an option that allows to reduce the number of non-task EPs. 4) DpT-P/Dpc$T$-P is effective in the situations with sufficient free EPs for them. 5) The current Sg still need some additional techniques to reduce redundant waits for the decomposed task allocation. 6) The incremental combination of Pt, Te and Dp/DPc is basically effective. On the other hand, there were inherent trade-offs among the methods, particularly in cases with a high density of agents that reduces the number of free EPs.

Regarding the computational time, the methods Dp and Dpc require relatively large overheads due to the management of additional tasks and paths, while they also offer opportunities to improve our experimental implementation. In addition, several parts of the computation can be performed while agents are still taking moves that are typically longer than the computational times.

5 Conclusion

As an analysis of solution techniques with endpoints for MAPD problems, we integrated several solution techniques in stages and experimentally investigated their effects and influence. The results reveal the redundancies of the problems and move paths which can be reduced by the solution techniques. On the other hand, there are several trade-offs among the heuristics that are combined for the concurrency of tasks. Our future work includes better adjustment of the trade-offs of the integrated techniques considering the choice of some indicators, and application of our results toward analyzing and improving several solution methods, including algorithms that more relax the conditions of well-formed problems.

Acknowledgements. This study was supported in part by The Public Foundation of Chubu Science and Technology Center (the thirty-third grant for artificial intelligence research).

References

1. Barer, M., Sharon, G., Stern, R., Felner, A.: Suboptimal variants of the conflict-based search algorithm for the multi-agent pathfinding problem. In: Proceedings of the Seventh Annual Symposium on Combinatorial Search (SoCS 2014), vol. 5, no. 1, pp. 19–27 (2014). https://ojs.aaai.org/index.php/SOCS/article/view/18315
2. Grenouilleau, F., van Hoeve, W.J., Hooker, J.: A multi-label A* algorithm for multi-agent pathfinding. In: Proceedings of the Twenty-Ninth International Conference on Automated Planning and Scheduling, pp. 181–185 (2019)
3. Hart, P., N.N., Raphael, B.: A formal basis for the heuristic determination of minimum cost paths. IEEE Trans. Syst. Sci. Cybern. **4**(2), 100–107 (1968)
4. Hart, P., N.N., Raphael, B.: Correction to a formal basis for the heuristic determination of minimum-cost paths. SIGART Newsl. (37), 28–29 (1972). https://dl.acm.org/doi/10.1145/1056777.1056779
5. Li, J., Tinka, A., Kiesel, S., Durham, J.W., Kumar, T.K.S., Koenig, S.: Lifelong multi-agent path finding in large-scale warehouses. In: Proceedings of the Thirty-Fifth AAAI Conference on Artificial Intelligence, pp. 11272–11281 (2021)
6. Liu, M., Ma, H., Li, J., Koenig, S.: Task and path planning for multi-agent pickup and delivery. In: Proceedings of the 18th International Conference on Autonomous Agents and Multiagent Systems, pp. 1152–1160 (2019)
7. Ma, H., Harabor, D., Stuckey, P.J., Li, J., Koenig, S.: Searching with consistent prioritization for multi-agent path finding. In: Proceedings of the Thirty-Third AAAI Conference on Artificial Intelligence and Thirty-First Innovative Applications of Artificial Intelligence Conference and Ninth AAAI Symposium on Educational Advances in Artificial Intelligence, pp. 7643–7650 (2019)
8. Ma, H., Li, J., Kumar, T.S., Koenig, S.: Lifelong multi-agent path finding for online pickup and delivery tasks. In: Proceedings of the 16th Conference on Autonomous Agents and Multiagent Systems, pp. 837–845 (2017)
9. Okumura, K., Machida, M., Défago, X., Tamura, Y.: Priority inheritance with backtracking for iterative multi-agent path finding. Artif. Intell. **310**, 103752 (2022). https://www.sciencedirect.com/science/article/pii/S0004370222000923?via%3Dihub
10. Okumura, K., Tamura, Y., Défago, X.: winPIBT: expanded prioritized algorithm for iterative multi-agent path finding. CoRR abs/1905.10149 (2019). http://arxiv.org/abs/1905.10149
11. Sharon, G., Stern, R., Felner, A., Sturtevant, N.R.: Conflict-based search for optimal multi-agent pathfinding. Artif. Intell. **219**, 40–66 (2015)

12. Shimokawa, M., Matsui, T.: Improvement of task allocation in TP algorithm for MAPD problem by relaxation of movement limitation and estimation of pickup time. Trans. Jpn. Soc. Artif. Intell. **37**(3), A-L84 1–13 (2022)
13. Silver, D.: Cooperative Pathfinding, pp. 117–122 (2005)
14. Čáp, M., Vokřínek, J., Kleiner, A.: Complete decentralized method for on-line multi-robot trajectory planning in well-formed infrastructures. In: Proceedings of the Twenty-Fifth International Conference on Automated Planning and Scheduling, pp. 324–332 (2015)
15. Yamauchi, T., Miyashita, Y., Sugawara, T.: Standby-based deadlock avoidance method for multi-agent pickup and delivery tasks. In: Proceedings of the 21st International Conference on Autonomous Agents and Multiagent Systems, pp. 1427–1435 (2022)

Towards Norm Entrepreneurship in Agent Societies

Amritha Menon Anavankot, Stephen Cranefield[(✉)],
and Bastin Tony Roy Savarimuthu

Department of Information Science, University of Otago, Dunedin, New Zealand
amritha.menon@postgrad.otago.ac.nz,
{stephen.cranefield,tony.savarimuthu}@otago.ac.nz

Abstract. One of the principal focuses of normative multi-agent systems in a distributed environment is coordination among agents. Most work in this area has studied norms that are provided to agents as part of their specification or distributed from centralized agents. Diverging from this line of thought, we focus on peer-to-peer interaction by providing the agents with the freedom to initiate norm creation in demanding situations like a potential interference. To achieve this, we blend probabilistic planning with norms in a multi-agent system and investigate the notion of *norm entrepreneurship*. A common approach in prior work is to reduce an interference coordination problem to a simple game theory model involving the simultaneous performance of a single action by each agent. Instead, in our work a norm entrepreneur proposes a local coordination plan (potential norm) which is a sequence of actions from each agent to cope with an interference in their normal course of action. This work will also investigate how proposed local coordination plans can be propagated to form norms at a later stage.

Keywords: Agent coordination · norm entrepreneurs · normative MAS

1 Introduction

Consider the etiquette that we tend to follow on our daily commute. On sidewalks, we stay mindful not to jostle past others close by. While walking with someone, we go single file on a crowded walkway. While listening to a personal collection of podcasts in a train, we make sure to be on earbuds rather than on speakers. Of many such codes of conduct that we follow in a community, some are unwritten, expected forms of behaviours, while others became formally codified to become legally enforceable. Social norms, which are the unwritten rules of conduct, help to maintain order and predictability in a society. They offer standards on behaviours that are considered acceptable or unacceptable among the members in a social group and provide a mechanism that people use to coordinate with each other in society.

P. Mathieu et al. (Eds.): PAAMS 2023, LNAI 13955, pp. 188–199, 2023.
https://doi.org/10.1007/978-3-031-37616-0_16

So how do norms emerge in a community? More than 10 decades have passed since Sumner [1] wrote a treatise on "Folkways" and "Mores", which are unwritten rules that are expected to be followed in a community. Sumner states that:

"The folkways are habits of the individual and customs of the society which arise from efforts to satisfy needs. The step an individual takes for an immediate motive is repeated when similar situations arise. This repetition of certain acts produces a habit in the individual. As this habit becomes widely acceptable in a society, people tend to comply with them even though they are not enforced by any authority and it thus evolves as a norm in the group."

We might presume that behind such norms in a group, there is an entrepreneurial mindset. We propose to borrow and adapt this entrepreneurial mindset from human society to multi-agent systems, where agents interact in a shared environment to achieve individual or common goals. One noteworthy strand of work on norms in social groups by various disciplines like anthropology, social science, economics etc. is regarding "norm entrepreneurs"[1] and their impact on society. A norm entrepreneur (NE) broadly has been considered as a person interested in changing social norms or as lawmakers or government agencies who could influence the dynamics of norm-following behaviours in a society. Finnemore & Sikkink [4] state that many international norms began as domestic norms and become international through the efforts of entrepreneurs of various kinds, which indicates how entrepreneurs become carriers of a norm and influence the society to follow them.

Our work proposes to adopt this concept of norm entrepreneur to a multi-agent system. We introduce a framework in a decentralized multi-agent environment where agents are at liberty to be norm entrepreneurs and propose solutions to any interference they come across while acting in the environment. Over a period of time, the coordinating solutions they propose may emerge as norms in the society. Our focus is on a peer-to-peer, bottom-up approach like folkways, where ideas to solve a problem emerge from an individual and later evolve to become norms.

2   Background and Motivation

Sociologists say that norms emerge in a society as a result of two factors: (i) as a result of unintended consequences of human action, and (ii) by human design. According to Opp [5], norms are mostly an unintended result of uncoordinated human interaction, i.e. norms may emerge spontaneously like many customs of everyday life. To illustrate this approach he analyses an example of how an unplanned non-smoking norm emerges in a society. Speaking about norm emergence by human design, he refers to the norms created intentionally like laws, contracts between businesses and likewise. Centola & Baronchelli [6]

---

[1] In her paper 'On the regulation of social norms', Kubler [2] states that Sunstein [3] coined this term.

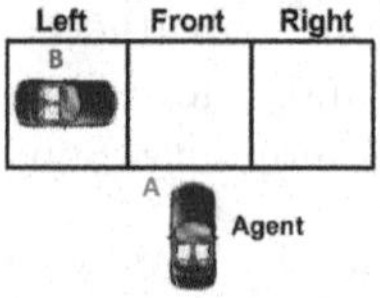

Norm	Pre-condition (θ)	Modality
n_1	$left(>)$	$obl(stop)$
n_2	$left(<)\&front(<)$	$obl(stop)$
n_3	$front(>)\&right(>)$	$obl(stop)$
n_4	$front(\wedge)$	$obl(stop)$

Fig. 1. A single-step coordination problem from Morales *et al.* [9]

present experimental results that show how social conventions emerge spontaneously. This work is inspired by their statement that social conventions emerge as unintended consequences of individual efforts to coordinate locally with one another.

2.1 Research Gap

Boella *et al.* [7] define a normative multi-agent system as:

"... a multi agent system together with normative systems in which agents on the one hand can decide whether to follow the explicitly represented norms, and on the other the normative systems specify how and in which extent the agents can modify the norms."

In most of the existing literature on normative multi-agent systems, norms are either provided to agents as part of their specification or created in a normative system through a norm synthesis process. Norm synthesis requires a governing mechanism or a special centralized agent to generate and distribute the norms. Some noteworthy work along this strand are the approaches of Shoham & Tennenholtz [8], Morales *et al.* [9–12] and Riad & Golpayegani [13]. These works commonly model the coordination problem as a simultaneous matrix game, as illustrated in Fig. 1 ([9]). In this approach, norms are modelled as a single joint action. However, coordination is often more complicated than that. Therefore, we consider the following questions. How can we coordinate the agents in an MAS without requiring specially empowered and benevolent agents to manage a norm synthesis process? Also, how can we represent agent coordination in a more general fashion than representing it as a single joint action choice by agents?

3 Norm Entrepreneurship Framework

Throughout this paper we will refer to a grid-world example (Fig. 2). We consider a park where two agents A and B move around trying to reach their respective goal locations. Figures 2a and 2b show two scenarios, where A and B indicate the current locations of the two agents and G_A and G_B show their goal locations. Initially the agents generate their own Markov Decision Process (MDP) policies to follow to reach their goals, minimizing the cost of movement. Agents are not assumed to be part of a team and the policies do not consider the presence of other agents. The park includes features that require agents to handle potential interference along their way. These features are represented in Fig. 2a by the following colours:

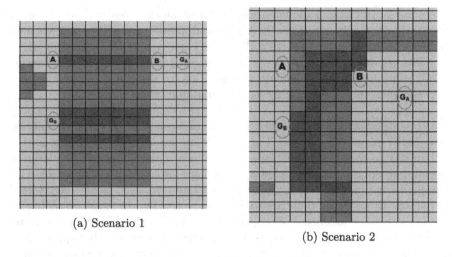

(a) Scenario 1

(b) Scenario 2

Fig. 2. Bridge crossing scenarios (best viewed in colour)

- Blue cells: water
- Brown cells: a bridge
- Grey cells: open space

In Fig. 2a, after moving around the park, two agents reach opposite sides of a bridge and are required to cross the bridge to reach their specific goals. This is an interference in their normal course of action since one of these agents may have to wait until the other crosses the bridge, or it will have to expend extra time in using the alternative bridge. When agents encounter interference scenarios such as this, we propose that one or both of them may become an norm entrepreneur and propose a coordination plan to be negotiated and then followed. If successful, this plan will be generalised to a wider range of situations, and may propagate and become a norm at a later stage. Figure 3 illustrates this framework.

3.1 Identifying Potential Interference

Assumptions: Agents use probabilistic path planning to generate a plan to reach their respective goal without considering other agents, given a model of the park as a finite horizon MDP with possible actions up, down, left, right and stay. Transitions from one cell to another are modelled as negative rewards (−1 when the destination cell is unimpeded, −0.5 the cost of staying in a cell and −100 while moving to a cell with an obstacle). An agent's goal is modelled as an absorbing state (with all actions leading to the same state with a cost of 0). Each agent performs probabilistic planning using the value iteration algorithm to produce a value $V_a(c)$, specific to that agent (a), for each cell c in the grid. This is the expected cumulative reward of following the optimal policy to reach the goal. These values are used to produce an optimal policy that maps each cell to an action.

Agents move through the environment following their optimal policies until they reach a potential interference. A potential interference is detected when an agent is observed within a certain distance. Once a norm entrepreneur agent recognises a potential interference, the agent generates a *region of coordination* (ROC) and infers[2] an approximate goal location for the other agent within the ROC and then generates possible *local coordination plans*.

Local Coordination Plan: The crux of our framework is the Local Coordination Plan (LCP) phase, depicted in Fig. 3. Existing studies propose the following mechanisms to avoid or handle interference in a multi-agent system: design a collision free environment, provide a mechanism for collision avoidance or a re-planning their course of action when they confront a collision using a centralized mechanism. However, all these approaches are restricting the agent's mobility by avoiding a collision in advance as opposed to the real world where humans devise strategies to handle such situations as and when they occur. Our approach of generating a *local coordination plan* addresses this research gap. Once an agent starts to move along the optimal path, it will recognize situations where other agents hamper its course of action. As two or more[3] agents come across such interference, a norm entrepreneur may propose a coordination plan to handle the hindrance locally, within the ROC.

The proposal of a local coordination plan has two cases. One is where a local coordination plan that emerged as a potential norm is reused as a local coordination plan. In the second case, the NE agent computes a new local coordination plan and tries to convince the other agent to follow it by providing supporting statements. In Fig. 2a, Agent A identifies a potential interference as soon as A and B reach opposite sides of the bridge. Agent A then proceeds with entrepreneurship. Figure 2b is another bridge crossing scenario similar to that of Fig. 2a. If, for brevity, we consider only local coordination plans that are optimal for A, both scenarios have LCPs that are similar at an abstract level: A can follow an optimal path to cross the water while B incurs extra cost by using another crossing point. However, in Scenario 2, there is a less costly solution for B: it can incur the cost of waiting near the narrowest portion of the bridge while not obstructing A's exit, until A has moved off it, and can then move optimally towards its goal.

3.2 Entrepreneurialism

In Fig. 3, we can see multiple local coordination plans that are numbered, which the NE agent has computed as the first step to solve the potential interference. The agent does this by executing a heuristic search over a space of joint actions in the local region of the environment where it identified the potential interference. We call this local region, the region of coordination (ROC). When an agent

---

[2] This paper does not propose a specific mechanism for goal inference, but this is an active area of research [14].

[3] We currently consider only two-agent scenarios.

Norm Entrepreneurship

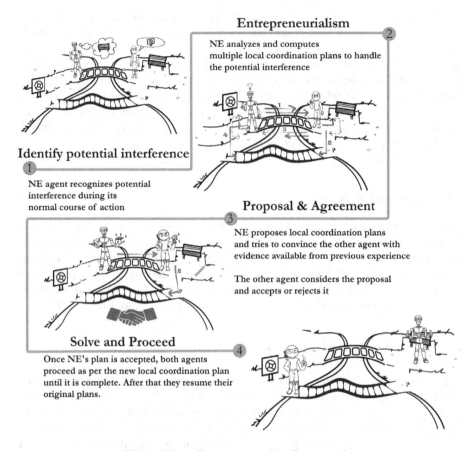

Fig. 3. Norm Entrepreneurship Framework

detects another agent within a fixed size zone around it, it may choose to move on to the entrepreneurship phase and computes multiple local coordination plans within the ROC to handle the situation and chooses one or more to propose to the other agent.

Heuristic Search: A multi-objective heuristic search is carried on a defined region of coordination. We adapt the NAMOA* algorithm for multi-objective heuristic graph search [15]. The objectives we consider are the welfare of each agent separately and their social welfare. This then generates multiple plans. They are the set of Pareto-optimal solutions to the local planning problem, i.e. each plan has a cost represented as a vector of values, one for each objective, and only non-dominated plans are returned.

3.3   Proposal and Agreement

The NE agent either proposes a candidate coordination norm it has used before and wishes to promote or it computes possible local coordination plans, selects one or more to propose as solutions, and tries to convince the other agent to follow one by providing supporting statements. The other agent considers the proposal and has the choice to accept, reject or negotiate. Proposing specific mechanisms for LCP selection, argumentation and negotiation are outside the scope of this paper. In Fig. 3, we can see that the NE agent has proposed the local coordination plan numbered 2. If he other agent accepts the proposal, it will take the alternative bridge to cross and reach its destination, thereby swerving from its original plan.

3.4   Solve and Proceed

Once a coordination plan is accepted, both the agents proceed with this plan until it is executed completely and the agents exit the region of coordination[4]. They then resume their optimal policy. When a local coordination plan has been successfully used, the norm entrepreneur can abstract it to a pattern of coordination landmarks that can match a wider range of scenarios and in later encounters this abstracted coordination plan may be promoted by the NE.

4   Norm Propagation

According to Savarimuthu and Cranefield [16], from a societal viewpoint, the important stages of norms are the formation stage, propagation stage and the emergence stage. The norm formation stage considers how agents can create norms in a society and how they can identify the norms that have been created. The norm propagation stage is where norms are spread and enforced in the society. The emergence stage is characterized by determining the extent of the spread of a norm in the society. Since norms are considered as behavioural regularities that guide agents' decisions in a social environment [17], we address the question of how a local coordination plan proposed by a norm entrepreneur agent could emerge as a norm.

We consider that once a coordination proposal is accepted by another agent during the proposal and agreement stage and then generalised into a pattern of coordination landmarks, that pattern is considered to be a candidate norm. Agents can reuse and spread this candidate norm through the society in similar situations that may arise later during their travels. The norm emerges through repeated future encounters with norm entrepreneurs who will promote their abstracted coordination plan. The fact that an agent accepted a candidate norm proposed by a norm entrepreneur becomes evidence to help convince other

---

[4] We leave consideration of an agent reneging on an agreed plan as a topic for future work.

agents. Additional conditions may be proposed by the NE to share the coordination costs. For example, a norm could take the following form: *in a situation matching pattern X, an agent approaching from the north or east should incur the greater coordination costs in following the abstracted LCP for X*.

A norm is said to have emerged when a candidate norm is accepted by a high proportion of agents. Once a norm thus emerges, agents do not need to compute solutions in interference situations similar to those they might come across at a later stage. Instead, they could just execute the norms that have emerged already. The emergence of a norm depends on a coordination plan being abstracted sufficiently to apply to multiple situations that involve similar coordination problems. Thus, we aim to be able to generalise local coordination plans, and we propose that the first step in this process is to define a *regret landscape* for each agent, given its optimal plan and the coordinating plan.

Regret Landscape: According to decision theory, regret is the value of difference between choice made and the optimal choice. When a norm entrepreneur agent identifies a potential interference, it computes a solution to resolve the interference. This solution might have a suboptimal plan being offered to either or both of the agents. Hence, there is regret compared to the hypothetical case of following the optimal plan unimpeded.

We define a *regret landscape* that shows the cost that an agent must bear when required to deviate from its optimal path as part of a local coordination plan. From its initial individual planning, an agent knows its valuation for all the cells in the region of coordination, and has an optimal path between its start (s) and end (e) positions within that region. It can also calculate the shortest path from s to each other cell in the region. Suppose the agent finds itself at some cell c that it reached while following an LCP. It can compare the value of c to the value of the cell c' that it would have reached by expending the same amount of effort when following the optimal plan. We define the regret that it would have from having to detour through c rather than following its optimal path. As we compute a regret landscape that is independent of any specific LCP, we assume that the agent reached c optimally, and will then proceed optimally to the goal—essentially we treat c as a required waypoint.

We use the following notation to define the regret $R_a(c)$ for an agent a:

- $\text{cost}(c, c')$, is the cost of moving between adjacent cells c and c'.
- $V_a^\delta(p)$ denotes the value that a achieves by exerting cost δ while moving along a path $p = \langle c_0, ..., c_n \rangle$ of cells c_i of increasing value, and stopping at c_n if it is reached.

$V_a^\delta(p)$ is defined as follows:

$$
V_a^\delta(p) = \begin{cases} V_a(c_n) & \text{if } \delta \geq \sum_{1 \leq i \leq n} \text{cost}(c_{i-1}, c_i) \\ V_a(c_m) + \frac{\delta - \sum_{1 \leq i \leq m} \text{cost}(c_{i-1}, c_i)}{\text{cost}(c_m, c_{m+1})}(V_a(c_{m+1}) - V_a(c_m)) & \text{otherwise} \\ [5pt] \text{where } m = \max(\{i \mid i < n \wedge \delta \geq \sum_{1 \leq j \leq i} \text{cost}(c_{j-1}, c_j)\}) \end{cases}
$$

The first case above says that you take the value of the final cell in the path if δ is sufficient to reach the end of the path (or beyond).

The second case finds the largest index in the path for which δ is greater than the sum of costs along the path up to cell c_m. If an effort of δ is greater than the effort required to reach c_m on the optimal path but not enough to reach c_{m+1}, an interpolated additional value is added to $V_a(c_m)$.

Consider an agent a that finds itself in location c after beginning its journey within the region of coordination at s. The value of being at c is $V_a(c)$. Now we need to compare this to the agent's utility if it had followed its optimal path op from s to e. The agent (on that optimal path) would have utility $V_a^{(spc(s,c))}(op)$ after incurring the cost $spc(s,c)$, where spc is the shortest path cost function.

Therefore, the regret is:

$$R_a(c) = V_a^{spc(s,c)}(op) - V_a(c) + \max\left(spc(s,c) - \mathrm{cost}(op), 0\right)$$

The last term in the definition considers the case where the cost already incurred by agent a to reach c (assumed to be optimal) exceeds the cost needed to conclude its journey from s to e along op. Here, $\mathrm{cost}(op)$ is the cost of travelling along op.

Considering all cells as candidates for c (a potential waypoint that may be off the optimal path), we can compute a *regret landscape* for each agent, as shown in Figs. 4a and 4b, corresponding to Figs. 2a and 2b, respectively. Figure 2a and Fig. 2b show the regret landscapes for agent A (the norm entrepreneur) and agent B. The higher the saturation of a colour, the higher the regret. In Fig. 4a (left), agent A has two paths to cross the water: one through the optimal path (white colour) and the other via the upper bridge, which is suboptimal (orange colour). If an agreed local coordination plan allows A to follow the optimal path, Fig. 4a (right) shows that B can still travel optimally by taking the lower bridge. In Fig. 4b, there is no coordination plan that is optimal for both agents. If A proceeds optimally, B must either take a long detour up, left and then down, or it can wait near the optimal path until A is out of the narrow section, and then move along its optimal route. However, the social welfare maximising solution is for A to take the slightly longer route up, right then down, and for B to follow its optimal plan.

Incremental Regret: Given an agent a's regret landscape and a path p that represents its sequence of actions in a local coordination plan, we seek to identify the specific steps of p at which a has an increment of regret. To accommodate the *stay* action, we represent p as a sequence of elements $c_i^{n_i}$ $(1 \leq i \leq \mathrm{len}(p))$ denoting a spending n_i consecutive time steps located at cell c_i. The *incremental regret* at c_i is defined as follows:

$$IR_a(c_i^{n_i}) = \begin{cases} 0 & \text{if } i = 1 \\ R_a(c_i) - R_a(c_{i-1}) + (n_i - 1)\,staycost & \text{otherwise} \end{cases}$$

where *staycost* is the (domain-specific) cost of staying in the same location for one time step rather than following an optimal path.

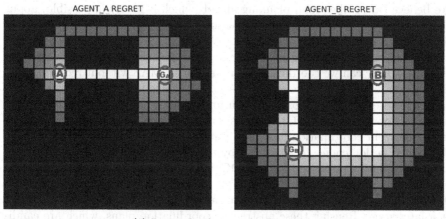

(a) Regret landscapes for Figure 2a

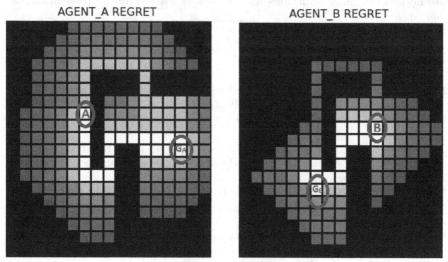

(b) Regret landscapes for Figure 2b

Fig. 4. The agents' regret landscapes for Figs. 2a and 2b (best viewed in colour)

The next step in our research is use the agents' incremental regret to investigate abstractions of a local coordination that could form a more widely applicable norm. For example, non-zero values for incremental regret indicate landmarks [18] where an agent must incur an additional cost for coordination with the other agent.

5 Conclusion

This paper set forth a framework to establish norms to handle interference among agents during their social interactions in a decentralized environment.

We believe that rather than planning ahead (which is nearly impossible) about how to handle every inter-agent interaction that agents could confront during their course of action in an environment, a better way could be to allow agents to solve interference as and when they occur. Thus we answer our first question in Sect. 2.1 ("How can we coordinate the agents in an MAS without requiring specially empowered and benevolent agents . . . ") by introducing norm entrepreneur agents. These agents propose a resolution of the interference within a local region of coordination (ROC). We answer our second question ("How can we represent agent coordination in a more general fashion than representing it as a single joint action choice by agents?") by the norm entrepreneur's generation of local coordination plans within the ROC, with one or more of these joint plans selected and proposed to the other agent. We use *regret landscapes* as a first step to abstracting these generated plans and reusing them in similar situations at a later stage. Reusing these abstracted coordination plans, which are candidate norms, in similar situations will eventually lead to norm propagation and emergence.

References

1. Sumner, W.: Folkways: A Study of the Sociological Importance of Usages, Manners, Customs, Mores, and Morals, Ginn (1906)
2. Kubler, D.: On the regulation of social norms. J. Law Econ. Organ. **17**, 449–476 (2001)
3. Sunstein, C.R.: Social norms and social roles. Columbia Law Rev. 903–968 (1996)
4. Finnemore, M., Sikkink, K.: International norm dynamics and political change. Int. Organ. **52**, 887–917 (1998)
5. Opp, K.-D.: When do norms emerge by human design and when by the unintended consequences of human action?: The example of the nosmoking norm. Ration. Soc. **14**, 131–158 (2002)
6. Centola, D., Baronchelli, A.: The spontaneous emergence of conventions: an experimental study of cultural evolution. Proc. Natl. Acad. Sci. **112**, 1989–1994 (2015)
7. Boella, G., Torre, L., Verhagen, H.: Introduction to the special issue on normative multiagent systems. Auton. Agents Multi-Agent Syst. 1–10 (2008)
8. Shoham, Y., Tennenholtz, M.: On the synthesis of useful social laws for artificial agent societies. In: Proceedings of the Tenth National Conference on Artificial intelligence (AAAI-92) (AAAI Press, 1992), pp. 276–281 (1992)
9. Morales, J., López-Sánchez, M., Rodríguez-Aguilar, J., Wooldridge, M., Vasconcelos, W.: Automated synthesis of normative systems. In: 12th International Conference on Autonomous Agents and Multiagent Systems (2013)
10. Morales, J., López-Sánchez, M., Rodríguez-Aguilar, J., Wooldridge, M., Vasconcelos, W.: Minimality and simplicity in the on-line automated synthesis of normative systems. In: 13th International Conference on Autonomous Agents and Multiagent Systems, pp. 109–116 (2014)
11. Morales, J., López-Sánchez, M., Rodríguez-Aguilar, J.A., Wooldridge, M.J., Vasconcelos, W.W.: Synthesising liberal normative systems. In: Proceedings of the 2015 International Conference on Autonomous Agents and Multiagent Systems (ACM, 2015), p. 433.441 (2015)

12. Morales, J., Wooldridge, M., Rodríguez-Aguilar, J., López-Sánchez, M.: Synthesising evolutionarily stable normative systems. Auton. Agents Multi-Agent Syst. **32**, 635.671 (2018)
13. Riad, M., Golpayegani, F.: Coordination, Organizations, Institutions, Norms, and Ethics for Governance of Multi-Agent Systems XIV. In: Theodorou, A., Nieves, J.C., Vos, M.D. (eds.), pp. 78–93. Springer, Cham (2021). https://doi.org/10.1007/978-3-031-16617-4
14. Vered, M., Mirsky, R., Pereira, R.F., Meneguzzi, F.: Editorial: advances in goal, plan and activity recognition. Front. Artif. Intell. **5**, 861669 (2022)
15. Mandow, L., Perez de la Cruz, J.L.: Multiobjective A* Search with consistent heuristics. J. ACM **57** (2010)
16. Savarimuthu, B.T.R., Cranefield, S.: Norm creation, spreading and emergence: a survey of simulation models of norms in multi-agent systems. Multiagent Grid Syst. **7**, 21–54 (2011)
17. Balke, T., et al.: Normative multi-agent systems. In: Andrighetto, G., Governatori, G., Noriega, P., van der Torre, L.W.N. (eds.) Schloss Dagstuhl - Leibniz-Zentrum für Informatik, pp. 171–189 (2013)
18. Aldewereld, H., Grossi, D., Vázquez-Salceda, J., Dignum, F.: Designing normative behaviour via landmarks. In: Boissier, O., et al. (eds.) AAMAS 2005. LNCS (LNAI), vol. 3913, pp. 157–169. Springer, Heidelberg (2006). https://doi.org/10.1007/11775331_11

Velluscinum: A Middleware for Using Digital Assets in Multi-agent Systems

Nilson Mori Lazarin[1,2(✉)], Igor Machado Coelho[1], Carlos Eduardo Pantoja[1,2], and José Viterbo[1]

[1] Institute of Computing - Fluminense Federal University (UFF), Niterói, RJ, Brazil
{imcoelho,viterbo}@ic.uff.br
[2] Federal Center for Technological Education Celso Suckow da Fonseca (Cefet/RJ), Rio de Janeiro, RJ, Brazil
{nilson.lazarin,carlos.pantoja}@cefet-rj.br

Abstract. Distributed Ledger Technologies (DLT) characteristics can contribute to several domains, such as Multi-agent Systems (MAS), facilitating the agreement between agents, managing trust relationships, and distributed scenarios. Some contributions to this integration are in the theoretical stage, and the few existing practical contributions have limitations and low performance. This work presents a MAS approach that can use digital assets as a factor of agreement in the relationship between cognitive agents using the Belief-Desire-Intention model. To validate the proposed methodology, we present the middleware Velluscinum that offers new internal actions to agents. The middleware was tested by adapting the Building-a-House classic example to cryptocurrency and agreements mediated by a distributed ledger.

Keywords: Middleware · Multi-agents · Digital Ledger Technology

1 Introduction

Multi-agent Systems (MAS) are systems composed of multiple agents, which can be cognitive, through the use of the Belief-Desire-Intention (BDI) [4] model that enables the programming of mental attitudes like beliefs, desires, and intentions. These agents are called cognitive since they have a reasoning cycle capable of analyzing the information perceived in the environment in which they are inserted, the knowledge acquired through communication with other agents, and making self-conclusions. These agents can interact or compete to resolve a task; in this relationship, conflicts and uncertainty can occur, so it is essential to provide mechanisms for all agents to cooperate by guaranteeing reliability in the acquired information and used resources [23,25].

Distributed Ledger Technologies (DLT) technologies have applications far beyond the financial sector, and their characteristics of decentralization, security, trust, and low cost of operation have a great capacity to contribute in various domains [9]. They are classified as permissionless or permissioned: in the first

P. Mathieu et al. (Eds.): PAAMS 2023, LNAI 13955, pp. 200–212, 2023.
https://doi.org/10.1007/978-3-031-37616-0_17

case, the access is unrestricted, the members can join and leave the network at any time, and finally, each node has a read-only copy of the data; the second case provides an additional access control layer, allowing some specific operations by authorized participants [18].

Adopting DLT technologies in MAS can facilitate the agreement between agents, taking what is registered in the Ledger as accurate, and also can be helpful to manage trust relationships, Open MAS, and distributed scenarios. This integration contains a great set of open challenges with great potential [6]. Whether in facilitating the execution of semi-autonomous interorganizational business processes [11] or even allowing intelligent agents to generate economic value for their owner [14], for example.

Many contributions that proposed the fusion of MAS and DLT are still in the theoretical stage [6]. When performing a mapping review, we found only one paper [16] implementing DLT in MAS using BDI agent. However, this implementation is in the environmental dimension of the MAS, making it necessary to create an institution in the organizational dimension. In this implementation, the agents can access only one wallet in the DLT, limiting the competitiveness or autonomy of agents. In addition, the DLT platform used has high latency and low performance.

Thus, this paper presents a middleware for using digital assets in the relationships between cognitive agents to represent the transfer of funds, registration of ownership of artifacts, declaration of promises or agreements, and dissemination of knowledge. The middleware comprises several new internal actions that operate in the agents' dimension, allowing them to manipulate assets and wallets directly in the DLT. So, the agents can create and transfer divisible and indivisible assets and manage digital wallets on a permissioned DLT. In addition, as a proof of concept, a case study integrating MAS and DLT is presented. We adapted the well-known Build-a-House example [1] for using digital assets in a BigchainDB Network. The contribution of this work is a middleware to be integrated in the JaCaMo [2] distribution, a well-known platform for agent-oriented development.

This work is organized as follows: a theoretical basis of DLT is presented in Sect. 2; an analysis of related works is presented in Sect. 3; in Sect. 4 is presents a proposal for the use of digital assets in the relationship between intelligent agents; the case study of the integration of the well-known examples with DLT is presented in Sect. 5; finally, conclusions and future work are presented in Sect. 6.

2 Theoretical Foundation

A DLT can be considered an append-only decentralized database because it provides a storage mechanism. However, compared with a traditional database, its performance is much lower because it has a low download rate and a high latency [13]. On the other hand, there are several models of permissioned DLTs, but they do not have a significant difference in performance compared to a permissionless [8,22].

New approaches based on distributed databases have been used to improve the performance of permissioned DLT. In this case, the properties of distributed databases are combined with blockchain networks, are thus security-oriented, and adopt transaction-based replication [10,17,21]. When considering the number of transactions that a DLT can successfully execute per second (*Transactions Per Second – TPS*), some benchmark works carried out demonstrate that: DLT permissionless (e.g., Bitcoin or Ethereum) ranges between 3.45 and 4.69 TPS [15,24]; DLT permissioned (e.g., HyperLedger Fabric) vary between 4.28 and 10.51 TPS [7,15]; DLT permissioned distribution database-based (e.g., BigchainDB) varies between 50.60 and 175 TPS [7,10].

The performance of DLT can be a limiting factor for their adoption in MAS since the delay in including a new block in the network can affect the behavior of intelligent systems. In addition, the cost of carrying out a transaction on some permissionless DLT can be another restrictive factor for wide use. These issues led to the choice of using BigchainDB, as it is a high-performance permissioned network. Rather than trying to improve the performance of DLT, BigChainDB adds the characteristics of a blockchain to a distributed database. In this way, it has unified the characteristics of low latency, high transfer rate, high storage capacity, and a query language of a distributed database, with the characteristics of decentralization, Byzantine fault tolerance, immutability, and creation or exchange of digital assets [13].

BigchainDB structures the data as an owner-controlled asset and only allows two types of transactions that are made up of the following fields [13]: *ASSET* is immutable information that represents a register in the DLT; *METADATA* is additional information that can be updated with each new transaction; *INPUT* specifies which key an asset previously belonged to and provides proof that the conditions required to transfer ownership of that asset have been met; *OUTPUT* specifies the conditions that need to be met to change ownership of a specific asset; *TRANSACTION-ID* is a digest that identifies the transaction, computed considering all transaction fields.

There is no previous owner in a *CREATE* transaction, so the *INPUT* field specifies the key registering the asset. Furthermore, in the *OUTPUT* field of this transaction, a positive number called *AMOUNT* is defined. If $AMOUNT = 1$, the asset is indivisible, thus representing a non-fungible token. If $AMOUNT > 1$, this asset is divisible, thus representing a token and how many instances there are. In a *TRANSFER* transaction, the INPUT contains proof that the user can transfer or update that asset. In practical terms, this means that a user states which asset is to be transferred with the *INPUT* field and demonstrates that it is authorized to transfer this asset [13].

3 Related Works

A mapping review was conducted by looking for related works integrating BDI agents with DLT. This research was made in three phases. The first phase used the following search string *(("DLT" OR "Distributed Ledger Technologies" OR*

"Blockchain") *AND* (*"BDI"* *OR* *"belief-desire-intention"*) *AND* (*"multi-agent oriented programming"* *OR* *"Jason"* *OR* *"Jacamo"*)) in GoogleScholar found 97 works. In the second phase, a refinement was carried out by reading the paper's titles and abstracts. Twenty works were classified involving DLT and MAS. In the third stage, the complete reading of the papers. Below are the only three papers that involved DLT and MAS practical applications.

Calvaresi et al. [6] presents an integration between the MAS and the Hyperledger Fabric. Via a smart contract, the reputation management of agents of a MAS is carried out. In the proposed model, prior registration is required to interact with other agents in the system or operate the ledger, making the use of a third membership service mandatory. Furthermore, an agent cannot create an asset in the ledger, but only execute a pre-existing contract. Finally, the proposed system does not use BDI agents.

Papi et al. [16] presents an integration model between JaCaMo and Ethereum. Creating a centralized entity and standards allows BDI agents to request the execution of a smart contract on the blockchain. A proof of concept is presented, where agents negotiate, hire, and pay for services from other agents through the centralizing entity. However, it does not allow each BDI agent to own a wallet. In addition, it is mandatory using an artificial institution (following the *Situated Artificial Institution* [5] model) that is recognized by all agents and other entities in the system because the notion of money transfer depends on the interpretation of each agent. Finally, the delay in effecting transactions is another limitation.

Minarsch et al. [14] presents a framework for *Autonomous Economic Agents* (AEA) to operate on Ethereum on behalf of an owner, with limited or no interference from that owner entity and whose objective is to generate economic value for its owner. Allows developers to distribute agents as finished products to end users, reducing barriers to widespread MAS adoption. However, AEA uses an abstraction based on behaviors and handler code. It does not have BDI-based fundamentals and does not support content based on ontology, agent persistence, and agent mobility services.

This work presents a middleware for integrating MAS with BigChainDB, a distributed database with blockchain characteristics. Unlike Calvaresi et al., this paper eliminates the need for a certifying authority. Each agent can generate a wallet to interact with the DLT. Unlike Papi et al., creating a virtual institution is unnecessary, and each agent can manage digital assets directly via new internal actions provided by the middleware. Finally, unlike Minarsch et al., this work allows BDI agents to generate economic value for their owners.

4   Proposed Middleware

This paper presents some approaches for using divisible and indivisible assets as concordance factors in intelligent agents' relationships. New internal actions are proposed to integrate BDI agents with a DLT. In addition, as a proof of concept, a middleware was developed, enabling agents to create and transfer assets and to manage digital wallets in the permissioned blockchain BigchainDB.

4.1 Indivisible Assets Supporting the BDI Agents' Relationship

Agents can create and transfer indivisible assets that are unique and immutable records in the DLT, cryptographically signed and protected by crypto-conditions. With this, they can represent ownership registrations and transfers of artifacts, publicize beliefs and plans, or even record promises and commitments. Below are some possible approaches for using indivisible assets by intelligent agents.

Indivisible Asset Such as Property Record: Artifacts provide some function or service for agents to achieve their goals. An artifact can be a computational device that populates the MAS's environment dimension [20] or a physical device capable of acting or perceiving the real world [12]. An artifact can be used individually or collectively by agents. So, DLT can add a layer of ownership to artifacts, making it easier to implement access control and security. Using indivisible assets as a property record, the artifact itself can use the DLT as a reliable basis for defining permissions, always consulting the last transaction of the asset.

Figure 1 presents an example where agent Bob registers an asset in the DLT, representing an artifact. Subsequently, it transfers ownership to agent Alice through a transaction. Then, agent Alice transfers to agent Eve, the current owner. The asset's immutable characteristics are recorded at creation: the artifact name and a serial number. The asset has metadata that is added to each new transaction.

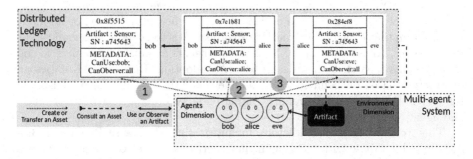

Fig. 1. Using indivisible asset such as property record.

When creating the asset (1), the metadata represents that the artifact can be observed by all agents and used only by agent Bob. When the asset was transferred to agent Alice (2), the artifact could only be observed and used by agent Alice. Finally, in the last transaction (3), the artifact can be observed by all agents and used only by agent Eve, the current owner of the artifact.

Indivisible Asset Such as Promise or Agreement: By analyzing the results of interactions between agents or information received from other agents, trust models seek to guide how, when, and with which agents it is safe to interact [19]. DLT technologies can add a layer of trust to the relationship between intelligent agents. In this case, a history of an agent's reputation can is built through an asset. Any agent that receives the asset will be able to analyze the history of agreements or promises made by the agent.

Figure 2 presents an example of agent bob committing to a particular task. After creating the asset (1) representing the commitment, the agent transfers (2) it to agent alice. When agent bob fulfills his commitment and agent alice is satisfied, he returns the asset (3) to Bob. Later, agent bob promised to eve can assume the same commitment (4).

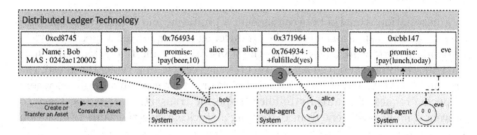

Fig. 2. Using indivisible asset such as promise.

4.2   Divisible Assets to Support the Agents' Relationship

A divisible asset can represent a cryptocurrency in DLT, so that can be created several tokens. All divisible assets are created in a wallet, are cryptographically signed, and initially, the wallet concentrates all the asset units, being able to transfer units of this asset to other wallets [13]. Intelligent agents can use divisible assets to trade with other agents inside or outside the MAS. Figure 3 presents an example of a transaction involving divisible assets. Agent bob creates 100 units of the asset BobCoin (1) and performs two transfers: in the first (2), 25 Bobcoins are sent to agent alice; in the second (3), another 25 BobCoins are sent to agent eve. Agent alice, in turn, transfers 5 Bobcoins to agent eve (4) and another 5 Bobcoins to agent charlie (5). Likewise, agent eve transfers 10 Bobcoins to agent charlie (6). Finally, what remained: agent bob has 50; agent alice has 15; agent eve has 20; agent charle has 15; totaling the 100 Bobcoins created and distributed by DLT.

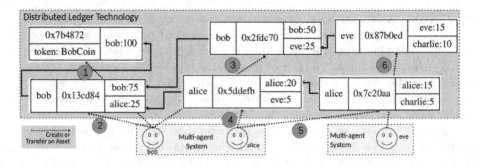

Fig. 3. Using divisible assets to support the agents' relationship

4.3 Stamping a Transaction

In a negotiation scenario between agents, a producer, and a consumer, the consumer agent transfers an asset to the producer agent, requesting a specific service. In turn, the producing agent verifies the transaction's validity on the DLT. Once the transaction is valid, the agent executes the service. In a typical scenario, the producer agent should store in its belief base or, worst case, in a database where a specific request has already fulfilled a specific transaction. It is necessary to prevent a malicious agent from requesting a service, using the same transaction several times.

A transaction is considered open if the OUTPUT pointer does not point to the INPUT pointer of the next transaction. It represents in this way that the transaction has not yet been spent. In addition to implementing internal actions to operate in DLT from the agents' dimension, this paper also presents the concept of stamping a transaction.

Definition 1 (Stamp Transaction). *Stamping a transaction is a self-transfer and unification process. Self-transfer, therefore, the units received from a divisible asset are transferred to itself, spending the received transaction (filling the OUTPUT pointer with the address of its wallet). Unification because this process joins the units from the received transaction with those already in the wallet. A transaction with two or more INPUT pointers and a single OUTPUT pointer is generated in this process.*

4.4 Middleware Velluscinum

Middleware Velluscinum[1] extends the jason-lang [3] through integration with BigchainDB [13], providing new internal actions to enable the use of digital assets to support the relationship between intelligent agents. Figure 4 presents the integration of two MAS with a DLT. The actions offered by the middleware are available directly to the dimension of the agents that populate the MAS. They bridge the Multi-agent Oriented Programming (MAOP) paradigm [1] and the BigchainDB communication driver [13].

---

[1] https://velluscinum.chon.group/.

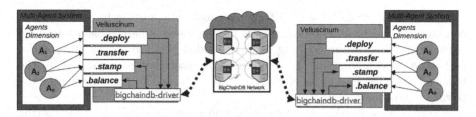

Fig. 4. Proposed middleware approach

In this way, intelligent agents can create or transfer digital assets, stamp transactions or manage their wallets on the DLT directly from their dimension. The built-in internal actions provided by the middleware are described below:

- **.buildWallet**(w) - generates a digital wallet and returns the belief $+w(P,Q)$;
- **.deployNFT**(S,P,Q,I,M,b) - registers an asset and returns the belief $+b(A)$;
- **.transferNFT**(S,P,Q,A,R,M,b) - transfer an asset and returns $+b(T)$;
- **.deployToken**(S,P,Q,I,V,b) - creates V units from an asset, returns $+b(C)$;
- **.transferToken**(S,P,Q,C,R,V,b) - transfer V units of C and returns $+b(T)$;
- **.stampTransaction**(S,P,Q,T) - stamps a transaction (T);
- **.tokenBalance**(S,P,Q,C,q) - check the wallet Q and return $+q(C,V)$.

Where:

- b is a belief that represents a result of an operation in DLT;
- w is a belief that represents an agent's wallet;
- q is a belief that represents the balance of C in the agent's wallet.
- A is a literal that represents a indivisible asset;
- C is a literal that represents a divisible asset;
- P e Q are literals that represent the agent's key pair;
- R is a literal that represents the public key of a recipient agent;
- S is a literal that represents the address of a DLT node;
- T is a literal that represents a transaction performed in the DTL;
- V is a literal that represents the number of parts of a C;
- I is a key-value array that represents the immutable data of an asset;
- M is a key-value array representing asset or transaction metadata;

5   Case Study

To validate the proposed approach, we present the adaptation of a well-known example of relationships between intelligent agents for the use of digital assets. The Building-a-House example [1] presents a multi-agent system scenario with an interorganizational workflow for building a house on the land of a contracting agent. The agent hires builder agents during an auction to achieve this overall objective. Furthermore, coordination is needed to carry out the tasks related to the construction of the property.

The original example uses artifacts to manage the auction for each stage of construction. In this integration, we use the approach of indivisible assets as an agreement. Thus, before creating artifacts, added plans to deploy an asset for each stage of construction. It represents a contract that is transferred to the winner before the execution of the task, and returned to the owner after the payment confirmation.

Figure 5 presents the necessary adaptations for all agents and the specific adaptations for the owner agent to integrate the example with the proposed approach. The adaptations are detailed below: Before the execution of the MAS, a digital currency (JacamoCoin) and a wallet for the owner agent are created. In addition, currency units are transferred to the owner's wallet; In the source code common to all agents in the system, a belief is added containing JacamoCoin's ASSET-ID and the address of a DLT node (common.asl, lines 2–3). This way, when starting the MAS, the agent already has a balance, and all agents agree with the cryptocurrency in that MAS; A belief is added to the owner agent, containing its wallet's private and public key (giacomo.asl, lines 2–3); In the creation plan of the artifact responsible for the auction were added actions to generate an asset representing a contract referring to the task to be auctioned (giacomo.asl, lines 50–56); In the auction result display plan was added actions to request the information necessary to transfer the digital asset to the winner (giacomo.asl, lines 71–75); In the contract execution plan, was added information about the digital asset in the message sent to the winners (giacomo.asl, lines 126–129); A plan responsible for carrying out the transfer of the digital asset that represents the contract between the owner and the contractor was added (giacomo.asl, lines 144–152); Finally, a plan to carry out the payment of the task after its execution by the contractor was added (giacomo.asl, lines 155–164).

The owner agent initiates the execution phase of the house construction project by requesting the winners to carry out the tasks. At this stage, organizations verify the validity of the asset representing the contract in the DLT. This action is performed through the transaction stamp. Once the contract is confirmed, the company starts executing the task. Upon completion of the execution, as defined in the contract, the company requests payment in JacamoCoins (digital currency accepted in the SMA - divisible assets approach to support the relationship between agents). Finally, when the agent informs about the payment of the task, the company confirms receipt (transaction stamp approach). If everything is correct, the company returns the asset representing the contract to the owner.

Fig. 6 presents the adaptations necessary for all organizations that enable the integration of the example with the proposed approach. The adaptations are detailed below: An action was added to request payment after executing each auction task (org_goals.asl, lines 5;8;10;12;15; 17;19;21); The necessary information for triggering the contract execution plan has been changed. In addition, before executing the tasks, a plan for validating the contract with the DLT is activated (org_code.asl, lines 13 and 15); A plan was added to provide for the creation of a virtual company wallet, along with the DLT (org_code.asl, lines

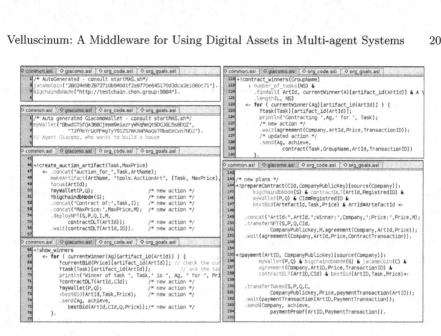

Fig. 5. Generic and specific changes to the giacomo agent to adhere to the Building-a-House [1] example with the proposal of digital assets as support for the relationship between intelligent agents.

Fig. 6. Generic changes were needed by organizations to adhere to the Building-a-House [1] example with the proposal of digital assets to support the relationship between intelligent agents.

40–45); A plan was added to note in the agent's mind the ASSET-ID of the contract he won in the auction and also to inform the owner which wallet will receive the contract (org_code.asl, lines 47–51); A plan was added with the necessary actions to validate contracts with the DLT (org_code.asl, lines 53–57); A plan has been added to make it possible to request payment after executing a task (org_code.asl, lines 59–64); Finally, a plan was added to validate a payment and transfer ownership of the contract to the owner (org_code.asl, lines 66–72).

6 Conclusion

This paper presents an approach for using digital assets in the relationships between cognitive agents, enabling the representation of the transfer of funds, registration of property, declaration of promises, and dissemination of knowledge. Integration of a well-known example of MAS with DLT was presented using middleware for the agents' dimension. In addition, it was possible to: evaluate the functioning of the system and verify that each agent can sign its transaction through its asymmetric key pair; use the DLT as an open and reliable basis to feed agents' beliefs; and enable the manipulation of assets directly by the agents. Future works can analyze the need for new internal actions for the agent dimension, more complex scenarios involving transactions between different multi-agent systems, and the possibilities and implications of a specific permissive DLT for intelligent agents.

References

1. Boissier, O., Bordini, R.H., Hübner, J.F., Ricci, A., Santi, A.: Multi-agent oriented programming with JaCaMo. Sci. Comput. Program. **78**(6), 747–761 (2013). https://doi.org/10.1016/j.scico.2011.10.004
2. Boissier, O., Hübner, J.F., Ricci, A.: The JaCaMo framework. In: Aldewereld, H., Boissier, O., Dignum, V., Noriega, P., Padget, J. (eds.) Social Coordination Frameworks for Social Technical Systems. LGTS, vol. 30, pp. 125–151. Springer, Cham (2016). https://doi.org/10.1007/978-3-319-33570-4_7
3. Bordini, R., Hübner, J., Wooldridge, M.: Programming Multi-Agent Systems in AgentSpeak using Jason. Wiley Series in Agent Technology, Wiley, Hoboken (2007)
4. Bratman, M.: Intention, Plans, and Practical Reason. Harvard University Press, Cambridge, Cambridge, MA (1987)
5. de Brito, M., Hübner, J.F., Boissier, O.: Situated artificial institutions: stability, consistency, and flexibility in the regulation of agent societies. Auton. Agent Multi-Agent Syst. **32**(2), 219–251 (2017). https://doi.org/10.1007/s10458-017-9379-3
6. Calvaresi, D., Calbimonte, J.P., Dubovitskaya, A., Mattioli, V., Piguet, J.G., Schumacher, M.: The good, the bad, and the ethical implications of bridging blockchain and multi-agent systems. Information **10**(12) (2019). https://doi.org/10.3390/info10120363
7. Contreras, A.F.: Benchmarking of blockchain technologies used in a decentralized data marketplace. Grado en Ingeniería Informática, E.T.S de Ingenieros Informáticos (UPM), Madrid, España, June 2019. https://oa.upm.es/55775/
8. Dabbagh, M., Choo, K.K.R., Beheshti, A., Tahir, M., Safa, N.S.: A survey of empirical performance evaluation of permissioned blockchain platforms: challenges and opportunities. Comput. Secur. **100**, 102078 (2021). https://doi.org/10.1016/j.cose.2020.102078

9. El Ioini, N., Pahl, C.: A review of distributed ledger technologies. In: Panetto, H., Debruyne, C., Proper, H.A., Ardagna, C.A., Roman, D., Meersman, R. (eds.) OTM 2018. LNCS, vol. 11230, pp. 277–288. Springer, Cham (2018). https://doi.org/10.1007/978-3-030-02671-4_16
10. Ge, Z., Loghin, D., Ooi, B.C., Ruan, P., Wang, T.: Hybrid blockchain database systems: design and performance. Proc. VLDB Endow. 15(5), 1092–1104 (2022). https://doi.org/10.14778/3510397.3510406
11. Kampik, T., Najjar, A.: Simulating, off-chain and on-chain: agent-based simulations in cross-organizational business processes. Information 11(1) (2020). https://doi.org/10.3390/info11010034
12. Manoel, F., Pantoja, C.E., Samyn, L., de Jesus, V.S.: Physical artifacts for agents in a cyber-physical system: a case study in oil & gas scenario (EEAS). In: The 32nd International Conference on Software Engineering and Knowledge Engineering, SEKE 2020, pp. 55–60. KSI Research Inc. (2020)
13. McConaghy, T., et al.: Bigchaindb: a scalable blockchain database. white paper, BigChainDB (2016)
14. Minarsch, D., Favorito, M., Hosseini, S.A., Turchenkov, Y., Ward, J.: Autonomous economic agent framework. In: Alechina, N., Baldoni, M., Logan, B. (eds.) Engineering Multi-Agent Systems. EMAS 2021. LNCS, vol. 13190, pp. 237–253. Springer, Cham (2022). https://doi.org/10.1007/978-3-030-97457-2_14
15. Nasir, Q., Qasse, I.A., Abu Talib, M., Nassif, A.B.: Performance analysis of hyperledger fabric platforms. Secur. Commun. Netw. 2018, 1–14 (2018). https://doi.org/10.1155/2018/3976093
16. Papi, F.G., Hübner, J.F., de Brito, M.: A blockchain integration to support transactions of assets in multi-agent systems. Eng. Appl. Artif. Intell. 107, 104534 (2022). https://doi.org/10.1016/j.engappai.2021.104534
17. Podgorelec, B., Turkanović, M., Šestak, M.: A brief review of database solutions used within blockchain platforms. In: Prieto, J., Pinto, A., Das, A.K., Ferretti, S. (eds.) BLOCKCHAIN 2020. AISC, vol. 1238, pp. 121–130. Springer, Cham (2020). https://doi.org/10.1007/978-3-030-52535-4_13
18. Rajasekaran, A.S., Azees, M., Al-Turjman, F.: A comprehensive survey on blockchain technology. Sustain. Energy Technol. Assess. 52, 102039 (2022). https://doi.org/10.1016/j.seta.2022.102039
19. Ramchurn, S.D., Huynh, D., Jennings, N.R.: Trust in multi-agent systems. Knowl. Eng. Rev. 19(1), 1–25 (2004)
20. Ricci, A., Viroli, M., Omicini, A.: Programming MAS with artifacts. In: Bordini, R.H., Dastani, M.M., Dix, J., El Fallah Seghrouchni, A. (eds.) ProMAS 2005. LNCS (LNAI), vol. 3862, pp. 206–221. Springer, Heidelberg (2006). https://doi.org/10.1007/11678823_13
21. Ruan, P., et al.: Blockchains vs. distributed databases: dichotomy and fusion. In: Proceedings of the 2021 International Conference on Management of Data, pp. 1504–1517. SIGMOD '21, New York, NY, USA (2021). https://doi.org/10.1145/3448016.3452789
22. Shalaby, S., Abdellatif, A.A., Al-Ali, A., Mohamed, A., Erbad, A., Guizani, M.: Performance evaluation of hyperledger fabric. In: 2020 IEEE International Conference on Informatics, IoT, and Enabling Technologies (ICIoT), pp. 608–613. IEEE, Doha, Qatar, February 2020. https://doi.org/10.1109/ICIoT48696.2020.9089614
23. Sichman, J.S., Demazeau, Y., Boissier, O.: When can knowledge-based systems be called agents. In: Simpósio Brasileiro de Inteligência Artificial, vol. 9, pp. 172–185. SBC, Rio de Janeiro (1992)

24. Tikhomirov, S.: Ethereum: state of knowledge and research perspectives. In: Imine, A., Fernandez, J.M., Marion, J.-Y., Logrippo, L., Garcia-Alfaro, J. (eds.) FPS 2017. LNCS, vol. 10723, pp. 206–221. Springer, Cham (2018). https://doi.org/10.1007/978-3-319-75650-9_14
25. Wooldridge, M.J.: Reasoning about Rational Agents. MIT Press, Cambridge (2000)

Parking Problem with Multiple Gates

Francesco Noviello, Munyque Mittelmann$^{(\boxtimes)}$, Aniello Murano,
and Silvia Stranieri

University of Naples Federico II, Naples, Italy
francesco.noviello@studenti.unina.it,
{munyque.mittelmann,aniello.murano,silvia.stranieri}@unina.it

Abstract. This work focuses on investigating parking problems with
time constraints using a game-theoretic approach, specifically in a multi-
gate scenario. The cars are treated as agents in a multi-player game where
they compete for parking spots at entry gates that have no limit. We propose a priority-based algorithm for allocating parking spaces to address
the problem. This algorithm guarantees a Nash equilibrium solution in
quadratic time, which depends on the number of cars rather than on
the number of gates. Additionally, we compare the performance of the
proposed algorithm to a Greedy allocation method. The experimental
results indicate the effectiveness of the proposed algorithm. Overall, the
study highlights the potential of game-theoretic approaches for solving
parking problems.

Keywords: Resource Allocation · Multi-Agent Systems · Nash
Equilibrium · Smart Parking

1 Introduction

The parking process is one of the serious social problems that daily involves
our cities, where the demand for parking spaces often exceeds the available
supply [14]. In this process, drivers compete against each other in order to
get a parking slot, and parking problems in cities and urban areas are becoming increasingly important and have been one of the most discussed topics by
both the general public and professionals. The difference between parking supply
and demand has been considered the main reason for metropolis parking problems, and lacking it shows close relation with traffic congestion, traffic accidents,
and environmental pollution. Although an efficient parking system can improve
urban transportation, the city environment, and the quality of life for citizens,
the problem is often overlooked in urban planning and transportation.

There are many causes for the deficit of available parking slots w.r.t. the
demand, including the high activity concentration with a high rate of cars in
the same area (such as commercial, medical, and governmental buildings) or
miscalculation of parking demand expected. Conventionally, in urban planning,
parking problems are solved with solutions based on different ideas, such as
planning solutions, in which the number of parking spaces is calculated by urban

P. Mathieu et al. (Eds.): PAAMS 2023, LNAI 13955, pp. 213–224, 2023.
https://doi.org/10.1007/978-3-031-37616-0_18

planners, or managed parks shared by buildings. Therefore, with the growth of Artificial Intelligence applications to automotive and the increased request for smart solutions to park, this problem is the inspiration for this work. In particular, we investigate the multi-gate parking problem with time constraints using a game-theoretic approach.

Related Work. The literature on smart parking solutions is extensive and varied. In [20], we provide a large survey on smart parking modeling, solutions, and technologies as well as identify challenges and open issues. Algorithmic solutions have been also proposed in the VANET research field, see for example [5–8,30–33]. Less common is the use of game-theoretic approaches to address the parking problem. An exception is [18], which is probably the closest to us, indeed we also propose a parking solution based on the Nash equilibrium. However, differently from us, they provide a numerical solution (rather than an algorithm or a tool), and, more importantly, they consider a scenario with both private and public parking slots, and the drivers' payoffs strongly rely on such a topology. Smart parking mechanisms based on a multi-agent game setting have been also proposed in the literature. In [22], drivers' behavior is simulated by modeling the environment on the basis of cellular automata. In [9] the model is based on the interaction between the user (driver) and the administrator, but focusing more on the architecture rather than the model setting and the strategic reasoning. Similarly, [15] provides an E-parking system, based on multi-agent systems aimed to optimize several users' preferences. In [28], the authors manage the parking problem with a cooperative multi-agent system, by relying on a priority mechanism. In [29], the authors also focus on an equilibrium notion, but they study the Rosenthal equilibrium rather than the Nash one, which describes a probabilistic choice model. Finally, [21] also considers the concept of Nash equilibrium applied to cars, but it is used to talk about traffic rather than parking.

Also related to our research are the problems of multi-agent resource allocation, which is a central matter when considering the distribution of resources amongst agents that can influence the choice of allocation [13]. In particular, the sequential allocation mechanism is a solution widely studied in the literature [3,4,10,16,17,19] and has been considered in several real-life applications (for instance, to organize draft systems [11] and to allocate courses to students [12]). In this work, we propose a solution for the multi-gate parking problem based on the sequential allocation mechanism. We take advantage of the particularities of the setting (e.g. the time constraints and the agents' priorities) to provide an algorithm that finds a Nash equilibrium on quadratic time.

In [26], the parking problem is analyzed as a competitive multiplayer game, where each car is an interacting agent with the goal of finding an available slot that meets its own constraints, the goal of the parking problem is to park as many cars as possible while satisfying their requirements, such as parking in bounded time, respecting one's resilience, and obtains a Nash Equilibrium for the game. But this work studies a scenario with one gate and proposes a solution for this case, not considering that parking areas (e.g., for hospitals, offices, and malls) have more gates than one. Thus, the multi-gate setting has not been considered.

Our work is also related to the literature on multi-agent resource allocation and sequential mechanisms. Allocation problems are a central matter in MAS in which resources need to be distributed amongst several agents, who may also influence the choice of allocation [13].

Our Contribution. This study builds upon the work [26], by extending it to the multi-gate scenario. We employ a game-theoretic approach to model the multi-agent parking problem, which enables the analysis of strategic solutions, as demonstrated through the identification of Nash equilibrium. We then propose an algorithm based on agent resilience that can identify a Nash Equilibrium for parking slot allocation in quadratic time, which depends only on the number of cars and not on the number of gates. The performance of the algorithm is compared to a Greedy solution, and the results show that the Nash algorithm satisfies a higher number of parking requests and leads to higher social welfare, indicating greater agent satisfaction. Specifically, the Nash-based algorithm out-performs the Greedy solution when the number of cars is equal to the number of parking slots (in this study, 20000). Therefore, we conclude that the proposed algorithm is preferable for accommodating agents' demands.

Outline. We start by formally introducing the parking problem in Sect. 2. In Sect. 3, we propose an algorithm for prioritized multi-agent parking selection and analyze it in terms of complexity and a game theoretic solution concept. In Sect. 4 we present experimental results. Section 5 concludes the paper.

2 Parking Problem

We begin this section by presenting the Parking Game Structure model, PGS for short, which forms the foundation for defining and examining our suggested method to solve the parking issue. Formally the Parking Game Structure is defined as follows:

Definition 1. *The Parking Game Structure (PGS) is a tuple* $\mathcal{G} = (G, Agt, S, F, T, R)$, *where:*

- $G = \{g_1, g_2, ..., g_n\}$ *is set of gates;*
- $Agt = \{Agt_k\}_{k \in G}$, *where* $Agt_k = \{a_1, a_2, ..., a_{l_k}\}$ *be the set of agents at the gate* $k \in G$ *(i.e., the* cars *waiting for parking at* k), *with* $\bigcap_{i=1}^{n} A_i = \emptyset$. *We let* $l_k = |Agt_k|$ *be the number of cars at the gate* k; $l_k = |Agt_k|$ *be the number of cars at the gate* k;
- $S = \{s_1, s_2, ..., s_m\}$ *is the set of parking slots;*
- $F = \{F_k\}_{k \in G}$, *where* $F_k = (f_1, f_2, ..., f_{l_k})$ *is the list of* resilience *values for the agents in* Agt_k, *with* $f_i \in [0, 1]$ *for each* $i \in Agt_k$;
- $T = \{T_k\}_{k \in G}$, *where* $T_k = (t_1, t_2, ..., t_{l_k})$ *is the list of* time limits *for the agents in* Agt_k, *where* $t_i \in \mathbb{N}$ *represents the time the agent* i *has available for parking starting from gate* g_k;

– $R = \{R_k\}_{k \in G}$, where $R_k = (r_1, r_2, ..., r_m)$ is the list of reaching-times for the gate k, where $r_i \in \mathbb{N}$ represents the time needed to reach the parking slot i from gate g_k, for each $i \in S$.

The resilience values for the agents have a twofold usage: first, they create an ordering system among the agents, which is essential in determining their prioritization; second, these indexes significantly impact the final preemption order, which can have a significant effect on the overall outcome. The intuition is that the higher the resilience the less the priority for the agent.

For the purpose of simplicity, we make the assumption that all the resilience indexes are unique, meaning $f_i \neq f_j, \forall 1 \leq i < j \leq n$. The indexes in the set F can either be manually set or automatically determined. In the case of agents, the resilience index represents their capability. Therefore, a lower index value indicates a higher priority.

A *strategy* for an agent involves choosing an appropriate slot. A *strategy profile* is a set of n strategies, one for each player, represented as an n-tuple $\bar{s} = (\bar{s}_1, ..., \bar{s}_n)$. It is important to note that it is possible for multiple players to choose the same strategy. Next, the *costs associated* with the strategy profile $\bar{s}$ will be defined as a tuple of costs, denoted as $\bar{c} = (\bar{c}_1, ..., \bar{c}_n)$. We let $B > 0$ be a constant value denoting the highest cost any agent may have for parking.

Definition 2. *Let $a_i \in Agt$ be an agent and $\bar{s} = (\bar{s}_1, ..., \bar{s}_n)$ be a strategy profile. The cost $\bar{c} = (\bar{c}_1, ..., \bar{c}_n)$ is such that:*

$$\bar{c}_i(\bar{s}) = \begin{cases} f_i(t_i - r_i); & \text{if } (i)(t_i - r_i) \geq 0 \ \& \\ \quad (ii)(\nexists k \neq i : f_k < f_i \land s_k = s_i \land (t_k - r_k) \geq 0) \\ B, & \text{otherwise} \end{cases}$$

The cost value c_i is considered finite if agent a_i has sufficient time to reach the parking slot s_i and the slot has not been occupied by another agent a_k with lower resilience ($f_k < f_i$). In this case, the finite value of c_i reflects the amount of time remaining for the agent after reaching the assigned slot, relative to the total amount of time available to him. On the other hand, if the cost value is assigned as highest, B, it represents the worst outcome for agent a_i, meaning that they were unable to park at slot s_i. The utility of agent i for the strategy profile $\bar{s}$ is

$$u_i(\bar{s}) = B - \bar{c}_i(\bar{s})$$

That is, $u_i(\bar{s})$ is the difference between the highest cost B and her actual cost c_i given the strategies $\bar{s}$. Finally, the *social welfare* is the sum of utilities of among all agents in the system.

A strategy profile s is a Nash Equilibrium [27] if for all players i and each alternate strategy s'_i, we have that

$$u_i(s_i, s_{-i}) \geq u_i(s'_i, s_{-i})$$

In other words, no player i can change his chosen strategy from s_i to s'_i and thereby improve his utility, assuming that all other players stick the strategies they have chosen in s. Observe that such a solution is self-enforcing in the sense that once the players are playing such a solution, it is in every player's best interest to stick to his or her strategy.

Then, the total cost, denoted as π, of a strategy $\bar{s}$ is defined as the sum of all the cost values in the tuple $\bar{c}$, that is $\pi(\bar{s}) = \sum_{i \in} c_i$.

Example 1. Let us now consider an example to illustrate the concepts and then formally introduce the PGS. In Fig. 1, we consider a parking lot with 9 available slots, placed at various places in the park, and 9 cars looking to park, where t_i indicate agent i's available time to park, f_i indicates her resilience, and the values on slots indicate the reaching-time. For simplicity of the example, we assume all slots have the same reaching time from all gates.

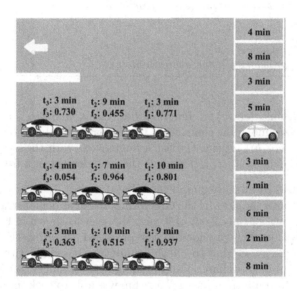

Fig. 1. Parking game with 3 gates, 9 cars waiting to park, and 9 available slots

3   Nash-Based Parking Selection

We now describe the proposed algorithm for the parking slot selection game. Algorithm 1, called *nash*, first creates an ordered list of cars by iterating on each gate, appending in a local list *priorityQueue* the highest priority car of each gate. Then, it calls the assign algorithm, Algorithm 2, to be used on this ordered list.

This works by selecting the highest priority car, the first in the list, setting the outcome as B and, for each available slot evaluating the payoff with $c(\cdot)$, which evaluates cost according to Definition 2.

If the slot assignment must meet the cars' time restriction, the outcome value is updated and set as the best-computed cost, and the slot with the best result is assigned to the car. Once assigned, the slot is removed from the set of available ones.

Algorithm 1. *nash(carsQueue, availableSlots)*

Input: a vector of lists of cars *carsQueue*, a list of slots *availableSlots*
Output: a list of strategies (the strategic profile) *strategy*

1: **repeat**
2:　　*prirorityQueue* ← ∅
3:　　**for** i ← 1 to |*carsQueue*| **do**
4:　　　**if** *carsQueue*[i] ≠ ∅ **then**
5:　　　　*car* ← *priorityCar(carsQueue*[i]*)*
6:　　　　*priorityQueue* ← *append(prirorityQueue, car)*
7:　　　　*carsQueue*[i] ← *remove(carsQueue*[i]*, car)*
8:　　　**end if**
9:　　**end for**
10: **until** *max(carsQueue)* = 0
11: **return** *assign(priorityQueue, availableSlots)*

In the algorithms, $max(v)$ is a function that returns $\max_{1\leq i\leq |v|}(|v[i]|)$, that is, the maximum size among the elements of the vector v. The function $append(a,b)$ (similarly $remove(a,b)$) returns the list a augmented with the element b (resp. obtained by removing b). $get(a,i)$ returns the i-th element of a list a.

Example 2. Let us recall the example introduced in Sect. 1. The cars would have been associated with the slots by the Greedy algorithm as demonstrated in Fig. 3, resulting in parking for only 7 out of 9 cars. However as shown in Fig. 3, parking for all cars in the queue is provided by the proposed algorithm (Fig. 2).

In this example we see that the Nash equilibrium-based algorithm performed better in terms of social welfare, despite taking slightly longer to execute. Additionally, the Nash equilibrium-based algorithm was able to park the same number of cars as the greedy algorithm, mitigating any potential disadvantages of the longer computation time.

3.1 Algorithm Analysis

First, we show that Algorithm 1 always finds a strategy profile that is Nash equilibrium.

Theorem 1. *Algorithm 1 computes the Nash equilibrium for the game.*

Proof. Assume by contradiction that $\bar{s} = (\bar{s}_1, .., \bar{s}_n)$ is the solution provided from our algorithm and it is not a Nash equilibrium. Next, for the definition of Nash equilibrium, there must be an agent, say agent a_i, whose strategy s_j is not optimal, with the strategies of the other players being fixed.

Hence, there exists another strategy s'_j for the agent a_i, such that the payoff of s'_j is better than the one for s_j (given the same strategies for the other players).

Algorithm 2. *assign(carQueue, availableSlots)*

Input: a vector of ready cars *carQueue*, a list of slots *availableSlots*
Output: a list of strategies (the strategic profile) *strategy*

1: *strategy* ← ∅
2: **while** *carQueue* ≠ ∅ and *availableSlots*¬∅ **do**
3:      *actualCar* ← *get(carQueue, 1)*
4:      *outcome* ← B
5:      *tmpSlot* ← *get(availableSlots, 1)*
6:      **for** *i* ← 1 to |*availableSlots*| **do**
7:          *slot* ← *get(availableSlots, i)*
8:          *po* ← *c(actualCar, slot)*
9:          **if** *po* ≥ 0 *and po* < *outcome* **then**
10:             *outcome* ← *po*.
11:             *tmpSlot* ← *slot*
12:         **end if**
13:         *strategy* ← *append(strategy, assignSlot(actualCar, tmpSlot))*
14:         *availableSlots* ← *remove(availableSlots, tmpSlot)*.
15:         *carQueue* ← *remove(carQueue, actualCar)*
16:     **end for**
17: **end while**
18: **return** *strategy*

But if this exists, then it would be found during execution of the algorithm and it would be chosen as the final strategy for agent a_i. But this contradicts the hypothesis that $\bar{s} = (\bar{s}_1, .., \bar{s}_n)$ is the solution provided, so this strategy is a Nash Equilibrium.

Now, let us evaluate the complexity of the algorithm.

Theorem 2. *The complexity of Algorithm 1 is quadratic with respect to the number of agents involved in the game, in the worst case.*

Proof. Let us take into account the worst possible scenario, by considering the case in which no vehicle obtains a parking slot. For an arbitrary algorithm A, we denote as $C(A)$ as its computational complexity. The proof proceeds by analysing the complexity of the most expensive operations, from the inner ones to the outer ones.

In *nash* function, Algorithm 1, the ordering of cars is performed for each gate, so many times as $|G|$, on total number of cars, $|Agt|$. Assuming that $|G| = g$ and $|Agt| = n$, we can deduce that $C(nash) = O(g) \times O(n) + C(assign) = O(g \times n) + C(assign)$. In *assign* function, Algorithm 2, the loop for assignment of slot for each car is repeated many times as $|S| \times |Agt|$. Assuming that $|S| = m$ and $|Agt| = n$ and that in worst case m and n are of the same order, we can deduce that $C(assign) = O(m) \times O(n) = O(n) \times O(n) = O(n^2)$.

Given that, $C(nash) = O(g \times n) + C(assign) = O(g \times n) + O(n^2) = O(n^2)$. In other words, the algorithm's performance is proportional to the square of the

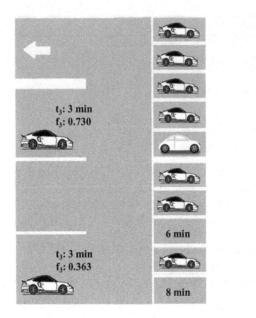
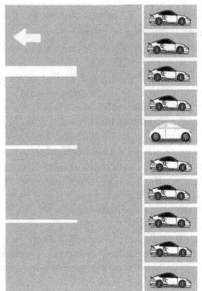

Fig. 2. Greedy solution for Example 1   **Fig. 3.** Nash solution for Example 1

input size (cars' number) and his growth factor will be influenced by the specific number of gates present but will maintain a quadratic nature.

4   Experimental Results

In the experiments, each setting was executed 100 times. The results presented here are the average between those executions. All experiments have been executed on an AMD Ryzen™ 7 5700U with Radeon™ Graphics CPU processor of 1,80 GHz, with 16 Gb RAM capacity.

The algorithm proposed in the previous section was compared with a greedy selection of parking slots. In the Greedy algorithm, the cars in each gate park according to their original order in the queue and select the first slot matching their time requirements. This approach disregards the specific requirements and constraints of the other parked vehicles. Thus, it may not lead to an optimal allocation of parking spaces.

The experiments considered 20000 slots, a fixed number of agents, and a variable number of gates ranging from 5 to 50 gates, as indicated on the x-axis of the graphs. In the graphs do not show Nash outperforming Greedy in terms of parked cars, except for case agents equal to slot, because this is consistent with previous results, which found that Nash results in either the same or more parked cars compared to Greedy. However, the Nash algorithm is shown to park cars in a shorter time interval compared to the Greedy algorithm, demonstrating that

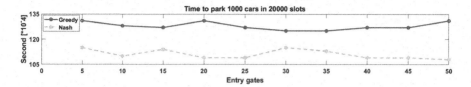

Fig. 4. Time to compute allocation for 1000 cars and 20000 slots

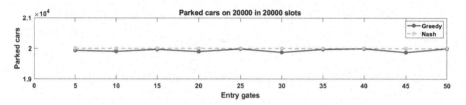

Fig. 5. Number of parked cars from an input of 20000 cars and 20000 slots

the algorithm is highly efficient. Nonetheless, as the number of cars increases, so does the required time.

In the following, a comparison of the performance of two methods for solving GPGs and PSGGs, respectively, is presented. The greedy solution and the algorithm are executed 100 times, with random values for time limits and resilience. The experiments considered 20000 slots, a fixed number of agents, and a variable number of gates ranging, as indicated on the x-axis of the graphs below. It should be noted that each graph is labeled to provide the necessary context and avoid any ambiguity in interpreting the data. The presented results in Fig. 4, indicate that the Nash approach outperforms the Greedy approach in terms of parking time, and takes hundreds of seconds to execute. Figure 5 presents the case in which the numbers are the same for cars and slots, we see that Nash algorithm outperforms the Greedy approach in terms of the number of successfully parked cars and of taken time, as in Fig. 6, because Nash takes less than half a second whereas Greedy takes 0,65–0,70 s. In Fig. 7, we can see that both algorithms park the same number of cars (that is, 20000 cars) in 1,5 s on the average time for Nash and in 2–2,5 s for Greedy. However, the Nash algorithm is shown to park cars in a shorter time interval compared to the Greedy algorithm, demonstrating that the algorithm is highly efficient.

In the same way as the number of parked cars was scored, we now display the results for social welfare, for the case where the number of agents and slots is equal to 20000. In Fig. 8, it can be seen that the Nash algorithm obtained higher social welfare than the Greedy one.

The results demonstrate that when there are one thousand cars intending to park in twenty thousand slots, the Nash algorithm takes hundreds of seconds to execute. However, with larger numbers of cars, the Nash algorithm is again better in terms of the taken time, managing to park more cars in less time, although in seconds or tens. This makes it clear that the Nash algorithm is preferable to the

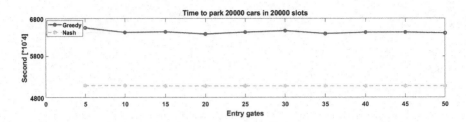

Fig. 6. Time to compute allocation for 20000 cars and 20000 slots

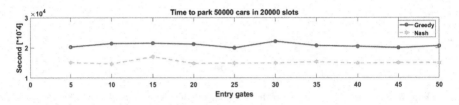

Fig. 7. Time to compute the allocation for 50000 cars and 20000 slots

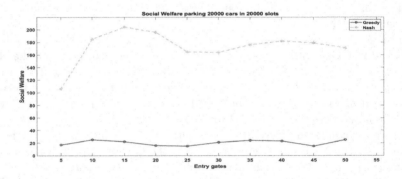

Fig. 8. Social Welfare obtained by the solution for 20000 cars and 20000 slots

Greedy algorithm, particularly in situations involving large numbers. Moreover, the time used in the configurations is proportional only to the total number of cars, not to the number of slots or gates present. In fact, as the number of gates varies, the time does not vary significantly.

5   Conclusion

This work presents a game-theoretic approach to formalize the multi-agent parking problem in a multi-gates scenario, allowing for the analysis of strategic solutions using Nash equilibrium. In particular, the proposed approach incorporates time constraints to represent slots' accessibility, and takes into account the agents' resilience in a competitive parking environment. We propose a multi-player game model that aims to solve the parking problem, and we develop an algorithm based on agent resilience and sequential allocation that aims to find a Nash equilibrium. This algorithm finds a Nash equilibrium for the allocation of parking slots in quadratic time and outperforms the Greedy solution in terms of the number of parking requests satisfied and social welfare. Moreover, the Nash algorithm is particularly effective when the number of cars is equal to the number of slots, making it preferable for accommodating agent demands, with performances significantly better. For future research, we aim to explore the use of formal methods and strategic reasoning to evaluate solutions for the parking problem [1,2,34]. Similar approaches have been considered in the context of synthesis and verification of allocation mechanisms [23–25].

Acknowledgments. This research is supported by the PRIN project RIPER (No. 20203FFYLK), the PNNR FAIR project, the InDAM project "Strategic Reasoning in Mechanism Design", and the EU ICT-48 2020 project TAILOR (No. 952215).

References

1. Aminof, B., Giacomo, G.D., Murano, A., Rubin, S.: Planning under LTL environment specifications. In: Benton, J., Lipovetzky, N., Onaindia, E., Smith, D.E., Srivastava, S. (eds.) Proceedings of the ICAPS, pp. 31–39. AAAI Press (2019)
2. Aminof, B., Murano, A., Rubin, S., Zuleger, F.: Verification of agent navigation in partially-known environments. Artif. Intell. **308**, 103724 (2022)
3. Aziz, H., Kalinowski, T., Walsh, T., Xia, L.: Welfare of sequential allocation mechanisms for indivisible goods. In: Proceedings of the ECAI 2016, pp. 787–794 (2016)
4. Aziz, H., Walsh, T., Xia, L.: Possible and necessary allocations via sequential mechanisms. In: Proceedings of the IJCAI 2015 (2015)
5. Balzano, W., Lapegna, M., Stranieri, S., Vitale, F.: Competitive-blockchain-based parking system with fairness constraints. Soft Comput. **26**(9), 4151–4162 (2022). https://doi.org/10.1007/s00500-022-06888-1
6. Balzano, W., Murano, A., Stranieri, S.: Logic-based clustering approach for management and improvement of VANETs. J. High Speed Netw. **23**(3), 225–236 (2017)
7. Balzano, W., Murano, A., Vitale, F.: V2V-EN - vehicle-2-vehicle elastic network. Procedia Comput. Sci. **98**, 497–502. Elsevier (2016)
8. Balzano, W., Stranieri, S.: ACOp: an algorithm based on ant colony optimization for parking slot detection. In: Proceedings of the AINA (2019)
9. Belkhala, S., Benhadou, S., Boukhdir, K., Medromi, H.: Smart parking architecture based on multi agent system. IJACSA **10**, 378–382 (2019)
10. Bouveret, S., Lang, J.: A general elicitation-free protocol for allocating indivisible goods. In: Proceedings of the IJCAI 2011 (2011)
11. Brams, S.J., Straffin Jr., P.D.: Prisoners' dilemma and professional sports drafts. Am. Math. Mon. **86**(2), 80–88 (1979)
12. Budish, E., Cantillon, E.: Strategic behavior in multi-unit assignment problems: theory and evidence from course allocations (2007)
13. Chevaleyre, Y., et al.: Issues in multiagent resource allocation. Informatica (Slovenia) **30**(1), 3–31 (2006)
14. Ibrahim, H.: Car parking problem in urban areas, causes and solutions. In: 1st International Conference on Towards a Better Quality of Life (2017)

15. Jioudi, B., Amari, A., Moutaouakkil, F., Medromi, H.: e-Parking: multi-agent smart parking platform for dynamic pricing and reservation sharing service. IJACSA **10**(11) (2019)
16. Kalinowski, T., Nardoytska, N., Walsh, T.: A social welfare optimal sequential allocation procedure. arXiv preprint arXiv:1304.5892 (2013)
17. Kalinowski, T., Narodytska, N., Walsh, T., Xia, L.: Strategic behavior when allocating indivisible goods sequentially. In: Proceedings of the AAAI 2013 (2013)
18. Kokolaki, E., Karaliopoulos, M., Stavrakakis, I.: On the efficiency of information-assisted search for parking space: a game-theoretic approach. In: IWSOS (2013)
19. Levine, L., Stange, K.E.: How to make the most of a shared meal: plan the last bite first. Am. Math. Mon. **119**(7), 550–565 (2012)
20. Lin, T., Rivano, H., Le Mouël, F.: A survey of smart parking solutions. IEEE Trans. ITS **18**(12), 3229–3253 (2017)
21. Lu, X.S., Guo, R.Y., Huang, H.J., Xu, X., Chen, J.: Equilibrium analysis of parking for integrated daily commuting. Res. Transp. Econ. (2021)
22. Małecki, K.: A computer simulation of traffic flow with on-street parking and drivers' behaviour based on cellular automata and a multi-agent system. J. Comput. Sci. **28**, 32–42 (2018)
23. Maubert, B., Mittelmann, M., Murano, A., Perrussel, L.: Strategic reasoning in automated mechanism design. In: Proceedings of the KR, pp. 487–496 (2021)
24. Mittelmann, M., Maubert, B., Murano, A., Perrussel, L.: Automated synthesis of mechanisms. In: Proceedings of the IJCAI, pp. 426–432. ijcai.org (2022)
25. Mittelmann, M., Maubert, B., Murano, A., Perrussel, L.: Formal verification of bayesian mechanisms. In: Proceedings of the AAAI. AAAI (2023)
26. Murano, A., Stranieri, S., Mittelmann, M.: Multi-agent parking problem with sequential allocation. In: Proceedings of the ICAART 2023 (2023)
27. Nisan, N., Roughgarden, T., Tardos, E., Vazirani, V.V.: Algorithmic Game Theory. Cambridge University Press, Cambridge (2007)
28. Okoso, A., Otaki, K., Nishi, T.: Multi-agent path finding with priority for cooperative automated valet parking. In: ITSC, pp. 2135–2140 (2019)
29. Pereda, M., Ozaita, J., Stavrakakis, I., Sanchez, A.: Competing for congestible goods: experimental evidence on parking choice. Sci. Rep. **10**(1) (2020)
30. Rad, F., Pazhokhzadeh, H., Parvin, H.: A smart hybrid system for parking space reservation in VANET (2017)
31. Safi, Q.G.K., Luo, S., Pan, L., Liu, W., Hussain, R., Bouk, S.H.: SVPS: cloud-based smart vehicle parking system over ubiquitous VANETs. Comput. Netw. **138**, 18–30 (2018)
32. Senapati, B.R., Khilar, P.M.: Automatic parking service through VANET: A convenience application. In: Das, H., Pattnaik, P.K., Rautaray, S.S., Li, K.-C. (eds.) Progress in Computing, Analytics and Networking. AISC, vol. 1119, pp. 151–159. Springer, Singapore (2020). https://doi.org/10.1007/978-981-15-2414-1_16
33. Stranieri, S.: An indoor smart parking algorithm based on fingerprinting. Futur. Internet **14**(6), 185 (2022)
34. Yazdanpanah, V., Stein, S., Gerding, E.H., et al.: Multiagent strategic reasoning in the IoV: a logic-based approach (2021)

UAV Swarm Control and Coordination Using Jason BDI Agents on Top of ROS

Iago Silvestre[1], Bruno de Lima[1], Pedro Henrique Dias[1],
Leandro Buss Becker[1,3(✉)], Jomi Fred Hübner[1,4], and Maiquel de Brito[2]

[1] Universidade Federal de Santa Catarina (UFSC), Florianópolis, Brazil
`das@contato.ufsc.br`
[2] Universidade Federal de Santa Catarina (UFSC), Blumenau, Brazil
[3] University of Manchester, Manchester, UK
`leandro.bussbecker@manchester.ac.uk`
[4] University of Bologna, Bologna, Italy

Abstract. This paper describes and evaluates the use of Jason BDI agents to make the high-level control and the coordination of a swarm of autonomous unmanned aerial vehicles (UAVs). The UAVs in the swarm work together searching and extinguishing fire spots in a simulated forest firefighting scenario. This problem was presented by the 2022 SARC–BARINET aerospace competition, which makes use of the ROS/Gazebo simulation environment. ROS is also used here to perform the low-level UAV's control. Our solution requires a minimum of 2 UAVs and can be easily scaled. We were able to successfully complete the given mission using up to 8 UAVs. Additional experiments devoted for performance-data collection were conducted using swarms with 4, 6, and 8 UAVs. Obtained results are presented and discussed along the paper.

Keywords: BDI agents · Coordination · UAV Swarm in firefighting

1 Introduction

Nowadays, the demand for autonomous systems is increasing [10]. Typical examples of such systems include, but are not limited to, self-driving cars, drones, vessels, and robots. According to [1,5], multi-agent systems (MAS) represent a suitable way to design autonomous systems. MAS can cope with autonomy, decentralization of decision and action, distribution of the decision process and resources usage, and effective cooperation.

This paper describes the use of MAS to control and coordinate a swarm of UAVs that aim to search and extinguish fire spots in the simulation scenario

This work was partially supported by the Brazilian funding agencies FAPESC, CAPES, and CNPq. Part of Leandro Buss Becker's work, while at Manchester, was supported by The Royal Academy of Engineering through its Chair in Emerging Technologies scheme. Jomi Hübner was supported by CNPq, grant 402711/2022-0.

P. Mathieu et al. (Eds.): PAAMS 2023, LNAI 13955, pp. 225–236, 2023.
https://doi.org/10.1007/978-3-031-37616-0_19

presented by the 2022 SARC–BARINET aerospace competition[1]. In the proposed solution, each UAV is controlled by an autonomous agent that executes on top of the Robot Operating System (ROS)[2], which is in charge of performing low-level control procedures. The agents cooperate with each other to search for and to extinguish fire spots. The agent implementation is done in Jason [2], a well-known Belief-Desire-Intention (BDI) programming language, inspired by AgentSpeak(L) [13].

As advantages of the proposed agent-based solution, it is possible to highlight the following: (1) the higher facility it offers for programming the UAVs when compared with traditional programming approaches based on imperative programming; (2) the high scalability of the solution, i.e., we can easily increase the number of UAVs to be used in a given mission; (3) the fact that the proposed solution is hardware-independent, i.e., it can be easily transferred to other types of aircraft, even with distinct flight characteristics, like VTOL ones, which by the way have much better flight performance in this type of application if comparing to the adopted quadcapter. Our team was awarded as one of the three best competitor's teams on the 2022 SARC–BARINET aerospace competition.

The reminder parts of this paper are organized as follows. Section 2 presents technical background information that are important for a clear understanding of the developed solution. Section 3 details the solution and the experiments conducted for performance evaluation. Section 4 addresses relevant related works. The conclusions and possible future work directions are presented in Sect. 5.

2   Technical Background

This section presents the technologies that are part of the solution presented in this paper, as follows:

- **Jason.** One of the best known approaches to the development of cognitive agents is the BDI (Beliefs-Desires-Intentions) architecture [3]. In the area of agent-oriented programming languages in particular, AgentSpeak [13] has been one of the most influential abstract languages based on the BDI architecture. In this architecture, the program is defined in terms of Beliefs, Desires and Intentions. Beliefs represent information about the environment (given by sensors) and other agents (given by communication). Desires are potential objectives of the agent (given by the developer or other agents, in our case). Intentions are desires the agent is actually pursuing and has one or multiple plans of actions on how to achieve them.
  Jason [2][3] is an interpreter for an extended version of AgentSpeak. It implements the operational semantics of that language, and provides a platform for the development of MAS. Some important characteristics of Jason in comparison with other BDI agent systems are that it is implemented in Java (thus multi-platform) and is available Open Source.

---

[1] https://sarc.center/sarc-barinet-aerospace-competition.
[2] https://www.ros.org/.
[3] http://jason.sf.net.

- **ROS/Gazebo.** In this project, the interface between the body of the agents and its reasoning system is provided by the Robot Operating System (ROS) [7]. ROS is a set of software libraries, tools, and conventions designed to simplify the development of robotic applications. Gazebo [6] is a 3D robot simulation environment that integrates with ROS. It allows developers to test and debug their robot software in a virtual environment before deploying it to the physical robot. ROS uses a messaging system to facilitate communication between different nodes (programs) in a robot system. Topics are a type of message-passing system where nodes can publish messages to a specific topic and subscribe to messages from that topic. This allows nodes to exchange information such as sensor data, motor commands, or other state information. On the other hand, services provide a way for nodes to request a specific action or response from another node. The service client sends a request to the service server, which processes the request and returns a response. Services are typically used for tasks that require a specific action to be performed, such as setting a parameter or requesting a diagnostic check.

- **Jason-ROS Interface.** The agents of our team are extensions of the default Jason agents. Such extension is provided by the *embedded-mas* framework[4]. It implements a Jason-ROS interface that integrates ROS resources to the processes of perception and action of the agents (Fig. 1). This integration is done through an interface that establishes communication between Jason agents and ROS through the WebSocket protocol, using rosbridge[5] as a transport layer. The agents are programmed through the usual high-level constructs provided by Jason, such as beliefs, goals, and plans. In each reasoning cycle, the perception system of the agent reads the topics of interest, whose values are converted into perceptions. These perceptions are gathered with the ones acquired through other means (e.g. non-ROS sensors). They are all handled by the belief updating process of the agent to possibly compose its belief base. The perception process is passive: the agent does not need to act to acquire perceptions from ROS topics. Rather, the reading of topics is managed by the agent execution machinery and the topic values are automatically converted to perceptions. After updating the beliefs, the practical reasoning process leads the agents to act towards their goal achievements, as usual in BDI agents. The actions triggered by the agents are converted either in topic writings or in service calls, depending on the application requirements. These actions are integrated to the repertory of actions of the agent. They are thus part of the agent implementation instead of being handled as actions triggered upon environmental elements. The actions run atomically as part of the reasoning cycle of the agent and can be configured to be blocking (the reasoning cycle moves on when ROS finishes the action processing) or non-blocking (the reasoning cycle moves on as soon as the action execution is delegated to ROS). A single agent can be linked to the topics and services

---

[4] http://github.com/embedded-mas/embedded-mas.
[5] http://wiki.ros.org/rosbridge_suite.

of as many ROS nodes as the application requires. The integration provided by the *embedded-mas* framework decouples the implementation of the agent behaviour (coded in Jason) from the implementation of the hardware control (implemented in the ROS nodes). The perception and action systems of the agent are linked to ROS topics and services via configurations that can be adjusted according to the ROS available resources. Thus, the same agent code can be linked to different ROS nodes by simply changing the mapping between perceptions and topics, as well as between actions and topics and services.

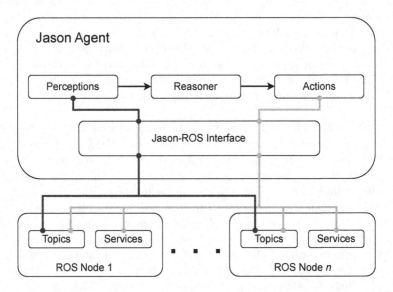

Fig. 1. Jason-ROS integration: the agent obtains perceptions from values read in ROS topics while its repertory of actions includes those performed though topic writings and service requests.

- **SARC-BARINET.** is a competition where teams present solutions towards solving a selected problem involving multiple UAVs. The theme of the 2022 edition consisted of fire detection and fighting in forests using multiple UAVs. The MRS UAV system[6] was used to spawn and control the drones used in the ROS-Gazebo simulation. This platform was developed by the Czech Technical University in Prague, with the main purpose of developing an UAV control and estimation system to support replicable research through realistic simulations. The MRS UAV System platform was developed using ROS Noetic, and was designed to be used for both indoors and outdoors applications and offers two feedback control designs, one for aggressive maneuvers and one for stable and smooth flight.

---

[6] https://github.com/ctu-mrs/mrs_uav_system.

Regarding the Flight Controller, the MRS UAV System developers chose to use the Pixhawk flight controller, more specifically the PX4, due to several reasons: both the hardware and software is open-source, the controller is sufficiently modular to use on a variety of multirotor platforms and Pixhawk supports both hardware- and software-in-the-loop simulations. Additionally the MRS UAV system uses the MAVROS package to provide a communication driver for the MAVLink communication protocol, used in situations where the drone is being remotely controlled.

3   The Proposed Solution

The application described in this paper regards multiple UAVs working collaboratively on searching and extinguishing fire spots in forests. It requires autonomy of each UAV, decentralization of decision and action, distribution of the decision process and resources usage, and effective cooperation. As previously addressed, all these features are provided by agents and Multi-Agent Systems. Thus, the proposed MAS solution is based on BDI agents.

In this application, BDI agents have "physical bodies" since some beliefs come from physical sensors, as well as some of the required actions are enabled by physical actuators. Thus, building the proposed solution involves (i) using BDI concepts to develop a distributed strategy for firefighting and (ii) integrating the perception and action processes of the agents with the sensors and actuators of the UAVs.

The development of the application involves the following points, described in the next sections: (i) developing the distributed strategy, (ii) implementing it with BDI agents, and (iii) making a performance evaluation.

3.1   Team Strategy

Each UAV is controlled by a BDI agent that has information about the state of the environment (the forest, trees, fire spots, other agents, etc.) and about the application (e.g., plans to follow a trajectory, join other agents, wandering). The agents coordinate with each other to perform the following tasks:

— **Task 1: Searching fire spots.** The area is divided among the agents and each agent is responsible to verify the existence of fire there. For n agents, the scenario is divided in n equally sized areas as shown in Fig. 2a. Inside each area, the corresponding agent flies following a trajectory that covers all its area. In the example of Fig. 2b, 8 waypoints are required for the area to be covered. The distance between the vertical arrows is defined by the range (on the ground) of the fire sensor. It is thus impacted by the altitude flight of the UAV. When the fire sensor detects an occurrence of fire, the agent acts to extinguish the fire. If the last waypoint is achieved, it finishes its mission.

— **Task 2: Extinguish fire.** When one agent finds a first spot of fire it asks other agents to come help him to extinguish that fire. We are assuming that usually a single UAV is not capable to extinguish some fire and m agents are

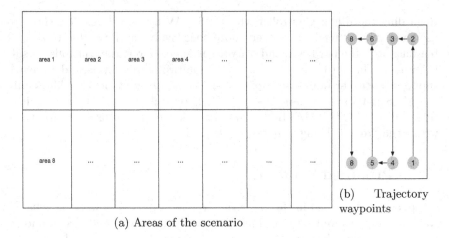

(a) Areas of the scenario

(b)   Trajectory waypoints

Fig. 2. Areas of the scenario and waypoints of the trajectory to find fire in each area

required for that task. m is computed based on the size of the area with fire and the capacity of extinguishing fire of each UAV. The agent who found the fire spot broadcasts the fire location to other agents asking for help. The $m - 1$ nearest UAVs answer the request. The agents can then work on the fire. After extinguishing the fire, all involved agents resume looking for fire spots. To elect the $m - 1$ agents, a decentralized protocol as follow is conceived:

1. the agent i who found the fire broadcasts a "fire found" message to others;
2. all agents who received the message answer with their current location if (i) they are executing task 1 and (ii) are not participating in other protocol like this; otherwise, they answer "not available";
3. the agent i waits answers for some time or until $n - 1$ answers were received;
4. based on its own location and locations received from others, agent i computes the $m - 1$ nearest UAVs, we named these UAVs "helpers";
5. agent i sends a message to helpers asking them to come;
6. agent i sends a message to others (non helpers) that they are dismissed.

— **Task 3: Finishing the mission.** When the agent has verified the entire area and extinguished all the fire, it broadcasts a message informing others that it has finished and flies to its landing location.

3.2   Design and Implementation of the Agents

The agent design is essentially based on two tasks: finding fire spots and extinguishing fire. The agent starts searching fire spots as described in Sect. 3.1. At any time, it can begin to extinguish fire found by itself or by others. In the former case, the agent changes its goal to handle that fire spot and performs the following steps: asking for help, forming a team, and extinguishing the fire (as shown in the initial lines of the code in Fig. 3). In the latter case, the agent is interrupted by a call from another agent who found a fire spot. The agent then changes its goal to help the other agent. This change depends on the other agent decision about the team allocated to that fire.

Figure 3 shows an excerpt of the AgentSpeak code of the agent. It implements part of the protocol to ask other agents to come and help to extinguish some fire. It shows the main BDI agent constructs integrated with the hardware to implement the agent UAVs. For example, `current_position(CX, CY, CZ)` is a belief that is continuously updated from values coming from the UAV sensor. While programming the agent, the developer can ignore all the details related to obtaining these values and can focus on using this belief to better decide about an action to perform.

The program also uses goals (prefixed by ! in the Jason language) to represent desired states of the environment and plans to represent strategies to achieve goals. For instance the goal `!help(N,X,Y)` can be achieved by four steps: suspend the current goal of following a trajectory; go to the fire location at (X,Y), extinguish fire there, and resume the following trajectory plan.[7] Using AgentSpeak makes also possible to implement UAVs that combine reactive and proactive behaviour. An example of reactive behaviour is the prompt reaction to the detection of fire (through the plan `+detected_fire`). This reaction itself has a proactive component as it adds a new goal `!handle_fire` to the agent. The UAV can also select different plans to achieve a goal depending on the circumstances, and can even change the chosen plan if the circumstances change, as in the case of the goal `!check_near`.

The agents acquire two perceptions from the environment by "listening" to two ROS topics. These perceptions are the current UAV position and the presence of fire in the spot the agent is currently inspecting. While the position is provided by the Gazebo simulator, the fire detection was implemented by our team and was deployed as an additional C++ ROS-node. It subscribes for the respective UAV camera, process its image and publishes the result into a topic that will be incorporated to the perception system of the agent. There is one different topic for each UAV, so that the agent must properly decode such messages, recalling that the agent code is the same for all UAVs. The repertory of actions of the agent are three, as follows. The action *goto*, used by the agent to move to another point (X, Y, Z), and the action *land*, used by the agent to land, are realized through the calling of ROS services. The action *drop*, used by the agent to drop anti-fire powder at the coordinates (X, Y), is realized through the writing in a ROS topic.

3.3   Application Scalability

The number of UAVs used in our solution can be easily scaled. This requires simply changing a few parameters, as follows.

---

[7] The full agent code is available for download at https://github.com/iagosilvestre/start-UFSC.

```
+detected_fire                        // whenever a fire spot is detected by me
  :  current_position(CX, CY, CZ)       // and I am in location Cx,Cy,Cz
     & .intend(follow_trajectory(CW))  // and I am currently finding fire
  <- !handle_fire(CX, CY).              // add new goal to handle that file


+!handle_file(CX, CY)  // when I acquire the goal to handle fire at CX, CY
  <- .suspend(follow_trajectory(CW));     // stops the finding intention
     .broadcast(tell, found_fire(N));                  // notify others
     !elect_helpers(CX,CY);     // add new goal to select-wait for helpers
     !extinguish_fire(CX, CY);        // add new goal to extinguish fire
     .resume(follow_trajectory(CW)).        // return to finding fire


+!help(N,X,Y)          // when I was elect to help agent N for fire at X,Y
  <- .suspend(follow_trajectory(CW));
     !goto_fire(X, Y);            // add new goal to go to the fire spot
     !extinguish_fire(X, Y);      // add new goal to extinguish the fire
     .resume(follow_trajectory(CW)).        // return to finding fire


+!goto_fire(X, Y)          // when I have the goal to go to the fire spot
  <- !check_near(X, Y, 50)./// continuously check whether I am at the spot


+!check_near(X, Y, Z) :  near(X, Y, Z)     // I am arrived to the fire spot
  <- .print("Arrived at ", X, Y, Z).


+!check_near(X, Y, Z)                       // I am going to the fire spot
  <- //execute an internal action to take the UAV to (X,Y,Z)
     defaultEmbeddedInternalAction("roscore1","goto", [X, Y, Z]);
     !check_near(X, Y, Z).


+found_fire(N)[source(A)] <- ...       // handle A ask to help with fire
+!follow_trajectory(CW)   <- ...       // plan to follow trajectories
+!elect_helpers(CX,CY)    <- ...       // plan to elect helpers
+!extinguish_fire(CX, CY) <- ...       // plab to extinguish fire at Cx, Cy
```

Fig. 3. AgentSpeak code excerpt from the firefighting application

Firstly, it is necessary to adjust the ROS/Gazebo launch script (*session.yml*), which is responsible for spawning each UAV, launching its UAV core program, and initializing its takeoff process. In the SARC-BARINET competition scenario there is no takeoff process included and, instead, the UAVs are activated during their drop from the KC-390 cargo aircraft. The ROS/Gazebo launch script consists of a *tmuxinator* script which contains a variety of windows responsible for various parts of the simulation, the windows that need to be altered in order to scale the simulation are the spawn, control and takeoff. In these parts of the script some lines need to be replicated for the added UAVs.

In regarding the multi-agent system (MAS), there are three files that need to be adjusted to scale the simulation. The first one is related with the project configuration for our MAS (*main.jcm*). It contains information about the amount and type of agents that will be part of a simulation run. Another file to be configured is the agent itself (*uav.asl*), which was partially reproduced in Fig. 3. It must be simply adjusted the belief representing the number of UAVs used in that specific run of the simulation (this can also be specified in the *main.jcm* project configuration file). Another aspect has to do with predefined rules used to compact the GPS (positioning) information provided by the ROS layer. There must be one rule defined for each UAV, and there is no problem on defining more rules then needed by the application, that is, one could define 24 rules (for 24 UAVs), but only using a fraction of that. Lastly it must be adjusted the part of the agent that performs the interface with ROS. In the *DemoEmbeddedAgentROS.java* file, all the ROS topics that will come from each UAV - to be further converted to beliefs - must be specified. Similarly to what was done with the rule, there is no problems on defining topic for more UAVs than used in a given simulation run. Such topics has to do with the UAV position and the UAV camera, in charge of the fire detection.

3.4 Experiments and Obtained Results

Experiments were performed in a workstation with an AMD Ryzen 5 3500x CPU with 6 cores at 3.60 GHz, 16 GiB of RAM memory, and the NVIDIA GeForce RTX 2060 Super graphics card. Linux Ubuntu 20.04 with ROS Noetic was used.

The developed implementation successfully accomplished the given mission using up to 8 UAVs. When using 10 UAVs or more it caused the ROS/Gazebo environment to crash at some point along the simulation.

The solution submitted for the SARC-BARINET competition used 6 UAVs. Performing the complete firefighting simulation with these 6 UAVs took 52 min of simulated time to complete. Increasing the number of UAVs to 8 reduced the simulated time to 43 min, an improvement of 21% when compared to the scenario with 6 UAVs. Reducing the number of UAVs to 4 caused the simulated time to increase to 1 h and 20 min, a 54% increase when compared to the scenario with 6 UAVs. A demonstration video using six (6) UAVs is let available.[8]

For performance-data collection, we executed 120 s simulation scripts. The *ps* command at 2 s intervals was used to log CPU utilization. As the simulation scripts are launched they spawn 21 processes related with ROS/Gazebo and one process related with the Jason agent. For the ROS/Gazebo processes, during the 6 UAVs simulation, the average CPU utilization was 295%, and this values remained constant over time. For the Jason process, the average CPU utilization was 28%. For Jason the CPU usage decreased slightly over time. Overall, Jason required 9.5% of the CPU portion used by ROS/Gazebo.

Analyzing the data from the 8 UAVs simulation, we could observe that our solution offered acceptable scalability in respect to performance. The average CPU utilization was fairly constant at 317.7%, slightly higher than the results obtained during the 6 UAVs simulation. For the Jason process, the average CPU utilization increased to 48.5%, and similarly to the 6 UAVs simulation, the Jason

---

[8] https://www.youtube.com/channel/UCuMtLsiR-Amuw9AizYQLCnw.

CPU usage decreased slightly over time. For this 8 UAVs scenario, Jason required 15.3% of the CPU portion used by ROS/Gazebo.

4 Related Works

Jason was already used for UAV's control and coordination in previous related works. For instance, in [8] it was demonstrated the used of Jason within an embedded computing platform for controlling both simulated and real quadcopters autonomous flights. In such work, Jason was communicating directly with the low-level control functions, a solution that should be seeing as being hardware-dependant. The work also presented an interesting analysis comparing agent-based versus imperative programming. Afterwards, in [15], Jason was used on top of ROS to control the same autonomous UAV. Therefore, the authors proposed a Jason/ROS integration mechanism [14]. Such work also addressed another interesting aspect related with the agent architecture, which has to do with adopting an active perception mechanism. This allowed specific perceptions to be actively gathered only when needed by the agent, saving computing resources for not doing such task indefinitely and unnecessarily.

Given that the integration between BDI agents and ROS is a topic of special interest here, additional related works are further addressed. Some of them use ROS resources to implement the data structures and algorithms required by a BDI implementation [9,12]. The behaviour of the agents is coded within ROS nodes, which also record and manage beliefs, desires, and intentions, as well as plan and execute actions. Closer to the approach adopted in the present work, some works propose to code the behaviour of the agent using agent-oriented programming languages, such as AgentSpeak [11], Jason [4,14], and GWEN-DOLEN [4]. These approaches, however, differ from the approach adopted in the present work in respect to how the agent execution system is linked to ROS. In such related works the connection between the agent execution system and ROS is managed by external interfaces, whereas in our approach it is part of the agent execution system. Besides, in [11] the perception and belief management are implemented in ROS, while in our work it is part of the agent architecture. The approach of [4] considers ROS as part of the environment in which the agent acts. In this case, the actions upon ROS are treated as actions upon elements external to the agents (*external actions*). In our approach, actions upon ROS are *internal actions* that compose the implementation of the agent and run atomically as part of its reasoning cycle. In the approach presented in [14], Jason agents have their execution system integrated with an *agent node*, which has topics to record perceptions to be handled and actions triggered by the agents. These topics are linked to the hardware via a ROS node named *bridge*, which can be configured according to the application hardware. While our approach also allows for this configuration, it does not rely on this kind of bridging nodes. The agent execution system is directly connected to the hardware nodes and can read topics to get perceptions, as well as write in topics and request services to perform actions.

5   Conclusions

Among the features of our solution, we would like to highlight the following:

1. hardware *decoupling*: the proposed software stack allow us the select different models of UAVs without huge impacts on the strategy development;
2. *agent based* design and implementation, which implies in autonomy for the UAVs and other features, as follows;
3. *decentralization* and distribution: we designed the team without a central point of control and thus each agent is able to perform its tasks alone;
4. *cooperation*: when required, agent can coordinate their plans to work together for solving complex tasks.

Providing the complete application solution, including a real UAV hardware integration, remains as a future work. Therefore one should attempt that we currently tested – and approved – our solution using an idealistic (unreal) simulation scenario, where meteorological conditions are always favorable and where there are no hardware failures.

Besides, the adopted collaboration strategy has space for further improvements. If considering other factor like battery capacity and amount of anti-fire powder available, more advanced optimization methods should come into play.

References

1. Boissier, O., Bordini, R.H., Hübner, J., Ricci, A.: Multi-agent Oriented Programming: Programming Multi-Agent Systems Using JaCaMo. MIT Press, Cambridge (2020). https://mitpress.mit.edu/books/multi-agent-oriented-programming
2. Bordini, R.H., Hübner, J.F., Wooldrige, M.: Programming Multi-Agent Systems in AgentSpeak using Jason. Wiley Series in Agent Technology, Wiley, Hoboken (2007). https://doi.org/10.1002/9780470061848, http://jason.sf.net/jBook
3. Bratman, M.E., Israel, D.J., Pollack, M.E.: Plans and resource-bounded practical reasoning. Comput. Intell. **4**, 349–355 (1988). https://doi.org/10.1111/j.1467-8640.1988.tb00284.x
4. Cardoso, R.C., Ferrando, A., Dennis, L.A., Fisher, M.: An interface for programming verifiable autonomous agents in ROS. In: Bassiliades, N., Chalkiadakis, G., de Jonge, D. (eds.) Multi-Agent Systems and Agreement Technologies. LNCS, pp. 191–205. Springer International Publishing, Cham (2020). https://doi.org/10.1007/978-3-030-66412-1_13
5. Dennis, L.A., Fisher, M.: Verifiable Autonomous Systems: Using Rational Agents to Provide Assurance about Decisions Made by Machines. Cambridge University Press, Cambridge (2023)
6. Koenig, N., Howard, A.: Design and use paradigms for gazebo, an open-source multi-robot simulator. In: 2004 IEEE/RSJ International Conference on Intelligent Robots and Systems, vol. 3, pp. 2149–2154 (2004). https://doi.org/10.1109/IROS.2004.1389727
7. Koubaa, A.: Robot Operating System (ROS): The Complete Reference, vol. 2, 1st edn. Springer, Cham (2017). https://doi.org/10.1007/978-3-319-54927-9

8. Menegol, M.S., Hübner, J.F., Becker, L.B.: Evaluation of multi-agent coordination on embedded systems. In: Demazeau, Y., An, B., Bajo, J., Fernández-Caballero, A. (eds.) PAAMS 2018. LNCS (LNAI), vol. 10978, pp. 212–223. Springer, Cham (2018). https://doi.org/10.1007/978-3-319-94580-4_17

9. Moro, D.D., Robol, M., Roveri, M., Giorgini, P.: Developing BDI-based robotic systems with ROS2. In: Dignum, F., Mathieu, P., Corchado, J.M., de la Prieta, F. (eds.) PAAMS 2022. LNCS, vol. 13616, pp. 100–111. Springer, Cham (2022)

10. Müller, M., Müller, T., Talkhestani, B.A., Marks, P., Jazdi, N., Weyrich, M.: Industrial autonomous systems: a survey on definitions, characteristics and abilities. Automatisierungstechnik **69**(1), 3–13 (2021). https://doi.org/10.1515/auto-2020-0131

11. Onyedinma, C., Gavigan, P., Esfandiari, B.: Toward campus mail delivery using BDI. J. Sens. Actuator Netw. **9**(4), 56 (2020). https://doi.org/10.3390/jsan9040056

12. Polydoros, A.S., Großmann, B., Rovida, F., Nalpantidis, L., Krüger, V.: Accurate and versatile automation of industrial kitting operations with SkiROS. In: Alboul, L., Damian, D., Aitken, J.M. (eds.) TAROS 2016. LNCS, pp. 255–268. Springer, Cham (2016). https://doi.org/10.1007/978-3-319-40379-3_26

13. Rao, A.S.: AgentSpeak(L): BDI agents speak out in a logical computable language. In: Van de Velde, W., Perram, J.W. (eds.) MAAMAW 1996. LNCS, vol. 1038, pp. 42–55. Springer, Heidelberg (1996). https://doi.org/10.1007/BFb0031845

14. Silva, G.R., Becker, L.B., Hübner, J.F.: Embedded architecture composed of cognitive agents and ROS for programming intelligent robots. IFAC-PapersOnLine **53**(2), 10000–10005 (2020). 21st IFAC World Congress

15. Silva, G.R., Hübner, J.F., Becker, L.B.: Active perception within bdi agents reasoning cycle. In: Proceedings of the 20th International Conference on Autonomous Agents and MultiAgent Systems, pp. 1218–1225. AAMAS 2021, International Foundation for Autonomous Agents and Multiagent Systems, Richland (2021)

Traffic Assignment Optimization Using Flow-Based Multi-maps

Alvaro Paricio-Garcia$^{(\boxtimes)}$ and Miguel A. Lopez-Carmona

Universidad de Alcala, Madrid, Spain
{alvaro.paricio,miguelangel.lopez}@uah.es
http://www.uah.es

Abstract. Traffic Assignment is a commonly used method for traffic modeling under congestion conditions. Many of the existing approaches find approximate solutions to the user equilibrium and the system optimum in terms of global travel time, though they can be computationally expensive. Previous works have shown that usage of Traffic-Weighted Multi-Maps (TWM) may help to reduce congestion in a wide range of scenarios. In this paper, we use TWM for traffic flow routing near the system optimum with an efficient computational performance. TWM is created using the k-shortest paths for the flows, and genetic algorithms are used to find the best TWM distribution for the flow paths to minimize global travel time (system optimum). The approach is illustrated with a non-trivial use case over a synthetic traffic network. Experimental results show that the TWM approach delivers efficient traffic routing, achieving low travel times under congestion conditions.

Keywords: Dynamic Traffic Assignment · Traffic Control · Intelligent Traffic Systems · Evolutionary Algorithms · Multimap Routing · Decision Making · Multi-agent systems

1 Introduction

Traffic congestion avoidance is a key concern of modern urban mobility systems. There is an important effort for finding effective solutions for congestion mitigation at reasonable costs. Congestion not only implies a huge waste of productive time, but also an enormous waste of energy and fuel, and is the cause of a considerable volume of gas emissions.

Traffic assignment methods are used to model transportation systems, abstracting them as a problem of demand and supply as pointed out in [8]. In traffic assignment, vehicle trips (demand) are assigned to the traffic network (supply) by strategically performing route choices. It is an NP-hard, convex problem (Traffic Assignment Problem) that requires approximate methods [12,13].

This work has been supported by Catedra Masmovil for Advanced Network Engineering and Digital Services (MANEDS) at Universidad de Alcala, CATEDRA2022-005.

Previous works [10, 11] have shown that it is possible to reduce travel times using an innovative technique called TWM (Traffic-Weighted Multi-Maps) based on complementary views (maps) of the traffic network, where each view has modified edge/link weights from the original network map. They are distributed to traffic groups to create differentiated routing. This technique may be applied to many use cases as multi-objective travel optimization, congestion reduction, incident management, per fleet differential routing, and some others.

This paper focuses on how to create TWM based on shortest-paths and how to assign them optimally for travel time minimization. GA algorithms are used for this purpose to create TWM distributions for the different traffic flows *(flow paths)*.

The paper compares different flow path routing alternatives, showing that it is possible to find optimal distributions of TWM for the traffic demand using the GA algorithm. This optimization method is highly effective in terms of computing resources, as optimal TWM distribution is achieved per flow path and not on a per vehicle or edge basis.

Our experiments are developed in a synthetic grid network with random link weights that connect three traffic sources with two receiving nodes. This scenario is more complex than others described in previous works [1, 4, 8] showing the feasibility of the approach.

The next section contains a review of state-of-art and previous works. Section 3 describes the TWM and flow path model, and the optimization strategies are discussed in Sect. 4. Section 5 describes the experimental use cases and results, and finally, Sect. 6 points out conclusions and future research lines.

2   Previous Works

There is a huge amount of literature on traffic assignment concepts and methods [1, 5, 6, 8]. Traffic assignment deals with the distribution of a given traffic demand in a network following ideal driver's behaviors. Static traffic assignment is based on Wardrop's first and second principles [14] that describe the situations of user equilibrium and system optimum. Dynamic traffic assignment (DTA) deals with the time-varying conditions of traffic, leading to dynamic user equilibrium (DUE). Also, stochastic models are used to model user's perception and uncertainty of travel time leading to stochastic user equilibrium (SUE). Generalized cost models are derived to deal with other aspects rather than travel time [13].

GA is a commonly used method for problem optimization when analytical approaches are not feasible, or their complexity is high. It has already been used to solve traffic assignment optimization problems as in [1]. Bazzan uses a GA to find the optimal distribution of the free-flow K-Shortest Paths to the vehicles. This method is applied to the synthetic network proposed by [8]. Considered optimization objectives are network total travel time and individual's mean travel time. The advantage of these methods is that computation times are low as there is no need to compute the k-shortest paths (KSP) iteratively.

However, the complexity of the proposed GA depends on the number of vehicles (demand) and assumes that vehicles are always going to follow the KSP delivered by the algorithm.

This previous model has been generalized to cope with multi-objective GA analysis as described in [4]. Both works do not detail how the routes are delivered to the vehicles, assuming that there is a centralized system, and assuming a complete driver's adherence to proposed routes, effectively using the recommended paths.

Our work relates to these previous studies in the flow-oriented and GA approaches used to solve the optimal process, though it has significant differences: a) instead of distributing KSP routes, it uses traffic-weighted multi-maps (TWM) that allow a feasible implementation for traffic routing having the benefits described in [10]; b) flow paths are defined as an abstraction of the O/D+KSP-based routing; c) flow paths determine a bonus-malus strategy encouraging the use of certain routes; d) there is not a central-server assumption calculating and delivering routes: they can be calculated and delivered by the vehicle or by a route server; e) the proposed GA algorithms are simpler as they do not use a per-vehicle optimization but a per flow path basis: only traffic demand matrices are required instead of knowing individual trips in advance; and last, f) a more complex scenario is analyzed with 6 flows and 64-nodes plus 244-edges synthetic network.

TWM was first introduced in [11] and a full model was presented in [10]. TWM raises the question of decoupling the physical traffic network and the view of the network, allowing it to distribute different views for different user needs. In that way, traffic users are grouped in fleets depending on different criteria and features, and each one receives a specific network map. A TWM is a collection of maps that differ in the edge/link weights which have been modified following a certain cost function. The standard cost function considers edge weight as the free-flow travel time. There can be other cost functions that consider specific conditions: type of traffic (buses, taxis, etc.), emission-free zones, restricted areas, stochastic distributions, time of the day, and others.

One of the key benefits of TWM is that it is a feasible proposal, compliant with most of the existing traffic management systems, as it consists of selective delivery of maps to the vehicles. These maps (TWM) can be used in server-side routing or vehicle-side routing.

TWM has been evaluated with microscopic simulation (using SUMO [2]) in synthetic networks [11] and in the complex real urban network such as the Alcala de Henares network discussed in [10]. Use cases described so far are congestion avoidance, dynamic incident management, and emergency corridor clearance.

3   TWM and Flow Path Model

This paper extends the model outlined in [11] and extended in [10] with the flow path concept and the necessary items to minimize total travel time finding an optimal TWM distribution.

The topological traffic representation of the urban network Θ is described by a graph of nodes η_n connected by unidirectional edges, each edge ϵ_e is formed by the set of links (lanes) that connects nodes η_i and η_j with a weight β_e.

Traffic is formed by G groups of vehicles $[\Omega_g]$ where vehicles are represented by their routing agents $[v_a^g]$. They generate a set of trips which are individually defined by the vehicle agent v_a^g, the starting timestamp t_a^0, the starting node O_a, the destination node D_a and the set of intermediate stops $[P_a^g]$.

Edge weights $[\beta_e]$ represent physical conditions and constraints in the network and are calculated with cost functions. They are the coefficients used by TWM for traffic routing. Edge weights are used in traffic assignment calculation together with edge load status. The lowest edge cost β_e^0 corresponds to the free-flow travel time and is used as a calculation reference.

We define a multi map TWM, denoted by $[\mu_m]$, as the collection of m-weighted views (maps) of the traffic network Θ, which can be used by the traffic groups that use it. Each map μ_m is an edge-weighted $[\beta_e]$ representation of the traffic network Θ (view m) which is calculated considering: a) network topology; b) traffic groups or fleets $[\Omega_g]$; c) time constraints for usage; and d) network traffic status data.

Traffic demand is usually expressed as an OD matrix which represents traffic flows $[f_i]$, where each flow f_i is formed by the individual trips moving from a traffic source O_i to a destination D_i. They can be physical network nodes, traffic area zones (TAZ) or traffic centroids.

Every routing agent v_a chooses a route r_a which is formed by the ordered sequence of nodes and connecting edges $[\epsilon_e]_a$ that link trip origin and destination (O_a, D_a). The routing agent uses the network map μ_m, the traffic status information given by edge traffic density $[\rho_e]$ defined in terms of edge capacity $[C_e]$ and edge occupation $[W_e]$, and a volume-delay function to calculate the edge costs [9]. The cost of the route r_a is the sum of the costs of the traversed links $C(r_a) = \sum c(\epsilon_e), \forall \epsilon_e \in r_a$ [5].

Given a set of F traffic flows $[f_i]_F$ a routing function is defined to obtain the k-shortest paths (routes, KSP) per flow $R_F^K = [(r_{11}, ..., r_{1K}), ..., (r_{F1}, ..., r_{FK})]$. These R^K routes are referred to as the *flow paths of the traffic demand*. These routes are calculated considering the "all-or-nothing" conditions [8] where network load status is ignored. We use the Dijkstra algorithm, but other strategies may be used for the flow path calculation such as A*, hyperpaths or disjoint-paths [3,7,9,15].

The R_F^K flow paths are then used to generate a set of weighted-maps TWM $[\mu_{i,k}]$ using a *"flow path to TWM"* function that takes as inputs: the default network map μ_0 (physical map), the flow paths R_F^K and a weight transformation function to define $[\beta_e]_{i,k}$. We use a linear scaling factor α applied to the edges included in each selected KSP $r_{i,k}$.

4   Flow Path Optimization Strategies

Multiple strategies are feasible to optimize total travel time using TWM maps distribution to the flow assignment problem. We introduce here: a) optimal TWM assignment per vehicle (OTV), b) optimal TWM assignment per flow with linear constraints (LCTV) and c) unconstrained optimal TWM assignment per flow (UCTV). There are other approaches not related to flow distribution such as calculating optimal TWM weights but are out of the scope of this work.

4.1   Optimal TWM Assignment per Vehicle (OTV)

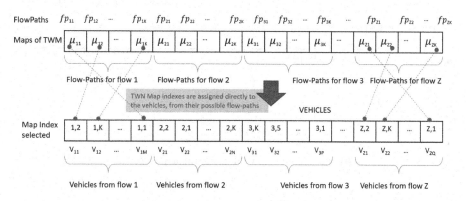

Fig. 1. Optimal TWM assignment per vehicle

This is a basic optimization problem like Bazzan's approach exposed in [1]. The problem to be optimized here is to deliver to each vehicle the best map assignment from the flow path based TWM $\mu_{i,n} \in TWM$ to minimize total travel time. Each vehicle belongs to a concrete flow f_i, so any of its associated flow paths R_i^K can be assigned. The optimization consists of assigning the best TWM map indexes $n \in [1...K]$ to apply the $\mu_{i,n}$ for each vehicle as shown in Fig. 1 so that the global travel time TTS is minimum. The GA function generates a chromosome $\aleph_1$ formed by the index of the corresponding μ_i map in the TWM.

Example: considering $K = 3$ shortest-paths and $[[v_{1,1}; v_{1,2}; v_{1,3}] ; [v_{2,1}; v_{2,2}]]$ vehicles which belong to the flows $[f_1; f_2]$, the returned $\aleph_1$ chromosome $\aleph = [3; 1; 2; 5; 7]$ indicates which maps indices μ_i will be distributed to and used by each vehicle.

This approach has important disadvantages: a) the number of variables to optimize depends on the traffic demand (number of vehicles), requiring enormous computing resources; b) flows and flow paths provide a macroscopic view of the traffic demand, and thus optimizing microscopic TWM assignment won't be accurate for traffic planning as it would depend on concrete trips. This use case is used as a reference to compare other optimization strategies.

4.2 Linear Constrained Optimal TWM Assignment per Flow (LCTV)

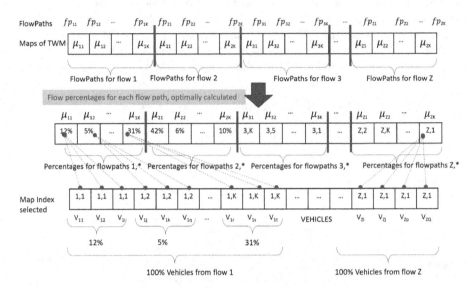

Fig. 2. Optimal TWM assignment per flow

It is possible to overcome the limitations found in our first algorithm if we consider map assignment per flow. We now consider that each flow f_i is subdivided into K flow paths f_{ik} which use their corresponding map $\mu_{i,n}$. The problem now is to distribute the vehicles to the sub-flows in an optimal way considering TTS. They are expressed as a percentage of traffic coming from flow f_i. Every vehicle will then receive the corresponding flow path map. Flow assignment is shown in Fig. 2.

The GA function generates a chromosome $\aleph_2$ formed by [0..1] number series representing each one the percentage of vehicles from each flow that is contained in each flow path. Constraints applied are a) normalization, each value must be in the [0..1] range; and b) traffic conservation, the sum of all the flow path percentages belonging to the same flow must be 1. $sum(\aleph(x_i)) = 1$ $K*(numFlows-1) < i < K*(numFlows)$. These constraints are applied directly in the GA fitness function.

Example: if the number of flows is 2 with $f_1 = 600, f_2 = 400$ vehicles, and $K = 3$ shortest-paths the chromosome will have size 6. If the GA function returns $\aleph_2 [(0.1; 0.2; 0.7); (0.5; 0.1; 0.4)]$, $\aleph_2$ that represents the traffic flow paths distribution. $[f_{1,1}; f_{1,2}; f_{1,3}; f_{2,1}; f_{2,2}; f_{2,3}] = [60; 120; 420; 200; 40; 160]$ using $TWM = [\mu_1; \mu_2; \mu_3; \mu_4; \mu_5; \mu_6]$ respectively.

4.3   Unconstrained Optimal TWM Assignment per Flow

It is possible to remove the linear constraints imposed in the GA fitness function, to apply them after the solver has ended. GA solving with constraints reduces the target population as it discards individuals who do not fit them. Unconstrained solver normalizes obtained values to [0..1], to calculate the corresponding TWM distribution together with traffic conservation calculation.

5   Case Studies

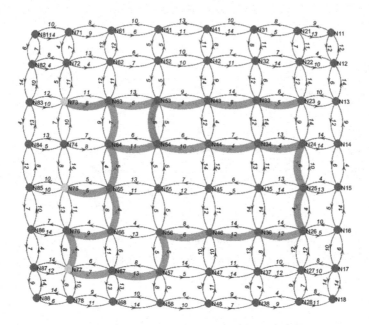

Fig. 3. Grid64 reference network with O/D flows and KSP-1.

We use a synthetic scenario over a grid network with unidirectional traffic flows that connect three traffic sources and two traffic sinks. Design criteria for the scenario are taken from the Ortuzar-Willumsen scenario described in [1,8], though we use a bigger network as the mentioned one is too small to generate a relevant diversity of KSP. TWM-based routing strategies and KSP variation are evaluated in terms of system optimum for total travel time (TTS).

Table 1. O/D Matrix

Source/Destination	N_{73}	N_{75}	N_{77}
N_{23}	1000	500	1000
N_{26}	500	1000	500

Table 2. Total travel time 30 flow paths and $\alpha = 0.5$ ($K = 5, F = 6$)

Free-Flow	Random	OTV	LCTV	UCTV
1355000	1131000	1099000	1117600	949980

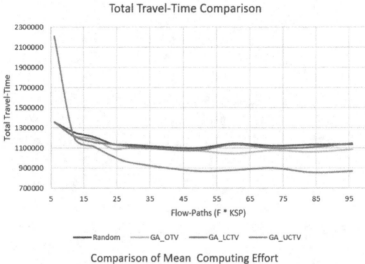

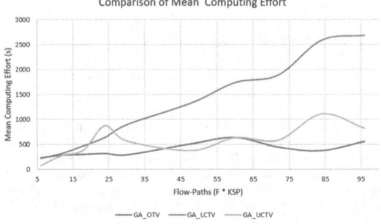

Fig. 4. TTS and computing effort for OTV, LCTV, and UCTV with different flow paths.

5.1 Scenario Description

The scenario selected for traffic simulations is an 8×8 grid (referred to GRID64) formed by bi-directional links with uniform random weights in the $[4, 12]$ range, as shown in Fig. 3. Nodes are named N_{xy} from their coordinates. The network contains three traffic sources (N_{73}, N_{75}, N_{77}) that generate traffic to the traffic sinks (N_{23}, N_{26}), having a total of 6 traffic flows with the distribution shown in Table 1.

5.2 Analysis of Routing Strategies

Experiments are developed using different number of k-shortest paths and consider the following routing strategies:

1. Free flow routing.
2. Flow path routing with randomly assigned TWM.
3. Flow path routing with OTV.
4. Flow path routing with LCTV.
5. Flow path routing with UCTV.

The flow path routing with randomly assigned TWM does no optimization at all but adds entropy to the traffic, thus making the vehicles select alternative routes without any other recommendation. It has an impact on total traveltime with invaluable cost. We use it to compare results with the optimization strategies.

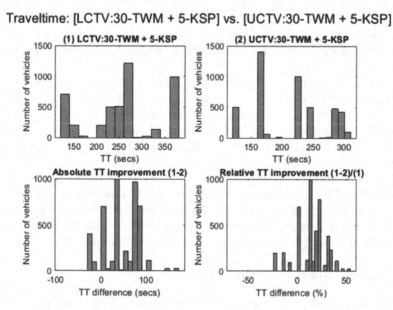

Fig. 5. Individual travel time using LCTV and UCTV.

All the experiments have been evaluated with Matlab R22b on a windows10 iCore7 with 16 Gb RAM. GA algorithms used Matlab's global optimization toolbox.

Table 2 shows results obtained for 5-KSP experiments which provide 30 flow paths for the $6\,\Omega/D$ flows considered and alpha-factor $\alpha = 0.5$. Each map $\mu_{f,k}$ has a weight reduction of $\alpha * \beta_{ij}$ in the weight edges of the corresponding KSP route $r_{f,k}$.

As it can be perceived, the usage of random TWM maps has an important effect (17%) on static traffic assignment as alternative routes are used. This cannot be considered a real scenario as the drivers will prefer the best routes based on their objective and subjective path evaluation. Usage of the optimal per-vehicle distribution (OTV) offers an improvement of (19%), but it is optimal property depends on knowing in advance real individual trips and full drivers' adherence, and under high traffic volumes it becomes computationally expensive. Thus, it cannot be considered as a feasible approach.

Flow path-oriented approaches provide more realistic results as they do not depend on individuals but on flow composition. Linear-Constrained per flow path optimization (LCTV) offers an improvement of 18% whilst unconstrained GA resolution provides an enhancement of 30%.

Figure 4 compares the different algorithms considering a different numbers of $KSP = \{1, 2, 3, 4, 5, 8, 10, 12, 14, 16\}$ leading to TWM of size $\{6, 12, 18, 24, 30, 48, 60, 72, 84, 96\}$ respectively. UCTV provides the best results, being more effective than individual optimization. The comparison also shows that the optimization converges quickly when the KSP number increases, leading to a flat behavior. Total travel time cannot be improved even if more flow paths and TWM are considered.

The pay-off for UCTV is computing time as can be observed in Fig. 4: OTV and LCTV hardly increase computing effort, whilst UCTV increases linearly with flow path number.

From the microscopic perspective Fig. 5 shows individual travel time histograms using LCTV and UCTV for map assignment (TWM = 30). The relative improvement of the travel time diagram clearly shows how usage of UCTV has a positive effect on individual travel time, considering the static VDF function on the loaded traffic network. Only a small amount of individuals are negatively affected.

The results obtained show that UCTV is a viable choice for TWM distribution attending a pre-known traffic demand. It provides a good trade-off between pseudo-optimal convergence and computing efforts. This algorithm is flow-oriented and thus variations in vehicle route choices may be compensated between them, having a minimal impact on the overall objective.

6   Conclusions and Future Works

The algorithms presented show how total travel time in a traffic network can be reduced using ad-hoc generated TWM maps that encourage selectively k-shortest paths usage for the traffic flows. Total travel time is evaluated using static traffic assignment. TWM maps are generated considering the best routes under free-flow conditions for each flow in the network. Travel time minimization can be achieved by creating an optimal TWM distribution to the flow vehicles, and several algorithms have been considered. Unconstrained GA provides the best balance between performance, effectiveness, and k-routes complexity.

The study offers many interesting future works: a) multi-objective optimization, considering not only TTS but also other indicators; b) flow paths can be split not only by k-shortest paths, but also by vehicle fleets considering them as sub-flows; c) creating of ad-hoc TWM for just-congested areas; and d) using not only alpha-scaling of KSP but also an optimization of the TWM weights. This last item would lead to a double-step algorithm where 1) optimal TWM is created considering whole traffic demand, and 2) optimal TWM distribution is done. Presented algorithms are fast and flexible, so dynamic traffic assignment may be easily implemented with the TWM and flow path approach.

References

1. Bazzan, A.L.C., Cagara, D., Scheuermann, B.: An evolutionary approach to traffic assignment. In: 2014 IEEE Symposium on Computational Intelligence in Vehicles and Transportation Systems, pp. 43–50. IEEE, Orlando (2014). https://doi.org/10.1109/CIVTS.2014.7009476
2. Behrisch, M., Bieker, L., Erdmann, J., Krajzewicz, D.: SUMO - simulation of urban mobility: an overview. In: Omerovic, S.U.o.O.A., Simoni, R.I.R.T.P.D.A., Bobashev, R.I.R.T.P.G. (eds.) SIMUL 2011, The Third International Conference on Advances in System Simulation, pp. 63–68. ThinkMind, Barcelona (2011)
3. Bell, M.G.H.: Hyperstar: a multi-path Astar algorithm for risk averse vehicle navigation. Transp. Res. Part B Methodological **43**, 97 (2009). https://doi.org/10.1016/j.trb.2008.05.010
4. Chira, C., Bazzan, A.L.C., Rossetti, R.J.F.: Multi-objective evolutionary traffic assignment. In: IEEE 18th International Conference on Intelligent Transportation Systems, ITSC 2015, Gran Canaria, Spain, 15–18 September 2015, pp. 1177–1182 (2015). https://doi.org/10.1109/ITSC.2015.194
5. Chiu, Y.C., et al.: Dynamic traffic assignment: A primer. E-Circular. Washington DC. USA, Transportation Research Board (2011)
6. Chow, J., Recker, W.: Informed Urban Transport Systems: Classic and Emerging Mobility Methods toward Smart Cities, 1st edn. Elsevier, Amsterdam (2018). https://doi.org/10.1016/C2016-0-02361-6
7. Reinhardt, L.B., Pisinger, D.: Multicriteria and multi-constrained non-additive shortest path problems. Comput. Oper. Res. **38**, 605 (2011). https://doi.org/10.1016/j.cor.2010.08.003
8. de Dios Ortúzar, J., Willumsen, L.G.: Modelling Transport, 3rd edn. Wiley, Hoboken (2001)
9. Pan, J., Sandu Popa, I., Zeitouni, K., Borcea, C.: Proactive vehicular traffic rerouting for lower travel time. Veh. Technol. IEEE Trans. IEEE **62**, 3551–3568 (2013). https://doi.org/10.1109/TVT.2013.2260422
10. Paricio, A., Lopez-Carmona, M.A.: Urban traffic routing using weighted multi-map strategies. IEEE Access IEEE **7**, 153086–153101 (2019). https://doi.org/10.1109/ACCESS.2019.2947699

11. Garcia, A.P., Lopez-Carmona, M.A.: Multimap routing for road traffic management. In: Demazeau, Y., Matson, E., Corchado, J., De la Prieta, F. (eds.) PAAMS 2019. LNCS, vol. 11523, pp. 188–199. Springer, Cham (2019). https://doi.org/10.1007/978-3-030-24209-1_16
12. Patriksson, M.: The Traffic Assignment Problem: Models and Methods. Dover Publications Inc, Mineola (2015)
13. Szeto, W., Wang, S.: Dynamic traffic assignment: model classifications and recent advances in travel choice principles. Cent. Eur. J. Eng. **2**, 1–18 (2011). https://doi.org/10.2478/s13531-011-0057-y
14. Wardrop, J., Whitehead, J.: Correspondence. some theoretical aspects of road traffic research. Proc. Inst. Civil Eng. ICE Virtual Libr. **1**, 767–768 (1952). https://doi.org/10.1680/ipeds.1952.11362
15. Ji, Z., Kim, Y.S., Chen, A.: Multi-objective alpha-reliable path finding in stochastic networks with correlated link costs: a simulation-based multi-objective genetic algorithm approach (SMOGA). Expert Syst. Appl. **38**, 1515 (2011)

A Monitoring Agent for Advancing Elderly Care Through Mobile Health Technology

Aaron Pico, Joaquin Taverner[✉], Emilio Vivancos, Aaron Raya,
Vicente Botti, and Ana Garcia-Fornes

Valencian Research Institute for Artificial Intelligence (VRAIN)
Universitat Politècnica de València, Valencia, Spain
{apicpas,joataap,vivancos,araylop,vbotti,agarcia}@upv.es

Abstract. Social isolation is a problem that affects more and more elderly people. Their limited social contact and low autonomy make it difficult for them to access the attention and care they need and deserve. This often results in a progressive deterioration of their physical and cognitive health. In this paper, we propose an agent model to monitor and provide assistance to socially isolated people. Our proposal has two main components: a mobile application, which is in charge of interaction with the user and data acquisition; and an intelligent agent model. The system uses different input devices to monitor the emotional state of the elderly person. This information is used by the agent to detect significant changes in the emotional state of the person. This information is very useful for the therapist to make a better diagnosis of the patient. Then, the agent will determine the best action to improve the emotional well-being of the elderly person. These actions may be aimed at generating personalized recommendations or triggering alerts to family members or social-healthcare staff. In addition, the information acquired by the application is used to provide diagnostic support to healthcare professionals and analyze progressive cognitive impairment.

Keywords: Emotion monitoring · affective agent · elderly care · social isolation

1 Introduction

The aging of the population is a major challenge faced by most western countries, with a decrease in birth rates and an increase in life expectancy contributing to a significant shift in the population pyramid [9]. This shift is causing economic, social, and health problems as older adults are more prone to suffer from chronic or complex diseases and disabilities that require continuous care [14]. As a result, the demand for health services and care is increasing, leading to overwhelmed social and health systems and making access to care more difficult and expensive [5]. Consequently, many elderly people are suffering from social isolation.

P. Mathieu et al. (Eds.): PAAMS 2023, LNAI 13955, pp. 249–259, 2023.
https://doi.org/10.1007/978-3-031-37616-0_21

Social isolation is considered one of the main risk factors for the health and physical condition of elderly people [11]. The lack of social contact has been linked to an increased risk of developing cognitive impairment, dementia, or Alzheimer's disease which can seriously affect the autonomy and emotional well-being of the elderly people [19]. Active monitoring by social and health professionals can be a possible approach to prevent these negative outcomes. However, due to the scarcity of resources, many elderly people do not receive the necessary care and support, leading to a deterioration in their quality of life and an increased burden on caregivers.

Artificial intelligence have used several approaches to address the problems associated with care-giving and social isolation, from exercise assistants to robot companions [1,7,16,17]. Unfortunately, when attempting to generalize the use of these solutions in domestic environments, numerous difficulties arise that make their widespread use unfeasible. Among these difficulties we can highlight the high cost of the systems, the level of intrusion and nuisance caused by the devices used, and the risks associated with privacy [3]. In this article, we propose a solution that has been designed to avoid these drawbacks to a large extent.

Our proposal has as main objectives to monitor the affective state of elderly persons, to propose them activities that improve their affective state and to facilitate the diagnosis and therapy prescribed by health professionals. But these objectives must be achieved by using inexpensive and extremely simple to use devices that do not alter the person's normal behavior guaranteeing his/her privacy.

The proposed conceptual framework has two main components: an application to monitor and interact with elderly people, and an agent to detect significant occasional affective state changes, and record information to detect progressive emotional impairment. The detection of occasional mood changes is used to alert in real time family members or social-healthcare professionals about the current emotional state of the elderly person so that social-healthcare professionals can verify and take appropriate measures. The long-term analysis of the recollected information provides an incredibly useful tool for health professionals in diagnostic of progressive impairments of emotional health. To facilitate the use of our system at home, the application can be installed on different devices, such as smartphones or tablets, which are easily accessible both in terms of cost and availability.

The rest of the paper is organized as follows. In Sect. 2 we analyze the most relevant computational proposals focused on improving problems related to social isolation in elderly people. Section 3 introduces the proposed framework for mood change detection and cognitive impairment monitoring. Finally, the main conclusions and future works are presented in Sect. 4.

2   Related Work

In recent years, the problem of social isolation has attracted the interest of the research community in the area of artificial intelligence [2,7,10]. The use of virtual assistants or conversational chatbots can provide assistance to elderly people by monitoring their health status, reminding them of their medication, and detecting falls or other medical emergencies [12,17]. In addition, these assistants can provide information and make recommendations focused on promoting physical activity, and offer mental health support. These technologies can also help to manage chronic diseases, reduce the need for hospitalization, and improve overall health outcomes [6,13]. For example, in [7], the use of a chatbot is proposed to address problems associated with social isolation. The results showed that people who used the chatbot have a high degree of satisfaction and even established social bonds with the chatbot. However, the authors also mention the importance of the proper development of these systems, as well as the challenges that remain open, since many participants showed their dissatisfaction when the chatbot generated texts that produced misunderstandings.

Another interesting proposal is found in [16], where the authors explore the potential of the most popular virtual assistants (e.g., Alexa, Siri, Google Assistant, or Cortana) to help elderly people suffering from social isolation to establish social links with their relatives. The results showed that these assistants covered a broad spectrum of social needs, such as email communication or online gaming. However, these systems lack other important functionalities when assisting elderly people, such as the personalization of recommendations to the specific needs of the individual or the monitoring of his/her emotional and health state. In this sense, the proposals made in the field of intelligent agents seem to be more feasible. For example, in [17], the E-Bot robot is proposed. This robot uses electrocardiograms to determine the health status of a person. The data is reported to doctors or caregivers through the Amazon AWS service.

Emotions have also been explored for the development of agents to provide assistance to elderly people. For example, the proposal made in [1], focuses on the development of a conversational agent model that provides emotional support to elderly people living in loneliness. The proposed model is based on active listening to the person and provides a response related to what the person has mentioned in order to improve his/her emotional state, but without applying emotional recognition techniques. Emotion recognition is a key factor in robots that assist people in social isolation. Recognizing emotions can help assistive systems to detect anomalous patterns and provide responses aimed at improving emotional well-being. In this sense, the work developed in [4], addresses the recognition of emotion through electroencephalogram to develop a robot whose behavior depends on the emotions recognized in the person. The robot is able to modify different parameters of its navigation to adapt the accompaniment to the privacy needs of the person, that is, the robot can approach or move away from the person dynamically depending on the person's emotional needs. However, the use of electrocardiogram for emotion recognition is very expensive, intrusive, and limits the person's behavior.

Regardless of the system used to recognize the person's emotional state, the method of representing the emotional state will greatly determine the reasoning capabilities of the intelligent agent. There are two different approaches widely used to represent emotions in computational models: the categorical and dimensional representations. In categorical representations, emotions are represented as a finite set of emotion labels. The best known categorical model is Ekman's basic emotion model [8], which uses six emotion labels: happiness, surprise, anger, fear, disgust, and sadness. In contrast, dimensional models represent emotions by using several dimensions, like the pleasure, arousal, or dominance. One of the best known dimensional model is the Circumplex Model of Affect [18], where emotions are described by its pleasure and arousal components (see Fig. 1).

3   Proposal

In this section we present a new agent model for monitoring and help elderly people suffering from social isolation. The agent monitors the emotional state of the elderly person, detects significant changes in his/her emotional state, and tracks the affective state to facilitate cognitive impairment detection. The detection of significant emotional changes allows the agent to recommend an activity focused on improving the emotional state or, if necessary, to alert family members or social-healthcare staff. To achieve these goals, our model consists of two main components: a mobile application in charge of communicating with the user, and an intelligent agent that, through a reasoning process, monitors the user's emotional state, suggests activities to the elderly person, analyzes long-term emotional changes, and alerts family members or social-healthcare staff in case of need. Figure 2 shows the conceptual model of our proposal.

3.1   Emotion Representation

In our approach, emotions are represented in a dimensional model based on pleasure and arousal. Figure 1 shows an example of the emotional representation used in this work. In this model, each piece of emotional information coming from different inputs devices is expressed as a vector $\vec{e}$ composed of the coordinates of pleasure and arousal. This way, the direction of the vector $\vec{e}$ represents the emotion, and the module of the vector represents the intensity. We have defined four regions of intensity for the emotions following a similar approach to the one proposed in [20]: neutral, weak, medium, and strong. With this dimensional representation, the emotional data provided by the different methods of data acquisition can be represented in a common dimensional space to identify changes and anomalies as well as to monitor progressive emotional impairment.

3.2   Mobile App Design

The proposed mobile application is in charge of four main functions. The first function of the app is to act as an interface with the persons to facilitate their cooperation in identifying the activity they are carrying out, as well as to facilitate the self-assessment of their affective state. For this purpose, the application has an *Activity control* module, in charge of monitoring the interactions that

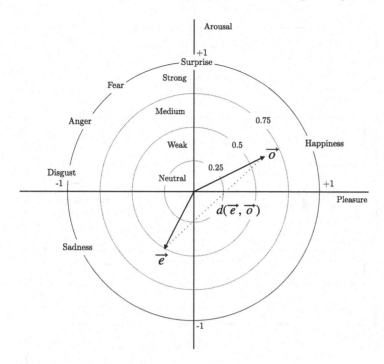

Fig. 1. Internal representation for emotions

the user performs with the application. The second function of the app is to provide support for the acquisition of affective information from different capture devices. A module called *Image processing* processes the images captured by a camera while a module called *Signal processing* processes the information coming from the other physiological capture devices. The third function of the app consists in filtering and merging all data obtained from the different capture devices. A *Face emotion recognition* module detects the facial emotions recognized in the captured images while a *Data fusion and emotion representation* module determines the emotion detected using the captured data and provides the emotion components using the dimensional model of pleasure and arousal. Finally, the app also provides a *Database management system* to store the mood and activities carried out by the person over time.

Activity monitoring is a key aspect in this type of systems. When measuring emotional state, it is necessary to contextualize the state with information related to the activity being performed by the person, since physiological measurements differ depending on the activity. For example, heart rate can have a significant difference when comparing activities such as watching TV and playing sports. Contextualizing the signals acquired by the different devices with the activity being performed allows a greater fine-tuning and personalization of the agent's parameters to make better recommendations. However, recognizing the context of the activity being performed by a user is a challenge in itself. We

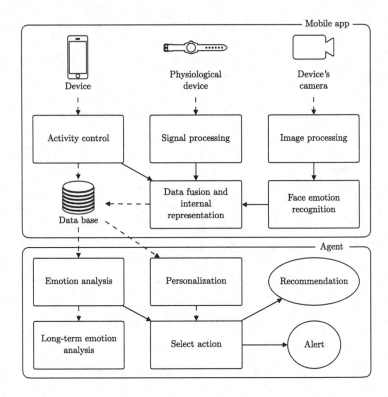

Fig. 2. Conceptual model.

have discarded some automation solutions to detect the activity that the person is performing because their high economic cost and great intrusion in the person's environment. For example, we have discarded the use of image analysis, to infer the activity that the person is performing because, this would require the installation of multiple cameras in the home and an artificial intelligence system to automatically infer the activity performed by the person. This would involve a high level of privacy risk and intrusion into personal life, and a substantial increase in the cost of the system. Instead of this, our application will ask for the collaboration of the person who, by selecting an icon representative of the activity, will indicate the activity that he/she is going to perform. For this purpose, in the *Activity control* module, we have defined a list of possible activities A. In our model, each activity $a \in A$ is represented by a tuple $\langle l, \delta, \Delta p, \Delta a, T \rangle$ where l represents the label of the activity, δ is a value between $[-1, 1]$ that indicates the degree of preference that the person has for the activity a, Δp and Δa represents the average increase in pleasure and arousal respectively, that activity a produces, and finally, T is a list of n tuples $\langle \vec{e}_0, t_0, \vec{e}_f, t_f \rangle$ where $\vec{e}_0$ and $\vec{e}_f$ are the emotion vectors composed by the pleasure and arousal coordinates representing the emotional estate at the beginning of the activity a at time t_0 and at the end of the activity a at time t_f, respectively. The list of n tuples T is used to update the values of Δp and Δa associated with one activity a as:

$$\Delta p = \frac{1}{n} \sum_{i=1}^{n} e_{f,i}^{p} - e_{0,i}^{p} \tag{1}$$

$$\Delta a = \frac{1}{n} \sum_{i=1}^{n} e_{f,i}^{a} - e_{0,i}^{a} \tag{2}$$

where n is the number of tuples in the list T, e_i^p and e_i^a represents the pleasure and arousal components of the ith emotional state $\vec{e}$, respectively.

To facilitate the usability of this application by elderly people, the icons have been designed with a large size (see Fig. 3a). For capturing the emotional state, we propose a multi-modal approach. First, while the application is open, the device's camera is used to capture the emotion through an analysis of the facial expression. For this purpose, the *Image processing* module performs a pre-processing of the image, that is executed in the device itself, consisting of the detection of facial landmarks. The landmarks are submitted anonymously to a web service that estimates the most probable pleasure and arousal values associated to the submitted facial expressions. This process is represented by the *Face emotion recognition* module in Fig. 2.

Secondly, the application allows the use of different peripheral physiological measurement devices to measure pulse, tension, or skin conductance. These measurements can be carried out by inexpensive devices that are easily carried by the person without causing discomfort or altering their behaviour. For example, using a smart band, the person's pulse can be measured. The different physiological signals captured by these devices are filtered and merged by the *Signal processing* module, which returns the detected emotional state represented by its pleasure and arousal dimensions. In this way, it is possible to have a real-time monitoring of some physiological parameters of the person which can be used to estimate the changes in his/her emotional state. This analysis facilitates the detection of anomalies in the emotional state as explained below. Finally, to reinforce the information provided by these devices and by the camera, the elderly is asked to self-report his/her emotional state using a simple list of emotions represented on the device screen (see Fig. 3b). All this information is processed by the *Data fusion and internal representation* module to store the pleasure and arousal components of the emotional state of the person in the database. The emotion detected from facial and heart rate analysis is compared with that self-reported by the elderly person. This allows us to analyze the accuracy of our estimation but also to detect difficulties in the elderly person's self-diagnosis.

3.3   The Agent Design

The proposed framework use a BDI (beliefs, desires, intentions) agent [15] to monitor the emotional state and generate recommendations and alerts. This agent has an *Emotion analysis* module, which is in charge of detecting specific changes in the emotional state; a *Long-term emotion analysis* module, which monitors long-term emotional impairment; an *Select action* module which, using

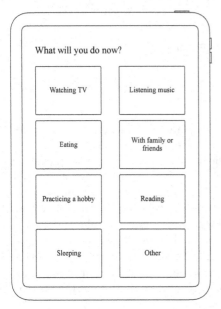

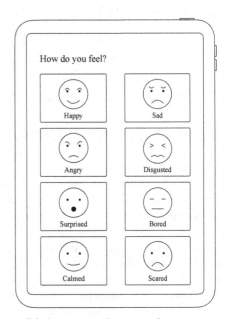

(a) Capturing the type of activity.   (b) Capturing the type of emotion.

Fig. 3. Mock-up of the application for emotion monitoring in different activities.

the emotional state, determines if an action need to be performed (i.e., recommendation or alert); and a *Personalization* module, that customizes the system parameters to the user's preferences and needs.

The state of the elderly person is analyzed in the *Emotion analysis* module in real time to identify significant emotional state changes. An emotional state at an instant t is recognized as a significant emotional change if the distance of the vector of the emotion detected at time t (i.e., $\vec{e}_t$) and the vector of the emotion detected at time $t-1$ (i.e., $\vec{e}_{t-1}$) is greater than a predefined threshold associated to the activity performed by the person. This threshold and the interval between emotion analysis must be personalized for each activity and person by the professional therapist in charge of the person according to his/her physical and emotional characteristics. The result of the *Emotion analysis* and the *Activity control* processes allows the agent to detect alterations in the elderly person's emotional state. This information is used by the *Long-term emotion analysis* module to detect possible progression of cognitive impairment.

The *Select action* module of the BDI agent evaluates a catalog of available plans P. Each plan $\rho \in P$ has a triggering event te (e.g., the detection of a significant change in the emotional state), a precondition pe (e.g., an undesirable or unexpected emotional state) and a sequence of actions s (e.g. notify a family member). The agent selects the most suitable action from a set of actions which are grouped into: actions focused on alerting the family member or social-health personnel responsible for the care of the elderly person; and actions focused on recommending an activity. If the agent determines that the best action is to suggest an activity to the elderly person, the agent will use a target emotional state $\vec{o}$ established by the therapist (see Fig. 1). This emotional state is represented as a vector composed by its pleasure and arousal components. Then, the activity α that maximizes the utility determined by the following function is selected:

$$\alpha := \arg\max_{a \in L} (u_a) \tag{3}$$

where u_a is the utility function for the activity a defined as:

$$u_a := \delta_a \cdot \frac{1}{d(\vec{\tau}_a, \vec{o})} \tag{4}$$

where δ_a represents the degree of preference that the user has for the activity a, $d(x,y)$ is a function of distance, $\vec{o}$ is a vector composed by the pleasure and arousal components of the target emotional state (see Fig. 1), and $\vec{\tau}_a$ is a vector representing the effect that the activity a produces on the individual's pleasure and arousal. The vector $\vec{\tau}_a$ is estimated as:

$$\vec{\tau}_a = (\Delta p_a + \vec{e}_p, \Delta a_a + \vec{e}_a) \tag{5}$$

where Δp_a and Δa_a represent the increment of pleasure and arousal of the activity a and are obtained by Formulas 1 and 2, respectively, and $\vec{e}_p$ and $\vec{e}_a$ are the pleasure and arousal components of the individual's current emotional state.

The *Personalization* module is used by the agent to adapt its behavior to the user's needs and preferences. First of all, in this module the professional therapist in charge of the person will define the initial values of the thresholds that determine when an emotional change is significant. This threshold will be updated later by the agent according to the person emotional state records (i.e., the average emotions modification obtained for each activity a). Secondly, this module is in charge of determining the information displayed on the screen of the mobile device. As mentioned above, the information is displayed using large icons to facilitate usability. However, this limits the number of activities that can be displayed on the screen. Therefore, to personalize the activities displayed on the screen, we have defined the set of activities $S \subseteq L$, which consists of n activities, where n is the number of activities that can be displayed at the same time on the screen. The set S is obtained from the estimation of the activities that maximize the utility function defined in Eq. 4.

Finally, an important aspect to consider when using this type of applications is the privacy risk assessment, especially when storing sensitive information such as information related to the user's emotional state. To guarantee the user's privacy, in our model the facial landmarks are anonymously submitted to a web service and the detected emotions are stored in a encrypted database on the device itself. These emotional information records are used by the *Long-term emotion analysis* module of the agent to detect specific changes or progressive health deterioration, but data can only be accessed by the authorized health therapist in charge of the person to analyze the evolution of the elderly person and facilitate diagnosis.

4 Conclusion

In this paper we have proposed a model of an agent to assist elderly people suffering from social isolation. The agent can use different inputs to monitor (e.g., tone-voice analysis, skin conductance, heart rate, or facial emotion recognition) the emotional state and the activity being performed by the elderly person. The emotional data coming from the different inputs is stored in a common dimensional space composed of pleasure and arousal dimensions. This common representation space allows identifying anomalous patterns in the emotional behavior of the elderly person, as well as monitoring the progression of cognitive impairment. With this information, the agent is able to recommend the most appropriate activity to promote a healthy emotional state. The evolution of the emotional state is a very useful tool for the therapist who will be able to detect abrupt emotional changes, elicitation of extreme emotions, and other emotional alterations. The agent is offered as an application that can be installed on most current mobile devices.

This project is currently in its early stages of development. Once the implementation of all the modules has been completed, it will be necessary to establish some initial rounds to calibrate the personalization of the agent's modules. This personalization must be done with the help of the professional therapist in charge of the elderly person before carrying out a validation phase with the elderly person. One of the limitations of our proposal is the difficulty of recognizing emotions in elderly people despite the use of multimodal methods, as in our proposal. But the estimation that we can obtain with this proposal will always be much better to take decisions than the absence of knowledge of the emotional state. Among the limitations of the proposed model, we can highlight that it requires the elderly person to be able to select at least the activity to be performed on the application screen.

Acknowledgements. This work is partially supported by Generalitat Valenciana CIPROM/2021/077, Spanish Government by projects PID2020-113416RB-I00 and TED2021-131295B-C32, and TAILOR, a project funded by EU Horizon 2020, under GA No 952215.

References

1. Baecker, A.N., Geiskkovitch, D.Y., González, A.L., Young, J.E.: Emotional support domestic robots for healthy older adults: conversational prototypes to help with loneliness. In: Companion of the 2020 ACM/IEEE International Conference on Human-Robot Interaction, pp. 122–124 (2020)
2. Baker, S., et al.: Combatting social isolation and increasing social participation of older adults through the use of technology: a systematic review of existing evidence. Australas. J. Ageing **37**(3), 184–193 (2018)
3. Balapour, A., Nikkhah, H.R., Sabherwal, R.: Mobile application security: role of perceived privacy as the predictor of security perceptions. Int. J. Inf. Manage. **52**, 102063 (2020)

4. Chang, Y., Sun, L.: EEG-based emotion recognition for modulating social-aware robot navigation. In Proceedings of the 43rd Annual International Conference of the IEEE Engineering in Medicine & Biology Society (EMBC), pp. 5709–5712. IEEE (2021)
5. Cristea, M., Noja, G.G., Stefea, P., Sala, A.L.: The impact of population aging and public health support on EU labor markets. Int. J. Environ. Res. Public Health **17**(4), 1439 (2020)
6. Demir, E., Köseoğlu, E., Sokullu, R., Şeker, B.: Smart home assistant for ambient assisted living of elderly people with dementia. Procedia Comput. Sci. **113**, 609–614 (2017)
7. Dosovitsky, G., Bunge, E.L.: Bonding with bot: user feedback on a chatbot for social isolation. Front. Digit. Health **3**, 138 (2021)
8. Ekman, P., et al.: Basic Emotions. Handbook of Cognition and Emotion **98**(45–60), 16 (1999)
9. Hämmig, O.: Health risks associated with social isolation in general and in young, middle and old age. PLoS ONE **14**(7), e0219663 (2019)
10. Jelodar, H., Orji, R., Matwin, S., Weerasinghe, S., Oyebode, O., Wang, Y.: Artificial intelligence for emotion-semantic trending and people emotion detection during COVID-19 social isolation. arXiv preprint arXiv:2101.06484 (2021)
11. Malcolm, M., Frost, H., Cowie, J.: Loneliness and social isolation causal association with health-related lifestyle risk in older adults: a systematic review and meta-analysis protocol. Syst. Control Found. Appl. **8**(1), 1–8 (2019)
12. Marco-Detchart, C., Carrascosa, C., Julian, V., Rincon, J.: Robust multi-sensor consensus plant disease detection using the choquet integral. Sensors **23**(5), 2382 (2023)
13. Martinez-Martin, E., del Pobil, A.P.: Personal robot assistants for elderly care: an overview. Pers. Assistants: Emerg. Comput. Technol. **132**, 77–91 (2018)
14. McMaughan, D.J., Oloruntoba, O., Smith, M.L.: Socioeconomic status and access to healthcare: interrelated drivers for healthy aging. Front. Public Health **8**, 231 (2020)
15. Rao, A.S., Georgeff, M.P.: Modeling rational agents within a BDI-architecture. Readings Agents, 317–328 (1997)
16. Reis, A., Paulino, D., Paredes, H., Barroso, J.: Using intelligent personal assistants to strengthen the elderlies' social bonds. In: Antona, M., Stephanidis, C. (eds.) UAHCI 2017. LNCS, vol. 10279, pp. 593–602. Springer, Cham (2017). https://doi.org/10.1007/978-3-319-58700-4_48
17. Rincon, J.A., Marco-Detchart, C., Julian, V., Carrascosa, C., Novais, P.: Towards a low-cost companion robot for helping elderly well-being. In: Yin, H., Camacho, D., Tino, P. (eds.) IDEAL 2022. LNCS, vol. 13576, pp. 179–187. Springer, Cham (2022). https://doi.org/10.1007/978-3-031-21753-1_18
18. Russell, J.A.: A circumplex model of affect. J. Pers. Soc. Psychol. **39**(6), 1161 (1980)
19. Shafighi, K., et al.: Social isolation is linked to classical risk factors of Alzheimer's disease-related dementias. Plos one **18**(2), 0280471 (2023)
20. Taverner, J., Vivancos, E., Botti, V.: A multidimensional culturally adapted representation of emotions for affective computational simulation and recognition. IEEE Trans. Affect. Comput. **14**(1), 761–772 (2023)

Extrinsic Emotion Regulation by Intelligent Agents: A Computational Model Based on Arousal-Valence Dimensions

Aaron Pico, Joaquin Taverner$^{(\boxtimes)}$, Emilio Vivancos, Vicente Botti,
and Ana Garcia-Fornes

Valencian Research Institute for Artificial Intelligence (VRAIN),
Universitat Politècnica de València, Valencia, Spain
{apicpas,joataap,vivancos,vbotti,agarcia}@upv.es

Abstract. Emotion regulation is an important aspect of emotional well-being that involves effectively managing and modifying one's or other emotions. However, there is a lack of computational models to guide the design and implementation of emotion regulation by intelligent agents. To address this gap, we propose a computational model for an intelligent agent which, using an emotion representation based on the arousal-valence dimensions, facilitates emotion regulation in persons. Based on the theoretical emotion regulation model proposed by J. Gross, our model of intelligent affective agent uses a dynamic planner to select a regulation strategy to facilitate the individual to maintain their emotional balance. The agent selects the most appropriate emotion regulation strategy taking into account the specific personality traits of the individual. The effects of each regulatory strategy on a particular individual are updated by the agent according to the emotional changes detected in the individual physiological parameters in previous uses of the strategy. The proposed model of agent is of great importance to facilitate the learning and use of emotion regulation techniques for promoting emotional well-being of people.

Keywords: Emotion regulation · affective computing · intelligent agents · affective agents

1 Introduction

Emotion regulation can be informally defined as an important aspect of emotional well-being that involves the ability to manage and modify one's or other's emotions effectively. Emotion regulation is crucial in mental health and can help individuals deal with emotional disorders such as stress, anxiety or depression. In addition, emotion regulation has practical applications in fields such as education, marketing, and entertainment.

© The Author(s), under exclusive license to Springer Nature Switzerland AG 2023
P. Mathieu et al. (Eds.): PAAMS 2023, LNAI 13955, pp. 260–271, 2023.
https://doi.org/10.1007/978-3-031-37616-0_22

James J. Gross is a well known psychologist who developed the process model of emotion regulation [15]. That theory is widely used and identifies different stages in the generation of emotions that can be modulated by various types of strategies. In his proposal, he establishes a framework to classify the different strategies, allowing a better identification and specification of the actions involved in emotion regulation [13].

In computing, emotion regulation is part of the affective computing field. Affective computing is an interdisciplinary field that aims to develop computational intelligent systems capable of recognizing, interpreting, and simulating human emotions [27]. Despite the importance of emotion regulation, to the best of our knowledge, there are no computational models of emotion regulation which can guide the design and implementation of emotion regulation by intelligent agents.

In this study, we propose a preliminary work of a computational model for an intelligent agent which, using an arousal and valence based emotion representation, facilitates emotion regulation in persons. Our proposed model, based on Gross' theory, is a significant advancement in the development of computational models for emotion regulation. It contributes to the development of affective intelligent systems that can effectively facilitate the user's emotion regulation.

2   Background

We will first define the theoretical foundation and assumptions on which our model of agent for emotion regulation is founded. Our approach to emotional regulation is based on the theories proposed by James J. Gross [12] and the definition and representation of emotions proposed by James A. Russel [30]. According to Gross, emotion regulation refers to a range of cognitive, behavioral, and physiological processes used by individuals to manage the generation, experience, and expression of their emotions. The ability to regulate emotions plays an important role in maintaining emotional balance, promoting mental well-being, and enabling effective decision-making in the different situations that people face. Effective emotion regulation provides the capacity to adjust one's emotional responses in a flexible and adaptive manner, according to both environmental factors and personal goals [11,23]. This regulation process can be carried out by a person to control or direct his/her own emotions, which is known as intrinsic emotion regulation or self-regulation [10]. It can also be carried out by a person to influence the emotional state of a third person, which is known as extrinsic emotion regulation [24]. Although in this article we use the generic term emotion regulation, we will only focus on extrinsic emotion regulation.

2.1   Process Model of Emotion Regulation

A widely used and referenced model of emotion regulation is the Emotion Regulation Process Model proposed by the psychologist James J. Gross [12,14], which postulates that it is possible to influence the different stages of the emotion generation process by means of certain actions or strategies. That model distinguishes between antecedent-focused strategies and response-focused strategies (see Fig. 1). Antecedent-focused strategies for emotion regulation involve the regulation of emotions before the emotions are triggered, as noted in [18]. These strategies can be implemented by either modifying the trigger of the emotion or altering one's cognitive processes. On the other hand, response-focused strategies are aimed at managing the response elicited by the emotion. This model categorizes these strategies into different families based on the stage they influence. These families include:

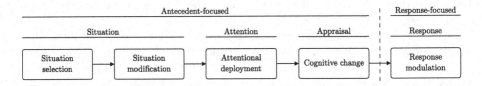

Fig. 1. The process model of emotion regulation [14].

- Situation selection: Strategies within situation selection focus on deciding what situations a person faces. For example, avoiding confronting situations that evoke negative emotions such as sadness. However, to apply this strategy effectively, it is necessary to have the ability to predict the emotional response that the situation will produce, which is difficult in many situations [13,32].
- Situation modification: These strategies involve altering a situation to achieve a more desirable emotional response. This type of modification pertains specifically to altering the external physical environment. Sometimes, it may be difficult to distinguish between selection and modification strategies since the changes made in one situation may be perceived as creating a new situation instead [12–14].
- Attentional deployment: Strategies within this family are aimed to redirect attention between elements of the external environment or between personal thoughts [7,33]. Distraction and concentration are the most common strategies. Distraction consists in redirecting attention from the emotional aspect of the situation to another, avoiding its emotional charge. Concentration would be its counterpart and refers to draw attention to emotional features of a situation [34].
- Cognitive change: Cognitive change strategies consist in altering the individual's evaluation or appraisal of a situation. The most commonly reported technique is reappraisal, which consists in altering person's internal interpretation or understanding of the situation. Another strategy is decentering, which consists in seeing an event from a broader perspective, observing one's inner experiences as transient and separate from one's self [2,19].

– Response modulation: Response modulation involves influencing the emotional response in its behavioral, experiential, or physiological components. A well documented strategy in this family is expressive suppression, which consists in inhibiting the externalization of emotional expressions. Exercise, sleep, and alcohol or drug use are also considered ways of response modulation.

2.2   Affective State Representation

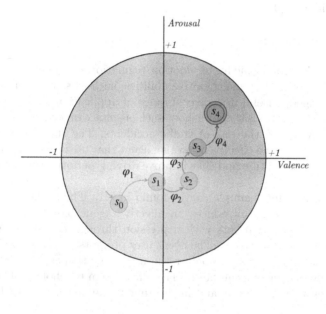

Fig. 2. Emotion regulation process

The concept of emotional balance is crucial when considering emotional stability [26]. Emotional balance refers to an individual's natural emotional state in the absence of events (external or internal). This state varies from person to person and is influenced by factors such as cognitive development, personality, and past experiences. positive emotions than negative ones. They are also better able to cope with stress and adversity, and have a greater sense of resilience.

In order to adequately represent and reason with a person's emotional state and detect the need to use emotion regulation, it is necessary to use an emotional state representation model. One of the most commonly used methods of emotion representation is the dimensional mode proposed by J. Rusell [30]. That model represents emotions in a two-dimensional space, in which valence is placed on the horizontal axis and arousal is placed on the vertical axis (see Fig. 2). Valence is a subjective measure of emotional experience that indicates whether the emotion is pleasant or unpleasant to the person. Arousal, on the other hand, refers to the level of activation or stimulation felt by the person in response to an emotional stimulus. In addition, a pair of arousal and valence values can be associated with a category of emotions. For example, the emotion of happiness is associated with a high level of positive valence and a low level of positive arousal, while the emotion of fear is associated with a high level of arousal and a negative valence.

The measurement of a person's valence and arousal values can be estimated in several ways. Some physiological parameters, which can be measured by smart wearables like wristbands or watches, have been proven to be effective measures of the levels of arousal and valence experienced by a person in response to an emotional stimulus [9].

3   Related Work

The ability of agents to facilitate emotion regulation can help mitigate negative emotions that undermine cognitive abilities, such as stress and frustration, making these agents useful in a diverse range of applications. For example, the research conducted in [16], shows how such agents can help drivers manage frustration and reduce the risk of traffic accidents. The study used a driving simulator [22] to test the effectiveness of an agent that uses cognitive reappraisal to reduce driver frustration and thus improve driving performance, with positive results.

Another interesting example can be found in [21]. The authors propose the Help4Mood model, that introduces an affective agent based on the FAtiMA architecture [5] to aid patients with depression through cognitive change and response modulation strategies. The agent uses prompts on the screen and tests to interact with the user and monitor the user's emotional state [20]. Results shows that affective agents can be specially effective in psychological therapy by providing therapeutic support and facilitating communication with healthcare professionals.

Emotion regulation has also aroused interest in the field of natural language processing. In [17], the ER-Chat is presented as an end-to-end dialogue framework that utilizes transformers to adapt the dialogue to different contexts and emotional states. The model focuses on emotion regulation by considering contextual factors and generating empathic responses to regulate the user's emotions. ER-Chat is trained on the EmpatheticDialogues data-set [29], which includes emotion and intent labels. The evaluation results demonstrate higher performance and user acceptability in the experiments with the chat bot.

In addition, chat bots can serve as moderators for promoting emotion regulation in groups, making them a valuable tool. For instance, GremoBot (Group emotion Bot) [25] is a prototype that uses reappraisal and attentional deployment strategies to improve group work performance. The GremoBot estimates the group's sentiment and tone, and, if it detects a lack of interaction or negative sentiment, it will apply techniques to restore the group's focus and encourage positive reinterpretation of the situation. Predefined phrases and emojis are used to make communication with users more friendly.

Emotion regulation also facilitates the creation and strengthening of social relationships. In [6], a model for developing intelligent virtual agents that use emotion regulation to establish and strengthen social relationships is proposed. The model enables the agent to generate and reason about emotions. Emotion regulation is implemented through instrumental and relationship-oriented actions. The model was evaluated in a video game experiment concluding that, agents with emotion regulation are perceived as providing more intimacy, help, emotional security, and self-validation functions.

As we have seen, in the literature we find several projects that develop systems that implement emotional regulation techniques for different purposes. But if we examine the proposals, we do not find any computational model to plan the emotional regulation actions necessary to achieve emotional balance which dynamically personalizes the regulation strategies to the human needs.

4 Emotion Regulation Agent

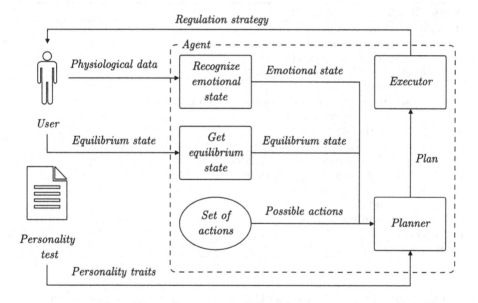

Fig. 3. Emotion regulation system

In this study, we propose a computational model which employs a arousal and valence based emotion representation and facilitates emotion regulation in persons (see Fig. 3). The theoretical foundation of our computational model is the process model of emotion regulation proposed by Gross [14]. This theoretical model identifies the different stages in the generation of emotion that can be modulated by several strategies, each one focusing on a specific stage. However, the emotion regulation strategies proposed by Gross are not specific enough for application in a computational model. Therefore, emotion regulation strategies should be divided into more specific sub-strategies so that they can be converted into real actions to be applied by the agent and their emotional impact can be estimated.

In our proposal, an agent has a catalog of actions A. The agent will prepare a plan defined as a list of actions $\{\alpha_1, \alpha_2, \cdots, \alpha_n\}$ (where $\alpha_i \in A$) that are sequentially executed. An action α consists of a tuple $\langle \varphi, S \rangle$ where φ is an emotion regulation strategy and S is the expected emotional state achieved after applying the regulation strategy φ. An expected emotional state S is composed by the tuple $\langle \delta, \psi \rangle$ where δ is the expected emotion vector, composed by arousal-valence components, and ψ represents the threshold of acceptance or tolerance for the emotional state S (i.e., a tolerance value that makes it possible to estimate whether a given emotion is in line with the expected emotion). Circles around each state $S_0, S_1, \cdots S_4$ in Fig. 2 represent the tolerance threshold ψ for each state S_i.

Algorithm 1. Agent behavior

```
 1: while true do
 2:     e ← recognize_emotional_state()
 3:     ε ← get_equilibrium_state()
 4:     if abs(e − ε) > ϑ then
 5:         π ← plan(e,ε,A)
 6:         while not (empty(π) or succeeded(e,ε)) do
 7:             α ← first element of π
 8:             execute(α)
 9:             π ← tail of π
10:             e ← recognize_emotional_state()
11:             if not succeeded(e,α_S) then
12:                 π ← plan(e,ε,A)
13:             end if
14:         end while
15:     end if
16: end while
```

Our computational model associates each emotion regulation strategy with the possible changes that can produce in the emotional state of the user, and the costs of applying that regulation strategy. An intelligent agent uses a planning algorithm to select the best strategy based on the user emotional state, the effect of the regulation strategies, the cost of applying each regulation strategy, and an equilibrium emotional state that is adjusted to the user's emotional balance. This is an iterative process in which a dynamic planner analyzes the real effect that each applied emotion regulation strategy has produced in the user until the desired equilibrium emotional state is reached.

Algorithm 1 defines the agent's behavior. The *recognize_emotional_state*() function returns the arousal and valence values of the emotion recognized in the user, *get_equilibrium_estate*() returns the state in which the user is in an emotional balance, the *plan*() function represents the dynamic planner, *succeeded* determines if the action has produced the expected emotional state, and ε and ϑ represent the user's balance state and the balance state tolerance, respectively.

4.1 Emotion Regulation Planner

The core of our model lies in the planning of the actions to be performed by the agent to apply a regulation strategy represented by the *plan* function in Algorithm 1. The planning process will begin when it is detected that the emotional state deviates from the equilibrium state. Then, the aim of the agent will be to reach the emotional balance again, moving the emotional state towards the equilibrium state of the person. The planner is based on the person's personality, emotional state, and the impact of each regulation strategy on arousal and valence, and selects a set of actions to be performed during the regulation process until the state of emotional balance is reached.

An example of a planning of regulation strategies to reach the equilibrium state can be seen in Fig. 2. The circles represent the expected states S_i after applying the regulation strategies $S_{i,\psi}$ (with a tolerance threshold), the lines represent the change in the affective state resulting from the application of the regulation strategies suggested by the planner. Our proposed model uses a dynamic planner, so that the process to reach the target emotional state is an iterative process in which, if any of the intermediate steps does not achieve the expected effect, a replanning process takes place to redefine the plan adding or removing actions. The success or failure of an action α_i can be estimated by calculating the difference between the user's emotional state e and the target emotional state S_δ of the action α_i and comparing it with the threshold S_ψ of acceptance, or tolerance, assigned to each of the sub-states (see Fig. 2) using the formula:

$$succeeded\,(\theta_1, \theta_2) = \begin{cases} \text{true, if } \|\theta_1 - \theta_2\| \leq \psi \\ \text{false, otherwise} \end{cases} \tag{1}$$

where θ_i are vectors composed by arousal and valence components.

The different actions α_i to apply emotion regulation strategies are associated with a cost. This cost is an estimation of the resources needed to carry out the action associated with the regulation strategy, such as the time required for the person to perform the action, or the cost of modifying his/her situation. This cost, together with the utility of each action determined with the Formulas 2 and 3, is used by the planning algorithm to select the strategy to be employed in each step of the emotional regulation process.

4.2   Personality Traits and User Customization

It is important to keep in mind that the effects of the different regulation strategies may vary from one person to another, depending on their personality, emotional state, context, and culture. Therefore, it is essential to identify which strategies work best for the user in each specific situation. In addition, to estimate the impact that different strategies have on the emotional state of people, it is important to customize the model to each particular user.

As a first approach to customizing the system for a specific user, in this work we use the personality defined by the Five Factor Model (FMM) [8]. The FFM, is a commonly used framework that describes personality along five dimensions: openness, conscientiousness, extroversion, agreeableness, and neuroticism. Each of these dimensions can influence how people experience and regulate their emotions.

Research has shown that personality traits may be related to different preferences or facility for emotion regulation strategies. People who score high on the attribute of openness are good at applying cognitive change strategies. In contrast, people with a high degree of conscientiousness tend to use attentional deployment strategies [1,28]. This information can be used to select specific techniques that may work best for individuals with different personality traits. It can also help us to estimate more accurately the influence that a technique will have on the emotional state of the user, taking into account his/her personality. To this end, we propose the following equations which define the increment that a specific regulation strategy produce in the arousal and valence:

$$\Delta a = \sum_{t \in T} (\sigma_t \cdot \Phi_{tsa}) \tag{2}$$

$$\Delta v = \sum_{t \in T} (\sigma_t \cdot \Phi_{tsv}) \tag{3}$$

where, for arousal a or for valence v, T is the set of personality traits, σ_t represents the user's level of a particular personality trait t, Φ_{ts} represents the weight or influence that a specific personality trait t has on a particular strategy s.

We estimate the personality traits of the user by a Big Five personality traits test [4]. With this test, we customize the values of the coefficients of each personality trait σ in the range from -1 to 1. For example, for the attribute of extroversion, a value of 1 means that the person is completely extroverted, while a value of -1 indicates that he/she is completely introverted. On the other hand, the weight Φ will be the maximum value that a specific personality trait can alter one of the arousal and valence axes when a particular strategy is applied. These weights are assigned to the different emotion regulation strategies and can be estimated by experimentation such as done in [3] and [31]. This customization is also improved through a learning approach, where the model continuously adapts these weights to the user's emotional responses and feedback. This model learns from previous experiences how different emotion regulation strategies influence the user affective state.

5   Conclusion and Future Work

In this article we have presented a preliminary work that will need to be validated by experiments conducted by a multidisciplinary team composed of specialists in artificial intelligence and psychologist.

The agent model described in this work facilitates emotion regulation based on the arousal-valence dimensions of emotions and the process model of emotion regulation. Each regulation strategy is associated with the changes that can produce in the arousal and valence values. This allows an agent to assist the user in reaching a target affective state or maintaining emotional balance. The proposed agent divides the different regulation strategies into more specific sub-strategies to assign their emotional impact in a precise manner. It is important to note that the effects of different actions to regulate emotions may vary from one person to another, depending on different factors as the personality of the person. Therefore, our model evaluates the result of each action taken during the regulation process and determines what the next action should be to achieve emotional equilibrium. This process dynamically personalize the user experience, and learn from previous experiences what is the result of applying the emotion regulation actions in an specific user. The dynamic planner estimates the best actions for emotion regulation based on the user personality, his/her current emotional state, his/her equilibrium emotional state, and the cost and impact on arousal-valence of each strategy.

While the proposed model for emotion regulation provides a promising framework for assisting users in regulating their emotions, there are still several areas that can be explored for future work. For instance, one area for future work is to investigate the role of context in emotion regulation. Different regulation strategies require different levels of understanding of the situation. Thus, one possible approach is to extend the current emotion regulation model to be context-aware, taking into account the specific context of the user and selecting the most appropriate regulation strategies accordingly.

We are currently working on the specification of several aspects of our model. For example, it is necessary to define the actions to be performed or proposed by the agent in order to facilitate the application of each emotion regulation technique. Likewise, the participation of the therapist in charge of each person will be necessary to review and personalize the actions according to the specific characteristics of the person, such as culture, social context, cognitive conditions,... Moreover, given the uncertainty of the result of applying a regulation technique to a specific user, in the future we can study the possibility of considering this uncertainty, for example, by using a probabilistic Markov planner.

The ethical and moral implications surrounding the use of intelligent agents to regulate human emotional states need the establishment of comprehensive guidelines, standards, and protocols to ensure the safe and responsible utilization of such systems. It is essential to strike a balance between the potential benefits of emotional regulation and the ethical challenges that may arise.

Acknowledgements. This work is partially supported by Generalitat Valenciana CIPROM/2021/077, Spanish Government by projects PID2020-113416RB-I00 and TED2021-131295B-C32, and TAILOR, a project funded by EU Horizon 2020, under GA No 952215.

References

1. Barańczuk, U.: The five factor model of personality and emotion regulation: a meta-analysis. Personality Individ. Differ. **139**, 217–227 (2019)
2. Bernstein, A., Hadash, Y., Lichtash, Y., Tanay, G., Shepherd, K., Fresco, D.M.: Decentering and related constructs: a critical review and metacognitive processes model. Perspect. Psychol. Sci. **10**(5), 599–617 (2015)
3. Borges, L.M., Naugle, A.E.: The role of emotion regulation in predicting personality dimensions. Pers. Ment. Health **11**(4), 314–334 (2017)
4. Costa, P.T., Jr., McCrae, R.R.: The Revised Neo Personality Inventory (neo-pi-r). Sage Publications Inc, Thousand Oaks (2008)
5. Dias, J., Mascarenhas, S., Paiva, A.: FAtiMA modular: towards an agent architecture with a generic appraisal framework. In: Bosse, T., Broekens, J., Dias, J., van der Zwaan, J. (eds.) Emotion Modeling. LNCS (LNAI), vol. 8750, pp. 44–56. Springer, Cham (2014). https://doi.org/10.1007/978-3-319-12973-0_3
6. Dias, J., Paiva, A.: I want to be your friend: establishing relations with emotionally intelligent agents. In: Proceedings of the 2013 International Conference on Autonomous Agents and Multi-agent Systems, pp. 777–784 (2013)
7. DiGirolamo, M.A., Kibrislioglu Uysal, N., McCall, E.C., Isaacowitz, D.M.: Attention-focused emotion regulation in everyday life in adulthood and old age. Emotion **23**, 633–650 (2022)
8. Digman, J.M.: Personality structure: emergence of the five-factor model. Annu. Rev. Psychol. **41**, 417–40 (1990)
9. Egger, M., Ley, M., Hanke, S.: Emotion recognition from physiological signal analysis: a review. Electron. Notes Theor. Comput. Sci. **343**, 35–55 (2019)
10. English, T., Eldesouky, L.: We're not alone: understanding the social consequences of intrinsic emotion regulation. Emotion **20**(1), 43 (2020)
11. English, T., Lee, I.A., John, O.P., Gross, J.J.: The role of social context and goals: emotion regulation strategy selection in daily life. Motiv. Emot. **41**, 230–242 (2017)
12. Gross, J.J.: The emerging field of emotion regulation: an integrative review. Rev. Gen. Psychol. **2**(3), 271–299 (1998)
13. Gross, J.J.: Emotion regulation. Handb. Emot. **3**(3), 497–513 (2008)
14. Gross, J.J.: Emotion regulation: current status and future prospects. Psychol. Inq. **26**(1), 1–26 (2015)
15. Gross, J.J.: The extended process model of emotion regulation: elaborations, applications, and future directions. Psychol. Inq. **26**(1), 130–137 (2015)
16. Harris, H., Nass, C.: Emotion regulation for frustrating driving contexts. In: Proceedings of the SIGCHI Conference on Human Factors in Computing Systems, pp. 749–752 (2011)
17. Katayama, S., Aoki, S., Yonezawa, T., Okoshi, T., Nakazawa, J., Kawaguchi, N.: ER-chat: a text-to-text open-domain dialogue framework for emotion regulation. IEEE Trans. Affect. Comput. **13**(4), 2229–2237 (2022)
18. Kever, A., Pollatos, O., Vermeulen, N., Grynberg, D.: Interoceptive sensitivity facilitates both antecedent-and response-focused emotion regulation strategies. Pers. Individ. Differ. **87**, 20–23 (2015)

19. Kobayashi, R., Shigematsu, J., Miyatani, M., Nakao, T.: Cognitive reappraisal facilitates decentering: a longitudinal cross-lagged analysis study. Front. Psychol. **11**, 103 (2020)
20. Martínez-Miranda, J., Bresó, A., García-Gómez, J.M.: Look on the bright side: a model of cognitive change in virtual agents. In: Bickmore, T., Marsella, S., Sidner, C. (eds.) IVA 2014. LNCS (LNAI), vol. 8637, pp. 285–294. Springer, Cham (2014). https://doi.org/10.1007/978-3-319-09767-1_37
21. Martínez-Miranda, J., Bresó, A., García-Gómez, J.M.: Modelling two emotion regulation strategies as key features of therapeutic empathy. In: Bosse, T., Broekens, J., Dias, J., van der Zwaan, J. (eds.) Emotion Modeling. LNCS (LNAI), vol. 8750, pp. 115–133. Springer, Cham (2014). https://doi.org/10.1007/978-3-319-12973-0_7
22. Mets, M.A., Kuipers, E., de Senerpont Domis, L.M., Leenders, M., Olivier, B., Verster, J.C.: Effects of alcohol on highway driving in the STISIM driving simulator. Human Psychopharmacol. Clin. Exp. **26**(6), 434–439 (2011)
23. Nalepa, G.J., Kutt, K., Giżycka, B., Jemioło, P., Bobek, S.: Analysis and use of the emotional context with wearable devices for games and intelligent assistants. Sensors **19**(11), 2509 (2019)
24. Nozaki, Y., Mikolajczak, M.: Extrinsic emotion regulation. Emotion **20**(1), 10 (2020)
25. Peng, Z., Kim, T., Ma, X.: GremoBot: exploring emotion regulation in group chat. In: Conference Companion Publication of the 2019 on Computer Supported Cooperative Work and Social Computing, pp. 335–340 (2019)
26. Pereira, G., Dimas, J., Prada, R., Santos, P.A., Paiva, A.: A generic emotional contagion computational model. In: D'Mello, S., Graesser, A., Schuller, B., Martin, J.-C. (eds.) ACII 2011. LNCS, vol. 6974, pp. 256–266. Springer, Heidelberg (2011). https://doi.org/10.1007/978-3-642-24600-5_29
27. Picard, R.W.: Affective Computing. MIT Press, Cambridge (1997)
28. Esti Hayu Purnamaningsih: Personality and emotion regulation strategies. Int. J. Psychol. Res. **10**(1), 53–60 (2017)
29. Rashkin, H., Smith, E.M., Li, M., Boureau, Y.L.: Towards empathetic open-domain conversation models: a new benchmark and dataset. arXiv preprint arXiv:1811.00207 (2018)
30. Russell, J.A.: A circumplex model of affect. J. Pers. Soc. Psychol. **39**(6), 1161 (1980)
31. Scheffel, C., Diers, K., Schönfeld, S., Brocke, B., Strobel, A., Dörfel, D.: Cognitive emotion regulation and personality: an analysis of individual differences in the neural and behavioral correlates of successful reappraisal. Pers. Neurosci. **2**, e11 (2019)
32. Sheppes, G.: Emotion regulation choice: theory and findings. Handb. Emot. Regul. **2**, 126–139 (2014)
33. Todd, R.M., Cunningham, W.A., Anderson, A.K., Thompson, E.: Affect-biased attention as emotion regulation. Trends Cogn. Sci. **16**(7), 365–372 (2012)
34. Webb, T.L., Miles, E., Sheeran, P.: Dealing with feeling: a meta-analysis of the effectiveness of strategies derived from the process model of emotion regulation. Psychol. Bull. **138**(4), 775 (2012)

Optimization of Complex Systems in Photonics by Multi-agent Robotic Control

Quentin Pouvreau[1,2]([✉])[ID], Jean-Pierre Georgé[1][ID], Carole Bernon[1][ID], and Sébastien Maignan[1]

[1] IRIT, Université de Toulouse, CNRS, Toulouse INP, UT3, Toulouse, France
{quentin.pouvreau,jean-pierre.george,carole.bernon,
sebastien.maignan}@irit.fr
[2] ISP System, Vic-en-Bigorre, France
http://www.irit.fr, http://www.isp-system.fr

Abstract. The optimization of complex industrial systems represents a class of difficult problems, due to their embodiment in the physical world, and whose search spaces are disrupted, non-linear and potentially vast. Their parametrization relies on the combination of many variables, each change generally impacting the whole system. Mathematical approaches are limited by the fact that the models are too coarse or non-existent, and by the imprecision of the measurements and the machining of components of such systems. The action cost of the system calls into question population-based heuristics and swarm intelligence where each individual must be tested. We propose a multi-agent approach allowing a global/black-box modeling of the system in terms of input variables and objectives, as well as an agnostic and continuous adaptive optimization, based on sensor feedbacks from the running system.

Keywords: Collective Problem Solving · Self-Organization · Continuous Multi-Objective Optimization · Robotic Control · Photonics

1 Problem Description

This study deals with continuous optimization problems arising from complex robotic industrial applications. Such problems have a wide variety of external constraints like limited resolution time or number of moves, predetermined components positions, etc. Regardless of the specifics of the applications, we choose to consider these problems as black-box systems to be optimized, given sensor feedback.

We propose a self-adaptive multi-agent system (MAS) for optimization able to tackle multiple robotic applications, with two main advantages:

1. A natural representation of the domain, easily observable and explainable, where each agent represents a variable of the problem and can perceive and interact with the real topology of the problem.

P. Mathieu et al. (Eds.): PAAMS 2023, LNAI 13955, pp. 272–283, 2023.
https://doi.org/10.1007/978-3-031-37616-0_23

2. A collective resolution process during which the agents continuously adapt to feedback, whether from a sensor or an expert interacting with the system, and can therefore integrate perturbations, imperfections, etc.

The application domain we focus on is the Photonics domain as illustrated in Fig. 1. The main goal is to correctly align optical components to get certain beam properties. Input parameters of the problem are translation and rotation axes values of the optical components. We aim at developing an algorithm able to find a set of satisfactory solutions in a minimum number of iterations, and able to deal with measurement and machining imprecisions.

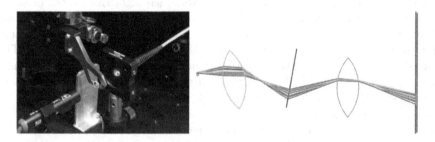

Fig. 1. Example of a real photonic application on which ISP System is working with the robot (left) and a schematic of a set of lenses that need to be positioned (right)

In this paper, we consider that optimizing a Photonics system is a continuous multi-objective optimization (MOO) problem. The following section presents the main approaches used in this field before focusing on the most suitable ones. The next section then describes the MAS we propose, followed by experiments. Finally we discuss the results and conclude.

2 Positioning

Exact methods are able to find optimal solutions but at the expense of high computation time and are thus not suited for large-scale optimization problems [5]. Moreover, it is often not possible to precisely model real systems taking into account all their particularities. The field of geometrical optics is subject to several types of aberrations between theoretical calculations and practical observation. Defects of optical components have also to be taken into account. This limits the relevance of learning approaches, which need repeatability.

Metaheuristic optimization algorithms are widely used to solve MOO problems, as they can find multiple optimal solutions in a single run, and improve the ratio between accuracy and computational cost. They are problem-independent optimization techniques that provide, if not an optimal solution, a set of satisfactory solutions by iteratively exploring and exploiting the search spaces stochastically [10]. The following sections focus on these algorithms.

2.1 Population-Based Heuristics

These approaches constitute a large part of the state of the art of optimization metaheuristics. The general principle is to simultaneously process a population of solutions distributed (randomly or not) in the search space. The population can evolve and select the best solutions iteratively according to the Darwinian principle, or converge towards an optimum by following a set of influence rules.

These algorithms can also be used in hybrid solutions alongside more classical algorithms or exact methods [7] to balance their weaknesses.

Being exhaustive on the state of the art in this area (e.g., Genetic Algorithms [4] and Swarm Intelligence algorithms [8] together have more than 3000 publications per year [12]) is difficult [11], however, such algorithms must evaluate a relatively large number of candidates in order to create a good population of solutions. To do so, the robot/bench must configure the entire experimental framework for each proposed new candidate solution in the population. The cost of activating a real robotic system is heavy compared to the algorithmic time. The computation of all candidate solutions is therefore prohibitive. A more suitable strategy would be an adaptive algorithm modifying and proposing for testing a unique configuration for each feedback (i.e. an optimization process forming a unique trajectory in the search space).

2.2 Multi-Agent Problem Solving

The MAS paradigm relies on a decentralized approach, based on self-organization mechanisms [14], where the computational task is distributed over the agents, which are virtual or physical autonomous entities. Each agent has only a local view of the problem it solves, corresponding to a local function. The global function of a problem then results from the *composition* of all these local functions. This feature allows to easily distribute the computational tasks in the solving process and thus to reduce the computational costs. This is why MAS approaches are preferred when centralized approaches have limited flexibility.

MAS are used in a wide variety of application areas of distributed optimization including power systems, sensor networks, smart buildings, smart manufacturing [13], etc. Many of these algorithms are based on a combinatorial logic such as the well-known Distributed Constraint Optimization Problem (DCOP) framework [1].

DCOP was originally developed under the assumption that each agent controls exactly one variable. This model was designed for problems where the difficulty lies in the combination of multiple constraints. Only a few works have tried to extend the DCOP model to continuous optimization problems [2,3]. Fundamentally DCOP requires a problem to be easily decomposable into several cost functions (to be able to evaluate partial assignments) and the relations between the states of the variables are supposed to be known. These major assumptions do not hold for complex continuous optimization problems, where the complexity of the models and their interdependencies mean that this detailed knowledge is not available in most real-life cases.

3   A MAS for Optimizing Complex Systems

When solving complex continuous problems, existing techniques usually require a transformation of the initial formulation, in order to satisfy certain requirements of the technique to be applied. Besides the fact that the correct application of these changes can be a demanding task for the designers, imposing such modifications changes the problem beyond its original and natural meaning. What we propose here is an agent-based modeling where the original structure/meaning of the problem is preserved. Indeed, it represents the formulation that is the most natural and the easiest to handle for the expert. We call it *Natural Domain Modeling for Optimization* (NDMO) [6].

3.1   Natural Domain Modeling

In order to represent the elements of a generic continuous optimization model, we have identified five classes of interacting entities: *design variables, models, outputs, constraints*, and *objectives*. In short: given the values of the design variables, some models will compute output values, and following models will compute further outputs and so on until the constraints and objectives can be computed, in a kind of computational network. Three types of elements are *agentified*: design variables (which must be optimized and thus constitute the solving process), constraints and objectives (i.e. the requirements or problem statements).

To take into account these requirements, the solving process relies on a specific measure called *criticality*. This measure represents the state of dissatisfaction of the agent with respect to its local goal. The role of this measure is to aggregate in a single comparable value all relevant indicators concerning the agent's state. Having this single indicator simplifies the reasoning of the agents. Each agent is responsible for estimating its own criticality and providing it to the other agents. However, the system designer has the task of providing the agents with adequate means to compute their criticality, as for example with a "barrier" or "logistics" function (Eq. 1 and Fig. 2).

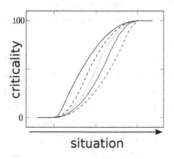

$$crit(x) = \frac{C}{1 + a * e^{-rx}} \quad (1)$$

Where C is the maximum critical value, a is a translation factor of the function determining the y-intercept and r enables to adjust the acceleration of the criticality curve and in a second hand determines the maximum tolerated distance to the objective.

Fig. 2. Typical criticality shapes

3.2   Internal State and Behavior of the Agents

The approach we propose is a single-solution (also called trajectory) algorithm. It iteratively modifies the solution's parameters and consequently selects a trajectory in the search space. Our implementation is based on the AMAK framework [9]. Regarding a complex system to optimize, some inputs affecting its behavior are considered design variables of the problem and outputs of interest can have an objective value or some constraints or both. As explained above we agentify design variables, objectives and constraints. Design variables are handled by solver agents. In the same way that we want to be as close as possible to the objectives, we must move away as much as possible from the constraints, and then objectives and constraints are handled by objective agents. Before going into details, the main principle of the resolution process is to make the agents cooperate to reduce the highest criticality at each iteration. From their combined actions will emerge the trajectory to more satisfactory solutions (Fig. 3).

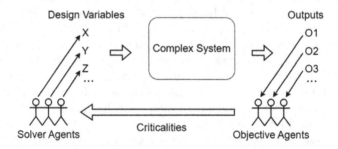

Fig. 3. Agentification process of a complex system to optimize

Objective Agents. Each objective agent is responsible for one objective/constraint and normalizes the associated feedback (the gap to expert-given ideal value) into criticality (see Eq. 1 and Fig. 2). It then propagates this criticality to all the solver agents who will act to lower it as much as possible.

Solver Agents. A solver agent has no criticality but has a value, corresponding to the design variable it is assigned to, and a memory. This memory is composed of a predefined number of previous observations cycles. Each entry of this memory contains the agent's value at the corresponding cycle, the set of objective agents criticalities, the entropy of the system, i.e. the number of solver agents having acted. The goal of a solver agent is to respond to the criticalities of the objective agents by adapting its value. Solver agents generally choose to help the most critical of the objectives so a cooperation may emerge. However, this mechanism is moderated by the local variations of the problem. To this end, a solver agent has a Perception-Decision-Action lifecycle:

- **Perception:** the agent records an observation of the last cycle in its memory and updates data needed during the decision phase.
- **Decision:** the agent may decide in 4 possible ways
  - If the agent has an empty memory or has never acted, then it acts in a *stochastic* way.
  - Otherwise the agent enters a *reactive* decision phase detailed below.
  - If the agent did not decide, it enters a *cognitive* decision phase detailed below.
  - Potentially, the agent can operate a *stochastic stop* to look whether its impact is real and not just a result of other agents impacts.
- **Action:** The agent changes or not its value according to its decision.

The resolution of the problem results from the capacity of the agents to make the right decision, therefore this phase is at the heart of the process. The difficulties encountered are mainly due to the problem itself: almost all the design variables have an impact on all the objectives, namely all the criticalities, and this in a non-linear way. The parameters are therefore strongly interconnected: the current value of one agent displaces the target value of one or several others. The system is therefore complex and the agents can collectively interfere with each other. At this point, the optimization problem becomes a cooperation problem.

The decisions of an agent are subject to a stochastic momentum mechanism, i.e. an agent will repeat its action for a random number of cycles equal to the momentum. The maximum value of the momentum is configurable. This mechanism of momentum allows to desynchronize the agents in order to avoid them being trapped in what we call non-cooperative synchronizations (essentially, when agents try to "help" at the same time, thus hindering each other). More importantly, this desynchronization individualizes the average perception of each agent over several cycles, allowing them to isolate their average impact on criticalities. Thus, if a solver agent sees that its impact on the most critical objective is negligible, it may decide to help another objective, potentially releasing a constraint on the improvement of the most critical.

Reactive Decision. If an agent observes that its target criticality decreases beyond a configurable threshold, it will increase its momentum. This rule is generally useful to converge quickly when the search space is locally regular or even linear. On the contrary, if the highest criticality increases beyond the same threshold, the agent will reduce its momentum so the next cognitive decision will come sooner, with updated data including these "error" cycles. The goal of this reactive method is to avoid more expensive processes when the current region of the search space is not ambiguous.

Cognitive Decision. When the momentum of its last decision drops to zero, the agent will process the data it has recorded during the successive perception phases. This more cognitive process consists in interpolating the variation of the current target criticality according to its own value. The goal is to identify

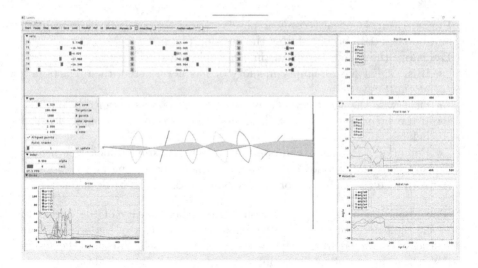

Fig. 4. Screenshot of simulator running

an objective to help according to its criticality and the impact that the agent believes it has on it. The momentum mechanism has another advantage with this decision process since the agent operates what we could call a stochastic pseudo-scan of its local search area. In cases where this second decision process does not lead to a decision, the agent acts randomly.

4   Simulation and Experiments

The MAS is connected to an optical simulator and has to update the state of this system, apply the changes decided by the agents and compute the feedback. The simulator we have developed is presented in Fig. 4. It is a 2D-world composed of a light source, several lenses (L_i with i in $[1, N]$) and a screen. The light source emits a number of rays (R_j with j in $[1, M]$) of conical shape. If a ray crosses a lens, it is refracted according to the Snell-Descartes laws: $n1.sin(\theta_1) = n2.sin(\theta_2)$ (where *theta* is the angle measured from the normal to the surface hit by the ray, and n_i is the refractive index of the respective medium). Thus, assuming that a ray passes through all the lenses in the system, we have a mathematical sequence of operations applied to its position and orientation: $R_j(pos_{j,i}, \theta_{j,i}) = L_i(R_j(pos_{j,i-1}, \theta_{j,i-1}))$ with i in $[1, N]$ and j in $[1, M]$.

The test cases are generated so that all rays pass through all lenses as follows: a set of lenses with various characteristics (thin or cylindrical shape, refractive index, focal length) are randomly placed on the axis between the light source and the screen. A set of rays is generated parallel to the axis X so that each ray passes through all the lenses and reaches the screen. The lenses are then iteratively and randomly moved and rotated, changing the direction of the rays. After a certain number of cycles, the state of the system is defined as the reference to be reached by the agents. The following iterations are used to artificially deteriorate the state of the system to what will be the starting point of the experiment.

A lens L_i is represented by its type (thin or cylindrical), its position $P_i(x, y)$ and its rotation angle T_i, its refractive index n_i and its focal length F_i. For cylindrical lenses, the radius of each face is also defined: $R1_i$ and $R2_i$. Among these parameters, only P_i and T_i can change during the execution and are controlled by the agents. So we have 3 solver agents per lens[1]: X and Y for the position on 2 axes and Rt for the rotation in the plane, as represented in Fig. 5.

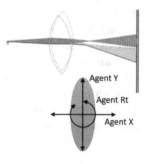

A ray is a more complex structure since it is represented by a path. A path is an ordered list of positions and directions describing the points of intersection with the various lenses it passes through $\{p_{j,k}(x, y)\}$ and the direction of the ray at these points represented by an angle to the X axis $\{ang_{j,k}\}$, with k the index of the intersection.

Fig. 5. Lens control diagram (theoretical objective beam in hashed gray)

The rays are not directly known by the agents. Only the last position and direction of each ray (when it reaches the screen) are used to compute sensor measures to send to the MAS. For example two measures can be computed from the mean square deviation of the positions and angles of the rays:

$$R_{pos} = \sqrt{\left(\sum((p_{j,last}(y) - p_{j,last}^{ref}(y))^2)/M\right)} \tag{2}$$

$$R_{ang} = \sqrt{\left(\sum((ang_{j,last} - ang_{j,last}^{ref})^2)/M\right)} \tag{3}$$

As seen in Sect. 3.2, an objective agent is associated with each sensor measure and updates its criticality depending on the gap with its objective value.

Other measures such as the width of the beam, or the power (percentage of rays arriving on the screen) can be calculated from this set of intersections of the rays with the screen. Our goal is to construct values that are as representative as possible of what can be perceived on a real system with one or more specific sensors.

5   Results

For each experiment presented in this section, for observability issues necessary to validate the tested hypotheses, each parameter evolves at a fixed step, and a curve of the most critical objective is represented at each iteration.

Each of the first two graphs (Fig. 6) represent an experiment run one hundred times, allowing to observe the variability of the resolutions on a single lens (cylindrical and thin). We notice that when the system is far enough from the solution

---

[1] Note that in reality, in 3 dimensions, there will be 6 agents for the 6 degrees of freedom.

(in the first cycles where the criticalities oscillate under 100), the convergence is slower. We observed the agents decisions are mostly cognitive and stochastic at this point. The main reason is that agents try to know what is the right direction. The momentum mechanism is crucial here. Then when the acquired information becomes sufficient to perceive a direction, the criticality decreases more and more quickly. The agents then make a series of reactive decisions that maintain this so-called acceleration phase. When the criticalities reach a level where their competition is strong, thus stopping the convergence, the agents reach an equilibrium in cognitive and reactive decisions which will help to continue converging towards the solution. However, this final phase includes the most non-cooperative synchronizations.

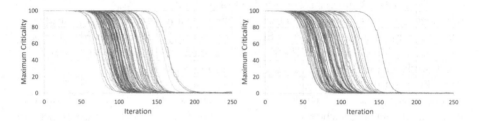

Fig. 6. Highest criticality over 100 repetitions of 2 problems with 1 lens (cylindrical on the left and thin on the right)

5.1   Problem Specific Knowledge

We made the hypothesis that the convergence of the system towards satisfactory states tends to accelerate when we provide agents with additional information that they take into account seamlessly without having to change their algorithms.

This hypothesis was tested by introducing a criticality on the deviation from the desired position of the quartile rays (in the order of the screen intersections). For example if Q_1 is more critical than Q_3 it means that the beam is too high compared to the target. The added information is that depending on which quartile is more critical, the collective will tend to redirect the beam faster than with the overall criticality of the positions.

The collective tries to help the most critical agent first, so it will lower the beam position before continuing the optimization of other objectives. This observation, validated empirically, led to better results when the quartile ray position criticalities are added (Figs. 7 and 8).

Indeed, we notice that the convergence of the system tends to be accelerated in the first phase of the resolution. The addition of criticality for purely informative purposes for the solver agents improves the worst resolution cases. However, we must be careful not to disturb their cooperation, because these additional criticalities are new criteria between which to arbitrate.

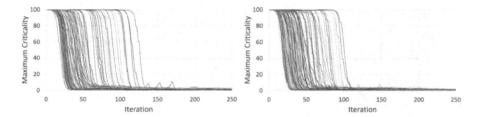

Fig. 7. Highest criticality over 10 repetitions of 10 1-lens problems without (left) and with criticality on quartiles (right)

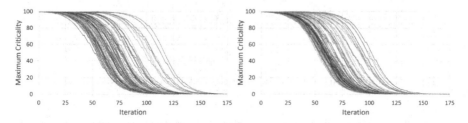

Fig. 8. Highest criticality over 100 repetitions of a 1-lens problem without (left) and with criticality on quartiles (right)

5.2   Increasing Complexity by the Number of Lenses

For an optical system, we consider that the increase of the complexity of a problem goes hand in hand with the increase of the number of lenses that compose it. Indeed, each lens has 3 axes of alignment, and therefore 3 design variables to the problem, which means 3 additional agents. Thus, for 10 lenses, we have a total of 30 agents who must cooperate in a 30 dimensional search space where each step deforms this space.

The following experiments have been performed with strongly reduced fixed steps because the instability of the system is greatly increased, due to the discontinuities of the beam in the chaining of the lenses. This causes peaks in criticality curves that can be remarked for 3-lens problems (Fig. 9) and even more for 7-lens problems (Fig. 10). However, a strong homeostasis capacity allows the agents to

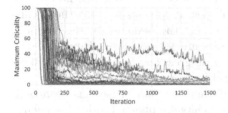

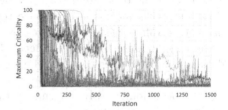

Fig. 9. Highest criticality over 10 repetitions of 10 3-lens problems

Fig. 10. Highest criticality over 10 repetitions of 10 7-lens problems

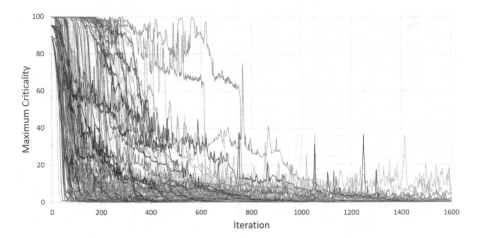

Fig. 11. Highest criticality for 10 repetitions of 10 problems with 10 lenses

successively degrade and improve the solution to globally converge to more satisfying configurations. This is the result of the trade-off between exploration and exploitation in the agents' behavior. We can see that the system also manages to converge with 10 lenses (Fig. 11). The increase in complexity is not the heart of the problem. The difficulty lies in the cooperation of an increasing number of interacting elements in an environment with many interconnections. The optimization problem has become at this stage a problem of systemic cooperation. The more efficient it is, the better the MAS will be in its resolution.

6   Conclusion and Perspectives

This article proposed a multi-agent approach to naturally model a real-world complex optimization problem as a cooperative solving problem and to satisfy as much as possible objectives given by experts at a reasonable computational cost. This is made possible by the agentification of the constraints and objectives of the problem and by making these agents cooperate in order to adapt the parameters of the system.

Experiments performed and results obtained show that this approach is generic enough to be applied to a wide range of complex systems, notably in Photonics with various search space topologies. It also shows that the agents manage to differentiate themselves by observing the behavior of the complex system in response to their changes. Results are yet to be confirmed on real data, and a deployment of this solution is in progress on physical robotic industrial systems, both in Photonics and control loop tuning domains.

The behaviour of solver agents, notably their decision phase, has been kept as simple as possible for now. Some improvements are planned inside the agents by implementing further learning algorithms able to work on sparse data, or by adding criticalities to have a constraint/stagnancy repulsive behavior.

Acknowledgements. This work is financially supported by the Occitanie Region (www.laregion.fr) as part of the READYNOV 2019–2020 research program. Quentin Pouvreau is co-funded by the French National Association for Research and Technology (ANRT) (www.anrt.asso.fr) and by *ISP System*.

References

1. Fioretto, F., Pontelli, E., Yeoh, W.: Distributed constraint optimization problems and applications: a survey. J. Artif. Intell. Res. **61**, 623–698 (2018)
2. Hoang, K.D., Yeoh, W.: Dynamic continuous distributed constraint optimization problems. In: Aydogan, R., Criado, N., Lang, J., Sanchez-Anguix, V., Serramia, M. (eds.) PRIMA 2022: Principles and Practice of Multi-Agent Systems, PRIMA 2022, vol. 13753, pp. 475–491. Springer, Cham (2022). https://doi.org/10.1007/978-3-031-21203-1_28
3. Hoang, K.D., Yeoh, W., Yokoo, M., Rabinovich, Z.: New algorithms for continuous distributed constraint optimization problems. In: Proceedings of the 19th International Conference on Autonomous Agents and MultiAgent Systems (2020)
4. Holland, J.H.: Adaptation in Natural and Artificial Systems: An Introductory Analysis with Applications to Biology, Control, and AI. MIT press, Cambridge (1992)
5. Hussain, K., Mohd Salleh, M.N., Cheng, S., Shi, Y.: Metaheuristic research: a comprehensive survey. Artif. Intell. Rev. **52**, 2191–2233 (2019)
6. Jorquera, T., Georgé, J.P., Gleizes, M.P., Régis, C.: A natural formalism and a multiagent algorithm for integrative multidisciplinary design optimization. In: IEEE/WIC/ACM International Conference on Intelligent Agent Technology - IAT, Atlanta, USA (2013)
7. Jourdan, L., Basseur, M., Talbi, E.G.: Hybridizing exact methods and metaheuristics: a taxonomy. Eur. J. Oper. Res. **199**(3), 620–629 (2009)
8. Kennedy, J., Eberhart, R.: Particle swarm optimization. In: Proceedings of ICNN 1995-International Conference on Neural Networks. IEEE (1995)
9. Perles, A., Crasnier, F., Georgé, J.P.: AMAK - a framework for developing robust and open adaptive multi-agent systems. In: 16th International Conference on Practical Applications of Agents and Multi-Agent Systems (PAAMS). Communications in Computer and Information Science book series (CCIS), Spain (2018)
10. Sharma, M., Kaur, P.: A comprehensive analysis of nature-inspired meta-heuristic techniques for feature selection problem. Arch. Comput. Methods Eng. **28**, 1103–1127 (2021)
11. Sörensen, K.: Metaheuristics-the metaphor exposed. Int. Trans. Oper. Res. **22**(1), 3–18 (2015)
12. Wang, Z., Qin, C., Wan, B., Song, W.W.: A comparative study of common nature-inspired algorithms for continuous function optimization. Entropy **23**(7), 874 (2021)
13. Yang, T., et al.: A survey of distributed optimization. Ann. Rev. Control **47**, 278–305 (2019)
14. Ye, D., Zhang, M., Vasilakos, A.V.: A survey of self-organization mechanisms in multiagent systems. IEEE Trans. Syst. Man Cybern.: Syst. **47**(3), 441–461 (2016)

GTG-CoL: A New Decentralized Federated Learning Based on Consensus for Dynamic Networks

M. Rebollo$^{(\boxtimes)}$, J. A. Rincon⊕, L. Hernández⊕, F. Enguix⊕, and C. Carrascosa⊕

Valencian Research Institute for Artificial Intelligence (VRAIN),
Universitat Politècnica de València (UPV),
Camino de Vera s/n, 46022 Valencia, Spain
mrebollo@upv.es, {jrincon,lhernand,carrasco}@dsic.upv.es,
fraenan@inf.upv.es

Abstract. One of the main lines of research in distributed learning in the last years is the one related to Federated Learning (FL). In this work, a decentralized Federated Learning algorithm based on consensus (CoL) is applied to Wireless Ad-hoc Networks (WANET), where the agents communicate with other agents to share their learning model as they are available to the range of the wireless connection. When deploying a set of agents is very important to study previous to the deployment if all the agents in the WANET will be reachable. The paper proposes to study it by generating a simulation close to the real world using a framework that allows the easy development and modification of simulations based on Unity and SPADE agents. A fruit orchard with autonomous tractors is presented as a case study.

Keywords: Complex networks · Distributed AI · Multi-Agent Systems (MAS) · Neural Networks

1 Introduction

Wireless Ad-hoc Networks (WANET) are formed by a set of mobile units (agents) that are equipped with a wireless connection antenna allowing them to communicate between them in a decentralized fashion [2]. This kind of device may have a short communication range due to the antenna capabilities and the need for battery-saving. For this reason, if the agents are moving, the possible other agents they will be able to connect will define a *Geographical Threshold Graph (GTG)* [1,4] according to the maximal scope given by the agents' antennas. This is the case of collaborative sensors in tractors (autonomous or not) perceiving the crop field they are populating.

When situated in rural areas far from connectivity availability and with the problems of being executed during a long period without a person controlling

P. Mathieu et al. (Eds.): PAAMS 2023, LNAI 13955, pp. 284–295, 2023.
https://doi.org/10.1007/978-3-031-37616-0_24

them or assuring their battery supply, these fields define a new interesting problem where AI techniques can be applied to adapt to those problems.

On the other hand, recent years have increased the research on cooperating distributed systems, particularly important in the distributed learning area. This area has seen the appearance last years of the Federated Learning (FL) algorithm as a way of sharing efforts for learning while maintaining the data being used privately. One of the approaches of Decentralized Federated Learning based on consensus in multi-agent systems is the *CoL* [3] algorithm.

The paper aims to study the application of Consensus in Multi-agent systems (and so, Co-Learning) to this *Geographical Threshold Graphs* to allow us to model the above-mentioned situation. Apart from the theoretical analysis, the paper presents the application of these graphs to *FIVE*, a Framework for developing Intelligent Virtual Environments inhabited by SPADE agents [6]. This framework allows for quickly defining or modifying a simulation, where a deployment of a set of mobile agents can be tested in a simulation of a crop field before deploying them in the actual environment.

The following section presents *GTG-CoL* as the application of *CoL* algorithm for *Geographical Threshold Graphs*. After that, the Orchard Digital Twin designed for validating the WANET designs is presented. The paper finishes with some conclusions and comments about future work.

2   GTG-CoL

2.1   Problem Definition

We apply CoL in WANETs where a vast area has limited connectivity. At design time, it is essential to ensure that the system will eventually form a strong-connected component for distributed systems to propagate the information along the participants using gossiping mechanisms. We want to apply FL to train neural networks without central servers, sharing the weights and biases with the direct neighbors. First, we present our decentralized FL algorithm, *CoL*, and how it can be applied to WANETs. Next, we develop how it can be assured at design time that a strong-connected component emerges from the MAS.

2.2   Co-Learning Algorithm

The Co-Learning *(CoL)* algorithm [3] is a decentralized FL algorithm that uses a consensus in multi-agent systems approach to share the weights of the neural network model each agent is learning, taking into account that all agents share the same neural network structure (see Fig. 1). This allows the agents to share the model being learned to aggregate with the others' models so that a new aggregated model can be used instead of his local one. In this case, the sharing is made only with the local neighbors of each agent, applying the consensus equations to obtain the aggregated model. Based on consensus properties, those weights can be propagated, and all the agents will converge to their average.

286   M. Rebollo et al.

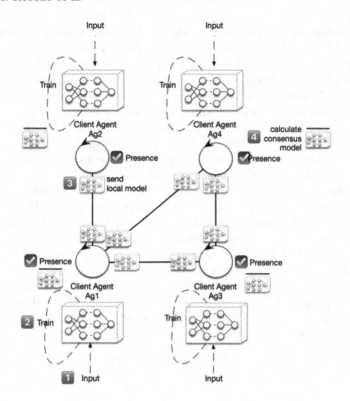

Fig. 1. MAS for FL through a consensus process.

Algorithm 1. $CoL_{a_i}(e, k, c)$ - Co-Learning Algorithm for agent a_i

---
1: **while** !doomsday **do**
2:     **for** $f \leftarrow 1, e$ **do**
3:       $W \leftarrow Train(f)$
4:     **end for**
5:     **for** $j \leftarrow 1, k$ **do**
6:       $X_i(0) \leftarrow W_j$
7:       **for** $t \leftarrow 1, c$ **do**
8:         $X_i(t+1) \leftarrow X_i(t) + \varepsilon \sum_{a_j \in N_i} [X_j(t) - X_i(t)]$
9:       **end for**
10:     **end for**
11: **end while**

Algorithm 1 details the steps an agent ai following the *Co-Learning* process will make when the neural network model is formed by k layers (agent ai storing their weights in W) These steps can also be observed in Fig. 1: first of all, it will train the neural network during e epochs (steps 1 and 2, input and training, in Fig. 1). This training results in the set of k matrices stored in W. For each one of them, the agent makes c iterations of the consensus algorithm, leading to k

new matrices that will be used in the training process again (step 4, calculate consensus model, in Fig. 1). This consensus is calculated with the models received from a_i neighbors, whom a_i has previously sent its own local model (step 3, send local model, in Fig. 1).

The process is executed in parallel as many times as parameters the artificial neural network has. Applying *CoL* algorithm to agents in WANET can be made by adapting it to take into account the switching topology of the network, that is, the set of neighbors of each agent N_i may change dynamically (as the agent could only communicate with the ones inside the range of his antenna. So, in the model, $N_i(t)$ has to be considered.

2.3   Network Characterization for WANETs

The network topology does not affect the result of the consensus process but does the convergence speed. A strong assumption is that all the participants must eventually form one connected component. Olfati-Saber and Murray [5] have demonstrated the algorithm's convergence under switching topology.

Carrascosa et al. [3] have studied different network topologies. This work concludes that random geometric graphs (RGG) are the most appropriate topology for a set of agents to coordinate. Existing networks following the same structure are known as Geographical Threshold Graphs (GTG), so this is the network topology preferred for the agent connection. For the theoretical study, and Without losing generality, we project the geographical space occupied by the orchard into a square area in a $[0,1)^2$ space. The agents will follow a set of rectilinear paths at regular distances. As a test bed, we define three different configurations:

- Test 1: one orchard with all robots running over parallel end-to-end lines.
- Test 2: two orchards next to each other, with agents moving in perpendicular directions
- Test 3: Test 2 + one extra agent that moves following a random walk.

Any actual configuration can be composed of these three scenarios. The movements of the agents on the orchard define a switching topology in the network, varying the set of neighbors for each agent at time $t, N_i(t)$ due to the entrance or leaving the detection range. Figures 2 to 4 show the network at two instants ($t = 20$ and $t = 70$). Therefore, we can consider the entire graph $G = \cup G(t)$ a weighted graph, where $G(t)$ is the network at time t and the weight w_{ij} indicates how much time agents a_i and a_j have been connected. This is the third graph depicted in the figures mentioned above.

Test 1. One Orchard. It is defined by one set of agents moving in the same direction. Different speeds and an offset can be introduced. The connection radius between agents in adjacent lines must be large enough to reach at least one neighbor. Figure 2 shows the location of the agents at two different times and the corresponding GTG with a radius $r = 0.3$. We accumulate all the connections and define the network as the union of all the networks at all analyzed epochs. The links' weight indicates how often two agents have been inside their reception radius. The plot on the left depicts the final network structure, an open ring connecting the two closest neighbors.

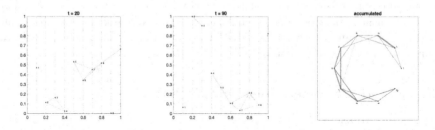

Fig. 2. Network evolution with robots moving along lines in an orchard

Test 2. Two Perpendicular Orchards. It follows a similar configuration. It considers two adjacent fields, with lines of trees (and paths) distributed in perpendicular directions. As shown in Fig. 3, the right-most agents in the vertical part act as bridges with all the agents with horizontal movements. The number of mutual connections will depend on the speed of agents, but eventually, all agents are susceptible to being connected. The aggregated final network can be considered as two open rings, where all the agents are connected with a subset of the right-most agents of the other ring depending on the radius $r = 0.3$.

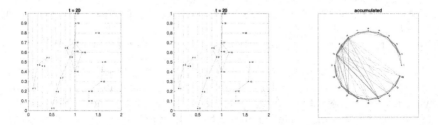

Fig. 3. Network evolution with robots in two orchards moving along with perpendicular lines

Test 3. Two Perpendicular Orchards and A Free Agent. The last model extends test 2 with an agent that moves freely across the orchard. It can represent a drone or other kind of vehicle without constraints. This agent follows a random walk inside the boundaries of the complete orchard. This agent is marked in red in Fig. 4. Depending on the agent's movements and its range, the resulting aggregated topology can vary, but some common properties emerge from this pattern, as seen in the following section.

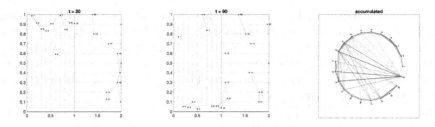

Fig. 4. Network evolution with robots in two orchards moving along with perpendicular lines and one drone moving freely following a random walk (in red) (Color figure online)

Each tractor can be viewed as a periodic task, where the period is the time they take to go and return to the same place (start of their path). If we calculate the hyperperiod as the least common multiple of the periods of such trips, one could study only that hyperperiod to see if all agents are connected or not.

To compare the three scenarios, we have analyzed the average degree and the average shortest paths of each type of aggregated network. They are relevant measures because the efficiency of the CoL process depends on them (not the resulting value, which is independent of the network topology). Networks with high degrees need to exchange information with more neighbors, which requires higher computational capabilities. On the other hand, longer paths provoke more extended periods until the consensus converges and a final training is obtained for the neural network.

Figure 5 shows the variation of these magnitudes as the connection radius increases. The evolution for tests one and two are similar: the path length decreases, and the degree increases with the radius. Nevertheless, in the third plot, we can see that the effect of the free agent is to keep both values almost constant. Its effect is to regularize the network degree and ease the connectivity of regions physically separated in the ground.

Finally, the efficiency of the network has been studied to analyze the failure tolerance (see Fig. 6). On the left, we can see no significant differences in the behavior under random failures. This is a consequence of being a GTG, where the spatial constraints avoid the existence of hubs, and the degree distribution

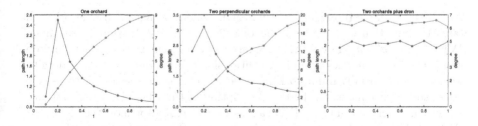

Fig. 5. Evolution of the avg. degree and the avg. shortest path length.

follows a Poisson distribution instead of a power law one. However, the situation is different for deliberate attacks. When we block the best-connected agents, the efficiency of the network degrades quicker than in test 1. This is because the right-most agents of perpendicular orchards, or the free agent, play as a bridge, with a slightly higher degree than average. That is why these agents are critical and precise in special surveillance.

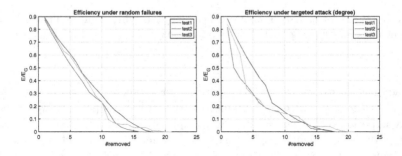

Fig. 6. Efficiency of the scenarios under random failures and deliberate attacks

3 Orchad Digital Twin for Validating WANET Designs

The approach presented here supposes using a Digital Twin of the orchard where the WANET is being deployed, so at design time, it can be tested and assured if the system deployed would be strongly connected.

A new version of the FIVE toolkit will be used to see in the virtual environment the dynamic evolution of the connections between the different agents as they are moving and entering or exiting the range of other agents' wireless antennas.

The simulations generated will be executed during the hyperperiod of the different agents, considering that the agents' periods are the time they need to return to their initial position.

3.1 FIVE

The FIVE (Flexible Intelligent Virtual Environment designer)[1] framework facilitates the creation and modification of a 3D Intelligent Virtual Environment (IVE) that is inhabited by SPADE (Smart Python Agent Development Environment) agents [6] effortlessly and expeditiously. This section presents a detailed overview of the FIVE framework and elaborates on the methodology used to model the environment. So, first, a description of the FIVE Designer system is presented, describing how an IVE can be easily created or modified. Next, the FIVE Execution System shows how the designed IVEs can be executed.

---

[1] https://github.com/FranEnguix/five.

FIVE Designer. The FIVE framework enables the creation of 3D environments using an integrated text-based map editor. Additionally, it offers the generation of custom agent avatars equipped with sensors, such as cameras. Defining a simulation is straightforward and efficient, requiring only modifying four text files to create the IVE and the agents (see Fig. 7). Among these files, the first three red files (`map.txt`, `map_config.json` and `map.json`) are responsible for generating the IVE, which includes light objects, agent spawn points, and other relevant elements. On the other hand, the last blue file (`configuration.json`) is utilized for generating the agents.

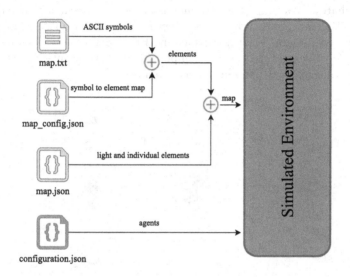

Fig. 7. Files involved in the generation of the IVE and the agents.

Once the constituent elements of the simulated IVE have been defined, the next step involves specifying the behavior of the inhabitant agents situated within the IVE. To achieve this, the FIVE framework incorporates a template for the inhabitant agents, composed of a SPADE agent with a Finite State Machine (FSM) behavior that governs the agent's execution cycle.

After setting up the files and defining the behaviors of the agents to meet our requirements, the next step is to initiate the execution of the framework modules. The subsequent section will provide a comprehensive overview of the modules and outline the steps for successfully running the simulation.

FIVE Execution System. The FIVE Execution System is a modular system that offers the flexibility to distribute computational load across multiple machines. It consists of three main components:

- The XMPP (Extensible Messaging and Presence Protocol) server, which enables communication between the agents and the environment.

- The FIVE Server Agent, which is developed using the Unity[2] engine.
- A collection of SPADE inhabitant agents that populate the IVE.

To launch an application, the execution order must be: first, execute the XMPP server (if the application is going to connect to a new one). Then, execute the FIVE Server Agent. And finally, to execute the SPADE inhabitant agents.

The inhabitant agents and the Server Agent connect to the XMPP Server, as they will communicate through this protocol, and the FIVE Server agent interacts with the SPADE inhabitant agents via XMPP presence control and messages conveyed through a custom open-source protocol.

The inhabitant agents send commands to the environment (FIVE Server Agent), such as moving their avatar to a new position or capturing an image with their equipped camera. For this reason, the FIVE Server Agent should be the next module to be executed. These components can be executed independently on different machines at different local networks.

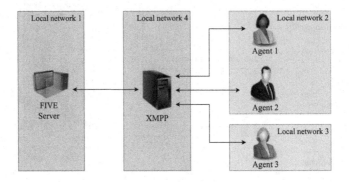

Fig. 8. Example of FIVE architecture deployed.

Figure 8 illustrates a FIVE simulation deployed across 4 distinct local networks. The colored rectangles depict different local networks, and the arrows denote network sockets. Each agent portrayed in the figure operates on a different machine. *Agent 1* and *Agent 2* are situated on the same local network (*Network 2*), and all agents are connected to the XMPP server.

The agents, based on SPADE, exercise control over the virtual avatars that populate the IVE that the FIVE Server manages. The framework supports network failure tolerance, which allows for easy reconnection of agents to the FIVE simulator, thereby enabling the resumption of their activities.

FIVE Server agent is in charge of the perception of inhabitant agents. As it has been extended for WANETs, the agents' antenna ranges can be configured, and this range is used to perceive which other agents are in his range and send it to the inhabitant agent. Each inhabitant agent will be subscribed to the presence of all the agents in the multi-agent system. The agent will have a set of active

---

[2] https://unity.com.

neighbors ($N_i(t)$ in the CoL algorithm) that will change every time he receives the perception from the FIVE Server. Then, the agent will attend only to the presence of his current active neighbors.

4   Case Study: A Simulation of Fruit Orchard Smart Areas

In this case study, the agents control tractors moving through fruit orchards located next to each other. As the tractors move through the orchards, they can communicate with only the tractors inside their antenna range. As the tractors are moving, they can communicate with other agents depending on this range.

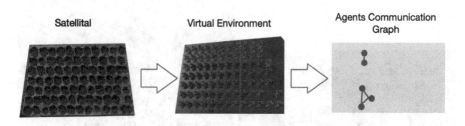

Fig. 9. Several views of a fruit orchard.

Figure 9 shows three views of the same fruit orchard. On the left, there is a satellite capture. In the middle of the figure, we can see the representation of this orchard in FIVE. On the right is the schematic representation of the communications between the tractors.

Tractor 2 has double the speed of the rest. Two isolated groups appear if they follow the distribution shown in 9. Allowing tractor 2 to change the orchard line, the team achieves the connection in one strong component and the data propagation among all participants. Figure 10 shows the result of this scenario.

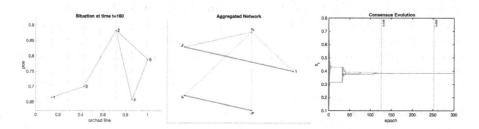

Fig. 10. Result of the simulation allowing robot 2 to change between second and fifth lines in the orchard. Left: situation at $t = 160$. Center: aggregated network. Right: Evolution of the consensus over two hyperperiods

The simulation has an hyperperiod $t = 126$. The plot on the left depicts the situation of the yard in $t = 160$. The one in the middle shows the aggregated network generated after the hyperperiod. A stronger connection appears between stable teams $\{1, 3\}$ and $\{4, 5\}$. Tractor 2 acts as a bridge between groups. Finally, the plot on the right is a sample of the consensus process over one common variable. The hyperperiod and twice the hyperperiod value are marked vertically. The mean absolute error at $t = 126$ is $MAE = 0.0016$, and when the second hyperperiod completes, at $t = 252$, $MAE = 8.8^{(-6)}$. So this is the time we can estimate the team needs to complete one training epoch of the neural network, exchange the weights and combine the models using CoL.

Fig. 11. Overhead and side views of the fruit orchard.

Figure 11 shows presents two different views of the simulated fruit orchard in FIVE: the left image shows an overhead representation, whereas the right image shows a side view where an agent is represented as a tractor. These images show the same instant as the agent communication graph shown in Fig. 9. So, in this last Figure, the representation in the Virtual Environment of the dynamic communication graph can be observed as the edges (drawn in pink color) appear and disappear, showing the availability of communication between agents in the antenna range of other agents. As observed in these figures, if all agents move at only one line, two different components in the system will not communicate between them. Changing the design of the system, making that agent 2 moves along two different lines, would achieve the connection between both components.

5   Conclusions

The paper has presented the work of applying *CoL* algorithm, a consensus-based decentralized federated learning algorithm, to Wireless Ad-hoc Networks. This kind of system generates a Geographical Threshold Graph formed by the agents moving and being able to connect only with other agents inside their wireless antenna range. When designing these kinds of systems is very important to be able to ensure that all agents are reachable at some time during the execution of the system. The paper proposes a method for testing this, generating a close-to-reality simulation of the environment (Digital Twin) and executing the agents during the hyperperiod of the duration of their routes (outward and return).

The paper proposes using the FIVE framework for easy creating and modifying the simulations and SPADE agents, as they are integrated into the framework. It has also presented a fruit orchard simulation, where the ideas commented on are exemplified.

In future work, we plan to study the optimization of communication, trying to reduce the number of messages between the agents and the size of such messages.

Acknowledgements. This work has been developed thanks to the funding of projects: Grant PID2021-123673OB-C31 funded by MCIN/AEI/ 10.13039/ 501100011033 and by "ERDF A way of making Europe", PROMETEO CIPROM/ 2021/077, TED2021-131295B-C32 and Ayudas del Vicerrectorado de Investigacion de la UPV (PAID-PD-22).

References

1. Bradonjić, M., Hagberg, A., Percus, A.G.: The structure of geographical threshold graphs. Internet Math. **5**(1–2), 113–139 (2008)
2. Bradonjic, M., Kong, J.: Wireless ad hoc networks with tunable topology. In: Proceedings of the 45th Annual Allerton Conference on Communication, Control and Computing. Citeseer (2007)
3. Carrascosa, C., Rincón, J., Rebollo, M.: Co-learning: consensus-based learning for multi-agent systems. In: Advances in Practical Applications of Agents, Multi-Agent Systems, and Complex Systems Simulation. The PAAMS Collection, pp. 63–75 (2022)
4. Masuda, N., Miwa, H., Konno, N.: Geographical threshold graphs with small-world and scale-free properties. Phys. Rev. E **71**(3), 036108 (2005)
5. Olfati-Saber, R., Murray, R.M.: Consensus problems in networks of agents with switching topology and time-delays. IEEE TAC **49**(9), 1520–1533 (2004)
6. Palanca, J., Terrasa, A., Julian, V., Carrascosa, C.: SPADE 3: supporting the new generation of multi-agent systems. IEEE Access **8**, 182537–182549 (2020). https:// doi.org/10.1109/ACCESS.2020.3027357

A Novel Framework for Multiagent Knowledge-Based Federated Learning Systems

Bruno Ribeiro⬛, Luis Gomes⬛, Rafael Barbarroxa⬛, and Zita Vale(✉)⬛

GECAD Research Group on Intelligent Engineering and Computing for Advanced Innovation and Development, LASI—Intelligent Systems Associate Laboratory, Polytechnic of Porto, R. Dr. António Bernardino de Almeida, 431, 4200-072 Porto, Portugal
{brgri,lfg,rroxa,zav}@isep.ipp.pt

Abstract. Multiagent systems promote a decentralized and distributed approach that enable the division of complex problems into smaller parts. The use of multiagent systems also enables the representation of physical entities, such as persons, pursuing their own goals in an active and proactive society. Currently developments are promoting the idea of having machine learning models in agents to enable intelligent decisions in agents-side. However, machine learning, required assess to large datasets that cannot be available locally to individual agents, demanding the sharing of data or the use of public available datasets to training models for a given agent. To address this issue, this paper proposes the use of federated learning to enable the existence of a collaborative learning model that respects the data privacy, security, and ownership and can be in compliance with the European General Data Protection Regulation (EU GDPR). This paper proposes a novel framework called Python-based framework for agent-based communities powered by federated learning (PEAK FL) that will provide all the necessary tools to build powerful federated learning solutions based on agent communities. This framework provides the users the ability to implement and test hybrid solutions (multiagent-based federated learning systems) in a simple-to-use way, removing the unnecessary boilerplates.

Keywords: multiagent systems · federated learning · distributed learning · collaborative learning · knowledge-based approach

1 Introduction

In today's society privacy and security of data are two properties that the technologies must have in order for the users to use them. After the increase of privacy and security concerns among the general public, European Union created the General Data Protection Regulation (EU GDPR) [1] to protect users from malicious usage of their data. With that, a new technology emerged called federated learning (FL). FL uses machine learning (ML) to collaboratively train a model to perform a task with great precision [2]. The difference lays down on the privacy and security of the data. Traditional ML trains the model in centralized data, whereas FL trains the model in decentralized data, avoiding breaking the privacy of the users. In FL instead of sharing and centralizing the data, the model is shared between the clients so they can train them with their data locally. Then a central server aggregates the updates of each client to update the global model. This is done for several iterations until the global model achieves the desired accuracy. In an FL environment, the client can be either a device, a user, or a company.

A lot of research in the FL domain has been put towards the development of solutions to certain limitations of the technology, like communication overhead, heterogeneity of devices, security risks, and lower model accuracy when compared to traditional ML, especially in non-identically and independently distributed (non-IID) data [3, 4]. To decrease communication overhead without decreasing the model accuracy, the authors of [5] by modeling the problem as a multi-objective one, used a multi-objective optimization algorithm to solve it. Regarding heterogeneity of devices, the authors of [6] propose a new solution to alleviate the constraints that other known solutions to this problem contain, like computation and memory constraints, while achieving great model accuracy. In this survey [7] security risks of federated learning are studied, and analyzed, and solutions to those risks are provided. Despite these achievements, there is still no one solution to all problems. However, there is a methodology that has the necessary capabilities to solve the overhead communication, the heterogeneity of the devices and security risks in a decentralized and distributed way. The methodology is Multi-Agent Systems (MAS).

MAS relies on several individual agents in order to achieve some kind of main shared objective [8]. In the context of this paper, an agent is an autonomous, intelligent, and adaptable piece of software that is cable of making decisions based on the information that it gathers from the environment [9, 10]. MAS can operate in competitive, cooperative, or collaborative environments, but in regard to FL systems, the environment is cooperative. This means that each agent has an individual objective (a specific machine learning task) but they work together towards their local objectives (share the model to be trained) [11, 12].

Normally, the problems MAS tries to solve cannot be solved by only one single system. This is because there are problems where the knowledge to solve the main problem is distributed in space and time, requiring several autonomous entities to work together toward the solution, like an FL system. One example of this is in this paper [13] the authors propose a solution based on MAS in order to do the management of computational resources of a computing network, alleviating the overhead in the communication and minimize the percentage of unused resources. In this other paper [14], a MAS framework is proposed in order to facilitate the development of simulations and emulations of real-time complex energy systems showing the capacities the MAS have to make systems interoperable, flexible, and expandable. In [15] the mobility aspect of the agents in a MAS is explored in order to optimize the performance of their individual objectives, achieving good results in the overall system. The described works show some of the benefits that the MAS can have on distributed and decentralized problems.

Regarding the actual combination of MAS and FL there are some works already. In [16] the authors propose a MAS solution for FL systems based on agents in order to add some flexibility and scalability to the system. In [17] propose a new solution that assures privacy while maximizing the accuracy of the model in a two-agent environment. Other approaches use reinforcement learning agents to solve specific FL tasks. In [18] the authors use multiagent reinforcement learning to create a more efficient client selection algorithm for FL systems. In [19] its proposed an intelligent cyber-physical system based on multiagent reinforcement learning in order to increase the security of an FL system. There are already related works regarding the use of MAS in FL environments which highlight the improvements that MAS can have on FL. However none of them proposes and provides a framework that helps the users to create, test and monitor these hybrid systems.

Other researchers use knowledge-based approaches like clustering to help the clients to form the most appropriate federations according to their data. In [20] the authors developed a solution that organized several clients in an FL system, according to their individual objectives, in order to maximize the training efficiency. In [21] the authors propose a solution based on clustering that helps the clients make better decisions regarding the federations that will provide more efficiency according to their model parameters. These studies do not use MAS to cluster, however, there are studies that show that MAS can have great results in clustering problems [22, 23].

These and other works, show the benefits that MAS can have when solving a distributed problem, and FL is no different. The MAS has the interoperability, communication capabilities, and flexibility needed to allow FL systems to work flawlessly with possible gains in computation effectiveness and communication overhead. This is because the MAS would give a knowledge-driven approach to the FL system, making the decisions made per client and server, more precise and more effective towards their goals, than the data-driven approach made by the FL alone.

This paper proposes a functionality extension to the Python-based framework for heterogeneous agent communities (PEAK) [24] by using the Flower framework [25]. This extension will help the developers to build intelligent and autonomous agent-based FL systems by combining the functionalities of both frameworks. The FL implementations made with Flower can be directly implemented in the PEAK extension. To test the proposed approach, it is created a federation with ten agents that will work together to train a shared genetic programming model to solve an image classification problem. The model was implemented using the Flower framework only, showing the interoperability of the PEAK FL can use that implementation to integrate it with the agents, without the need to change anything in the model.

This paper is structured in the following manner: Sect. 1 where the context of the paper, the state of the art and the main objective are described; Sect. 2 where the solution proposed is described in detail; Sect. 3 has the description of the case study, the results and the discussion; and finally Sect. 4 has the summary of the solution proposed and the main conclusions of the paper.

2   Python-Based Multiagent System Solution for Federated Settings

PEAK is a software library written in Python that allows users to build powerful, flexible, and expandable agents [24]. More than that, PEAK helps users to create an ecosystem around communities of these powerful agents. An example of this ecosystem can be seen in Fig. 1. The powerfulness of these agents comes from their intrinsic capacities for communication and integration with other systems. Their communication skill relies on

Extensible Messaging and Presence Protocol (XMPP) [26] which works like an instant messaging application (e.g., social media apps). This protocol allows humans to interact with the agents directly and to integrate functionalities like a list of personal contacts, the creation of social groups, to share of resources like images and sound files, and so on. Because the agents are written in Python, they have all the capabilities related to this programming language. Python has become a very popular language given that it is easy to write and understand. Nowadays there are a lot of artificial intelligence libraries in Python that can easily be integrated with PEAK agents to add more skills, intelligence, and robustness. Another benefit is the ability to integrate the agents with the IoT and smart-devices environment, allowing the agents to interact with the real world, and have a meaningful impact on users.

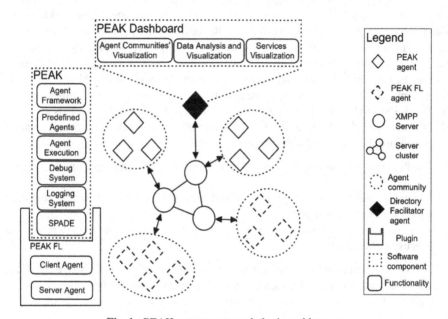

Fig. 1. PEAK components and plugin architecture

It is important to define what are an agent community and the PEAK ecosystem. An agent community is a group that is made of agents that are digitally close/connected to each other. This means that they can easily communicate/interact with the whole community and create societies around it. These groups can represent different things but normally the agents share some characteristic or objectives, e.g. in a federated learning system the agents would create a group to train a shared model together. It's not obligatory for the agents to belong to a community, they can interact with other agents without the need for one. The PEAK ecosystem is a larger concept that represents all the agent communities created with PEAK and the agents inside them (Fig. 1). PEAK has several features, but the most important can be summarized in the following points:

- Gives the user the proper tools (e.g., functions and classes) to create powerful and flexible agents capable of socializing, learning, creating structured communities and so on;
- Permits the creation, monitorization and visualization of the PEAK ecosystem;
- Allows the monitorization and visualization of the communities structures and agents' interactions;
- Allows for extendability by permitting adding extra functionalities and new paradigms in the agent structure and in the system.

PEAK Dashboard is a separate project from PEAK itself. This is a web application that allows the visualization and monitoring of the PEAK ecosystem. The PEAK Dashboard can connect to any PEAK ecosystem, the only requirement for the dashboard to work is having the predefined agent Directory Facilitator (DF) in PEAK activated in the ecosystem. This is because DF, in addition to being an administrator in the system, has the ability to see the inside structure of the agents' communities and also their services, communications, and data. To be able to provide those pieces of information to the PEAK dashboard or any other external service, DF has a REST API. This gives the PEAK ecosystem the ability to integrate it with other services or platforms. The main functionalities that PEAK Dashboard provides are:

- Visualization and monitorization of the communities structures in the PEAK ecosystem;
- Visualization of the data being produced and published by the agents in the ecosystem in the form of plots and graphs;
- Visualization of the services being provided by the agents in the ecosystem and the ones using the services.

All of these functionalities are available in the dashboard in an interactive interface. Another important point to be mentioned is the fact that the dashboard can also be extendible, changed or even new ones can be created that can work with PEAK.

2.1 PEAK Federated Learning

In order to facilitate the creation, design, and development of Federated Learning systems based on agents, this paper proposes a new plugin for the PEAK framework, called PEAK Federated Learning (PEAK FL). This plugin can be seen as an extension of PEAK (Fig. 2). PEAK was chosen because of its ability to extend its functionalities and integrate with other systems, especially Python artificial intelligence libraries. Likewise, a lot of federated learning frameworks exist written in Python, and some research was done in order to choose the best FL frameworks to combine with PEAK. The one that seemed most appropriate was Flower. Flower is one of the most used frameworks, especially by researchers, given that the framework was built with the purpose to be modular, extendible, and easily modified to suit easily to the purposes of the user. In this case, it was used the modularity capabilities of both frameworks in order to combine them together, as will be described later in this section. What the PEAK FL plugin does is it gives more functionalities to the base PEAK agents so they can create and participate, either as a server or client, in federations with the purpose to train a global machine learning model. To be able to understand how the architecture behind PEAK FL it is necessary to see how Flower and PEAK work behind the scenes.

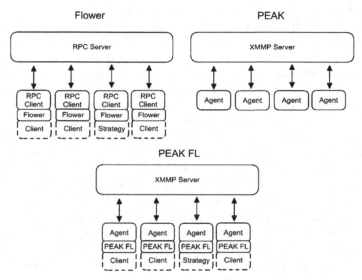

Fig. 2. Communication layers of PEAK, Flower, and PEAK FL.

Flower is a framework that aims to help users to build, test, and experiment with FL systems [25]. The framework was built to be extendable and easily adaptable. In Flower, there are two main concepts to be aware of. The first one is client and the second one is strategy. The client is a member that will participate in the federation in order to train and evaluate an artificial intelligence model for a specific shared problem. The server's strategy is the algorithm behind the synchronization, client selection, client configuration, and fitness and evaluation aggregation operations. Regarding the actual implementation, there are two classes that represent these two concepts, which have the same name, Client and Strategy. The users, to build an FL system with Flower, must implement the Strategy used by the server and the Client. Only then, they can execute the FL system.

For clients and server to be able to communicate with each other, Flower uses a communication protocol called RPC. What the communication layer will do is to use the implementation of the Strategy and Client and create the respective instances of the clients and the server, and manage the synchronization and communications between them. The authors of Flower did this by abstracting the Strategy and Client classes from the communication layer. This means that given an implementation of a Client and a Strategy, it is possible to change the communication layer with a working implementation (e.g., MQTT) and the FL system would work as well. In the case of PEAK FL, the communication layer used was the PEAK itself. In PEAK, it is possible to consider the agents as part of the communication layer, given that one of the main features of a

PEAK agent is communication skills. But the PEAK itself does not have the necessary functionality to synchronize and manage the FL process. That is where the PEAK FL comes in, it implements an additional layer in the agents, that instructs them how to use the Flower implementations of the classes Client and Strategy (Fig. 2). One important aspect to mention is that any implementation made in the Flower Client and Strategy can be used directly in a PEAK FL agent without any change.

So, in order to be able to use the flower classes integrated into the agents it is necessary to add extra functionality (that is where the plugin part of the PEAK FL comes in). In Flower, the communication layer is responsible to synchronize and send the right information to the right destiny. The original PEAK agent cannot do that intrinsically, so two new agents were created the FlowerClientAgent and the FlowerServerAgent. The FlowerServerAgent will be responsible to create a group for the federation, waiting for the necessary clients to join, and also to synchronize the process order of the FL system according to the Flowers implementation. For this to work the FlowerServerAgent needs to implement two more classes the AgentProxy (based on the ClientProxy of Flower) and the AgentManager (based on the ClientManager of the flower). The AgentProxy can be described as a virtual representation of the FlowerClientAgents on the server side. This allows the FlowerServerAgent to perform actions in the FlowerClientAgents remotely. The AgentManager allows the management of the agents in the federation. One implementation of a Strategy might not need every client to train the model for example, so the AgentManager will give access to the list of agents available in the federation. Finally, the FlowerClientAgent will only wait for instructions and execute them when asked by the FlowerServerAgent.

3   Case Study

To showcase a simple example of how the PEAK FL can be used to implement, test and monitor an FL system the following case study was developed.

The dataset used to train de model is the Rectangles dataset. The dataset has 51,200 28 × 28 pixels images of rectangles and squares, with different dimensions and localizations. The idea is to identify which rectangles in the images have a larger width or length. Originally the dataset is divided into training and test sets of sizes 12,000 and 50,000, respectively. However, given the nature of the FL, only a fraction of the dataset was used. In total, there are 10 clients, everyone with a dataset with 200 images chosen randomly from the original dataset.

In this case study, it was chosen a genetic programming model called Flexible Genetic Programming (FGP). This model has shown to be a great solution for several image classification problems. The model is called flexible because of each individual's program structure. The structure was purposely built thinking about image classification problems. The set of the function set is function related to image processing. More details about the model can be found in [27]. Because the FGP's authors already had the FGP parameters defined, it was decided to use the same ones, except for the population size and the number of generations which were adapted to the present case study (100 and 10, respectively).

This model was implemented in the Fower framework producing only the necessary files and documents to run the model on Flower. Those exact same documents were used in the PEAK FL framework directly, without changing the implementation, to show the interoperability that PEAK FL has in what regards to creating FL systems with Flower. Little implementation was needed in the agent front, only the necessary behavior to join the community of the agents.

Regarding the FL the agents will join a group called "Federation" where all the clients will join to begin a 30-round FL session. There are in total 10 agent clients and one agent server. Figure 3 analyzes the evolution of the individuals throughout the execution of the case study. The x-axis represents the individuals in the hall of fames ordered from the first to the last one. The graph resembles a Pareto distribution in which achieved a stable overall error very close to the beginning of the execution. Every client ended up with an error of 0%, except for the clients three and seven that ended up with 0.4%. The error is the classification error rate.

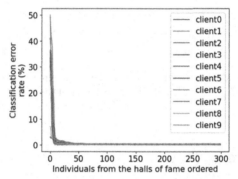

Fig. 3. Pareto distribution of the classification error rate evolution of the local halls of fame throughout the case study execution.

Figure 4 shows, on the left side, the contributions that each client made to each other. A lot of individuals were shared and used between them, indicating that all the clients benefitted with the FL system. The right side of Fig. 4 shows a graph that is used to showcase the evolution of the impact that each client had on the global hall of fame, the hall of fame belonging to the server. After round six the contributions are constant because they reach a stable evolution point where better individuals could not be made, given that their errors are almost null. Finally, Fig. 5 is a print screen taken in real-time of the ecosystem created by the case study in the PEAK Dashboard.

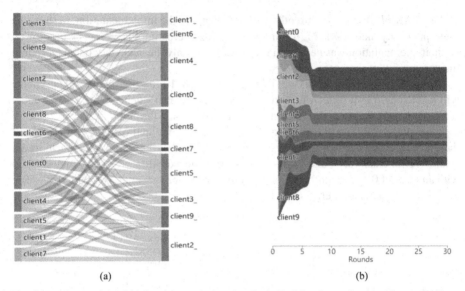

(a)   (b)

Fig. 4. On the (a) right side shows a graph showing the hall of fame contributions that each client made; on the (b) left side shows a graph of the evolution of the contributions that each client throughout the rounds.

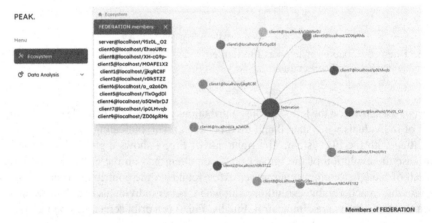

Fig. 5. Print screen of the Ecosystem of the PEAK Dashboard interface.

4   Conclusions

This paper proposes a novel approach to integrate federated learning in multiagent systems by using PEAK framework. PEAK Federated Learning plugin is proposed and tested by using federated learning framework Flower. The result is a framework that helps the developers to design, implement, test and monitor multiagent-based federated learning systems in a easy-to-use way. It eliminates the unnecessary boilerplates to speed up the development of these systems, while allowing the interoperability between

Flower and PEAK Federated Learning. PEAK Federated Learning achieves this without changing the user interface of PEAK and Flower frameworks.

To test this novel approach, and the proposed plugin, a case study was created where a group of ten client agents had to train a genetic programming model to solve an image classification problem. The federation ended up with good solutions overall, meaning that the federation was a success, with almost every agent reaching a classification error rate of 0%. In future work, other models will be tested and other applications of multiagent systems will be explored using the proposed solution.

Acknowledgements. This article is a result of the project RETINA (NORTE-01-0145-FEDER-000062), supported by Norte Portugal Regional Operational Programme (NORTE 2020), under the PORTUGAL 2020 Partnership Agreement, through the European Regional Development Fund (ERDF). The authors acknowledge the work facilities and equipment provided by GECAD research center (UIDB/00760/2020) to the project team.

References

1. European Union, General Data Protection Regulation. https://gdpr.eu/
2. Li, Q., et al.: A survey on federated learning systems: vision, hype and reality for data privacy and protection. IEEE Trans. Knowl. Data Eng. **35**, 3347 (2023)
3. Zhu, H., Xu, J., Liu, S., Jin, Y.: Federated Learning on Non-IID Data: A Survey. ArXiv (2021)
4. Mahlool, D.H., Abed, M.H.: A comprehensive survey on federated learning: concept and applications. In: Lecture Notes on Data Engineering and Communications Technologies (2022)
5. Morell, J.Á., Dahi, Z., Chicano, F., Luque, G., Alba, E.: Optimising communication overhead in federated learning using NSGA-II. In: Jiménez Laredo, J.L., Hidalgo, J.I., Babaagba, K.O. (eds.) EvoApplications 2022. LNCS, vol. 13224, pp. 317–333. Springer, Cham (2022). https://doi.org/10.1007/978-3-031-02462-7_21
6. Mendieta, M., Yang, T., Wang, P., Lee, M., Ding, Z., Chen, C.: Local learning matters: rethinking data heterogeneity in federated learning. In: Computer Vision and Pattern Recognition 2022 (2021)
7. Liu, P., Xu, X., Wang, W.: Threats Attacks and Defenses to Federated Learning: Issues, Taxonomy and Perspectives. Cybersecurity **5**(1), 1–19 (2022)
8. Balaji, P.G., Srinivasan, D.: An introduction to multi-agent systems. In: Srinivasan, D., Jain, L.C. (eds.) Innovations in Multi-Agent Systems and Applications – 1, Studies in Computational Intelligence, vol. 310, pp. 1–27. Springer, Berlin, Heidelberg (2010). https://doi.org/10.1007/978-3-642-14435-6_1
9. Santos, G., et al.: Semantic services catalog for multiagent systems society. In: Dignum, F., Corchado, J.M., De La Prieta, F. (eds.) PAAMS 2021. LNCS (LNAI), vol. 12946, pp. 229–240. Springer, Cham (2021). https://doi.org/10.1007/978-3-030-85739-4_19
10. Santos, G., Pinto, T., Vale, Z., Corchado, J.M.: Semantic interoperability for multiagent simulation and decision support in power systems. In: De La Prieta, F., El Bolock, A., Durães, D., Carneiro, J., Lopes, F., Julian, V. (eds.) PAAMS 2021. CCIS, vol. 1472, pp. 215–226. Springer, Cham (2021). https://doi.org/10.1007/978-3-030-85710-3_18
11. Cardoso, R.C., Ferrando, A.: A review of agent-based programming for multi-agent systems. Computers **10**, 16 (2021)

12. Fourez, T., Verstaevel, N., Migeon, F., Schettini, F., Amblard, F.: In: Dignum, F., Mathieu, P., Corchado, J.M., De La Prieta, F. (eds.) Advances in Practical Applications of Agents, Multi-Agent Systems, and Complex Systems Simulation, The PAAMS Collection (2022), vol. 13616, pp. 166–178. Springer, Cham (2022)
13. Bajo, J., De la Prieta, F., Corchado, J.M., Rodríguez, S.: A low-level resource allocation in an agent-based cloud computing platform. Appl. Softw. Comput. **48**, 716 (2016)
14. Santos, G., Gomes, L., Pinto, T., Faria, P., Vale, Z.: MARTINE's real-time local market simulation with a semantically interoperable society of multi-agent systems. Sustain. Energy Grids Netw. **33**, 100995 (2023)
15. Pereira, H., Ribeiro, B., Gomes, L., Vale, Z.: Smart grid ecosystem modeling using a novel framework for heterogenous agent communities. Sustainability **14**, 15983 (2022)
16. Rincon, J., Julian, V., Carrascosa, C.: FLaMAS: federated learning based on a SPADE MAS. Appl. Sci. **12**, 3701 (2022)
17. Znaidi, M.R., Gupta, G., Bogdan, P.: Secure distributed/federated learning: prediction-privacy trade-off for multi-agent system. ArXiv (2022)
18. Zhang, S.Q., Lin, J., Zhang, Q.: A multi-agent reinforcement learning approach for efficient client selection in federated learning. Proc. AAAI Conf. Artif. Intell. **36**, 9091 (2022)
19. Xu, M., et al.: Multiagent federated reinforcement learning for secure incentive mechanism in intelligent cyber-physical systems. IEEE Internet Things J. **9**, 22095 (2022)
20. Ghosh, A., Chung, J., Yin, D., Ramchandran, K.: An efficient framework for clustered federated learning. IEEE Trans. Inf. Theory **68**, 8076 (2022)
21. Long, G., Xie, M., Shen, T., Zhou, T., Wang, X., Jiang, J.: Multi-center federated learning: clients clustering for better personalization. World Wide Web **26**, 481 (2023)
22. Fiosina, J., Fiosins, M.: Density-based clustering in cloud-oriented collaborative multi-agent systems. Hybrid Artif. Intell. Syst. **2013**, 639–648 (2013)
23. Chaimontree, S., Atkinson, K., Coenen, F.: A multi-agent based approach to clustering: harnessing the power of agents, agents and data mining. Interaction **2021**, 16–29 (2012)
24. Ribeiro, B., Pereira, H., Gomes, L., Vale, Z.: Python-based ecosystem for agent communities simulation. In: Pablo Gracia, B., et al. (eds.) 17th International Conference on Soft Computing Models in Industrial and Environmental Applications (SOCO 2022). SOCO 2022, vol. 531, pp. 62–71. Springer, Cham (2023). https://doi.org/10.1007/978-3-031-18050-7_7
25. Beutel, D.J., et al.: Flower: A Friendly Federated Learning Research Framework. ArXiv (2020)
26. Internet Engineering Task Force, Extensible Messaging and Presence Protocol.https://xmpp.org/
27. Bi, Y., Xue, B., Zhang, M.: Genetic programming with image-related operators and a flexible program structure for feature learning in image classification. IEEE Trans. Evol. Comput. **25**, 87 (2021)

Exploring Planner-Guided Swarms Running on Real Robots

Michael Schader$^{(\boxtimes)}$ and Sean Luke

George Mason University, Washington, DC 22030, USA
{mschader,sean}@gmu.edu

Abstract. Robot swarms have been proposed as a way to take advantage of the scalability, robustness, and adaptability of natural large-scale multiagent systems in order to solve engineering challenges. However, accomplishing complex tasks while remaining flexible and decentralized has proven elusive. Our prior work on planner-guided robot swarms successfully combined a distributed swarm algorithm implementing low-level behaviors with automated parallel planners and executives selecting high-level actions for the swarm to perform as a whole, but had only been tested in simplistic grid-world simulations. Here we demonstrate our approach on physical robots augmented with experiments in continuous-space simulation, showing that it is an effective and efficient mechanism for achieving difficult task objectives to which swarms are rarely applied.

Keywords: Multi-robot systems and real world robotics · Real-time multi-agent systems · Agent cooperation and negotiation

1 Introduction

The field of swarm robotics prizes three cardinal virtues. The first virtue is scalability, thanks to potentially large numbers of inexpensive robots. The second is robustness, the ability to withstand the loss of members and to accommodate the addition of new ones. The third is adaptability, the appropriate response to changing conditions in the environment. These virtues take inspiration from natural systems such as ant colonies, flocks of birds, schools of fish, and so on. To achieve these goals, swarm robotics designs have historically taken the form of potentially large numbers of simple and usually homogenous robots, with limited and typically local interaction and communication, and with loosely coupled or entirely separated decision-making.

However, the highly decoupled and distributed nature of a typical robot swarm, valued for these virtues, has also proven difficult to control. As the survey of Brambilla et al. [5] noted, "[d]ue to the lack of a centralized controller, it is in general very difficult to effectively control a swarm once it starts operating." Because they are loosely coupled, swarms by design cannot easily coordinate to do synchronized, interleaved, or nontrivial collaborative tasks. Rather,

P. Mathieu et al. (Eds.): PAAMS 2023, LNAI 13955, pp. 307–319, 2023.
https://doi.org/10.1007/978-3-031-37616-0_26

swarm robotics dogma often turns to *emergent behavior*, arguing that swarms can achieve complex macro-level behavior through the micro-interactions of many agents. But while it is feasible, through simulation, to predict the resulting macrophenomena arising from these interactions, a critical inverse problem— identifying which micro-behaviors will achieve a desired macrophenomenon—is generally unsolved and perhaps unsolvable. Collective behavior involving synchronization and coordination has proven elusive. In short: researchers have succeeded in getting swarms to forage, patrol, distribute themselves, and to form shapes, but swarms have not shown promise in working together to build a house.

The tension here is between coordination and decentralization. The classic method for identifying, solving, and executing synchronized and collaborative robot tasks is to use a (normally centralized) task planner and executive with tight coupling. But when doing so, a swarm degenerates into a single-agent system with multiple effectors (the swarm robots), hurting scalability due to network complexity, and damaging robustness by relying on a single point of failure. Global knowledge held by every agent would not scale well and would limit adaptability, and requiring long-distance communication among robots would violate the swarm-style focus on having only local interactions.

We are interested in endowing swarm architectures with sophisticated collaboration and synchronization. To this end, we have developed *planner-guided robot swarms* as a novel solution to these problems. In our method, the mission for the swarm is specified in automated planning terms. Each agent has its own planner, and all use the same algorithm and inputs, yielding identical results. The swarm is treated as a set of one or more *virtual agents*, each composed of many real ones and responsible for the parallel execution of the actions in the plan steps. An *a priori* mapping of virtual agent actions to real agent behaviors is the bridge that leads to emergent behavior in service of the mission objectives. Our approach does not require tight synchronization among swarm members but is still robust to retrograde behavior among out-of-sync robots. The method also seeks to ensure that their plans will ultimately synchronize and align.

In our previous work in this area [21,22], we assumed ideal and simplistic conditions in a trivial simulated grid-world, with predictable communications and none of the sensor noise or action failures associated with actual physical robots. In this paper we remedy this, showing that potentially large groups of physical robots can collectively perform synchronized and planned actions. The robots are able to do these tasks while overcoming physical crowding and interference, significant difficulties in localization and wayfinding, and physical challenges inherent in object detection grasping and manipulation. We further show that the method scales and that it can adapt to dynamic changes in the environment and in the nature of the robot swarm.

We begin with a review of relevant robot swarm research. We then explain our planner-guided method, describing both physical robot and continuous-space simulation implementations. We present the results of experiments performed on real robots as a proof of concept and in simulation as a stress test of time and complexity, showing that our approach lives up to the virtues of scalability, robustness, and adaptability.

2   Previous Work

Planning for Robot Groups. Several researchers have worked to use symbolic planning to direct groups of robots. Audrito et al. [2] explored specifying high-level goals using MA-PDDL, the multiagent variant of Planning Domain Definition Language, and automatically translating them into single-agent behaviors using "Aggregate Programming" (AP) to express low-level activities. Jang et al. [10] experimented in simulation with solving underwater survey mission planning challenges with sophisticated versions of PDDL that included time and numeric variables, soft constraints, and probabilistic actions. Chen et al. [8] used Linear Temporal Logic (LTL), a first-order logic calculus with temporal operators, to define overall objectives, then from that definition synthesized a symbolic plan for robot swarm members to follow. In follow-up work [7], they extended this approach to work in a decentralized fashion. The two-layer mechanism has similarities to our work; however the initial LTL specification and automatically generated plans are constrained to "location and formation-based swarm behaviors", primarily formation control, rather than addressing a general set of possible agent actions. Moarref et al. [15] also used LTL to generate decentralized symbolic plans for individual swarm members to follow, and demonstrated some success in simulation.

Decentralized Swarm Control. Much literature has applied or extended traditional decentralized swarm approaches: here we only list a few relevant examples. Bachrach et al. [3] used the "Proto" programming language, designed for directing large groups of agents by treating them like an amorphous medium, to guide swarm robot movements with potential fields. This synthesis of low- and mid-level actions produced robust emergent behaviors, but it did not address high-level goals and decisions. Rossides et al. [20] adapted the particle swarm optimization technique to work with swarms of actual rather than virtual members. They were able to demonstrate using a swam to localize a radio source in physically realistic simulations. The method only applies to swarm movement rather than any other activities. Suárez et al. [23] implemented the "bat algorithm" on real robots, showing that the bio-inspired technique could be used for three-dimensional map-building and navigation. Vardy [25] showed that simple odometry could serve as the basis for swarming behaviors such as aggregation, and in later work [26] developed an algorithm for object clustering also based on simple low-level capabilities.

Physical Swarm Robots. Also related to our work is physical demonstrations of noteworthy swarm robot capabilities. Many have explored the classic emergent behavior of foraging along with some variants. Lu et al. [12] and Nouyan et al. [16] implemented collaborative foraging algorithms on both simulated and physical robots. Talamali et al. [24] combined 200 Kilobots (small limited-capability swarm robots) with augmented reality to implement virtual pheromones and

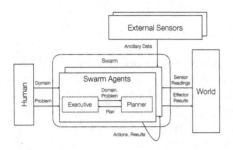

Fig. 1. Planner-guided swarm architecture.

Fig. 2. Component relationships.

to investigate collective foraging. Other researchers have demonstrated different swarm behaviors. Adkikari [1] and Farrugia et al. [9] created physical robot swarms that demonstrated collaborative object transport, the former achieving superlinear performance with a 30-robot team. Chamanbaz et al. [6] implemented a consensus algorithm on physical rovers and floating buoys that allowed the robots to move from one location to another in a coordinated fashion. Petersen et al. [19] created a system for physical and simulated robots to construct preplanned structures from specialized square blocks.

3   Method

In our planner-guided swarm approach (Fig. 1), a human programmer uses the Planning Domain Definition Language (PDDL) [14] to specify a *domain*, the predicates, actions, and objects available in the world; and a *problem*, the initial conditions and goal state of the situation at hand. These definitions are issued to each agent before it enters the swarm, and are the only centralized element in the architecture. Once online, each agent uses its planner to produce a plan, a series of possibly parallel macro-actions that will accomplish the objectives. If the actions are parallelizable, the agents will distribute themselves (randomly or round-robin, depending on circumstances) to one of several groups, each responsible for one of the concurrent actions. Each agent's executive then begins performing the micro-behaviors associated with its chosen action. As the agents in the swarm interact with the world, collecting sensor inputs and manipulating objects, they exchange information with each other when in close proximity. Optional external sensors, separate from the swarm itself, may provide additional input to agents that are nearby. When the agents determine that a plan step has been completed, they advance to the next one, until the goal has been achieved.

3.1   Software Framework

In our implementation (see Fig. 2) the key figure is the *agent*. Each agent uses a built-in planner to generate a *plan*, which encapsulates the result of processing a PDDL domain and a PDDL problem. A plan has one or more *steps*, each of which have one or more *actions*. An action has its own *completion criteria* allowing it to determine when it has been accomplished. A step is complete when all its actions have been accomplished, and a plan is complete when all its steps are complete. Based on the action mapping M_{act}, each action is associated with a single *behavior* which guides the agent to perform certain activities. Last, the predicate mapping M_{pred} associates *predicates* with the plan, one for each predicate specified in the PDDL domain definition, allowing the agent to assess the state of the world in planning terms. When the predicates listed as goal conditions in the PDDL problem statement are all true, the agent is done with the mission.

3.2 Mapping Actions to Behaviors

The action mapping M_{act} ties together the high-level specifications in the PDDL domain and problem statements and the low-level behaviors of each swarm agent. While a classical task planner produces a collection of *actions* that are triggered by initial preconditions, are finite in length, and produce expected postconditions (effects), swarm agent *behaviors* may run forever and do not yield postconditions. Thus to map an action into a behavior, we must define a stopping criterion after which we expect the action postconditions have been fulfilled by the behavior. Those conditions can be tied to the agent's knowledge of its own activities (such as successfully picking something up), information received from other agents about their activities, data from the agent's sensors, or external data from global sensors helping the swarm.

3.3 Predicate Mappings

The predicate mapping M_{pred} enables replanning by closing the loop between the observed state of the world and the conditions asserted in the problem statement. Although classical planning assumptions do not accommodate changes caused by actors other than the plan-executing agents, rerunning the planner with revised initial conditions provides an effective way to adjust behavior in response to unexpected updates to the environment. The inputs specified in the mapping come from the same categories as those for the action completion criteria: self-knowledge, exchanged information, onboard sensor readings, and external sensor data.

3.4 Algorithm

The general algorithm for each planner-guided swarm agent is as follows:

```
1: procedure RunDecentralizedAgent(domain, problem)
2:     currentState ← problem.initialConditions
3:     while plan is nil or not plan.isComplete do
4:         if plan is nil then
5:             plan ← MakePlan(domain, problem)
```

```
6:              stepNum ← 1
7:              successes ← ∅
8:          step ← plan.steps[stepNum]
9:          if step.isComplete then
10:             stepNum ← stepNum + 1
11:             continue
12:         action ← step.actions[groupNum]
13:         if action.isComplete then with probability P_switchGroups
14:             groupNum ← randomly chosen group number
15:             continue
16:         ⟨behavior, parameters, criteria⟩ ← M_act{action}
17:         result ← Execute(behavior, parameters, criteria)
18:         if result = success then
19:             Add new token to successes
20:         TransmitTokens(successes)
21:         for agentSuccesses in ReceiveTokens() do
22:             add tokens in agentSuccesses to successes
23:         newState ← Evaluate(predicates in M_pred)
24:         if currentState ≠ newState then
25:             plan ← nil
26:             problem.initialConditions ← newState
27:             currentState ← newState
28:             continue
```

The functions referenced in this algorithm are:

MakePlan(). Run the planner on the supplied domain and problem to generate a new plan, along with any predicates needed to determine its completion status.

Execute(). Move as needed and change the world with effectors as per the active behavior and its parameters. This could include activities like driving toward a destination, wandering randomly, picking things up, pressing buttons, assembling structures, and leaving stigmergic messages.

TransmitTokens(). Transmit success tokens and state information to neighboring agents. This is how the agents share knowledge of their activities.

ReceiveTokens(). Process success token messages received from others. This is the means of coordination that enables the swarm agents to collectively decide when to advance to the next plan step.

Evaluate(). Update the state of the world to determine action completion as well as any need for replanning. Each agent evaluates the predicates defined in the planning domain to determine if the environment has changed in a way contrary to the classical assumptions that only a unitary agent can affect the world, thus resyncing the planner to observed reality.

4 Experiments in Simulation and Physical Robot Validation

In this paper we demonstrate our method on physical robots and in a realistic robot swarm simulation, showing its effectiveness and scalability in controlling real groups of robots despite noise, failure, and the complexity of physical constraints.

Fig. 3. Locobot with brick.

Fig. 4. Robots at work on a Brick Layering scenario. Red and yellow bricks are at their destinations in the top right; green and white ones are still in the field. (Color figure online)

We perform three experiments on both physical robots and in simulation. The first is a baseline experiment which demonstrates that the method scales to large numbers of agents (we tested up to 64). The second experiment tests if the method is robust to unexpected changes in the number of agents in the swarm, both tolerating loss of agents and accepting new ones. The third experiment tests if the method can deal with noise and unexpected state changes in the robot environment.

Our simulations were created with the MASON multiagent simulation toolkit [13] using two-dimensional continuous-space. For the physical robot implementation we used the Trossen Robotics PX100, a robot platform based on the open-source LoCoBot design (Fig. 3). We positioned four AprilTag [17] two-dimensional barcodes on the sides of the experiment area to add visual localization assistance to the onboard odometry, and incorporated YOLOv5 object detection [11] trained on a custom set of images of colored Duplo bricks on the floor.

All code for the abstract swarm operations, including PDDL definitions, parallel planning, success token management, and completion criteria, was shared between the physical robot and simulation implementations. We used our own custom implementation of the GraphPlan algorithm [4] built using the PDDL4J planning toolkit [18].

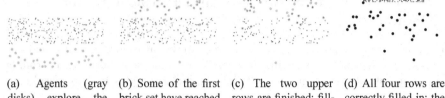

(a) Agents (gray disks) explore the field for bricks (colored rectangles).

(b) Some of the first brick set have reached their destination, others are en route.

(c) The two upper rows are finished; filling in the next row is underway.

(d) All four rows are correctly filled in; the agents have declared the job complete.

Fig. 5. Stages of the Brick Layering scenario in simulation.

Base Scenario. The experiments we performed are built on a common core challenge we call *Brick Layering* (Figs. 4 and 5). The initial state has bricks of four different colors scattered throughout the large field portion of the environment. The goal state has the bricks arranged by color in rows in the target area: red nearest the wall, followed by yellow, then green, and finally white (dark gray in simulation). To achieve the objective, the swarm must move the bricks in the correct sequence, filling in the farthest layers first, or their own movements will disrupt the pattern.

PDDL Definition. The planning domain for Brick Layering has one set of predicates to specify if each area is empty, i.e. (area1-empty), (area2-empty), etc.; and another to tell what color brick each contains, such as (area1-contains ?item), (area2-contains ?item), and so on, in which ?item is a placeholder for one of the four brick types. The domain also contains actions to fill or empty each area with a particular kind of brick, as in (fill-area1 ?item), (empty-area2 ?item), and the like. The planning problem has initial conditions with all four areas being empty, and a goal state of each area containing the correct color bricks. Driven by these dependencies, the planner produces the following straightforward single-group plan to be executed in sequential order: (fill-area1 red-brick), (fill-area2 yellow-brick), (fill-area3 green-brick), (fill-area4 white-brick).

Action Mapping. The crosswalk M_{act} between plan actions and swarm member behaviors is based on translating fill-area and empty-area directives into foraging activities. The agents' low-level collect() behavior has parameters for item, source-area, and destination-area. The completion criterion is for the count of fill-area or empty-area events to equal the preconfigured size of each area: four in the physical robot scenario and 64 in simulation. As an example, the plan action (fill-area1 red-brick) maps to the agent behavior collect(red-brick, field, area1), which means, "navigate to the field, then wander looking for a red brick; when you find one, pick it up, navigate to area1, and drop it off; repeat until area1 is full".

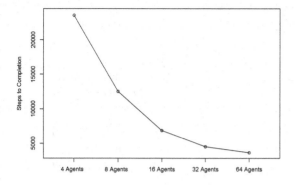

Robots	Minutes to completion	Speedup vs one
1	45.1	1.00
2	24.1	1.87
3	17.6	2.56
4	16.4	2.75

Fig. 6. Scalability in simulation: steps to completion for full runs with various numbers of agents.

Fig. 7. Scalability results with physical robots.

Predicate Mapping. The mapping M_{pred} between domain predicates and agent knowledge is largely based on the counts of actions accomplished. For example, the truth value of (area4-contains white-brick) is determined by taking the count of (fill-area4 white-brick) events, subtracting the number of (empty-area4 white-brick) events, and seeing if the result equals the size of area4. The only other mechanism in this mapping is used in the third experiment, in which an external sensor determines if red bricks are in area1 or not.

4.1 Experiment 1: Scalability

In the first experiment we examined how the planner-guided swarm method works with different numbers of agents. Ideally, the more robots that are used, the faster the mission will be accomplished, up to the point of negative returns due to crowding and interference among too many individuals. One aspect of this challenge that makes scaling up difficult is contention for the last few bricks of a color, requiring the robots to implicitly or explicitly coordinate their collection actions. Another is the common destination region for robots carrying bricks of the same color, forcing them to navigate around each other on the way to and from each delivery.

In simulation, we set the brick count to 256 and conducted runs with 4, 8, 16, 32, and 64 agents. Average steps to completion ranged from 23,537 with four agents down to 3643 with 64 agents (Fig. 6), showing that our method works and scales from a few agents up to common swarm population sizes. We performed 1000 runs of each treatment in simulation with 100% completion, and verified that all step counts were statistically significant using a two-tailed t-test at $p = 0.05$ with the Bonferroni correction.

For physical validation, we performed full runs of the scenario with sixteen bricks using one, two, three, and four robots, in a much smaller and physically constraining space, so crowding was much more of an issue compared to simulation. We measured the time to completion for each group size and observed

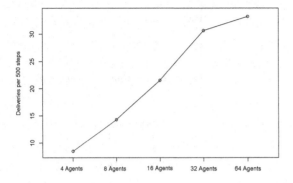

Robots	Deliveries per minute	Speedup vs one
1	0.53	1.00
2	0.73	1.39
3	0.81	1.53
4	1.26	2.39

Fig. 8. Robustness in simulation: deliveries per 500 steps for run segments with varying numbers of agents.

Fig. 9. Robustness results with physical robots.

that every increase led to faster mission completion (Fig. 7). Two robots were 87% faster than one robot, and three robots were 2.5 times as fast as one. With four robots, the speedup increased only to 2.75, showing diminishing returns as expected based on the diameter of the robots and the area of the field. These results showed the scalability of our approach with real robots.

4.2   Experiment 2: Robustness

In the second experiment, we evaluated the planner-guided swarm's ability to continue progressing with a mission (albeit more slowly) when some swarm members are removed, and to speed up progress when new swarm members are added. If working as intended, the swarm will maintain its knowledge of the state of the world regardless of membership changes, tolerating the loss of departing individuals and rapidly incorporating new arrivals. Even the gradual complete replacement of the original swarm members should pose no problem since all are fungible and there is no hierarchy.

In simulation we performed repeated runs with 256 bricks, adding or removing randomly-selected agents every 500 steps to exercise groups with 4, 8, 16, 32, and 64 individuals, while measuring the rate of brick delivery over time (Fig. 8). We evaluated 1000 periods of each population size in simulation, and verified that all delivery rates were statistically significant using the two-tailed t-test at $p = 0.05$ with the Bonferroni correction. Periods with more agents were consistently more productive than those with fewer; average rates ranged from 8.5 deliveries per 500-step period up to 33.7. This showed the planner-guided swarm's ability to robustly tolerate removals and take advantage of additions.

For physical validation, we launched the sixteen-brick scenario with three robots, then added or removed randomly-selected robots every two minutes to test with 1, 2, 3, and 4 individuals. In spite of this swapping in and out of swarm members, the group continued to progress in the plan, ultimately succeeding. From telemetry we determined the time periods when each number of robots

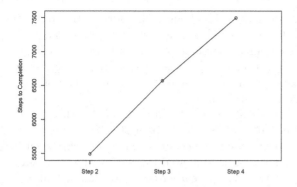

Notif.	Mins to	Add'l mins
step	compl.	needed
2	29.2	5.1
3	31.9	7.8
4	33.7	9.6

Fig. 10. Adaptability in simulation: steps to completion for 32-agent runs with different change notification times.

Fig. 11. Adaptability results with physical robots.

was active and counted the bricks delivered during each period. Delivery rates ranged from 0.53 bricks per minute for one robot up to 1.26 for four (Fig. 9), consistent with speedups expected when using more robots.

4.3 Experiment 3: Adaptability

In the third experiment, we explored how a planner-guided swarm can respond to changed circumstances. For this we added a new component to the scenario: a sensor positioned near the brick dropoff area that could observe how many bricks of each color were present. During each run, some time after the first two rows were filled in, we would remove the uppermost layer of red bricks and return them to the field, undoing some of the group's work. After a variable delay, the sensor would inform the swarm members of this change to the world. In response, the individuals would replan based on their updated knowledge of the conditions, remove already-placed bricks as needed to expose the empty top section, then proceed with the usual layering sequence. We would expect the swarm to accommodate the unexpected change and still complete the mission, with earlier notification leading to faster completion than later notification due to the varying amount of rework needed.

In simulation we ran 32 agents through the same series of environmental change scenarios with 256 bricks. For notification after plan steps two, three, and four, the average time steps to completion were 5491, 6569, and 7494 respectively, demonstrating that the sooner the swarm learns about a changed situation, the faster it can replan and ultimately complete the assignment (Fig. 10). We performed 1000 runs of each treatment in simulation with 100% completion, and verified that all step counts were statistically significant using the two-tailed t-test at $p = 0.05$ with the Bonferroni correction.

For physical validation, we used eight bricks and two robots. We started the scenario and allowed the group to complete plan steps one and two, building the red and yellow brick layers. We then removed the first layer and redistributed the red bricks to the field. The sensor noted this change and informed the robots. Upon learning the news, each robot replanned, deciding to disassemble the second layer to gain access to the first, then begin building the four layers again. The revised plans prepended the action (empty-area2 yellow-brick) to the filling steps in the original. Making the same decisions independently, the robots completed the challenge despite the change to their environment.

During successive real robot runs, we delayed notification of this change to the end of plan step three, and then to the end of plan step four. This led to additional preliminary steps being added, i.e. (empty-area3 green-brick) for the step three change and (empty-area4 white-brick) followed by that for the step four change. Across these runs, we observed that the earlier the robots learned about the removal of the top layer, the sooner they could replan and the more quickly they finished the mission (Fig. 11).

5   Conclusion

We built on our prior work with planner-guided robot swarms, demonstrating the approach on physical robots and in continuous-space simulation for the first time. We showed that the technique is scalable, robust, and adaptable in real swarm and multi-robot conditions. In future work will build a planner-guided swarm out of larger numbers of physical robots. With it we will experiment with more sophisticated types of collaboration among agents, and evaluate various navigation and communication methods. This will help pave the road from research to real-world applications for this powerful, general approach to swarm engineering.

References

1. Adhikari, S.: Study of Scalability in a Robot Swarm Performance and Demonstration of Superlinear Performance in Conveyor Bucket Brigades and Collaborative Pulling. Ph.D. thesis, The University of Toledo (2021)
2. Audrito, G., Casadei, R., Torta, G.: Fostering resilient execution of multi-agent plans through self-organisation. In: 2021 IEEE International Conference on Autonomic Computing and Self-Organizing Systems Companion (ACSOS-C), pp. 81–86. IEEE (2021)
3. Bachrach, J., Beal, J., McLurkin, J.: Composable continuous-space programs for robotic swarms. Neural Comput. Appl. 19(6), 825–847 (2010)
4. Blum, A.L., Furst, M.L.: Fast planning through planning graph analysis. Artif. Intell. 90(1–2), 281–300 (1997)
5. Brambilla, M., Ferrante, E., Birattari, M., Dorigo, M.: Swarm robotics: a review from the swarm engineering perspective. Swarm Intell. 7(1), 1–41 (2013)
6. Chamanbaz, M., et al.: Swarm-enabling technology for multi-robot systems. Front. Rob. AI 4, 12 (2017)
7. Chen, J., Sun, R., Kress-Gazit, H.: Distributed control of robotic swarms from reactive high-level specifications. In: 2021 IEEE 17th International Conference on Automation Science and Engineering (CASE), pp. 1247–1254. IEEE (2021)

8. Chen, J., Wang, H., Rubenstein, M., Kress-Gazit, H.: Automatic control synthesis for swarm robots from formation and location-based high-level specifications. In: 2020 IEEE/RSJ International Conference on Intelligent Robots and Systems (IROS), pp. 8027–8034. IEEE (2020)
9. Farrugia, J.L., Fabri, S.G.: Swarm robotics for object transportation. In: 2018 UKACC 12th International Conference on Control (CONTROL), pp. 353–358. IEEE (2018)
10. Jang, J., Do, H., Kim, J.: Mission planning for underwater survey with autonomous marine vehicles. J. Ocean Eng. Technol. 36(1), 41–49 (2022)
11. Jocher, G., et al.: ultralytics/yolov5: v3.1 - Bug Fixes and Performance Improvements (2020). https://doi.org/10.5281/zenodo.4154370
12. Lu, Q., Griego, A.D., Fricke, G.M., Moses, M.E.: Comparing physical and simulated performance of a deterministic and a bio-inspired stochastic foraging strategy for robot swarms. In: 2019 International Conference on Robotics and Automation (ICRA), pp. 9285–9291. IEEE (2019)
13. Luke, S., Cioffi-Revilla, C., Panait, L., Sullivan, K., Balan, G.: MASON: a multiagent simulation environment. SIMULATION 81(7), 517–527 (2005)
14. McDermott, D., et al.: PDDL: the planning domain definition language (1998)
15. Moarref, S., Kress-Gazit, H.: Decentralized control of robotic swarms from high-level temporal logic specifications. In: 2017 International Symposium on Multirobot and Multi-agent Systems (MRS), pp. 17–23. IEEE (2017)
16. Nouyan, S., Groß, R., Bonani, M., Mondada, F., Dorigo, M.: Teamwork in self-organized robot colonies. IEEE Trans. Evol. Comput. 13(4), 695–711 (2009)
17. Olson, E.: Apriltag: a robust and flexible visual fiducial system. In: 2011 IEEE International Conference on Robotics and Automation, pp. 3400–3407. IEEE (2011)
18. Pellier, D., Fiorino, H.: PDDL4J: a planning domain description library for Java. J. Exp. Theoret. Artif. Intell. 30(1), 143–176 (2018)
19. Petersen, K.H., Nagpal, R., Werfel, J.K.: Termes: An autonomous robotic system for three-dimensional collective construction. Rob.: Sci. Syst. VII (2011)
20. Rossides, G., Metcalfe, B., Hunter, A.: Particle swarm optimization–an adaptation for the control of robotic swarms. Robotics 10(2), 58 (2021)
21. Schader, M., Luke, S.: Planner-guided robot swarms. In: Demazeau, Y., Holvoet, T., Corchado, J.M., Costantini, S. (eds.) PAAMS 2020. LNCS (LNAI), vol. 12092, pp. 224–237. Springer, Cham (2020). https://doi.org/10.1007/978-3-030-49778-1_18
22. Schader, M., Luke, S.: Fully decentralized planner-guided robot swarms. In: Dignum, F., Corchado, J.M., De La Prieta, F. (eds.) PAAMS 2021. LNCS (LNAI), vol. 12946, pp. 241–254. Springer, Cham (2021). https://doi.org/10.1007/978-3-030-85739-4_20
23. Suárez, P., Iglesias, A., Gálvez, A.: Make robots be bats: specializing robotic swarms to the bat algorithm. Swarm Evol. Comput. 44, 113–129 (2019)
24. Talamali, M.S., Bose, T., Haire, M., Xu, X., Marshall, J.A., Reina, A.: Sophisticated collective foraging with minimalist agents: a swarm robotics test. Swarm Intell. 14(1), 25–56 (2020)
25. Vardy, A.: Aggregation in robot swarms using odometry. Artif. Life Rob. 21(4), 443–450 (2016)
26. Vardy, A.: Orbital construction: swarms of simple robots building enclosures. In: 2018 IEEE 3rd International Workshops on Foundations and Applications of Self* Systems (FAS* W), pp. 147–153. IEEE (2018)

Integrating Policy Summaries with Reward Decomposition for Explaining Reinforcement Learning Agents

Yael Septon[1], Tobias Huber[2]([⊠]), Elisabeth André[2], and Ofra Amir[1]

[1] Technion - Israel Institute of Technology, Haifa, Israel
yael123@campus.technion.ac.il, oamir@technion.ac.il
[2] University of Augsburg, Augsburg, Germany
{tobias.huber,andre}@informatik.uni-augsburg.de

Abstract. Explainable reinforcement learning methods can roughly be divided into local explanations that analyze specific decisions of the agents and global explanations that convey the general strategy of the agents. In this work, we study a novel combination of local and global explanations for reinforcement learning agents. Specifically, we combine reward decomposition, a local explanation method that exposes which components of the reward function influenced a specific decision, and HIGHLIGHTS, a global explanation method that shows a summary of the agent's behavior in decisive states. Results from two user studies show significant benefits for both methods. We found that the local reward decomposition was more useful for identifying the agents' priorities. However, when there was only a minor difference between the agents' preferences, the global information provided by HIGHLIGHTS additionally improved participants' understanding.

Keywords: Explainable AI · Reinforcement Learning · Neural Networks

1 Introduction

Artificial Intelligence (AI) agents are being deployed in a variety of domains such as self-driving cars, medical care and home assistance. In this work, we focus on explaining the behavior of agents that operate in sequential decision-making settings, which are trained in a deep reinforcement learning (RL) framework. Explainable reinforcement learning methods can broadly be divided into two classes based on their scope: local and global explanations. *Local* explanations analyze specific actions of the agent, for example, by generating saliency maps [8] that depict the agent's attention, or by showing the utility the agent expects to obtain from different actions by decomposing its reward function [10]. *Global*

This research was partially funded by the DFG through the Leibniz award of Elisabeth André (AN 559/10-1) and by the Israeli Science Foundation (grant #2185/20).

explanations attempt to describe the high-level policy of an agent. For example, by extracting logical rules that describe the agent's strategy [4], by approximating the policy with a simpler decision tree [11], or by creating a "summary" of the policy demonstrating the agent's behavior in different scenarios [2].

While local explanations provide detailed information about single decisions of an agent, they do not provide any information about its behavior in different contexts. Similarly, while global explanation methods provide a high-level view of a policy, they do not provide decision-specific insights. Due to the potential complementarity of such approaches, it is important to examine the effectiveness of combining them, rather than studying each approach in isolation. Huber et al. [9] combined local and global explanation methods by integrating strategy summaries with saliency maps. Their user study showed that the combination of local and global explanations is promising. However, the saliency maps they used as local explanation were lacking. One potential reason for this is that saliency maps are a post-hoc explanation technique that is created after the RL agents are fully trained. Recent literature suggests that such post-hoc explanations do not always faithfully reflect the agent's learned decision model [7,13]. Therefore, we explore the use of reward decomposition, an intrinsic explanation method that is build into the agent's decision model, as local explanation in this work.

We conducted two user studies in which participants were randomly assigned to one of four different conditions that vary in the combination of global and local information: (1) being presented or not presented with a local explanation (reward decomposition), and (2) being presented with a global explanation in the form of a HIGHLIGHTS policy summary [1] or being presented with frequent states the agent encounters (a baseline for not providing global explanations). We used a Highway and a Pacman environment and trained agents that varied in their priorities by modifying the reward function. Participants were asked to determine the priorities of these agents based on the explanations shown in their assigned study condition.

Our results show that the use of reward decomposition as a local explanation helped users comprehend the agents' preferences. In addition, the HIGHLIGHTS global explanation helped users understand the agents' preferences in the environment of Pacman. While we found that the benefit of presenting reward decomposition was greater than that of providing HIGHLIGHTS summaries, the combined explanations further helped users to distinguish between the agents' priorities when there only was a minor difference between the agents' preferences.

2 Approach

We assume a Markov Decision Process (MDP) setting and use Double DQN [14] to train our agents. The exact architecture of the networks we used was specific for each environment and will be described in the corresponding sections.

2.1 Reward Decomposition

Van Seijen et al. [15] proposed the Hierarchical Reward Architecture (HRA) model. HRA takes a decomposed reward function as input and learns a separate

Q-function for each reward component. In a game like Pacman, such reward components could correspond to dying or reaching specific goals. Because each component typically only depends on a subset of all features, the corresponding Q-function can be approximated more easily by a low-dimensional representation, enabling more effective learning.

This can be incorporated in the MDP formulation by specifying a set of reward components C and decomposing the reward function R into $|C|$ reward functions $R_c(s, a, s')$. The objective for the HRA agent remains the same as for traditional Q-learning: to optimize the overall reward function $R(s, a, s') = \sum_{c \in C} R_c(s, a, s')$. HRA achieves this by training several Q-functions $Q_c(s, a)$ that only account for rewards related to their component c. For choosing an action for the next step, the HRA agent uses the sum of these individual Q-functions: $Q_{HRA}(s, a) := \sum_{c \in C} Q_c(s, a)$. However, when updating the Q-functions each function $Q_c(s, a)$ only considers the reward $R_c(s, a, s')$, which corresponds to its' reward component c, for the current and expected future reward. If the underlying RL agent uses neural networks, the different Q-functions $Q_c(s, a)$ can share multiple lower-level layers of the network. In this case, the collection of Q-functions that each have one type of reward can be viewed as a single agent with multiple *heads*, such that each head calculates the action-values of a current state under his reward function.

HRA was originally proposed to make the learning process more efficient. However, Juozapaitis et al. [10] suggested the use of *Reward Decomposition (RD)* as a local explanation method. Showing the individual Q-values $Q_c(s, a)$ for each reward component c can explicitly expose the different types of rewards that affect the agent's behavior.

This increase in explainability should not result in a decreased performance. Van Seijen et al. [15] already showed that HRA can even result in increased performance for Pacman. We additionally conducted a sanity check in the Highway environment to verify that HRA results in comparable learning to that obtained without decomposing the reward function.

2.2 Policy Summaries

Agent Strategy Summarization. [2] is a paradigm for conveying the global behavior of an agent. In this paradigm, the agent's policy is demonstrated through a carefully selected set of world states. The goal of strategy summarization is to choose the subset of state-action pairs that best describes the agent's policy. In a formal way, Amir and Amir [1] defined the set $T =< t_1, ..., t_k >$ as the trajectories that are included in the summary, where each trajectory is composed of a sequence of l consecutive states and the actions taken in those states, $< (s_i, a_i), ..., (s_{i+l-1}, a_{i+l-1}) >$. Since it is not feasible for people to review the behavior of an agent in all possible states, k is defined as the size of the summary.

We use a summarization approach called HIGHLIGHTS [1] that extracts the most "important" states from execution traces of the agent. The importance of a state s is denoted as $I(s)$ and is defined differently between environments.

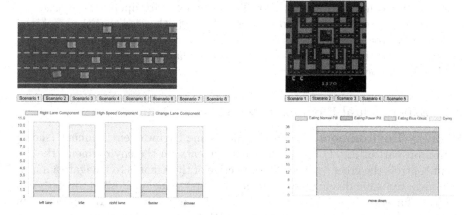

Fig. 1. Screenshots from our two experiments. The upper part of each screenshot shows a specific state ("Scenario 2") extracted from an agent's behavior. The bottom part shows the reward bars corresponding to the state shown above. For each action (shown on the x-axis) the Q-values of the different reward components (depicted in different colors) are shown (y-axis). For Pacman, only the reward bar for the agent's chosen action is shown. Users could switch to different states by choosing a scenario from the list. The states (scenarios) were chosen based on the summary method (HIGHLIGHTS or frequency-based). For conditions without local explanation, the reward bars were omitted and each scenario showed a short video.

The general idea is that a state is important if the outcome of the chosen action is expected to substantially affect the agent's utility.

2.3 Integrating Policy Summaries and Reward Decomposition

We combined HIGHLIGHTS as a global explanation with reward decomposition as a local explanation. We used HIGHLIGHTS to find the most important states during the agents' gameplay. For each state that was chosen by the HIGHLIGHT algorithm, we created reward decomposition bars that depict the decomposed Q-values for actions in the chosen state (see Fig. 1). We chose to combine these two types of explanations because we believe they complement each other. Reward decomposition reflects the intentions of an agent while HIGHLIGHTS gives a broader perspective on the agent's decisions.

HIGHLIGHTS summaries are typically shown as videos. However, the reward decomposition bars are static and vary for each state. Therefore, when integrating the two methods, we used HIGHLIGHTS to extract the important states but displayed them using static images rather than videos.

3   Empirical Methodology

To evaluate the benefits of integrating HIGHLIGHTS with reward decomposition as well as their respective contributions to users' understanding of agents' behavior, we conducted two user studies in which participants were asked to evaluate the preferences of different agents. We hypothesized that the combined explanations would best support participants' ability to correctly identify agents' preferences and that both the local and global explanations would be better than the baseline information.

3.1 Experimental Environments and Agent Training

Highway Environment. We used a multi-lane Highway environment (shown in the top part of Fig. 1) for our first experiments. In the environment, the RL agent controls the green vehicle. The objective of the agent is to navigate a multi-lane highway while driving alongside other (blue) vehicles. Positive rewards can be given for each of the following situations: changing lanes (CL), speeding up (SU), and moving to the right-most lane (RML) (the environment assumes the convention of driving on the right). Therefore we use three reward components, corresponding to the aforementioned situations, for the reward decomposition. We trained the agents as described in Sect. 2. The network input is an array of size 25 (5X5) that represents the state. The input layer is followed by two fully connected hidden layers of length 256. The last of these two layers is connected to three heads. Each head consists of a linear layer and outputs a Q-value vector of length of 5 that contains the following: lane left, idle, lane right, faster, slower. We trained four RL agents which differ in their policies:

(1) The Good Citizen - The highest reward for being in the right lane, next to change lane, and lastly to speed up
(2) Fast And Furious - The highest reward for speeding up, then changing lanes, and lastly being in the right-most lane
(3) Dazed and Confused - The highest reward for changing lanes, next to be in the right-most lane, and lastly to speed up
(4) Basic - Reward for being in the right-most lane

Common to all agents, when crashing a negative reward of -3 is given, and no future rewards can be obtained due to ending the episode. The precise settings of the rewards for the different agents that we used are summarized in Table 1. Each agent was trained for 2,000 episodes and each episode consists of 80 steps (or fewer if the agent crashed). Our implementation is based on two open source repositories: the Highway environment and an implementation of double DQN.[1]

The state importance definition for HIGHLIGHTS in the Highway environment is: $I(s) = \max_a Q^\pi_{(s,a)} - \min_a Q^\pi_{(s,a)}$, as used in the original HIGHLIGHTS implementation [1]. According to this formulation, a state is considered important if there is a large gap between the expected outcome of the best and worst action available to the agent in the state. To extract the policy summaries, we ran 2,000 simulations of the trained agent and saved the traces.

---

[1] https://github.com/eleurent/highway-env, https://github.com/eleurent/rl-agents.

Table 1. Highway environment. Settings of the four agents.

Agent	CL reward	SU reward	RML reward	Agent reward	CL reward	SU reward	RML reward
The Good Citizen	3	1	8	Dazed and Confused	8	1	5
Fast and Furious	5	8	1	Basic	0	0	15

Pacman Environment. In the second experiment, we used the Atari 2600 game MsPacman (Pacman for simplicity) contained in the Arcade Learning Environment [3]. For training the agents we build upon the Double DQN implementation in OpenAI baselines [5]. The network architecture is the same as used in [12], which consists of 3 convolutional and 2 fully connected layers, and uses preprocessed pixel values as input. We implemented reward decomposition (HRA) by sharing the convolutional layers but training individual fully connected layers for each reward component. Our implementation can be found online.[2]

In the game, Pacman has to traverse a labyrinth while avoiding ghosts (see top of Fig. 1). Based on the rules of the game, we used four different reward components ($|C| = 4$) for the RL agent controlling Pacman: the agent receives a reward of 1 for eating normal pills (NP) and a reward of 5 for eating Power Pills (PP). Additionally, after eating a PP, the ghosts turn blue and Pacman can eat them. The agent receives a reward of 20, 40, 80, or 160 for each blue ghost (BG) it eats successively. Finally, the agent receives a reward of -10 for dying. To get agents with distinct strategies, we used different weights for the reward components (see Table 2). Each agent was trained for 5 million steps. In the Pacman environment, the values of the individual rewards do not directly correlate to the agents' preferences. For example, the labyrinth contains a huge amount of normal pills compared to power pills and ghosts. Therefore, the agent with no specific reward component weights focuses very strongly on normal pills even though the reward value for individual normal pills is the lowest. To determine what the agents preferred, we observed the Q-values and actions of each fully trained agent for several full games before running the experiment. In total, we trained three different Pacman agents with the following preferences:

(1) Normal Pill Agent - Highest preference for eating normal pills, next eating power pills and lastly eating blue ghosts
(2) Power Pill Agent - Highest preference for eating power pills, next eating normal pills and eating blue ghost has the same preference
(3) Blue Ghost Agent - Highest preference for eating blue ghosts, next eating normal pills, lastly eating power pills.

We used HIGHLIGHTS-DIV to generate summaries for the Pacman agents. Compared to the basic HIGHLIGHTS algorithm, this approach additionally utilizes a similarity metric (Euclidean distance in our case) to avoid very similar

---

[2] https://github.com/hcmlab/baselines/tree/reward_decomposition.

Table 2. How each of the reward components was weighted for our Pacman agents.

	NP weights	PP weights	BG weights	Dying
Normal Pill Agent	1	1	1	1
Power Pill Agent	0.01	1	0.01	0.01
Blue Ghost Agent	0.1	0.1	10	0.01

states within the summaries [1]. Following Huber et al. [9], we calculated the importance as $I(s) = \max_a Q^\pi_{(s,a)} -$ second-highest $Q^\pi_{(s,a)}$. According to this formulation, a state is considered important if there is a large gap between the expected outcome of the best and second best action available to the agent in the state. This was done since the Arcade Learning Environment implementation of Pacman contains several redundant actions. These redundant actions are often completely ignored by the agents and always have low Q-values. To extract policy summaries, we ran the trained agent for 1,000 episodes after the training and recorded the traces.

3.2   Study Design

Experimental Conditions. We conducted two user studies to evaluate the impact of combining global and local explanations, as well as the effect of each method individually. Since local explanations are given for specific states, there must be some choice of which states to show the information for. Hence, as a baseline approach, rather than using HIGHLIGHTS to select states, we used frequency sampling to generate summaries that choose states for the summary by uniform sampling from the traces of the agent, as used in the study by Huber et al. [9]. Since each state has the same probability of being chosen, in practice states that appear more frequently are more likely to appear in the summary. Therefore, this is equivalent to selecting states based on the likelihood of their appearance. We assigned participants randomly to one of four different conditions:

- HIGHLIGHTS Summaries (H): In this condition, participants were shown summary videos that were generated by the HIGHLIGHTS algorithm. We used a context window of 10 states that were shown before and after the chosen state and an interval size of 10 states to prevent directly successive states in the summary.
- Frequency sampling summaries (FS): This condition contained videos similar to condition H, but the states in the middle of the trajectories were chosen based on frequency sampling. Moreover, to ensure that the summary is not particularly good or particularly bad we created 10 different summaries of this form for the Highways environment and 5 for Pacman.
- HIGHLIGHTS + reward decomposition (H+RD): Since interpreting reward decomposition takes some time, we did not show videos in this condition. Instead, participants were only shown the most "important" state of each

trajectory. This means that they did not get the context of that state as the video summaries provide. However, the chosen states were the same states that appeared in the middle of the videos in condition H. Each chosen state was shown using an image alongside a bar plot that represents the Q-values of the different reward components. In the Highway environment, the bar plot was shown for each available action in the chosen state, as shown in Fig. 1. Since Pacman contains ambiguous actions, we only showed the bar plot for the agents' chosen action in this environment.

- Frequency sampling summaries + reward decomposition (FS+RD): This condition was the same as condition H+RD but the shown states were the same states that were uniformly sampled for the middle of the trajectories in the FS condition.

Following [9], we set the size of the summaries for Pacman to $k = 5$. For the Highway environment, we used $k = 8$. Therefore, all participants were shown a summary of the agent's behavior that is composed of 5 or 8 different videos or images regarding the specific agent depending on the environment.

Procedure. At first, participants were given an explanation regarding the environment (Highway or Pacman). Second, they were given a brief explanation about reinforcement learning and specifically about q-values in layperson vocabulary. In particular, they were told that the agents are maximizing their future total score by taking into account both immediate points as well as points for future actions. Lastly, depending on the condition, participants were given information about the type of explanation they will see and an example explanation. At the end of each instructions phase, the participants were asked to complete a quiz and were only allowed to proceed after answering all questions correctly. Participants were compensated as follows: they received a $3 base payment and an additional bonus of 10 cents for each correct answer in the Highway environment and a 30 cent bonus for identifying the preferences of each of the agents correctly in the Pacman environment.

Task. The participant's task was to assess the preferences of the different agents. To avoid learning effects, the ordering of the agents was randomized. Specifically, participants were asked to rank which of each pair of reward components (e.g., high speed vs. driving in the right lane in the Highway environment or eating power pills vs. eating normal pills in the Pacman environment) the agent prioritizes or whether it is indifferent between the two options. If participants have a correct mental model of the agents' strategy, they should be able to rank the different reward components according to the agents' priorities.

Participants were then asked to rate their confidence in each of their answers on a Likert scale from 1 ("not confident at all") to 5 ("very confident") and to describe their reasoning in a free-text response. Lastly, participants rated their agreement on a 7-point Likert scale with the following items adapted from the explanation satisfaction questionnaire proposed by Hoffman et al. [6] :

1. The videos\graphs helped me recognize agent strategies
2. The videos\graphs contain sufficient detail for recognizing agent strategies

3. The videos\graphs contain irrelevant details
4. The videos\graphs were useful for the tasks I had to do in this survey
5. The specific scenarios shown in the videos\images were useful for the tasks I had to do in this survey.

Participants. We recruited participants through Amazon Mechanical Turk (N = 164 for each environment). We excluded participants who did not answer the attention question correctly, as well as participants who completed the survey in less than two standard deviations from the mean completion time in their condition. After screening, we had 127 and 159 participants in the Highway environment and the Pacman environment respectively (mean age = 36 years for both environments, 58 and 88 female in the Highway environment and the Pacman environment respectively, all from the US, UK, or Canada).

4   Results

To measure participants' ability to asses the agents' preferences, we calculated the mean fraction of correct reward component comparisons, i.e., their correctness rate, for each condition (see Fig. 2). We tested our hypotheses using the non-parametric, one-sided Mann-Whitney U test. Only when comparing the individual explanation conditions H and FS+RD, we used a two-sided test since we did not have a hypothesis as to which method will be better.

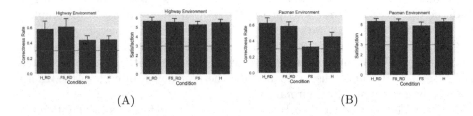

(A)   (B)

Fig. 2. Participants' mean correctness rate in identifying the preferences averaged over all agents and participants' explanation satisfaction by conditions in the Highway (A) and in the Pacman (B) environment. The error bars show the 95% CI.

We found that reward decomposition improved participants' ability to asses the agents' preferences in both environments. In the Highway environment, the combination of FS+RD led to significantly improved performance compared to FS (FS+RD vs. FS: $U=736$, $p=0.014$; FS+RD vs. H: $U=791$, $p=0.017$). Similarly, H+RD led to significantly improved performance compared to FS and H ($U=532$, $p=0.014$ and $U=571$, $p=0.018$, respectively). Similarly, in the Pacman environment, the combination of FS+RD significantly improved participants' performance compared to FS or H ($U=1187$ and $U=1176$ respectively, $p<0.001$ for both) and participants in the H+RD condition performed better compared to FS and H ($U=1286$ and $U=1332$ respectively, $p<0.001$ for both). Some of the participants explicitly referred to reward decomposition as being helpful for the task, e.g., "In each of the scenarios the graph clearly shows the preference for normal pills followed by eating power pills. Eating ghosts was a minor section on the graph".

The HIGHLIGHTS summaries only contributed to participants' mental model of the agents in the Pacman environment. Here, there was a significant difference between condition H and condition FS (U=935, p=0.002). In some explanations given by participants, it seemed that the HIGHLIGHTS summary displayed information that was useful for inferring preference, e.g., one participant wrote "the pacman would go for a power pill, eat it and turn around" when explaining their answers about the Power Pill agent preferences.

In both environments, the combined explanation did not outperform reward decomposition alone. There were no significant differences between H+RD and FS+RD in either of the environments when aggregated across all agents. However, in the Highway environment, our results indicate that the combination of H+RD helped asses the agent's preferences when the difference between the reward types was minor. For example, when assessing the agent "Fast and Furious" that was trained according to the rewards of 8 points for speed up vs. 5 points for changing lanes, participants who were shown H+RD succeeded about half of the times (M=0.55, 95% CI=(0.41, 0.69)) compared to participants in conditions FS+RD, FS or H that had a lower success rate (M=0.44, 95% CI=(0.34, 0.54); M=0.18, 95% CI=(0.03, 0.33); M=0.26, 95% CI=(0.1, 0.42), respectively). Similarly, for the BG agent in Pacman, there was only a small difference between the Q-values for the blue ghosts and normal pills. Participants in conditions H (M=0.3, 95% CI=(0.2, 0.5)) and H+RD (M=0.31, 95% CI=(0.17, 0.46)) were better at correctly identifying the blue ghost as more important than the participants in conditions FS+RD (M=0.2, 95% CI=(0.17, 0.46)) and FS (M=0.12, 95% CI=(0, 0.23)). This indicates that even though our overall results do not show that the combination of H+RD is significantly better, there were cases in which this combination helped.

In general, while participants' objective performance was better with RD compared to video-based policy summaries, this did not lead to an increase in subjective measures. In the Highway environment, participants' confidence and satisfaction ratings were above the neutral rating (> 3) but there was no difference between the conditions. In the Pacman environment, the confidence and satisfaction values of participants were also above neutral (see Fig. 2). However, here the explanation conditions FS+RD, H+RD, and H had higher mean satisfaction ratings (M between 5.34 and 5.39) than the baseline condition (condition FS with M=4.93).

5   Discussion

In previous work, HIGHLIGHTS summaries were integrated with saliency maps, but a user study showed that saliency maps did not provide much benefit to users' understanding of agent behavior [9]. We hypothesized that reward decomposition may be more beneficial for several reasons. First, saliency maps describe what features of the state the agent pays attention to, but it is often hard to infer how this information affects the agent's decisions, especially for laypeople. Reward decomposition has the benefit of explicitly describing what values the agent expects to get in a way that reflects its preferences for different reward components. Moreover, saliency maps are a post-hoc method and may not be faithful to the underlying model [7,13] while reward decomposition values are learned through the agent's training and reflect its true decision-making policy. Another difference between our integration of global and local information and the one used in the study by Huber et al. [9] is the use of static images rather than videos. We chose this approach based on the findings from their study which identified the use of videos as one possible limitation, as the local information is harder to discern when looking at dynamic videos.

Our studies showed a fairly limited contribution of HIGHLIGHTS summaries to participants' performance compared to prior works [1,9], with improved performance observed only in some scenarios in the Pacman environment. A possible explanation for the limited contribution of HIGHLIGHTS is that the experimental task may have been particularly suited to reward decomposition. Since reward decomposition was already highly effective in conveying agent preferences, the selection of states for the summary was less important. We further hypothesize that HIGHLIGHTS summaries were not better than frequency-based summaries in the Highway environment since the environment is somewhat limited in terms of agent behaviors.

6   Conclusion and Future Work

This paper presented a new approach for describing the behavior of RL agents, which integrates HIGHLIGHTS, a global policy summary, with local reward decomposition. We conducted user studies in two environments to evaluate the contribution of this approach to people's ability to analyze agent preferences. Our results show that reward decomposition was particularly helpful for this task and that HIGHLIGHTS also led to improvement in participants' performance, but only in certain situations.

The fact that the intrinsic reward decomposition method in our work outperforms the post-hoc saliency maps used in a similar experiment [9] empirically reaffirms the recommendation by Rudin [13] to use intrinsic explanation methods whenever possible. Furthermore, based on the difference between our study and the one by Huber et al. [9], who showed their local saliency maps on videos instead of static states, future combinations of local explanations and global policy summarization should provide the local explanation on static states. This allows users to discern the information within the explanation.

The finding that HIGHLIGHTS only improved participants' performance in the Pacman environment indicates that the usefulness of policy summaries may depend on the complexity of behaviors that agents may deploy in a domain. Future work should explore how the characteristics of different environments affect the usefulness of alternative explanation methods.

Another notable finding is that the use of different explanation methods did not result in substantial differences in subjective measures like explanation satisfaction. This finding emphasizes the importance of using objective performance measures for XAI, while also showing the need for future work on how we can increase the usability of explanatory systems.

Acknowledgements. We thank Julian Stockmann and Simone Pompe for their help with implementing HRA for MsPacman.

References

1. Amir, D., Amir, O.: Highlights: summarizing agent behavior to people. In: Proceedings of the 17th International Conference on Autonomous Agents and MultiAgent Systems, pp. 1168–1176 (2018)
2. Amir, O., Doshi-Velez, F., Sarne, D.: Summarizing agent strategies. Auton. Agent. Multi-Agent Syst. **33**(5), 628–644 (2019)
3. Bellemare, M.G., Naddaf, Y., Veness, J., Bowling, M.: The arcade learning environment: an evaluation platform for general agents. J. Artif. Intell. Res. **47**, 253–279 (2013). https://doi.org/10.1613/jair.3912
4. Booth, S., Muise, C., Shah, J.: Evaluating the interpretability of the knowledge compilation map: communicating logical statements effectively. In: IJCAI, pp. 5801–5807 (2019)
5. Dhariwal, P., et al.: OpenAI baselines. https://github.com/openai/baselines (2017)
6. Hoffman, R.R., Mueller, S.T., Klein, G., Litman, J.: Metrics for explainable AI: challenges and prospects. arXiv preprint arXiv:1812.04608 (2018)
7. Huber, T., Limmer, B., André, E.: Benchmarking perturbation-based saliency maps for explaining Atari agents. Front. Artif. Intell. **5** (2022). https://doi.org/10.3389/frai.2022.903875, https://www.frontiersin.org/articles/10.3389/frai.2022.903875
8. Huber, T., Schiller, D., André, E.: Enhancing explainability of deep reinforcement learning through selective layer-wise relevance propagation. In: Benzmüller, C., Stuckenschmidt, H. (eds.) KI 2019. LNCS (LNAI), vol. 11793, pp. 188–202. Springer, Cham (2019). https://doi.org/10.1007/978-3-030-30179-8_16
9. Huber, T., Weitz, K., André, E., Amir, O.: Local and global explanations of agent behavior: integrating strategy summaries with saliency maps. Artif. Intell. **301**, 103571 (2021). https://doi.org/10.1016/j.artint.2021.103571
10. Juozapaitis, Z., Koul, A., Fern, A., Erwig, M., Doshi-Velez, F.: Explainable reinforcement learning via reward decomposition. In: IJCAI/ECAI Workshop on Explainable Artificial Intelligence (2019)
11. Liu, G., Schulte, O., Zhu, W., Li, Q.: Toward interpretable deep reinforcement learning with linear model U-Trees. In: Berlingerio, M., Bonchi, F., Gärtner, T., Hurley, N., Ifrim, G. (eds.) ECML PKDD 2018. LNCS (LNAI), Part II, vol. 11052, pp. 414–429. Springer, Cham (2019). https://doi.org/10.1007/978-3-030-10928-8_25
12. Mnih, V., et al.: Human-level control through deep reinforcement learning. Nature **518**(7540), 529–533 (2015)
13. Rudin, C.: Stop explaining black box machine learning models for high stakes decisions and use interpretable models instead. Nat. Mach. Intell. **1**(5), 206–215 (2019). https://doi.org/10.1038/s42256-019-0048-x

Y. Septon et al.

Y. Septon et al.

332   Y. Septon et al.

14. Van Hasselt, H., Guez, A., Silver, D.: Deep reinforcement learning with double q-learning. In: Proceedings of the AAAI Conference on Artificial Intelligence, pp. 2094–2100 (2016)
15. Van Seijen, H., Fatemi, M., Romoff, J., Laroche, R., Barnes, T., Tsang, J.: Hybrid reward architecture for reinforcement learning. arXiv preprint arXiv:1706.04208 (2017)

A Multi-Agent Based Dynamic Network Slice Tarification Framework

Joshua Shakya[1,2]([✉]) [ID], Morgan Chopin[1] [ID], and Leila Merghem-Boulahia[2] [ID]

[1] Orange Innovation, Châtillon, France
{joshua.shakya,morgan.chopin}@orange.com
[2] University of Technology of Troyes, Troyes, France
{joshua.shakya,leila.merghem_boulahia}@utt.fr

Abstract. 5G networks promise to satisfy diverse kinds of advanced use cases, by providing tailored services to different kinds of customers, through the concept of Network Slicing (NS). Although NS, i.e. multiple virtual networks running on a shared infrastructure, is expected to offer substantial advantages in terms of flexibility and cost-efficiency, there are several key issues that have yet to be addressed. One of the open challenges that have emerged is regarding the economic interaction between Mobile Network Operators (MNOs) and the multitude of tenants (e.g. vertical industries) that MNOs intend to serve. With the paradigm shift from a product-based to a service-based model, MNOs need to come up with sophisticated pricing strategies for their heterogeneous set of customers. To address this issue, we propose a dynamic slice tarification algorithm based on Reinforcement Learning (RL) that adapts slice prices in accordance with the microeconomic laws of supply and demand. To model the system and prove the performance of our approach, we use a Multi-Agent Simulation (MAS) of our NS scenario. We train and evaluate our approach on a monopolistic scenario with one MNO and a number of tenants.

Keywords: Multi-Agent Simulation · 5G Network Slice Pricing · Reinforcement Learning · Markov Decision Process · Q-learning

1 Introduction

The key feature of 5G and Beyond networks compared to its predecessors is the support of a wide array of new applications, generating opportunities for novel business models and profit-making strategies. One of the key technologies that enable this transformation is Network Slicing (NS). NS [1,2] is the concept of running multiple independent logical networks (slices) dedicated to different *tenants* on top of a common shared physical infrastructure owned by a *Mobile Network Operator(MNO)*. It is a win-win situation for both parties as NS, on one hand, allows MNOs to monetize their services for a potential revenue surplus, whereas on the other hand, it allows tenants to demand resources that are specialized to meet their specific service requirements. Subsequently, the market space for NS

P. Mathieu et al. (Eds.): PAAMS 2023, LNAI 13955, pp. 333–345, 2023.
https://doi.org/10.1007/978-3-031-37616-0_28

ecosystem is extended to include not only Business-To-Customer (B2C) models (contract between MNOs and service end-users) but also Business-To-Business (B2B) models (contract between MNOs and service providers/tenants).

In a NS environment, different slices are dedicated to specialized types of services with different QoS requirements. For example, (a) a slice dedicated to 8K streaming and Immersive Virtual Reality (VR) requires stable and high peak data rates, on the other hand, (b) a slice dedicated to automatic driving requires ultra-reliability and low-latency. Although static pricing still applies in a NS scenario, since the demands are heterogeneous and dynamic in nature, it urges MNOs to come up with more innovative business models. Firstly, the resource needs vary according to the service demanded by the tenants. Since different slices have different metrics to optimize, taking our example, bandwidth for slice (a) and latency for slice (b), the consumption of network resources and the costs incurred for the operation of the two slices are generally different from one another. Secondly, end-user demands are not constant and the load on the network varies according to their demands. The load is affected by the demand patterns of diverse groups of users, their peak usage hours, etc. Finally, different tenants value services differently, therefore have a certain threshold for the price they are willing to pay for a service. In a more 'tenant focused' model, MNOs base their pricing strategy on how much the tenant believes the service is worth.

1.1 Related Works

Despite having significant benefits, the topic of dynamic pricing for NS is not mature yet. However, there are several interesting studies done in the field. For instance, authors in [4,5] model the pricing/purchasing problem as a Stackelberg game. Then, authors in [4] propose a multi-agent dueling deep Q-network algorithm to achieve optimal pricing schemes while ensuring MNOs profit and acceptable levels of users' utility. Similarly, authors in [5] develop an optimization framework that seeks a balance between Network Service Provider (NSP)'s profit and network social welfare (i.e. user utility - resource cost). Authors in [6] formulate the problem of setting differential prices for different classes of customers using the fundamental principles of economics. They then present a Drift-Plus-Penalty algorithm to maximize the provider's profit and evaluate the algorithm on a network with two classes of customers. Other authors, for example, in [7,8] employ auction theory in their solution. Authors in [7] present the overall enhancements brought in by their algorithm that adapts the policy for the most rewarding bid according to different resource pool sizes, traffic loads, and Slice Provider's behavior. Authors in [8] perform extensive simulations to showcase their auction-based method for increasing network revenue, efficiency in slice resource allocation, and satisfying slice requirements.

Regardless of the contributions, from the existing literature, it can be remarked that although models exist that partly covers the NS scenario, a comprehensive end-to-end model that encompasses all the aspects (business, network, infrastructural, etc.) has not been proposed yet. Furthermore, most of the proposed work provides static solutions without considering the dynamicity of involved entities, with some assumptions or priori information about the behaviors of actors that are approximations of real behavior. In addition, there is limited literature in the area of dynamic pricing for NS using approaches such as Reinforcement Learning (RL) even though RL and Multi-Agent RL (MARL) have been proven as potent contenders for dynamic pricing in several domains. Therefore, we believe that it is necessary to develop a practical framework that simulates NS in a realistic manner where proposed algorithms can be integrated for training and evaluation. Furthermore, as NS involves a number of dynamic entities such as MNOs, tenants, end-users, etc., the framework should be able to demonstrate the collective behavior of actors (emergent phenomena) across all layers, given their individual non-linear dynamics.

1.2   Contributions

To address these issues, in this paper, in contrast to the existing literature, we model the interactions between MNOs and tenants using a multi-agent approach without a priori information about the system dynamics. We consider a scenario where a MNO can adaptively decide the prices of network slices based on several objectives such as profit maximization, preservation of service quality, and tenant satisfaction. We take into account various stochastic dynamics of NS scenario including the end-users' dynamic traffic generation, and variable valuation of services by different tenants. We regard the pricing problem as a sequential decision problem and formulate a Markov Decision Process (MDP) problem where a MNO observes the network state transition and proposes optimal price to maximize its profit whilst maintaining other objectives. To solve the problem, we use classical Q-learning algorithm and evaluate its performance in a realistic multi-agent environment. Although in a typical scenario, NS is performed end-to-end, in this paper, we focus only on slicing in the Radio Access Network (RAN) layer.

To the best of our knowledge, this is the first work that models the economic interactions in a NS scenario by adopting a multi-agent approach. Furthermore, we propose a preliminary Q-learning algorithm that effectively tackles our dynamic pricing problem. All in all, our key contributions are three-fold and can be summarized as:

- **Formulation of Multi-Agent Simulation (MAS) framework:** We design a novel MAS framework that allows simulating NS in 5G RAN in a representational and efficient manner. The framework represents the dynamicity and interactions between different actors involved in NS efficiently. This framework also serves as a testbed for evaluating Artificial Intelligence (AI) and/or Operational Research (OR) algorithms in a realistic environment.
- **Proposal of RL-based pricing solution:** We formulate a MDP that models our MAS, then propose and integrate a RL-based dynamic pricing algorithm into our framework. Our RL solution monitors the demands of different slices and aids MNOs in the proposition of optimal pricing policies, that can be used as a decision-support tool.

- **Extensive evaluation and experimentation:** We assess the proposed RL solution on our MAS framework, which is a lifelike representation of a real-world slicing scenario in 5G RAN. Leveraging realistic MAS and RL, we demonstrate through experimentation, the applicability of our solution in real 5G systems.

The rest of the paper is structured as follows. In Sect. 2, the problem is formally defined. In Sect. 3, the methodology is thoroughly explained including a multi-agent model of NS in 5G RAN, a MDP formulation of the multi-agent model to find the optimal pricing strategy, and our adaptation of Q-learning algorithm to address the dynamic pricing problem. In Sect. 4, we evaluate the performance achieved, followed by a conclusion in Sect. 5.

2 Problem Description

In this paper, we investigate the Dynamic Network Slice Tarification (DNST) problem which arises in the context of 5G slicing and is defined as follows:

A set of tenants request to a MNO the deployment of their slice. Instead of proposing a fixed price for the deployment, the MNO seeks for a *dynamic pricing strategy*, i.e. proposes a price that varies over time and aims to take into account its own preference as well as the preference of the tenant. More formally, at each time-step, the MNO attempts to propose a tailored price for each of the tenants by respecting both preferences (its own and that of the tenant) that are modeled using utility functions defined as:

- The MNO's utility function is based on two criteria: (1) the immediate profit gained by the MNO after a slice request is accepted and agreed on by a tenant (2) the current load of the network. As the quality of service degrades with the increase in load, the MNO wants to avoid an overloaded network.
- The tenant's utility function is based on its valuation of the service: the tenant wants to pay a price that is equivalent to its consumption.

The objective is then to compute the best dynamic pricing strategy to be adopted by the MNO.

3 Methodology

We propose to model the DNST problem as a Markov Decision Process (MDP) that relies on a MAS framework of NS in 5G RAN. We then apply a Q-learning algorithm to learn the optimal dynamic pricing strategy. In this section, we start by describing the MAS part of the model, then we provide the MDP formulation and conclude with a description of the Q-learning algorithm.

3.1 Multi-agent 5G RAN Network Slicing Simulation Framework

Our multi-agent modelization is composed of a set $\mathcal{A} = \{1, \ldots, N\}$ of N *agents* spread across two layers (Business and Network) which is further divided into subsets according to the agent types as follows. (also see Fig. 1).

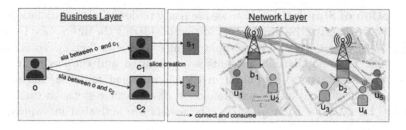

Fig. 1. Schema of a Multi-Agent NS Scenario with one MNO and two tenants.

Network Layer:

Slices. Let $\mathcal{A}_s \subseteq \mathcal{A}$ be the set of slices. Each slice agent $s \in \mathcal{A}_s$ is associated with a positive cost value $p_s \in \mathbb{R}_+$, a traffic profile for its end-users at each time-step t given by a minimum (resp. maximum) traffic value $\texttt{traffic}(s^t_{min})$ (resp. $\texttt{traffic}(s^t_{max})$), and a requirement vector $r_s = (r^1_s, \ldots, r^m_s) \in \mathbb{R}^n_+$, which points to a list of m technical requirements to be guaranteed for slice s such as latency, data-rate, reliability, and availability. Finally, let $\texttt{load}^t_s \in \{0, 1, ..., 10\}$ be the level of load of slice s at time t which measures the saturation of a slice. The higher the load of a slice is, the lower is the quality of service.

Base Stations. Let $\mathcal{A}_b \subseteq \mathcal{A}$ be the set of base stations (BS). Each $b \in \mathcal{A}_b$ has a peak capacity usage $\texttt{cap}_s(b) \in \mathbb{R}_+$ that sets an upper limit of traffic for end-users subscribed to slice $s \in \mathcal{A}_s$. Each $b \in \mathcal{A}_b$ also has a coverage radius $\texttt{rad}(b) \in \mathbb{R}$ that allows end-users within this radius to connect to b.

End-Users. Let $\mathcal{A}_u \subseteq \mathcal{A}$ be the set of End-User (EU) agents. Each EU agent $u \in \mathcal{A}_u$ is associated with a traffic value $\texttt{traffic}^b_s(u^t)$ lying in the interval $[\texttt{traffic}(s^t_{min}), \texttt{traffic}(s^t_{max})]$ and limited by $\texttt{cap}_s(b)$ that defines the traffic generated by u subscribed to s via b at time-step t.

Business Layer:

Mobile Operators. Let $\mathcal{A}_o \subseteq \mathcal{A}$ be the set mobile network operators (MNO). The role of a MNO agent is to propose a price offer to the tenants that request a network slice $s \in \mathcal{A}_s$. The choice of a price β^t at time-step t is based on a utility function $u_o : \mathbb{R}^2 \to \mathbb{R}$. A MNO strictly prefers a price β^t to another price $(\beta')^t$ or is indifferent if and only if $u_o(\beta^t, \texttt{load}^t_s) \geq u_o((\beta')^t, \texttt{load}^t_s)$.

Tenants/Clients. Let $\mathcal{A}_c \subseteq \mathcal{A}$ be the set of tenants. The terms *tenants* and *clients* are used interchangeably for rest of the paper. We model the preferences of each tenant over the proposed prices by MNOs using a utility function $u_c : \mathbb{R}^2 \to \mathbb{R}_+ \cup \{-\infty\}$. A tenant strictly prefers a price β^t to another price $(\beta')^t$ or is indifferent if and only if $u_c(\beta^t, \texttt{load}^t_s) \geq u_c((\beta')^t, \texttt{load}^t_s)$. We say that a tenant accepts a price offer β if $u_c(\beta^t, \texttt{load}^t_s) \neq -\infty$, and rejects it otherwise.

In our multiagent modelization, the *environment* is a cartesian plane that represents a city. Each end-user $u \in \mathcal{A}_u$ and base station $b \in \mathcal{A}_b$ agent is spatially referenced using coordinates $(x_u, y_u) \in \mathbb{R}^2$ and $(x_b, y_b) \in \mathbb{R}^2$, respectively.

Description of Simulation: Now we are ready to describe our simulation. For simplicity, we describe the simulation process considering the interaction between one MNO agent $o \in \mathcal{A}_o$ and one tenant agent $c \in \mathcal{A}_c$ (see Fig. 2). To initialize the simulation, a population of agents are generated and the environment is set-up. Localized agents are placed in the environment and the time-step is initialized. The simulation process unfolds in discrete time-steps: at each time-step $t = 1, \ldots, T$, for some $T \in \mathbb{N}_+^*$, the agents are activated in sequence as follows:

1. A tenant agent requests a network slice $s \in \mathcal{A}_s$ to a MNO agent that monitors resource availability and accepts the slice based on their Admission Control (AC) policy and the requirement vector r_s. As we consider that there are dedicated resources provisioned for incoming slices such that all the requirements are satisfied, all the slice requests are admitted by the MNO agent.

2. Each EU $u \in \mathcal{A}_u$ moves from its current position (x_u, y_u) to (x'_u, y'_u) using a prescribed Random Waypoint Mobility algorithm. Then, the EU agent u, if it is located within the coverage area, connects to the closest BS $b \in \mathcal{A}_b$ given by the equation:

$$b = \arg\min_{b' \in \mathcal{A}_b} \text{dist}(u, b') \tag{1}$$

   where $\text{dist}(u, b)$ is the Euclidean distance between u and b. EU agent u then sends traffic to the BS b following some rules. If SLA has been established between MNO and tenant, in our setting, each EU agent has the liberty to consume network resources limited by the traffic profile of its subscribed slice $s \in \mathcal{A}_s$ and less than the peak capacity usage $\text{cap}_s(b)$. Therefore, the traffic $\text{traffic}_s^b(u^t)$ generated at time-step t of an agent $u \in \mathcal{A}_u$ is between $\text{traffic}(s_{min}^t)$ and $\min\{\text{traffic}(s_{max}^t), \text{cap}_s(b)\}$ if u is connected to the slice s via the BS b, 0 otherwise. We also assume that the traffic generated is largely dependent on individual EU agents' consumption patterns and fluctuates throughout the day.

3. Once the EU agents have terminated their actions, the network status is updated which triggers MNO agent to propose a price $\beta_c^t \in \mathbb{R}_+$ (price/time-slot) to tenant $c \in \mathcal{A}_c$ based on the dynamic pricing strategy solution described in Sect. 3.2.

4. The tenant agent $c \in \mathcal{A}_c$ now decides whether it accepts the proposed price β_c^t by the MNO based on its utility function u_c. Whenever a slice request is accepted and agreed on by both parties, a Service Level Agreement (SLA) is stipulated, which defines the technical constraints r_s to be guaranteed and the hourly tarif β_c^t for the slice object to be paid by the tenant agent c with the condition that the constraints are met at all times during the operation of the slice. In this regards, the SLA between $o \in \mathcal{A}_o$ and $c \in \mathcal{A}_c$ for slice s can be defined by the tuple

$$SLA_c^o = (r_s, \beta_c^t) \tag{2}$$

This sequential decision-making continues until a limit of T time-steps. We refer the readers to [3] for a demonstration of the simulation.

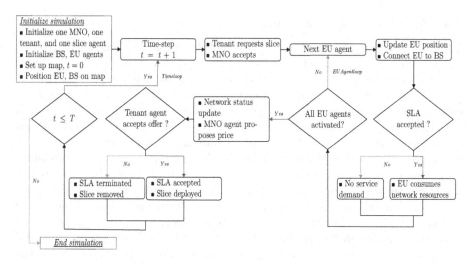

Fig. 2. Illustration of the simulation process with one MNO and one tenant agent.

3.2   MDP Formulation

In this section, we provide a discrete-time MDP with finite horizon formulation of our MAS as follows. It should be noted that the MDP represents one *MNO-tenant pair*.

State Space: Let $S = \{\mathfrak{s}_1, \ldots, \mathfrak{s}_n\}$ be the set of states. We define each state $\mathfrak{s}_i \in S$ of the MDP as a finite combination of a simulation time-step $t \in \{1, \ldots, T\}$ and the tenant's slice load $\texttt{load}_s^t$ at time-step t i.e.,

$$\mathfrak{s}_i = (t, \texttt{load}_s^t) \in S \tag{3}$$

In addition, we include in S a distinguished rejection state denoted by $\mathfrak{s}_{reject}$, which indicates a state where the tenant does not accept a price offer. The total number of states is then equal to $|S| = 11T + 1$, recall that the number of different load levels is $|\{0, \ldots, 10\}| = 11$.

Action Space: Let $A \subseteq \mathbb{N}$ be a set of discretized prices that can be proposed by the MNO. Every $\mathfrak{a} \in A$ corresponds to a price offer.

Reward Function: The reward function is based on an aggregation operator that represents the preferences of the MNO and tenant through their respective utility functions u_o and u_c and given by the expression:

$$R(\mathfrak{s} = (t, \texttt{load}_s^t), \mathfrak{a}) = AGG(u_o(\mathfrak{a}, \texttt{load}_s^t), u_c(\mathfrak{a}, \texttt{load}_s^t)) \tag{4}$$

Transition Model: The transition model is driven by our MAS, where the next state $\mathfrak{s}' = (t', \texttt{load}_s^{t'})$ is obtained from the simulation where $t' = (t+1) \mod T$. Depending on the action $\mathfrak{a}$, the state transitions into the rejection state $\mathfrak{s}_{reject}$ if and only if $u_c(\mathfrak{a}) = -\infty$.

3.3 Adaptation of Q-Learning

To solve our problem, we use an adaptation of the classical Q-learning algorithm. The Q-table is a $|S| \times |A|$ table containing the Q-values of each state-action pair $Q(\mathfrak{s}, \mathfrak{a})$. The Q-value represents the goodness of proposing action price $\mathfrak{a}$ when the state of the system is in $\mathfrak{s}$. The pseuso-code of the adapted Q-learning algorithm is depicted in Algorithm 1. The algorithm is executed for I iterations where each $i \in \{1, \ldots, I\}$ represents a call to our simulation, each call to the simulation runs for T time-steps. First, the Q-values of all state-action pairs are initialized to 0. Then, until the number of iterations reaches its maximum value, the simulation is executed and the state $\mathfrak{s}$ is observed, followed by the calculation of policy using an exploration/exploitation strategy ($\epsilon - Greedy$). Then, an action price is chosen from the set of prices A at each time-step according to the policy and the reward of selecting price $\mathfrak{a}$ at state $\mathfrak{s}$ is calculated. Following this, the transition function driven by our MAS is used to move into the next state and the Q-value is updated. The final Q-table obtained after I iterations gives us the optimal pricing strategy. For a more detailed study on RL and Q-learning, we refer the reader to [9].

Algorithm 1. Q-learning based pricing algorithm

Require:
  A set of states S ▷ States are tuples of time-step and load
  A set of actions A ▷ Actions are the proposed prices
  Reward function $R : S \times A \to R$ ▷ Reward function given in equation 4
  Transition model $\Psi : S \times A \to S$ ▷ Transition model driven by simulation
  Learning rate $\alpha \in [0, 1]$
  Discount factor $\gamma \in [0, 1]$
  Exploration-Exploitation strategy $\epsilon \in [0, 1]$
  procedure QLEARNING($S, A, R, \Psi, \alpha, \gamma, \epsilon$)
      Initialize $Q(s, a) \leftarrow 0, i = 0$
      for $i = 1, \ldots, I$ **do**
         for $t = 1, \ldots, T$ **do**   ▷ represents a call to the simulation
            Observe state $\mathfrak{s}_t = (t, \text{load}_t^s)$ from the simulation
            Calculate π according to Q and strategy (ϵ)
            Selection price $\mathfrak{a}_t$ within price bounds using $\pi(\mathfrak{s}_t)$
            Compute the reward $\mathfrak{r}_t \leftarrow R(\mathfrak{s}_t, \mathfrak{a}_t)$
            Transition to new state $\mathfrak{s}_{t+1} \leftarrow \Psi(\mathfrak{s}_t, \mathfrak{a}_t)$ ▷ driven by simulation
            Update $Q(\mathfrak{s}_t, \mathfrak{a}_t) \leftarrow (1 - \alpha) \cdot Q(\mathfrak{s}_t, \mathfrak{a}_t) + \alpha \cdot (\mathfrak{r}_t + \gamma \cdot \max_{\mathfrak{a}_{t+1}} Q(\mathfrak{s}_{t+1}, \mathfrak{a}_{t+1}))$
      return Q

---

4 Evaluation

In this section, we perform experimentation to evaluate the efficacy of our proposed solution.

4.1 Testbed Configuration

We consider a monopolistic NS scenario with 200 EU agents i.e. $|\mathcal{A}_u| = 200$, one MNO $o \in \mathcal{A}_o$ and two tenants $c_1, c_2 \in \mathcal{A}_c$. The first tenant c_1 requests the deployment of a slice $s_1 \in \mathcal{A}_s$ to provide 8K streaming and Immersive VR services. The second tenant c_2 asks for a slice $s_2 \in \mathcal{A}_s$ to provide Automatic Driving services. Each EU is assigned randomly to a tenant with the same probability, and at each time step moves whilst connecting to a base-station $b \in \mathcal{A}_b$ and generating traffic stochastically within a given range $[\texttt{traffic}(s^t_{i_{min}}), \texttt{traffic}(s^t_{i_{max}})]$ which is influenced by the hour of the day (see Table 1) and limited by $\texttt{cap}_{s_i}(b)$. We assume $\texttt{cap}_{s_i}(b) = 10$ for all $b \in \mathcal{A}_b$. Traffic values are normalized between 0 to 10, and represent different types of traffic depending on the type of slice. We set the simulation time horizon to $T = 24$ to represent 24 h of a day.

Table 1. Detailed configuration of tenants and their respective slices.

Tenant	p_{s_i}	Peak hour (p.h.)	Mid hour (m.h.)	Off hour (o.h.)	p.h. traffic range (traffic($s^{ph}_{i_{min}}$) – traffic($s^{ph}_{i_{max}}$))	m.h. traffic range (traffic($s^{mh}_{i_{min}}$) – traffic($s^{mh}_{i_{max}}$))	o.h. traffic range (traffic($s^{oh}_{i_{min}}$) – traffic($s^{oh}_{i_{max}}$))	p.h. threshold ($\theta^{ph}_{c_i}$)	m.h. threshold ($\theta^{mh}_{c_i}$)	o.h. threshold ($\theta^{oh}_{c_i}$)
c_1	1	10:00-16:00	08:00-10:00, 16:00-21:00	00:00-08:00, 21:00-00:00	8-10	4-7	0-3	8	5	3
c_2	2	09:00-12:00, 13:00-18:00	12:00-13:00, 18:00-21:00	00:00-09:00, 21:00-00:00	7-10	3-6	0-2	18	10	6

We define the utility functions of the MNO o and each tenant c_i, $i = 1, 2$, as:

$$u_o(\beta^t, \texttt{load}^t_{s_i}) = \beta^t - \texttt{load}^t_{s_i} \tag{5}$$

$$u_{c_i}(\beta^t, \texttt{load}^t_{s_i}) = \begin{cases} |\beta^t - p_{s_i} * \texttt{load}^t_{s_i}|, & \text{if } \beta^t \le \theta^t_{c_i} \\ -\infty, & \text{otherwise} \end{cases} \tag{6}$$

where $\theta^t_{c_i}$ is a time-variant threshold for the tenant that determines the acceptance/rejection of a price offer and p_{s_i} is the positive cost value associated with slice s_i (see Table 1).

The aggregator in the reward function is initialized as a linear aggregator $R(\mathfrak{s} = (t, \texttt{load}^t_{s_i}), \mathfrak{a}) = \omega_1 \cdot u_o(\mathfrak{a}, \texttt{load}^t_{s_i}) - \omega_2 \cdot u_{c_i}(\mathfrak{a}, \texttt{load}^t_{s_i})$ with weights ω_1 and ω_2 respectively. The weights ω_1 and ω_2 are set to $\frac{1}{3}$ and $\frac{2}{3}$ respectively, indicating relatively higher importance on the tenant's preference. The value for $\gamma \in [0, 1]$ that determines the importance of future rewards has been set to 0.9, considering future rewards with greater weight. Although a lower learning rate leads to a longer learning time, the value for $\alpha \in [0, 1]$ has been set to 0.1 to avoid sub-optimal convergence. The value of ϵ is initialized to 1 with a decay rate of 0.01 until it reaches a fixed value of 0.1. This is to allow the agent to take completely random decisions in the beginning to explore the state space maximally, and then settle down to a fixed exploration rate of 0.1. It should be noted that all the parameter values are adaptable and can be modified to fit different needs.

Based on the scenario defined above, the simulation was run for 10^6 iterations, each iteration being an execution of a simulation process with $T = 24$. The algorithm converged at $\sim 10^3$ iterations after which the scenario was re-simulated and the trained agent was evaluated on it. All the experiments were performed on a machine with Intel(R) Core(TM) i5-10310U processor and 16GB of RAM. Some of the observations are now explained.

4.2   Revenue Comparison: Static Pricing Vs. Dynamic Pricing

The main outcome of our simulation is the optimal prices proposed at each time-step t for each tenant. In order to evaluate the revenue gain from the dynamic pricing approach, we first set fixed prices (price that remains constant throughout T irrespective of peak, mid, and off hours) for tenant c_1 and c_2 at 5 (i.e. $\beta_{c_1}^t = 5, \forall t \in T$) and 11 (i.e. $\beta_{c_2}^t = 11, \forall t \in T$) respectively. The prices were chosen using a mid-level load $\text{load}_t^{s_1} = 4$ and $\text{load}_t^{s_2} = 5$ for c_1 and c_2 respectively and using the formula $\text{load}_{s_i}^t * p_{s_i} + 1.$. Then, the static prices are compared with the dynamic pricing strategy proposed by our Q-learning algorithm, for an execution of simulation with $T = 24$, as shown in Fig. 3. From the figure, with the dynamic prices, we can clearly observe the peak, mid, and off hours for each of the tenants and the price variation with respect to the hours.

Then, to evaluate the revenue gain incurred by the solution from c_1 and c_2, we execute 365 calls to the simulation, each call an execution of our simulation with $T = 24$ (to represent a year), and apply both static and dynamic prices. The revenue/month with both of the approaches is shown in Fig. 4 which demonstrates the overall revenue increase of the MNO through the use of dynamic pricing by an average of $\sim 35\%$ per month.

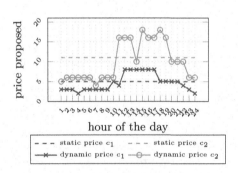

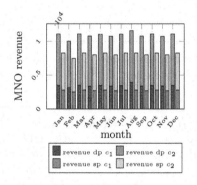

Fig. 3. Comparing static pricing vs. dynamic pricing for an execution of simulation with T=24

Fig. 4. Comparing revenue/month using static pricing (sp) and dynamic pricing (dp) for 365 executions of simulation with T=24

4.3   Differential Pricing for Different Types of Tenants

Fig. 5 and Fig. 6 shows the optimal prices β_{c1}^t and β_{c2}^t proposed by our dynamic pricing approach for tenants $c1$ and $c2$ alongside their loads $(\text{load}_{s1}^t, \text{load}_{s2}^t)$ and thresholds $(\theta_{c1}^t, \theta_{c2}^t)$ for an execution of our simulation with $T = 24$.

From the graphs, we notice that the trend of β_{c1}^t and β_{c2}^t follows the trend of load_{s1}^t and load_{s2}^t respectively; however, the thresholds of the respective tenants θ_{c1}^t and θ_{c2}^t are not exceeded. The graphs also demonstrate clearly the variation of prices during peak, mid, and off hours for each tenant. It can also be observed that the average price for c_2 is higher than that for c_1, this is because $p_{s_2} > p_{s_1}$ (associated with higher deployment/operational costs). Overall, it can be remarked that the pricing scheme is able to propose tailored prices for each $c \in \mathcal{A}_c$ depending on their discretized loads at different hours, thresholds, etc.

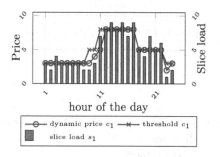 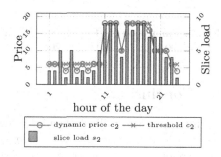

Fig. 5. Load, threshold, and dynamic prices for c_1 for an execution of simulation with T=24

Fig. 6. Load, threshold, and dynamic prices for c_2 for an execution of simulation with T=24

4.4 Impact of Number of End-Users on Load

It is clear from the experiments above that the level of load load_s^t on the slices is a crucial factor in determining the optimal pricing policy. Since the load_s^t is an aggregate of individual EU traffic $\mathrm{traffic}_s^b(u^t)$ for each EU u connected to slice s through b at time t, we studied the effects of the number of EUs on load_s^t. Figure 7 and Fig. 8 shows our simulation with $|\mathcal{A}_u| = 100$ and $|\mathcal{A}_u| = 200$ respectively and Fig. 9 shows their impacts on load_s^t. We can see that the number of EUs has a direct impact on the load; however, the general trend remains similar (similar trends of off, mid, and peak hours). This observation is possible through our multi-agent framework, where the aggregation of individual behavior (in our case, individual EU traffic behaviors) leads to global behavior (in our case, effect on the load and eventually on the pricing scheme), showing the efficiency of our framework in representing realistic scenarios.

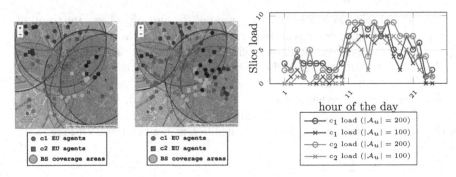

Fig. 7. Simulation $|\mathcal{A}_u| = 100$

Fig. 8. Simulation $|\mathcal{A}_u| = 200$

Fig. 9. Load profiling for c_1 and c_2

5   Conclusion

In this paper, we studied a Dynamic Network Slice Tarification (DNST) problem where a MNO can adaptively decide network slice prices taking into account its own preference and the preference of the respective tenant.

To address the problem, we first model Network Slicing (NS) in 5G RAN using a multi-agent approach, thus creating a framework for training and evaluating our solutions. Then we formulate a finite discrete MDP of our multi-agent simulation and employ an adapted Q-learning algorithm to solve the DNST problem. Simulation of a preliminary monopolistic scenario shows the effectiveness of our solution on MNO's profitability as well as tenants' satisfaction. Decisions are made using real-time load from our Multi-Agent Simulation (MAS) framework, thus our solution can be used in online-decision support.

For future research, firstly, the model can be extended to a multi-MNO multi-tenant ecosystem, creating a more realistic competitive marketplace. Secondly, the comparison with existing approaches was not in our current scope; therefore, we intend to prioritize it in our future work as it would be an asset to evaluate the performance of our approach. Finally, further analysis should be performed towards determining the optimal balance of different objectives to satisfy and studying the system behavior in case of limited resources where MNO has different priority levels for different tenants.

References

1. Zhang, S.: An overview of network slicing for 5G. IEEE Wirel. Commun. **26**(3), 111–117 (2019)
2. Khan, L.U., Yaqoob, I., Tran, N.H., Han, Z., Hong, C.S.: Network slicing: recent advances, taxonomy, requirements, and open research challenges. IEEE Access **8**, 36009–36028 (2020)
3. Shakya, J., Ghribi, C., Chopin, M., Merghem-Boulahia, L.: Agent-based simulation for placement and pricing of 5G network slices. In: 2023 IEEE 20th Consumer Communications & Networking Conference (CCNC), pp. 883–884. IEEE (2023)

4. Ou, R., Boateng, G.O., Ayepah-Mensah, D., Sun, G., Liu, G.: Stackelberg game-based dynamic resource trading for network slicing in 5G networks. J. Netw. Comput. Appl. **214**, 103600 (2023)
5. Wang, G., Feng, G., Qin, S., Wen, R., Sun, S.: Optimizing network slice dimensioning via resource pricing. IEEE Access **7**, 30331–30343 (2019)
6. Chen, S., Krishnamachari, B.: Differential pricing of 5G network slices for heterogeneous customers. In: 2020 10th Annual Computing and Communication Workshop and Conference (CCWC), pp. 0705–0711. IEEE (2020)
7. Vincenzi, M., Lopez-Aguilera, E., Garcia-Villegas, E.: Maximizing infrastructure providers' revenue through network slicing in 5G. IEEE (2019)
8. Jiang, M., Condoluci, M., Mahmoodi, T.: Network slicing in 5G: an auction-based model. In: 2017 IEEE International Conference on Communications (ICC), pp. 1–6. IEEE (2017)
9. Wiering, M.A., Van Otterlo, M.: Reinforcement learning. Adapt. Learn. Optim. **12**(3), 729 (2012)

An IDE to Support the Development of Embedded Multi-Agent Systems

Vinicius Souza de Jesus[1]([✉]) [ID], Nilson Mori Lazarin[1,2] [ID],
Carlos Eduardo Pantoja[1,2] [ID], Gleifer Vaz Alves[3] [ID],
Gabriel Ramos Alves de Lima[2] [ID], and Jose Viterbo[1] [ID]

[1] Institute of Computing - Fluminense Federal University, Niterói, Brazil
{vsjesus,viterbo}@id.uff.br, {nilson.lazarin,pantoja}@cefet-rj.br
[2] Federal Center for Technological Education Celso Suckow da Fonseca,
Rio de Janeiro, Brazil
gabriel.ramos@aluno.cefet-rj.br
[3] Federal University of Technology - Paraná, Ponta Grossa, Brazil
gleifer@utfpr.edu.br

Abstract. Embedded MAS development requires knowledge in different areas, such as agent-oriented programming, object-oriented programming, low-level programming, and basic electronics concepts. The literature has a consolidated Embedded MAS development architecture divided into four layers: Reasoning, Serial, Firmware, and Hardware. However, one of the main difficulties that MAS designers face is the need to use and configure different *Integrated Development Environments* (IDE) and make several integrations to embed the MAS. Even using all these technologies, embedding and monitoring the Embedded MAS is done using physical wired connections, making them limited and impracticable depending on the application. Therefore, this work aims to present an IDE to develop Embedded MAS that centralizes the entire development in a single IDE with all required integrations and configurations done. Moreover, the embedding and monitoring MAS of the IDE are done remotely without physical wired connections. Finally, aiming to show the IDE's applicability and functionalities, this work presents a case study set on a road junction with different Embedded MAS.

Keywords: Embedded MAS · Development · IDE

1 Introduction

The Multi-Agent System (MAS) [19] comprises autonomous, proactive agents with decision-making capacity, social abilities to interact with other agents and cooperate to achieve a common goal. A MAS can be applied in virtual or physical environments. The virtual environment is a controlled environment that allows

---

The original version of this chapter was revised: The second affiliation has been corrected to "Center for Technological Education Celso Suckow da Fonseca, Rio de Janeiro, Brazil" and the third affiliation has been corrected to "Federal University of Technology - Paraná, Ponta Grossa, Brazil". The correction to this chapter is available at https://doi.org/10.1007/978-3-031-37616-0_38

© The Author(s), under exclusive license to Springer Nature Switzerland AG 2023, corrected publication 2023
P. Mathieu et al. (Eds.): PAAMS 2023, LNAI 13955, pp. 346–358, 2023.
https://doi.org/10.1007/978-3-031-37616-0_29

the application of MAS for specific tests. However, the physical environment is unpredictable and can change at any time, forcing the agents to update the information captured from the environment frequently to avoid acting based on outdated information. For applying a MAS in a physical environment, the agents use several sensors and actuators grouped in a physical device to capture information and act/modify this environment. When a MAS is applied to a physical device can be classified as an Embedded MAS [5].

Several architectures for developing an agent, such as SOAR [11] and Belief-Desire-Intentions (BDI) [6], represent the cognitive reasoning processes that enable decision-making. The SOAR focuses more on the information storage process, and the BDI on decision-making. This work uses the BDI regarding its agents' decision-making process. In this process, Beliefs are the information that an agent accepts as truth, including information acquired through interactions with other agents or perceptions of the environment. Desires represent an agent's motivation to achieve a specific goal. Finally, Intentions represent the agent's commitment to performing some actions to achieve those goals [6].

As the BDI allows agents to make decisions based on their beliefs, which can be perceptions of the environment, this architecture is interesting to be applied in an unpredictable environment such as the physical one. For embedding a MAS in a physical environment, there is a consolidated architecture that is divided into four layers [13]: the Reasoning layer is responsible for cognition, and it usually is composed of MAS with BDI agents. the Serial layer for the interface between the MAS and the microcontrollers [8,12]; the Firmware layer for the programs of microcontrollers; Finally, the Hardware layer is composed of sensors and actuators. Therefore, to develop an Embedded MAS, the MAS designer needs to deal with different areas of knowledge, such as agent-oriented programming to develop the MAS (Reasoning Layer), object-oriented programming to develop the middleware that allows the exchange of information between the MAS and the microcontroller (Serial layer), low-level programming to develop the firmware of the microcontroller (Firmware Layer), and electronics for operating the sensors and actuators (Hardware layer). Moreover, the MAS designer must use one Integrated Development Environment (IDE) per programming language involved in this development procedure and provide integration between all of them.

Some frameworks in the literature aim to assist in developing MAS supported by IDEs, such as the *Jason framework* [4] that has an *AgentSpeak* [14] language interpreter for programming BDI agents and can be incorporated into the *Eclipse IDE*. In addition, the *Visual IDE's* [7] work allows the programming of MAS in code blocks to facilitate the codification for MAS designers who do not dominate the agent-oriented language to develop MAS. Finally, the *ARGO agents* [13] is a customized agent architecture capable of controlling microcontrollers.

However, these works do not cover the entire Embedded MAS development architecture presented, providing support only for the Reasoning layer. Consequently, to obtain support for the other layers, it is necessary to use different IDEs, sometimes one IDE per layer. In addition, the embedding and monitoring process requires physical wired connections, making the embedded process limited for instance in devices like Unmanned Aerial Vehicles (UAV) and Remotely

Operated Vehicles (ROVs). Besides, the monitoring process with these devices in operation is impracticable. For example, the *UAV* is an aerial and unmanned vehicle, so its operation is controlled and monitored remotely since maintaining a physical wired connection limits the mobility and the maximum area of exploration to the length of the wire.

Therefore, the objective of this work is to present an IDE to support the development of Embedded MAS considering all architecture's layers that need programming (Reasoning, Serial, and Firmware) with all necessary integration and configuration between these elements. So, the MAS designer can develop and program in three different layers of the architecture using a single IDE. In addition, the IDE allows to embed MAS and monitor their agents' minds (all Beliefs, Desires, and Intentions of each agent) remotely and wireless.

For this, the *Jason framework* was used to develop MAS (Reasoning Layer), as it is consolidated in the literature. For the Serial layer, the *Javino* [12] is the serial interface used, allowing messages to be exchanged with guaranteed content integrity. And in the Firmware layer, the *Arduino Command Line Interface (CLI)* was used to compile, upload and deploy the microcontroller program, allowing it to capture and send commands to the sensors and actuators. Finally, the integration and configuration of all these technologies were made and incorporated into a single IDE named *Cognitive Hardware on Network - Integrated Development Environment (ChonIDE)*.

To show the applicability of *ChonIDE*'s functionalities, a case study was elaborated and set on a road junction traffic scenario. The scenario is composed of an autonomous vehicle and a traffic light where the autonomous vehicle must be able to perceive the colors of the traffic light signal and, using its cognitive process, decide to move or stop the vehicle based on the colors of the traffic light. And the traffic light must change the colors according to the current traffic laws.

The main contributions of this paper are: **i.** allows the development and monitoring of the Embedded MAS using a single IDE, with all the required integrations of the different technologies made; **ii.** enables the development and monitoring of the Embedded MAS remotely without using a physical wired connection, which allows applying MAS in devices such as *ROVs* and *UAVs* that were previously done in a limited way; **iii.** assists in facilitating the Embedded MAS development by allowing MAS designers to embed and monitoring MAS even if they do not know how to deal with all layers of the architecture since it already has the technologies integrated and configured into the *ChonIDE*.

This work is organized as follows: Sect. 2, presents the related work; in Sect. 3, *ChonIDE* is presented, its functionalities and interaction with the designer; Sect. 4 discusses the case study where Embedded MAS is developed on a road junction scenario; finally, in Sect. 5, the final considerations and future works are presented.

2   Related Works

Considering the Embedded MAS development with agents capable of proactively and autonomously making decisions, some works in the agents' literature implement the BDI architecture and have mechanisms to enable embedding MAS. Two frameworks stand out with several solutions to embed MAS and are part of many works in the literature, such as *ARGO agents* [13], *Physical Artifacts* [5], *Bioinspired protocols* [10], integration with the Robotic Operating System (ROS) [17]. The first framework is *Jason* (previously presented), and the second is *JaCaMo* [3] which combines three other frameworks: *Jason* is responsible for supporting the agents' development, *CArtAgO (Common ARTifact Infrastructure for AGents Open Environments)* [15] for the agents' interaction with the environment, and *Moise+* [9] for coordinating the organizational part of the agents in the MAS.

The *Jason framework* has a specific text editor for programming languages incorporated in its distribution called *jEdit*[1] that allows the programming of cognitive agents *(Jason + jEdit)*. In addition, the *Jason framework* has a plug-in for the *Eclipse IDE*[2] that provides tools for MAS development as a particular perspective that enables the creation, deletion, and import of MAS development projects and agents through the MAS interface in *Eclipse IDE (Jason + Eclipse)*.

However, these solutions only consider the Reasoning layer. As both use the *Jason framework*, it is possible to integrate the customized architecture of agents, named *ARGO agents*, into the presented solutions *(Jason + JEdit/Eclipse + ARGO)*. These *ARGO agents* can communicate and control microcontrollers, allowing them to capture information and act in the physical environment. For this, these agents have a serial interface called *Javino* in their constitution. *Javino* [12] has a process for verifying the integrity of messages and guaranteeing lossless delivery of information between the *ARGO agents* and microcontrollers.

As *Javino* is a generic serial interface that can communicate with different microcontrollers, the ARGO Agents (which has Javino in its architecture) can control different microcontrollers. Although several microcontrollers are available on the market, in this work, the Arduino microcontroller was used due to its applicability, versatility, and low monetary cost. For the *Arduino* microcontroller, several text editors and IDE support developing, compiling, uploading, and deploying its firmware. However, the *Arduino IDE* is a well-used tool because the producers built it themselves, it is free, and it has a web[3] and a desktop[4] version to install on the MAS device *(Arduino IDE)*. Moreover, the *Arduino IDE* allows the import of external libraries, which facilitates the integration with the *Javino* serial interface *(Arduino IDE + Javino)*.

Considering the *JaCaMo framework* integrates with several IDE, which stands out: the integration with the *Eclipse IDE*[5] that provides a whole perspective that allows MAS programming using all three frameworks (*Jason, CArtAgO,* and *Moise+*) jointly and simultaneous *(JaCaMo + Eclipse)*. In addition, there is an approach for agent-oriented visual programming that aims to enable MAS

---

[1] https://jason.sourceforge.net/doc/tutorials/getting-started/readme.html.
[2] https://jason.sourceforge.net/mini-tutorial/eclipse-plugin/.
[3] https://docs.arduino.cc/learn/starting-guide/the-arduino-web-editor.
[4] https://www.arduino.cc/en/software.
[5] https://jacamo.sourceforge.net/eclipseplugin/tutorial/.

designers without programming experience but with specific knowledge of BDI agents can develop a MAS. Considering this approach, an IDE integrated with the *JaCaMo framework* named *Visual IDE* [7] was implemented, which has a visual programming system for agents that simplify the agent-oriented programming concepts using a blocks-based visual development environment *(JaCaMo + Visual IDE)*. Another IDE highlighted in the agents' area is a WEB IDE which uses the *JaCaMo* framework to allow interactive programming of MAS named *JaCaMo WEB* [2]. The interactive programming allows the MAS designer to modify the agents' source code at runtime without stopping and compiling the MAS. So, the MAS keeps running while the MAS designer changes the source code, maintaining MAS availability *(JaCaMo WEB)*.

Finally, *JaCaMo framework* has a plugin for *Visual Studio Code (VS Code)*[6]. Considering that the *JaCaMo framework* has *Jason* in its constitution, it is possible to integrate *ARGO agents* with *JaCaMo*. Since *VS Code* has a plugin for programming, uploading, and deploying firmware for *Arduino* microcontrollers, it is theoretically possible to centralize the development of an Embedded MAS in *VS Code* by performing all of the described integrations *(VS Code + ARGO + Arduino)*. However, to program the microcontroller firmware, it is necessary to have a physical wired connection between the MAS designer's computer (where the firmware is being developed) and the microcontroller, limiting the embedding and making it impracticable to monitor in some devices.

Aiming at the Embedded MAS development *ChonIDE* is a IDE for supporting the development of Embedded MAS with functionalities that include some layers (Reasoning, Serial, and Firmware) of the Embedded MAS development architecture, such as coding, compilation, uploading, and deployment of microcontroller firmware and agent source code. Furthermore, *ChonIDE* has a monitoring module that allows the designer to monitor the MAS log and the minds of all agents using *MindInspector* from *Jason framework*. All these functionalities can be done in remote solutions that do not require a physical wired connection., allowing embedding in devices such as *UAVs* and *ROVs* that require unrestricted mobility for locomotion. In Table 1, there are comparisons of the functionalities to develop Embedded MAS provided by *ChonIDE* and other IDE. These comparisons show which layers of the Embedded MAS architecture each IDE supports the development and whether the embedding and monitoring procedure is done remotely or not.

3   ChonIDE: The IDE for Embedded MAS

As seen previously, one of the main difficulties in the Embedded MAS development is dealing with concepts from different areas of knowledge (e.g., agent-oriented programming, object-oriented programming, and low-level programming with structured languages). In addition, the Embedded MAS designer needs to use one different IDE per programming language, making integrations and configurations between all of them.

---

[6] https://code.visualstudio.com/.

Table 1. Comparison between *ChonIDE* and other IDEs.

	Reasoning Layer	Serial Layer	Firmware Layer	Wireless Embedding	Monitoring
Jason + *JEdit*	✓	X	X	X	X
Jason + *Eclipse*	✓	X	X	X	X
Jason + *JEdit* + *ARGO*	✓	✓	X	X	X
Jason + *Eclipse* + *ARGO*	✓	✓	X	X	X
Arduino IDE	X	X	✓	X	X
Arduino IDE + *Javino*	X	✓	✓	X	X
JaCaMo + *Eclipse*	✓	X	X	X	X
JaCaMo + *Visual IDE*	✓	X	X	X	X
JaCaMo WEB	✓	X	X	X	X
VS Code + *ARGO* + *Arduino*	✓	✓	✓	X	X
ChonIDE	✓	✓	✓	✓	✓

Thereat, aiming to facilitate and assist in the Embedded MAS development, this work presents a IDE named *Cognitive Hardware on Network - Integrated Development Environment (ChonIDE)*. *ChonIDE* is a development environment that integrates technologies and tools to support the development of Embedded MAS, considering the three layers that require programming (e.g., Reasoning, Serial, and Firmware) in a single *WEB* platform. The *ChonIDE* works by establishing a network connection (wireless or wired) between the designer's computer and the physical device, so all functionalities can be performed remotely. Moreover, *ChonIDE's* main functionalities, such as embedding, starting, stopping, and monitoring the agents' minds, are activated by simply pressing buttons on the graphical interface. As the *ChonIDE* is a *WEB* platform, the MAS designer can develop an Embedded MAS using any device, such as a laptop, computer, or smartphone, without requiring configuration and integrations.

For the development of an Embedded MAS using *ChonIDE*, the MAS designer needs a physical device composed of sensors and actuators to interact with the environment, one or more microcontrollers to manage the operation of the sensors and actuators, and, finally, a single board computer (e.g., Raspberry) with a network adapter (can be wired or wireless) for connecting the physical device on the LAN to able *ChonIDE* to embed and monitor the MAS. With the physical device prototypes connected on the same LAN of *ChonIDE*, the MAS designer can embed and monitor the MAS operation of any prototype and send *Instructions* addressed to each one separately using the prototype identification on the LAN. The *Instructions* are to import a new MAS, start and stop them. Considering the microcontroller's firmware of the prototypes, the *Instructions* are to compile, upload, and deploy new firmware. The return of the execution of each of the Instructions is presented in a Log interface in *ChonIDE*.

Therefore, the information flow of the architecture of *ChonIDE* works as follows: the graphical interface of *ChonIDE* (*WEB* platform) is responsible for interactions with the MAS designer. These interactions are converted into the *Instructions* (previously presented) to be executed on the physical device. The *Instructions* are sent via network communication (wireless or wired) to the physical device, and *ChonOS* (installed on the physical device) is responsible for interpreting and executing them. Figure 1 shows the interaction of *ChonIDE* with the physical prototype.

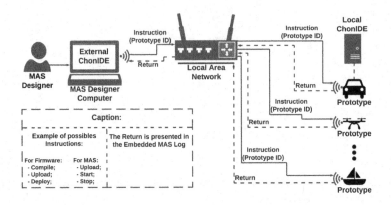

Fig. 1. Illustration of ChonIDE interactions.

To support the layers (Reasoning, Serial, and Firmware) that require programming, *ChonIDE* has a generic coder that allows programming in C (Firmware layer) and *AgentSpeak* (Reasoning layer). For the Serial layer, the integrations and configurations for the microcontroller of the physical device to communicate with the MAS agents are already done by the *Javino* serial communication interface. So, to control the microcontroller, the MAS designer only needs to use the *ARGO* agents with their internal actions (e.g., port, act, and percepts).

To facilitate the embedding of MAS using *ChonIDE*, this work uses a specialized GNU/Linux distribution, which has a set of services dedicated to embedding MAS. This distribution, named *Cognitive Hardware on Network - Operational System (ChonOS)*[7], has services such as network management, serial interface (using *Javino*), and a specific *Jason's* version for Embedded MAS. This *Jason's* version used by *ChonIDE*, in addition to the *ARGO agent*, has another customized agent architecture named Communicator Agents. The Communicator agents can interact with agents of other MAS using a network infrastructure. These agents allow the MAS designer using *ChonIDE* to create MAS capable of communicating and moving agents between different MAS. Moreover, the network manager service can check that no known networks are available; in this case, it changes the Wireless adapter configuration from client to access point mode to allow the MAS designer to connect with the physical prototype.

Like other IDEs, *ChonIDE* allows programming the source code of BDI agents, adding new agents, modifying their names, choosing their architecture

---

[7] http://chonos.sf.net.

(e.g., Communicator, ARGO, or Standard Jason Architecture), and removing any MAS agents. Before starting the MAS execution, *ChonIDE* verifies if the developed source code is already in the physical device. If it is not found, *ChonIDE* uploads the MAS source code to the physical device and starts the MAS execution automatically. However, if the MAS source code is already found on the physical device, *ChonIDE* just starts the MAS execution. Moreover, the stop functionality stops the MAS execution, keeping the MAS source code on the physical device for another future execution. With all these functionalities, the MAS designer can develop a MAS remotely and embed it in a physical device without any wire connection.

To allow the MAS designer to monitor the execution of the MAS, *ChonIDE* has two functionalities: The first allows seeing the agents' minds at runtime with their beliefs, desires, and intentions provided by the *MindInspector* [4] of the *Jason* framework used by *ChonIDE*. The second is a *MAS log* interface that centralizes the logs and error messages generated by the MAS, allowing the MAS designer to identify and correct some errors or possible unwanted behavior of some agents. In addition, the MAS log also presents the information written on the console by the agents using internal actions such as *.print*. Like the embedding functionalities, these monitoring functionalities are enabled remotely without wired connections. Therefore, *ChonIDE* allows the application of Embedded MAS in physical devices such as the *UAV* that its operation is controlled and monitored remotely, which with previous technologies was done in a limited way since they use wire connections.

Finally, to support the development in the *Firmware* layer, the generic coder of the *ChonIDE* also allows the programming of the microcontroller's firmware. To assist in developing the firmware, *ChonIDE* has three functionalities: The first allows compiling the source code and seeing the return message from the compilation process for the MAS designer to see and correct any error that occurs with the developed source code. The second allows importing external libraries, which is essential when using some sensors or actuators that require a particular library to control them. The third allows uploading and deploying the firmware on the microcontroller and can also be done remotely without a physical wired connection. In Fig. 2, ChonIDE's graphical interface is highlighted.

4   Case Study

To show the heterogeneity and applicability of *ChonIDE*, the case study is composed of MAS applied to physical devices that require mobility and remote monitoring (e.g., autonomous vehicle) and to a stationary device (e.g., traffic light). The proposed test scenario considers a road junction with an autonomous vehicle and semaphore prototypes. The scenario selection is mainly motivated by the following: i. Road junctions represent high risks of traffic accidents, as mentioned in [18]. ii. Previous work developed towards formalising and implementing autonomous vehicles endowed with road traffic rules, specifically road junction rules, as seen in [1,16].

354   V. Souza de Jesus et al.

(a) MAS' functionalities.   (b) Firmware' functionalities.

Fig. 2. ChonIDE's graphical interface.

This case study presents the feasibility of deploying what has been proposed in previous works (e.g., [1,16]) The agents (autonomous vehicles) with the corresponding knowledge of road traffic rules are embedded in a MAS. The traffic light must execute its change logic of the traffic signal color agreed, beginning with red, then changing to green, and finishing with yellow to restart, forming a cycle. Moreover, the traffic light has a mechanism to inform the autonomous vehicle of the current signal color. So, the autonomous vehicle should be able to receive the current traffic light and have knowledge about the traffic rules; it is agreed that in the red and yellow signal colors of the traffic lights, the vehicle must stop, and only at the green signal color should it go on. Based on this, the autonomous vehicle uses its decision ability process to respect the traffic rules and decide whether it should proceed through the junction or stop.

4.1 Deployment

The road junction scenario consists of two Embedded MAS applied in two physical prototypes (one for each). For implementing these Embedded MAS, it was used the Embedded MAS architecture presented, and the development started from the Hardware layer, passing through the Firmware layer, and going up until reaching the Reasoning layer. Therefore, the semaphore prototype was built using a single-board computer with a Wi-Fi network card (e.g., Raspberry PI) responsible for storing the MAS, a microcontroller (e.g., Arduino UNO) for interaction with the hardware components, and three LEDs on the green, red and yellow colors to represent traffic signals. Figure 3a has a schematic that shows how the traffic light prototype circuit was built.

The other physical prototype built was the autonomous vehicle prototype that is composed of a single-board computer with a Wi-Fi adapter (e.i. Banana PI), a light sensor called *Light Dependent Resistor* LDR; an HC-SR04 Ultrasonic Sensor for identifying obstacles; a set of five LEDs to light the vehicle; a buzzer; a set of *Direct Current* (DC) motors with an H bridge L298N for locomotion; a *Arduino UNO* microcontroller for controlling the hardware components. In Fig. 3b, it is possible to see the autonomous vehicle prototype built.

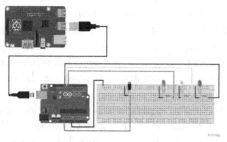

(a) Schematic of semaphore prototype.   (b) Autonomous vehicle prototype.

Fig. 3. Prototypes.

With the prototype built, *ChonIDE* was first used to develop the firmware of the prototype's microcontroller. After that, the MAS designer only needs to focus on developing the MAS. Considering this, the *ChonIDE* is used to develop and embed the MAS in the autonomous vehicle prototype. The MAS is composed of two agents: an *ARGO agent* controls the physical hardware of the vehicle, receiving perceptions of the environment through sensor measurements and acting with the activation and deactivation of the actuator such as motors, *Light-Emitting Diode* (LED), and buzzers. Finally, a *Communicator agent* requests and receives information about the current traffic signal color to the traffic light Embedded MAS.

Like the implementation of the autonomous vehicle Embedded MAS, the traffic light Embedded MAS also uses the *ChonIDE* to develop the microcontroller's firmware and the Embedded MAS. So the traffic light Embedded MAS is also implemented using two agents: an *ARGO agent* responsible for respecting the traffic laws by activating the traffic signals in the correct colors, knowing the current color of the signal, and informing the *Communicator agent*. The *Communicator agent* is responsible for receiving requests from the autonomous vehicle Embedded MAS and responding to the current signal color of the traffic light based on its *ARGO agent's* knowledge.

4.2 Reproducibility

The documentation and instructions for the reproduction of the presented traffic intersection test scenario can be found in the experiment repository of this work[8]. The procedure for reproducing the test scenario can be summarized into four main activities: construction of prototypes, installing *ChonOS*, firmware programming of the microcontrollers inserted in the prototypes, and finally, embedding and monitoring the MAS in the prototypes.

For the prototypes' construction, there is a step-by-step with the necessary electronic components and the diagrams for orientation in the prototypes' building in the experiment repository (See footnote 8). With the prototype built, the

---

[8] https://chonide.chon.group/.

MAS designer must install the GNU/Linux *ChonOS* distribution on the proto-types' single-board computers following the installation manual available on the official *ChonOS* website (See footnote 7). With *ChonOS* installed on the proto-types, it is possible to access *ChonIDE* with all its functionalities. Given this, the MAS designer can use the *ChonIDE* resources to deploy the firmware of the pro-totypes' microcontrollers where the source codes are available in the experiment repository (See footnote 8). Finally, for the entire experiment's reproduction, the MAS designer must access the experiment repository to retrieve the source code of all MAS agents of the test scenario and use ChonIDE to embed and monitor the developed MAS (See footnote 8).

5   Final Remarks

In this work, an Embedded MAS development architecture divided into four layers was used: The *Reasoning* layer; the *Serial* interface layer between the MAS and the physical device; the *Firmware* layer to program the microcontroller behavior, the *Hardware* layer composed of sensors and actuators. With this, it is possible to observe that one of the difficulties in embedding MAS is that it requires knowledge in different areas (Electronics, Low-Level Programming, Object-Oriented, and Agent-Oriented Programming).

Given this difficulty and others, such as the need to use different IDEs (usu-ally one for each layer), this work presents a *WEB IDE* to help the development of an Embedded MAS named *ChonIDE*. *ChonIDE* has graphical interfaces and functionalities to support the three layers that require programming (Reasoning, Serial, and Firmware) of the architecture used, allowing the MAS designer to develop the Embedded MAS using only a single IDE, the *ChonIDE*. In addition, *ChonIDE's* embedding and monitoring procedure does not need to use physical wired connections with the physical device, which allows applying MAS to phys-ical devices with remotely controlled and monitored operations, such as *ROVs* and *UAVs*, which with the previous technologies this sort of connection was somehow restricted.

As future work, it is intended to add to the coding interface a real-time syntax checker, the auto-completion function, keywords identification to pro-duce a visual differentiation in writing these words, and functionalities to debug the Embedded MAS. Moreover, it is expected to provide integration with the *JaCaMo* framework to allow the programming of agents' interaction with the environment's Artifacts and the organizational part of the agents in the MAS. With the integration with JaCaMo done, it is expected that the integration with ROS will be facilitated and can be incorporated into *ChonIDE*. Finally, create an interface for Embedded MAS designers to send suggestions and comments to produce qualitative and quantitative feedback from *ChonIDE* to evaluate how much *ChonIDE* simplifies the development of Embedded MAS.

References

1. Alves, G.V., Dennis, L., Fisher, M.: Formalisation and implementation of road junction rules on an autonomous vehicle modelled as an agent. In: Sekerinski, E., et al. (eds.) FM 2019. LNCS, vol. 12232, pp. 217–232. Springer, Cham (2020). https://doi.org/10.1007/978-3-030-54994-7_16
2. Amaral, C.J., Hübner, J.F.: Jacamo-web is on the fly: an interactive multi-agent system IDE. In: Dennis, L.A., Bordini, R.H., Lespérance, Y. (eds.) EMAS 2019. LNCS (LNAI), vol. 12058, pp. 246–255. Springer, Cham (2020). https://doi.org/10.1007/978-3-030-51417-4_13
3. Boissier, O., Bordini, R.H., Hübner, J.F., Ricci, A., Santi, A.: Multi-agent oriented programming with JaCaMo. Sci. Comput. Program. **78**(6), 747–761 (2013)
4. Bordini, R.H., Hübner, J.F., Wooldridge, M.: Programming Multi-Agent Systems in AgentSpeak using Jason. Wiley, Hoboken (2007)
5. Brandão, F.C., Lima, M.A.T., Pantoja, C.E., Zahn, J., Filho, J.V.: Engineering approaches for programming agent-based IoT objects using the resource management architecture. Sensors (Basel, Switzerland) **21**, 8110 (2021)
6. Bratman, M.E.: Intention, Plans and Practical Reasoning. Cambridge Press, Cambridge (1987)
7. Burattini, S., et al.: Agent-oriented visual programming for the web of things (2022)
8. Guinelli, J.V., Pantoja, C.: A Middleware for using PIC microcontrollers and jason framework for programming multi-agent systems. In: Anais do Workshop de Pesquisa em Computação dos Campos Gerais WPCCG, vol. 1. Ponta Grossa (2016). http://www.wpccg.pro.br/volume001.html
9. Hübner, J.F., Boissier, O., Kitio, R., Ricci, A.: Instrumenting multi-agent organisations with organisational artifacts and agents. Auton. Agent. Multi-Agent Syst. **20**(3), 369–400 (2010)
10. Jesus, V.S., Pantoja, C.E., Manoel, F.C.P.B., Alves, G.V., Viterbo, J., Bezerra, E.: Bio-inspired protocols for embodied multi-agentsystems. In: 13th International Conference on Agents and Artificial Intelligence (ICAART 2021) (2021)
11. Laird, J.E., Newell, A., Rosenbloom, P.S.: SOAR: an architecture for general intelligence. Artif. Intell. **33**(1), 1–64 (1987)
12. Lazarin, N.M., Pantoja, C.E.: A robotic-agent platform for embedding software agents using raspberry Pi and Arduino boards. In: Proceedings of the 9th Software Agents, Environments and Applications School (WESAAC), pp. 13–20. Niterói (2015)
13. Pantoja, C., Junior, M., Lazarin, N.M., Sichman, J.: ARGO: a customized Jason architecture for programming embedded robotic agents. In: Fourth International Workshop on Engineering Multi Agent Systems (EMAS 2016). Singapore (2016)
14. Rao, A.S.: AgentSpeak(L): BDI agents speak out in a logical computable language. In: Van de Velde, W., Perram, J.W. (eds.) MAAMAW 1996. LNCS, vol. 1038, pp. 42–55. Springer, Heidelberg (1996). https://doi.org/10.1007/BFb0031845
15. Ricci, A., Viroli, M., Omicini, A.: CArtA gO: a framework for prototyping artifact-based environments in MAS. In: Weyns, D., Parunak, H.V.D., Michel, F. (eds.) E4MAS 2006. LNCS (LNAI), vol. 4389, pp. 67–86. Springer, Heidelberg (2007). https://doi.org/10.1007/978-3-540-71103-2_4
16. Schwammberger, M., Alves, G.V.: Extending urban multi-lane spatial logic to formalise road junction rules. Electron. Proc. Theor. Comput. Sci. **348**, 1–19 (2021). https://doi.org/10.4204/EPTCS.348.1

17. Silva, G.R., Becker, L.B., Hübner, J.F.: Embedded architecture composed of cognitive agents and ROS for programming intelligent robots. IFAC-PapersOnLine **53**(2), 10000–10005 (2020). https://doi.org/10.1016/j.ifacol.2020.12.2718

18. Wada, Y., Asami, Y., Hino, K., Nishi, H., Shiode, S., Shiode, N.: Road junction configurations and the severity of traffic accidents in Japan. Sustainability **15**(3), 2722 (2023). https://doi.org/10.3390/su15032722

19. Wooldridge, M.J.: Reasoning about Rational Agents. MIT press, Cambridge (2000)

Bioinspired Artificial Cockroach Colony Strategy Combined with 2-Type Fuzzy Logic for the Priority-Based Sanitization of Railway Stations

Fabrizio Tavano[1,2]([✉]) [ID], Riccardo Caccavale[1] [ID], Mirko Ermini[2],
Eugenio Fedeli[2], Luca Ricciardi[2], Alberto Finzi[1] [ID], and Vincenzo Lippiello[1] [ID]

[1] Università degli Studi di Napoli "Federico II", via Claudio 21, 80125 Naples, Italy
{fabrizio.tavano,riccardo.caccavale,alberto.finzi,
vincenzo.lippiello}@unina.it
[2] Rete Ferroviaria Italiana, Piazza della Croce Rossa 1, 00161 Rome, Italy
{mi.ermini,e.fedeli,l.ricciardi}@rfi.it

Abstract. Recent studies show that in railway stations, there is a high probability of being infected during the periods of a pandemic: passengers gathered in the corridors and platforms of stations, eating at restaurants, and getting on trains facilitate the transmission of diseases. The pandemic caused by the SARS-CoV-2 has spawned an important crisis that has affected the railway sector in a significant way, for example, by inducing people to prefer cars instead of trains. RFI S.p.A., in collaboration with the University of Naples "Federico II", is studying methods to reduce the risks of contagion in railway stations, and robotics is demonstrated to be very helpful in attacking this issue. In this study, we propose a multi-robot online sanitization system that exploits the information about the position of people. The new method combines the Bioinspired Artificial Cockroach Colony Strategy with the 2-type Fuzzy Logic to coordinate together a team of robot sanitizers. The solution's performances are compared with those of four different methods deployed in the same scenario, using real data shared by RFI S.p.A., showing better results.

Keywords: Cockroach Colony Strategy · 2-type Fuzzy Logic · Multi-Robot · Sanitization

1 Introduction

Recent studies have highlighted that shared areas of the railway stations may be locations where there is contagion by viruses and bacteria during the periods of

Supported by the Italian Infrastructure Manager Rete Ferroviaria Italiana S.p.A. The source code of the system is available at the following link: https://github.com/Tavano1/MultiRobot_Sanitization_Railway.

P. Mathieu et al. (Eds.): PAAMS 2023, LNAI 13955, pp. 359–374, 2023.
https://doi.org/10.1007/978-3-031-37616-0_30

a pandemic, like in the case caused by SARS-CoV-2 diffusion [31]. The propagation of SARS-CoV-2 disease particularly damaged the railway sector because the transportation demand had registered a drastic reduction. People prefer to travel only if strictly necessary, using private cars in alternative to public services such as railway transportation [29]. Studies demonstrate the importance of the use of robotics to contrast the diffusion of the pandemic in several applications [30]. In this work, answering the Infrastructure Manager Rete Ferroviaria Italiana's request, we propose a sanitization strategy that coordinates a team of robots in a dynamic railway station without interrupting the preexisting human activities. Since every important Italian station is equipped with a WiFi Meraki Cisco System Network, our aim is to exploit such infrastructure to monitor the positions of mobile devices (tablets and phones) and to evaluate the most crowded areas of the station to be sanitized. Specifically, our approach is to define a heatmap, whose colored zones indicate the presence of contamination (prioritized zones) caused by the aggregation of visitors, which can be used by robots as guidance during sanitization activities. This approach may also be applied in every indoor public location as shopping centers and industrial sheds, if WiFi Service is available with visitors' positioning information, with a correct number of robots.

2   Related Works

The sanitization of an environment may be seen as a problem of coverage path planning. In this sense, there are several studies in literature where the authors suggest cleaning and sanitization as possible applications. Classical approaches to the coverage are [17,20], where the environment is divided into different zones, and every robot covers the assigned subareas using paths with a boustrophedon or spiral shape. Other studies are focused on finding paths that ensure the cleaning of prioritized zones with higher assigned frequencies than the others [19,23,28]. In contrast, we are interested in considering a dynamic environment in which every zone may increment its priority to be cleaned during the day, following the spreading of contamination caused by people's movements and the natural contaminant's diffusion law. Specifically, we rely on Ant Colony Strategy (ACS) to guide multiple robots toward our dynamic context. In [32], a coverage planning method in fields with multiple obstacle areas was presented. The method implies that the field is divided into blocks around the in-field obstacles, such that the blocks contain no obstacles. This study applies ACS to add adaptability to the problem of coverage path planning, but in contrast to our method, the ACS is applied only to find the optimal block traversal sequence formulated as a TSP problem in a static environment. In [10] based on the ant colony algorithm, every robot uses the distance matrix to get the optimization sequence of the sub-areas after the decomposition of the coverage environment. The robot covers the local sub-area through boustrophedon motion. In contrast, in our approach, every robot needs to decide on a new position at every step, considering the dynamic environmental conditions. Similarly to our approach, in [25], a group of ant-robots utilizes the principle of pheromone-based coordination: each robot deposits pheromones on boundaries of its territory to inform the others about the already covered areas. When full coverage is achieved, each robot patrols its territory by persistently moving on the territory border. In [8] the authors use a multi-robot coverage approach based on honey bee colony behavior. Specifically, they propose a honey bee-inspired pheromone signaling method: if a robot receives a pheromone, it decides where to move by selecting a target destination in the opposite direction of the received pheromone. In [2], the authors combine the effectiveness of the two pheromone-based approaches detailed above while overcoming the major weaknesses of each approach taken alone. These approaches use pheromone communication as a repulsive signal to increment the spreading of the robots and favor the exploration of new areas, as in our case. In contrast, they consider the coverage problem from the point of view of the patrolling and surveillance task in a static environment, not the cleaning in a dynamic context. Together with the pheromone mechanism, an ACS may include another procedure: the daemon actions [13]. Daemon actions are an optional component of the ACS meta-heuristic and can be used to implement centralized actions which single ants cannot perform. Examples are the collection of global information that can be used to decide whether depositing additional pheromones is useful to bias the search process from a non-local perspective. An example is in [26], where a mobile robot team cooperates to detect obstacles. When a robot faces an obstacle during navigation, it will store its location in the global memory, and all the robots can access it. In our case, we deploy a similar strategy: we define a centralized WiFi server that creates a heatmap representing the current global state of the station, also exploiting the 2-type Fuzzy logic to assign attractive regions to the robots depending on contaminated areas in the map. The Fuzzy logic method is useful when processes are too complex for analysis by conventional quantitative techniques or when the available sources of information are interpreted in a qualitatively inaccurate or uncertain way [9] or the mathematical and statistical description of the time-variability is unknown in a variable time system [18], as in our case. Examples of studies in which type-2 Fuzzy is used together with the ACS technique are in [12,24,26]. In [21] the authors describe the preference of cockroaches to choose for their paths the shadowed zones in order to feel safer. Inspired by this work, we modeled our robots as cockroach-like agents that prefers at every step of their path the attractive regions with higher heatmap's priority distribution. In [21,22] the paper shows that in the exploration phase, the cockroaches prefer to visit zones where there are no other members of the colony. To this end, they may also generate a repulsive pheromone to move away other members. In this work we apply a similar strategy, we program our agents to generate a repulsive pheromone to discourage agents aggregations. In [11], the authors provide evidence that the cockroaches in their exploration prefer to choose destination-shadowed shelters with more food and no other members of the colony. In this sense, the robots will find more attractive the areas assigned to each of them by their daemon server, where they find more density of priority and higher distances between the robots. Following these studies, we propose a novel method

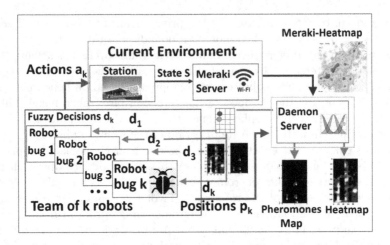

Fig. 1. Graphical representation of the proposed architecture including multiple robotic agents (left) and a single server (the Daemon Server on the right) exploiting WiFi data to generate a heatmap of priorities (red to yellow spots) and the destination nodes for each robot thanks to the Fuzzy Logic System. It updates also the PheromonesMap. (Color figure online)

of sanitization of large and dynamic environments based on a multi-robot bio-inspired artificial cockroach colony strategy that uses two levels of the 2-type fuzzy logic systems to coordinate a team of robots. The sanitization follows the rapid and continuous propagation of the contaminations represented in the heatmap, where different colors are associated with different levels of priority of zones. We considered for our simulations the biggest and most important station in Italy, Roma Termini, in the capital. We used for our tests one day of real data about the positions and motion of people in Roma Termini, stored by the current WiFi Infrastructure Network Meraki Cisco System, shared by the Italian Infrastructure Manager Rete Ferroviaria Italiana. We compared our solution with two examples of conventional coverage path planning strategies commonly proposed in the literature for sanitization [17,20] and two solutions studied specifically for our case of study, capable of adapting their strategies to a dynamic environment where the contamination expands [4–7].

3   Architecture of the System and the Environment

3.1   The Heatmap

The architecture we propose for sanitizing the railway stations is shown in Fig. 1. The server has the role of the daemon as defined in [13,26]. It is responsible for building the heatmap, storing the information about the distribution of the pheromones in the environment in a different gridmap that we call PheromonesMap, building a graph representation of the environment, and assigning to each robot a different destination node. In this manner, it assigns every (cockroach-like) agent with a different attractive contaminated destination zone thanks to the 2-type Fuzzy logic. Every robot will receive this data, and at every timestep, it decides its next area to be cleaned in the gridmap thanks to the 2-type Fuzzy system. The heatmap is a gridmap whose hot/cold points represent high/low priority areas to be sanitized depending on the estimated distribution of people in the environment. Each matrix element of the heatmap is a real number in the interval $[0, 1]$, where 1 stands for the maximum priority, while 0 means that no cleaning is needed (see heatmap in Fig. 2 (left), where this matrix is displayed as a color-coded image, black pixels are 0 priority areas, while colors from red to yellow are for increasingly higher priorities). The heatmap (cleaning priority) is computed from the position of a group of people (clusters) by modeling the possible spreading of viruses or bacteria using a Gaussian model of dispersion [15]. Specifically, we exploit the periodic convolution of a Gaussian filter $\mathcal{N}(\mu, \sigma^2)$ at every step, where μ, σ^2 are suitable parameters that can be regulated depending on the meters/pixels ratio, the timestep, and the considered typology of spreading. In our case, we set the μ and σ values according to the spreading parameters proposed in [3,16]. The values are respectively 0 and 0.9, with a diameter of spreading equal to 5 pixels as in [5–7]. The heatmap after the Gaussian filter application is shown in Fig. 3, (d)). More formally, we define with M our gridmap that represents the environment in which a robot $k \in K$ can move following their policy to decide, at every step, their new position $x_{i,j} \in X$, where X is the set of all free-obstacle grids in the map and K represents the set of robots. We also define s as one possible heatmap with its own distribution of priority in M. A graphical representation of the environment is shown in Fig. 3. Using the planimetry shared by Rete Ferroviaria Italiana, we selected a region of 100×172 m (orange rectangle in 3(a)). The areas of shops, restaurants, and walls represent the fixed obstacles on the map. From this portion, we realize a black and white gridmap (3(b)). We consider that the WiFi server receives an updated distribution of people every 1 h from the Meraki Cisco System (an example of Meraki heatmap is in Fig. 3 upside). The information from the Meraki is then converted into a heatmap for the robots by associating each location with a priority value proportional to the density of people. Since the information from the Meraki is georeferenced, the retrieved value is finally rotated, translated, and scaled in order to match the reference frame of the robots (see Fig. 3(c)). In our simulations, the heatmap has a dimension 100×172 pixels, with a resolution of 1 pixel per $1\,m^2$, and the timestep corresponds to 1 min so that the Meraki will share its information about the presence of people every 60 timesteps. Agents can move by one pixel in any direction. Hence we define the set A that includes 8 actions a_i (4 linear and 4 diagonal). At every timestep, we consider that a robot will sanitize an area of 9 pixels, corresponding to a surface of $3\,m^2$ of the station.

3.2 The Algorithm

The server is responsible for receiving, at every timestep, the current position from every robot. It verifies people's movements in the environments thanks to the information received from Meraki Cisco System WiFi Infrastructure. At

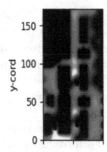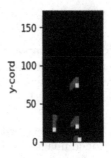

Fig. 2. Example of Heatmap (left) and PheromonesMap (right) during the sanitization process. The yellow lines in PheromonesMap represent the deposited pheromones along the paths of 4 robots in the gridmap. (Color figure online)

Every hour (60 timesteps in our simulation), the server builds the heatmap considering the received information about the people's distribution. At every timestep, a Gaussian filter is applied to the heatmap to simulate the effects of the spreading and attenuation of the contaminants inside the environment. The server also updates the information about the presence of pheromones on a gridmap named PheromonesMap (Ph in the Algorithm 1 and 2), with dimensions 100×172 pixels like the heatmap, applying values 1 to the cells corresponding to the 3×3 robot's cleaned area of the gridmap, around the robot's position at every robot's step. The pheromone is represented by a real number in the range $[0, 1]$. It has the value of 1 at the first moment it is applied in PheromonesMap. An example of PheromonesMap is shown in Fig. 2 (right side). At every step, the server implements pheromone evaporation, the process by which the pheromone trail intensity on the grids automatically decreases over time. Specifically, the server at every timestep subtracts a constant value equal to 0.1 at every non-zero cell of PheromonesMap. The heatmap and the PheromonesMap are sent to every robot of the team at every timestep. At every 60 timesteps, the server also builds a graph representation of the environment, $G = (N, Ar)$ where $N = \{0, 1, \ldots, i\}$ is the set of vertexes and $Ar = \{(i, j) : i, j \in N, i \neq j\}$ is the set of arcs. The server uses the heatmap s to realize G. Specifically, it provides a partition with fixed steps of 40 pixels along the coordinates x and y of s (Fig. 3(e)) to obtain 15 different zones as in [5]. A different node then represents a single zone. The server calculates the total amount of priority inside every single zone $q_i \in Q$ where $i \in N$ and Q is the set of q_i for each zone ($\mathbf{card}(Q) = \mathbf{card}(N)$). Every node is associated with the q_i of its relative zone. Each node is connected to the others. Every arc has a cost $d_{i,j}$ with $(i, j) \in Ar$: the Euclidean distance between the centers of the zones in the heatmap represented by the starting and destination nodes in G. The server uses a 2-type Fuzzy decision layer with taboo search [1,27] to establish the destination nodes $dest_k \in Dest$ of each robot k, where $k \in K$ and $Dest$ is the set of all destination nodes with cardinality $\mathbf{card}(K)$. Every robot receives its destination node at every 60 timesteps. The activities of the server are described in the Algorithm 1. In the simulation, the term max_step (line 2)

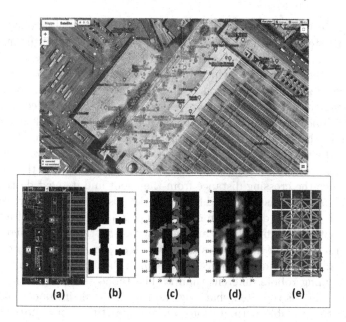

Fig. 3. Example of the distribution of people inside the Roma Termini station as retrieved from the Cisco Meraki WiFi network (up) and the process of the realization of the heatmap and the relative full connected graph (down): the planimetry of the station Roma Termini shared by Rete Ferroviaria Italiana S.p.A. (a), the black-white image (b); the heatmap (d); the heatmap after the Gaussian convolution filter applied for 50 steps (d); partitioning of the heatmap to obtain the corresponding graph (e).

is a parameter that we set to 840, considering 14 h of real data and a duration of 1 min for a timestep. The server, at every timestep, receives the positions of the robots (line 3). At every 60 timesteps: the server rebuilds the heatmap (line 5), adding new priorities in the gridMap M depending on the movements of people, builds the Graph (line 6), puts to zero the cells of the PheromonesMap for its initialization (line 7), verifies the numbers of robots inside each node (line 8), applies the 2-type Fuzzy system with taboo search to obtain the destination nodes for each robot (line 9), sends the destination node to every robot (line 10). At every timestep: the server updates the PheromonesMap (line 12) applying the pheromones to the current positions of the robots and implementing the evaporation process, updates the heatmap applying the Gaussian filter and puts to 0 the pixels of the zones currently cleaned by the robots (line 13), and sends to the robots the updated heatmap, the updated PheromonesMap, and their current positions of the robots to all the team (lines 14–16). The set of the 2-type Fuzzy decision system exploited by the server is shown in Table 1. The Fuzzy system is executed to evaluate each graph node in order to find for every robot $k \in K$ its destination node $dest_k \in Dest$. It receives, as input 1, $d_{i,j,k}$, that is $d_{i,j}$ with $(i,j) \in Ar$, the distance between a node i in N with the current node j where the specified robot k is positioned. Input 2 is the concentration of the priorities for the node q_i with $i \in N$. Input 3 is $nr_i \in Count\_Rob$, the number of robots currently situated in the node i, where $Count\_Rob$ is the set of the numbers of robots per node with dimension $\mathbf{card}(N)$. The Fuzzy system gives as output a real value in the range $[0,1]$, which represents how much the considered node i is convenient such as destination node $dest_k$ for a determined robot k. The $\mathbf{card}(N)$ evaluations of the Fuzzy system for a robot k are collected in a list, and $dest_k$ will be the maximum value of the list. Specifically, the Fuzzy rule base is designed for the Fuzzy system to assign a higher real-value output for a node i, considering the robot k, the higher the priority density q_i, the lower the number of robots nr_i to favor the spread of the colony, and the lower the number of $d_{i,j,k}$ to reduce the crossing distance from the robot and its next destination. A taboo search approach is developed to reduce the possibility that more robots are assigned with the same destination node as in [1,27]. In particular, after a node i is assigned with a specific robot k and becomes $dest_k$, the server assigns in G to that chosen node i very high values of distances $d_{i,j}$ in Ar for each $j \in N$, $j \neq i$ and sets a value 0 to priority's concentration q_i in the next Fuzzy evaluation lists for the remaining robots different than k. The taboo search with the cycles of Fuzzy evaluations is repeated changing the robots' order in its execution, considering all the possible permutations without repetitions $p = \mathbf{card}(K)!$. The server obtains p different $Dest$, and selects that with the higher sum of q_i for each node $i \in Dest$. In the Fuzzy system, For every input, we define a different domain that represents the universe of discourse, as shown in Table 1. For each domain, we report the minimum, the maximum value, and the number of samples generated for it (Min, Max, Num) [14]. We created then for each input three different Gaussian intervals type-2 Fuzzy sets denominated Small, Medium, and Large ($SmlH$, $MedH$, $LrgH$ with H the number of input in the Tables) with uncertain standard deviation values [14] as illustrated in the Table 1. For each Gaussian set, we report in the table the parameters, consisting of the mean, the standard deviation center, the standard deviation spread, and the height of the set (respectively $Mean$, Std_Center, Std_Spread, $Height$). For the output, we defined one domain and ten different Gaussian intervals type-2 Fuzzy sets with uncertain standard deviation values. The sets and their parameters are illustrated in the same Table 1. So we have defined our rules as reported in Table 2. We used an interval type-2 Mamdani Fuzzy inference system. The type reduction plays a key role in achieving crisp values from Type-2 Fuzzy sets. In our case, we used the type reduction algorithm: Enhanced Iterative Algorithm with Stopping Condition [14]. At every step, each robot k decides autonomously which zone $x_{r,l}$, with r,l coordinates in the gridmap M, is necessary to be cleaned inside the heatmap s. The process is described in Algorithm 2. At the beginning of the simulation, every robot is located at random position as in [5–7] (line 2). The robot k receives the new destination node $dest_k$ at the beginning of the hour, at every 60 timesteps (line 5). At every minute, it receives the updated heatmap s, the PheromonesMap Ph from the server, and the current positions of the other robots in the map $(x_1, \ldots, x_k)$ (lines 7, 8, and 9). Every robot k will decide autonomously at every timestep its next position x_{new}. It may choose one of 8 different zones $x'_{r,l}$, because it may do 8 different chess-like movements $ai \in A$: up, down, left, right, and towards the diagonal positions. To make its decision, it finds an evaluation output as a real value in the range $[0, 1]$ by the 2-type Fuzzy Logic for each possible next step. The Fuzzy decision system developed for the robot uses the following inputs: the amount of pheromone $Amount\_pher$ (input 1) considering 3×3 grid-zone around its next possible position choice $x'_{r,l}$ in the PheromonesMap, the total amount of priority $Amount\_prior$ (input 2) in the 3×3 grid-zone around its next possible position selection $x'_{r,l}$ in the heatmap, $dist\_dest_k$ (input 3), defined as the Euclidean distance in the gridmap M of the new considered position $x'_{r,l}$ from the center of the heatmap's zone represented by the destination node $dest_k$. Moreover, the robot evaluates the distances of the new considered position $x'_{r,l}$ from the current position $(x_i, \ldots, x_k)$ of the other robots and selects the minimum of them, $Dist\_x_{min}$ (line 10), that represents the input 4. We have studied a rule base in order to obtain a higher evaluation number if the higher is the total amount of priority $Amount\_prior$ to maximize the removal of priorities at every step, if the lower is the amount of pheromone $Amount\_pher$, where higher concentration corresponds to a less attractive movement selection, if the lower is the value $dist\_dest_k$, and if the higher is $Dist\_x_{min}$ to maximize the spread of the colony. The decision is taken thanks to the 2-type Fuzzy Logic process and the taboo search. Thanks to the 2-type Fuzzy logic, we list an evaluation output for every next new possible position selection x' (one of 8 positions corresponding to 8 chess-like possible movements $a_i \in A$). The list's maximum value will be the robot's next new position x_{new} (line 11). It applies the action to the environment (line 12). Finally, it sends the new position to the server (line 13). For every input, we defined a different domain that represents the universe of discourse, as shown in Table 3. We then created, for each input, three different Gaussian interval type 2 Fuzzy sets denominated Small, Medium, and Large ($SmlH$, $MedH$, $LrgH$ with H the number of input in the Table) with uncertain standard deviation values [14]. For the Gaussian sets, we report in the Table the parameters in Table 3 as in the server case. Also, we defined the output's domain and ten different Gaussian intervals type-2 Fuzzy sets with uncertain standard deviation values as in the case of the server-side Fuzzy system, whose values are shown in Table 1. So we have defined our rule base as reported in Table 4. We used an interval type-2 Mamdani Fuzzy inference system and the type reduction algorithm: Enhanced Iterative Algorithm with Stopping Condition [14] as in the server case.

4 The Case Study

In this Section, we compare our approach with four different methods studied for the sanitization task. Thanks to the collaboration with Rete Ferroviaria Italiana, we received an entire day of recording of the Meraki system (6 September 2021) to be exploited for our experiments. The results are shown in Fig. 4. The first method (orange line) is a spiral-based [17] exploration of the environment, divided into k non-overlapping sub-areas of equal dimensions, each assigned to

Algorithm 1. Server-side cockroach colony algorithm

```
1: procedure SERVER(k, M)
2:     for stp < max_step do
3:         (x_1,...,x_k) = receive_positions()
4:         if stp == 0 OR stp%60 == 0 then
5:             s = apply_real_recorded_data(M,ClusterPeople)
6:             G,N,Ar,Q = build_graph(M, s)
7:             Ph = initialize_Pheromones_Map(M)
8:             Count_Rob = Count_Robots_Per_Nodes(M,G,N,(x_1,...,x_k))
9:             Dest = Fuzzy_Taboo_Search(G,N,Ar,Q,(x_1,...,x_k),Count_Rob)
10:            send_Destination_Nodes(Dest)
11:        end if
12:        Ph = update_Pheromones_Map(M,(x_1,...,x_k) )
13:        s = update_heatmap(s, N(mu,sigma^2), M,(x_1,...,x_k))
14:        send_heatmap(s)
15:        send_Pheromones_Map(Ph)
16:        send_Current_Robots_Positions((x_1,...,x_k))
17:    end for
18: end procedure
```

Algorithm 2. Agent-side cockroach colony algorithm.

```
1: procedure AGENT(i, M)
2:     x_i = random_position()
3:     for stp < max_step do
4:         if stp == 0 OR stp%60 == 0 then
5:             dest_i = receive_destination_Node()
6:         end if
7:         s = receive_heatmap()
8:         Ph = receive_Pheromones_Map()
9:         (x_1,...,x_k)=receive_positions()
10:        Dist_x_min=min_distance((x_1,...,x_k))
11:        x_new = select_action2typeFL(s, x_i,dest_i,Dist_x_min,Ph)
12:        emulate_action(s, x_new, M)
13:        send_position(x_new)
14:    end for
15: end procedure
```

a single robot. Sub-areas are partitioned by rectangular decomposition, and a spiral path is used to cover such partitions. The second method (dashed violet line) is boustrophedon-based [20] exploiting a modified version of the boustrophedon environment decomposition for partitioning and boustrophedon paths are employed for coverage. The third method (blue line) uses a model-free Deep Reinforcement Learning (MARL) [4,6]. The fourth method (green line) is based on a distributed method based on the Hierarchical MPC-MILP approach combined with the Artificial Potential Fields technique [5]. It considers the information about the railway transportation service (arrivals and departures of the

Table 1. Gaussian interval type-2 Fuzzy sets for the inputs and the output of the Server-side 2-type Fuzzy Logic System

Variable	Gaussian_Set	Domain			Mean	Std_Center	Std_Spread	Height
		Min	Max	Num				
Input 1	Sml1	0	150	1000	0	8	5	1
	Med1	0	150	1000	75	8	5	1
	Lrg1	0	150	1000	150	8	5	1
Input 2	Sml2	0	450	1000	0	45	15	1
	Med2	0	450	1000	225	45	15	1
	Lrg2	0	450	1000	450	45	15	1
Input 3	Sml3	0	4	1000	0	0.15	0.05	1
	Med3	0	4	1000	2	0.15	0.05	1
	Lrg3	0	4	1000	4	0.15	0.05	1
output	LB	0	1	1000	0	0.02	0.01	1
	LM	0	1	1000	0.11	0.02	0.01	1
	LA	0	1	1000	0.22	0.02	0.01	1
	MB	0	1	1000	0.33	0.02	0.01	1
	MM	0	1	1000	0.44	0.02	0.01	1
	MA	0	1	1000	0.55	0.02	0.01	1
	HB	0	1	1000	0.66	0.02	0.01	1
	HM	0	1	1000	0.77	0.02	0.01	1
	HA	0	1	1000	0.88	0.02	0.01	1
	HAA	0	1	1000	1	0.02	0.01	1

Table 2. Rule base for the Server-side 2-type Fuzzy Logic System

Input 1	Input 3	Input 2	Output	Input 1	Input 3	Input 2	Output
Sml1	Sml3	Sml2	LA	Sml1	Med3	Sml2	LA
Med1	Sml3	Sml2	LM	Med1	Lrg3	Sml2	LM
Lrg1	Med3	Sml2	LB	Lrg1	Lrg3	Sml2	LB
Sml1	Med3	Med2	MA	Sml1	Sml3	Med2	MA
Med1	Lrg3	Med2	MM	Med1	Sml3	Med2	MM
Lrg1	Lrg3	Med2	MB	Lrg1	Med3	Med2	MB
Sml1	Sml3	Lrg2	HAA	Sml1	Med3	Lrg2	HA
Med1	Sml3	Lrg2	HM	Med1	Lrg3	Lrg2	HM
Lrg1	Med3	Lrg2	HB	Lrg1	Lrg3	Lrg2	HB

trains in the station) together with the historical data regarding the movements of people inside the environment stored by Meraki Cisco System to predict the future cluster's positions. The grey line represents the priorities' evolution caused by the contaminants' spread and attenuation following the Gaussian diffusion law, considering zero robots. Every method is applied considering a team of 4

Table 3. Gaussian interval type-2 Fuzzy sets for the inputs and the output of the Agent-side 2-type Fuzzy Logic System

Variable	Gaussian_Set	Domain			Mean	Std_Center	Std_Spread	Height
		Min	Max	Num				
Input 1	Sml1	0	9	1000	0	0.8	0.4	1
	Med1	0	9	1000	4	0.8	0.4	1
	Lrg1	0	9	1000	9	0.8	0.4	1
Input 2	Sml2	0	9	1000	0	0.8	0.4	1
	Med2	0	9	1000	4	0.8	0.4	1
	Lrg2	0	9	1000	9	0.8	0.4	1
Input 3	Sml3	0	200	1000	0	15	10	1
	Med3	0	200	1000	100	15	10	1
	Lrg3	0	200	1000	200	15	10	1
Input 4	Sml4	0	200	1000	0	15	10	1
	Med4	0	200	1000	100	15	10	1
	Lrg4	0	200	1000	200	15	10	1

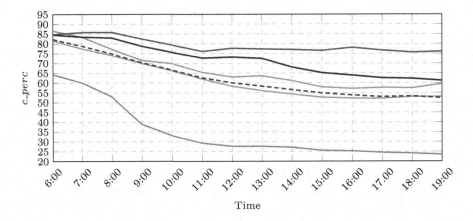

Fig. 4. Comparison between the proposed Bio-inspired Cockroach Colony method (red) and the alternative MARL framework (blue), MPC-MILP technique (green), the spiral-based (violet dashed line) and boustrophedon-based (orange) CPP ones considering c_perc value. In all settings, a team of 4 robots is deployed. The grey line shows the behavior of c_perc with zero robots. (Color figure online)

robots. To compare these methods, we defined the following metric c_perc [5–7] that represents the cleaning rate (in percentage) of the map as follows:

$$c\_perc = ((x_{tot} - s_{curr})/x_{tot}) \cdot 100 \tag{1}$$

where the term s_{curr} is the total amount of priority that the team of robots has removed, and the term x_{tot} represents the total free-obstacle area of the environment. As we can see in Fig. 4, the Cockroach Colony approach (red line)

Table 4. Rule base for the Agent-side 2-type Fuzzy Logic System

Input 1	Input 3	Input 2	Input 4	Output	Input 1	Input 3	Input 2	Input 4	Output
Sml1	Sml3	Sml2	Lrg4	LA	Sml1	Sml3	Lrg2	Sml4	HAA
Med1	Sml3	Sml2	Lrg4	LM	med1	Med3	Sml2	Sml4	HM
Lrg1	Med3	Sml2	Lrg4	LB	Lrg1	Med3	Sml2	Sml4	HB
Sml1	Med3	Med2	Lrg4	MA	Sml1	Lrg3	Sml2	Lrg4	LA
Med1	Lrg3	Med2	Med4	MM	Med1	Lrg3	Med2	Lrg4	LM
Lrg1	Lrg3	Med2	Med4	MB	Lrg1	Sml3	Med2	Lrg4	LB
Sml1	Sml3	Lrg2	Med4	HA	Sml1	Sml3	Med2	Lrg4	MA
Med1	Sml3	Lrg2	Med4	HM	Med1	Med3	Lrg2	Med4	MM
Lrg1	Med3	Lrg2	Sml4	HB	Lrg1	Med3	Lrg2	Med4	MB
Sml1	Med3	Sml2	Sml4	LA	Sml1	Lrg3	Lrg2	Med4	HA
Med1	Lrg3	Sml2	Sml4	LM	Med1	Lrg3	Sml2	Med4	HM
Lrg1	Lrg3	Sml2	Sml4	LB	Lrg1	Sml3	Sml2	Sml4	HB
Sml1	Sml3	Med2	Lrg4	MA	Sml1	Sml3	Sml2	Sml4	LA
Mdm1	Sml3	Med2	Lrg4	MM	Med1	Med3	Med2	Sml4	LM
Lrg1	Med3	Med2	Lrg4	MB	Lrg1	Med3	Med2	Sml4	LB
Sml1	Med3	Lrg2	Lrg4	HA	Sml	Lrg3	Med2	Lrg4	MA
Med1	Lrg3	Lrg2	Med4	HM	Med1	Lrg3	Lrg2	Lrg4	MM
Lrg1	Lrg3	Lrg2	Med4	HB	Lrg1	Sml3	Lrg2	Lrg4	MB
Sml1	Sml3	Sml2	Med4	LA	Sml1	Sml3	Lrg2	Lrg4	HA
Med1	Sml3	Sml2	Med4	LM	Med1	Med3	Sml2	Med4	HM
Sml1	Med3	Sml2	Sml4	LB	Lrg1	Med3	Sml2	Med4	HB
Sml1	Med3	Med2	Sml4	MA	Sml1	Lrg3	Sml2	Med4	LA
Med1	Lrg3	Med2	Sml4	MM	Med1	Lrg3	Med2	Med4	LM
Lrg1	Lrg3	Med2	Sml4	MB	Lrg1	Sml3	Med2	Sml4	LB
Sml1	Sml3	Lrg2	Lrg4	HA	Sml1	Sml3	Med2	Sml4	MA
Med1	Sml3	Lrg2	Lrg4	HM	Med1	Med3	Lrg2	Sml4	MM
Lrg1	Med3	Lrg2	Lrg4	HB	Lrg1	Med3	Lrg2	Sml4	MB
Sml1	Med3	Sml2	Lrg4	LA	Sml1	Lrg3	Lrg2	Lrg4	HAA
Med1	Lrg3	Sml2	Med4	LM	Med1	Lrg3	Sml2	Lrg4	HM
Lrg1	Lrg3	Sml2	Med4	LB	Lrg1	Sml3	Sml2	Lrg4	HB
Sml1	Sml3	Med2	Med4	MA	Sml1	Sml3	Sml2	Lrg4	LA
Mdm1	Sml3	Med2	Med4	MM	Lrg1	Lrg3	Lrg2	Sml4	MB
Lrg1	Med3	Med2	Sml4	MB	Sml1	Lrg3	Lrg2	Sml4	HA
Sml1	Med3	Lrg2	Sml4	HA	Med1	Sml3	Lrg2	Sml4	HM
Med1	Lrg3	Lrg2	Sml4	HM	Lrg1	Sml3	Sml2	Sml4	HB
Lrg1	Lrg3	Lrg2	Sml4	HB	Sml1	Med3	Sml2	Lrg4	LA
Med1	Med3	Med2	Med4	LM	Med1	Med3	Sml2	Lrg4	LM
Lrg1	Med3	Med2	Med4	LB	Lrg1	Lrg3	Med2	Lrg4	LB
Sml1	Lrg3	Med2	Med4	MA	Sml1	Lrg3	Med2	Lrg4	MA
Med1	Lrg3	Lrg2	Med4	MM	Med1	Sml3	Med2	Med4	MM
Lrg1	Sml3	Lrg2	Sml4	MB					

overcomes the other methods. The average of c_perc in the day is 79.26 for the Cockroach method, while it is 71.91 for the MARL. The methods based on the movements of the robots with fixed shapes (spiral-based and boustrophedon-based) are less performing because their sanitization technique does not take into account the evolution of the contamination in a dynamic environment. Moreover, the proposed Cockroach Colony approach outperforms the MARL method every hour, especially after 10:00, arriving to gain 15% at 19:00. In the proposed method, robots generally don't clean the same zones during the action of cleaning. There are fewer overlapping in their paths following the updating of contaminant concentration depending on the movements of people during the day. They remain well distributed on the map because the WiFi server, at every hour, gives each of them a different target zone to be reached for the cleaning. Each robot deposits its repulsive pheromone on the path, so there is less interference between the members at every step while they move, attracted by a higher concentration of priorities.

5   Conclusions and Future Works

In this study, we have proposed a new strategy for on-line sanitization of railway stations based on a bio-inspired Cockroach Colony Strategy combined with 2-type Fuzzy logic decision systems in a dynamic environment. The results highlighted the better performances of our new technique in terms of cleaning percentage. Although, in this work, we focused only on the definition and testing of the high-level strategy, we wish to continue this research by integrating this method with lower-level navigation strategies to consider the avoidance of moving obstacles. We also plan to investigate heterogeneous teams as in [7], considering different roles for the agents but also hierarchies inside the insect colony.

Acknowledgements. The research leading to these results has been supported by the Italian Infrastructure Manager Rete Ferroviaria Italiana S.p.A, and by the HARMONY project (Horizon 2020 Grant Agreement No. 101017008). The authors are solely responsible for its content.

References

1. Atli, O., Kahraman, C.: Fuzzy resource-constrained project scheduling using taboo search algorithm. Int. J. Intell. Syst. **27**(10), 873–907 (2012)
2. Broecker, B., Caliskanelli, I., Tuyls, K., Sklar, E.I., Hennes, D.: Social insect-inspired multi-robot coverage. In: Proceedings of the 14th International Conference on Autonomous Agents and Multiagent Systems (AAMAS) (2015)
3. Buonanno, G., Morawska, L., Stabile, L.: Quantitative assessment of the risk of airborne transmission of SARS-CoV-2 infection: prospective and retrospective applications. Environ. Int. **145**, 106112 (2020). https://doi.org/10.1016/j.envint.2020.106112. https://www.sciencedirect.com/science/article/pii/S0160412020320675
4. Caccavale, R., Calà, V., Ermini, M., Finzi, A., Lippiello, V., Tavano, F.: Multirobot sanitization of railway stations based on deep Q-learning. In: 8th Italian Workshop on Artificial Intelligence and Robotics, AIRO 2021, pp. 34–39 (2022)

5. Caccavale, R., et al.: Combining hierarchical MILP-MPC and artificial potential fields for multi-robot priority-based sanitization of railway stations. In: The 16th International Symposium on Distributed Autonomous Robotic Systems 2022. Springer Proceedings in Advanced Robotics (2023)

6. Caccavale, R., Ermini, M., Fedeli, E., Finzi, A., Lippiello, V., Tavano, F.: A multi-robot deep Q-learning framework for priority-based sanitization of railway stations. Appl. Intell. 1–19 (2023). https://doi.org/10.1007/s10489-023-04529-0

7. Caccavale, R., Ermini, M., Fedeli, E., Finzi, A., Lippiello, V., Tavano, F.: Toward a heterogeneous multi-robot framework for priority-based sanitization of railway stations. In: Dovier, A., Montanari, A., Orlandini, A. (eds.) AIxIA 2022. LNCS, vol. 13796, pp. 387–401. Springer, Cham (2023). https://doi.org/10.1007/978-3-031-27181-6_27

8. Caliskanelli, I., Broecker, B., Tuyls, K.: Multi-robot coverage: a bee pheromone signalling approach. In: Headleand, C.J., Teahan, W.J., Ap Cenydd, L. (eds.) ALIA 2014. CCIS, vol. 519, pp. 124–140. Springer, Cham (2015). https://doi.org/10.1007/978-3-319-18084-7_10

9. Castillo, O., Neyoy, H., Soria, J., Melin, P., Valdez, F.: A new approach for dynamic fuzzy logic parameter tuning in ant colony optimization and its application in fuzzy control of a mobile robot. Appl. Soft Comput. 28, 150–159 (2015)

10. Chibin, Z., Xingsong, W., Yong, D.: Complete coverage path planning based on ant colony algorithm. In: 2008 15th International Conference on Mechatronics and Machine Vision in Practice, pp. 357–361. IEEE (2008)

11. Daltorio, K.A., et al.: A model of exploration and goal-searching in the cockroach, Blaberus discoidalis. Adapt. Behav. 21(5), 404–420 (2013)

12. Di Caprio, D., Ebrahimnejad, A., Alrezaamiri, H., Santos-Arteaga, F.J.: A novel ant colony algorithm for solving shortest path problems with fuzzy arc weights. Alex. Eng. J. 61(5), 3403–3415 (2022)

13. Dorigo, M., Di Caro, G.: Ant colony optimization: a new meta-heuristic. In: Proceedings of the 1999 Congress on Evolutionary Computation-CEC99 (Cat. No. 99TH8406), vol. 2, pp. 1470–1477. IEEE (1999)

14. Haghrah, A.A., Ghaemi, S.: PyiT2FLS: a new python toolkit for interval type 2 fuzzy logic systems (2019)

15. Hanna, S.: Transport and dispersion of tracers simulating COVID-19 aerosols in passenger aircraft. Indoor Air 32(1), e12974 (2022). https://doi.org/10.1111/ina.12974

16. Harmon, M., Lau, J.: The facility infection risk estimator^{TM}: a web application tool for comparing indoor risk mitigation strategies by estimating airborne transmission risk. Indoor Built Environ. 31(5), 1339–1362. https://doi.org/10.1177/1420326X211039544

17. Miao, X., Lee, H.S., Kang, B.Y.: Multi-cleaning robots using cleaning distribution method based on map decomposition in large environments. IEEE Access 8, 97873–97889 (2020)

18. Mittal, K., Jain, A., Vaisla, K.S., Castillo, O., Kacprzyk, J.: A comprehensive review on type 2 fuzzy logic applications: past, present and future. Eng. Appl. Artif. Intell. 95, 103916 (2020)

19. Murtaza, G., Kanhere, S., Jha, S.: Priority-based coverage path planning for aerial wireless sensor networks. In: 2013 IEEE Eighth International Conference on Intelligent Sensors, Sensor Networks and Information Processing, pp. 219–224 (2013). https://doi.org/10.1109/ISSNIP.2013.6529792

20. Nasirian, B., Mehrandezh, M., Janabi-Sharifi, F.: Efficient coverage path planning for mobile disinfecting robots using graph-based representation of environment. Front. Robot. AI **8**, 4 (2021)

21. Obagbuwa, I.C., Adewumi, A.O., Adebiyi, A.A.: A dynamic step-size adaptation roach infestation optimization. In: 2014 IEEE International Advance Computing Conference (IACC), pp. 1201–1205. IEEE (2014)

22. Obagbuwa, I.C., Abidoye, A.P.: Binary cockroach swarm optimization for combinatorial optimization problem. Algorithms **9**(3), 59 (2016). https://doi.org/10. 3390/a9030059. https://www.mdpi.com/1999-4893/9/3/59

23. Pasqualetti, F., Durham, J.W., Bullo, F.: Cooperative patrolling via weighted tours: performance analysis and distributed algorithms. IEEE Trans. Rob. **28**(5), 1181–1188 (2012). https://doi.org/10.1109/TRO.2012.2201293

24. Poornaselvan, K., Kumar, T.G., Vijayan, V.P.: Agent based ground flight control using type-2 fuzzy logic and hybrid ant colony optimization to a dynamic environment. In: 2008 First International Conference on Emerging Trends in Engineering and Technology, pp. 343–348. IEEE (2008)

25. Ranjbar-Sahraei, B., Weiss, G., Nakisaee, A.: A multi-robot coverage approach based on stigmergic communication. In: Timm, I.J., Guttmann, C. (eds.) MATES 2012. LNCS (LNAI), vol. 7598, pp. 126–138. Springer, Heidelberg (2012). https:// doi.org/10.1007/978-3-642-33690-4_13

26. Riyadh, K.: A novel prototype model for swarm mobile robot navigation based fuzzy logic controller. Int. J. Comput. Sci. Inf. Technol. (IJCSIT) **11**(2) (2019)

27. Song, X., Zhu, Y., Yin, C., Li, F.: A hybrid strategy based on ant colony and taboo search algorithms for fuzzy job shop scheduling. In: 2006 6th World Congress on Intelligent Control and Automation, vol. 2, pp. 7362–7365. IEEE (2006)

28. Stump, E., Michael, N.: Multi-robot persistent surveillance planning as a vehicle routing problem. In: 2011 IEEE International Conference on Automation Science and Engineering, pp. 569–575 (2011). https://doi.org/10.1109/CASE.2011.6042503

29. Tardivo, A., Zanuy, A.C., Martín, C.S.: COVID-19 impact on transport: a paper from the railways' systems research perspective. Transp. Res. Rec. **2675**(5), 367–378 (2021). https://doi.org/10.1177/0361198121990674

30. Tavakoli, M., Carriere, J., Torabi, A.: Robotics, smart wearable technologies, and autonomous intelligent systems for healthcare during the COVID-19 pandemic: an analysis of the state of the art and future vision. Adv. Intell. Syst. **2**(7), 2000071. https://doi.org/10.1002/aisy.202000071

31. Yin, Y., Li, D., Zhang, S., Wu, L.: How does railway respond to COVID-19 spreading? - countermeasure analysis and evaluation around the world (2020). https://doi.org/10.21203/rs.3.rs-107167/v1. https://europepmc.org/article/PPR/PPR237958

32. Zhou, K., Jensen, A.L., Sørensen, C., Busato, P., Bothtis, D.: Agricultural operations planning in fields with multiple obstacle areas. Comput. Electron. Agric. **109**, 12–22 (2014)

Embedding Autonomous Agents into Low-Power Wireless Sensor Networks

Danai Vachtsevanou[1]([✉]), Jannik William[2], Matuzalém M. dos Santos[3],
Maiquel de Brito[3], Jomi Fred Hübner[3], Simon Mayer[1], and Andres Gomez[4]

[1] Universität St.Gallen, St. Gallen, Switzerland
{danai.vachtsevanou,simon.mayer}@unisg.ch
[2] ETH Zürich, Zürich, Switzerland
jwilliam@student.ethz.ch
[3] Federal University of Santa Catarina, Florianpolis , Brazil
{maiquel.b,jomi.hubner}@ufsc.br
[4] TU Braunschweig, Braunschweig, Germany
gomez@ida.ing.tu-braunschweig.de

Abstract. Low-power sensors are increasingly becoming available,
equipped with more energy-efficient processing and networking capabilities. Still, in order to accommodate the independent deployment
and intermittent availability of such constrained devices, engineers often
manually reconfigure system behavior for integrating sensors and actuators into complex and context-aware systems. The Multi-Agent Systems paradigm enables engineering systems where components can be
deployed more independently and operate towards achieving their design
objectives. In this process, they act autonomously and interact with others to perform context-aware decision-making without human intervention at run time. In this paper, we present autonomous agents implemented as low-power nodes that perceive and act in a shared environment through sensors and actuators. The autonomous agents on
these constrained devices locally reason and act on the environment,
and wirelessly interact with each other to share knowledge and enable
more context-aware system behavior. The capabilities of our low-power
autonomous nodes are demonstrated in a light-control scenario with two
Belief-Desire-Intention agents. Our experiments demonstrate that running autonomous and social agents in low-power platforms incurs little
overhead, indicating their feasibility.

1 Introduction

Research on autonomous agents and Multi-Agent Systems (MAS) provides
solutions to engineering complex systems, where components – modeled as
autonomous agents – can flexibly perceive and act in distributed, open, and
heterogeneous environments. Such environments are prominent in the Internet
of Things (IoT), where engineers integrate low-power devices into complex systems while catering to the independent deployment, intermittent availability,
and heterogeneity of components. IoT engineers typically perform integration

© The Author(s), under exclusive license to Springer Nature Switzerland AG 2023
P. Mathieu et al. (Eds.): PAAMS 2023, LNAI 13955, pp. 375–387, 2023.
https://doi.org/10.1007/978-3-031-37616-0_31

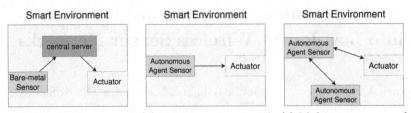

Smart Environment   Smart Environment   Smart Environment

(a) Centralized approach (b) Single-agent approach (c) Multi-agent approach

Fig. 1. Low-power sensors are typically employed in a centralized approach, where decisions are made by a powerful centralized server. Individual autonomous agents have been used to increase the intelligence of low-power sensors and allow local decision-making to directly control actuators. Scaling such single-agent systems to cooperative multi-agent systems introduces new challenges that we address in this paper.

and maintenance manually. On the other hand, exploiting MAS methods for programming IoT applications offers the flexibility to achieve new user goals and handle unexpected events. It also opens up possibilities for examining hybrid goal-driven and event-driven use cases, for example, where goal delegation allows the system to remain robust in the event that autonomous components become unavailable, possibly due to resource constraints.

The Belief-Desire-Intention (BDI) model [5] has been proposed to enable the engineering of agents whose procedural knowledge is defined in terms of beliefs, desires, and intentions, and where agents can flexibly balance between proactive and reactive behavior [13]. Additionally, agent procedural knowledge may include communicative actions, influenced by speech-act theory [16]. These actions enable agents to interact with each other, for example, to change another agent's beliefs. However, our ability to deploy BDI agents in IoT applications for leveraging their desirable properties is hindered by the limited resources of low-power devices, which constrain the system's reasoning cycle and therefore reduce the agents' proactivity, reactivity, and social ability [2]. At the same time, the programming tools (language and run-time environments) that are typically used to develop BDI agents for desktop computers or servers are not well-suited for low-power devices [10]. As a result, low-power sensors are typically used only in conjunction with a powerful centralized server, as depicted in Fig. 1a. Moving towards a multi-agent approach (Fig. 1c), where these sensors more flexibly interact and coordinate with each other – that is, where they are treated more like autonomous entities than dependent nodes – presents new challenges in providing tooling and a system architecture that meet the limitations of highly resource-constrained devices.

This paper explores the potential of using autonomous agent technologies for programming low-power devices in the context of the IoT, with the overarching research aim to isolate the minimal set of BDI properties an agent must have in order to function in low-power devices. This minimal set has been initially proposed in [18] (Fig. 1b). We extend that system to a network of BDI agents and propose a fitting system architecture. Our results show that this architecture enables programming and running social BDI agents on low-power wireless networks while retaining small overhead with respect to memory and energy consumption.

Our proposed system architecture is implemented in the context of a (simple) light-control application where BDI agents that are deployed on low-power devices interact with each other to sense and control the environment and manage illuminance in a room. Our agents is deployed on the DPP3e [14], an ultra-low-power platform that has been custom-designed for next-generation IoT networks. DPP3e includes not only advanced sensing and processing capabilities but also a specialized communication protocol called *Low-power Wireless Bus* (LWB) [7], which uses concurrent transmissions to enable energy-efficient all-to-all communication. This allows every agent in the network to efficiently send *and* receive information, enabling their social behavior.

2   System Architecture

In [15], a lightweight single-agent framework is suggested, which is based on a simplified variant of Jason [3] (an interpreter for an extended version of AgentSpeak). The high-level workflow of the framework is to program the deliberation of the agent using the features of AgentSpeak, and implement perception and action functions together with other hardware-dependent code (like a real-time OS, sensor drivers, and hardware interrupts) in C/C++. The main objective of our work is to bring this embedded BDI framework and its simplified agents to an ultra-low power platform with tight processing, memory, and communication constraints; in the following, we discuss our proposed modifications to that system's Translation Engine (Sect. 2.1) and the BDI Runtime (Sect. 2.2). On the basis of these changes, we then introduce the concept of *Decision Cycles* to better balance agent responsiveness and resource requirements (Sect. 2.3).

2.1   Translation Engine

The Translation Engine presented in [15] converts AgentSpeak programs into optimized C++ code that represents the initial beliefs, goals, and plans of the agent. It is able to connect actions and perception functions available in the hardware with the naming convention used in the AgentSpeak program. The resulting code can be compiled and deployed to a microcontroller. In the process, the translation engine takes special care to optimize the memory and run-time performance of the embedded agent. For instance, while creating C++ classes to represent AgentSpeak beliefs and actions, the engine converts belief and action labels (e.g., is_dark) to corresponding identifiers that are 8-bit integer numbers, limiting the agents to 256 distinct beliefs and actions, respectively. Furthermore, only propositions are allowed (instead of the predicates in Jason), thus no variables can be used in the agent program to be translated. These limitations were carefully selected to still allow us to develop reasonably complex agents (considering low-power embedded devices).

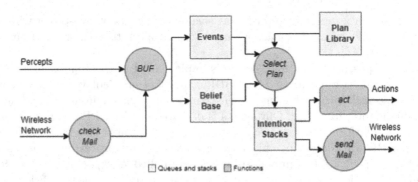

Fig. 2. The practical reasoning cycle of the Embedded-BDI runtime is derived from a simplified version of the Jason interpreter. For multi-agent programs, the runtime must be able to receive messages from the wireless networks and combine any external beliefs with its own perceptions.

In this work, we make use of the translation engine that has undergone a set of modifications. The original engine translates propositions based on their first appearance in the AgentSpeak program of an agent. This approach is effective with single agents, as these use the propositions only for internal operations. However, if multiple agents communicate with each other using their internal propositions, it can lead to misunderstandings, as the same proposition might be mapped to different identifiers in different agents (or vice versa).

The adopted solution is the use of hashed proposition names. As hashes produce reproducible output given a fixed input, the same proposition names get translated equally in every agent program. This solution does not depend on a global state or require all agents to be compiled at the same time. However, special considerations on hash size and function have to be made to minimize the probability of hash collisions. If two propositions do produce the same output, this would happen at compile time, and would be easily detected.

2.2 BDI Runtime

The second core component of the framework is a BDI Runtime that implements a simplified reasoning cycle from the Jason interpreter. Figure 2 summarizes our simplified reasoning cycle, which is run in an infinite loop by the microcontrollers: At the beginning of each reasoning cycle, the agent updates its belief base with percepts from the environment. These percepts are generated using sensor values and the belief update function (BUF) component, coded in C++. We consider that all possible beliefs are known in the translation phase and thus the belief base is a fixed size mapping between beliefs and boolean values. For instance, BUF verifies whether a light sensor value is smaller than a threshold and, if so, the belief is_dark is mapped to true, otherwise it is mapped to false.

The belief base may also be updated due to messages received through the wireless sensor network. Messages encode speech acts [16] that convey a *content* that acts on the mental states of the receiver based on an *illocutionary force*, i.e. the intention of the sender. In our previous work, we did not support the use of illocutionary forces. Now, we employ the illocutionary forces `tell` and `untell` – used with the intention of changing the receiver's beliefs. For example, an agent can send the content `sunny` in a `tell` or `untell` message so that the receiver believes that `sunny` is true or false, respectively.

Any change to the belief base due to percepts or received messages generates an event that is added to the event queue via the BUF component. Then, an event is selected from the event queue, and all applicable plans are selected, i.e. plans from the agent's plan library that are relevant to the event, and most probable to succeed based on the agent's current beliefs. The agent then selects an active intention and executes a single instruction. The instruction could include adding or deleting a belief or achievement-goal, or executing an action (including broadcasting actions).

2.3 From Reasoning Cycle to Decision Cycle

When agents are deployed on unconstrained devices, the reasoning cycle is usually executed at a high frequency. In case the agent has long term goals, it usually keeps executing reasoning cycles, even after an action was decided. We argue that this becomes a problem with respect to computational overhead in resource-constrained devices. Rather, it would be beneficial to execute the reasoning cycle until it has decided on an action and then suspend execution for a certain time. This lets the agent be responsive, once there is information available to support a decision. At the same time, this mechanism saves resources because empty reasoning cycles are avoided.

A possible solution is to suspend the execution of reasoning cycles if there are no events pending and if all intentions and all messages have been processed. There are however some programming patterns (e.g., maintenance goals [3]) that implies that the set of intentions is never empty. In AgentSpeak, this is implemented with the following pattern:

```
+!goal : ctxt1 <- act1 ; !!goal.
+!goal : ctxt2 <- act2 ; !!goal.
```

The chosen plan handles the goal by performing an action (here, `act1`), and then the goal remains relevant through the goal addition (here, `!!goal`) at the end of the plan. Thus the event and intention bases are never empty at the same time. This implies that the condition for the agent to suspend reasoning never happens. The proposed solution is based on *decision cycles*, in which the agent decides the actions to perform and eventually executes them. We typically want to execute actions caused by maintenance goals at most once in a decision cycle. We propose to only check the event base for *external* events, i.e., events not related to achievement goals. A decision cycle is thus composed of sensing, several reasoning cycles until there are no more external events, and (communicative) action. There needs to be more research done on this topic, as it is only tested with our use case scenario.

Listing 1. The AgentSpeak program of an agent that maintains the illuminance conditions in a room (cf. [18]).

```
 1    +user_turn_on <- !!preserve_light.
 2
 3    +!preserve_light: bright_inside & user_turn_on <- !!preserve_light.
 4    +!preserve_light: dark_inside & user_turn_on <- !brighten; !!preserve_light.
 5    -!preserve_light: user_turn_on <- !!preserve_light.
 6
 7    +sunny_outside : user_turn_on <- +eco_mode_available.
 8    +cloudy_outside: user_turn_on <- -eco_mode_available; +standard_mode_available.
 9    +night_outside : user_turn_on <- -eco_mode_available; +standard_mode_available.
10
11    +!brighten: eco_mode_available <- turn_off_lights; raise_blinds; -eco_mode_available.
12    +!brighten: standard_mode_available  <- turn_on_lights; -standard_mode_available.
13
14    +user_turn_off <- !!preserve_dark.
15
16    +!preserve_dark: night_outside & user_turn_off <- lower_blinds; !!preserve_dark.
17    +!preserve_dark: bright_inside & user_turn_off <- turn_off_lights; lower_blinds;
18                                            !!preserve_dark.
19    -!preserve_dark: user_turn_off <- !!preserve_dark .
```

3   Light Control in a Building Automation MAS

To ground our approach, we present an application scenario where a MAS features two BDI agents (Fig. 1c): An indoor_agent perceives the illuminance conditions within a building (percepts: {bright,dark}_inside), and adjusts the conditions by acting on a lamp (actions: {turn_on,turn_off}_lights) or on a set of blinds (actions: {raise,lower}_blinds). The agent also perceives the illuminance preferences of room occupants (percepts: user_turn_{on,off}). Additionally, an outdoor_agent perceives the outdoor illuminance conditions (percepts: {sunny,cloudy,night}_outside).

Lst. 1 shows the program of the indoor agent – formerly presented in [18] as part of a single-agent application – which acts on the environment based on users' preferences. In contrast to previous work, the agent now only perceives the building's interior, with external weather information shared by the outdoor agent through agent-to-agent interaction.

The scenario begins with both agents launched. The indoor agent observes the indoor illuminance conditions, while the outdoor agent is initially in sleep mode. Upon perceiving the occupant's preference for high illuminance conditions, the indoor agent continuously strives to maintain a high illuminance level (lines 1–5) and will, by default, turn on the lights to increase brightness if the room is dark (lines 12 and 13). Accordingly, if the indoor agent perceives that the occupant now prefers low illuminance conditions in the room, it will adopt the goal of maintaining such conditions (line 14). Therefore, if it is bright inside the room, the agent will turn off the lights, and additionally lower the blinds to eliminate any possible source of illumination (lines 16–18).

In the second scenario phase, the outdoor agent starts observing the outdoor environment and broadcasts messages to synchronize other agents' beliefs with the current weather conditions. The behavior of the agent is based on the AgentSpeak program shown in Lst. 2. The indoor agent is still committed to maintaining optimal illuminance conditions, however, now the agent's decision-making is more contextual since it takes into consideration the communicated weather conditions. For instance, when brightening the room, the agent reasons that a more eco-friendly option is available when the weather is sunny (Lst. 1, line 7), and decides to raise the blinds (Lst. 1, line 11) instead of turning on the lights.

```
1  !communicate. // initial goal
2  +!communicate : sunny_outside <-
3     .broadcast(tell, sunny_outside);
4     .broadcast(untell, cloudy_outside);
5     .broadcast(untell, night_outside);
6     !!communicate.
7  +!communicate : cloudy_outside <-
8     .broadcast(untell, sunny_outside);
9     .broadcast(tell, cloudy_outside);
10    .broadcast(untell, night_outside);
11    !!communicate.
12 +!communicate : night_outside <-
13    .broadcast(untell, sunny_outside);
14    .broadcast(untell, cloudy_outside);
15    .broadcast(tell, night_outside);
16    !!communicate.
```

Listing 2. The AgentSpeak program of an agent that perceives and broadcasts information about the weather conditions.

4 Experimental Evaluation

In this section, we evaluate the proposed BDI framework (labeled "Multi-Agent Version" hereafter) using the previously described light control application from [18] (labeled "Single-Agent Version"). The experimental setup is described first, along with the used hardware components and infrastructure. The light-control experiment is then presented in detail, along with its environmental traces. We then perform a low-level performance evaluation of the BDI framework and present our analysis.

4.1 Experimental Set-Up

In the Single-Agent Version of the experiment, we have used the commercial Edge platform by Sparkfun, which is based on the Ambiq Apollo3 Blue microcontroller. We integrated the embedded-BDI framework [15] with FreeRTOS and utilized ARM's Cordio BLE stack for asynchronous communication. Whenever an agent wanted to perform an action, it would transmit a bluetooth advertisement and trigger different actuators. In this work, we use the DPP3e platform [14], which features a separation of application and communication processors. This allows for the independent development of the different domains, and can also save valuable memory in the application domain since it no longer needs to maintain a communication stack.

The DPP3e's application domain features an Ambiq Apollo 3 Blue Plus. Instead of using BLE advertisements, the DPP3e's communication domain uses the LWB protocol, enabling efficient all-to-all communication. Two DPP3e's are used to form a two-agent system, as described in Sect. 3.

One agent is located indoors, the other outdoors; each is equipped with a light sensor. The outdoor agent wirelessly transmits the values of the {sunny,cloudy,night}_outside beliefs to the indoor agent. A third DPP3e board is connected to a Raspberry Pi and acts as a gateway, limited to forwarding commands to the lights and blinds via the wired network. The UART output of all boards is logged for debugging and postprocessing. Figure 3 shows the set-up for the multi-agent experiment.

The experiment is conducted in the evening when the outdoor illuminance is decreasing. The following light thresholds have been set: sunny/cloudy threshold is 4000 lux, cloudy/night threshold is 500 lux, and

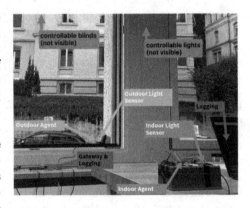

Fig. 3. A user can set the indoor agent's goal either to brighten or darken a room. Depending on the information broadcast by the outdoor agent, the indoor agent can select among different actuators to achieve its goal.

the indoor threshold: 19 lux. The decision cycle period was set to 15 s, which aligned with the communication period. These were however not synchronized (worst-case, it could be, that communication happens right before the decision cycle, leading to almost 15 s delay, until an action is sent).

4.2   Experimental Results

The measurements of the energy consumption were performed by an Otii Arc and are summarized in Table 1. The reasoning part corresponds to a full decision cycle including message fetching from the wireless communication domain. The energy and execution time values thus are significantly higher. The task that consumed the most energy is sensing. This is also significantly higher than in the single-agent experiment since longer integration times are chosen. Another significant energy consumer is the wireless communication, which now requires almost three orders of magnitude more energy, although they cannot be directly compared, as here, the communication is bidirectional.

The original embedded BDI framework [15] was explicitly developed for resource-constrained devices. The AgentSpeak functionality is fundamentally the same in both versions, so the translation yields the same C++ code size. The single-agent version implements the entire sense-reason-transmit functionally on a single chip (Apollo3 Blue), using 748 KB of read-only memory. The multi-agent version is run on the DPP3e's application domain (Apollo3 BluePlus), implementing only the sensing-reason functionality on 311 KB of read-only memory.

Smart Light Control. The experiment lasted for 765 s. The initial conditions were, that the lights were off and the blinds down and the user preference was to brighten the room. This initially triggered the action of raising the blinds. The indoor illuminance is actually below the threshold, but the sunny condition prevents the agent to turn on the light. After 169 s, the outdoor conditions indicate, that it is cloudy. Since the outdoor agent has a near worst-case alignment of the decision cycle and communication cycle, it needs 14 s, until the beliefs are sent over the LWB. The indoor agent requires two full decision cycles to come to the conclusion to turn on the lights, meaning, the breaking condition got triggered to our disadvantage. This results in a total delay of 44 s from acquiring the belief, until the action gets triggered. There were two cycles required, because after acquiring the belief `cloudy_outside`, `+!brighten` was already processed, before `standard_mode_available` got added to the belief base (so there was no context matching the belief base for a plan for `+!brighten`). Therefore, the action gets triggered only in the next decision cycle. At 513 s, the user preference changed to darken. As `+user_turn_off` executes `!!preserve_dark`, the breaking condition gets triggered before a plan for `+!preserve_dark` can be executed. This results in a delay of one decision cycle, until the actions get triggered, resulting in a 15 s delay from the LWB communication period.

4.3   Analysis

The experiments showed, that it is possible to implement a low-power BDI agent on an embedded device, which can perform a basic home automation task (Fig. 4). The agents show reactive and proactive behavior, where it reacts to user input and proactively adapt to the environment. Compared to the traditional tasks of sensing and communication, reasoning takes up very little time and energy, so the cost of adding intelligence and autonomy to a simple system is very minimal. The results also showed the differences between the single and

Table 1. The multi-agents version requires longer mean execution times (t_{mean}) and higher mean energies (E_{mean}) because it tasks are more complex, e.g. sensing with dynamic integration times, a variable number of reasoning cycles, and full bidirectional wireless communication.

Single-Agent Version					
Task	E_{mean}	E_{std_dev}	t_{mean}	t_{std_dev}	# samples
Sensing	15.1 mJ	4.4 µJ	569.4 ms	63 µs	114
Reasoning Cycle	1.2 µJ	<0.1 µJ	334.3 µs	2.9 µs	114
Communication	47.8 µJ	<0.1 µJ	15.2 ms	31 µs	147
Multi-Agent Version					
Task	E_{mean}	E_{std_dev}	t_{mean}	t_{std_dev}	# samples
Sensing	39.7 mJ	160.7 µJ	1113.4 ms	4.5 ms	190
Decision Cycle	54.8 µJ	17.5 µJ	1.609 ms	490.2 µs	115
Communication	25.9 mJ	4.0 mJ	419.9 ms	64.6 ms	115

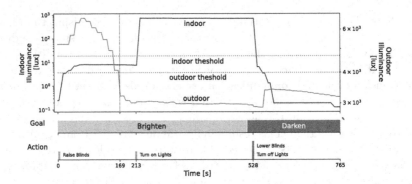

Fig. 4. Upon adopting the `brighten` goal, the indoor agent first raises the blinds to increase the illuminance. Once the low threshold for natural light is crosses, the agent decides to turn on the artificial lights to maintain the `brighten` goal. After the user chooses to darken the room, both actuators are turned off.

multi-agent systems. The single agent had practically no communication delay, whereas there was a worst-case delay of 15 s in the multi-agent system. There is however the advantage of the meshed communication in LWB, which BLE does not allow efficiently (BLE is point-to-point, which is not directly compatible with MAS). The computational delay could however be greatly improved, because of the introduction of the *full decision cycle*. This allows to do a "burst" of reasoning cycles directly one after the other and thus directly decide on an action.

Though low-power BDI agents have significant potential, there are still several limitations in our current implementation. Developing applications for low-power multi-agent systems still requires significant manual effort to synchronize BDI functions with hardware-dependent code and communication stacks. Furthermore, the specific characteristics of the communication protocol can limit the performance of the overall system, as shown by the latencies stemming from periodic communication.

5   Related Research

Developing efficient autonomous agents for low-power devices is crucial for applying BDI-based agent technology in the IoT domain. Previous research bridges the resource gap between low-power platforms and the resources required by agents by connecting low-power devices to more powerful ones [1,9,11,17], but this approach may not be energy-efficient for many IoT applications. Our approach focuses on deploying agents exclusively on constrained devices.

Other approaches deploy the agents solely on constrained platforms. Agents are programmed in C++ [12], assembly-like languages [8], or using on-chip synthesis of finite-state machine models [4]. These agents have social abilities through wireless communication (e.g. [4,8]), but are limited with respect to their autonomy, proactivity, and reactivity. Our aim is to retain the expressiveness of an agent programming language and the high-level constructs of the BDI model to preserve agent properties in IoT applications.

Towards combining the expressiveness of an agent programming language and the energy efficiency of a more low-level language, Bucheli et al. propose translating BDI specifications programmed in AgentSpeak [3] to C programs for low-power devices [6]. However, their translation is application-specific, while our work employs a general-purpose framework. Also, while their work is evaluated in simulated environments [6], we propose evaluating our framework in real applications with explicit energy and communication concerns.

Our previous work [18] focused on running AgentSpeak programs for single-agent systems with isolated domain vocabularies, which limits any social interaction between agents. While the feasibility of autonomous agents in wireless sensors was demonstrated, agents can only broadcast asynchronous messages to actuators. Due to its asynchronous nature, an agent can broadcast a message to an actuator as soon as it decides on an action. While this minimizes the latency between decision and actuation, unidirectional communication is not feasible for multi-agent systems. In this work, we address some challenges to enable multiple agents to run on a *network* of low-power wireless sensors. We extend the simplified embedded BDI reasoning cycle to include belief updates from/to the wireless network, enabling agents to disseminate their beliefs using a shared domain vocabulary.

6   Conclusions

In this paper, we presented a general-purpose BDI multi-agent programming framework that runs on low-power devices for wireless sensor networks. By integrating an energy-efficient all-to-all wireless protocol, we can develop social BDI agents capable of sharing beliefs in a scalable and efficient manner. We have implemented a real-world light control application on a state-of-the-art hardware platform and shown the feasibility of low-power multi-agent systems. Our experimental findings prove the low overhead of a constrained set of BDI features in Jason for low-power sensors while preserving the core properties of autonomous agents: Agents are capable of perceiving and acting on their environment, deliberating about goals and making decisions while balancing between their proactive and reactive behavior, and, finally, interacting and collaborating with other agents by exchanging messages.

Acknowledgements. This work has been partially funded by the GFF-IPF Grant of the University of St.Gallen, and the Swiss National Science Foundation, grant No. 189474 (Hypermedia Communities of People and Autonomous Agents). The authors would like to thank L. Meier, G. Ramanathan, N. Stricker, and K. Razavi for their contributions to this work.

References

1. Bahri, O., Mourhir, A., Papageorgiou, E.I.: Integrating fuzzy cognitive maps and multi-agent systems for sustainable agriculture. Euro-Mediterr. J. Environ. Integr. **5**(1), 1–10 (2020)
2. Boissier, O., Bordini, R.H., Hübner, J.F., Ricci, A., Santi, A.: Multi-agent oriented programming with JaCaMo. Sci. Comput. Program. **78**(6), 747–761 (2013)
3. Bordini, R.H., Hübner, J.F., Wooldridge, M.: Programming Multi-agent Systems in AgentSpeak Using Jason. Wiley, Hoboken (2007)
4. Bosse, S.: Distributed agent-based computing in material-embedded sensor network systems with the agent-on-chip architecture. IEEE Sens. J. **14**(7), 2159–2170 (2014)
5. Bratman, M.E., Israel, D.J., Pollack, M.E.: Plans and resource-bounded practical reasoning. Comput. Intell. **4**, 349–355 (1988)
6. Bucheli, S., Kroening, D., Martins, R., Natraj, A.: From AgentSpeak to C for safety considerations in unmanned aerial vehicles. In: Dixon, C., Tuyls, K. (eds.) TAROS 2015. LNCS (LNAI), vol. 9287, pp. 69–81. Springer, Cham (2015). https://doi.org/10.1007/978-3-319-22416-9_9
7. Ferrari, F., Zimmerling, M., Mottola, L., Thiele, L.: Low-power wireless bus. In: Proceedings of ACM SenSys Conference (2012)
8. Fok, C.L., Roman, G.C., Lu, C.: Agilla: a mobile agent middleware for self-adaptive wireless sensor networks. ACM Trans. Auton. Adapt. Syst. (TAAS) **4**(3), 1–26 (2009)
9. Lazarin, N.M., Pantoja, C.E.: A robotic-agent platform for embedding software agents using raspberry pi and arduino boards. 9th Softw. Agents, Environ. Appl. School, **152** (2015)
10. O'Hare, G.M.P., et al.: Embedding agents within ambient intelligent applications. In: Agents and Ambient Intelligence - Achievements and Challenges in the Intersection of Agent Technology and Ambient Intelligence. IOS Press (2012)
11. Pantoja, C.E., de Jesus, V.S., Manoel, F., Viterbo, J.: A heterogeneous architecture for integrating multi-agent systems in AMI systems (S). In: Proceedings SEKE Conference. KSI Research Inc. (2018)
12. Purusothaman, S.R.R.D., Rajesh, R., Bajaj, K.K., Vijayaraghavan, V.: Implementation of Arduino-based multi-agent system for rural Indian microgrids. In: Proceedings ISGT Asia Conference, pp. 1–5 (2013)
13. Rao, A.S., Georgeff, M.P.: BDI agents: from theory to practice. In: Proceedings of the First International Conference on Multiagent Systems (1995)
14. Rufer, L., Stricker, N., et al.: Demo abstract: Dpp3e: a harvesting-based dual processor platform for advanced indoor environmental sensing. In: Proceedings IPSN Conference. IEEE (2022)
15. Santos, M.M.d.: Programação orientada a agentes BDI em sistemas embarcados. Master's thesis, Universidade Federal de Santa Catarina (2022)
16. Searle, J.R., Searle, J.R.: Speech Acts: An Essay in the Philosophy of Language, vol. 626. Cambridge University Press, Cambridge (1969)

17. Wanyama, T., Far, B.: Multi-agent system for irrigation using fuzzy logic algorithm and open platform communication data access. Int. J. Comput. Inf. Eng. **11**(6), 690–695 (2017)
18. William, J., et al.: Increasing the intelligence of low-power sensors with autonomous agents. In: Proceedings of the 20th ACM Conference on Embedded Networked Sensor Systems, pp. 994–999 (2022)

Safe Autonomous Decision-Making with *vGOAL*

Yi Yang[✉][iD] and Tom Holvoet[iD]

imec-DistriNet, KU Leuven, 3001 Leuven, Belgium
{yi.yang,tom.holvoet}@kuleuven.be

Abstract. Safety is one of the crucial features of autonomous systems. Safe decision-making is a critical and challenging task in developing such systems. To address this challenge, we proposed *vGOAL*, a GOAL-based specification language designed for ensuring safe autonomous decision-making. In this paper, we present an interpreter for *vGOAL*, serving as an agent-based decision-making component for autonomous systems. Our main contributions are the design and implementation of the *vGOAL* interpreter, which automatically and efficiently generates safe decisions in real-time, while simultaneously performing safety checking, error handling, and conflict resolution for competing requests. As the Robot Operating System is a popular framework for developing robotic application systems, we integrate the *vGOAL* interpreter with it via rosbridge. To demonstrate the effectiveness of *vGOAL*, we validated its performance using a real-world autonomous logistic system comprising three autonomous mobile robots.

Keywords: Autonomous Decision-Making · Safety Assurance · *vGOAL* · Interpreter

1 Introduction

Autonomous systems are increasingly gaining interest due to their ability to operate independently in hazardous or remote environments, or in situations where the complexity and speed of environmental interactions are beyond human capacity, making direct human control infeasible [12]. Despite their appeal for autonomous operation, their application is often hampered by the (rightul) need for safety assurance.

The controller of autonomous systems plays a critical role in ensuring the safety of these systems. In agent-based autonomous systems, the controller includes a high-level discrete agent-based decision-maker and a low-level continuous controller, which function independently and collaboratively to make decisions in response to the environment [12]. However, ensuring safety of autonomous systems is difficult due to the unpredictability of the real world, which makes it not only hard but theoretically impossible to guarantee that an autonomous system will always behave safely [10]. It is crucial but challenging to define the concept of safe autonomous decision-making. In this paper, we adopt the definition of safe autonomous decision-making proposed in [10], which defines an autonomous decision-maker as safe if it refrains from intentionally pursuing unsafe behaviors based on its beliefs and goals. In this paper, we aim to achieve safe autonomous decision-making through the high-level discrete agent-based decision-maker of an agent-based autonomous system with safety assurance.

In recent decades, agent programming languages (APLs), such as AgentSpeak [4], Jason [5], Gwendolen [11], and GOAL [14], have received considerable attention for programming autonomous agents. Consequently, APLs can be practical in addressing the challenge of safe autonomous decision-making. To verify safety properties of APLs, static verification techniques have been widely applied. Among these, model checking is the most successful and influential method for evaluating hardware and software systems, and verifying APLs due to its automated verification process [19]. Specifically, model checking has been applied to verify AgentSpeak(L) [3], Gwendolen, GOAL, SAAPL [20], and ORWELL [8,13,25], while it suffers from the state-space explosion. In contrast, theorem proving has been used to verify a subset of GOAL [2,17], mainly due to the complexity of its specification and verification processes. Two key points need to be highlighted. First, while the verification of APLs aims to verify formal properties, including safety properties, it does not have the specific purpose of verifying safety. Second, a verified APL program cannot guarantee safety against unforeseen real-time errors that may occur in the real world.

It is desirable for the agent-based decision-making component to be safe-by-generation. However, APLs including AgentSpeak (Jason), Gwendolen, and GOAL, are currently unable to fulfill this requirement. To address this limitation, we proposed a specification language called *vGOAL* [26] with the aim of achieving safe autonomous decision-making through generation. *vGOAL* is a first-order logical specification language based on the internal logical reasoning mechanism of GOAL.

To efficiently generate verifiable safe decision-making for autonomous systems, [22] presents a high-level overview of a three-stage formal approach: formal specification using *vGOAL*, safe decision generation using a *vGOAL* interpreter, and PCTL model checking using a *vGOAL* translator and a PCTL model checker (Storm [9] or PRISM [18]). Safe autonomous decision-making pertains to *vGOAL* and the *vGOAL* interpreter. [26] provides a comprehensive description of *vGOAL* including its formal syntax and formal semantics. Building on [26], we present the design and implementation of the interpreter for *vGOAL* in this paper, explaining how to achieve safe autonomous decision-making through generation.

This paper is organized as follows. In Sect. 2, we provide the necessary background on the *vGOAL* interpreter. In Sect. 3, we present the architecture and key implementation details of the interpreter for achieving safe autonomous decision-making. In Sect. 4, we provide a practical demonstration of the key features of the *vGOAL* approach, as well as the efficiency of the *vGOAL* interpreter, through the utilization of a real-world autonomous logistic system. In Sect. 5, we discuss the advantages of using *vGOAL*, identify the limitations of the current version of the *vGOAL* interpreter, and provide an outline of future work.

2   Background

This section provides the necessary theoretical foundation for developing safe autonomous decision-making with $vGOAL$. First, we examine the formalization and verification of safety and invariants in model checking provided in [1]. Second, we provide a succinct overview of the key features of the formal syntax and operational semantics of $vGOAL$ provided in [26], which are essential to implement an interpreter for $vGOAL$. Finally, we briefly introduce rosbridge [7], which is essential for the integration of ROS.

2.1   Safety Properties and Invariants in Model Checking

Informally speaking, safety properties are essential conditions that a system must satisfy to maintain a safe state. They can be classified into two categories: state-based and non-state-based safety properties. State-based safety properties are characterized by invariants, which define the conditions that must hold in every state of the system to ensure safety.

To facilitate model checking, it is necessary to restrict the safety properties to those that can be expressed in a regular language, known as regular safety properties. It should be noted that every invariant qualifies as a regular safety property.

There are two important theoretical results. First, for a transition system, checking an invariant for the propositional formula Φ amounts to checking the validity of Φ in every state that is reachable from some initial state. Second, checking a regular safety property on a finite transition system (TS) can be reduced to invariant checking on the product of TS and a nondeterministic finite automaton A for the bad prefixes. In summary, invariant checking is simple but essential to checking safety against a transition system. For the details of aforementioned definitions and theorems, we refer readers to [1].

2.2 $vGOAL$

Originating from GOAL, $vGOAL$ was specifically designed to specify safe autonomous decision-making mechanisms. $vGOAL$ is a first-order logical specification language. The key implementation of the interpreter for $vGOAL$ is the implementation of the operational semantics of $vGOAL$. Its operational semantics reflects how an n-agent autonomous system generates decisions for each agent in a modular manner.

For each agent, the generation of each decision involves six reasoning stages, five of which involve logical derivation and minimal model generation over a first-order theory constrained by the formal syntax of $vGOAL$. Specifically, the formal syntax of $vGOAL$ imposes three restrictions on the first-order logic used in the reasoning cycles. First, each rule contains no negative recursion. Second, each variable has a finite domain. Third, each variable is quantified. These restrictions guarantee that a $vGOAL$ specification that strictly follows the formal syntax of $vGOAL$ has a minimal model [25]. Therefore, the implementation of automated logical derivation and automated minimal model generation over first-order theories is crucial to implement an interpreter for *vGOAL*. For the details of the formal syntax and operational semantics of *vGOAL*, we refer readers to [26].

2.3 Rosbridge

Rosbridge has become a popular tool for accessing robot interfaces and algorithms in ROS due to its simple, socket-based programmatic interface [7]. In recent years, efforts have been made to facilitate communication between the Gwendolen agent programming language and ROS via Rosbridge. In this regard, [6] have proposed an interface that enables Gwendolen to interact with ROS via Rosbridge, allowing for the development of verifiable autonomous agents.

3   Interpreter for *vGOAL*

This section provides an overview of the architecture and implementation of the *vGOAL* interpreter. Specifically, the interpreter serves as a safe high-level discrete agent-based decision-making component and works collaboratively and closely with the low-level continuous controller of the autonomous system. In our implementation, we have chosen ROS-based controllers as the low-level continuous controllers. Consequently, the implementation of the *vGOAL* interpreter consists of two primary components: the implementation of the operational semantics of *vGOAL*, and an interface with ROS. The syntax and operational semantics of *vGOAL* are necessary to thoroughly understand this section; we refer readers to [26] for a detailed explanation. By developing a *vGOAL* interpreter including these two components, we aim to provide a safe agent-based decision-making component implemented by the *vGOAL* interpreter that efficiently makes safe-by-generation decisions.

3.1   Architecture

The architecture of the *vGOAL* interpreter is depicted in Fig. 1. This figure provides an overview of how the interpreter generates safe decisions and interacts with ROS. The *vGOAL* interpreter consists of two main components: a data processing component and a decision-making generation component. The data processing component acts as an interface for data exchange with ROS, and the decision-making component generates safe decisions for all agents within the autonomous system.

The data processing component has two main functions. First, it processes the *vGOAL* specification and the real-time sensor information obtained from ROS via rosbridge into the state of the autonomous system. Second, it translates the generated safe decision obtained from the decision-making component to the information understood by ROS.

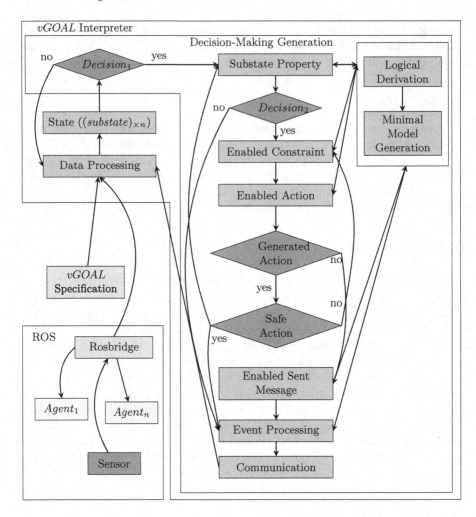

Fig. 1. The Architecture of the *vGOAL* Interpreter

The decision-making generation component involves the implementation of the reasoning cycle of *vGOAL*, the safe action evaluation, and the decision-making evaluation. The decision-making generation component works independently for each agent. The central element of the decision-making generation component is the implementation of the reasoning cycle of *vGOAL*, involving six stages: substate property generation, enabled constraints generation, enabled action generation, enabled sent message generation, event processing, and communication. The first five stages of the reasoning cycle involve the logical derivation and the minimal model generation over the first-order theories constrained by the *vGOAL* syntax. Therefore, the first-order logical derivation and minimal model generation are core to implementing the reasoning cycle.

Moreover, a safety-checking process and a decision-making evaluation process are integrated into the decision-making generation component. The safety-checking process ensures safe-by-generation decisions, and a decision-making evaluation process guarantees an agent receives safe real-time decisions when needed. We briefly describe how to generate safe decisions using the $vGOAL$ interpreter. A complete $vGOAL$ specification includes system specifications and agent specifications, whereas a $vGOAL$ specification used to generate real-time safe decisions only contains the system specification. System specifications describe the rules applied to the whole autonomous system, and the agent specifications describe the current beliefs and goals of the agents within the autonomous system. System specification is predefined by users, while agent specifications are obtained at runtime from ROS, providing the interpreter with the real-time information available.

The data processing component of the $vGOAL$ interpreter integrates the $vGOAL$ specification with real-time sensor data to establish the current state of the autonomous system. Within this context, the state of an individual agent within the system is regarded as a substate, which contributes to the overall state of the autonomous system in a modular fashion. Specifically, a substate consists of the belief base and goals of an agent.

The decision-making generation component will first evaluate if any agent of the autonomous system needs a decision. If no agent needs any decision at the moment, the decision-making component will not generate any decisions; otherwise, the decision-making component proceeds for each agent. It generates the substate properties. After that, it evaluates whether the agent needs a decision at the given moment. If the agent needs a decision, the decision-making component tries to generate a safe decision. Finally, the decision-making component will process events and perform communication.

If an agent needs a safe decision, the decision-making component will first try to generate a feasible action for an agent. If there is no generated action, the decision-making component will try to generate sent messages to obtain more information to make decisions. If there is a generated action, the decision-making component will evaluate whether it is a safe decision. If it is a safe decision, the decision-making component will not generate any sent messages, and it will go to the fifth stage of the reasoning cycle to process events, such as responding to received messages. If it is not a safe decision, the decision-making component will go to the second stage of the reasoning cycle to regenerate another decision.

Once all agents within the autonomous system complete the decision-making generation process, the data processing component receives all safe actions generated by the decision-making component. These actions are translated into commands that can be understood by ROS and transmitted to ROS via rosbridge.

3.2   Implementation

The $vGOAL$ interpreter is implemented in Python, and the source code is available at [24]. We briefly describe the key aspects of the implementation of the $vGOAL$ interpreter to explain how it generates safe decisions in a logical manner.

Logical Approach. The $vGOAL$ language is a specification language that is entirely logical in nature. In $vGOAL$, system specifications and agent specifications, including communication and error specifications, are expressed in logical form. Thus, the $vGOAL$ interpreter is expected to be capable of managing communication and errors in a logical manner, without altering any of the existing implementations.

The implementation of the automated logical derivation and automated minimal model generation over the first-order theory constrained by the syntax of $vGOAL$ is core to implementing the purely logical approach, as five stages of the reasoning cycle involve the automated logical derivation and automated minimal model generation.

To improve efficiency, we implemented the automated logical derivation and automated minimal model generation for each stage in a tailored manner while maintaining a similar underlying approach. All implementations share the same core approach, which is to fully instantiate a first-order theory constrained by the syntax of $vGOAL$ to its logically equivalent first-order theory. Each implementation is then further customized to include the desired beliefs and to process specific keywords based on the $vGOAL$ syntax.

Decision Generation. To generate real-time decisions, the $vGOAL$ interpreter receives real-time sensor information at fixed intervals, e.g., every 0.5 s. However, generating decisions for all agents at each update is unnecessary and computationally costly, especially when agents are performing durative actions. To improve efficiency, we implemented two decision evaluation processes to evaluate whether real-time decisions are necessary at the given moment.

The first process checks if any agent needs a decision by comparing their current and last beliefs and checking for redistributed goals. If there are no updates or goals, the interpreter waits for the next sensor update. The second process evaluates each agent to determine if it requires a decision by checking for goals, durative actions, and errors. An agent needs a decision only when it has goals and is not performing durative actions or encounters an error.

Durative Action Evaluation. When generating a safe action, the decision-making component computes and records the resulting next substate. Subsequently, the decision-making component evaluates the real-time substate against its calculated next substate. The durative action remains incomplete until the current substate aligns with the previously computed next substate.

Safety Checking. In the context of agent decision-making under the $vGOAL$ specification, the overall safety of the system is determined by the safety of each individual agent within the system. However, the safety of one agent is independent of the safety of other agents. Therefore, a safety-checking process that evaluates each agent's decisions is sufficient to ensure the system's safety, as long as each agent only makes safe decisions. Moreover, we only consider state-based safety properties, i.e., invariants, in the current version of the *vGOAL* interpreter.

Safety checking must be performed for each generated action, as every action has the potential to alter the agent's belief base. To be considered a safe action, the resulting beliefs have to contain all specified invariants. Additionally, the decision-making component of the agent generates its desired next substate for the purpose of evaluating durative actions. By employing the substate property generation process and the desired next substate, the substate properties of the agent can be computed and used to check if it contains all specified invariants. Therefore, the safety-checking process of the *vGOAL* interpreter is essentially an efficient invariant-checking process, requiring little additional computation costs and achieving a safe-by-generation decision-making mechanism.

Error Handling. The error handling process of the *vGOAL* interpreter comprises two main aspects: error detection and error processing. Error detection simply checks whether the current substate violates any safety requirements, which is integrated into the evaluation process concerning decision generation. The *vGOAL* specification includes error specifications. The decision-making component of the interpreter logically deals with error processing without modifying any existing implementations.

Interface with ROS. To integrate the *vGOAL* interpreter with ROS, the interface with ROS involves rosbridge, the abstraction of the continuous data and discrete data, and the translation between the discrete data and the agent specifications of *vGOAL*. The abstraction and the translation are user-defined. Importantly, the *vGOAL* interpreter can collaborate with other continuous controllers as long as the appropriate interface is provided.

4 Case Study

To demonstrate the *vGOAL* approach, we employ a real-world autonomous logistic system as a case study. The case study involves three autonomous mobile robots collaborating to complete transportation tasks. Detailed information regarding the case study and its complete *vGOAL* specification is available at [24]. Additionally, we have provided three demonstration videos on [23]: an error-free run, a run involving a non-fatal error, and a run involving a fatal error, to illustrate the *vGOAL* approach. The case study serves as evidence that the *vGOAL* approach can effectively handle unexpected situations and generate safe decisions, even in challenging environments. This section comprises two parts. First, we describe the key aspects of the case study, validating the significant features of the *vGOAL* approach, including safety checking, error handling, and conflict resolution for competing requests. Second, we discuss the empirical results of the $vGOAL$ interpreter's efficiency.

Data Abstraction and Translation. Data abstraction and translation are crucial for the collaboration of the $vGOAL$ interpreter and ROS. Sensor data is abstracted from continuous to discrete values, e.g., battery level from continuous data, ranging from 0% to 100%, to three values, L_1, L_2, and L_3. Safe actions generated by $vGOAL$ must also be translated into commands recognized by ROS, such as five types of *move* in $vGOAL$ mapped to one action in the low-level implementation.

Action. The case study includes four durative actions: *pick up, move, drop off*, and *charge*. In $vGOAL$, *move* has five types, which can affect an agent's belief base differently depending on their starting and destination locations and whether they succeed or fail.

Safety. We define two state-based safety properties, i.e., invariants: $safe_1$ denoting a safe battery level, and $safe_2$ denoting a safe location. Each state of each agent always has to satisfy these two invariants.

Error. This case study includes four error types: E_1, *dock* errors; E_2, *pick up* errors; E_3, *drop off* errors; and E_4, *charge* errors. In this setting, E_1, E_2, and E_3 are non-fatal, while E_4 is fatal. Non-fatal errors prompt the agent to abandon its current delivery goal, request permission for P_5, and generate a decision to move to P_5. Fatal errors lead to goal redistribution and inactivate the agent.

Location. The experimental area for robots is abstracted into nine subareas, specifically ranging from P_1 to P_9. Among these, P_2, P_3, P_4, P_5, P_6, P_7, and P_8 are exclusive locations that require permission for access, as they are critical resources in the case study.

Competitive Requests Resolution. We define one dummy agent, C, to control the critical resources. For example, two agents, A_1 and A_3, request location permission for P_3 at the same time, but only one agent will receive permission from C. The $vGOAL$ interpreter sends the *move* action to A_1, while A_3 continues requesting permission from C. C assigns permission for P_3 to A_3 after A_1 leaves P_3.

Execution Time. Using a MacBook Air 2020 with an Apple M1 and 16 GB of RAM, we conducted over 100 runs of the case study. Each run lasted six to eight minutes, during which the ROS sent real-time sensor information every 0.5 s. As a result, the $vGOAL$ interpreter received 720 to 960 times sensor information per run to generate real-time decisions. All experiments witnessed the safe behavior of all robots, with each robot unfailingly achieving its goals in the absence of any errors.

In our experiments, we observed two distinct phenomena. First, the sensor updates are mostly repeated compared with the last sensor information. Second, the *vGOAL* interpreter typically generates either zero or one real-time decision. These phenomena have three main causes. First, durative actions take time to complete. Second, sensor updates occur frequently during the robot's actions. Third, permissions are required for exclusive locations when generating *move* actions.

Table 1 shows the average execution time for decision-making in representative cases of the case study, based on 400 randomly selected practical records. It includes information on belief and goal updates in any agent of the autonomous system, the number of active agents, the number of generated decisions, and error types (no errors, fatal errors, and non-fatal errors) for each decision-making generation process, the time overhead of safety checking, along with the execution time.

The table highlights five crucial observations. First, the *vGOAL* interpreter handles repeated information quickly (in under 0.1 ms). Second, the execution time increases almost linearly with the number of active agents. Third, generating zero or one decision takes roughly the same execution time for the same number of active agents. Fourth, safety checking during decision-making generation incurs a nearly linear time cost that is negligible compared with the execution time required for generating decisions. Finally, the order of specifications affects execution time; e.g., encountering a fatal error causes slightly less execution time for one decision than a non-fatal error due to the order of error specification.

Table 1. Execution Time for Decision-Making Using the *vGOAL* Interpreter

Repeated	Active Agent	Decision	Error	Safety Checking(s)	Execution Time(s)
Yes	–	–	–	0	4.28E-5
No	3	2	No	2.10E-6	0.82
No	3	1	No	1.02E-6	0.64
No	3	0	No	0	0.69
No	2	1	No	1.02E-6	0.49
No	2	0	No	0	0.48
No	1	1	No	1.02E-6	0.38
No	1	1	Fatal	1.02E-6	0.36
No	1	1	Non-Fatal	1.02E-6	0.41
No	1	0	No	0	0.35

5   Conclusion and Future Work

This paper presents the *vGOAL* interpreter as a safe high-level discrete decision-making component of agent-based autonomous systems. Our contributions are the design and implementation of the interpreter. Using a real-world autonomous logistic system, we demonstrate that the *vGOAL* approach can automatically and efficiently generate safe decisions in real-time, while simultaneously performing safety checking, error handling, and conflict resolution for competing requests. It is important to note that while we demonstrate the application of $vGOAL$ in one specific domain, its wide-ranging applicability extends to various other domains. Compared with three comparable APLs (GOAL, Gwendolen, AgentS-peak), $vGOAL$ has three advantages. First, it generates safe decisions, requiring no extra formal verification. Second, it logically handles errors and allows users to specify error handling in the specifications, requiring no modification to the existing implementation. Third, its Python implementation makes it easier to integrate with ROS-based robotic applications. To generate safe autonomous decisions, the $vGOAL$ interpreter necessitates solely sound $vGOAL$ specifications and a data interface connecting ROS and $vGOAL$, prerequisites shared by the three comparable APLs. Consequently, the $vGOAL$ interpreter requires no additional domain-specific conversion. However, the current version of the interpreter has two limitations: it only checks invariants, and it may not be capable of making safe real-time decisions for high-speed robots.

Our future work includes three areas. First, we will make the safety-checking process applicable to more general safety properties. Second, we plan to employ program verification to prove the correctness of the $vGOAL$ interpreter. Finally, we will explore integrating safe and intelligent motion planning components into the $vGOAL$ interpreter using recent safe shielding techniques, as recent safe shielding techniques enable reinforcement learning-based control of autonomous systems in continuous state spaces while ensuring safety [15,16,21].

Acknowledgements. This research is partially funded by the Research Fund KU Leuven.

References

1. Baier, C., Katoen, J.P.: Principles of Model Checking. MIT Press, Cambridge (2008)
2. de Boer, F.S., Hindriks, K.V., van der Hoek, W., Meyer, J.J.C.: A verification framework for agent programming with declarative goals. J. Appl. Log. 5(2), 277–302 (2007)
3. Bordini, R.H., Fisher, M., Pardavila, C., Wooldridge, M.: Model checking AgentS-peak. In: Proceedings of the Second International Joint Conference on Autonomous Agents and Multiagent Systems, pp. 409–416 (2003)
4. Bordini, R.H., Hübner, J.F.: BDI agent programming in AgentSpeak Using *Jason*. In: Toni, F., Torroni, P. (eds.) CLIMA 2005. LNCS (LNAI), vol. 3900, pp. 143–164. Springer, Heidelberg (2006). https://doi.org/10.1007/11750734_9
5. Bordini, R.H., Hübner, J.F., Wooldridge, M.: Programming Multi-agent Systems in AgentSpeak Using Jason. Wiley, Hoboken (2007)
6. Cardoso, R.C., Ferrando, A., Dennis, L.A., Fisher, M.: An interface for programming verifiable autonomous agents in ROS. In: Bassiliades, N., Chalkiadakis, G., de Jonge, D. (eds.) EUMAS/AT -2020. LNCS (LNAI), vol. 12520, pp. 191–205. Springer, Cham (2020). https://doi.org/10.1007/978-3-030-66412-1_13

7. Crick, C., Jay, G., Osentoski, S., Pitzer, B., Jenkins, O.C.: Rosbridge: ROS for non-ROS users. In: Christensen, H.I., Khatib, O. (eds.) Robotics Research. STAR, vol. 100, pp. 493–504. Springer, Cham (2017). https://doi.org/10.1007/978-3-319-29363-9_28

8. Dastani, M., Tinnemeier, N.A., Meyer, J.J.C.: A programming language for normative multi-agent systems. In: Handbook of Research on Multi-Agent Systems: Semantics and Dynamics of Organizational Models, pp. 397–417. IGI Global (2009)

9. Dehnert, C., Junges, S., Katoen, J.-P., Volk, M.: A storm is coming: a modern probabilistic model checker. In: Majumdar, R., Kunčak, V. (eds.) CAV 2017. LNCS, vol. 10427, pp. 592–600. Springer, Cham (2017). https://doi.org/10.1007/978-3-319-63390-9_31

10. Dennis, L., Fisher, M.: Verifiable autonomy and responsible robotics. In: Softw. Eng. Robot., pp. 189–217. Springer, Cham (2021). https://doi.org/10.1007/978-3-030-66494-7_7

11. Dennis, L.A., Farwer, B.: Gwendolen: a BDI language for verifiable agents. In: Proceedings of the AISB 2008 Symposium on Logic and the Simulation of Interaction and Reasoning, Society for the Study of Artificial Intelligence and Simulation of Behaviour, pp. 16–23. Citeseer (2008)

12. Dennis, L.A., Fisher, M., Lincoln, N.K., Lisitsa, A., Veres, S.M.: Practical verification of decision-making in agent-based autonomous systems. Autom. Softw. Eng. **23**, 305–359 (2016)

13. Dennis, L.A., Fisher, M., Webster, M.P., Bordini, R.H.: Model checking agent programming languages. Autom. Softw. Eng. **19**(1), 5–63 (2012)

14. Hindriks, K.V.: Programming rational agents in GOAL. In: El Fallah Seghrouchni, A., Dix, J., Dastani, M., Bordini, R.H. (eds.) Multi-Agent Programming, pp. 119–157. Springer, Boston, MA (2009). https://doi.org/10.1007/978-0-387-89299-3_4

15. Hunt, N., Fulton, N., Magliacane, S., Hoang, T.N., Das, S., Solar-Lezama, A.: Verifiably safe exploration for end-to-end reinforcement learning. In: Proceedings of the 24th International Conference on Hybrid Systems: Computation and Control, pp. 1–11 (2021)

16. Jansen, N., Könighofer, B., Junges, J., Serban, A., Bloem, R.: Safe reinforcement learning using probabilistic shields (2020)

17. Jensen, A.B., Hindriks, K.V., Villadsen, J.: On using theorem proving for cognitive agent-oriented programming. In: 13th International Conference on Agents and Artificial Intelligence, pp. 446–453. Science and Technology Publishing (2021)

18. Kwiatkowska, M., Norman, G., Parker, D.: PRISM: probabilistic symbolic model checker. In: Field, T., Harrison, P.G., Bradley, J., Harder, U. (eds.) TOOLS 2002. LNCS, vol. 2324, pp. 200–204. Springer, Heidelberg (2002). https://doi.org/10.1007/3-540-46029-2_13

19. Weiss, G.: Multiagent Systems. MIT Press, Cambridge (2013)

20. Winikoff, M.: Implementing commitment-based interactions. In: Proceedings of the 6th International Joint Conference on Autonomous Agents and Multiagent Systems, pp. 1–8 (2007)

21. Yang, W.C., Marra, G., Rens, G., De Raedt, L.: Safe reinforcement learning via probabilistic logic shields. arXiv preprint arXiv:2303.03226 (2023)

22. Yang, Y.: Verifiably safe decision-making for autonomous systems. In: Proceedings of the 2023 International Conference on Autonomous Agents and Multiagent Systems, pp. 2973–2975 (2023)

23. Yang, Y.: vGOAL demo video (2023). https://kuleuven-my.sharepoint.com/:f:/g/personal/yi_yang_kuleuven_be/EiB5CHUuIk9Ij-qDnKmOLk8BST7v3xlPydf ryfL5HcXRmg?e=NiqYu8

24. Yang, Y.: vGOAL interpreter source code (2023). https://github.com/YiYangKUL/vGOAL
25. Yang, Y., Holvoet, T.: Making model checking feasible for GOAL. In: 10th International Workshop on Engineering Multi-Agent Systems (2022)
26. Yang, Y., Holvoet, T.: vGOAL: a GOAL-based specification language for safe autonomous decision-making. In: 11th International Workshop on Engineering Multi-Agent Systems (2023)

PAAMS 2023 - Demonstrations

Towards Exception Handling in the SARL Agent Platform

Matteo Baldoni⬡, Cristina Baroglio⬡, Roberto Micalizio⬡,
and Stefano Tedeschi(✉)⬡

Dipartimento di Informatica, Università degli Studi di Torino, Turin, Italy
{matteo.baldoni,cristina.baroglio,roberto.micalizio,
stefano.tedeschi}@unito.it

Abstract. We demonstrate how exception handling can be realized in
the SARL agent platform. We see exception handling as a mechanism
binding some agents, entitled to raise given exceptions, to the ones entitled to handle them. To this end, we define dedicated *exception spaces*
through which defining the agents' behavior in presence of exceptions.

Keywords: Exception Handling · Engineering MAS · SARL

1 Introduction

Broadly speaking, exception handling amounts to equipping a software system
with the capabilities needed to tackle, at runtime, classes of abnormal situations, identified at design time. An *exception* is an "event that causes suspension
of normal program execution" [9]. The purpose of an exception handling mechanism is to provide the tools to (i) identify when an exception occurs, and (ii)
apply suitable handlers, capable of treating the exception and recovering. *Raising* an exception is a way to signal that a given piece of the program cannot be
performed normally; whereas, *handling* an exception refers to the set of instructions to be performed to restore the normal execution flow [6]. Exception handling mechanisms usually rely on some relationship between the side raising the
exception and the side handling it. In programming languages, for instance, the
exception raised by a function is expected to be caught by the function invoker.
In the actor model [8], a similar relationship is captured by the relation parent-
child among actors: the exception raised by an actor is reported to its parent.
Multi-Agent Systems (MAS), on the contrary, are particularly challenging under
this respect because such kinds of relationships are not part of the paradigm:
agents are autonomous entities which just exchange each other messages. Moreover, in a distributed system, the component in which a failure occurs, the one
entitled to raise the corresponding exception, and the one(s) entitled to handle it may amount to different agents. Our claim is that exception handling in
MAS has to leverage on dedicated structures binding the agents raising given
exceptions with the ones entitled to handle them. We demonstrate this in SARL
[14], which currently does not include an exception handling mechanism, by

P. Mathieu et al. (Eds.): PAAMS 2023, LNAI 13955, pp. 403–408, 2023.
https://doi.org/10.1007/978-3-031-37616-0_33

specifying appropriate structures, exception spaces, whose conceptual meaning is to distribute responsibilities among agents about the raising and handling of specific exceptions.

2 Main Purpose

In SARL [14], a MAS is conceived as a collection of agents that interact by way of a set of shared *spaces*. A specific type of space, the *event space*, is natively defined in SARL, and supports event-driven interactions. Agents are equipped with *behaviors*, which map perceived events into sequences of *actions*. At the language level, SARL only supports exception throwing and catching within an agent's code, in a similar way to what is done in Java. This language feature, however, operates at a lower level of abstraction than the agent computational model. It deals with exceptions within the threads that constitute each single agent. Recently, the notion of *failure event* has been introduced [1]. Failure events represent any failure an agent could face while executing a behavior. They can be fired and captured by the same agent, and they can also be directed towards other agents.

Failure events alone, however, are not enough to implement an exception handling mechanism. The raising of a failure event, in fact, does not create any binding between the raiser and the catcher. Indeed, when an agent issues a failure event, it does not even know whether another agent will capture that. In our vision, the structure supporting exception handling has, first of all, to identify which agent is capable of raising a specific exception, and which other(s) will be capable of handling it. Note that, in a MAS the agents raising or handling exceptions may change according to the specific situation at hand. These are, in fact, tasks that can only be performed by agents having the right capabilities. For instance, consider a patient agent asking for a prescription to a doctor agent. In case of no answer (for instance because the request gets lost), it is the patient that can realize something has gone wrong, and raises an exception that the doctor can handle. Instead, in case the doctor cannot prescribe what requested, it is the doctor that can raise an exception. When the doctor raises the exception concerning the impossibility of making a prescription (because he/she lacks expertise), the patient is the one that should handle it. The example shows that raising exceptions and handling exceptions are tasks, and that such tasks should be under the responsibility of specific agents.

To realize this picture, we exploit the same interaction spaces through which SARL agents perceive events generated by others. In particular, we define an *exception space* as a dedicated space that agents can instantiate upon specific types of exceptions and where, by means of appropriate functionalities, they can register as either raisers or handlers of such exceptions. Broadly speaking, following [3], we may interpret the registration of an agent to an exception space as an assumption of responsibility about that exception. According to this view, the registration creates an expectation in other agents of the MAS that either the agent will raise the corresponding exception, when it is the case, or it will handle it, when raised by others.

Practically, the exception space interface is implemented in SARL's runtime platform[1], extending the *OpenLocalEventSpace* implementation of the event space. Specifically, our exception space interface for an exception of type T introduces three new actions:

- def registerAsRaiser(listener : EventListener): a *listener* agent registers as raiser of exceptions of type T. The agent should be equipped with some behaviors that allow the exception raising. Whenever an agent registers as exception raiser, all the agents participating in the exception space are notified through the emission of an *ExceptionRaiserRegistered* event.
- def registerAsHandler(listener : EventListener): a *listener* agent registers as handler of exception of type T. Whenever an agent registers as handler for some exception, an *ExceptionHandlerRegistered* event is fired and propagated to the participating agents. Note that many agents may be registered to handle the same exception. In this case, once the exception is raised, it is delivered to all the registered handler agents, each one implementing a suitable handling.
- def raiseException(ex : T, u : UUID): allows an agent registered as exception raiser to actually raise an exception instance *ex* of type T. The event is delivered to all the suitable registered exception handler agents (if any). If no handler is registered for the given exception, a *NoHandlerAvailable* event is fired back to the agent that raised the exception.

Every time an exception space instance is created, an *ExceptionSpaceCreated* event is fired to notify the other agents about the type of exceptions the space aims at treating. Along the execution, an instantiated exception space keeps track of the agents which register as raisers and handlers for the corresponding exception type, and propagates exceptions accordingly.

3 Demonstration

We consider a scenario from [5], involving a patient, a doctor, and a pharmacist: the patient complains of some symptoms with the doctor, expecting the doctor to provide a prescription to the pharmacist, who should then fill it and send the medicines to the patient. A possible exception in this scenario is related to the patient not receiving the expected medicines. The following listing shows an excerpt of the patient agent's code using the exception space we propose.

Patient, doctor and pharmacist interact in the same context. The patient creates an exception space instance for exception LostMedicines (Line 9). It also registers as raiser of the exception (Line 10) and notifies the other agents about the creation of the exception space by emitting a dedicated *ExceptionSpaceCreated* event (Line 11).

```
1  agent Patient {
2      uses DefaultContextInteractions , Behaviors , Logging , Schedules
3      var exSpace : ExceptionSpace<LostMedicines>
4      var prescriptionReceived = false
```

---

[1] The proposed implementation is available at http://di.unito.it/sarlexceptions.

```
5   on Initialize {
6     val type = new ExceptionSpaceSpecification.class
7       as Class<ExceptionSpaceSpecification<LostMedicines>>
8     exSpace =
9       defaultContext.getOrCreateSpaceWithID(type, UUID::randomUUID)
10    exSpace.registerAsRaiser(asEventListener)
11    emit(new ExceptionSpaceCreated(LostMedicines, exSpace.spaceID.ID))
12    emit(new GetMedication)
13  }
14  on GetMedication {
15    emit(new Consult)
16    in(5000) [
17      if (!prescriptionReceived) {
18        exSpace.raiseException(new LostMedicines, ID)
19      }
20    ]
21  }
22  on FillPrescription {
23    prescriptionReceived = true
24    emit(new FollowTherapy)
25  }
26  on FillPrescriptionAgain {
27    emit(new FollowTherapy)
28  }
29 }
```

In principle, both the doctor and the pharmacist may register as exception handlers. In this case, both agents would be notified about the exception in order to put in place suitable handling behaviors in accordance to their goals. The patient raises the exception if no medicines are received within a given amount of time since the prescription request (in the simulation 5 s). If the LostMedicines exception is raised (Line 18), the space instance propagates it to all the agents registered as handlers.

The listing below shows an excerpt of the pharmacist agent's code. The agent registers as handler of LostMedicines by reacting to the *ExceptionSpaceCreated* event emitted as soon as the space is instantiated (Lines 16–19).

```
1  agent Pharmacist {
2    uses DefaultContextInteractions, Behaviors, Logging
3    var exSpacePatient : ExceptionSpace<LostMedicines>
4    var exSpaceDoctor : ExceptionSpace<MissingPrescription>
5    var prescriptionReceivedFromDoctor = false
6    var medicinesSent = false
7    on Initialize {
8      val type = new ExceptionSpaceSpecification.class
9        as Class<ExceptionSpaceSpecification<MissingPrescription>>
10     exSpaceDoctor =
11       defaultContext.getOrCreateSpaceWithID(type, UUID::randomUUID)
12     exSpaceDoctor.registerAsRaiser(asEventListener)
13     emit(new ExceptionSpaceCreated(MissingPrescription,
14                                     exSpaceDoctor.spaceID.ID))
15   }
16   on ExceptionSpaceCreated [occurrence.ex == LostMedicines] {
17     exSpacePatient = defaultContext.getSpace(occurrence.id)
18     exSpacePatient.registerAsHandler(asEventListener)
19   }
20   on Prescribe {
21     prescriptionReceivedFromDoctor = true
22     // Prepare medicines
23     emit(new FillPrescription)
24     medicinesSent = true
25   }
26   on LostMedicines {
27     if(medicinesSent) {
```

```
28      emit(new FillPrescriptionAgain)
29    }
30    if (!prescriptionReceivedFromDoctor) {
31      exSpaceDoctor.raiseException(new MissingPrescription, ID)
32    }
33   }
34 }
```

When the pharmacist receives a LostMedicines exception event, an appropriate handling behavior is triggered (Lines 26–33). The agent checks if the medicines were already sent; in this case a second attempt is made, by filling the prescription (and sending the medicines) again. It is worth noting that medicines may not have been sent because the pharmacist did not previously receive the prescription from the doctor. Such an eventuality can be modeled by introducing an additional MissingPrescription exception and a corresponding exception space shared among pharmacist and doctor. Here the exception space is instantiated by the pharmacist upon initialization, who also registers as exception raiser. As a result, while handling the exception raised by the patient, the pharmacist may end in raising a further exception addressed to the doctor and concerning the missing prescription (Line 31).

The doctor will be programmed by following a similar approach. Upon instantiation, it will register as handler of both the exceptions raised by the patient and by the pharmacist. Upon raising, in turn, it will be notified about the occurrence of exceptions so as to activate proper handling behaviors. It is worth noting that the scenario can be easily extended to encompass further exceptions (e.g., raised by the doctor and handled by the patient if the request is made when the doctor is on vacation). For each exception deemed to possibly occur during the interaction a suitable exception space can be defined in order to establish a binding among the agent in charge of raising such exception and the agent(s) in charge of handling it.

4 Conclusions

Exception handling has been addressed by a number of papers in the MAS literature (see e.g., [5,7,10–13]). In this paper, we have demonstrated in SARL how exception handling can be achieved by exploiting dedicated structures, i.e., exception spaces, binding raisers and handlers, and interpreting these spaces as a distribution of responsibilities among the agents.

The exception spaces address situations, occurring during the agent interaction, which make the overall system fragile, with the aim of making the system more robust. In fact, the registrations as raiser/handler of an exception are public events, therefore any agent into a space knows what exceptions are possibly raised and handled and by what agents. This increases the awareness of the agents about their context: on the one side, by creating an exception space and registering as a raiser, an agent discloses to others what exceptions could be raised during an interaction. On the other side, being aware of an exception space, agents may assess whether they possess the right capabilities to carry out the interaction, even in case of the raise of an exception, and decide to register as handlers. Failure events are essentially weaker than exception spaces because they cannot create a binding among the agents. The use of failure events, in fact, is opaque to the agents: agents can neither know whether a specific failure event will be emitted, nor whether such an event will ever be intercepted by some other agent in the space.

As future work, it would be interesting to study the introduction of *accountability* in the SARL framework. Accountability allows agents to get runtime information to be used in their decision making in ways that go beyond the exception handling mechanisms. So far, indeed, accountability has been studied only for frameworks (e.g. JaCaMo [2–4]) that provide an organizational infrastructure: roles, norms, organizational goals and how they are structured into sub-goals that are associated with roles, etc.

References

1. Management of the failures and validation errors, SARL general-purpose agent-oriented programming language ("specification"). http://www.sarl.io/docs/official/reference/Failures.html. Accessed 20 Apr 2023
2. Baldoni, M., Baroglio, C., Micalizio, R., Tedeschi, S.: Reimagining robust distributed systems through accountable MAS. IEEE Int. Comput. **25**(6), 7–14 (2021)
3. Baldoni, M., Baroglio, C., Micalizio, R., Tedeschi, S.: Exception handling as a social concern. IEEE Int. Comput. **26**(6), 33–40 (2022)
4. Baldoni, M., Baroglio, C., Micalizio, R., Tedeschi, S.: Accountability in multi-agent organizations: from conceptual design to agent programming. JAAMAS **37**(1), 7 (2023)
5. Christie V., S., Chopra, A.K., Singh, M.P.: Bungie: improving fault tolerance via extensible application-level protocols. Computer **54**(5), 44–53 (2021)
6. Goodenough, J.B.: Exception handling: issues and a proposed notation. Commun. ACM **18**(12), 683–696 (1975)
7. Hägg, S.: A sentinel approach to fault handling in multi-agent systems. In: Zhang, C., Lukose, D. (eds.) DAI 1996. LNCS, vol. 1286, pp. 181–195. Springer, Heidelberg (1997). https://doi.org/10.1007/BFb0030090
8. Hewitt, C., Bishop, P., Steiger, R.: A universal modular actor formalism for artificial intelligence. In: Proceedings of the IJCAI 1973, pp. 235–245. Morgan Kaufmann (1973)
9. ISO/IEC/IEEE: Systems and software engineering – Vocabulary. 24765:2010(E) – ISO/IEC/IEEE International Standard (2010)
10. Kalia, A.K., Singh, M.P.: Muon: designing multiagent communication protocols from interaction scenarios. JAAMAS **29**(4), 621–657 (2015)
11. Mallya, A.U., Singh, M.P.: Modeling exceptions via commitment protocols. In: Proceedings of the AAMAS 2005, pp. 122–129. ACM (2005)
12. Miller, R., Tripathi, A.: The guardian model and primitives for exception handling in distributed systems. IEEE Trans. on Soft. Eng. **30**(12), 1008–1022 (2004)
13. Platon, E., Sabouret, N., Honiden, S.: An architecture for exception management in multiagent systems. IJAOSE **2**(3), 267–289 (2008)
14. Rodriguez, S., Gaud, N., Galland, S.: SARL: a general-purpose agent-oriented programming language. In: 2014 IEEE/WIC/ACM International Joint Conferences on Web Intelligence (WI) and Intelligent Agent Technologies (IAT), vol. 3, pp. 103–110 (2014)

Multi-agent Path Finding for Indoor Quadcopters

Matouš Kulhan and Pavel Surynek[✉][iD]

Faculty of Information Technology, Czech Technical University in Prague,
Thákurova 9, 160 00 Prague 6, Czechia
{kulhama7,pavel.surynek}@fit.cvut.cz

Abstract. We study the planning-acting loop for the multi-agent path finding problem (MAPF). MAPF is a problem of navigating agents from their start positions to specified individual goal positions so that agents do not collide with each other. We focus on executing MAPF plans with a group of Crazyflies, small indoor quadcopters, for which we developed a platform that integrates decision theoretic planning and plan execution modules. Our platform can be used for testing suitability of variants of MAPF for execution with real agents. We show how to modify the existing continuous-time conflict-based search algorithm (CCBS) to produce plans that are suitable for execution with the quadcopters. Our finding is that the CCBS algorithm allows for extensions that can produce safe plans for quadcopters, namely cylindrical protection zone around each quadcopter can be introduced at the planning level.

Keywords: multi-agent path finding · planning · acting · indoor quadcopters · Crazyflie · localization

1 Introduction

In *multi-agent path finding* (MAPF) [6–8] the task is to navigate agents $A = \{a_1, a_2, ..., a_k\}$ from their starting positions to individual goal positions so that agents do not collide with each other. The standard discrete version of MAPF takes place in an undirected graph $G = (V, E)$ whose vertices represent positions and edges define the topology of the environment - agents reside in vertices and move across edges, but no two agents can reside in the same vertex, nor two agents can traverse an edge in opposite directions.

Recent progress in MAPF brings the abstract problem closer to real life applications. Concretely a variant of MAPF that integrates continuous aspects of the real world has been devised - MAPF with continuous time (MAPF^R) where agents move smoothly usually along the straight lines between the finite number of vertices that are embedded in a metric space (continuous 2D or 3D space). Agents can be of any shape in MAPF^R and the collision between agents is defined as any overlap between their bodies. Collisions are avoided in the time domain by allowing an agent to wait in a vertex[1].

---

[1] Agents cannot wait outside vertices hence once the agent starts its (linear) movement between two vertices embedded in the metric space, the agent has to finish its movement and reach the other vertex before it can wait.

P. Mathieu et al. (Eds.): PAAMS 2023, LNAI 13955, pp. 409–414, 2023.
https://doi.org/10.1007/978-3-031-37616-0_34

410   M. Kulhan and P. Surynek

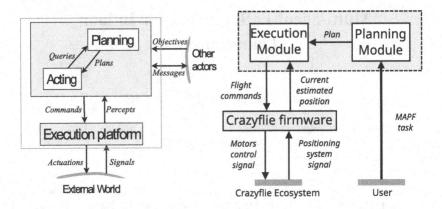

Fig. 1. Planning and acting in intelligent agents and its adaptation for Crazyflie quadcopters.

We implement the **planning-acting** scheme from [4] (Fig. 1 [4]) within a modular execution platform that integrates a decision theoretic planning module and an execution module. Using our platform, we demonstrate that planning algorithms for MAPF^R are suitable for constructing plans that are executable by real *robotic agents* - Crazyflies, small indoor quadcopters coupled with localization system. Thus we show that contemporary MAPF^R algorithms are ready for transfers into real-life applications.

In a broader perspective, our execution platform can be used to test suitability of variants of MAPF for execution with real agents, in our case with agents that support relatively complex 3D motion.

2   Related Work and Background

Previous attempts to bridge the theory and acting with real robots for MAPF include the use of mobile robots Ozobot EVO [3]. The planning phase was represented by the standard discrete MAPF. Hence the output decision theoretic plan had to be post-processed to form continuous command sequences before it was executed by the real robots.

In this work, we use the MAPF^R model and the existing Continuous-time Conflict Based Search (CCBS) algorithm [1] that extends the previous Conflict Based Search (CBS) [7] by resolving conflicts between agents in the time domain via allowing agents to wait. The original CBS uses lazy resolution. It first plans one path per agent by single-agent path-finding algorithm ignoring other agents. Then the algorithm branches to resolve collisions. For example if two agents a_i and a_j collide in vertex v at time step t, then in one branch of CBS we forbid agent a_i to enter vertex v at time step t, and we forbid a_j to enter v at time step t in the other branch.

CCBS follows the same framework as CBS. Instead of discrete path-finding algorithms, CCBS uses the SIPP [5] algorithm for single-agent path-planning that plans w.r.t. *safe time intervals* assigned to actions and allows an agent to wait in a vertex to avoid executing a move action within an unsafe interval that would lead to a collision.

If for example agents a_i and a_j collide when executing their movements, then in one branch a_i waits minimum amount of time before it starts its movement to safely pass around agent a_j and analogously a_j waits in the other branch (Fig. 2).

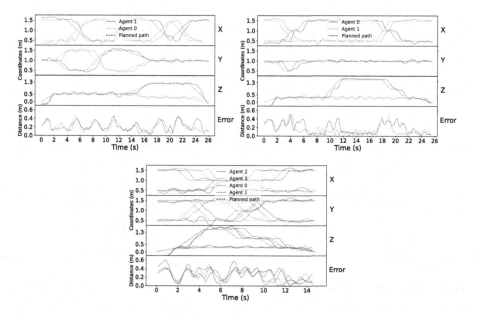

Fig. 2. Position and error over time for selected experiments (experiment 1, 2, and 4 are shown).

3   Planning and Acting for MAPF^R

We modified CCBS to support 3D grids and added collision detection mechanism for agents moving in 3D[2]. As the quadcopters usually cannot fly too close to each other and must keep relatively bigger vertical distances we model the agents as tall **cylinders**. Collision detection of two cylinders is done by splitting the task into two 2D collisions - a collision of the vertical projection of cylinders, that is between two circles and a collision between horizontal projection of cylinders, that is between two rectangles.

Acting Hardware - Crazyflie Ecosystem: For the demonstration of acting for MAPF^R we used Crazyflie 2.1, small indoor quadcopters (Fig. 4). Crazyflie comes with hardware ecosystem [2]: (i) Crazyflie Family, consisting of several versions of Crazyflie quadcopters, (ii) positioning systems, consisting of external sensors to determine the positions of Crazyflies - in this work we tested the Loco positioning system (see Fig. 5) based on measuring distance to anchors, specified accuracy of 10 cm, and (iii) technologies for remotely controlling the Crazyflies, this includes USB radio dongle Crazyradio PA and `cfplib`, a Python library for sending commands using the radio.

---

[2] The original implementation of CCBS supports 2D space with circular agents.

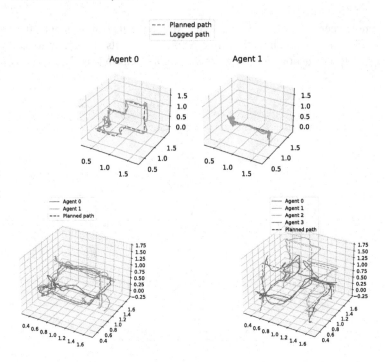

Fig. 3. Position and error over time for selected experiments (experiment 1, 2, and 4 are shown).

Acting Software - Crazyflie Plan Execution Module: Plan execution module is represented by our Python program using the cflib library. The module periodically receives the most current estimated position from each controlled Crazyflie and sends them individually generated flight commands based on the flight plan generated by CCBS. We propose and compare three different methods for generating these commands: (1) **BHL method** - uses High Level Commander, a firmware module, which receives abstract commands containing absolute position and duration and refines them into setpoints on board of the Crazyflie, (2) **BLL method** - generates the setpoints directly and sequentially send them to the Crazyflie (the pseudo-code of BLL is shown as Algorithm 1), (3) **VLL method** - checks if the Crazyflie is inside a bounding box around the desired coordinates and if not sends a command to move in the direction of these coordinates.

Fig. 4. Crazyflie 2.1   **Fig. 5.** Loco positioning system

Algorithm 1. BLL method for execution of MAPF^R plan $P(a_i)$ for agent a_i.

BLL-Execute($P(a_i)$):

1: $(x_\ell, y_\ell, z_\ell, t_\ell) \leftarrow$ first position of $P(a_i)$
2: **for** each position $(x, y, z, t) \in P(a_i)$ **do**
3:      $\Delta t \leftarrow t - t_\ell; v_x \leftarrow \frac{x - x_\ell}{\Delta t}; v_y \leftarrow \frac{y - y_\ell}{\Delta t}; v_z \leftarrow \frac{z - z_\ell}{\Delta t}$
4:      **while** current-time() $< t$ **do**
5:          $t_r \leftarrow$ current-time()$-t_\ell$
6:          $x_c \leftarrow x_\ell + v_x \cdot t_r; y_c \leftarrow y_\ell + v_y \cdot t_r; z_c \leftarrow z_\ell + v_z \cdot t_r$
7:          send-command(a_i, x_c, y_c, z_c)
8:          delay()
9:      **end while**
10:     $x_\ell \leftarrow x; y_\ell \leftarrow y; z_\ell \leftarrow z; t_\ell \leftarrow t$
11: **end for**

---

4   Experimental Evaluation

We performed experiments in a 2 m × 2 m × 2 m flying area within our indoor laboratory with 8 Loco positioning anchors, one in each corner of the flying area. The position of each Crazyflie was estimated every 10 ms. The first experiment focused on testing of the three plan execution methods and evaluating their accuracy w.r.t. the flight plan produced by CCBS. The three other experiments tested the plan execution with three different MAPF^R scenarios with a variable number of quadcopters.

In the first experiment the flight plan was successfully executed 13 times. Aggregated results are shown in Fig. 6. For each of the successful execution we plotted error, that is the deviation of the actual position from the planned position, and position of the

Method	Error	
	Max.	Avg.
BHL	0.644 m	0.223 m
BLL	0.662 m	0.241 m
VLL	0.601 m	0.282 m

Fig. 6. Results of experiment 1

agents over time. Three of these plots can be seen in Fig. 3. Video recording of all four experiments can be seen on: https://youtu.be/v2BTHKcCiCI.

Our key finding is that the proposed planning-acting system for $MAPF^R$ is capable of generating feasible flight plans and executing them using the Crazyflie Ecosystem with high success rate. Our current flight area can accommodate up to four crazyflies for which we are able to plan and safely execute even very complex scenarios. We expect that the number of quadcopters can be increased in a larger flying area.

5   Conclusion

We demonstrated that $MAPF^R$ planning algorithms are ready for being used for real agents. This shows the maturity of $MAPF^R$ technology and feasibility of deployments of real-life $MAPF^R$ planning-acting systems.

Our execution platform can be used not only by researchers for testing the suitability of MAPF variants for deployment on real agents but also by educators to demonstrate the difficulties of planning-acting loop on the well understandable MAPF domain.

For future work we plan to integrate an alternative localization system into our platform and we also plan to implement more intensive interaction between the planning and execution modules.

Acknowledgments. This research has been supported by GAČR - the Czech Science Foundation, grant registration number 22-31346S. We would like to thank anonymous reviewers for their valuable comments.

References

1. Andreychuk, A., Yakovlev, K.S., Surynek, P., Atzmon, D., Stern, R.: Multi-agent pathfinding with continuous time. Artif. Intell. **305**, 103662 (2022)
2. Bitcraze, A.B.: System overview (2022). https://www.bitcraze.io/documentation/system/
3. Chudý, J., Surynek, P.: ESO-MAPF: bridging discrete planning and continuous execution in multi-agent pathfinding. In: Proceedings of AAAI 2021, pp. 16014–16016. AAAI Press (2021)
4. Ghallab, M., Nau, D., Traverso, P.: Automated Planning and Acting. Cambridge University Press, Cambridge (2016)
5. Phillips, M., Likhachev, M.: SIPP: safe interval path planning for dynamic environments. In: Proceedings of ICRA 2011, pp. 5628–5635 (2011)
6. Ryan, M.R.K.: Exploiting subgraph structure in multi-robot path planning. J. Artif. Intell. Res. (JAIR) **31**, 497–542 (2008)
7. Sharon, G., Stern, R., Felner, A., Sturtevant, N.: Conflict-based search for optimal multi-agent pathfinding. Artif. Intell. **219**, 40–66 (2015)
8. Surynek, P.: A novel approach to path planning for multiple robots in bi-connected graphs. In: Proceedigns of ICRA 2009, pp. 3613–3619 (2009)

Energy Community Integration of a Smart Home Based on an Open Source Multiagent System

Bruno Ribeiro⬥, Ricardo Faia⬥, Luis Gomes⬥, and Zita Vale$^{(\boxtimes)}$⬥

GECAD Research Group on Intelligent Engineering and Computing for Advanced Innovation and Development, LASI—Intelligent Systems Associate Laboratory, Polytechnic of Porto, R. Dr. António Bernardino de Almeida, 431, 4200-072 Porto, Portugal
{brgri,rfmfa,lfg,zav}@isep.ipp.pt

Abstract. Smart grid is a revolutionary concept that came to renew the way the power systems are thought. However, for these systems to be possible it is necessary and recommended that the consumers have the right technology integrated in their houses, in other words, have smart homes. This paper describes the demonstration of a smart home solution based on multiagent systems for the optimization of the house energy usage.

Keywords: smart grid · smart devices · multiagent system · energy optimization

1 Introduction

With today's technology revolution the limit to its implementations is almost limitless. Technology is overpowering every aspect of our lives for the better or the worse. And it is no different in the energy systems domains. Smart grid is a new concept that revolves around the application of information technology in the traditional energy systems, making them more reliable, efficient, and flexible [1]. But in order to implement these smart grids it is necessary that the houses of the community in which will be implemented must have the necessary equipment to allow the efficient management of energy consumption. One way to do it is turning the consumers houses into smart homes by integrating smart devices. These devices can monitor the several electrical equipment in the house to allow deeper insights into the waste and losses of energy [2]. With the right systems and optimization algorithms it is possible to make the energy usage much more efficient, decreasing the energy wastes while maintaining the consumers comfort and scheduling.

This paper describes the solution made to the demonstration based on a smart home system that has as its goal to optimize the energy usage of the house. The house is equipped with smart devices (LED and battery control system) and will be managed autonomously by a multiagent system. The solution also provides an intelligent assistant that the user can communicate with either by chat or by voice. The data produced by the multiagent system can be monitored by a web application. The results are shown further in the paper.

© The Author(s), under exclusive license to Springer Nature Switzerland AG 2023
P. Mathieu et al. (Eds.): PAAMS 2023, LNAI 13955, pp. 415–421, 2023.
https://doi.org/10.1007/978-3-031-37616-0_35

2 Main Purpose

The main purpose of this demonstration is to create a decentralized solution supported by multiagent system that allows the intelligent monitorization and control of the energy resources of a smart home, considering the collaboration with other entities in the same energy community, the users' preferences and the minimization of the electricity energy costs. This system must have the capability of autonomously and intelligently manage the energy resources while providing an assistant for smart building users for controlling the environment.

Researchers have already studied several ways to use multiagent systems to make smart homes, buildings, and energy communities more efficient and economical in what regards to the energy usage [3]. There are works providing solutions to maximize the efficiency of energy resources to prevent wastes and unnecessary pollution to the atmosphere [4, 5]. Despite the effectiveness of these solutions normally they are focused to solve one main problem and neglect sometimes how integrate the consumers experience into the usage of these systems, making difficult for unexperienced users to work well with those solutions. What this demonstration will do is demonstrate that this system can be implemented in real world scenarios, using recent and open-source technology to allow a more easy, appealing, and friendly experience for the users, without decreasing the efficiency of the systems.

In this demonstration, it is shown that smart homes can become more efficient with the integration of multiagent systems, smart devices and optimization algorithms while maintaining an appealing and easy interface with the user, through the usage of an intelligent assistant. In addition, this demonstration shows that is already possible to implement this kind of system in real environments with today's technology.

3 Demonstration

In this demonstration there will be a home that possesses different types of smart devices, namely smart LEDs, smart plugs to monitor the energy consumption and generation of the house, and a smart controller of batteries that monitors and manages the usage of the energy storage system. These devices will be represented by agents so they can manage the devices individually. Two other agents are needed: one, the assistant, that will be responsible to interact with the user and orchestrate every other agent in the house based on the user's tasks, and the community manager agent that will use the smart devices agent data to optimize the energy using an optimization algorithm. To see the operations taken effect, the data produced by the agents and smart devices will be published in a dashboard so the user can see it in a more appealing and organized way. The assistant agent will be integrated with natural language processing (NLP), understanding (NLU) and generation (NLG) algorithms in order to communicate with the user in a common language. In Fig. 1 it is possible to see the overall system's implementation described.

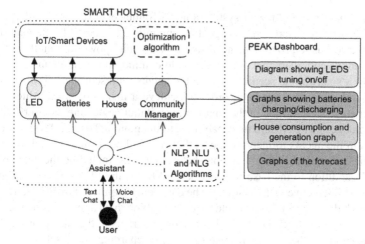

Fig. 1. Smart home system overview.

The LED agent will be responsible for regulating the intensity of the LEDs of the house, which are organized by rooms. The batteries agent will be responsible to charge and discharge the batteries when needed. The house agent will be responsible for monitoring the consumption and generation of the house, by having access to every outlet data and to the photovoltaic panels (PV) generation. The assistant will process the tasks that the user will ask (see Table 1 for all possible tasks) and interact with the right agent to fulfill them.

Table 1. Tasks available to the user. The X is a value given by the user.

Agent responsible to fulfill the task	List of tasks available
LED agent	• Turn on the lights of room X
	• Turn off the lights of room X
Battery agent	• Charge battery X1 with X2 kWh
	• Discharge battery X1 with X2 kWh
	• Get state of charge of battery X
House agent	• Get consumption (kWh) of the house
	• Get generation (kWh) of the PV
Community Manager	• Run optimization model
	• Get previous data

To implement the multiagent system a novel framework was used called Python-based framework for heterogeneous agent communities (PEAK) [6]. The main feature of this framework is to provide the necessary tools to build powerful, intelligent, sociable, autonomous and adaptable agents and build communities with them. This applies perfectly to a smart home scenario, where the agents represent the IoT/smart devices and they work as a community in order to achieve a main objective, which is optimize the energy consumption of the smart home without neglecting the users' comfort. Some advantages of PEAK are its capabilities to integrate IoT/smart devices, integrate AI models in the agents to increase their efficiency and performance, and monitor the communities created and the interactions between agents, including the data produced by them. In addition to the base framework, PEAK has the PEAK Dashboard plug-in that allows an interactive visualization of the data being monitored by PEAK in the web browser. With this plug-in it is possible to see everything that happens inside the ecosystem. In this case the PEAK Dashboard will show diagrams of the LEDs turning on and off, graphs showing the energy volume of batteries charging and discharging actions, the house consumption and generation throughout time, and a graph showing the optimization values calculated by the optimization algorithm. PEAK is implemented using Extensible Messaging and Presence Protocol (XMPP) which allows communication via chat by using a proper client. This is what allows the assistant to communicate with the user via chat.

To implement the NLP, NLU and NLG algorithms in the assistant, that will be responsible for interacting with the users, by text and voice, the Rasa framework was used. Rasa is framework for building chat and voice-based assistants that provide natural language models and the tools needed to fine tune these models to the user's needs [7]. This is the framework that allows the assistant to communicate via voice with the user.

The optimization algorithm used by the community manager is a mixed integer linear programming algorithm implemented using the MIP Python library using the free solver coin-or branch and cut (CBC) [8]. The algorithm will receive as input the forecasted of consumption including LED and other loads of the house, PV generation forecast, the maximum of charge, discharge and total battery power, market prices to buy and sell energy and the limits of the import and export energy to the house. The results will contemplate for each period of 15 min the exported and imported energy from the grid, the charge and discharge values of the battery and the costs of the operations (i.e., buy, sell and the costs at the end of the day).

For the simulation of the results of the system described, an example dataset was used. This dataset was fed to the optimization algorithm and the results can be seen in Fig. 2. In Fig. 2, (a) represents the optimization of the exported and imported energy, (b) represents the optimization of the energy consumption of the house devices, and (c) represents the optimization of the battery's usage. Figure 3 shows the PEAK Dashboard view of the house agents in the same community.

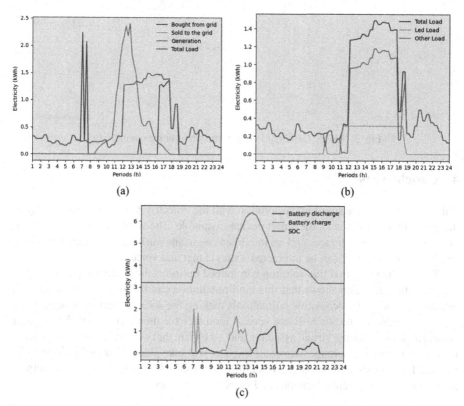

(a)   (b)

(c)

Fig. 2. Results of the optimization algorithm: (a) optimization of the exported and imported energy, (b) optimization of the house devices energy, (c) optimization of the batteries.

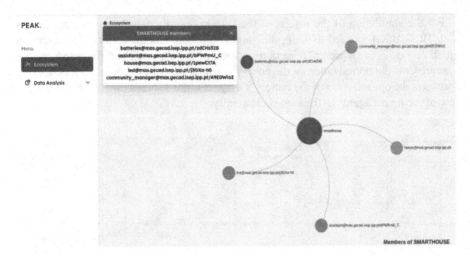

Fig. 3. PEAK Dashboard view of the smart home community.

4   Conclusions

This paper describes a smart home solution with the objective to optimize the energy of the house by making use of the smart devices available. The solution uses a multiagent system to control the devices and an intelligent assistant working as a human-machine interface. The assistant can be interacted with via text and voice.

The results show that this solution can indeed optimize the electrical equipment of the smart home. It also shows that this kind of solution can be developed with today's technology and easily accessible online tools making the solution very economic.

The live demonstration will use several monitors for monitoring, a tablet for user control and the use of the virtual assistant, and a webcam that will transmit a real building located in Portugal where the actions of the user will take place. This real building will be used for demonstration and the video transmission will enable to assess the impact of the multiagent systems decisions and management actions.

Acknowledgements. This article is a result of the project RETINA (NORTE-01-0145-FEDER-000062), supported by Norte Portugal Regional Operational Programme (NORTE 2020), under the PORTUGAL 2020 Partnership Agreement, through the European Regional Development Fund (ERDF). The authors acknowledge the work facilities and equipment provided by GECAD research center (UIDB/00760/2020) to the project team.

References

1. Dileep, G.: A survey on smart grid technologies and applications. Renew. Energy **146**, 2589–2625 (2020)
2. Al-Badi, A., Ahshan, R., Hosseinzadeh, N., Ghorbani, R., Hossain, E.: Survey of smart grid concepts and technological demonstrations worldwide emphasizing on the Oman perspective. Appl. Syst. Innov. **3**, 5 (2020)

3. Nezamoddini, N., Gholami, A.: A survey of adaptive multi-agent networks and their applications in smart cities. Smart Cities **5**, 318 (2022)
4. Silva, C., Faria, P., Ribeiro, B., Gomes, L., Vale, Z.: Demand response contextual remuneration of prosumers with distributed storage. Sensors **22**, 8877 (2022)
5. Pereira, H., Ribeiro, B., Gomes, L., Vale, Z.: Smart grid ecosystem modeling using a novel framework for heterogenous agent communities. Sustainability **14**, 15983 (2022)
6. Ribeiro, B., Pereira, H., Gomes, L., Vale, Z.: Python-Based ecosystem for agent communities simulation. In: 17th International Conference on Soft Computing Models in Industrial and Environmental Applications (SOCO 2022), pp. 62–71 (2023)
7. Bocklisch, T., Faulkner, J., Pawlowski, N., Nichol, A.: Rasa: open source language understanding and dialogue management. ArXiv (2017)
8. Toffolo, T., Santos, H.: MIP Python Library. https://python-mip.com/

Cognitive Assistant for Enhanced eHealth Monitoring

J. A. Rincon[1,2]($\boxtimes$) , C. Marco-Detchart[1] , and V. Julian[1,2]

[1] Valencian Research Institute for Artificial Intelligence (VRAIN),
Universitat Politècnica de València (UPV), Camino de Vera s/n,
46022 Valencia, Spain
{cedmarde,vjulian}@upv.es

[2] Valencian Graduate School and Research Network of Artificial Intelligence
(VALGRAI), Universitat Politècnica de València (UPV),
Camí de Vera s/n, 46022 Valencia, Spain
jrincon@dsic.upv.es

Abstract. The use of cognitive assistants for elderly individuals can greatly benefit their everyday lives, particularly with medication management and household tasks. These assistants can send reminders for medication and even dispense pills, as well as help with tasks such as adjusting the thermostat and grocery shopping. Furthermore, this technology has the potential to improve the quality of life for elderly individuals and help them maintain their independence. This paper introduces a cognitive assistant designed for monitoring cardiorespiratory signals in remote healthcare settings, specifically for use in rural or underserved areas. The proposed tool utilizes a combination of mechanical, electronic, and computer components to enable analysis and pre-diagnosis of potential diseases.

Keyword: EDGE AI, eHealth, Cognitive Assistants, Health Robotics

1 Introduction

Life expectancy has increased, straining healthcare. Aging leads to declining physical and cognitive abilities. Drugs are prescribed to manage blood pressure, pain, and age-related health issues. However, these medications can have adverse side effects, particularly in older adults, which increase the risk of cardiovascular events and mortality [7]. In light of these challenges, Steptoe et all [9] emphasize the importance of promoting the well-being of older adults. They argue that healthcare systems should focus not only on treating illness and disability but also on supporting positive psychological states in older populations.

With the integration of AI into robotics, the capabilities of robots are greatly enhanced. AI can enable robots to adapt to changing environments, make decisions based on real-time data, and learn from experience. Machine vision allows robots to "see" and identify objects, while audio capture enables them to "hear" and respond to commands. These perceptual systems, combined with AI, allow robots to perform a wide range of tasks, from assisting in surgery to monitoring patients in hospitals, to performing mundane tasks in homes and workplaces. As AI and robotics continue to evolve, it is likely that their applications in healthcare and other fields will only continue to expand. As the world's population continues to age, there is an increasing need for technology that can help elderly people live more independently and comfortably. Cognitive assistants [3] for elderly people are one such technology that is rapidly gaining popularity. These devices are specifically designed to cater to the needs of the elderly.

Accordingly, this work presents a cognitive assistant designed for monitoring cardiorespiratory signals, specially designed for use in rural areas or where 24-h health care is difficult to obtain. The proposed cognitive assistant utilizes a combination of mechanical, electronic, and computer components. This innovative tool aims to enable analysis and pre-diagnosis of potential diseases for individuals living in remote areas or living alone. By leveraging these cutting-edge technologies, the cognitive assistant will be a powerful solution for improving healthcare access and outcomes in underserved communities.

2   System Proposal

This section provides a detailed overview of the components of the cognitive assistant presented in this paper. The system comprises a combination of mechanical, electronic, and computer components, forming a powerful tool for analyzing and pre-diagnosing potential diseases in remote areas or for individuals living alone.

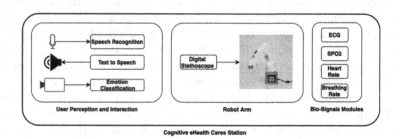

Fig. 1. General view of the proposed cognitive assistant.

The cognitive assistant comprises three main components (Fig. 1). The first component focuses on emotion detection [8], voice interaction [6], and speech recognition [10], which are critical for enabling the assistant to communicate effectively. The second component is the robotic arm, which possesses four degrees of freedom. Finally, the assistant features a set of non-invasive sensors that capture vital signs such as ECG signals, respiratory rate, SPO2, and beats per minute. These sensors are designed to ensure patient comfort while acquiring the relevant data. Once collected, the biosignals are processed and transmitted to the software component of the system. They can be analyzed and interpreted to provide medical professionals valuable insights into the patient's health.

The following subsections will describe the hardware and software components employed in the proposed prototype. These components have been selected and integrated to create a comprehensive healthcare solution, allowing for remote monitoring and interaction with medical professionals worldwide.

2.1 Hardware Description

The proposed cognitive assistant features a crucial component known as the four-degree-of-freedom arm, which serves the purpose of interacting with patients autonomously or via remote control. This paper will concentrate only on the autonomous interaction mode.

The arm is equipped with an end effector that can integrate a diverse array of sensors, such as portable echocardiography systems, digital stethoscopes, and SPO2 sensors. However, a digital stethoscope has been developed and integrated into the arm for this particular prototype. This stethoscope employs a microphone with an integrated amplifier, and a XIAO microcontroller is used to convert the amplified analogue signal into a 12-bit digital signal. The resulting digitised signal is then transmitted to the signal analysis and control system.

Phonocardiography [5] is a critical technique that provides a non-invasive method for evaluating the functional state of the heart through the analysis of heart sounds. It allows healthcare professionals to obtain valuable information about the heart's function and detect abnormalities, such as heart murmurs, which may indicate underlying cardiovascular disease. By providing a graphical representation of heart sounds, phonocardiography enables specialists to analyze the various components of the heart sound in an objective and repeatable manner, aiding in the accurate diagnosis and treatment of heart conditions. Furthermore, the use of digital stethoscopes in phonocardiography has expanded the capabilities of this technique, allowing for more accurate and efficient analysis of heart sounds. Overall, phonocardiography is essential in assessing and managing heart disease, a leading cause of morbidity and mortality worldwide. To enhance the diagnostic capabilities of the user, the assistant includes a module for ECG capture. This module is facilitated by the BMD101 cardio chip, which captures a derivative of the heart signal. To use this module, the user must position their hands on stainless steel electrodes, which act as an interface between the electrical activity of the heart and the cardio chip.

The assistant utilizes a Doppler radar to measure respiratory rate. Specifically, a 60 GHz radar is used for the respiratory and heart rate measurement. This type of radar is known as a millimetre-wave sensor and delivers superior performance compared to 24 GHz sensors. The 60 GHz millimetre-wave sensors can capture a vast amount of point cloud data, which is crucial for maintaining high accuracy when calculating heart and respiratory rates.

The reTerminal[1] is a human-machine interface installation designed in modularisation, offering multiple interfaces and components. This development system is based on Raspberry Pi, RPi CM4 32 GB, integrated with multi-touch IPS display, Wi-Fi & Bluetooth dual-band, Linux compatible system pre-installed. It

---

[1] https://www.seeedstudio.com/ReTerminal-with-CM4-p-4904.html

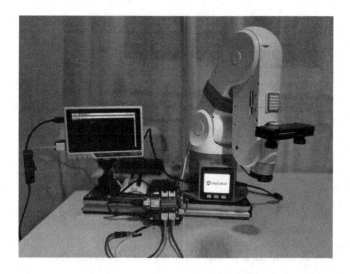

Fig. 2. An image of the proposed cognitive assistant prototype.

is a modular and robust system that allows the creation of applications in Iot robotics, among others (Fig. 2).

2.2 Software Description

This section describes the software utilized in the prototype, including a range of tools that enable monitoring of the robotic arm, analysis of camera images, and preliminary diagnosis based on sensor signals. An innovative approach to robotics is achieved through the integration of hardware and software via ROS2. The use of ROS2 as the middleware enables seamless communication with the MyCobot280 robot arm and facilitates control of its movements using high-level programming languages. Real-time feedback on the robot's movements is made possible through the visualization provided by RVIZ2, which is highly beneficial for debugging and refining control algorithms.

The physiological signal capturing subsystems, namely ECG and PCG, have incorporated embedded models in their devices. This integration of embedded models within the subsystems has effectively reduced the time required for data analysis. The development of these embedded models involved training using the tensor flow technology, and the resulting models were then transformed to be embedded within each microcontroller. During the training process, a series of data sets were utilized, with the dataset from The PhysioNet/Computing in Cardiology Challenge 2017 being employed specifically for pathology detection in ECG signals [2].

The dataset comprises recordings from a portable ECG device, captured using a single channel. Through the application of deep learning techniques, the recordings have been classified into four distinct categories: normal sinus rhythm (N), atrial fibrillation (A), other rhythm (O), or too noisy to be classified (U). Of

426   J. A. Rincon et al.

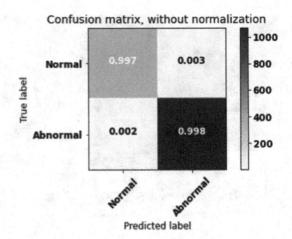

Fig. 3. Confusion matrix resulting from ECG classification.

the 8,528 total recordings in the dataset, 60% (5,076) are labelled "N," while 9% (758), 28% (2,415), and 3% (279) are labelled "A," "O," and "U," respectively. Given the dataset's significant class imbalance, the decision was made to combine the "A," "O," and "U" categories into a single class: Abnormal. As a result, the new dataset consists of only two classes: Normal and Abnormal. To train the classification model for these cardiac conditions, we utilized a RasNet [4] network. The classification process produced the confusion matrix in Fig. 3.

Table 1. Hyperparameters for Training the Model

Hyperparameter	Value
Start Learning Rate	1e−7
End Learning Rate	1e−6
Maximum Number of Steps	50
Smoothing	0.6
Batch Size	256
Epochs	5

Table 1 presents the hyperparameters associated with network training. As stated in the system description, the assistant examines potential cardiac sounds associated with heart sounds. It can record sounds related to heart valve movements, thereby enabling the detection of Normal, Murmur, Extracardiac Sound, Artifact, and Extrasystole. We utilized the Classifying Heart Sounds Challenge dataset [1], which contains two sub-datasets aimed at segmenting and classifying heart sounds, to perform our classification task.

3   Conclusions and Future Work

This paper describes a protoytpe of a cognitive assistant for eHealth applications that consists of three main components: emotion detection, voice interaction, and speech recognition for effective communication, a robotic arm with four degrees of freedom, and non-invasive sensors that capture vital signs such as ECG signals, respiratory rate, SPO2, and beats per minute. The sensors are designed for patient comfort while acquiring relevant data, which is then processed and analyzed by the software component to provide valuable insights into the patient's health for medical professionals. Overall, the cognitive assistant has the potential to revolutionize eHealth applications by providing efficient and accurate data collection and analysis, leading to improved patient outcomes.

As part of future work, we plan to integrate a new component that measures blood pressure, blood sugar and cholesterol using test strips and a remote monitoring system for cases where remote physician intervention is necessary.

Acknowledgements. Work partly supported by Universitat Politècnica de València Research Grant PAID-10-19 and PID2021-123673OB-C31 funded by MCIN/AEI/ 10.13039/501100011033 and by "ERDFA way of making Europe", Consellería d'Innovació, Universitats, Ciencia i Societat Digital from Comunitat Valenciana (APOSTD/2021/227) through the European Social Fund (Investing In Your Future).

References

1. Bentley, P., Nordehn, G., Coimbra, M., Mannor, S.: The PASCAL Classifying Heart Sounds Challenge 2011 (CHSC 2011)
2. Clifford, G.D., Liu, C., et al.: AF classification from a short single lead ECG recording: The PhysioNet/computing in cardiology challenge 2017. In: 2017 Computing in Cardiology (CinC), pp. 1–4. IEEE (2017)
3. Costa, A., Novais, P., Julian, V., Nalepa, G.J.: Cognitive assistants (2018)
4. He, K., Zhang, X., Ren, S., Sun, J.: Deep residual learning for image recognition. In: IEEE Conference on Computer Vision and Pattern Recognition, pp. 770–778 (2016)
5. Kao, W.C., Wei, C.C.: Automatic phonocardiograph signal analysis for detecting heart valve disorders. Expert Syst. Appl. **38**(6), 6458–6468 (2011)
6. Kowalski, J., et al.: Older adults and voice interaction: a pilot study with google home. In: CHI Conference on Human Factors in Computing Systems, pp. 1–6 (2019)
7. Maust, D.T., et al.: Antipsychotics, other psychotropics, and the risk of death in patients with dementia: number needed to harm. JAMA Psychiat. **72**(5), 438–445 (2015)
8. Rincon, J.A., Costa, A., Novais, P., Julian, V., Carrascosa, C.: A new emotional robot assistant that facilitates human interaction and persuasion. Knowl. Inf. Syst. **60**, 363–383 (2019)
9. Steptoe, A., Deaton, A., Stone, A.A.: Subjective wellbeing, health, and ageing. Lancet **385**(9968), 640–648 (2015)
10. Waibel, A., Lee, K.F.: Readings in Speech Recognition. Morgan Kaufmann, Burlington (1990)

Extended Green Cloud – Modeling Cloud Infrastructure with Green Energy Sources

Zofia Wrona[1]([✉])[ID], Maria Ganzha[1][ID], Marcin Paprzycki[2][ID],
and Stanisław Krzyżanowski[3]

[1] Faculty of Mathematics and Information Science,
Warsaw University of Technology, Warsaw, Poland
{zofia.wrona.stud,Maria.Ganzha}@pw.edu.pl
[2] Systems Research Institute Polish Academy of Sciences, Warsaw, Poland
marcin.paprzycki@ibspan.waw.pl
[3] CloudFerro Sp. z o. o., Warsaw, Poland
skrzyzanowski@cloudferro.com

Abstract. Recently, cloud computing has emerged as key way of delivering computing resources. Hence, research has focused on optimizing use of cloud resources. The following contribution presents an agent-based Extended Green Cloud Simulator, motivated by the Green Edge Processing project of the cloud company, CloudFerro. The simulator serves as a digital twin for agent-enabled carbon-intelligent cloud infrastructure that incorporates renewable energy sources and facilitates the modeling and evaluation of resource management strategies. Additionally, it offers a Graphical User Interface, System Engine, and Logging System which enable capturing, visualization, and analysis of key system statistics.

Keywords: multi-agent systems · digital twin · agent modelling · JADE

1 Introduction

The cloud computing has become the dominant way of delivering computing resources over the Internet. Its growing popularity originates from its flexibility, scalability, and affordability. Among cloud companies, CloudFerro is one of the key providers in the European space sector (e.g. storing and processing Copernicus data). Moreover, it offers services to the industry, international organizations, and scientific institutions. It also participates in research projects, including the Green Edge Processing (GEP)[1] that aims at creating a carbon-intelligent cloud infrastructure powered, in large part, by renewable energy sources. Specifically, GEP relies on the placement of servers within lightweight, containerized micro-server rooms, situated physically next to the green energy sources.

The implementation of the envisioned (and needed) infrastructure involves multiple challenges, due to the dynamic and unpredictable nature of the environment. For instance, (1) since green energy is provided by "external contractors",

---

[1] https://cloudferro.com/en/case-studies/green-edge-processing/.

P. Mathieu et al. (Eds.): PAAMS 2023, LNAI 13955, pp. 428–433, 2023.
https://doi.org/10.1007/978-3-031-37616-0_37

different policies, including dynamically varying pricing, are expected. (2) As the amount of available green energy fluctuates (e.g. depending on the weather conditions), the system has to self-adjust, to maintain stability of workload completion. (3) Additional complexity arises from the infrastructure itself, as servers are distributed throughout different locations, and new nodes (containers) can be added (or removed) to (from) the working ecosystem "at any time".

Addressing those (and other similar) concerns falls naturally into the domain of autonomous agents. Not surprisingly, in recent years, multi-agent systems (MAS) have been extensively studied in this domain [2,3]. As agents are able to collaborate, to achieve a common objective, and adapt to changing environmental conditions, they can be used to monitor and orchestrate the execution of cloud workloads, and to adjust their behavior to cope with fluctuating conditions. As such, the simulation of a MAS cloud infrastructure was the primary motivation behind the Extended Green Cloud System Simulator.

2 Main Purpose

The creation of the Extended Green Cloud System Simulator (EGCSS) addresses a real-life problem, arising in the context of the CloudFerro's novel data center infrastructure. The primary objective of the EGCSS is to model and facilitate simulations of the use of green energy sources in the distributed could center infrastructure. As such, it serves as a digital twin, designed to aid the development of an actual agent-based system, to be deployed by CloudFerro. This simulator should allow exploring, and evaluating, various approaches to managing different aspects of the system including, among others:

- *Energy management* – what strategies should be employed to manage (predict) availability of energy from different types of low-carbon resources (e.g. wind turbines vs. solar panels), caused by fluctuations in weather conditions?
- *Resource management* – how available computing resources should be distributed among locations and sources, and how should the system handle changes in its structure (i.e. adding, removing, or disabling components)?
- *Workload allocation* – in which way priorities should be set, considering the heterogeneous clients' jobs, and which types of allocation strategies (e.g. load balancing, job scheduling) facilitate the "best behavior" of the system?
- *System topology modeling* – to what extent are the system deployment and redeployment related to the available topology, i.e. how a particular topology influences the system's efficiency and scalability, for large-scale deployments?

As the simulator is intended for modeling the real-life extended cloud, its objective is to operate in a distributed manner. Furthermore, in order to make the system extensible and modifiable (particularly to allow users to define and test different strategies), all components have to be modular. In this way, the logic of the agents, system policies, system adaptations, and GUI components, become easily modifiable. To instantiate such a system, it was implemented in

Java, using the JADE[2] framework, which provides tools for agent system design, and supports the distribution of agents across multiple containers. The following section contains an overview of the conceptual framework of the system and describes implemented components, along with their intended use.

3 Demonstration

In order to meet the objectives set for the system, the EGCSS consists of the following modules:

- *Agent System* – module "containing the logic of the agents", offering a variety of generic behaviors and functionalities that can be used, by the user, to define specific system strategies.
- *Managing System* – module that extends the agent system with self-adaptive functionalities.
- *System Engine* – engine that allows running user-defined scenarios and strategies, configuring system properties to distribute the system on multiple hosts, as well as specifying the extended cloud topology
- *Socket Server* – NodeJS-based server that acts as a proxy between the backend and the GUI.
- *Graphical User Interface (GUI)* – interactive web interface, implemented in Typescript that allows monitoring and analysis of the state of the system.
- *Knowledge Database* – PostgreSQL time-scale database, instantiated to collect the system's statistics and to facilitate fast data storage and retrieval.
- *Logging System* – logging configuration, employed using log4j2 that allows system administrators to control the system's correctness.

Additionally, the system is connected with the external API – OpenWeatherMap API[3] that enables retrieval of real weather data for the simulations. The simplified architecture of the system is presented in Fig. 1.

3.1 Multi-agent System

The Extended Green Cloud System Simulator represents each network component, and each client, as a separate agent. In the current implementation, the orchestration of job execution is realized in the following manner.

The job is introduced to the cloud by the **Client Agent** (**CA**). Each **CA** has information about characteristics of a given job, including its time frame and resources required for its execution. The **CA** informs the cloud about a new job by sending the information to the **Scheduler Agent** (**SCHA**). The **SCHA** puts the job into a dedicated queue, based on its priority. The priority depends on the job's execution deadline and estimated required power. If the required power is too large, the **SCHA** can try to split the job into smaller

---

[2] https://jade.tilab.com/.
[3] https://openweathermap.org/api.

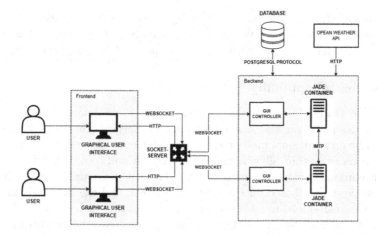

Fig. 1. Extended Green Cloud System Simulator system architecture

instances (i.e. of smaller powers) to increase its chance of execution. The **SCHA** retrieves periodically one job from the queue and broadcast it to **Cloud Network Agents** (**CNA**). The **CNA** plays the role of "location orchestrator". It gathers (and "manages") servers that are located in the same region (or belong to the same owner, etc.). Note that the way that servers should be grouped can be explored using the EGCS. When the **CNA** receives the job, it communicates with connected **Server Agents** (**SA**). The **SA**s are responsible for the jobs' execution. Each **SA** has a given maximum capacity (i.e. maximum amount of resources available for job execution) and is connected to one or more green energy sources. When the **SA** receives the job request, it communicates with all **Green Energy Source Agents** (**GSA**) in order to establish the availability of power. The **GSA** represents a renewable energy source. Currently, the system supports two types of sources – *wind farms* and *solar farms*. The **GSA** manages the provisioning of power for job execution. When the job request is received, the **GSA** evaluates its available power, by sending a request to **Monitoring Agent** (**MA**), which retrieves the weather forecast for a specific location. The **GSA** computes predicted available power on the basis of weather data and responds to the **SA** if it can power the job or not. When all responses are collected by **SA**, it selects one **GSA** for powering the job and responds to the **CNA**. The **CNA** performs a similar selection and passes its response to the **SCHA**. The **SCHA** repeats the procedure and gives the final information to the **CA**. In the case when there are no resources for the job's execution, it is either postponed (and the selection process is later repeated) or the **SCHA** reports failure. This may result in job being executed by the cloud center, using non-renewable resources.

When the job is being executed, the client is systematically informed about changes in its status. The **GSA**s are responsible for periodically monitoring the weather, in order to detect potential energy fluctuations. When the power fluctuation is detected, the system initiates the emergency behavior, which depends on the particular strategy. The default strategy is to transfer the jobs, that cannot be executed anymore by a given server, to another node (possibly, if necessary, e.g. due to the nature of the SLA contract, sending it to the cloud center).

3.2 System Adaptability

The system state is being monitored at all times, to assess if it operates as intended. To maintain the desired Quality of Service, the system has been extended by an additional module called the *Managing System*. It employs autonomic mechanisms that allow agents to self-adjust and reconfigure their behavior, in accordance with system conditions. From a theoretical perspective, the *Managing System* is based on the self-* paradigms, and the MAPE-K architectural model, introduced in IBM's autonomic computing manifesto [1]. From the technical side, it is implemented as a separate agent called **Managing Agent** (**MA**). The **MA** evaluates the parameters of the system (such as job execution success ratio), against the predefined thresholds. If any of the thresholds are violated (or, regularly, almost violated) it initiates an adaptation trigger. Then, it selects the adaptation action that is to be enacted on the system, and constructs a plan for its realization. In order to enact the adaptation, **MA** communicates with (a) specific agent(s), a configuration of which is to be adapted. Additionally, **MA** measures how the system has changed, as a result of a given adaptation, to make better decisions in the future. Apart from modifying the extended cloud configuration, the MA can change the ecosystem structure by adding additional *SA/GSA* or changing the connections between them.

3.3 System Strategies

The aim of the *EGCSS* is to support the assessment of different system strategies, employed in the extended cloud. Hence, users can deploy and evaluate individual system policies that define the system's rules and behaviors (e.g. algorithms used in job executors selection). Such strategies can be prepared for both the *Agent System* and the *Managing System*. The system policy can be changed by modifying the logic behind particular system agents. When all changes are applied, the user can build a system package, using Maven, and store it in a *.jar* file. Then, to execute the specified strategy, it is sufficient to place a *.jar* in the resource folder and pass its name as a parameter while running the system. Moreover, to specify the topology of the network, it is enough to create a dedicated *XML* file, and "import it" when running the simulation.

The initial assessment of the impact of a given strategy on the system can be done using a dedicated GUI. It displays the live statistics of each individual agent, the statistics of adaptations, and enables the user to trigger particular events in the system. The GUI offers also a dedicated dashboard that allows the analysis of long-term system activity. The dashboard is presented in Fig. 2.

During the demonstration, two types of strategies will be presented to the attendees. The strategies will consider two different types of topologies and will present how the system performance is influenced by adopting different policies.

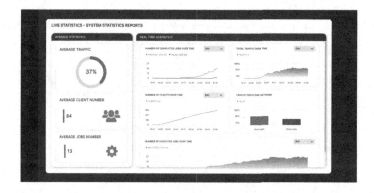

Fig. 2. Statistics dashboard GUI

4 Concluding Remarks

The objective of the developed EGCS is to facilitate the implementation of an extended cloud system. The tool allows testing a variety of strategies, in order to evaluate their impact on the quality and performance of the ecosystem, before deploying an actual agent-based infrastructure. The modular design of the proposed solution enables convenient modifications and extensions. In addition, the use of autonomous agents in the simulator facilitates modeling a dynamic system and effectively addresses concerns related to environmental unpredictability. It also emphasizes the potential for agent cooperation in resolving complex tasks.

The presented version of the system is in its early stage. For instance, it does not consider cost-related factors, which constitute another critical aspect of the extended cloud that can also be managed by employing distinct strategies. Furthermore, future plans involve expanding the adaptability and applicability of the strategies by injecting selected functionalities into the system at runtime. The current version of the system can be found at https://github.com/Extended-Green-Cloud.

Acknowledgements. Work of Maria Ganzha, Marcin Paprzycki and Stanisław Krzyżanowski was funded in part by the European Commission, under the Horizon Europe project aerOS, grant number 101069732 as well as NCBiR. The initial code of the project was prepared in collaboration with Piotr Witkiewicz and Mikołaj Stańczyk.

References

1. IBM: Architectural blueprint for autonomic computing. Technical report, IBM (2005)
2. Kozhevnikov, S., Svítek, M., Skobelev, P.: Smart grid system for real-time adaptive utility management in smart cities, pp. 4–9 (2022). https://doi.org/10.54808/IMCIC2022.01.4
3. De la Prieta, F., Rodríguez-González, S., Chamoso, P., Demazeau, Y., Corchado, J.M.: An intelligent approach to allocating resources within an agent-based cloud computing platform. Appl. Sci. **10**, 4361 (2020). https://doi.org/10.3390/app10124361

Correction to: An IDE to Support the Development of Embedded Multi-Agent Systems

Vinicius Souza de Jesus(iD), Nilson Mori Lazarin(iD),
Carlos Eduardo Pantoja(iD), Gleifer Vaz Alves(iD),
Gabriel Ramos Alves de Lima(iD), and Jose Viterbo(iD)

Correction to:
Chapter "An IDE to Support the Development of Embedded Multi-Agent Systems" in: P. Mathieu et al. (Eds.): *Advances in Practical Applications of Agents, Multi-Agent Systems, and Cognitive Mimetics. The PAAMS Collection*, LNAI 13955, https://doi.org/10.1007/978-3-031-37616-0_29

In the originally published chapter 29 the affiliation information was partly incorrect. The second affiliation has been corrected to "Center for Technological Education Celso Suckow da Fonseca, Rio de Janeiro, Brazil" and the third affiliation has been corrected to "Federal University of Technology - Paraná, Ponta Grossa, Brazil".

The updated original version of this chapter can be found at
https://doi.org/10.1007/978-3-031-37616-0_29

Author Index

P. Mathieu et al. (Eds.): PAAMS 2023, LNAI 13955, pp. 435–436, 2023.
https://doi.org/10.1007/978-3-031-37616-0

Printed in the United States
by Baker & Taylor Publisher Services